Excavations in North Sinai: Tell el-Borg II

Excavations in North Sinai

Tell el-Borg II

A deity, probably Amun-Re, from a royal, triumphal scene at Tell el-Borg

Edited by

James K. Hoffmeier

with contributions by

Louise Bertini, Thomas W. Davis, Scott D. Haddow, James K. Hoffmeier, Rexine Hummel, Hesham M. Hussein, Salima Ikram, Mark Janzen, Michelle A. Loyet, Claire Malleson, Carol McCartney, Stephen O. Moshier, and Gregory D. Mumford

Eisenbrauns | University Park, PA

Library of Congress Cataloging-in-Publication Data

Names: Hoffmeier, James Karl, 1951– editor. | Moshier, Stephen O., 1955– contributor.
Title: Tell el-Borg II : excavations in North Sinai / edited by James K. Hoffmeier ; with contributions by Stephen Moshier [and 12 others].
Description: University Park, Pennsylvania : Eisenbrauns, [2019] | Includes bibliographical references and index.
Summary: "The second and final volume of scientific and interdisciplinary reports on the excavations and research conducted at Tell el-Borg, north Sinai, between 1998 and 2008, focusing on cemetery areas"—Provided by publisher.
Identifiers: LCCN 2018058559 | ISBN 9781575069883 (cloth : alk. paper)
Subjects: LCSH: Tell el-Borg Site (Egypt) | Sinai (Egypt)—Antiquities. | Excavations (Archaeology)—Egypt—Sinai. | Cemeteries—Egypt—Sinai.
Classification: LCC DT73.T26 T48 2019 | DDC 939.4/8—dc23
LC record available at https://lccn.loc.gov/2018058559

Printed in the United States of America
Published by The Pennsylvania State University Press,
University Park, PA 16802–1003

Eisenbrauns is an imprint of The Pennsylvania State University Press.

The Pennsylvania State University Press is a member of the Association of University Presses.

It is the policy of The Pennsylvania State University Press to use acid-free paper. Publications on uncoated stock satisfy the minimum requirements of American National Standard for Information Sciences—Permanence of Paper for Printed Library Material, ANSI Z39.48–1992.

Dedicated to

K. Lawson Younger Jr. and Richard E. Averbeck

Dear colleagues and faithful friends

Contents

Acknowledgments ix

Abbreviations xi

Published Reports and Studies on the Work at Tell El-Borg xiii

CHAPTER 1. A Brief Summary of a Decade of Research in North Sinai and Tell el-Borg 1
James K. Hoffmeier

CHAPTER 2. Geological Investigation of the Ballah Depression, Northern Suez Canal Zone, Egypt 5
Stephen O. Moshier

CHAPTER 3. Public Space at Tell el-Borg: Field II, Areas 1–3 21
Gregory D. Mumford

CHAPTER 4. The Funerary Area: Field III, The "Eastern Cemetery" 166
Scott D. Haddow and James K. Hoffmeier

CHAPTER 5. Clay Coffins from Tell el-Borg 259
Mark Janzen

CHAPTER 6. The "Western Cemetery" 270
Scott D. Haddow and James K. Hoffmeier

CHAPTER 7. Field VI: The Domestic Space 278
Thomas W. Davis

CHAPTER 8. Mapping an Ancient Egyptian Highway of North Sinai: The Ways of Horus 348
Hesham M. Hussein

CHAPTER 9. Identification and Provenance of Elite Stones Found at Tell el-Borg . . 355
Stephen O. Moshier

CHAPTER 10. Lithics / Chipped Stone Implements from Tell el-Borg 365
Carol McCartney

CHAPTER 11. Report on the Charred Plant Remains at Tell el-Borg 380
Claire Malleson

CHAPTER 12. Faunal Report on the First Three Seasons of Excavations (2000–2002) 390
Michelle A. Loyet

CHAPTER 13. The Faunal Remains from the 2004–2007 Excavations at Tell el-Borg 404
Louise Bertini

CHAPTER 14. The Equid Remains from Tell el-Borg 414
Salima Ikram

CHAPTER 15. Reflections on a Decade of Research and Excavations at Tell el-Borg and Its Environs (1998–2008) 424
James K. Hoffmeier

Acknowledgments

Tell el-Borg I was published in 2014. This is the second volume (*Tell el-Borg II*) of the reports on the excavations at Tell el-Borg and the final scientific report. To produce a large technical volume such as an excavation report required the efforts of many. I am grateful that the fieldwork and field study were undertaken by such competent experts, some of whom have contributed to this volume. The names of the staff during our decade of work are recorded year by year in *Tell el-Borg I* (chapter 1). Without the financial support of the Miller Family Foundation between 1999 and 2009, this entire project would not have been possible. Once again, heartfelt thanks are offered to Harvey L. Miller for his friendship, encouragement, and support over this ten-year period and beyond.

Then, too, the production of this volume required technical help with preparation: creating various illustrations; making tables and charts; digitizing field drawings; selecting and enhancing illustrations; and in regard to the actual manuscript, much writing, editing, formatting, tagging, page layout, and proof-reading. Many assisted in this monumental task, including Trinity students Kenton Williams (one of my Ph.D. students) and David Larson (an M.A. student), who assisted with reading and editing. Joshua Olsen digitized and enhanced all the line drawings (top plans, sections, some objects). In the final stages, Ben Hoffmeier (my son) tagged the chapters and assisted with further editing, as did Cathy Hoffmeier (my wife), whose sharp eyes spent many hours proof-reading. Finally, Jim Eisenbraun himself did the page layout for this volume. All of these people worked diligently and professionally. Kudos to Jim Eisenbraun who took on the page layout task as one of his final projects as he was turning over the Eisenbrauns publishing operation to Penn State University Press. It was a pleasure working with Eisenbrauns; I greatly appreciate their professionalism.

Making this all possible were two grants. The first came from the Shelby White and Leon Levy Program for Archaeological Publications. Professor Lawrence Stager from Harvard University was a key person in the Levy-White program, and he encouraged me with this publication effort. In fact, we spoke about it on November 16, 2017, at the annual American Schools of Oriental Research meeting, where I advised him that the task was almost complete. Sadly, on December 31, 2017, Professor Stager passed away unexpectedly. He will be missed. I want to acknowledge his role in evaluating the *Tell el-Borg II* publication project and getting behind it. The two-year Levy-White grant is greatly appreciated and made this publication possible.

The second critical source of funding was the Antiquities Endowment Fund of the American Research Center in Egypt. This grant covered the cost of the subvention for the publisher. The former executive director of ARCE, Dr. Gerry Scott is to be thanked for his role in making these funds possible.

With this volume, we are trying something new. In volume I, we included a CD with *all* of the illustrations, plans, and site maps. This allowed the reader access to site field shots and small finds in color, and plans and maps could be enlarged to see important details. But because technology has changed so quickly in the three years since the first volume was published, we also have to adjust to a system that will allow readers to have access to the images via the internet. Our data has been stored on the OCHRE (Online Cultural & Historical Research Environment) database at the University of Chicago (http://ochre.lib.uchicago.edu/publish?project=Borg). Do to the sheer number of plans and section drawings from Field II, not all could be included within chapter 3 but all can be accessed through the OCHRE link. Thanks to Sandra Schloen and Dr. Miller Prosser, who designed and administer the OCHRE program at the Oriental Institute and for their assistance in setting up the Tell el-Borg database and creating the link so that readers can access this material. Here, too, I need to acknowledge that funds from the above-mentioned grants covered costs for OCHRE's services.

Throughout the course of the years of work in North Sinai, I was grateful that the administration at Trinity allowed my teaching schedule to be packaged in such a way that I was permitted to be in the field during the second half of the Spring semester, March and April. This arrangement meant that I was not always able to fulfill all my departmental duties, as a consequence of which various colleagues had to carry some of my responsibilities. So I am grateful to my chair, Professor Dennis R. Magary, for his patience and handling of the scheduling issues. Before coming to Trinity in 1999, my friendship between two colleagues had already begun. Back in the early 1990s, a professional connection was established with Richard E. Averbeck, who was then at Grace Theological Seminary (Indiana), and K. Lawson Younger Jr., who was on the faculty of LeTourneu University (Texas). We were interested in each other's research and read with interest one another's publications. Both were committed to cutting-edge research in Near Eastern and biblical studies. They collaborated on a couple of books that I organized and edited. In time, all three of us ended up at Trinity, and our friendship flourished over the past 19 years. Dick and Lawson have been wonderful friends and colleagues who encouraged me in my fieldwork and all my research. With my retirement this spring (2018) from Trinity, it is a fitting time to acknowledge how much I appreciate them as friends and colleagues by dedicating this volume to them. Thanks, Lawson and Dick, for investing in me and working with me on many areas of common interest. More to come in the future, I hope.

James K. Hoffmeier, Project Director
Professor of Near Eastern Archaeology and History
Trinity International University, Divinity School

Abbreviations

AJA	*American Journal of Archaeology*
ASAE	*Annales du service des antiquités de l'Égypte* (Cairo)
ÄuL	Ägypten unde Levante
BASOR	*Bulletin of the American Schools of Oriental Research*
BIFAO	*Bulletin de l'Institut Français d'Archéologie Orientale*
CdÉ	*Chronique d'Égypte*
CRIPEL	*Cahiers de recherches de l'institut de Papyrologie et d'Égyptologie de Lille*
EA	*Egyptian Archaeology*
EI	*Eretz Israel*
GM	*Göttinger Miszellen*
IEJ	*Israel Exploration Journal*
JAEI	*Journal of Ancient Egyptian Interconnections*
JARCE	*Journal of the American Research Center in Egypt*
JEA	*Journal of Egyptian Archaeology*
JEOL	*Jaarbericht ex Oriente Lux*
JNES	*Journal of Near Eastern Studies*
JSSEA	*Journal of the Society for the Study of Egyptian Antiquities*
KB	Ludwig Koehler & Walter Baumgartner, *Lexicon in Veteris Testamenti Libros* (trans. & updated by M.E.J. Richardson; Leiden: Brill, 2001).
KRI	Kenneth Kitchen, *Inscriptions, Historical and Biographical*, 7 Volumes (Oxford: Blackwell, 1968–1983).
MDAIK	*Mitteilungen des deutschen Instituts für ägyptische Altertumskunde in Kairo*
NEAEHL	Ephriam Stern (ed.), *New Encyclopedia of Archaeological Excavations in the Holy Land*, 4 Volumes (New York: Simon & Schuster, 1993).
OEANE	*Oxford Encyclopedia of Archaeology in the Near East,* 5 Volumes (ed. Eric Meyer; New York: Oxford University Press, 1997).
RdÉ	*Revue d'Égyptologie*
RITANC	Kennenth Kitchen, *Ramesside Inscriptions Translated and Annotated: Notes and Comments* (Oxford: Oxford University Press, 1993).
RT	*Receuil de travaux relatifs à la philology et à l'archéologie égyptiennes et assyriennes*
TBO	Tell el-Borg Object (Small find registration prefix)
TBO I–IV	Tell el-Borg Object (Small find registration system. In 2001, the Field # was included. This system was discontinued in subsequent seasons to simplify the registration for the INFRA database)
TBOX	Small find registration prefix for surface finds in 2000 season only.
TBP	Tell el-Borg Pottery (Pottery Registration prefix)
Urk IV	Kurt Sethe, *Urkunden der 18. Dynastie* 4 volumes (Berlin: Akademie-Verlag, 1961).
Wb	Adolf Erman & Hermann Grapow, *Wörterbuch der ägyptischen Sprache*, 5 volumes (Leipzig: J.C. Hinrichs'sche, 1926–1931).
ZÄS	*Zeitschrift für Ägyptische Sprache und Altertumskunde*

Published Reports and Studies on the Work at Tell El-Borg

Articles

James K. Hoffmeier, "Tell El-Borg in North Sinai," *Egyptian Archaeology* 20 (2002) 18–20.

James K. Hoffmeier and Mohamed Abd el-Maksoud, "A New Military Site on 'the Ways of Horus' — Tell el-Borg 1999–2001: A Preliminary Report," *Journal of Egyptian Archaeology* 89 (2003) 169–97.

James K. Hoffmeier, "Aspects of Egyptian Foreign Policy in the 18th Dynasty in Western Asia and Nubia." Pp. 121–41 in *Egypt, Israel, and the Ancient Mediterranean World: Studies in Honor of Donald B. Redford* (ed. Gary Knoppers and Antoine Hirsch; Leiden: Brill, 2004).

James K. Hoffmeier, "The North Sinai Archaeological Project's Excavations at Tell el-Borg (Sinai): An Example of the 'New' Biblical Archaeology?" Pp. 53–68 in *The Future of Biblical Archaeology* (ed. J. Hoffmeier and A. R. Millard; Grand Rapids, MI: Eerdmans, 2004).

James K. Hoffmeier, "Tell el-Borg on Egypt's Eastern Frontier: A Preliminary Report on the 2002 and 2004 Seasons," *Journal of the American Research Center in Egypt* 41 (2004) 85–111.

James K. Hoffmeier and Lyla Pinch-Brock, "A New Royal Chariot Scene from Tell el-Borg," in *Millet Memorial Volume = JSSEA* 22 (2005) 81–94.

James K. Hoffmeier and Ronald D. Bull, "New Inscriptions Mentioning Tjaru from Tell el-Borg, North Sinai," *Revue d'Égyptologie* 56 (2005) 79–86.

James K. Hoffmeier, "Recent Excavations on the 'Ways of Horus': The 2005 and 2006 Seasons at Tell el-Borg," *Annales du Service des Antiquités de l'Égypte* 80 (2006) 257–79.

James K. Hoffmeier, "Sulla via di Horus," *Pharaon* 2 no. 7/8 (2006) 6–13.

James K. Hoffmeier, "The Walls of the Ruler in Egyptian Literature and the Archaeology Record: Investigating Egypt's Eastern Frontier in the Bronze Age," *Bulletin of the American Schools of Oriental Research* 337 (2006) 1–20.

James K. Hoffmeier and Stephen O. Moshier, "New Paleo-Environmental Evidence from North Sinai to Complement Manfred Bietak's Map of the Eastern Delta and Some Historical Implications." Pp. 168–76 in *Timelines: Studies in Honour of Manfred Bietak* II (Leuven: Peeters, 2006).

James K. Hoffmeier and Earl Ertman, "Amarna Period Kings in Sinai," *Egyptian Archaeology* 31 (2007) 38–39.

James K. Hoffmeier and Kenneth A. Kitchen, "Reshep and Astarte in North Sinai: A Recently Discovered Stela from Tell el-Borg," *Ägypten und Levante* 17 (2007) 127–36.

James K. Hoffmeier, "Report of the Trinity International University at Tell el-Borg: The 2005 Season," *Annales du Service des Antiquités de l'Égypt* [Arabic edition] (2008) 109–30.

James K. Hoffmeier, "The Search for Migdol of the New Kingdom and Exodus 14:2: An Update," *Buried History* 44 (2008) 3–12.

James K. Hoffmeier and Earl Ertman, "A New Fragmentary Relief of King Ankhkheperure from Tell el-Borg (Sinai)?" *Journal of Egyptian Archaeology* 94 (2008) 206–302.

Stephen O. Moshier and Ali El-Kalani, "Late Bronze Age Paleogeography along the Ancient Ways of Horus in Northwest Sinai, Egypt," *Geoarchaeology* 23 (2008) 450–73.

James K. Hoffmeier, “Deities of the Eastern Frontier.” Pp. 197–216 in *Shefik Allam Feschrift* (ed. Z. Hawass; Cairo: SCA, 2010).

James K. Hoffmeier and Jacobus van Dijk, “New Light on the Amarna Period from North Sinai,” *Journal of Egyptian Archaeology* 96 (2010) 195–201.

James K. Hoffmeier, “The Gate of the Ramesside Period Fort at Tell el-Borg, North Sinai.” Pp. 207–17 in *Ramesside Studies in Honour of K. A. Kitchen* (ed. S. Snape and M. Collier; Bolton: Rutherford, 2011).

James K. Hoffmeier, “Reconstructing Egypt’s Eastern Frontier Defense Network in the New Kingdom (Late Bronze Age).” Pp. 163–94 in *The Power of Walls: Fortifications in Ancient Northeastern Africa* (ed. Friederike Jesse and Carola Vogel; Africa Praehistorica; Cologne: Heinrich-Barth-Institut, 2013).

James K. Hoffmeier, “‘The Ways of Horus’: The Main Road from Egypt to Canaan.” Pp. 485–510 in *Desert Road Archaeology in the Eastern Sahara* (ed. Heiko Reimer and Frank Förster; Colloquium Africanum 5; Cologne: Heinrich-Barth-Institute, 2013).

James K. Hoffmeier, Thomas W. Davis, and Rexine Hummel, “New Archaeological Evidence for Ancient Bedouin (Shasu) on Egypt’s Eastern Frontier at Tell el-Borg.” *ÄuL* 26 (2016) 285–311.

James K. Hoffmeier, “A Possible Location in Northwest Sinai for the Sea and Land Battles between the Sea Peoples and Ramesses III.” *Bulletin of the American Schools of Oriental Research* 380 (2018) 1–25.

James K. Hoffmeier, “The Curious Phenomenon of Moving Military Sites on Egypt’s Eastern Frontier,” *JSSEA* (The Edwin Brock Memorial Volume) 36 (in press).

Monographs

James K. Hoffmeier (ed.), *Excavations in North Sinai: Tell el-Borg I* (Winona Lake, IN: Eisenbrauns, 2014)

James K. Hoffmeier (ed.), *Recent Studies on North Sinai: Archaeological, Historical, Geological and Biblical Investigations* (Ägypten und Altes Testament 94; Münster: Zaphon, in press.).

CHAPTER 1

A Brief Summary of a Decade of Research in North Sinai and Tell el-Borg

James K. Hoffmeier
Trinity International University

Introduction to Tell el-Borg Volume II

Tell el-Borg, as it turns out, was an extremely important ancient military establishment on the eastern frontier of Egypt, just into the Sinai Peninsula. It functioned in this capacity throughout the New Kingdom. It is located about 10 km east of the Suez Canal at Qantara East (Sharq), and about 2.5 km north of the El-Arish Road. The coordinates are N 30° 55.516′ E 32° 24.621′. The project was sponsored by my own institution, Trinity International University (Deerfield, IL) and we worked under the auspices of the American Research Center in Egypt and in partnership with the Supreme Council for Antiquities (now the Ministry of State for Antiquities). The investigation and research at Tell el-Borg was largely carried out between 1999 and 2008.

Tell el-Borg I, published in 2014, contained a detailed history of the project at Tell el-Borg (Chapter 1), and we offered a textual and archaeological study of the "Ways of Horus," the military road between Egypt and western Asia, on which Tell el-Borg was situated. It also dealt with other related archaeological sites that had been investigated over the past two to three decades (Chapter 2). To understand this frontier zone required a clear picture of the paleo-environment of northwestern Sinai. This was the focus of geologist Stephen Moshier's groundbreaking fieldwork, which enabled us to reconstruct the ancient landscape of this region from 3,000 and 4,000 years ago (Chapter 3). Two New Kingdom forts were found at Tell el-Borg (Fields IV, V, and VIII), a testimony to the military nature of the site. These military features were situated at the critical junction of the Nile distributary and the land route to the Levant. Chapter 4 treated most of the inscribed materials discovered at the site, including the cache of inscribed limestone blocks and fragments uncovered in Field I, some of which were dredged up when the drainage canal was excavated in the early 1990s. Volume I also included the results of the magnetometer survey conducted by Tomasz Herbich of the Polish Academy of Sciences (Chapter 7). One of the anomalies exposed by Herbich's work resulted in the unexpected discovery of a moat in Field VI, which is reported here (Chapter 7). The Egyptian, Canaanite, Cypriote, and Mycenaean ceramics are studied in Volume I (Chapters 8, 9, 10, and 11). Finally, in keeping with the military nature of Tell el-Borg, Chapter 12 treated weapons, both metal and lithic, recovered from our excavations.

This second volume offers reports on areas excavated that were not discussed in Volume I. Field II was situated on the north side of the eastward-flowing Nile distributary. It is considered to be "public space" by Gregory Mumford (Chapter 3), who, among others, directed excavations in this critical zone; this chapter offers an incredibly detailed accounting of the excavations. Furthermore, Field II includes a stepped stone-lined pit (probably a well) and a possible temple foundation. The burial areas of the site and osteological remains are also reported in this volume. The so-called eastern cemetery in Field III (Chapter 4) and the western cemetery in Field VII (Chapter 6) were both largely excavated by Scott D. Haddow, who teams up with Hoffmeier to describe the architecture, small finds and osteological remains. Mark Janzen puts forth a study of the clay-coffin fragments that were retrieved and restored (expertly by Noël Siver) in Field III (Chapter 5). Field VI, the highest area of the tell is where the only clear habitat was documented at Tell el-Borg—namely, unique remains of burned-out huts from the 17th–16th centuries B.C., and in Area III, the highly deflated remains of a third mud-brick moat was uncovered (the other two were found in association with the forts in Fields IV, V, and VII; see *Tell el-Borg I*). Thomas Davis spearheaded the work in Field VI and discusses these intriguing finds in Chapter 7; Field VI is referred to as the "Domestic Space."

Of special interest to the military history of the northwest Sinai area was the discovery of a section of a mud-brick road in the sands between Tell el-Borg and Hebua II (to the north), apparently connecting the sites. Dr. Hesham Huessein, who worked for many years in this area of northwest Sinai and also ably served as an inspector from the North Sinai Inspectorate of the Ministry of Antiquities, made this significant discovery and reports on it in Chapter 8.

After presenting the results from Fields II, III, VI, and VII, the volume turns to specialist reports. Stephen O. Moshier presents the results of his study of the elite stones recovered at the site (Chapter 9). Another kind of stone, flint, and various implements made of flint or chert were widely found in our excavations. Carol McCartney, a specialist on chipped stone implements, offers her analysis of this material in Chapter 10. Claire Malleson examined plant remains, typically charred seeds obtained by floatation. The results of her work is found in Chapter 11. The next three chapters treat the faunal remains. Michelle Loyet processed the animal remains discovered during the 2000–2002 seasons (Chapter 12), while Louise Bertini studies the faunal remains from the 2004–2007 seasons. Then, in Chapter 14, Salima Ikram concentrates her analysis on the equid bones, interestingly found in the Field V fosse and the aforementioned moat in Field VI. Finally, I have a concluding essay that attempts to synthesize the discoveries of Tell el-Borg and their implications.

A Brief Review of the History of the Work at Tell el-Borg

A full review of the history of the investigations in northwestern Sinai, and the excavations at Tell el-Borg in particular, is provided in *Tell el-Borg I*, Chapter 1. There is therefore no need to repeat that information. It may be, however, that some readers of this monograph may not have access to the initial volume. Consequently, what follows is a brief orientation.

Preliminary efforts began with brief visits to the area just east of the Suez Canal at Qantara East in 1994 and 1995. My initial interests grew out of some preliminary reports about the discovery of an ancient canal on the eastern frontier by members of the Geological Survey of Israel.[1]

1. Amihai Sneh, Weissbrod Tuvia, and Itamar Perath, "Evidence for an Ancient Egyptian Frontier Canal," *American Scientist* 63 (1975) 542–48; William Shea, "A Date for the Recently Discovered Eastern

It was their theory that the defunct channel they found running east of Tell Abu Sefêh was part of the New Kingdom defense system of Egypt as depicted on the incredible battle reliefs of Seti I on the north outside wall of the Hypostyle Hall at Karnak. Owing to the rapid pace of development in the area since the 1970s, when the Israeli geologists verified the presence of this "canal" they had first noticed on aerial photographs, we were unable to find traces of the channel until 1998, when Stephen Moshier and I were reconnoitering the area with the aid of recently accessed CORONA satellite images (see *Tell el-Borg I*, 7–10). By this date, we were fairly certain that Tell Abu Sefêh was not Tjaru/Sile, Egypt's border town. This equation had been a long-standing one.[2] The excavations at Hebua, 8.5 km to the north of the traditional site, were showing that there was a massive New Kingdom military establishment there, while at the former site, no New Kingdom stratigraphy or ceramics were found. It seems unlikely, then, that Tell Abu Sefêh could be ancient Tjaru.[3]

My first goal was to see if indeed the low-lying shell-covered area between Hebua I and II could be the feature depicted at Karnak and whether the two sites identified as the Fortress Tjaru on the relief might correspond to Hebua I and II. The excavations at these two sites indeed demonstrated that Egypt's frontier forts were Tjaru,[4] and our coring into the subsurface mud and clay in 1995 showed that a Nilotic branch passed between the forts (*Tell el-Borg I*, 5–7 and 62–83), just represented on the Seti I relief.

In 1998, Moshier and I continued work to clarify the geological setting of the region. We actually hiked through a section of the East Frontier Canal about 15 km east of the Suez Canal (see *Tell el-Borg I*, 7–10, cf. figs. 10 and 55 there). During this visit, we first heard about a New Kingdom site several kilometers to the southeast of Hebua II—namely, Tell el-Borg. We returned with a small survey team in May 1999 to examine this site at the invitation of Dr. Mohamed Abd el-Maksoud, then director of the North Sinai Inspectorate. Surface study in the course of several days determined that Tell el-Borg was in fact a New Kingdom site, but badly pitted by recent robbing. Readily identifiable New Kingdom era sherds were scattered across the surface and pieces of granite, limestone, and other rocks not local to the region were visible, all indicators of a significant site. It was also clear that the Israeli and Egyptian armies had used this tell as a military base from the 1960s through the 1980s. On top of that, roads were now being laid and a drainage canal had been dug in connection with the As-Salam irrigation project, which also contributed to the destruction of the site. We wondered if there was any value in excavating, given the amount of damage, exposure, and deflation that was evident.

It should also be noted that another motivating factor for our work in north Sinai was to salvage archaeological remains that might otherwise be destroyed and forever lost. The governmental antiquities authorities encouraged the international community of archaeologists to assist with the salvage effort. We saw first-hand the kind of damage that was done before we arrived. Previously, some members of the Supreme Council for Antiquities had briefly excavated some soundings on the western side of the site, in our Field VII (see fig. 3.1).

Canal of Egypt," *BASOR* 226 (1977) 31–38.

2. Alan H. Gardiner, "The Ancient Military Road between Egypt and Palestine," *JEA* 6 (1920) 99–116.

3. For a full discussion of these sites and their history and relationship, see James K. Hoffmeier, "The Curious Phenomenon of Moving Military Sites on Egypt's Eastern Frontier," *JSSEA* (The Edwin Brock Memorial Volume) 36 (in press).

4. M. Abd el-Maksoud and D. Valbelle, "Tell Héboua-Tjarou l'apport de l'épigraphie," *Rd'É* 56 (2005) 7–8 and 18–21. Regarding Hebua II, see Mohamed Abd el-Maksoud, and Dominique Valbelle, "Tell Héboua II: Rapport Préliminaire sur le décor el l'épigraphie des elements architectoniques découverts au cours des campagnes 2008–2009 dans la zone centrale du Khétem de Tjarou," *Rd'É* 62 (2011) 1–39.

Despite our assessment that the site was badly damaged, we nonetheless decided to proceed. After the initial survey and mapping of the site in January 2000, full-scale excavations began in March 2000 and continued each Spring, save 2003 (due to problems with permits). The final season of excavations occurred in 2007. In 2007, the magnetometer survey of crucial areas was completed. Several anomalies were investigated, but we did not notice any substantial features that demanded further investigation. This factor was crucial in our decision to discontinue fieldwork at Tell el-Borg. In 2008, we conducted a final study season, and the focus shifted to publishing the final reports. The completion of *Tell el-Borg II* brings this phase to a close. From the outset of the project, we have sought to publish preliminary reports in a timely manner; when objects of historical or cultural significance were discovered, we quickly made the material available. A list of studies and preliminary reports is produced just before this chapter.

These papers are scattered about in refereed journals, in *Festschriften,* and in volumes of collected essays, which makes accessibility a challenge. It is fortuitous, then, that two years ago, Professor Wolfgang Zwickel of Johannes Gutenberg Universität, Mainz, suggested to me that he would like to publish a number of the articles about our work in north Sinai in the monograph series he edits, Ägypten und Altes Testament. This volume should appear sometime in 2019 under the tile, *Recent Studies on North Sinai: Archaeological, Historical, Geological and Biblical Studies* (series editors: Wolfgang Zwickel and Stefan Wimmer). Here, 20 previously published articles will be brought together and be accessible in a single volume.

By reading the chapters in this volume along with the data and interpretations offered in volume I, the reader will get a comprehensive understanding of the excavated remains from Tell el-Borg, comprehend the site's role in the east frontier-defense system, and appreciate its place on the military highway between Egypt and Canaan.

CHAPTER 2

Geological Investigation of the Ballah Depression, Northern Suez Canal Zone, Egypt

Stephen Moshier and Bahaa Gayed
WHEATON COLLEGE AND EGYPTIAN GEOLOGICAL SURVEY

INTRODUCTION

The archaeological expedition to Tell el-Borg provided an opportunity to investigate the physical geography of the region as it existed during the Bronze Age. Shallow, subsurface geology was accessible around the Tell el-Borg site in open irrigation canals of the Al-Salaam agricultural project. Completion of the agricultural project covered or removed many surface features relating to ancient depositional environments, even as we conducted our field surveys. Fortunately, declassified space imagery from decades before our work reveals many such features.

The first phase of our geological work (2000–2004) focused on a rectangular area anchored diagonally between the city of Qantara on the Suez Canal and the archaeological site (Roman) Tel Herr (fig. 2.1, upper rectangle). Our survey confirmed earlier proposals for the location of the Bronze Age Mediterranean coastline (a regional, tectonic lineament known as the Pelusium Line) and the presence of an inland lagoon, both now located several tens of kilometers south of the modern coastline.[1] Our most significant contribution was the discovery of an unknown river channel that flowed past the New Kingdom fort excavated at Tell el-Borg and emptied into the paleolagoon.[2] We proposed that the channel represented an early distributary of the Pelusiac Nile.

We document the second phase of our geologic work (2005–2007) in this chapter. Our objective was to study an area that is known as the former location of lakes and wetlands, known as the Ballah Lakes, which were essentially drained with the construction of the Suez Canal in the

1. A. Sneh et al., "Holocene Evolution of the Northeastern Corner of the Nile Delta," *Quaternary Research* 26 (1986) 194–206; Vincent Coutellier and D. J. Stanley, "Late Quaternary Stratigraphy and Paleogeography of the Eastern Nile Delta, Egypt," *Marine Geology* 77 (1986) 257–75; Bruno Marcolongo, "Évolution du paléo-environnement dans la partie orientale du Delta du Nil depuis la Transgression Flandrienne (8000 B.P.) par rapport aux modèles de peuplement anciens," *CRIPEL* 14 (1992) 23–31; Manfred Bietak, *Avaris the Capital of the Hyksos: Recent Excavations at Tell el-Dabʿa* (London: British Museum, 1996).

2. Stephen O. Moshier and Ali El-Kalani, "Late Bronze Age Paleogeography along the Ancient Ways of Horus in Northwest Sinai, Egypt," *Geoarchaeology* 23/4 (2008) 450–73; Stephen O. Moshier, "Geologic Setting of Tell el-Borg with Implications for Ancient Geography of the Northwest Sinai," in *Excavations in North Sinai: Tell el-Borg I* (ed. James K. Hoffmeier; Winona Lake, IN: Eisenbrauns, 2014) 62–83.

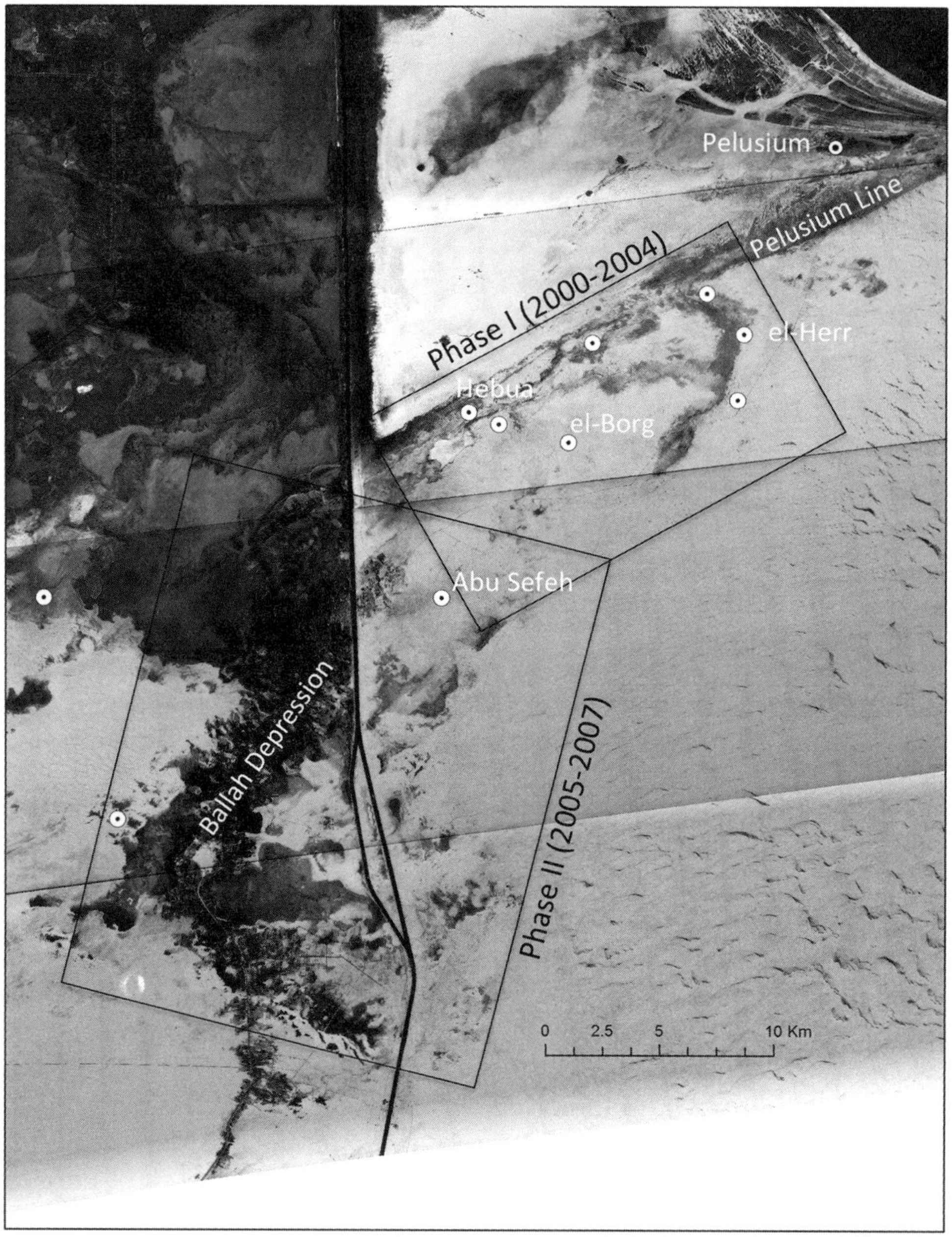

Fig. 2.1. Study areas for phase I, 2000–2004, (northern rectangle) and phase II, 2005–2007 (southern rectangle), plotted on georectified CORONA space image (ca. 1968). Circles mark selected archaeological sites.

late nineteenth century (fig. 2.1, lower rectangle). The small lakes occupied a depression that aligns with the position of the paleolagoon. A well-known map by Bietak[3] features the lakes as they may have existed in the Bronze Age, based upon the outlines of 0 m contours (sea level) from early to middle 20th-century topographic maps (see *Tell el-Borg I*, 39, fig. 50). We suspected that the "Borg-Pelusiac" channel continued south through the Ballah depression, based on the course mapped in the phase one study area, and connected somewhere with the Nile system north of modern Cairo.

3. Bietak, *Avaris: The Capital of the Hyksos*, 2, fig. 1.

Fig. 2.2. Field photograph in Ballah depression south of Qantara City, east of Suez Canal showing percussion drill rig.

Methods

Field methods included examination of subsurface materials obtained by shallow hand-dug pits (generally to about 1 m depth) and manual percussion drilling with a bailer to retrieve sediment (generally to about 5 m depth; fig. 2.2). Sediment texture, composition, and color were described in the field and thicknesses of distinct deposits were measured in order to compile detailed stratigraphic logs (see the Appendix, pp. 16ff.). Representative samples were collected and returned from the field for additional textural and compositional analysis. A digital elevation model for the study area was created using GIS and topographic data from several generations of government maps (from British surveys of the early 20th century to Egyptian government quadrangle maps of recent decades). Sediment mineralogy was determined for selected samples by X-ray Diffractometry at the Egyptian Geological Survey. Radiocarbon dates from *Cerastoderma glaucum*, a marine clam of the family Cariidae, were determined by Beta Analytic.

Surface Deposits and Natural Landforms

The study area in the Ballah depression appears flat from horizon to horizon, with scattered sand dunes; however, there are places where distinct changes in topography mark ancient shorelines. A surveyed transect extending 320 m from the top of one shoreline bank measured a drop of 3.5 m over a distance of 100 m, followed by a more gentle slope over the next 220 m to 5.5 m below the upper level of the bank (fig. 2.3). It is possible that some of the lakes may have approached or exceeded 6–8 m deep when bank-full. While largely drained, artificial levees have been constructed in the depression to impound water for aquiculture. One such reservoir existed at the time of our study between the natural shoreline and the eastern embankment of the Suez Canal south of el Qantara City (specifically, below the eastern approach ramp to the Egyptian-Japanese Friendship Bridge). Vintage maps (early to middle 20th century) refer to many of the lower areas as subject to frequent inundation (presumably by sea water during large storms). No natural, active drainage patterns are evident, although irrigation canals bisect the study area on the west side of the Suez Canal south of el Qantara (and more recently on the east side of the Suez Canal, northeast of el Qantara).

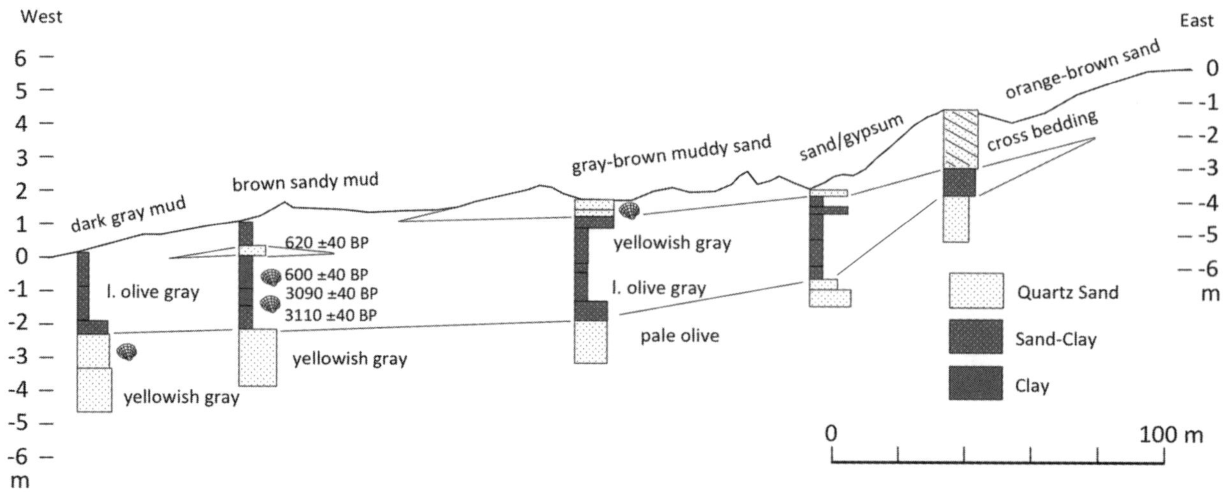

Fig. 2.3. Surveyed traverse and land elevation profile and subsurface stratigraphy approaching an ancient shoreline.

A surface geology map that includes phase one and phase two study areas was published in 1975, based upon aerial multispectral, thermal and visible light imagery, and ground mapping (reproduced in fig. 2.4).[4] Surface materials and environments mapped include deposits of clay, sandy clay, gravel, eolian sheet and dune sand, and marshes-sabkhas (signifying muddy wetlands and intermittently wet mudflats). The latter occupy the bottoms of former lakes and ponds. At many localities in the Ballah depression, we observed a thin cover of wind-reworked, very coarse gypsum and medium-coarse quartz sand over subsurface deposits.

Subsurface Deposits

Three general categories of subsurface sediment were encountered in the study area. They are similar to sediments reported from the contiguous study area to the north.

Basal Sand

An extensive deposit of unconsolidated quartz sand underlies the study area. Typically, the moderately well sorted, medium-to-coarse quartz sand appears very pale brown, yellowish-gray or yellow-brown (fig. 2.5). The deposit is found exposed at the surface or covered by muddy or coarse sand deposits (described below). This "basal sand" unit is the foundation for all archaeological structures at Tell el-Borg. The unit probably corresponds to the Pleistocene Al Qantarah Formation of the Geologic Map of the Northwest Sinai (Geological Survey of Egypt) and was formed by the reworking of alluvial-coastal deposits during Late Pleistocene transgression.[5]

4. E. M. El Shazly and M. A. Abdel Hady, *Geological and Geophysical Investigations of the Suez Canal Zone* (Cairo: Remote Sensing Research Project, Academy of Scientific Research and Technology, 1975).

5. Sneh, "Holocene Evolution," 194–206; Coutellier and Stanley, "Late Quaternary Stratigraphy and Paleogeography," 257–75.

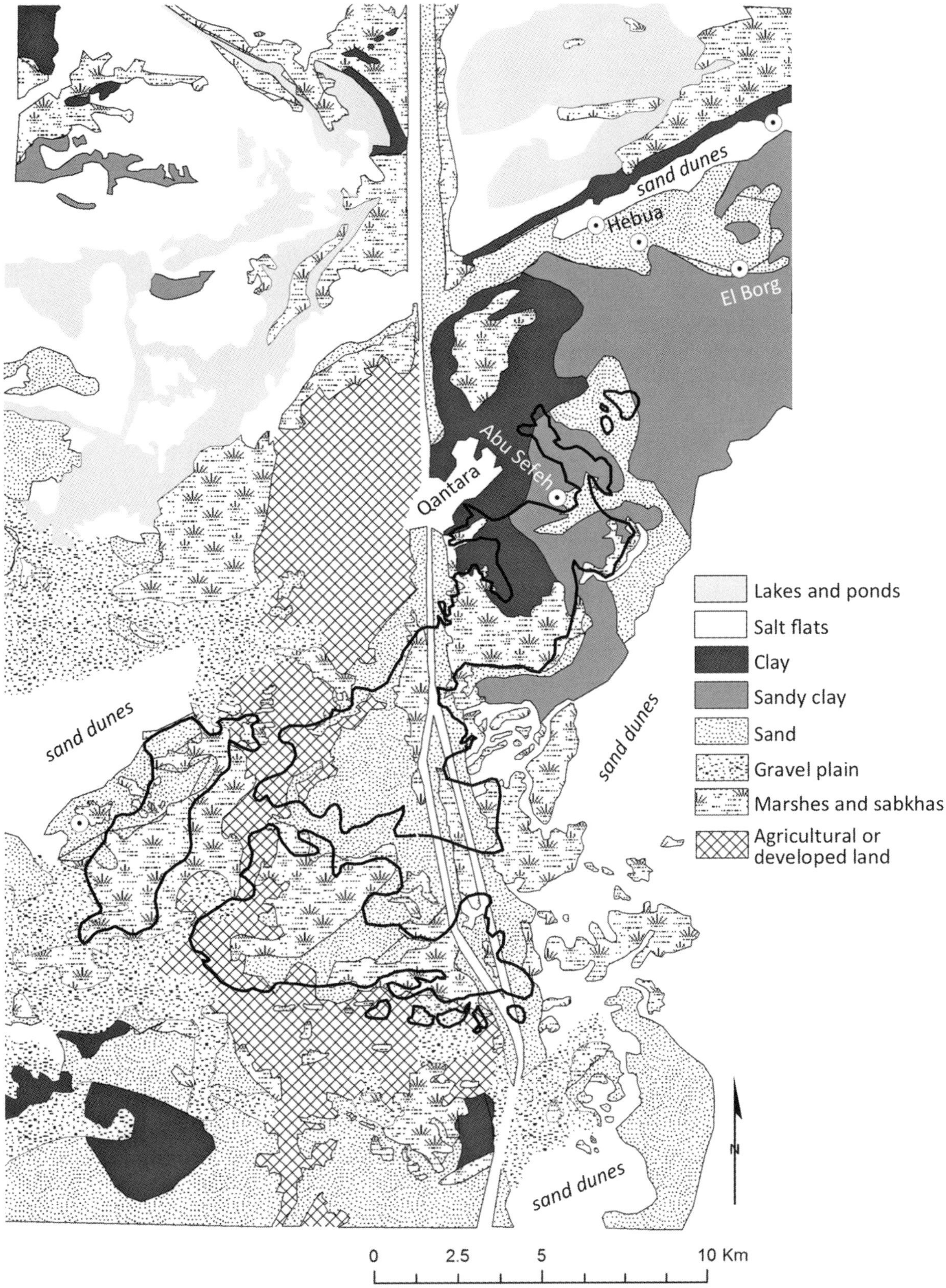

Fig. 2.4. Map of surface sediments and environments in the study area (after El Shazly and Abdel Hady; see n. 4) with outline of Ballah Lakes (0 m contour).

Fig. 2.5. Sediment from subsurface deposits: Basal sand (cm scale with mm divisions).

Fig. 2.6. Sediment from subsurface deposits: Mud with Cerastoderma glaucum shells.

Mud and Sandy Mud

Isolated muddy deposits contain proportions of sand, silt, and clay corresponding to the compositions of loam, sandy loam, sandy clay, and sandy clay loam (fig. 2.6). Color is typically medium gray with shades of olive, pale orange, or brownish-black. These deposits are generally no more than 3 m thick and pinch out against the natural embankment (shoreline) surrounding the depression. The most common macro-invertebrates in the sediment are cockle-bivalve mollusk *Cerastoderma glaucum* and small turriculate gastropd *Pirenella conica*. Both taxa tolerate a range of salinity conditions and are common inhabitants of Mediterranean and Mesopotamian estuaries, lagoons, and inland saline lakes, including modern Nile settings.[6] Mud and muddy sand deposits are interpreted as representing inland lake environments.

Coarse Sand (Sublitharenite)

Our subsurface probes recovered thick deposits of poorly sorted, medium-to-coarse and very coarse sand composed of quartz with lesser amounts of feldspar and rock fragments (fig. 2.7). Color of the sand is generally yellowish gray or light-to-dark olive gray. Quartz sand includes monocrystalline, polycrystalline, and microcrystalline varieties derived from intrusive igneous, volcanic, metamorphic, and sedimentary bedrock sources. Feldspar includes plagioclase and microcline, which are derived from both granite and porphyritic basalt. Pyroxene and amphibole are present (1–5%) and show remarkable lack of alteration by chemical weathering. Garnet is present in some samples, but very rare. Rock fragment lithologies include granite, serpentinite, sandstone, and limestone and reach the size of pebbles in some horizons. Point counts of sand in thin section mounts are recorded for selected deposits in the Appendix. Average contents of 84.6% quartz, 5.6% feldspar, and 9.7% rock fragments corresponds with the Folk sandstone classification of sublitharenite.[7]

6. Maria Pia Bernasconi and D. J. Stanley, "Molluscan Biofacies and Their Environmental Implications, Nile Delta Lagoons, Egypt," *Journal of Coastal Research* 10 (1994) 440–65.

7. Robert L. Folk, *Petrology of Sedimentary Rocks* (Austin, TX: Hemphill, 1974) 182.

Fig. 2.7. Coarse, fluvial sand (cm scale with mm divisions).

Intact *Cerastoderma glaucum* shells are less common in the coarse sand than in the muddy deposits. Fish remains recovered from coarse sand in two probes are fragments of the cranium (cephalo-nuchal shield) and pectoral spine of *Synodontis sp.*, a freshwater mochokid catfish found in the Nile River system.[8] A bone fragment similar to the operculum (hard bony flap covering and protecting the gills) of *Tilapia sp.* was also recovered.[9]

Coarse sand deposits are interpreted as representing fluvial channel environments. Identical coarse sand was observed in the "Borg-Pelusiac" channel in the phase-one study area. We interpret these sands as deposited in a contiguous fluvial system between the Ballah depression and the Bronze-Age coast paleo-lagoon setting to the north.[10]

Stratigraphic Framework

The lateral distributions of shallow subsurface deposits were correlated between clusters of 23 probes in the Ballah depression, between Tell Abu Sefêh, east of the Suez Canal, and an area west of "Ballah Island," where the canal bifurcates into two channels, south of el Qantara (fig. 2.8). Fence diagrams were drawn to visualize subsurface stratigraphy (figs. 2.9 and 2.10).[11] Correlations reveal widespread distribution of coarse sand, interpreted as deposited in fluvial channels, overlain by isolated deposits of mud and muddy sand, interpreted as deposited in shallow lakes. The probes along the shoreline transect (fig. 2.3) reveal how the lacustrine muds pinch out against the ancient shoreline.

Carbon-14 dates from *Cerastoderma glaucum* provide limited chronostratigraphic control for the deposits. Along the shoreline transect, shells in lacustrine mud yield conventional radiocarbon ages of 620 ±40 BP[12] at 0.8 m depth and 600 ±50 BP at 1.7 m depth. Calibrated to calendar

8. Douglas J. Brewer and Renée F. Friedman, *Fish and Fishing in Ancient Egypt* (Warminster: Aris & Phillips, 1989) 90–91.

9. Ibid., 89.

10. Moshier and El-Kalani, "Late Bronze Age Paleogeography along the Ancient Ways of Horus."

11. Fence diagrams are commonly used in stratigraphic studies to illustrate subsurface geology. They provide a perspective view from above, looking obliquely at the subsurface stratigraphy, akin to looking at a fence with panels showing correlations of deposits between fence posts, which represent the strata in the probes.

12. BP is abbreviation of Before Present, which in standard use means before A.D. 1950.

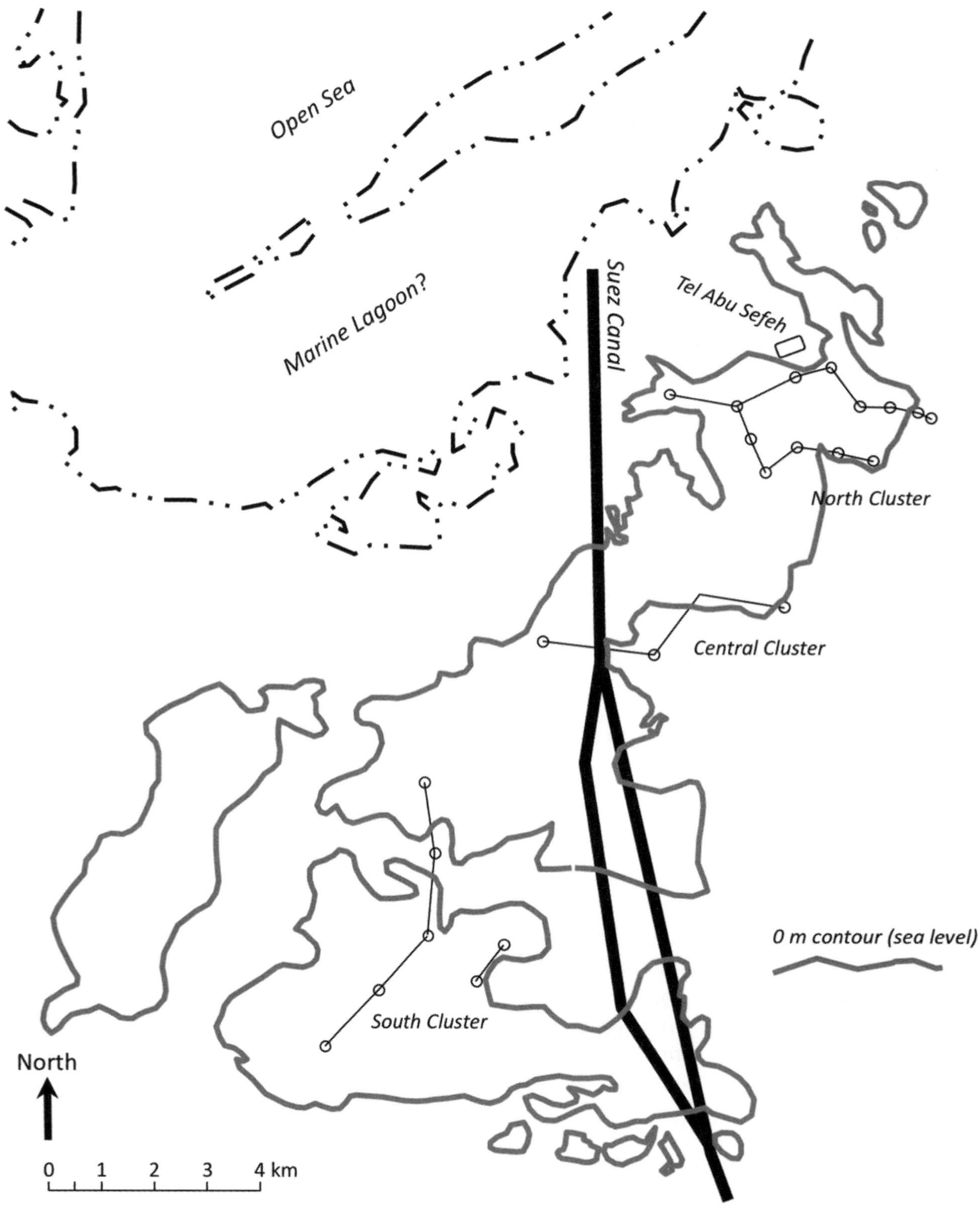

Fig. 2.8. Location of probes in the study area with ties between probes represented as stratigraphic cross-sections in figs. 9 and 10 (below). Approximation of Bronze Age coastline north of study area is depicted.

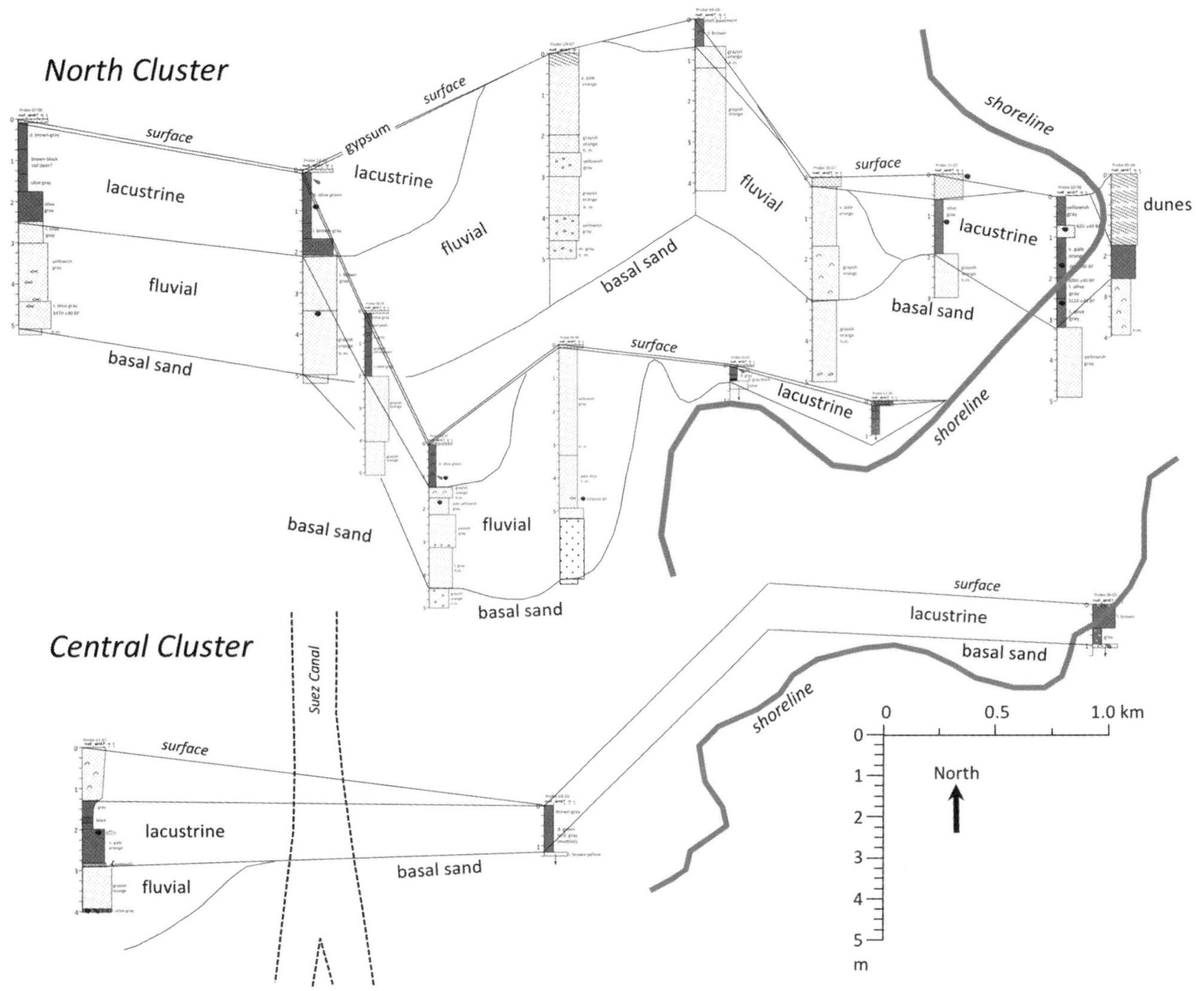

Fig. 2.9. Fence diagram cross-sections of subsurface deposits correlated between probes, north and central clusters.

dates, these results represent with 95% confidence (2 sigma) deposition between 660–540 BP and 660–530 BP, respectively. A significant shift to much older dates are represented in two shells recovered below 2 m: 3090 ±40 BP at 2.1 m depth and 3110 ±40 BP at 2.6 m depth. Calibrated to calendar dates, these results represent with 95% confidence (2 sigma) deposition between 3380–3220 BP and 3390–3240 BP, respectively. These two clusters of dates in the 3-m-thick deposit suggest an initial phase of widespread lacustrine deposition across the depression some 3300 years ago, followed by lake recession over the next two millennia, until a return to more widespread lacustrine conditions after 700 years BP.

Cerastoderma glaucum shells in coarse, fluvial sand between 4 and 5 m depth in two probes yielded conventional radiocarbon dates of 3350 ±50 BP and 3470 ±40 BP. Calibrated to calendar dates, these results represent with 95% confidence (2 sigma) deposition between 3700–3460 BP and 3640–3480 BP, respectively. It is likely that these sands were deposited in a fluvial channel

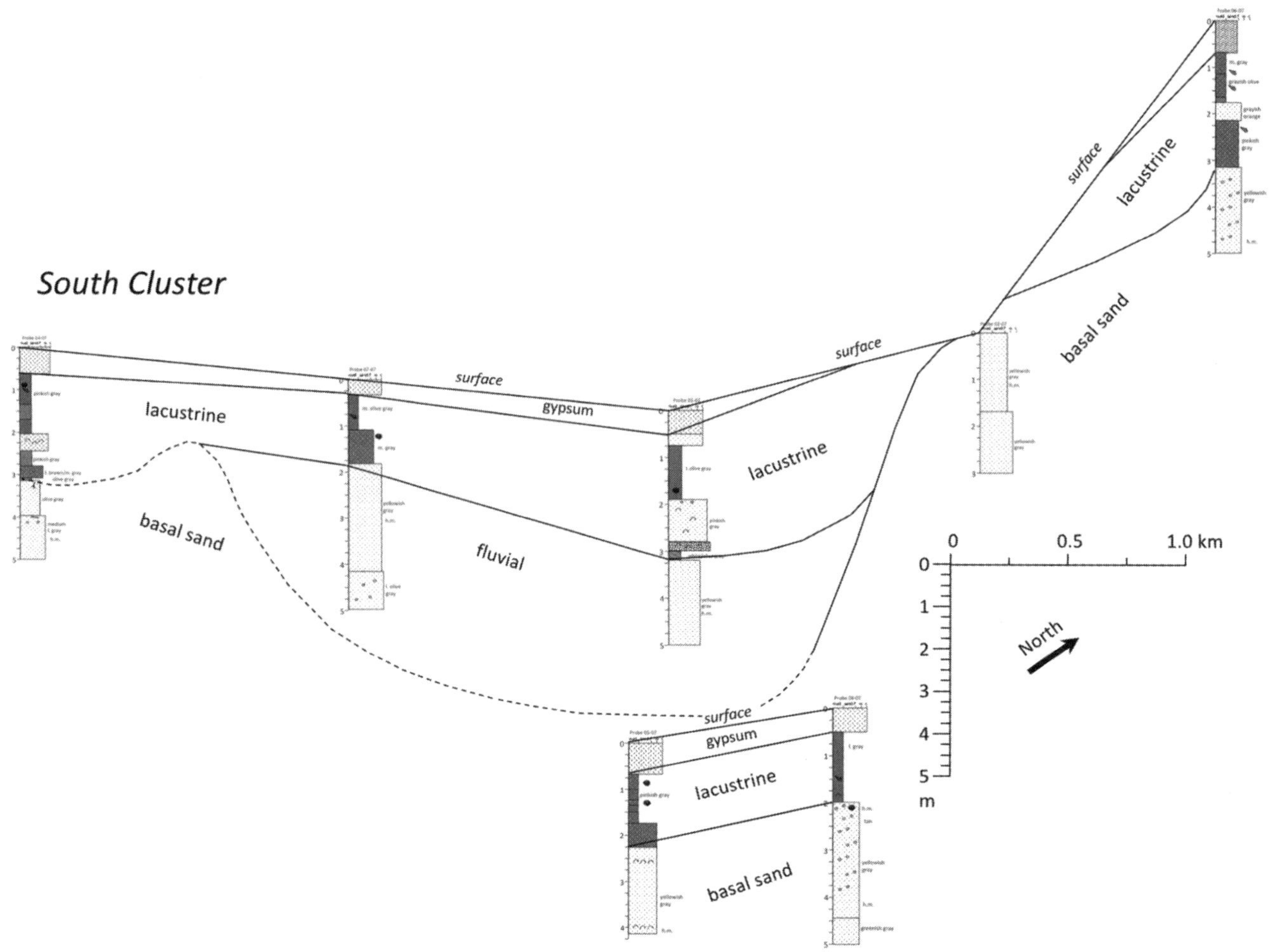

Fig. 2.10. Fence diagram cross-sections of subsurface deposits correlated between probes, south cluster.

that was generally contemporaneous with the initial phase of lacustrine deposition documented in the shoreline transect (described above).

Delineation of Early Pelusiac Branch and Ballah Lakes

Based upon the current topography and distribution of subsurface deposits, it is possible to trace the pathway of an ancient distributary of the Nile system that flowed through the Ballah depression and emptied into the paleolagoon near the site of Tell el-Borg. It is likely that the channel is one of the earliest distributaries of the Pelusiac branch that was active in the Eastern Nile Delta during ancient times.[13] A system of small lakes and wetlands, represented by the muddy deposits, existed along the course of the channel. Areas within closed map contours at 0 m (sea level) provide a reasonable but not definitive outline of the lake shorelines (as depicted in fig. 2.9,

13. Rushdi Said, *The River Nile: Geology, Hydrology and Utilization* (New York: Pergamon, 1993).

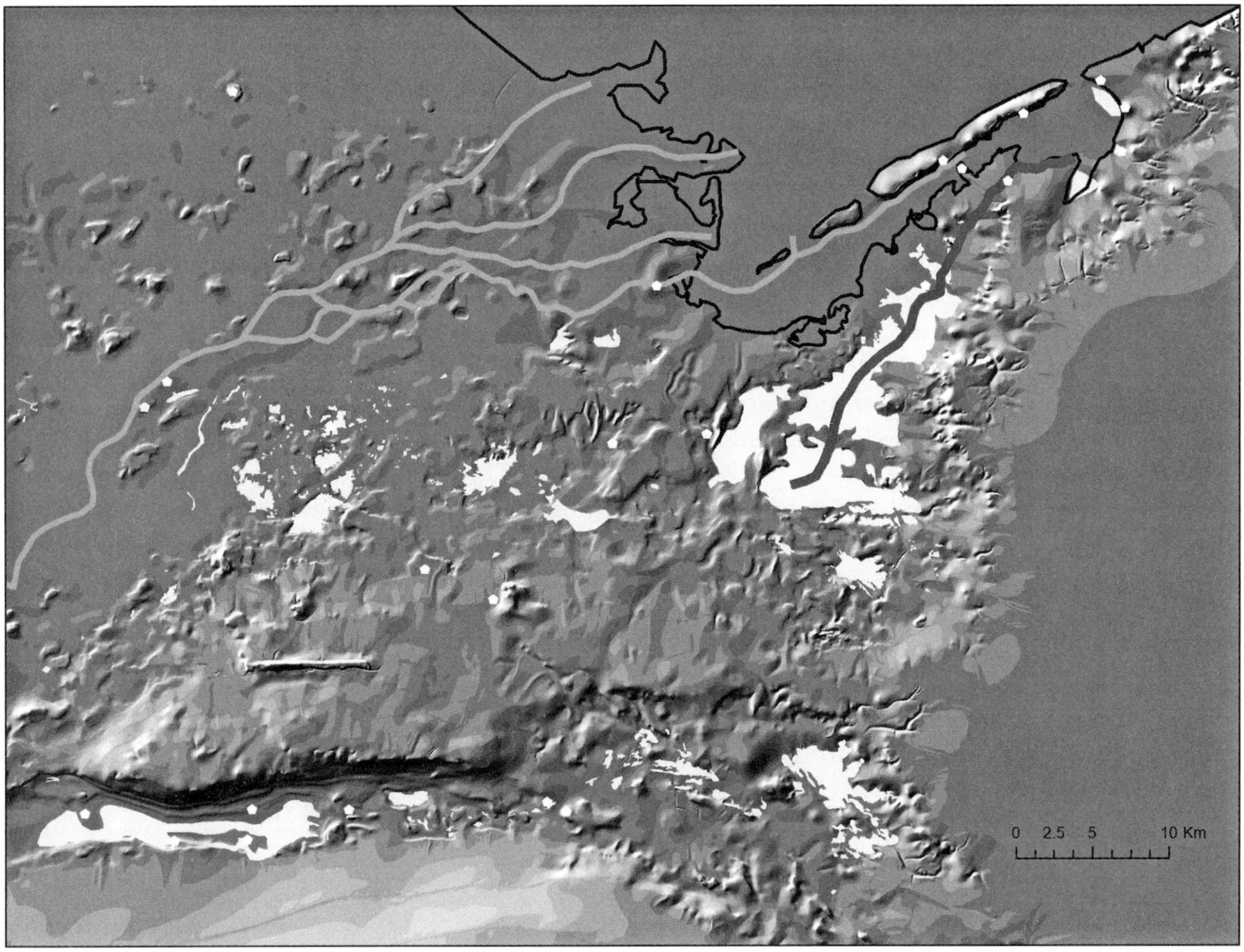

Fig. 2.11. Shaded relief map based upon digitized topographic map contours depicting physical geography during the Bronze-Age. Ballah Lakes delimited by 0 m contour, other lakes appear on historical topographic maps published during first half of 20th century. Borg–Pelusium channel based upon distribution of fluvial deposits discovered in this study. Western Pelusiac channels from Bietak (1996). Selected archaeological sites marked.

after the paleogeographic map of Bietak).[14] Figure 2.10 depicts the extended path of the Pelusiac-Borg channel, plotted on a shaded relief map derived from digitized topographic contours on vintage maps (avoiding modern changes to the land surface, including the Suez Canal, modern highways, and agricultural canal systems).[15] Pelusiac channels west of the study area, delineated by Bietak's survey of the eastern delta, are traced in fig. 2.11.

---

14. Bietak, *Avaris the Capital of the Hyksos*, 2, fig. 1.

15. Topographic data digitized from 1:50,000 and 1:25,000 maps produced by various British surveys of the early and middle 20th century, on file at the Center for Ancient Middle Eastern Landscapes, Oriental Institute, University of Chicago.

IMPLICATIONS FOR ARCHAEOLOGICAL SITES

The river course and associated lakes and wetlands within the Ballah depression leading to the Sinai coast were strategic for the siting of at least two significant ancient military installations: Tell el-Borg (New Kingdom, Dynasties 18–20) and Tell Abu Sefêh (Roman). It appears that the initial phase of fort construction at Tell el-Borg was abandoned due to flood destruction of the foundation, resulting in the second phase of construction shifted to higher ground. Excavations at Tell Abu Sefêh revealed a port with stone quays (piers for boats), presumably along a Ballah lakeshore or riverbank. Crocodile remains were found by one of the quays.[16]

Pottery recovered from the channel course at Tell el-Borg spans New Kingdom to Roman cultures. Active flow from the Nile continued in this channel until at least the time that the fort at Tell el-Borg was abandoned (or more generally when all of the Eastern Frontier forts were abandoned with the demise of the New Kingdom [ca. 1000 B.C.]). Historically normal to above normal Nile flow is recorded from 1570 B.C. to 1240 B.C. (3653 to 3190 BP) followed by low Nile flow from 1200 B.C. to 945 B.C. (3150 to 2895 BP).[17] At the beginning of the low Nile interval, corresponding with the 20th Dynasty, Pelusiac distributaries west of the study area at Avaris (Tell Dab'a) and Pi Rameses (Qantir) silted up resulting in abandonment of those settlements.

We suspect that the Pelusiac-Borg channel was canalized for boating between Roman settlements in the eastern Delta, such as from Tell Abu Sefêh (on a northern Ballah Lake) to Tell Herr to Pelusium, long after active Nile flow ceased. A final Pelusiac distributary built the delta plain of Tina, north of the Pelusium line (Bronze-Age coast), reaching the site of ancient Pelusium by either Egypt's Third Intermediate Period from about 1070 to 712 B.C. or during the Late Period from 712 to 332 B.C.[18] The distributary reaching Roman Pelusium was no longer active by the time longshore currents deposited wide strand-plain of sand along the coast of the Tina Plain in front of the river mouth during the 9th century A.D.[19]

APPENDIX: DRILLING RESULTS (PROBE LOGS)

PROBE 01–06 SHORE TRAVERSE (11 April 2006) 30.85072833°N, 32.37984333°E

0–1.0 m	Light gray sandy clay.
1.0–2.0 m	Light olive-gray to pale olive sandy clay. 1.00 m: XRD–Kaolinite, Montomorillonite, Illite, Calcite. 1.75 m: XRD–Montomorillionite, Kaolinite, Illite, Feldspar?
2.0–2.4 m	Light olive gray, muddy medium sand with rock fragments.
2.4–3.4 m	Yellowish gray, poorly sorted, fine to coarse sand with fragmented and whole mollusk shells.
3.4–4.7 m	Yellowish gray medium-coarse sand with rock fragments, few shells, fine-medium sand at bottom.

16. See James K. Hoffmeier, *Israel in Egypt: The Evidence for the Authenticity of the Exodus Tradition* (Oxford: Oxford University Press, 1999) 183, where this find is reported based on a verbal communication from Mohamed Abd el-Maksoud, the excavator.

17. Said, *The River Nile: Geology, Hydrology and Utilization*, 150.

18. D. J. Stanley, Maria P. Bernasconi, and Thomas F. Jorstad, "Pelusium, an Ancient Port Fortress on Egypt's Nile Delta Coast: Its Evolving Environmental Setting from Foundation to Demise," *Journal of Coastal Research* 24 (2008) 451–62.

19. Glenn A. Goodfriend and D. J. Stanley, "Rapid Strand-plain Accretion in the Northeastern Delta in the 9th Century A.D. and the Demise of the Port of Pelusium," *Geology* 27 (1999) 147–50.

PROBE 02–06 SHORE TRAVERSE (11 April 2006) 30.85057°N, 32.38039333°E

0–0.7 m Yellowish gray, sandy clay with scattered pebbles.
0.7–1.0 m Yellowish gray silt and fine sand. 0.7 m: *C. glaucum* shell Conventional radiocarbon age 620 ±40 BP, 2 sigma cal: BP 660–540.
1.0–2.0 m Very pale orange clay with shells. 1.70 m: *C. glaucum* shell Conventional radiocarbon age 600 ±50 BP, 2 sigma cal: BP 660–530.
2.0–2.5 m Light olive gray clay. 2.0 m: *C. glaucum* shell Conventional radiocarbon age 3090 ±40 BP, 2 sigma cal: BP 3380–3220.
2.5–3.2 m Light olive gray sandy clay with shells, increasing sand content with depth. 2.5 m: *C. glaucum* shell Conventional radiocarbon age 3110 ±40 BP, 2 sigma cal: BP 3390–3240 and root tube (?) nodules.
3.2–4.9 m Yellowish gray, clean, moderately sorted, medium sand with rock fragments (quartzite or chert), coarse sand at 4.90 m.

PROBE 03–06 SHORE TRAVERSE (11 April 2006) 30.85024333°N, 32.381345°E

0–0.3 m Mixed sand and shell fragments.
0.3–0.5 m Pale brown sand with *C. glaucum* shell hash (ave. 0.5 cm dia.).
0.5–0.85 m Pale brown muddy sand.
0.85–1.9 m Yellowish gray clay. 1.35 XRD- Calcite, Kaolinite, Montomorillonite
1.9–2.2 m Pale yellowish brown clay with sand. 1.9 m: XRD–Calcite, Kaolinite, Illite, Montomorillonite, (Gibbsite?).
2.2–3.05 m Light olive gray clay with sand and fine shell fragments. 2.2 m: XRD- Illite, Quartz?, Calcite? 2.75 m: XRD–Calcite, Quartz, Kaolinite?, Montomorillonite?
3.05–3.65 m Gray clayey sand.
3.65–4.9 m Pale olive, fine-medium sand, with rock fragments at 4.25 m. 4.9 m: Very pale orange well sorted medium sand.

PROBE 04–06 SHORE TRAVERSE (11 April 2006) 30.85001°N, 32.38205333°E

0–0.15 m Surface wind-blown sand.
0.15–0.5 m Mixed sandy clay with gypsum.
0.5–0.7 m Brown black muddy sand with shells.
0.7–1.50 m Gray sandy clay with small shells.
1.5–2.3 m Light olive gray clay with fine sand.
2.3–2.7 m Light olive gray clay with medium sand.
2.7–3.0 m Fine sand.
3.0–3.2 m Coarse sand with rock fragments.
3.2–3.5 m Coarse sand.

PROBE 05–06 SHORE TRAVERSE (11 April 2006) 30.849718°N, 33 32.38236°E

0–1.75 m Yellowish brown, wind-blown, coarse sand.
1.75–2.6 m Clayey sand.
2.6–3.9 m Fine sand with fragmented mollusk shells, coarse sand with heavy minerals at bottom.

PROBE 06–06 (12 April 2006) 30.84388°N, 32.35709°E

0–0.10 m Brown-gray, clayey sand with coarse gypsum crystals. *C. glaucum*.
0.1–3.3 m Yellowish gray, clean, well sorted, fine-medium sand with heavy minerals, rock fragments (black and tan).
3.3–7.0 m Pale olive, clean, fine-medium sand with heavy minerals and rock fragments. 4.6 m: *C. glaucum* shell Conventional radiocarbon age 3350 ±50 BP, 2 sigma cal: BP 3700–3460; catfish scales. 5.0 m- coarse sand with rock fragments.
7.0–7.1 m Medium sand.

PROBE 07–06 (12 April 2006) 30.853135 °N, 32.331165°E

0–0.1 m Hard surface sand and clay with gypsum.
0.1–0.75 m Dark brownish gray clay.
0.75–1.3 m Brownish black clay with ped-like structures (gravel size clots).

1.3–1.75 m Olive gray sandy clay. 1.30 m: XRD–Kaolinite?, Quartz?, Calcite?, Montomorillonite?. 1.45 m: XRD–Kaolinite, Illite, Calcite?
1.75–2.5 m Olive gray clayey medium sand.
2.5–3.0 m Light olive gray, fine-medium sand with minor clay. Quartz 83%, Feldspar 8%, Lithic Fragments 9%.
3.0–4.4 m Yellowish gray, clean, fine-coarse sand with granite, sandstone and limestone rock fragments and fish scales (scales at 3.7, 3.9–4.0 m, 4.4 m). Quartz 84.3–88.2%, Feldspar 1.4–6.5%, Lithic Fragments 6.7–10.4%.
4.4–5.2 m Olive gray, coarse-very coarse sand with granite, sandstone and limestone rock fragments, clay balls, bone or scale material. 4.7 m: *C. glaucum* shell Conventional radiocarbon age 3470 ±40 BP, 2 sigma cal: BP 3640–3480 (scales at 4.65 m, 4.7 m). Quartz 81.1–90.4%, Feldspar 0.0–4.0%, Lithic Fragments 6.7–18.5%.
5.2 m Grayish yellow, fine-medium sand with heavy minerals. Quartz 81.5, Feldspar 6.9%, Lithic Fragments 11.6%.

PROBE 08–06 (13 April 2006) 30.84519667°N, 32.3478°E
0–0.1 m Brown sandy clay with gypsum.
0.15–0.4 m Olive gray clay with shells.
0.4–0.7 m Olive gray sandy clay with carbon traces (roots) and blocky structure (soil peds?).
0.70–1.4 m Grayish olive green clay (5GY 3/2) with small (mm) shell fragments. 90 cm: XRD-Illite, Kaolinite, Montomorillonite, Quartz?, Feldspar?
1.40–2.05 m Light olive gray clay. 1.40 m: XRD- Kaolinite, Montomorillonite, Quartz, Calcite, Dolomite?
2.05–4.05 m Grayish orange, clean, medium-coarse sand with rock fragments and mollusk shells. 2.2 m: recovered watery clay-sand mix, probably thin clay bed in sand or clay matrix.
4.05–5.10 m Grayish orange, medium sand.

PROBE 09–06 (13 April 2006) 30.85814667°N, 32.36363167°E
0–0.7 m *C. glaucum* shell pavement over light brown sandy clay with shell fragments.
0.7–1.2 m Grayish orange, medium-coarse, well-rounded sand with common heavy minerals.
1.2–4.2 m Grayish orange, poorly sorted fine-coarse sand.

PROBE 01–07 (24 July 2007) 30.8096455°N, 32.30623967°E
Surface Windblown sand, brown, medium-coarse sand, poorly sorted.
0.1–1.3 m Wet, gray, fine sand, well sorted, with small shells. Coarser sand at top of interval.
1.3–1.7 m Gradational contact with overlying unit to sandy, gray clay.
1.7–1.85 m Gray (top) to black (base) pure clay.
1.85–2.0 m Gray sandy mud.
2.0–2.8 m Very pale orange muddy sand (loamy). 2.0 m: recovered wood fragment and *C. glaucum* shell.
2.8–3.0 m Fine-medium sand with heavy minerals. Porous pebble rock fragments with root tubules (paleosol).
3.0–3.6 m Grayish orange medium-coarse sand.
3.6–3.8 m Grayish orange fine-medium sand with scattered sandstone fragments.
3.8–3.9 m Grayish orange fine-coarse sand with heavy minerals.
3.9–4.0 m Light olive gray muddy, medium-coarse sand with heavy minerals, *C. glaucum* and *P. conica*

PROBE 02–07 (24 July 2007) 30.77218233°N, 32.2847525°E
0–1.7 m Yellowish gray fine-medium, well sorted sand.
1.7–3.0 m Yellowish gray medium-coarse, well sorted sand.

PROBE 03–07 (24 July 2007) 30.75784933°N, 32.283272°E
0–0.5 m Gypsum and quartz sand.
0.5–0.75 m Coarse sand with gypsum crystals.
0.75–1.9 m Light olive gray clay. 1.7 m: *C. glaucum* shells.

1.9–2.8 m Pinkish gray coarse-very coarse sand with shell fragments. 1.9 m: recovered 2 cobbles composed of cemented sediment.
2.8–3.0 m Pinkish gray very coarse and pebbly sand with shell fragments.
3.0–3.2 m White and olive gray silty clay in cm-laminae.
3.2–5.0 m Yellowish gray medium-coarse sand with heavy minerals.

PROBE 04–07 (25 July 2007) 30.7382995°N 32.26240833°E
0–0.8 m Gypsum and quartz sand, white, coarse, loose crystals.
0.8–1.3 m Pinkish gray clay with shells (*C. glaucum*, *P. conica*, *Donax sp.*?).
1.3–1.7 m Pinkish gray silty clay.
1.7–2.1 m Pinkish gray clay.
2.1–2.45 m Gypsum and muddy sand with shell fragments.
2.45–2.8 m Pinkish gray silty clay with fine sand.
2.8–3.1 m Light brown, muddy, fine-medium sand with cm-oval medium gray reduction patches.
3.1–3.15 m Very light olive gray silty clay.
3.15–3.95 m Olive gray fine sand with minor clay and root fragments.
3.95–5.0 m Medium light gray medium sand with heavy minerals and plant fragments. 4.15 m: abundant pebble rock fragments.

PROBE 05–07 (25 July 2007) 30.74977233°N, 32.29323517°E
0–0.7 m Gypsum and quartz sand.
0.7–1.0 m Pinkish gray sandy clay with small *C. glaucum* shells.
1.0–1.25 m Pinkish gray clay (minor sand).
1.25–1.3 m Pinkish gray sandy clay with small *C. glaucum* shells.
1.3–1.35 m Pinkish gray sandy clay with large *C. glaucum* shells.
1.35–1.45 m Pinkish gray clay.
1.45–1.55 m Pinkish gray sand clay.
1.55–2.1 m Pinkish gray medium sand with rock fragments and heavy minerals.
2.1–4.15 m Yellowish gray medium sand. Small *C. glaucum* and *P. conica* at 2.6 m and 4.15 m. Heavy minerals and rock fragments at 4.15 m.

PROBE 06–07 (25 July 2007) 30.7847875°N, 32.2824255°E
0–0.7 m Agricultural soil.
0.7–1.15 m Medium gray clay with medium-coarse sand.
1.15–1.6 m Grayish olive sandy clay with fragmented small gastropods and pockets of dark grayish black clay. 1.35 m: whole small *P. conica*.
1.6–1.75 m Silty clay.
1.75–2.15 m Grayish orange fine-medium sand with heavy minerals.
2.15–3.15 m Pinkish gray muddy fine sand with small *C. glaucum* and very small *P. conica*.
3.15–5.0 m Yellowish gray clean fine-medium sand with sandstone pebbles.

PROBE 07–07 (25 July 2007) 30.74798317°N, 32.27321433°E
0–0.35 m Gypsum and quartz sand.
0.35–1.05 m Medium olive gray clay. 0.75–0.85 m: hash of small gastropods and *C. glaucum*.
1.1–1.8 m Medium gray muddy sand with large *C. glaucum* shells.
1.8–4.2 m Yellowish gray medium-coarse sand with abundant rock fragments.
4.2–5.0 m Light olive gray very coarse sand with quartz pebbles.

PROBE 08–07 (25 July 2007) 30.75633083°N, 32.299014°E
0–0.5 m Gypsum and quartz sand.
0.5–2.0 m Very light gray clay with grayish orange pockets. 0.9 m: dense clay with small shell fragments and scattered rock fragments. 1.25 m: dense pure clay. 1.45–1.55 m: gastropod clay hash. 1.8 m: dense clay with shell fragments and minor sand and pebbles.
2.0–4.6 m Yellowish gray medium-fine sand with *C. glaucum* shells, heavy minerals and sandstone pebbles and gravel.
4.6–5.0 m Greenish gray fine-medium sand.

PROBE 09–07 (26 July 2007) 30.85640417°N, 32.35646433°E

0–2.0 m	Very pale orange coarse sand, wind blown at surface.
2.0–2.4 m	Grayish orange coarse sand with rock fragments and heavy minerals.
2.4–3.0 m	Very pale orange coarse-very coarse sand with small quartz pebbles.
3.0–3.9 m	Grayish orange coarse sand with rock fragments and heavy minerals.
3.9–4.6 m	Yellowish gray coarse sand with abundant small quartz pebbles.
4.6–5.0 m	Medium gray medium-coarse sand with abundant rock fragments and heavy minerals.

PROBE 10–07 (26 July 2007) 30.85128417°N, 32.36938067°E

0–0.25 m	Gypsum and quartz sand.
0.25–1.7 m	Very pale orange medium-coarse sand.
1.7–3.0 m	Grayish orange medium-coarse sand with shell fragments and rock fragments.
3.0–5.0 m	Grayish orange medium sand with heavy minerals and rock fragments. 4.7 m: cm-diameter flat limestone pebbles (local Eocene bedrock?).

PROBE 11–07 (26 July 2007) 30.85129724°N, 32.37546635°E

0–0.65 m	Gypsum, quartz sand and *C. glaucum.*
0.65–1.9 m	Olive gray silty clay with scattered *C. glaucum.* 1.15 m: abundant *C. glaucum.*
1.9–3.0 m	Grayish orange medium sand with abundant heavy minerals.

PROBE 12–07 (27 July 2007) 30.85107267°N, 32.34477533°E

0–0.1	Gypsum, quartz silt and *C. glaucum.*
0.1–1.3	Dark olive green clay with gastropods. 0.9 m: *C. glaucum* hash in clay.
1.3–1.7	Light brownish gray sandy clay.
1.7–2.1	Muddy sand with sandstone rock fragments and pebbles.
2.1–3.4	Light brownish gray coarse-very coarse sand.
3.4–5.0	Grayish orange coarse-very coarse sand with heavy minerals and *C. glaucum* fragments.
5.0–5.2	Grayish orange fine-medium sand.

PROBE 14–07 (27 July 2007) 30.83967067°N, 32.35082383°E

0–0.05 m	Gypsum and quartz sand.
0.05–1.35 m	Dense dark olive green clay with shell fragments.
1.35–1.65 m	Grayish orange coarse sand with heavy minerals and *C. glaucum* fragments.
1.65–2.2 m	Pale yellowish gray medium sand with *C. glaucum* fragments.
2.2–3.2 m	Pinkish gray very coarse angular sand with some calcareous sandstone gravel. (early lithification of sediment?) and red rock fragments.
3.2–4.4 m	Light gray coarse sand with very coarse rounded rock fragments and heavy minerals.
4.4–5.0 m	Grayish orange medium sand with very coarse rock fragments, small quartz pebbles and heavy minerals.

CHAPTER 3

Public Space at Tell el-Borg: Field II, Areas 1–3

Gregory D. Mumford
UNIVERSITY OF ALABAMA AT BIRMINGHAM

3.1. INTRODUCTION

Our attention was drawn to the area on the south side of the tell because of the large number of broken pieces of limestone, granite, and other elite stones, including what appeared to be a large block partially protruding from the sands. Furthermore, this area, known as Field II at Tell el-Borg, is located to the southeast of a late 2nd Intermediate Period to early Dynasty 18 settlement with reed structures (Field VI), to the southwest of a New Kingdom cemetery (Field III), and to the northwest of a Dynasty 18 fort (Fields IV and VIII) and a Dynasty 19 fort (Field V) (fig. 3.1).

Field II is associated with a low hill in the northwest area of Tell el-Borg, lying on its southeast slope. It is situated beside an ancient, silted-up river channel that ran from southwest to northeast, separating the New Kingdom settlement and cemetery from the forts on the high ground to the southeast (fig. 3.2).

By 2007, Field II expanded to encompass a roughly rectilinear area of 100–150 meters (southwest to northeast) by 300 meters (east–west) (figs. 3.1–3.3) and is subdivided into three areas of investigation (Areas 1–3). The surface and sub-surface features in Field II have been investigated by surface observation, topographic mapping, magnetometer survey (*Tell el-Borg I*, chapter 7), and excavation. Regarding excavation results, Field II has yielded multiple occupation phases and diverse activity areas spanning most of the New Kingdom, with minimal Roman activity alongside the riverbank. The excavation units have revealed a silted-up course and bank of a river channel (Area 2, Unit D: eastern end of trench), an adjacent mud-brick structure ("shrine") and its environs (Area 2, Units D–I), a zigzagging walling system (Area 2, Unit A), a massive granite block, probably from a cultic installation (Area 2, Unit A Trench 1), portions of an ovoid-shaped pit with fragments from decorated blocks (Area 2, Units J and Ja–d), the remnants of a large, well-floored courtyard (Area 2, Units J–K; Area 1, Unit I), multiple layers with occupation debris (Area 1, Units E, F, G, and H), a large granite block (Area 1, Unit B), and a stone-lined "well" (Area 1, Units C, D, E, and F).

The following sections cover different parts of Field II, starting with Area 1, Units A–H (the stone-lined well and outlying areas), Areas 1–2 Units I–K (the pit and courtyard area), Area 2,

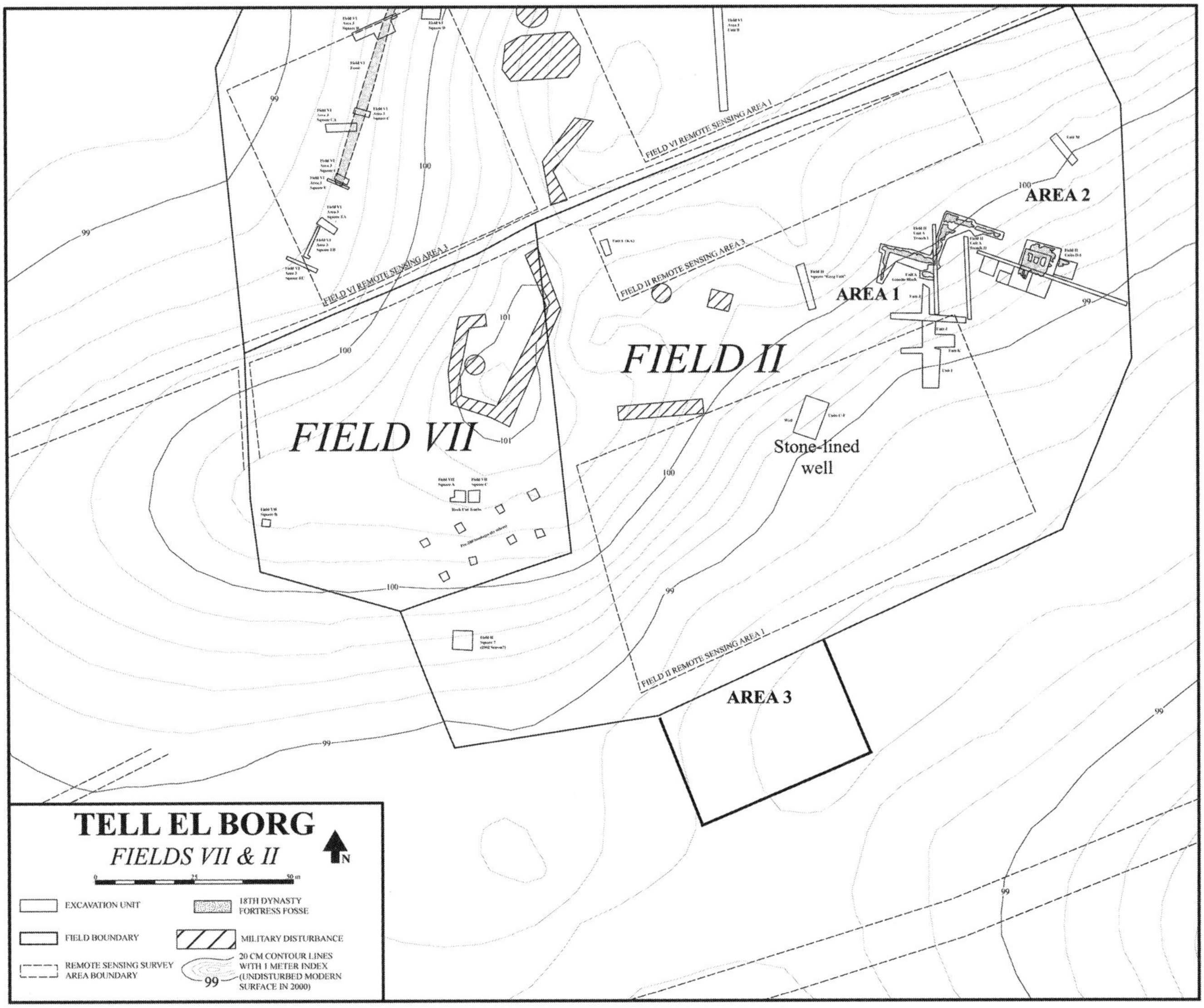

Fig. 3.1. Site Map 6, Field II, Areas 1–3 and Field VIII (prepared by D. Olney; digitized by J. Olsen).

Units A–I (the river channel and an adjacent structure and walling system), Area 3 (south end of Field II), and two outlying test units to the north (Unit L) and east (Unit M) in "Area 1" (perhaps more accurately labeled Areas "4" and "5"). The materials and analysis comprising this chapter have relied on the excavations and records of many persons: Louise Bertini (animal osteology [2004–2007]), Aaron Burke (Area 2, Unit I), Jeremy Cheek (Area 1, Unit H; assisting in Units E–F), Thomas Davis (Area 2, Units D–I; Area 3, Unit A), Rosa Frey (Area 1, Units A–C; Area 2, Units A–D), Scott Haddow (assisting in Area 1, Units D–I; Area 2, Unit E; human osteology), Tomasz Herbich (magnetometer survey in Fields II–VII), James Hoffmeier (director; field reports), Rexine Hummel (Field II pottery), James Knudstad (Areas 1–2 architectural plans), Michelle Loyet (animal osteology [1999–2002]), Ashraf Melika (Area 2, Units D–I), Stephen Moshier (Areas 1–3 magnetometer surveys), Gregory Mumford (Area 1, Units J–K; Area 2, Units E extension, and F–G), Lyla Pinch-Brock (small finds registration), and Linda Wilding (Unit A; database).

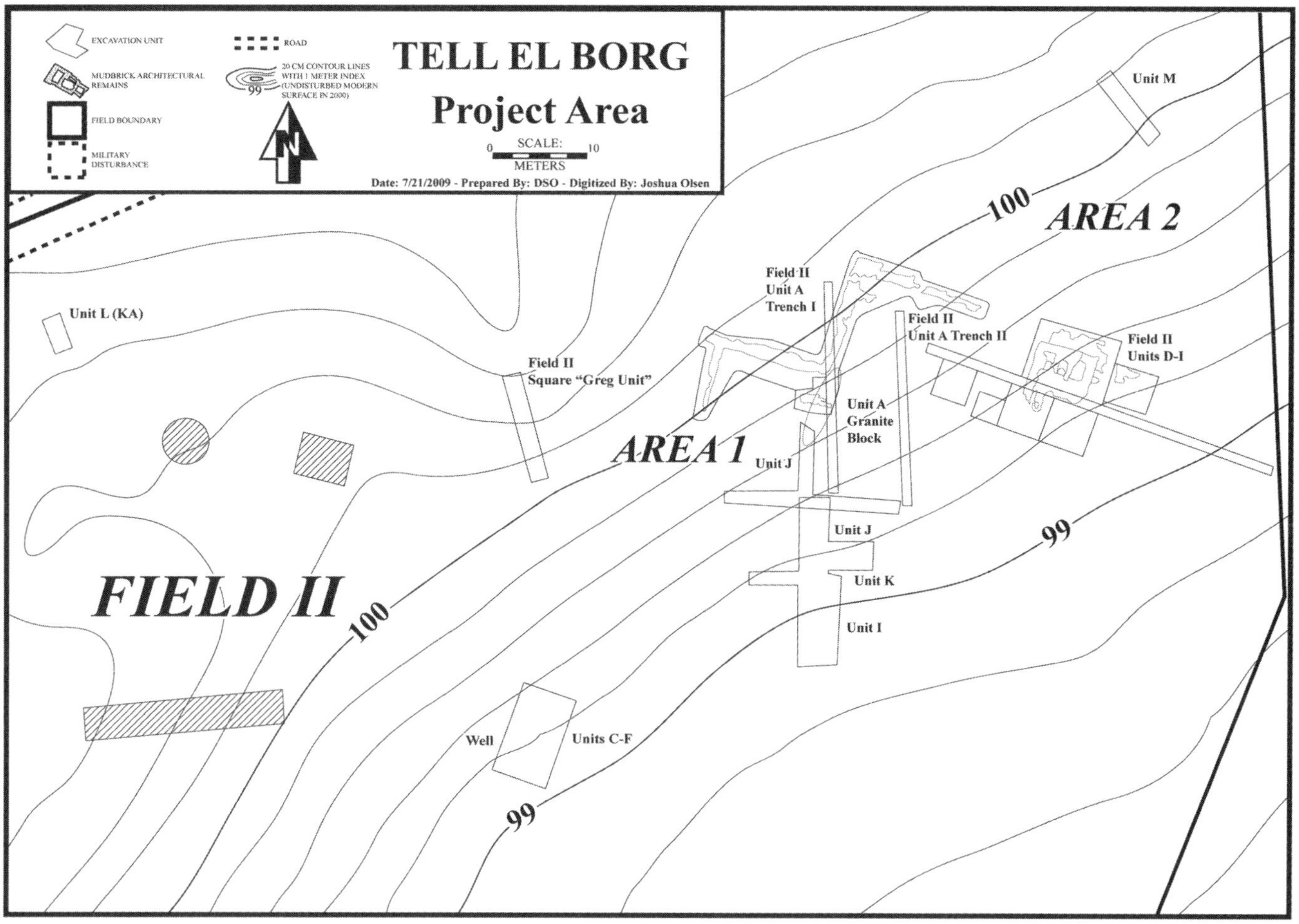

Fig. 3.2. Site Map 6, Field II detail of Areas 1–2 (prepared by D. Olney; digitized by J. Olsen).

Table 3.1 provides a general idea of the relative temporal relationships between physically separated areas, excavation units, and loci/layers within Field II. The ceramic evidence reveals early–mid Dynasty 18 to Ramesside period activity in Field II, with some evidence for Roman period and more recent disturbances. It should be noted that, in the initial excavation of various units, it was not always possible to differentiate the slope and undulations of multiple sand layers, especially where successive sand layers exhibited virtually identical colors and textures, often ranging from less than 1 cm to a few cm in thickness. Any temporal "mixing" of otherwise separate deposits (i.e., pottery and small finds) is indicated and reflected in the phasing within each excavation unit and area. The plotting—on sequential top plans—of the find-spot of many small finds, samples, some diagnostic potsherds, and other items, has allowed a reassessment of their phasing in relation to actual layer boundaries. In most cases, the period spanned by multiple sand layers is too short for any mixed pottery sequences to affect adversely the phasing of the stratigraphy throughout Field II. For example, the layers preceding the well in Units C–F may span a 50-to-100-year period in ten phases of deposition. The mixing of several sloping sand layers has created fewer differentiated deposits of pottery but still allows the dating of these 10 layers into several groupings of pottery dating from mid-Dynasty 18 to early Dynasty 19. The following discussion, plans, sections, and tables, in conjunction with additional data presented in

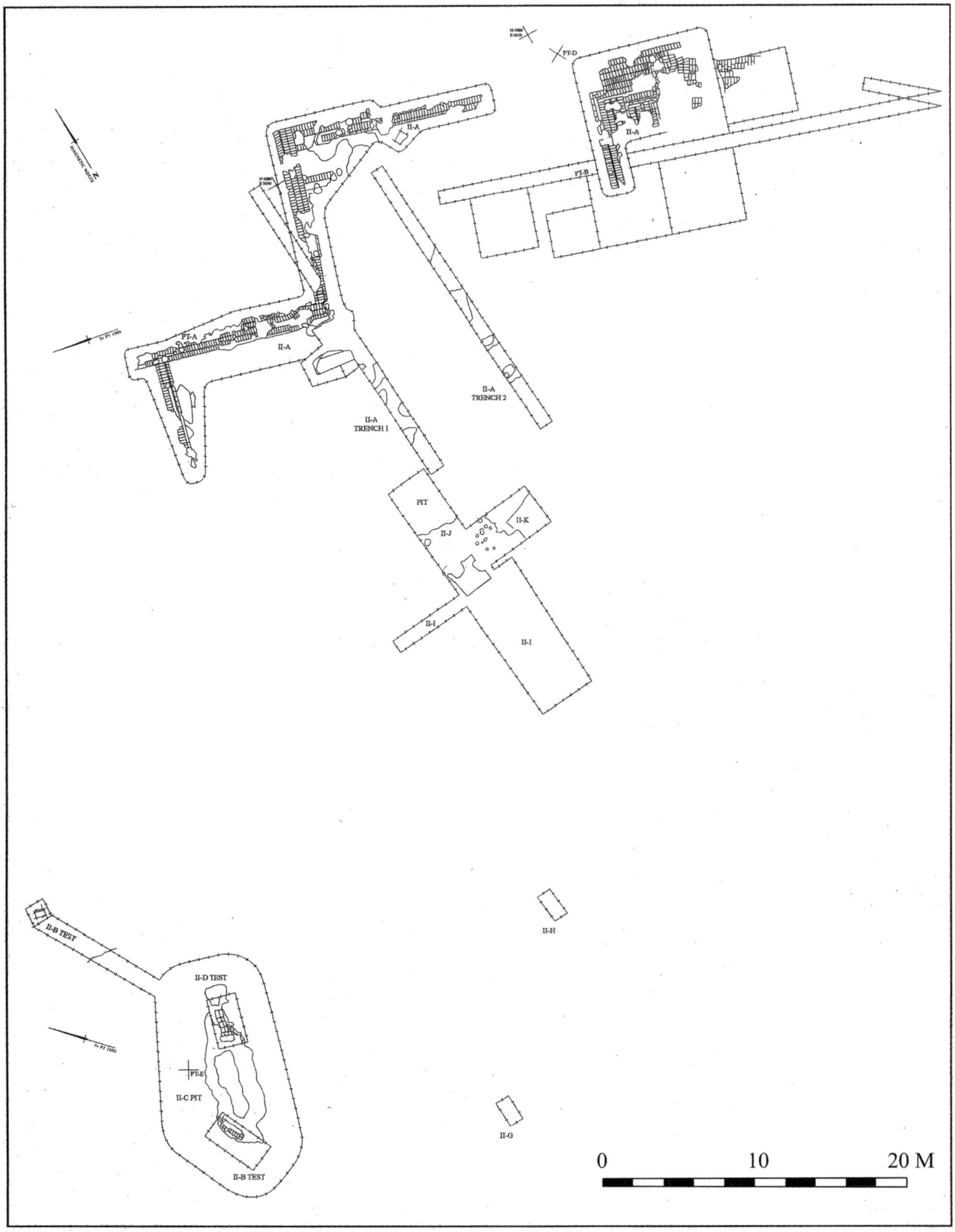

Fig. 3.3. Detailed view of Field II, Areas 1–2, including test pits G and H (prepared by D. Olney; digitized by J. Olsen).

the disk (Field II section), provide sufficient information for readers to search and reassess the suggested phasing.

Tables 3.2–3.42 summarize various excavation unit supervisors' records of material culture (small finds and other items) and Rexine Hummel's pottery information labels. In the following sections, the small finds' tables contain information extracted from excavation record books, small find cards, the "Tell Borg Object" (TBO) data recording system for registered small finds, drawings, and photographs. This data identifies each excavation unit (e.g., J for Unit J), locus (e.g., 3[N] for Locus 3, north side), pottery basket/sub-locus level/area (e.g., 1 for basket 1), local phase number (e.g., P9 for phase 9), site supervisor's small find or sample number (e.g., sf.2 for small find "2"; "[c]" for sample "c"), and, whenever possible, the official TBO registration number (e.g., TBO 0001). These tables also have descriptions of object types (e.g., lumps), materials (e.g., copper alloy), color and surface treatment (e.g., white slab with red pigment), dimensions (e.g., 1.7 × 0.8 × 1.5 cm), and comments (e.g., irregularly shaped lump). Similarly, the pottery tables provide pottery-label summaries for each locus and pottery basket, tabulating information about each excavation unit (e.g., E), locus and basket numbers (e.g., 19 b.1 for Locus 19 basket 1), local phase numbers (e.g., P3 for phase 3). This series of tables also gives the quantity of sherds in each pottery basket (e.g., scanty basket of sherds), the amount of rims, handles, and bases per pottery basket (e.g., "9", "–", and "4" for nine rims, no handles, and four bases), the percentages of Nile silts, desert marls, and other wares in each basket (e.g., 60%, 35%, and 5%), comments (e.g., small, worn body sherds; silt: red-slipped sherds; marl: gray-green slip), and a bottom row with sherd totals for pottery baskets (e.g., 132+ body sherds), diagnostic sherds (e.g., 101 rims; 9 handles; 22 bases), and the average proportion of ware types (e.g., 58% silt; 32% marls; 10% other wares). Both the small finds and pottery tables indicate where information is absent or missing for each locus and pottery basket, while an absence of small finds or pottery from an area or phase is reflected by a mention in the text, rather than generating an empty table.

Plates 3:1–6 at the end of this chapter illustrate a selection of the artifacts and materials found throughout Field II. A fuller presentation of drawings, photographs, plans, sections, and related data on materials from this area are available through the Tell el-Borg database on the internet: http://ochre.lib.uchicago.edu/publish?project=Borg. Illustrations in that database are designated in this chapter as OCHRE plates, followed by their number.[1]

These include (1) the stone-lined well (pls. 1–62), (2) the courtyard and Pit J (pls. 63–107), the zigzagging wall and granite block (pls. 108–12), the "shrine" and its environs (pls. 113–23), the Unit L test pit (pl. 124), the Unit M test trench (pls. 125–27), a reconstruction of Field II and surrounding fields (pl. 128), and a catalogue of photographs and drawings of items from Field II (pl. 129 nos.1–165). Each item in this catalogue is accompanied by its TBO number, field, area, locus, basket, material, and description, photograph, and drawing (where applicable) or detail photograph of each artifact/material type.

The original context for these items and materials may be located via the phase and locus summary table below or in the subsequent small find and pottery tables. Otherwise, it should be emphasized that the phasing noted throughout each discussion section and table (Phases 1–39) represents only a local phasing in each area, grouping of excavation units, or individual excavation units. Based upon the stratigraphy and datable potsherds and other materials, it has been possible to provide a rough relative sequence of periods within the New Kingdom (and later)

1. OCHRE = Online Cultural and Historical Research Environment, the name of the database of the Oriental Institute, University of Chicago.

Table 3.1. Strata and Loci in Field II, Areas 1–3

Dates	*Area 1: Units C–F loci*	*Area 1: Units G–H*	*Area 1: Units A–B, L–M*	*Area 1/2: Units I–K*	*Area 2: Units D–I*	*Area 2: Units A–C*	*Area 3: Unit A*
Early Dyn. 20?	**Post-well loci/layers (fill in well):** **P39:** D1, E100, F2-1, F1-(1-2), F6-1 **38–39:** D1, E101, F2-1, F1-(1-2), F3-1 **P38:** D2, F1-1, F4-(1-2) ***P37:*** *Lime layer-6* ***P36:*** *D2, F7-(1-2)* ***P35:*** *Lime layer-5* ***P34:*** *D4, F8-1*	G1 H1 G2 H2 G3 H3 G4 H4	**Surface** Unit L Unit M Loc.1-10	**Surface/pits:** I.1, J1, J2, K1 **Mottled sand** I.8-1, I.9-1, K2-1(E) **Large pit:** J3-1, J4-1 JA-C.2-4 J6-1, J7-1, J8-1,	**Surface:** Units D–I Locus 1 **Sterile pit:** D11-1	**Surface:** A1	A1 A2 A3
Late Dyn. 19	**P33:** D4, F9-(1-3) **P32:** D5, F11-(1-2) ***P31:*** *Lime layer-4* **P30:** D5, F12-(1-3) → (F15-F25) **P29:** D5, F12-(1-3) → (F15-F25) **P28:** D5, F12-(1-3) → (F15-F25) **P27:** D6, F12-(1-3) → (F15-F25) ***P26:*** *Lime layer-2* **P25:** D6, F15-(1-2) F25-2 **P24:** D7, F15-(1-2) F25-2 ***P23:*** *Lime layer-1*	G5 H5 G6,8 H6 G7,9 H7 G10 G11-1		JA-C.5-6 **Yellow sand** I.1-(1-6), I.2-1-2 J3-1(S), J5-(1-3), K2-1(W), K3-1(W), *Brick debris* J9-3, K3-1 I.3-1	**Tomb(?):** D, G Loci 4, 6, 8 **Floor pits:** I, E, D, 15,19, 20 **Floor pits:** D, E, I loci 16 and 17		
Early Dyn. 19	**P22:** D7, F16-1, F27-1 **P21:** D9, F17-1, F28-1 **P20:** D9, F18-1, F29-1 **P19:** D11, F18-F21-1, F32-1 **P17–18:** D11, F22-1, F33-1 **P16:** D12, F24-1, F34-1 **P16:** D12, F35-1 **P15:** D13, F37-1 **P15:** D13, F37-1→ F38-1 **P14:** D14, F39-1 **P13:** D14, F42-(1-5)	G11-2 **Slab** G12-1 G12-2 – – – –	**Blocks** Dyn.19	**Mud brick:** I.10, J10 **Sand layer:** J9-(1-2; 4), J11-1, K5-1 K4-1, I.4-1, I.5-1, I.11-1	**Wall:** F13-1 **Tower(?):** D, E, F Loci 2, 10, 12, 14, 19	**Zigzag wall** **Blocks** Dyn.19	
Late Dyn. 18 Early-mid. Dyn. 18	**Foundation loci for well:** **P12:** F45 (wall-curbing well) **P12:** F36-1 **P12:** F46-1 **P11:** Pit cutting			**Floor pits:** SanD–Filled **Mud brick:** I.10, J.0 **Floor:** I.5-1, I.12-1	**Occupation layer:** D, E, F 5, 11, 18		
	Pre-well occupation loci: **P10:** E102, F4-(3-5)/F7-3, F5-1 **P10:** E104, F8-2/F9-4, F5-1 **P10:** E104, F13/F14, F5-1 **P9:** E105, F/19/F20, F5-1/F10 **P8:** E104, F20/23, F10/F12/F40 **P7:** E106, F20/F25, F23/30, F12/40 **P6:**E106,F19/20/25,F23/30, F12/40 **P5:** E106, F20/25, F23-(1-3), F12-6 **P5:** E106, F20/25, F23-2-3, F40-1 **P4:** E107, F19/20, F30-1, F41-1 **P4:** E108, F25-1, F30-1, F41-1 **P3:** E109, F25-1, F30-1, F41/43-1 **P2:** E110, F25-1, F31-1, F44-1 **P1:** E110, F44-1			**Occupation layer:** I.6-1			
Basal/ Sterile layer	**P0:** Basal Sand, F45	*Phase-0* Basal Sand	*Phase-0* Basal Sand	*Phase-0* Basal sand Unit I.7-1	*Phase-0* Basal Sand Unit I.6-1	*Phase-0* Basal Sand	*Phase-0* Basal sand

Key to Table 3.1: P0, P1, P2, represent phase-0, phase-1, phase-2, etc.; E101, F5-1, F2-(1–5), G7, 8, are abbreviations for Unit E, Locus 101, Unit F, Locus 5, basket 1, Unit F, Locus 2, baskets 1–5, and Unit G, Loci 7 and 8. The omissions of basket numbers usually reflect "basket 1," leaving fuller listings of each basket number to tables 3.2–3.42 and the text. In general, the loci have been ordered from the earliest periods to the latest periods, but more complete details appear in the following sections.

Fig. 3.4. James Knudstad cleaning brick of "zigzag" wall by the granite block in Unit B (Photo: NSAP).

for each excavation unit and cluster of units across Field II. This relative chronological sequence is abbreviated in Table 3.1.

3.2. Field II, Area 1: Dynasty 18 Occupation and a Dynasty 19 Stone-Lined Well and Its Environs (Unit B)

During the 2000–2001 seasons at Tell el-Borg, survey and excavation work occurred in Area 1 of Field II. Investigations concentrated on granite blocks near the surface (Units/test trenches A-B), three modern pits exposing part of a New Kingdom (OCHRE pls. 3-4) stone-lined pit ("well") (Units C–F), and two test pits (Units G-H) in the adjacent low ground. Units I–J, which technically occur in Area 1, will be discussed in section 3.3 (Area 1/2) since they span the border between Areas 1 and 2. In 2000, Rosa Frey directed excavation work in Units C–D (OCHRE pls. 5–6), while Scott Haddow supervised the excavation of Unit E. In 2001, Gregory Mumford and Jeremy Cheek excavated Units E-(extension) and F–H, while James Knudstad planned the architectural features for the 2000–2001 seasons (OCHRE pls. 1–2).

3.2.1. Unit A in Field II
Excavator: Rosa Frey

The 2000 excavations at Tell Borg initiated work in Unit A in Field II, which subsequently spanned two subdivisions (i.e., Areas 1–2) of this portion of Tell el-Borg. Since Unit A is located mostly in what became Area 2 of Field II, it will be discussed after Area 1 (see below). Hence, Unit B will begin the sequence of excavation units examined in this section.

3.2.2. Granite Block (Unit B)
Excavator: Rosa Frey

Unit B lies 14.20 m to the north of the stone steps accessing the limestone lined well in Area 1. Unit B was laid out as a 1.50 × 1.50 m excavation unit surrounding a mostly buried granite block (*Tell el-Borg I*, figs. 22–23). This block (partially exposed) lay at the edge of a sand-filled pit and measured about 0.40 × 0.70 meters. When fully exposed, it measured 2.75 × 1.30 × 1.16 m and

Fig. 3.5. Granite block in Unit B near "zigzag" wall (Photo: NSAP).

weighs an estimated 12 tons (figs. 3.4–3.5). It is uninscribed and does not appear to be associated with the stone-lined well, and the pit in which it lay produced no potsherds. It represents one of many of the disturbed and redistributed New Kingdom stone blocks found across the surface of Tell el-Borg.

3.2.3. Stone-Lined "Well" (Area 1, Units C, D, E, and F)
Excavators: J. Cheek; R. Frey; S. Haddow; J. Knudstad; G. Mumford

Units C, D, E, E-extension, and F contain a sequence of Dynasty 18 occupation layers (OCHRE pls. 51–53), a Dynasty 19 foundation and an installation of a stone-lined "well" in a pit cutting through part of the Dynasty 18 layers, and the abandonment, in-filling, and reuse of a stone-lined well (OCHRE pls. 1–2, 6–11). In essence, the phases of activity in this area began with a series of ten mid-Dynasty 18 occupation and debris layers that accumulated successively over the sterile, basal sand at Tell el-Borg. The occurrence of a Dynasty 19 sherd in the upper levels of these ten phases is evidence that Phase-10 cannot have ended prior to the advent of Dynasty 19 (see below). At some point in early Dynasty 19, the inhabitants of the site excavated a 4.5 × 10 m ovoid pit to a depth of 2.5 m into the basal sand (OCHRE pls. 42 Unit C).[2] This pit was then floored and lined with a diverse collection of Dynasty 18 limestone architectural fragments (e.g., reused *talatat* blocks from a temple of Akhenaten, wall blocks, ceiling blocks, column bases, paving slabs), with some sand, clay, and mud-brick debris filling the space between the stone lining and the vertical face of the foundation pit (OCHRE pl. 43). The upper edge of the ovoid pit was lined with a narrow mud-brick wall, which curved around the outer perimeter of the ovoid pit (figs. 3.6–3.7). This stone installation was abandoned and filled-up with debris over time but included a series of six successive lime-plastered basins placed within the resulting depression.

2. A well in the "police barracks" at Tell el-Amarna consisted of a large pit accessed by mud-brick steps, located in a large courtyard: a "parade ground" (cf. J. D. S. Pendlebury, *The City of Akhenaten III* [London: Egypt Exploration Society, 1951] 133, pl. lii.2–4). Few details have been published concerning this well, and it seems to have been enlarged, possibly as a feature of the adjacent horse stable complex.

Fig. 3.6 (above). Mud-brick wall around top of ovoid pit, south view in Unit E (Photo: NSAP).

Fig. 3.7 (left). Mud-brick wall around southwest edge of stone-lined, ovoid pit (well), south view in Unit E (Photo: NSAP).

The function of the stone-lined ovoid pit has been discussed during the period of its investigation. The lack of lime plaster or any mortar sealing its side walls and base preclude its use as a cistern. The installation is defined by an ovoid pit cut into the basal sand, which also eliminates the possibility of passageways or chambers continuing beyond its visible surface boundary (i.e., there is no evidence to support its use as a tomb). Hence, the most likely function appears to be that of an open pool accessing shallow sub-surface, fresh—or perhaps a bit brackish—ground water. This feature appears to have had the same function as a similar stone-lined, stepped pit uncovered in Field IV; it was built against the outside wall of Fosse D of the earlier Dynasty 18 fort and dates to the Ramesside Period (see *Tell el-Borg I*, 262–74).

Excavation in the disturbed southern portion of the structure revealed that modern pitting had removed much of the paving stones and lining, but the otherwise apparently undisturbed deeper basal sand argues against a deep well shaft in this part of the pit.[3] The limestone block

3. A late Dynasty 18 well from Tell el-Amarna needed to extend fairly deep to reach the underlying water table. It has a roughly circular hole and lower ledge accessed by a rough stairway, with a second, lower, narrower shaft and stairway leading to the water table below (A. Galal, "A Large Well beside Building Q48.4," in *Amarna Reports V*, Egypt Exploration Society Occasional Publications 6 (ed. Barry Kemp; London: Egypt Exploration Society, 1989) 1–14, figs.1.1, 1.3a, 1.3b, and 1.6). Of note, a few reused architectural stone pieces did lie against this well shaft's side but represent steps placed in the well (Galal, "A Large Well beside Building Q48.4," 5, layer 1; 2, fig.1.1; 6–7, figs.1.3a–b; and 9, fig.1.4). More elaborate stone-lined wells appear in Egyptian temples, such as the mortuary temple of Ramesses III at Medinet Habu (Alexander Badawy, *A History of Egyptian Architecture: The Empire (the New Kingdom) from the Eighteenth Dynasty to the End of the Twentieth Dynasty 1580 – 1085 B.C.* (Los Angeles: University of Cali-

Fig. 3.8a–b. TBO II 36, amphora handle with cartouche of Nebkheperure, Tutankhamun (Photo: NSAP; drawing by Lyla Pinch-Brock).

lining maintained the integrity of the well's soft sand walls but allowed ground water to fill this installation; the placement of a mud-brick wall around the well's rim (see figs. 3.6–3.7 and OCHRE pls. 12a–b and 13) minimized the intrusion of wind-blown sand and grit into the open water below (for additional illustrations and plans for Field II, see OCHRE pls. 14–15a–b).

In the New Kingdom, prior to the cutting of the nearby Suez Canal (and the current As-Salaam irrigation canals), the water table was much higher in north Sinai, supporting a series of lagoons and marshes. Hence, it is likely that ground water could be obtained much closer to the New Kingdom ground surface than the 3.45-m-deep water table found 80 m to the east in Area 1, Unit D, Locus 7 (see below). After the abandonment and gradual in-filling of this shallow well, a successive plastering of six ovoid hollows suggests a change in activity in this area, either as a shallow water-catchment basin or, more likely, as a transitory shallow, basin-like installation requiring an impermeable, clean surface: the successive basins could hold a decreasing volume of approximately 12 to 6 cubic meters of liquid. Perhaps these shallow basins enabled the threshing of grain or the treading of grapes to produce wine in this famed wine-producing region near Tjaru. Indeed, grape seeds were discovered at Tell el-Borg (see Chapter 12, figs. 12.3a–b).

3.2.3.1. The Discovery of the Stone-Lined Shallow Well (Unit C)

In March 2000, the site guard, Hasan, drew Rosa Frey's attention to a 4 × 8 m depression containing a robber's pit and numerous sherds, six large limestone block fragments, and other debris around the perimeter of the pit (figs. 3.11–3.13; OCHRE pl. 16). He further noted that a set of limestone steps had been observed about 10 years earlier, when this feature was first disturbed. During the initial cleaning of Unit C, Frey assigned Locus 1 to the pit's upper sloping sides and Locus 2 to the base of the debris-filled depression (OCHRE pl. 17). The debris produced many limestone chips, several blocks, an immense amount of pottery (three full baskets of potsherds; two full baskets of field-sorted diagnostics), including Blue Painted pottery (Locus 1) and two stamped amphora handles with two royal cartouches stamped on them: (1) *nb ḫprw rʿ*, Nebkheperure—that is, Tutankhamun (TBO II 36; fig. 3.8a–b; for additional analysis of this, see Excursis I below) and (2) *ʿnḫ ḫprw rʿ*, Ankhkheperure—namely, Smenkhkare (TBO II 37; fig. 3.10a–b),[4] both in

fornia Press, 1968)146–47, fig. 97. Later examples appear at Tanis. However, these wells are much better built than the rough structure at Tell el-Borg.

4. For a photograph and drawing of this amphora handle impression, see *Tell el-Borg I*, fig. 173 and discussion on pp. 137–41. The reason for treating this find in the chapter discussing Field IV is because a

TBO II 61

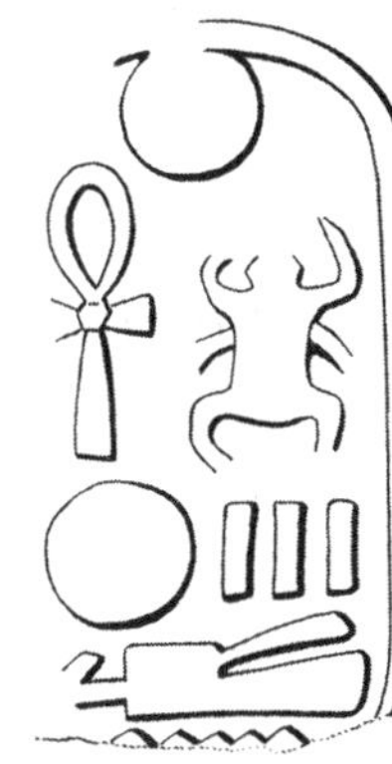

TBP 0207/TBO II 37
Ankhkhepperure wa en Re

Fig. 3.10a–b (above). TBO II 37, amphora handle with cartouche of Ankhkheperure, Smenkhkare (Photo: NSAP; drawing by Lyla Pinch-Brock).

Fig. 3.9 (left). TBO II 61, jar base bearing cartouche of Nebkheperure, Tutankhamun (Photo: NSAP).

Locus 2. In addition, a jar base with a second occurrence of Tutankhamun's cartouche (fig. 3.9) was found in the general vicinity of these two jar handles. Some modern items were also recovered (e.g., a rusted turnbuckle). The delineated strata exposed in the sides of the robber's pit revealed a series of six lime surfaces separated by debris layers (see below). Three robber's pits within the feature were exposed (fig. 3.13).

After removing the wind-blown sand and other materials, the initial depression (Unit C) was revealed to be a set of three debris-filled robber's pits, designated as Unit Ca, Cb, and Cc from south to north (fig. 3.13). Unit Ca measured approximately 7.20 × 4 m (north–south by east–west), while Units Cb and Cc extended 1.70 × 1.40 m and 1.80 × 1.40 m, respectively. The disturbed debris (Loci 1–3) from these units produced a broad range of items (Table 2): a disk with inlay, a sherd reshaped into a gaming piece, fragments from calcite unguent vessels, the lower parts of two amphoras, probably a chert utensil/awl(?) (pl. 3:6 no.1, TBO 098, registered perhaps mistakenly in "Area 2" of Field II "but otherwise from Unit C, Locus 3, basket 4), numerous potsherds (several full baskets with field-sorted diagnostics), a Cypriot juglet base, five/six subsurface fragments from limestone blocks, and five well-finished rectangular limestone blocks. A wall of dry-laid, roughly finished and reused limestone blocks was traced for at least six stepped courses along the east side of Units Cc and Cb. The best-dressed sides of each block were used to place the blocks side by side, minimizing the gaps between each reused piece. The excavators also relocated in Unit Cb the stone steps reportedly seen during the robbing of stone from this installation. The robber's pit had reached and partly destroyed the stone lining along the southern end of the well in Unit Ca (Locus 2) (see figs. 3.11–19).

nearly identical impression was found in the fosse of the 18th Dynasty fort. Because it was found near the top of the fill of Fosse D (Unit D 10, l. 2), the mention of this late Amarna-period royal figure suggests that the 18th Dynasty fort was in use until nearly the end of that period. For other discussions of TBO II 37, see J. K. Hoffmeier and M. Abd el-Maksoud, "A New Military Site on 'the Ways of Horus': Tell el-Borg 1999-2001: A Preliminary Report," *JEA* 89 (2003) 180–81; and J. K. Hoffmeier and J. van Dijk, "New Light on the Amarna Period from North Sinai," *JEA* 96 (2010) 199–200.

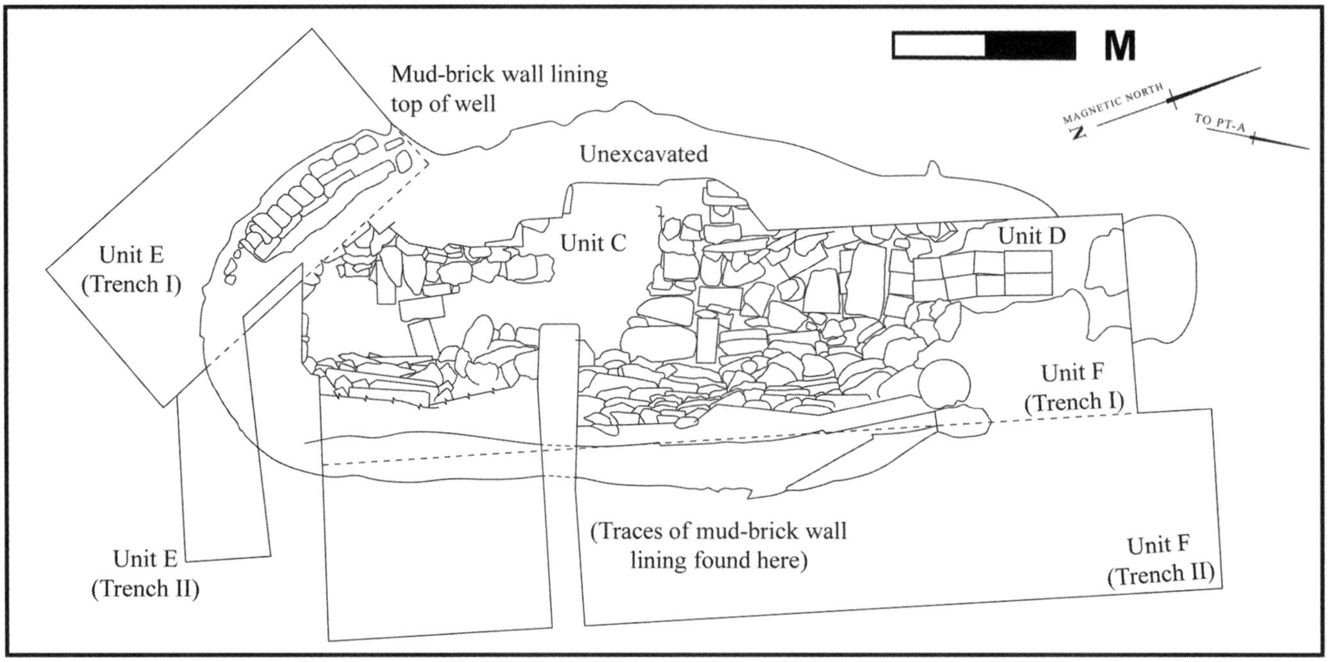

Fig. 3.11. Plan of stone-lined, ovoid well in Field II, Area 1 (Field drawing by James Knudstad; digitized by Joshua Olsen).

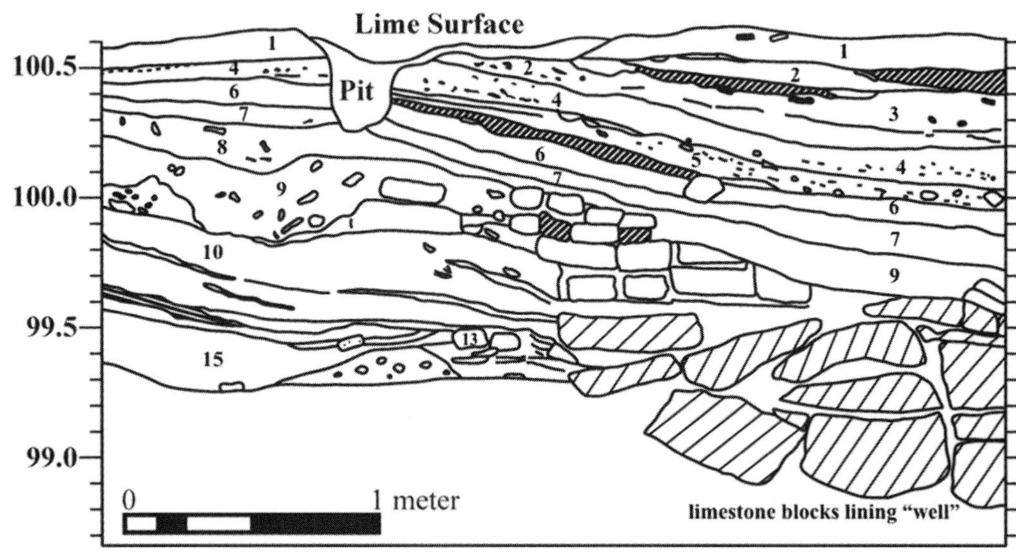

Fig. 3.12. East baulk of Unit D in stone-lined well (Field II) (drawn by Rosa Frey; digitized by Joshua Olsen).

The following sections will discuss the phases and nature of occupation in Units C–F.

3.2.3.2. Phase 0: Dynasty 18 Pre-Well Layer (Units D–F): Locus 45

The occupation in Field II is preceded by a deep layer of white basal sand that appears to be completely sterile and devoid of cultural and other materials. The upper portion of the basal sand does display some evidence of intrusive roots from vegetation that has since disintegrated into a black organic residue staining the sand. The upper portion of the basal sand was excavated as Locus 45 in Unit F, but yielded only sterile white sand (OCHRE pls. 47–49).

Table 3.2. Summary of Small Finds from Unit C (Post-Well Strata and Loci)

Unit	*Locus*	*Unit Book no.*	*TBO II no.*	*Object type*	*Material*	*Color and Surface Treatment*	*Dimensions (cm)*	*Comments: Frey's notes for Unit C*
Ca	Locus 1	30	TBO 0030	Two beads	Faience	1 is ivory colored; 1 is chalky white.	-	One is small and flat; Other is round & larger
Ca	Locus 2	31	TBO II 31	Perforated disk/tablet	Limestone	(white)	2.9 cm in diameter	Loom weight; from west pit area.
Ca	Locus 1	32	TBO II 32	Bead	Soapstone	Black and dark gray with small white specks	Small	No details
Ca	Locus 1	33	TBO II 33	Fragmentary ceiling block (reused as a door jamb)	Limestone	Traces of blue paint with six stars in relief.	-	Lower level of jumbled limestone block debris in robber's pit (Ca Locus 1)
Ca	Locus 2	34	TBO II 34	Block	Limestone	Fragment of relief decoration	-	Raised rectangular section; west pit fill.
Ca	Locus 2	35	TBO II 35	"Anchor" stone with a hole	Limestone	(white)	-	A tethering stone and/or an anchor
C	Locus 2	36	TBO II 36	Amphora handle	Ceramic	Stamped impression of a cartouche: nbkheperwre	-	Amphora handle bears cartouche of Tutankhamun
C	Locus 2	37	TBO 0037	Amphora handle	Ceramic	Stamped impression of a cartouche: ankh-kheperw-re W'-n-re	-	Smenkhkare
Ca	Locus 3	38	TBO II 38	Gaming piece	Ceramic	Sherd reshaped into a game piece	0.9 cm high by 1.4 cm in diameter	Potsherd reshaped into a game piece/counter.
Ca	Locus 1	42	TBO II 42	Base from a large mortar?	Stone	-	Large	Exterior chisel marks.
Ca	Locus 2	47	TBO II 47	Bead or scarab(?)	Frit (faience)	Red, blue, and colored faience	Small	Fragmentary amulet, possibly a scarab.
Ca	Locus 2	No SF number	TBO II 61	Amphora base	Ceramic	Stamped impression	-	Base of amphora bears a cartouche.
Ca	Locus 1	No SF number	-	Fragmentary basin	Limestone	3 pieces forming a corner from one basin	Maximum 71 × 43 × 15 cm	Basin depth = 6 cm (only one corner)
Ca	Locus 1	No SF number	-	14 fragments from blocks etc.	Limestone	Varying in size and shape	Max. 80 cm in length	No details
Ca	Locus 1	No SF number	-	Column base Fragment	Limestone	Half of a column base	About 83–85? cm in diameter	Described as almost half of a column base.
Ca	Locus 2	No SF number	-	Basin(?) fragment	Limestone	Limestone piece with a depression	Max. 20 cm preserved	Possibly originally part of a basin.
Cc	Locus 1	No SF number	-	Rectilinear block	Limestone	Well-dressed block	48–50 × 25–26 × 18–20 cm	Most tool marks appear as small hammered circular depressions; two opposite faces display smooth faces versus remaining rough sides
Cc	Locus 1	No SF number	-	Rectilinear block	Limestone	Well-dressed block	50–52 × 25–26 × 22 cm	Same as above
Cc	Locus 1	No SF number	-	Rectilinear block	Limestone	Well-dressed block	49 × 24–25 × 22–23 cm	Same as above
Cc	Locus 1	No SF number	-	Rectilinear block	Limestone	Well-dressed block	50 × 24–25 × 17–20 cm	Same as above
Cc	Locus 1	No SF number	-	Rectilinear block	Limestone	Well-dressed block	50–51.5 × 24–25.5 × 22.5–23 cm	Same as above (Best example with mason's marks)
Cb–Cc	Locus 1	No SF number	-	Block fragment	Limestone	-	Max. 44 x 30 × 7–8 cm	Originally from a larger block
Cb–Cc	Locus 1	No SF number	-	Block fragment	Limestone	-	Max. 63 × 36 × 12 cm	Originally from a larger block
Cb–Cc	Locus 1	No SF number	-	Block fragment	Limestone	-	Max. 44 × 43 × 10 cm	Originally from a larger block
Cb–Cc	Locus 1	No SF number	-	Block fragment	Limestone	-	Max. 54 × 36 × 17 cm	Found beside pit
Cb–Cc	Locus 1	No SF number	-	Roughly rectilinear block	Limestone	A roughly chiselled and roughly rectilinear block with a hole (jar stand?)	Max. 62.5 × 18–26 × 16–19 cm	19 cm diameter depression (6 cm deep)

Table 3.2. Summary of Small Finds from Unit C (Post-Well Strata and Loci)								
Unit	*Locus*	*Unit Book no.*	*TBO II no.*	*Object type*	*Material*	*Color and Surface Treatment*	*Dimensions (cm)*	*Comments: Frey's notes for Unit C*
Cb	Locus 1	No SF number	-	14 small – medium fragments	Limestone	-	-	No details
Cb	Locus 1	No SF number	-	Column base fragment	Limestone	Column base fragment	85 × 24 × 22 cm (diameter around 1 m)	No details
Cb	Locus 1	No SF number	-	Rectilinear block	Limestone	(white)	68 × 14–25 × 17–22 cm	Fragmentary and rough block.
Cb	Locus 1	No SF number	-	Square block	Limestone	(white)	44 × 37 × 16 cm	Fragmentary and rough block.
Cb	Locus 1	No SF number	-	2 large rectilinear blocks	Limestone	(white)	Large (similar to blocks above)	Fragmentary and rough block.

3.2.3.3. Phase 1: Dynasty 18 Pre-Well Layer (Units D–F): Loci E110 and F44 (OCHRE pls. 45–49)

The first phase is represented by a thin brown layer, which ranges up to 2 cm in thickness (Units E and F). This layer follows the undulating topography of the underlying basal sand. It was left mostly unexcavated, providing a firm capping consolidating and securing the soft basal sand overlooking the adjacent stone-lined pit ("well"). The excavation of Locus E110 and the lower half of Locus 44 (basket 1; phase 2) appear to have cut a little into this layer.

3.2.3.4. Phase 2: Dynasty 18 Pre-Well Layer (Units D–F): Loci E110, F25, F31, and F44 (OCHRE pls. 34, 45–46, 49)

The next layer (phase 2) represents the accumulation of wind-blown sand over the lower brown surface (phase 1). This material had collected within the hollows found throughout the underlying layer. This sand layer ranges from 6 to 20 cm thick and contains some inclusions: small gypsum nodules, pebbles, shell fragments, bone fragments, charcoal flecks, and some potsherds. It was excavated as the lower half of Locus F25 (basket 1), Locus F31 (basket 1), Locus F44 (basket 1), and Locus E110.

3.2.3.5. Phase 3: Dynasty 18 Pre-Well (Units D–F): Loci E109, F25, F30, and F41–43 (OCHRE pls. 33, 45–46, 49)

The subsequent sand layer (phase 3) is thicker, undulates across some low dunes, and ranges from 10 to 56 cm in depth. This sand layer is colored medium yellow. It is composed of fine-to-medium sand grains and contains some rough-to-dense clay nodules, shell fragments, gypsum nodules, some light yellow-gray sand patches, and potsherds. This matrix was excavated as the upper part of Locus F25 (basket 1), Locus F30 (basket 1), Locus F43 (basket 1), the lower half of Locus F41 (basket 1), and Locus E109.

3.2.3.6. Phase 4: Dynasty 18 Pre-Well (Units D–F): Loci E107–108, F19–20–25, F30, and F41 (OCHRE pls. 31–33, 45–46, 49)

The following layer is thinner, ranging from 17 to 25 cm and smooths out a little more the underlying undulating topography of phase 1. This sand layer contained multiple deposits of fine-to-medium gray sand, which had been deposited in at least three main layers (toward the south of Unit F). These layers contained some charcoal flecks, small ash lenses, shell fragments, and pieces of stone. In addition, the layer displays more diverse cultural and related debris, such as fragments

Fig. 3.13. Robber holes into the stone-lined pit, designated Units Ca, Cb, Cc (Photo: NSAP).

of bone, ostrich shells, small limestone chunks, mud-brick pieces (jumbled at different angles), and potsherds. A portion of a hard, white lime plaster surface was discernible toward the northern end of Unit F. Phase 4 was excavated as the lower part of Locus F19 (basket 1), Locus F20 (basket 1), the eastern, lower half of basket 2 of Locus F25, Locus F41 (basket 1), and Locus E107–E108. These loci produced potsherds, scattered animal bone fragments and teeth, a clam shell (F25), a copper alloy lump (F25), a sandstone pounder fragment (Locus F20), a ceramic disk ("token"; F25 sf.36; OCHRE pl. 61), and a flint blade with a serrated edge (F25 sf.35; OCHRE pl. 61) (see OCHRE pls. 61–62). It is uncertain whether the ceramic disk and serrated flint blade lay in phases 2, 3, or 4. Of note, a diagnostic bowl sherd (loc. F20) bearing interior red slip and burnishing, with a black stripe along the interior and exterior rim, indicates that this phase cannot pre-date early Dynasty 18.

3.2.3.7. Phase 5: Dynasty 18 Pre-Well (Units D–F): Loci E106, F19+F20+F25, F23+F30, and F40 (OCHRE pls. 30–31, 45–46, 49)

The phase 5 sand layer varies from 7 to 13 cm but is mostly a fairly uniform depth, with a tightly undulating upper surface in the low ground beside a small dune. This upper rippling was likely caused

Fig. 3.14. Two northern robber holes (Units Cb–Cc) cutting into the stone-lined pit (Photo: NSAP).

by wind action, rather than water. Phase 5 was excavated as Loci F19 (basket 1), F23 (basket 1), F25 (basket 2), F40 (basket 1), and Locus E106. This layer yielded a flint blade (Locus F40) and potsherds (see OCHRE pl. 61).

3.2.3.8. Phase 6: Dynasty 18 Pre-Well (Units D–F):
Loci E106, F19+F20+F25, F23+F30, and F40 (OCHRE pls. 30–31, 45–46, 49)

Phase 6 contained a 1–4 cm thick layer of undulating, wind-blown gray sand that had collected over the lower surfaces alongside a sand dune. This layer contained poorly sorted fine-to-medium grained sand. This phase was excavated as Loci F19 (basket 1), F23 (basket 1), F25 (basket 2), F40 (basket 1), and E106. These loci contained a copper alloy toggle pin(?) (loc.19; OCHRE pl. 62), a copper alloy arrowhead (loc.19), and potsherds (see OCHRE pl. 62).

3.2.3.9. Phase 7: Dynasty 18 Pre-Well (Units D–F):
Loci E106, F19+F20+F25, F23+30, and F40 (OCHRE pls. 30–31, 45–46, 49)

Phase 7 represents a 2–5 cm thick layer of gray sand that had been deposited evenly over an underlying, undulating, sand layer. The upper portion of this layer had been water laid and exhibited differential sorting of fine-to-coarse sand grains. The layer contained some sherds at its upper interface and pebbles and shells throughout the layer itself. The layer covered most of the underlying layer but did become thinner at the top of an adjacent slope. This phase includes Locus F20 (basket 1), Locus F23 (baskets 1–3), Locus F25 (basket 2), Locus F40 (basket 1), and Locus E106. These loci yielded only one flint blade (loc.40) and potsherds (see OCHRE pl. 62).

3.2.3.10. Phase 8: Dynasty 18 Pre-Well (Units D–F):
Loci E104, F19+F20, F23, and F40 (OCHRE pls. 24, 45–46, 49)

In phase 8, a 3–12 cm thick layer of gray-yellow sand was deposited over the water laid sand of phase 7. This sand had been differentially deposited with fine-to-coarse-grained sand. The layer contained black and brown staining from organic materials (vegetation), shell fragments, and some potsherds. In particular, nodules of gray clay (mud-brick fragments) tended to cluster within the upper portion of this layer, reflecting depositional activity at the end of phase 8. For instance, a mud brick lay on edge at the western side of Unit E and extended down into the underlying phase 7 from the top of phase 8. This phase includes Locus F12 baskets 4–6, Locus F20 (basket 1), Locus F23 (baskets 1–3), Locus F40 (basket 1), and Locus E105. These loci contained potsherds and sand stained by a piece of copper alloy (loc.23 basket 1) (see OCHRE pl. 62).

3.2.3.11. Phase 9: Dynasty 18 Pre-Well (Units D–F):
Loci E105, F19+F20, F12+F23, and F5+F10 (OCHRE pls. 25–29, 45–46, 49)

The sand layer in phase 9 ranged from 2–9 cm in depth, with the shallowest part of the layer lying on the top of an adjacent hillock, while more sand had gathered in the lower lying areas. This layer consisted of gray-yellow sand that had accumulated in multiple layers and contained some charcoal flecks and shell fragments. This phase includes Locus F12 (baskets 4–6), the eastern half of Locus F19 (basket 1), Locus F 20 (basket 1), Locus F23 (baskets 1–3), and Locus E 105. Locus 12 basket 6 yielded a copper alloy lump (see OCHRE pl. 62).

3.2.3.12. Phase 10: Dynasty 18 Pre-Well (Units D–F):
Loci E102+E104, F7+F8+F9+F13+F14, and F5+F10 (OCHRE pls. 19, 21–24, 45–46, 49)

The deposition of sand increased noticeably in phase 10, ranging from 10 to 29 cm in depth. At the top of this layer, the underlying, sloping landscape had become a generally flat surface.

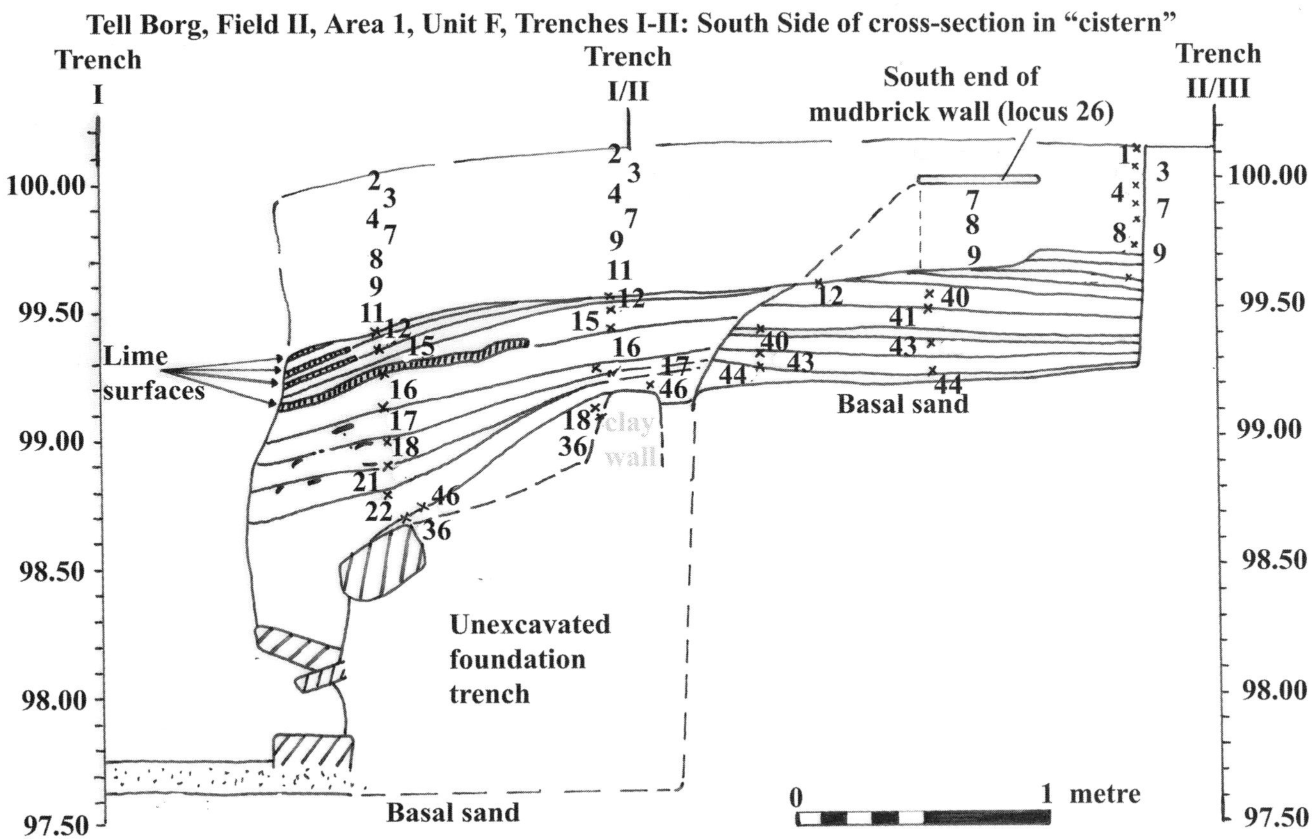

Fig. 3.15. North view of cross-section of well in Field II, Area 1 (Unit F) (drawn by G. Mumford; digitized by Joshua Olsen).

This layer consisted of very soft, medium-yellow sand with some sporadic reddish staining, some charcoal flecks, and some shell fragments. In addition, the layer yielded small gray and black areas of discoloration (decayed organic materials), gray clay nodules, gray mud-brick fragments, and a few potsherds. This phase includes Locus F5 (basket 1), Locus F7 (basket 3), Locus F8 (basket 2), the eastern half of Locus F9 basket 1, Locus F10 (basket 1), most of Locus F13 (basket 1), Locus F14 (basket 1), Locus E102, and Locus E104. These loci contained potsherds, a copper alloy cylindrical item (loc. F7 sf.37; OCHRE pl. 62), six copper alloy lumps (loc. F13 sf.24a–c, sf.26a–c; OCHRE pl. 62), a cylindrical copper alloy piece (loc. F14 sf.25; OCHRE pl. 62), a white faience vessel fragment (loc. F14 sf.29; OCHRE pl. 60), and a Cypriot White Slip sherd (loc. F9 baulk scraping).

3.2.3.13. Summary Discussion of Phases 0–10 Pre-Well Strata (Units D–F)

Prior to the excavation of a pit and subsequent installation of a stone-lined "well" in early Dynasty 19, Units C–F contained ten occupation and debris layers dating to Dynasty 18 (OCHRE pls. 45–49). These layers yielded mud-brick debris eroded from a nearby structure (phases 8 and 10). A few fragments of limestone and sandstone blocks (F12; F36; F44; E102) suggest the presence of imported stone, either from a local abandoned/destroyed structure or introduced from elsewhere for reuse at Tell el-Borg. A hand stone for grinding grain (F20) (OCHRE pl. 61), ash

Text continues on p. 41

Table 3.3. Summary of Small Finds from Units D–F (Pre-Well Strata and Loci)

Unit	*Locus*	*Basket or level*	*Unit Book no.*	*TBO no.*	*Object type*	*Material*	*Color & Surface Treatment*	*Dimensions*	*Comments: Mumford notes for Units E–F*
F	26	Wall	-	-	-	-	-	-	No small finds
F	36	1	Sf.41	No	Stone slab fragment	Limestone	White	9.3 x 4.5 x 3.2 cm	Corner fragment from a block
F	36	1	Sf.42	No	Longitudinal fragment of cylindrical stone	Limestone	White (burnt)	Originally 10 cm diameter; 7.8 x 5 x 5 cm	Partly chiselled- out hole at one end of stone.
F	46	1	-	-	-	-	-	-	No small finds
F	4	3	-	-	-	-	-	-	No small finds
F	4	4	-	-	-	-	-	-	No small finds
F	4	5	-	-	-	-	-	-	No small finds
E	102	1	(a)	No	Block fragment (carved lines)	Sandstone	Yellow; two vertical carved lines	20 x 8 x 6? cm	Two vertically carved lines on one face.
F	8	1	-	-	-	-	-	-	No small finds
F	5	1	-	-	-	-	-	-	No small finds
E	104	1	-	-	-	-	-	-	No small finds
F	9	4	-	-	-	-	-	-	No small finds
F	10	1–2	-	-	-	-	-	-	No small finds
F	12	4	-	-	-	-	-	-	No small finds
F	12	5	-	-	-	-	-	-	No small finds
F	12	6	Sf.41	TBO 0062	Slab	Limestone	White slab smooth on three sides	9 x 4.5 x 2.5 cm	White limestone slab
F	12	Basket no.(?)	(?)	TBO 0088	Copper lump	Copper alloy	Green (corroded)	Photograph reveals larger piece than site book drawings	**SF register:** Notes it may be from a vessel.
F	13	1	Sf.24a	No	Droplet/lump (smelting)	Copper alloy	Green (corroded)	0.7 x 0.5 x 0.4 cm	Droplet-shaped lump of copper
F	13	1	Sf.24b	No	Lump	Copper alloy	Green (corroded)	0.9 x 0.6 x 0.6 cm	Pear-shaped lump of copper
F	13	1	Sf.24c	No	Lump	Copper alloy	Green (corroded)	0.9 x 0.7 x 0.6 cm	Conical-shaped lump of copper
F	13	1	Sf.26a	No	Lump	Copper alloy	Green (corroded)	0.2 x 0.25 cm diameter	Tiny ball of copper
F	13	1	Sf.26b	No	Lump	Copper alloy	Green (corroded)	1 x 0.65 x 0.85 cm	Ovoid-shaped lump of copper
F	13	1	Sf.26c	No	Copper residue from casting	Copper alloy	Green (corroded)	3.0 x 0.9 x 0.8 cm	Irregularly shaped lump of copper
F	14	1	Sf.25	TBO 0422	Cylinder fragment from needle/awl?	Copper alloy	Green (corroded)	1.4 x 0.25 cm diameter	Fragment from a small nail/awl(?)
F	14	1	Sf.27	No	Palette/slab fragment	Ceramic	Brown	9.0 x 8.7 x 2.5 cm	A large sherd shaped into a slab
F	14	1	Sf.28	No	Small block	Limestone	White	8.4 x 10.9 x 6.9 cm	A small, broken limestone slab
F	14	1	Sf.29	No	Bowl base	Faience	White	3.1 x 1.6 x 0.3 cm; 9 cm. dia.	Slightly curved base from a bowl.
E	105	1	(a)	No	Lump	Copper alloy	Green (corroded)	0.2 x 0.2 cm	Tiny copper alloy nodule
E	105	1	(b)	No	Lump	Copper alloy	Green (corroded)	0.5 x 0.4 x 0.2 cm	Tiny, slab-like copper lump
E	105	1	(c)	No	Lump	Copper alloy	Green (corroded)	1.0 x 0.6 x 0.2 cm	Half-disk shaped copper lump
E	105	1	(d)	No	Lump	Copper alloy	Green (corroded)	1.0 x 0.8 x 0.3 cm	D-shaped slab of copper
E	105	1	(e)	No	Lump	Copper alloy	Green (corroded)	0.3 x 0.2 cm	Copper nodule
E	105	1	(f)	No	Lump	Copper alloy	Green (corroded)	0.8 x 0.7 x 0.2 cm	D-shaped slab of copper

Table 3.3. Summary of Small Finds from Units D–F (Pre-Well Strata and Loci)

Unit	Locus	Basket or level	Unit Book no.	TBO no.	Object type	Material	Color & Surface Treatment	Dimensions	Comments: Mumford notes for Units E–F
E	105	1	(g)	No	Lump	Copper alloy	Green (corroded)	0.3 × 0.2 × 0.2 cm	Copper nodule
E	105	1	(h)	No	Lump	Copper alloy	Green (corroded)	0.4 × 0.3 × 0.2 cm	Copper lump
E	105	1	(i)	No	Lump	Copper alloy	Green (corroded)	0.6 × 0.4 × 0.2 cm	Copper lump
F	19	1	Sf.31	TBO 0046	Togglepin or fastening pin	Copper alloy	Green (corroded)	8.6 × 0.5 cm diameter	Tapering at both ends with a broad central barrel
F	19	1	Sf.34	TBO 0044	Leaf-shaped arrow-head	Copper alloy	Green (corroded)	6.7 × 2.1 × 0.7 cm	A break reveals two sharp edges.
F	12	4	-	-	-	-	-	-	-
F	12	5	(c)	No	Lump/droplet (smelting)	Copper alloy	Green (corroded)	0.8 × 0.4 × 0.3 cm	Droplet shaped lump of copper
F	12	5	(b)	No	Lump	Copper alloy	Green (corroded)	0.7 × 0.6 × 0.4 cm	Irregularly shaped lump.
F	12	6	(a)	No	Lump	Copper alloy	Green (corroded)	0.7 × 0.5 × 0.3 cm	Irregularly shaped lump.
E	106	1	-	-	-	-	-	-	No small finds
F	20	1	Sf.33	No	Hand grinder	Fine sandstone	Brown	8.0 × 4.1 × 3.4 cm	One smoothed face
E	107	1	Sf.44	No	False spout or base fragment	Calcite(?) (another type of stone, faience, or ivory?)	Gray and white striated material	2.8 cm dia. Base; 1.1 cm diameter neck; 0.6 cm diam interior neck.	Footed disk-base from a faience or stone vessel. (salt-encrusted)
F	23	1	(a)	No	Copper alloy stained sand	Copper alloy	Green (corroded)	Less than 1 × 1 cm	Copper-stained sand
F	23	2	-	-	-	-	-	-	No small finds
F	23	3	-	-	-	-	-	-	No small finds
F	40	1	(a)	No	Stone blade or flake	Chert	Medium brown	4.7 × 1.6 × 0.6 cm	Flake/blade with no retouching
E	108	1	-	-	-	-	-	-	No small finds
F	41	1	-	-	-	-	-	-	No small finds
E	109	1	-	-	-	-	-	-	No small finds
F	30	1	(a)	No	Copper alloy in sand (smelting)	Copper alloy	Green (corroded)	1.8 × 1.2 × 0.7 cm	Copper alloy set in sand
F	30	1	(b)	No	Container? (ostrich shell fragment)	Ostrich eggshell	Gray	Less than 1 × 1 cm	Fragment from an ostrich eggshell
F	43	1	-	-	-	-	-	-	No small finds
F	31	1	-	-	-	-	-	-	No small finds
F	25	1 (E)	Sf.35	TBO 0030	Sickle blade with retouched edge	Chert	Brown; serrated edge	5.7 × 2.6 × 0.4 cm	Blade with a serrated edge along one side.
F	25	1 (E)	Sf.36	TBO 0042	Token(?) (gaming piece)	Ceramic	gray-brown	1.9 cm dia. 0.6 cm thick	Sherd with edges ground into a circular disk.
F	25	1 (E)	(a)	TBO 0208 (?)	Lump (possibly TBO .208 assigned in SF register)	Copper alloy	Green (corroded)	0.5 cm dia. 1 cm long	Green, corroded lump of copper alloy.
E	110	1	-	-	-	-	-	-	No small finds.
F	44	1	-	No	Fragments	Limestone Sandstone	Undecorated	Tiny-small (many)	Debris from architecture(?)
F	45	1	-	-	-	-	-	-	Basal sand

Table 3.4. Summary of Pottery from Loci and Layers Predating the Well in Units E–F

Unit	*Locus*	*Basket/ level*	*Pottery basket*	*Rims*	*Handles*	*Bases*	*Nile Silts*	*Desert marls*	*Other wares*	*Comments: Hummel pottery labels.*
E	102	1	Scanty basket of sherds	1	1	-	60%	40%	-	Silt: decorated with peach slip and red slip and burnishing; Marl: decorated with gray-green burnishing and peach burnishing.
F	4	3	Large basket of sherds	7	8	3	25%	75%	-	**Silt:** including Blue Painted pottery; **Marl:** store-jars.
F	4	4	Small basket of sherds	1	1	2	10%	90%	-	**Silt:** red slip; **Marl:** gray-green on amphorae; peach and green burnishing.
F	4	5	Small basket of sherds	1	-	1	90%	10%	-	**Silt:** red slip traces; **Marl:** decorated with cream-green slip.
F	5	1	Tiny basket of sherds	4	3	1	50%	50%	-	New Kingdom vessels including one Dynasty 19–20 form; **Silt:** mostly jars and red-slipped bowls; **Marl:** amphora sherd.
F	7	3	Medium-full basket of sherds	7	1	5	50%	50%	-	**Silt:** much red slip; **Marl:** gray-green slip; gray-green burnishing; flask with red-brown concentric circles.
F	8	2a	Large basket of sherds	25	10	12	59%	40%	1%	**Silt:** red-slipped bowls; **Marl:** gray-green slip; **Foreign fabrics:** a Cypriot, Base Ring II body sherd.
F	8	2b	Small basket of sherds	-	1	1	60%	40%	-	**Silt:** much red slip and burnishing; **Marl:** peach and gray-green burnishing.
E	103	1	Small basket of sherds	1	2	-	50%	50%	-	Salt-encrusted body sherds. **Silt:** some red slip; **Marl:** decorated with gray-green slip and cream-green burnishing
E	104	1	4 sherds in total	-	-	-	50%	25%	25%	**Marl:** decorated with cream slip and burnishing; **Other fabrics:** Canaanite amphora.
F	9	4	Scanty basket of Sherds	3	-	-	60%	40%	-	**Silt:** red slip; **Marl:** decorated with gray-green burnishing.
F	10	2	Small basket of sherds	5	1	2	60%	40%	-	**Silt:** red slip and burnishing; **Marl:** cream burnishing.
E	105	1	Small basket of sherds	4	2	-	75%	25%	-	**Silt:** including a red-burnished jar; **Marl:** a gray-green, burnished pitcher handle.
F	12	4	Small basket of sherds	5	2	3	25%	74%	1%	**Silt:** some red slip; Blue Painted sherd; **Marl:** much gray-green slip; cream-green burnishing; **Other fabrics:** a Cypriot Base Ring sherd.
F	12	5	Small basket of sherds	-	1	1	50%	50%	-	**Silt:** some red slip and burnishing; beer jar base; **Marl:** cream burnished flask; gray-green slips.
F	12	6	Small basket of sherds	1	1	-	50%	50%	-	**Silt:** much red slip; amphorae fragments; **Marl:** cream and gray-green slips.
F	13	1	Small basket of sherds	7	2	2	50%	50%	-	**Silt:** some red slip; **Marl:** peach burnishing with black painted decoration; gray-green slip.
F	14	1	Medium-full basket of sherds	4	1	2	45%	55%	-	**Silt:** some red slips; Blue Painted sherd; **Marl:** much cream-green slip with burnishing.
F	19	1	Small basket of sherds	10	-	3	55%	45%	-	**Silt:** red-slipped bowls; one early–mid-Dynasty 18, black-rimmed bowl sherd; **Marl:** much gray-green slip.
E	106	1	3 sherds in total	-	-	-	67%	33%	-	**Silt:** decorated with peach burnishing and cream slip; **Marl:** a gritty yellow sherd.

Table 3.4. Summary of Pottery from Loci and Layers Predating the Well in Units E–F

Unit	*Locus*	*Basket/ level*	*Pottery basket*	*Rims*	*Handles*	*Bases*	*Nile Silts*	*Desert marls*	*Other wares*	*Comments: Hummel pottery labels.*
F	23	1	Scanty basket of sherds	-	-	2	90%	10%	-	Small, worn sherds; **Silt:** beer jar base; **Marl:** cream slip and burnishing.
E	107	1	Small basket of sherds	4	-	2	60%	40%	-	**Silt:** simple bowls; **Marl:** decorated with gray-green slip.
F	20	1	Scanty basket of sherds	2	-	-	90%	10%	-	**Silt:** much red slip; an early–mid-Dynasty 18, black-rimmed bowl; **Marl:** cream-green slip.
F	40	1	Scanty basket of sherds	3	-	-	75%	24%	1%	**Silt:** red-slipped sherds; **Marl:** red-slipped lentoid flask with black stripes; **Other fabrics:** possible Canaanite amphora sherd.
E	108	1	Small basket of sherds	6	-	1	90%	10%	-	**Silt:** red slip and cream slip with black stripes; an early–mid-Dynasty 18, black-rimmed bowl; **Marl:** decorated with peach burnishing.
E	109	1	Scanty basket of sherds	1	-	1	25%	75%	-	**Silt:** decorated with black and red paint on cream slip; **Marl:** including one possible foreign fabric.
F	25	1	Small basket of sherds	7	-	2	50%	50%	-	**Silt:** red slips; incised, carinated bowl; **Marl:** decorated with painted stripes; much cream-green slip.
F	30	1	Amount of sherds in basket not stated	6	-	2	80%	20%	-	**Silt:** some red slip; **Marl:** gritty green; cream and peach slips; red slip and burnishing.
F	41	1	Small basket of sherds	4	-	2	70%	30%	-	Small, worn body sherds; **Silt:** traces of red slip; **Marl:** gray-green slip and cream slip.
E	110	1	Scanty basket of sherds	1	-	-	90%	10%	-	-
F	43	1	Small basket of sherds	4	1	2	70%	30%	-	Very small, salt-encrusted body sherds; **Silt:** red-slipped bowls; **Marl:** peach slip and burnishing; cream-green slip with black stripes; gray-green slipped and burnished strap-handle.
F	31	2	Scanty basket of sherds	-	-	1	60%	40%	-	**Silt:** red slip traces; large and small bowls with red slips; **Marl:** gray-green slips with burnishing.
F	44	1	Scanty basket of sherds	2	-	1	75%	24%	1%	**Silt:** red slips; **Marl:** peach slip with burnishing; cream and gray-green slips; **Other fabrics:** a possible Canaanite vessel base.
Total	-	-	**218+ body sherds**	126	38	54	**59%**	**40%**	**1%**	**Note:** The silt and marl percentages represent averages from the columns.

patches (hearths?), riverine and marine shells, animal bones, and a fragment from an ostrich eggshell (a food source and container?) (F30) suggest some hunting, food preparation, cooking, and other domestic activities. The stone tools (F25, pl. 3:6 no. 3, TBO 0030; F40) are apparently mostly Predynastic (see Chapter 11) but may have been reused in a New Kingdom context (OCHRE pls. 61 sf-35 and sf-40a). A crucible fragment with copper alloy staining (pl. 3.3 no.5: TBO 0088), 17 lumps of copper alloy (F12; F13; F25; E105) (pl. 3:5 no. 11, TBO 0208), droplets of copper from smelting (F12; F13), copper-stained sand (F13; F23; F30), copper alloy needles(?) (F14), a copper alloy fastening pin (F19) (pl. 3:5 no. 8, TBO 0046 awl?), and an arrowhead (F19) (pl. 3:5 no. 12, TBO 0044, arrow/spearhead?) suggest some copper-working and use in this area (OCHRE pl. 62 artifacts). The remains of a faience bowl base (F14), a faience/calcite(?) false-spout (E107) (OCHRE pl. 61 sf-44; pl. 3:6 no. 19, TBO 0120, Unit E, Locus 107), a ceramic token (F25) (OCHRE pl. 61 sf-36; pl. 3.3 no. 6: TBO 0042, token, counter, or gaming piece?), many Egyptian pottery vessels (99%), three sherds from Canaanite amphorae (0.5%) (F40; F44; E104), and two Cypriot Base Ring ware sherds (0.5%) (F8; F12) reveal other aspects of life, trade, and cross-cultural relations in the Dynasty 18 community in Field II (Tables 3.3–3.4; see Field II pottery chapter). Overall, these finds (see OCHRE pls. 61–62) indicate the presence of a nearby mud-brick structure or installation, household and industrial activities (e.g., food processing; copper smelting), and the possession of utilitarian and luxury items (e.g., copper tools and jewelry; imported pottery; faience containers). None of these items argue for the existence of a nearby temple or shrine during Dynasty 18 but also do not exclude this possibility—remote though it may be. The postulated shrine in Area 2 of Field II appears to be late Dynasty 18 to Ramesside in date.

3.2.3.14. Construction and Abandonment of the Stone-Lined Well

In cutting the large ovoid pit for a well (phase 11), the site's inhabitants needed to stabilize both the underlying 1 meter of occupation sand layers and the lower 1.5 meters of loose basal sand. The application of a gray sandy silt-and-clay mixture provided temporary stability but required an additional stone paving and lining to effect a long-term stability of the pit's walls (see figs. 3.11–3.14, 3.18–19). It is presumed here that there was a need for access to filtered(?) ground water in the public space and nearby "cultic" area, different from the water available 80 m and 400 m away in the adjacent river and lagoon, respectively. According to Stephen Moshier (see *Tell el-Borg I*, 63–68), the rate of flow in the nearby river channel fluctuated but the channel probably had at least one meter of water during the dry season. This is suggested by the alternating bands of water-laid clays and wind-blown sand at the western end of the Dynasty 18 baked-brick fosse (Field VIII, Units C–D7: *Tell el-Borg I*, 147–57, 197–98), thereby suggesting the requirement of more permanent, year-round access to water by the site's inhabitants. In addition, locational convenience and safety may have been additional issues for situating a water source in Field II rather than collecting water more than 400 m to the north from the crocodile-infested lagoon. The river channel between Fields II and IV appears to have been silting-up throughout the course of the late New Kingdom. Hence, the cutting and placement of another stone-lined well in the south corner of a Ramesside fort in Field IV (cutting into the underlying, abandoned, sand-filled Dynasty 18 fosse; see *Tell el-Borg I*, 262–67), argues that continuous access to water became an increasingly important issue for the Ramesside garrison at Tell el-Borg. Datable sherds from the well indicate that it continued into the late 19th Dynasty (see Excursus II at the end of this chapter, p. 150).

3.2.3.15. Phase 11: Dynasty 19 Well Foundation Trench (Units D–F)

Phase 11 is characterized by the ancient cutting of an ovoid foundation pit through the cultural layers spanning phases 1–10 and into the underlying basal sand (phase "0").

3.2.3.16. Phase 12: Dynasty 19 Foundation Trench Backfill (Units D–F): Loci F26 and F36 (OCHRE pls. 45–49)

Phase 12a consists of a partial in-filling of the foundation pit with gray-brown sand that formed a leveling foundation for a limestone paving placed a few centimeters above the base of the well's foundation. This layer remained unexcavated but had been exposed by later recent intrusive pitting and the robbery of various portions of the cistern's stone lining.

Fig. 3.16. Stone-lined pit (well), with reused blocks, looking south (Photo: NSAP).

Fig. 3.17. Northern entry of stone-lined pit (well) looking east from above (Photo: NSAP).

Fig. 3.18. Stone-lined pit/well, showing reused stone lining, looking east (Photo: NSAP).

Fig. 3.19. Stone-lined pit (well) looking northeast at northern, entry stairway (Photo: NSAP).

3.2.3.17. Phase 13: Dynasty 19 Stone Lining for Well (Units D–F): Locus F42 Baskets 1–5 (OCHRE pls. 41, 43, 45–49)

Phase 13 entailed the placement of limestone blocks and pieces over the backfill lining the base and sides of the foundation pit (figs. 3.16–3.19). The delineation of the paving blocks in the base of the well required excavating Locus F42, which lay partly above and between the limestone paving slabs. Locus F42 contained gray-brown, medium-to-coarse grained sand, limestone block chips and powder, a red stone chip, charcoal pieces, blackened bone fragments, and potsherds (including pieces from two decorated vessels) (see tables 3.5–3.6). It is uncertain how long the well remained functional, but it would have presumably needed some cleaning to remove the accumulation of wind-blown debris.

3.2.3.18. Phase 14: Dynasty 19 Post-Well Fill (Units D–F): Loci D14 and F39 (OCHRE pls. 40–41, 44, 47)

Phase 14 contains the initial accumulation of debris over the limestone flooring. This layer contained Loci F39 and D14, which consisted of brown, coarse-grained sand, limestone blocks and chips of various sizes, limestone debris, many small, flat-lying sherds, some medium to large pottery pieces, and a body sherd from a Blue Painted vessel (Locus 14 in Unit D) (see Excursus I discussion by Hummel). Locus D14–15(?) represented the lowest area dug in Unit D owing to the concentration of limestone blocks and debris in the constrained space between the foot of the steps and the adjacent southern baulk. However, this area did yield a full basket of potsherds.

3.2.3.19. Phase 15: Dynasty 19 Post-Well Fill (Units D–F): Loci D13, F37, and F38 (OCHRE pls. 39–40, 44, 47)

Phase 15 represents a new layer of debris accumulating in the stone installation. This layer consisted of medium-yellow sand with mostly medium-sized grains, some gray clay inclusions, some cobble-sized stone chips, pieces of burned bone, sporadic charcoal flecks, a few shells, and mostly flat-lying sherds at the base of this layer. Loci F38, F37, and D13 also contained a fire-cracked stone and a sandstone polishing stone (F37 sf.43; see OCHRE pl. 56). Locus D13 lay to the north in Unit D and contained dense gray-brown sandy soil, similar to Locus D12 (to the south), and had some charcoal flecks, lumps of mud, limestone debris, and a dense quantity of potsherds (one-third of a basket from a small area).

3.2.3.20. Phase 16: Dynasty 19 Post-Well Fill (Units D–F): Loci D12, F24, F34, and F35 (OCHRE pls. 36–39, 44, 47)

Phase 16 is the next layer of debris deposited in the stone installation. This layer contained Loci F35, F34, and D12, which included yellow-gray and medium-sized sand grains, gray mud-brick debris, bits of bone, large stones, some shells, sporadic charcoal flecks, two amphora bases, and potsherds of varying sizes. Locus D12 lay in the southern part of Unit D and filled the area between the top of the fourth and fifth steps. Excavation revealed that the steps had been installed first, with the rough limestone block wall being placed next, abutting and partly covering the steps.

3.2.3.21. Phase 17: Dynasty 19 Post-Well Fill (Units D–F): Loci D10, D11, F22, and F33 (OCHRE pls. 35–39, 44, 47).

Phase 17 forms the next debris layer. The lower half of Loci F22, F33, and D11 represent a layer with coarse- to medium-grained yellow sand, some pebble-sized stones, sporadic flecks of charcoal, and a few potsherds. Locus D11 lies in the southern part of Unit D, under Locus D9 (from which it is arbitrarily divided) and spans the area between the top of the third to fourth steps at the northeastern side of the well. This area contained a compact layer of yellow-brown sand, flecks of charcoal, potsherds, the lower part of an amphora, limestone debris, a small faience bead (TBO II 45; see OCHRE pl. 60), and several flakes of gold foil/jewelry (TBO II 49; fig. 3.20).

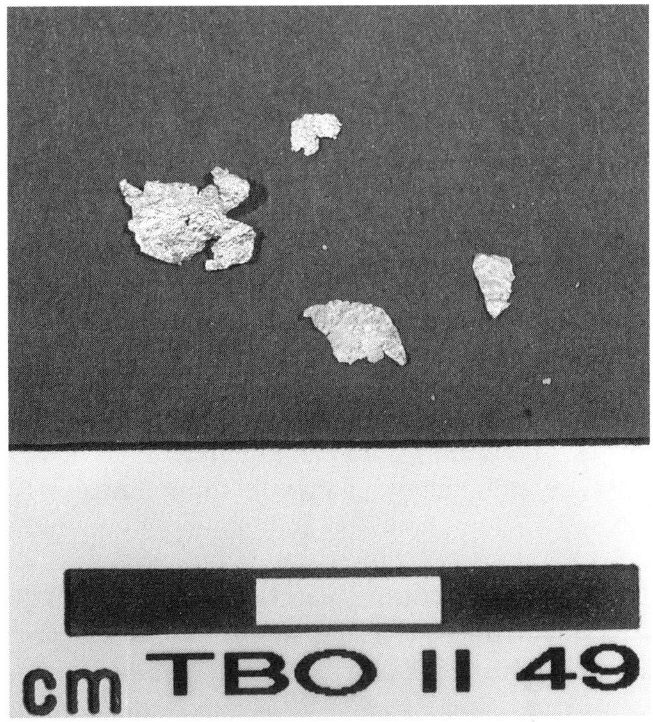

Fig. 3.20. Pieces of gold foil (TBO II 49) from Locus 11 in Unit D (Photo: NSAP).

3.2.3.22. Phase 18: Dynasty 19 Post-Well Fill (Units D–F): Loci D10, D11, F22, and F33 (OCHRE pls. 34–39, 44, 47)

Phase 18 represents a subsequent layer of debris deposition in the abandoned well. The upper half of Loci F22, F33, and D11 represent a layer with coarse- to medium-grained yellow sand, some pebble-sized stones, sporadic flecks of charcoal, a fragmentary animal tooth, and a few potsherds. Locus D10 lies only in the northern part of Unit D, under Locus D9, and yields a compact, darker, yellow-brown sandy matrix, some streaks of ash, lumps of mud and mud-brick debris, stone chips, and some pieces of bone. This fill lay against a 1-m stretch of gray-brown mud bricks in a crude wall overlying some limestone blocks in the northeastern part of the well's entryway. This portion of the mud-brick wall is notable for its unusual use of lime in the mortar for bonding its bricks, which rises three courses in height.

3.2.3.23. Phase 19: Dynasty 19 Post-Well Fill (Units D–F): Loci D9, D10, F18, F21, and F32 (OCHRE pls. 33–39, 44, 49)

Phase 19 is a new layer in the stone-lined well. It spans Loci F18, F32, and D9 and contains a medium-grained, light gray-brown sand with a piece of mud brick, small bits of sandstone, pebbles, sporadic shells, isolated charcoal flecks, some bone fragments (roasted), a purple quartzite pounder or polishing stone (F32 sf.39; see OCHRE pl. 56), mostly flat-lying potsherds, and a fragment from a Blue Painted vessel.

3.2.3.24. Phase 20: Dynasty 19 Post-Well Fill (Units D–F): Loci D9, F18, and F29 (OCHRE pls. 31–34)

Phase 20 is a subsequent layer of debris in the stone installation. This phase consists of Loci F18, F29, and D9, which represent a medium-grained, white-yellow sand layer with some pebble-sized stones, sporadic charcoal flecks, fragments of roasted bone, a tooth, a stone flake (F29 sf.40), and many flat-lying sherds near the base of this layer. Locus D9 in Unit D contained large limestone blocks in its lowest levels, many lumps of mud, some mud-brick debris, some pieces of bone, a piece of folded gold foil, and two full baskets of potsherds found lying at all angles. (Locus D9 is underlain by Loci D10–11, but belongs to the same layer as Locus D10.) A fragment of a green faience tile is also noted from Locus 9 in Unit D (pl. 3:4 no.12, TBO 0035).

3.2.3.25. Phase 21: Dynasty 19 Post-Well Fill (Units D–F): Loci D9, F17, and F28 (OCHRE pls. 31–34)

Phase 21 (Loci F17, F28, and D9) consists of a medium- to coarse-grained yellow sand layer with red stains (root marks?), sporadic charcoal flecks, a few fragments of bone, some pebble- and cobble-sized stones, small, mostly flat-lying sherds, and a sherd from a vessel decorated with black bands.

3.2.3.26. Phase 22: Dynasty 19 Post-Well Fill (Units D–F): Loci D8, F16, and F27 (OCHRE pls. 26–31)

Phase 22 (Loci F16, F27, and D8) contains medium- to coarse-grained sand with small- to medium-sized stones, some charcoal flecks, fragments of roasted bone (with some large pieces), and small to medium-sized potsherds. This layer lay below portions of a white lime plaster surface (no.1). Locus D8 lay in the northern part of Unit D and overlay Locus D9. It consisted of a dark brown matrix, charcoal lumps, some lumps of mud, a few bones, and a half basket of potsherds.

3.2.3.27. Phase 23: Dynasty 19 Lime Surface-1 (Units D–F) (OCHRE pl. 47).

Phase 23 contains patches of a 1–4 cm thick lime plaster surface, which appears in Units D and F. In Unit D, the remnants of this lime surface continue in the south baulk, separating Locus D7 from Locus D9. Unit F contained more traces of this lime plaster surface, yielding two patches separating Loci F15 and F25 from underlying Loci F16 and F27.

3.2.3.28. Phase 24: Dynasty 19, Initial Fill Above Lime Layer-1 (Units D–F): Loci D7, F15, and F25 (OCHRE pls. 23–25, 28-30, 32–33)

Phase 24 (Loci F15, F25, and D7) represents a thin layer between two residual lime plaster surfaces, of which the upper plaster surface (no. 2) was barely discernible in an internal section. This layer contains medium-grained yellow sand with some pebble-and cobble-sized stones, some bone bits, flecks of charcoal (F25 basket 2), ash and soot patches, and mostly flat-lying sherds at the base of this layer. Locus D7 sloped from north to south in Unit D and overlay Loci D8 (north) and D9 (south). Loci D7 and D8 are apparently fairly homogenous and belong to the same layer. Locus D7 contained a deposit of ash, lumps of clay, an oyster shell embedded into the underlying surface, and a full basket of potsherds (including large sherds at various angles).

3.2.3.29. Phase 25: Dynasty 19, Secondary Fill Above Lime Layer-1 (Units D–F): Loci D7, F15, and F25 (OCHRE pls. 23–30, 32–33)

Although phase 25 (Loci F15, F25, and D7) reflects a secondary, later layer overlying the phase 24 layer, it was not separated from phase 24 and was excavated as a single unit (the description of phase 25 duplicates phase 24).

3.2.3.30. Phase 26: Dynasty 19, Lime Layer-2 (Units D–F) (OCHRE pl. 47)

The remnant of lime plaster layer no. 2 appeared in the southern side of the internal baulk in Unit F, lying between Locus 12 and Locus 15. Lime layer no. 2 measured 1–2 cm in thickness and did not survive in the northern face of the 30-cm-wide internal baulk.

3.2.3.31. Phase 27: Dynasty 19, Initial Fill Above Lime Layer-2 (Units D–F): Loci D7, F12, F15, and F25 (OCHRE pls. 23–30, 32–33).

Phase 27 (Loci F12, F25, and D7) represents the accumulation of debris above and within the lime-plastered basin (no.1). The initial layer above lime plaster surface no. 2 consists of white-gray sand with charcoal flecks, fragments of bone, a burned limestone chunk, some copper alloy-stained sand, potsherds, a sherd from a Cypriot vessel, and a fragment from a grinding stone (burned limestone? F25 sf.38; see OCHRE pl. 58).

3.2.3.32. Phase 28: Dynasty 19 Secondary Fill Above Lime Layer-2 (Units D–F): Loci D6, F12, and F25 (OCHRE pls. 22, 26–31)

Phase 28 (Loci F12, F25, and D6) encompasses a subsequent layer of debris deposition above the second lime-plastered basin. The description of phase 28 basically duplicates phase 27.

3.2.3.33. Phase 29: Dynasty 19 Lime Layer-3 (Units D–F)

Traces of a lime plaster layer (no.3) were only visible in the south side of the internal baulk in Unit F. This lay in Locus 12, only 2–3 cm below lime layer no. 4 and 2 cm above lime surface no. 2. Lime layer-3 was less than 2 cm thick, and, like lime surface-2, did not survive in the northern face of the internal baulk (30 cm thick).

3.2.3.34. Phase 30: Dynasty 19 Fill Above Lime Layer-3 (Units D–F): Loci D6, F12, F15, and F25 (OCHRE pls. 22, 26–31)

Phase 30 (Loci F12, F25, and D6) is a debris layer above the third plastered, ovoid hollow ("basin"). The description of phase 30 basically duplicates phase 28. Locus 6 in Unit D produced a full basket of potsherds and some bones.

3.2.3.35. Phase 31: Dynasty 19 Lime Layer-4 (Units D–F)

The internal east–west baulk in Unit F, north of sondage 2, revealed a patch of lime plaster that separated parts of Locus F11 (basket 1) from underlying Locus F12 (baskets 2–3) and F25 (basket 1). The northern end of Locus F12 (basket 2) contained a patch of soot that matches a dark patch and lime plaster layer noted in the south baulk of Unit D. This lime surface in Unit D separated parts of Locus D5 from parts of underlying Locus D6.

3.2.3.36. Phase 32: Dynasty 19 Fill Above Lime Layer-4 (Units D–F): Loci D5 and F11 (OCHRE pl. 24)

Phase 32 (Loci F11 and D5) represents a medium-grained yellow-white sand layer with several cobble-sized sandstone chips, fire-cracked stones, some charcoal flecks, small to large fragments of bone, shells, an ostrich shell fragment, a stone flake (F11 sf.22; see OCHRE pl. 60), a burned fragment from a small limestone column base (F11 sf.23), flat-lying potsherds, and sherds from a Blue Painted vessel and a cream slip-coated vessel with black stripes. Locus D5 sloped from north to south, overlying Locus D6. Locus D5 produced a three-quarter full basket of potsherds, a tiny fragment of gold leaf (TBO II 40; fig. 3.21; pl. 61) and a dark gray stone bead (TBO II 41).

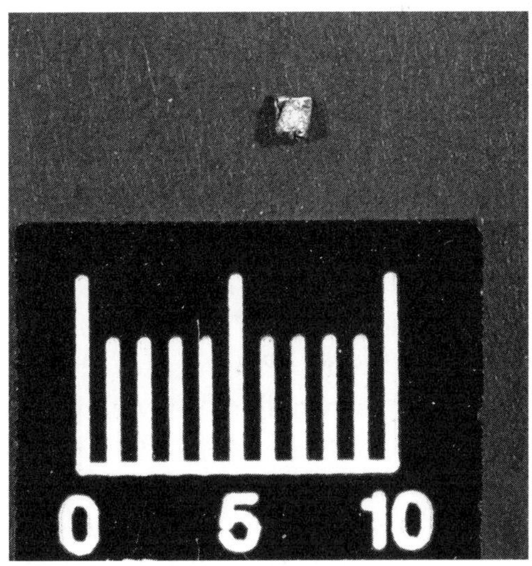

Fig. 3.21. A piece of gold foil (TBO II 40) from Unit D, Locus 5 (Photo: NSAP)

3.2.3.37. Phase 33: Dynasty 19 Fill Above Lime Layer-4 (Units D–F): Loci D4 and F9 (OCHRE pls. 21, 23–25)

Phase 32 (Loci F9 and D4) consists of Locus 9 baskets 2–3, the western half of Locus F9 basket 1, and Locus D4.

This layer contained medium-grained sand, some pebble-sized, sandstone chips, streaks of mud lumps, flecks of charcoal (especially along the south side), scattered fragments of animal bone and teeth, shells, two copper alloy lumps (F9 sf.20–21; see OCHRE pl. 60), small to large potsherds with worn and sharp edges, and sherds from a Mycenaean vessel, a Bichrome decorated vessel, a Cypriot vessel, and a Blue Painted vessel. Locus D4 in Unit D lay to the north, above Locus D5, and yielded a full basket of potsherds.

3.2.3.38. Phase 34: Dynasty 19 Fill Above Lime Layer-4 (Units D–F): Loci D3 and F8 (OCHRE pl. 22)

Phase 34 (Loci F8 and D3) is a coarse- to medium-grained yellow sand layer with pebble- and cobble-sized stones, fire-cracked rocks, charcoal flecks, some small mud lumps, small to large fragments of burned animal bones, fish bones, four copper alloy lumps, a copper alloy blade(?) tip (F8 sf.19; see OCHRE pl. 60), a blue faience bead (F8 sf.18; see OCHRE pl. 60), mostly flat-lying potsherds, and up to 50% of a Mycenaean pyxis (Mycenaean IIIB; from Loci F8 and F7). Locus D3 lay in the southern part of Unit D and contained a half basket of potsherds.

3.2.3.39. Phase 35: Dynasty 19 Lime Layer-5 (Units D–F): Loci D2 and F7 (OCHRE pls. 19, 21)

The eastern and southern baulks in Unit D and a patch in Unit F displayed the remnants of a lime plaster surface (no. 5) that sloped down into a shallow ovoid depression. In Unit F, a large lime patch separated part of Locus F7 (basket 2) from parts of underlying Loci F8, F9 (basket 2) and F11. In Unit D, remnants of a lime surface separated parts of Locus D2 from D3.

3.2.3.40. Phase 36: Dynasty 19 Fill Above Lime Layer-5 (Units D–F): Loci D2 and F7 (OCHRE pls. 19, 21)

Phase 36 (Loci F7 and D2) consists of a layer between and beyond the scattered patches of an underlying and overlying lime plaster surface (nos. 5 and 6, respectively). This layer was excavated as Locus F7 baskets 2–3 and Locus D2, which contain coarse- to medium-sized grained white-yellow sand, cobble- and pebble-sized stones, burned limestone chips, many flecks of charcoal, small to large fragments of roasted animal bones, mostly flat-lying small to medium-sized potsherds with worn and sharp edges, and the base of a store-jar.

3.2.3.41. Phase 37: Dynasty 19 Lime Layer-6 (Units D–F)

The eastern and southern baulks in Unit D, and the southern baulk in Unit F, revealed the remnants of a lime plaster surface (no. 6) sloping down into a shallow ovoid hollow. This lime layer ranged from 1 cm to 3 cm in thickness but survived only in isolated patches in Units D and F. In Unit F, these lime surface patches separated Locus F1 and parts of Locus F4 from part of underlying Locus F7; in Unit D, the lime patches separated Locus D1 and parts of Locus D2 from Locus D3 below. The base of the well's upper mud-brick wall lay 1 meter to the east of the lime patch (initially called "gray clay") in Locus F4 (basket 1).

3.2.3.42. Phase 38: Dynasty 19 Fill Above Lime Layer-6 (Units D–F): Loci D2, F3, and F4 (OCHRE pls. 19–21)

Phase 38 (Loci F4, F3, and D2) is a sub-surface layer that overlay the remnants of a lime plaster surface (no. 6), which sloped down into the last shallow ovoid hollow. This layer consists of mottled yellow sand, gray clay debris, and reddish-brown to brownish soil, with some pebble-sized stones, a quartz chip, sporadic charcoal flecks, fragments of roasted animal bones (including a pig jawbone), copper alloy lumps (F4 sf.15, 17; see OCHRE pl. 60), a copper alloy bead (F4 sf.16; see

Fig. 3.22 (left). A stamped amphora handle (TBO 0039) from Unit D, Locus 2 (Photo: NSAP).

Fig. 3.23 (below). South baulk of stone-lined "well" in Field II, Area 1 (Unit F) (drawn by G. Mumford).

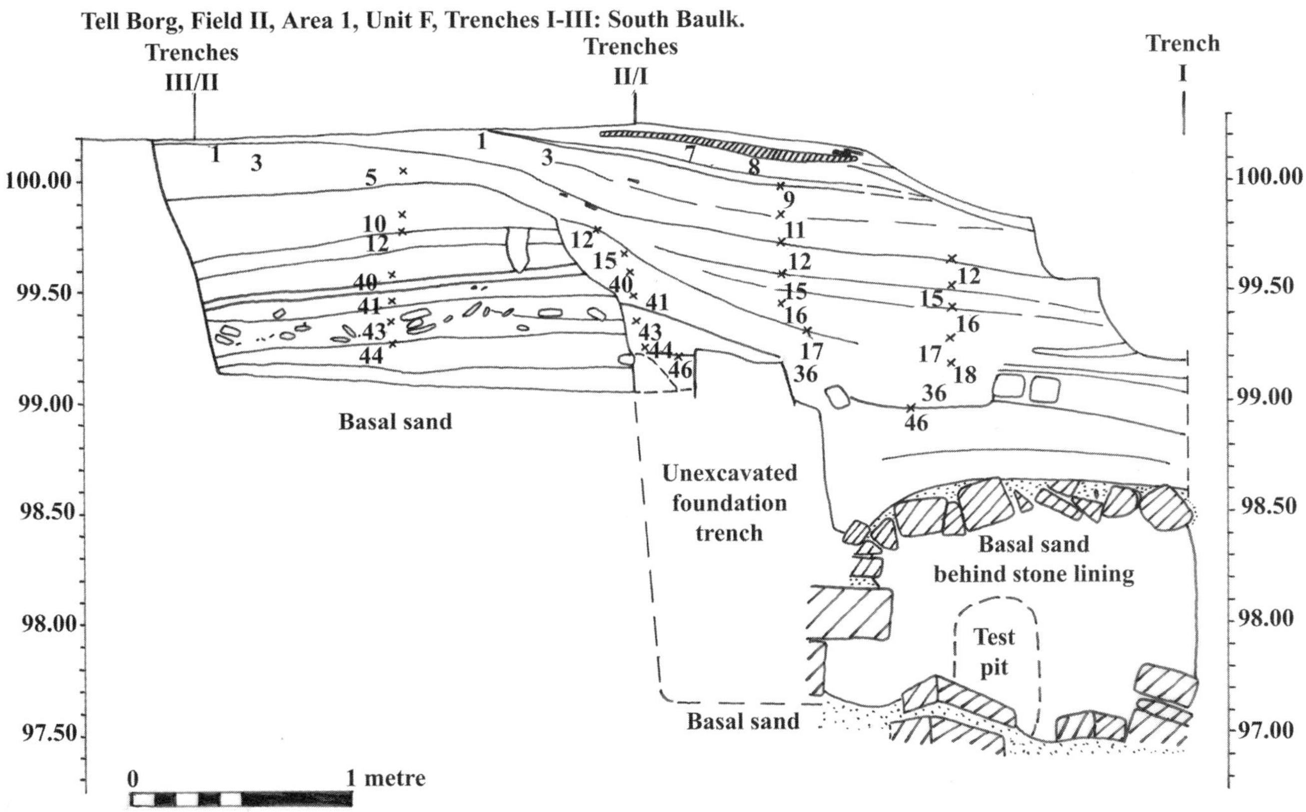

OCHRE pl. 60), a copper alloy nail (F3 sf.5), small to large potsherds with worn and sharp edges, and sherds from a Blue Painted vessel and a vessel with cream slip and black bands. Locus D2 lay along the south side of Unit D, above Locus D3, and produced one-third of a basket of potsherds, including a stamped amphora handle (TBO II 0039/TBP 223) (fig. 3.22; pl. 3.3 no.7).

3.2.3.43. Phase 39: Dynasty 19 Surface Layer Above Lime Layer-6 (Units D–F): Loci F1, F2, and F6 (OCHRE pls. 17, 47)

Phase 39 (Loci F1, F6, and D1) represents a surface layer of coarse- to medium-grained yellow-gray sand with some pebble- to cobble-sized stones, sporadic flecks of charcoal, a hammer stone (F1 sf.1; see OCHRE pl. 54), part of a sandstone polishing stone (F1 sf.3; see OCHRE pl. 54), and many copper alloy pieces: a fragment (F1 sf.2; see OCHRE pl. 55), a "staple" (F1 sf.4; see OCHRE pl. 55), a nail tip (F6 sf.7; see OCHRE pl. 55), a cylindrical item (F6 sf.8; see OCHRE pl. 55), a blade/arrowhead fragment (F6 sf.9; see OCHRE pl. 55; pl. 3:5 no.4, TBO 041), four lumps (F6 sf.10a–b, 12, 14; see OCHRE pl. 55), a blade (F6 sf.11; see OCHRE pl. 55), and a piece of partly rolled-up sheeting (F6 sf.13; see OCHRE pl. 55). Locus 1 in Unit D yielded a full basket of potsherds.

3.2.3.44. Phases 11–39 Discussion of Post-Well Fill (Units D–F)

Regarding the deliberate abandonment and disposal of refuse in the shallow well at some point in Dynasty 19 (see figs. 3.15 and 3.23), it is interesting to note that the site's inhabitants later reused the still noticeable depression forming within the boundaries of this sand-filled installation. The first lime plaster layer was laid in the ovoid depression, sloping downward from all sides into the hollow. The exact function of this lime surface remains uncertain, but its construction required moderate effort, while its design objectives apparently required a surface that stayed clean, firm, and impermeable; it incorporated an ovoid basin form with gradually sloping sides and easy access from the adjacent, contemporary ground surfaces. The primary function may have been associated with a liquid, whether as a pressing installation (e.g., a wine press?) or possibly a watering hole for animals. A wine press would not be unexpected, considering this region's reputation for wine production (i.e., wine of Tjaru). However, there is no evidence for an area to drain the liquid extracted from the grapes. On the other hand, the presence at Tell el-Borg of bones from large animals (e.g., cattle, horses, donkeys) suggests the need for a watering place, presumably secure from marauding crocodiles along the adjacent river and lagoon banks. Otherwise, if cereal grains were being cultivated nearby (see Clair Malleson's report on Field VI), the lime-plastered hollow and surviving mud-brick lining wall would form ideal conditions for separating grain (wheat and/or barley) from the chaff.

Although the first plastered basin installation had soon filled with debris, the inhabitants of the site valued it sufficiently that they later placed a second lime plaster layer over the debris, renewing the use of this hollow. On the other hand, this installation was not sufficiently vital that it was maintained continuously by cleaning out any accumulated debris. The period of dormancy between the first and second plastering suggests that the installation may have required seasonal or possibly a bit more sporadic use. For instance, the installation's use may have followed the cycle of the annual grape or cereal grain harvest; or, perhaps there was long-term use separated by enough time to allow for the 31–60 cm of debris accumulation in the first basin. Either enough debris had accumulated in the first basin, or sufficient time had passed, that the persons installing the second plaster surface did not deem it necessary to clear out the debris and reuse the first plastered basin. Of note, it appears that the lime surfaces also faced much abrasion: it was not being continuously preserved. It is possible that sufficient activity within each basin wore it out and introduced sufficient contamination that it was deemed easier to install a new, clean basin. Whatever the reason(s), the inhabitants seem to have preferred to install a new plastered basin. This pattern continued for four more lime-plastered layers/surfaces until the area within the abandoned well could no longer accommodate any further basins.

The material culture debris from phases 11–39 (OCHRE pls. 54–60) consists of many fragments of architectural pieces (mostly blocks) (pl. 3.1 no.4: TBO 27, possible stela top), a quartz chip (pl. 3.1 no.3: TBO 56), a fragment of diorite, a fragment of sandstone, four hammer-stones (or polishing stones), a hand-stone (for grinding grain?) (pl. 3:6 no.15, TBO 0018, a quartzite pounder/

Text continues on p. 56

Table 3.5. Summary of Small Finds from Units D–F (Post-Well Strata and Loci)

Unit	*Locus*	*Basket or level*	*Unit Book no.*	*TBO no.*	*Object type*	*Material*	*Color and Surface Treatment*	*Dimensions (cm)*	*Comments: Mumford notes for E–F*
D	Sur-face?	-	(?)	TBO II.48	Tile	Faience	Light green glaze	-	Found later in April 2001
E	101	1	-	-	-	-	-	-	No small finds
D	1	1	2001 cleanup	No	Lump	Copper alloy	Green (corroded)	1.2 x 1.4 x 0.8 cm	Irregularly shaped lump
F	1	1	Sf.2	-	Rectangular fragment	Copper alloy	Green (corroded)	1.4 x 0.6 x 0.3 cm	Possibly a blade fragment
F	1	1	(a)	No	Fragment	Diorite	Black	Small	All surfaces rough
F	1	2	Note book Sf.1	TBO II 51	Hammerstone	Fine-grained stone (granite?)	Yellow cortex; gray stone with smoothed edges	5.2 x 4.8 x 4.4 cm	Square in form with rounded corners and polished sides
F	1	2	Sf.3	TBO II 57	Grinding or polishing stone fragment	Sandstone	Yellow	4.2 x 3.3 x 2.2 cm	Edge piece with polished surface
F	1	2	Sf.4	TBO II 59 (?)	Staple(?) fragment (handle?)	Copper alloy	Green (corroded)	2.7 x 1.2 x 0.3 cm	U-shaped piece with a circular section
F	1	(?)	(?)	TBO 0426	U-shaped fragment	Copper alloy	Green (corroded)	No details	No details
F	2	1	(a)	No	Modern concrete fragments (surface)	Concrete	Gray	small pieces	Modern pieces of concrete from military bunkers
F	2	1	Sf.6	TBO II 58	Nail or pointed blade tip fragment.	Copper alloy	Green (corroded)	4.3 x 0.7 x 0.3 cm	Long, narrow blade with tip
F	6	1	Sf.7	TBO 0420	Needle point	Copper alloy	Green (corroded)	1.4 long x 0.3 cm diam	A thin, narrow, pointed item
F	6	1	Sf.8	TBO 0421	Fragment	Copper alloy	Green (corroded)	1.4 x 0.4 x 0.3 cm	A rectangular strip with one bulging end
F	6	1	Sf.9	TBO 0041	A triangular fragment (point?)	Copper alloy	Green (corroded)	2.4 x 1.3 x 0.2 cm	A triangular fragment
F	6	1	Sf.10a	(?)	Fragment	Copper alloy	Green (corroded)	1.1 x 1.0 x 0.4 cm	A tiny, triangular slab
F	6	1	Sf.10b	(?)	Fragment	Copper alloy	Green (corroded)	1.2 x 0.8 x 0.3 cm	A tiny, irregularly shaped slab
F	6	1	Sf.11	TBO 0455	Chisel? blade	Copper alloy	Green (corroded)	3 x1 x 0.7 cm	A small blade
F	6	1	Sf.12	(?)	Lump	Copper alloy	Green (corroded)	0.9 x 0.6 x 0.6 cm	An irregularly shaped lump
F	6	1	Sf.13	TBO 0014	Rolled sheeting (copper wrapped around a nail?)	Copper alloy	Green (corroded)	2.9 x 1.5 x 0.5 cm	A rolled-up sheet of copper
F	6	1	Sf.14	(?)	Lump	Copper alloy	Green (corroded)	1.1 x 0.4 x 0.3 cm	A copper slab-shaped lump
F	6	1	(a)	No	Rectangular block	Limestone	White	51 x 19 x 17 cm	A rectangular, weathered block
F	3	1	Sf.5	TBO 0007 (0456?)	Nail? blade? Awl? fragment. (Poss. TBO 0456)	Copper alloy	Green (corroded)	3.5 x 0.7 x 0.3 cm	A cylindrical item with a tapering end
F	3	1	(a-b)	No	2 lumps	Copper alloy	Green (corroded)	Small	2 tiny copper alloy nodules.
D	2	1	39	TBO II 39	Handle from an amphora	Ceramic	Stamped impression	-	-
E	103	1	-	-	-	-	-	-	No small finds
F	4	1	-	-	-	-	-	-	No small finds
F	4	2	Sf.15	(?)	Lump	Copper alloy	Green (corroded)	1.6 x 0.9 x 0.9 cm	An irregularly shaped lump
F	4	2	Sf.16	(?)	Bead	Copper alloy	Green (corroded)	0.7 x 0.7 cm dia.	A perforated barrel bead

Table 3.5. Summary of Small Finds from Units D–F (Post-Well Strata and Loci)

Unit	*Locus*	*Basket or level*	*Unit Book no.*	*TBO no.*	*Object type*	*Material*	*Color and Surface Treatment*	*Dimensions (cm)*	*Comments: Mumford notes for E–F*
F	4	2	Sf.17	(?)	Lump	Copper alloy	Green (corroded)	1.1 × 0.8 × 0.4 cm	An irregularly shaped lump
F	4	2	(a)	-	Chip	Translucent quartz	Milky white	1.5 × 0.7 × 0.5 cm	A tiny chip of quartz
F	7	1	-	-	-	-	-	-	No small finds
F	7	2	-	-	-	-	-	-	No small finds
F	7	3	Sf.37	TBO 0045	Cylindrical item (knife handle?)	Copper alloy	Green (corroded)	4.2 × 0.9 × 0.8 cm	A cylindrical item with an ovoid section
F	7	(?)	(?)	TBO 0102	Scraper	Very fine chert	Very worn		SF register: Cited in Unit F, Locus 7
F	8	1	Sf.18	TBO 0028	Bead with a 3 mm diameter perforation	Faience	Blue	0.7 cm long × 0.85 cm dia.	A barrel bead with 16 longitudinal, exterior grooves
F	8	1	Sf.19a	(?)	A blade? tip	Copper alloy	Green (corroded)	1.7 × 0.5 × 0.3 cm	A grooved, blade? tip
F	8	1	Sf.19b	(?)	Lump	Copper alloy	Green (corroded)	1.1 × 0.8 × 0.4 cm	A tiny slab with a rounded end
F	8	1	Sf.19c	(?)	Lump	Copper alloy	Green (corroded)	0.6 × 0.4 × 0.3 cm	A small nodule
F	8	1	Sf.19d	(?)	Lump	Copper alloy	Green (corroded)	0.6 × 0.4 × 0.4 cm	A small nodule
F	8	1	Sf.19e	(?)	Lump	Copper alloy	Green (corroded)	0.6 × 0.3 × 0.2 cm	A small nodule
D	4	1	-	-	-	-	-	-	-
F	9	1	Sf.20	(?)	Lump	Copper alloy	Green (corroded)	0.6 × 0.4 × 0.4 cm	Irregularly shaped lump
F	9	1	Sf.21	(?)	Lump	Copper alloy	Green (corroded)	1.0 × 0.7 × 0.6 cm	Irregularly shaped lump
F	9	2	-	-	-	-	-	-	-
F	9	3	-	-	-	-	-	-	-
D	5	1	40	TBO II 40	Thin sheet /leaf fragment (possibly from a "bead")	Gold	(gold)	Tiny	Gold leaf (also called a bead by the registrar)
D	5	1	41	TBO II 41	Bead	Stone	Dark gray	Small	Bead
D	5	1	Not in notes	TBO 0038	Pieces of jewelry	Faience, carnelian and mineral	-	-	Multiple beads
F	11	1	(a)	TBO 0023	Container? (ostrich shell fragment)	Ostrich eggshell	Gray	less than 1 × 1 cm	Fragment from an ostrich shell
F	11	2	-	-	-	-	-	-	No small finds
F	11	1/2?	Sf.22	(?)	Flake from a core (debitage)	Flint	Dark brown	3.6 × 2.0 × 1.2 cm	Wedge-shaped flake (some re-touching?)
F	11	1/2?	Note book Sf.23	TBO 0027	Registrar: part of a stele top with lines (field notes: column base frag.)	Limestone	gray-white	12.8 × 5.5 × 4.2 cm (5.5 cm high by 22 cm dia.)	Burnt and broken limestone piece
F	11	Basket no.2	Pottery Basket	TBO 0008	Jar handle with impression (TBP 270)	Ceramic	Stamp impression on handle	-	SF register: Unit F, loc.11, B.2
D	6	1	-	-	-	-	-	-	No details
F	12	1–3	-	-	-	-	-	-	No small finds
F	15	Sondage no.1	Sf. 30	(?)	Flake	Flint	Gray-brown	3.7 × 2.5 × 1.4 cm	Flake from a stone's exterior
F	15	1	-	-	-	-	-	-	No small finds
F	15	2	(a)	No	Container? (ostrich shell fragment)	Ostrich eggshell	Gray	less than 1 × 1 cm	Fragment from an ostrich shell

Table 3.5. Summary of Small Finds from Units D–F (Post-Well Strata and Loci)

Unit	*Locus*	*Basket or level*	*Unit Book no.*	*TBO no.*	*Object type*	*Material*	*Color and Surface Treatment*	*Dimensions (cm)*	*Comments: Mumford notes for E–F*
D	7	1	39	TBO II 39	Utensil(?), such as an ink palette	Osyster shell fragment	(white)	-	Red paint on interior
F	16	1	-	-	-	-	-	-	No small finds
F	17	1	-	-	-	-	-	-	No small finds
F	25	1 (W)	-	-	-	-	-	-	No small finds from west side
F	25	2 (W)	Sf.38	?	Pounder or grinding stone fragment	Fine grained, hard stone	Gray	8.8 x 6.6 x 6.1 cm	Grinding stone with smoothed base
F	27	1	-	-	-	-	-	-	No small finds
D	9	1	-	-	Foil	Gold	-	Small	Folded over
D	9	1	(?)	TBO II 35	Tile	Faience	Green (corroded)	-	-
F	18	1	-	-	-	-	-	-	No small finds
F	28	1	-	-	-	-	-	-	No small finds
F	29	1	Sf.40	?	Chipped stone	Quartz (glassy stone)	Brown-black	3.4 x 1.8 x 1.4 cm	Irregularly- shaped stone
F	29	1	(a)	No	Pebble	Semi-translucent	Semi-translucent, light brown	1.2 x 0.8 x 0.4 cm	Water-worn pebble
D	11	1	Cited in notes	(?)	Bead	Faience	-	Small	No details
D	11	1	No SF number	TBO II 49	Foil (jewelry)	Gold	-	Small	Folded over
D	11	1	Not in notes	TBO 0454	Obscure item (an awl or pin)	Copper alloy	Green (corroded)	Largest piece is 0.4 cm in diameter	10 cylindrical fragments from an awl/pin
F	21	1	Sf.32	-	Curved/bent needle tip(?)	Copper alloy	Green (corroded)	1.1 x 0.25 cm diameter	Bent or curved needle(?) tip.
F	32	1	Sf.39	TBO 0056	Fragment of a polishing or grinding stone	Quartzite	Red-purple	6.0 x 5.1 x 4.2 cm	Smoothed, polished edges (outside break)
F	22	1	-	-	-	-	-	-	No small finds
F	33	1	(?)	TBO 0018	Pounder	Quartzite	Color(?); one side smoothed	-	Reg. book: Noted TBO018
D	12	1	-	-	-	-	-	-	No details
F	24	1	-	-	-	-	-	-	No small finds
F	34	1	-	-	-	-	-	-	No small finds
F	35	1	-	-	-	-	-	-	No small finds
D	13	1	-	-	-	-	-	-	No details
F	37	1	Sf.43	TBO 0790	Grinding or polishing stone (hand-stone)	Sandstone	Yellow	8.2 x 7.7 x 6.1 cm	Stone with well-polished base
F	37	1	(a)	No	Flint	Flint	-	-	No details
F	38	1	-	-	-	-	-	-	No small finds
D	14	1	-	-	-	-	-	-	No details
F	39	1	-	-	Fragmentary block	Limestone	White	14.5 x 7.1 x 6.5 cm	Slab broken along 4 edges
F	42	1	(a)	No	Fragment	Sandstone (quartzite?)	Red	Small piece	No details
F	42	2–5	-	-	-	-	-	-	No small finds
C/D		-	-	TBO II 33	Ceiling block fragment	Limestone	White with a blue back-ground and gold stars in raised relief	16 x 18 cm	New Kingdom ceiling block

Table 3.6. Summary of Pottery from Loci/Layers in Well Foundations and Interior Fill

Unit	*Locus*	*Basket /level*	*Pottery basket*	*Rims*	*Handles*	*Bases*	*Nile Silts*	*Desert marls*	*Other wares*	*Comments: Hummel pottery labels*
E	100	1	Small basket of sherds	3	2	1	50%	50%	-	**Marl:** gray-green slips; peach slip
F	1	1	Medium-full basket of sherds	5	1	1	50%	50%	-	Small, worn sherds.
F	1	2	Large basket of sherds	8	9	9	40%	60%	-	New Kingdom, red-slipped, simple bowls; **Marl:** many marl amphorae.
F	2	1	Very large basket of sherds	27	8	6	45%	35%	20%	New Kingdom vessels; **Silt:** much red slip; **Other fabrics:** a Mycenaean base fragment.
F	6	1	Small to medium basket of sherds	5	5	2	50%	50%	-	**Silt:** red-slipped, simple bowls; **Marl:** peach and green burnishing.
E	101	1	Small basket of sherds	-	-	-	70%	30%	-	**Marl:** decorated with peach burnishing, green burnishing, and green slip.
F	3	1	Large basket of sherds	12	8	6	50%	49%	1%	**Silt:** much red slip; **Marl:** decorated with cream-green slip. **Other fabrics:** Cypriot White Shaved juglet handle (1450–1300 B.C.).
F	4	1	Medium-full basket of sherds	4	3	4	40%	40%	20%	**Silt:** red-slipped bowls; **Marl:** amphorae **Other fabrics:** no details.
F	4	2	Large basket of sherds	12	3	7	50%	50%	-	**Silt:** red slips and burnishing; Blue Painted pottery; **Marl:** decorated with gray-green and cream slips.
F	7	1	Large basket of sherds	12	4	3	45%	55%	-	**Silt:** many red-slipped bowls; **Marl:** cream-green slip; one Canaanite-style store-jar.
F	7	2	Large basket of sherds	20	11	16	45%	50%	5%	**Silt:** many red slipped bowls; **Other fabrics:** Canaanite amphora sherds; (a Mycenaean base joins vessel body from F8).
F	8	1	-	-	-	-	-	-	*	Pottery label absent. **Other fabrics:** Mycenaean IIIA vessel body (joins with base fragment from Locus F7).
F	9	1	Large basket of sherds	32	6	6	50%	49%	1%	**Silt:** much red slip; Blue Painted pottery; **Marl:** gray-green and green burnished pottery; **Other fabrics:** a Cypriot? Sherd; a Mycenaean sherd.
F	9	2	Large basket of sherds	12	8	8	40%	60%	-	**Silt:** much red slip on bowls; **Marl:** gray-green slip, peach slip, and gray-green burnishing on lentoid flask.
F	9	3	Small to medium basket of sherds	4	3	3	30%	70%	-	**Silt:** red slip; **Marl:** much gray-green slip and green burnishing.
F	11	1a	Medium to large basket of sherds	9	1	6	50%	40%	10%	**Silt:** red-slipped, simple bowls; **Marl:** cream-green slip, cream burnishing, peach slip. **Other fabrics:** unknown amphora ware.
F	11	1b	Large basket of sherds	23	6	6	50%	50%	-	**Silt:** much red slip and burnishing; Blue Painted sherd; **Marl:** e.g., burnished basket handle fragment.
F	11	2	Large basket of sherds	21	6	7	40%	59%	1%	**Silt:** red slip on large bowls; **Marl:** peach burnishing; cream-green slip; basket handle fragment; **Other fabrics:** a Cypriot White slip rim.
F	12	1	Medium basket of sherds	12	2	4	50%	50%	-	**Silt:** red slip on jars and bowls; **Marl:** green slip and burnishing; handle fragment joining piece from basket 2.
F	12	Sondage no.1	8 sherds in total	7	-	-	100%	-	-	**Silt:** red-slipped bowls.
F	12	Sondage no.2	Small basket of sherds	1	-	1	50%	49%	1%	**Silt:** some red slip; **Marl:** green and cream burnishing; **Other fabrics:** a possible Canaanite amphora sherd.

Table 3.6. Summary of Pottery from Loci/Layers in Well Foundations and Interior Fill

Unit	*Locus*	*Basket /level*	*Pottery basket*	*Rims*	*Handles*	*Bases*	*Nile Silts*	*Desert marls*	*Other wares*	*Comments: Hummel pottery labels*
F	12	2	Medium to large basket of sherds	4	4	3	25%	75%	-	**Silt:** red-slipped bowls; beer jar base; **Marl:** many amphora sherds; a basket handle fragment; green burnishing.
F	12	3	Medium basket of sherds	8	1	3	70%	28%	2%	**Silt:** red-slipped sherds; **Marl:** cream-green slip with black decoration; **Other fabrics:** a Cypriot White Slip bowl; a Cypriot White Shaved juglet (Late Bronze 2: 1450-1200 B.C.).
F	15	1	Small basket of sherds	3	1	1	50%	50%	-	**Silt:** much red slip and burnishing; Blue Painted sherd; **Marl:** gray-green burnished sherds.
F	15	2	1 sherd in total.	-	-	-	-	100%	-	Sondage 1: a body sherd from a Marl D flask(?) with gray-green slip decorated with red stripes in concentric circles.
F	16	1	Small to medium basket of sherds	3	1	-	50%	50%	-	**Silt:** red-slipped jar; **Marl:** much peach and green burnishing.
F	25	2	Small basket of sherds	-	2	3	75%	25%	-	Worn sherds; **Silt:** beer jar base; **Marl:** a handle and disk-base.
F	25	2a	Large basket of sherds	12	2	9	40%	60%	-	**Silt:** red-slipped and burnished bowls; **Marl:** much gray-green slip; white burnishing.
F	25	2b	Small basket of sherds	6	-	2	60%	40%	-	**Silt:** red-slipped and burnished bowl; **Marl:** gray-green slip and burnishing.
F	17	1	Small to medium basket of sherds	7	-	2	70%	30%	-	**Silt:** some red slip; black stripe on cream-slipped sherd; **Marl:** green-gray slip; burnished green and peach slips.
F	27	1	Medium-full basket of sherds	3	1	1	55%	45%	-	**Silt:** much red slip; **Marl:** much green-cream burnishing; black stripes on cream-green slip.
F	18	1	Small basket of sherds	5	-	1	75%	25%	-	Salt-encrusted vessels; **Silt:** much red slip and burnishing; Blue Painted sherd; **Marl:** black stripe on burnished, cream-green slip.
F	28	1	Sherd quantity in basket not stated	5	-	1	50%	50%	-	Salt-encrusted vessels; **Silt:** much red slip; **Marl:** burnished peach slip marls.
F	28	1a	Small basket of sherds	1	-	-	80%	20%	-	Small, worn body sherds; **Silt:** red-slipped and burnished bowl.
F	29	1	Small to medium basket of sherds	4	-	1	60%	40%	-	**Silt:** much red slip and burnishing **Marl:** much cream-green and peach burnishing.
F	21	1	Small basket of sherds	4	1	1	50%	50%	-	Salt-encrusted vessels; **Silt:** some red-slipped bowls; **Marl:** gray-green and peach slips.
F	32	1	Medium-full basket of sherds	5	4	2	50%	50%	-	Very small body sherds; **Silt:** red slip & burnishing; Blue painted sherd; **Marl:** much cream-green slip and burnishing; gray-green slip.
F	33	1	Medium basket of sherds	7	1	1	50%	49%	1%	Small and very worn body sherds; **Silt:** red slip & burnishing; Blue Painted sherd; **Marl:** white and cream-green slip and burnishing; **Other fabrics:** a possible Canaanite sherd.
F	24	1/pot	Medium-full basket of sherds	-	-	3	75%	25%	-	**Silt:** large fragments from a jar; **Marl:** large amphora base.
F	24	1	Scanty basket of sherds	-	1	-	80%	20%	-	**Silt:** Blue Painted sherd; **Marl:** amphora handle with gritty-green slip.
F	34	1	Large basket of sherds	14	5	3	40%	60%	-	**Silt:** much red slip; **Marl:** much gray-green slip with burnishing; incised handle.

Table 3.6. Summary of Pottery from Loci/Layers in Well Foundations and Interior Fill

Unit	*Locus*	*Basket /level*	*Pottery basket*	*Rims*	*Handles*	*Bases*	*Nile Silts*	*Desert marls*	*Other wares*	*Comments: Hummel pottery labels*
F	35	1	Small basket of sherds	5	-	1	60%	40%	-	**Silt:** much red slip; **Marl:** much gray-green slip with burnishing; peach and cream slips with burnishing; amphora sherds.
F	35	1/pot	Single vessel base with some sherds	-	-	1	-	100%	-	**Marl:** body sherds and base from a Marl D amphora with cream-green slip and burnishing.
F	37	1	Large basket of sherds	12	7	4	40%	60%	-	**Silt:** red-slipped and burnished bowls and jars; **Marl:** much gray-green slip on jars with some burnishing; cream slip with red and brown stripes.
F	38	1	Small basket of sherds	3	2	4	50%	50%	-	**Silt:** red slipped bowls; **Marl:** white slip and burnishing; peach and gray-green slips.
F	39	1	Large basket of sherds	15	6	7	50%	50%	-	**Silt:** some red slips and peach slip; some burnishing; **Marl:** much peach and cream-green slip.
F	39	1a	Medium-full basket of sherds	2	2	2	50%	50%	-	**Silt:** some red slip; **Marl:** white slip and a gray-green slips.
F	42	1	Large basket of sherds	6	3	1	39%	60%	1%	**Silt:** traces of red slip; **Marl:** highly burnished white slip; burnished white and green slip; **Other fabrics:** a Canaanite amphora base
F	42	2	Small basket of sherds	2	1	-	50%	50%	-	Small salt-encrusted sherds **Silt:** traces of red slip; **Marl:** gray-green and cream slips.
F	42	3	Large basket of sherds	11	5	6	40%	60%	-	**Silt:** much red slipped bowls; some peach and cream slips; **Marl:** gray-green slip with some burnishing
F	42	4	Scanty basket of sherds	1	-	-	60%	40%	-	Some small body sherds; **Marl:** cream slip on Marl D jar rim.
F	42	5	Scanty basket of sherds	-	-	-	60%	40%	-	Some Nile silt body sherds.
Ca	TBO II 37	1	TBP 207	-	1	-	-	-	-	Stamped jar handle with cartouche of Ankhkheperure
Ca	TBO II 36	1	TBP 222	-	1	-	-	-	-	Stamped jar handle with prenomen of Tutankhamun
F	26 Well curb-wall	1	Small basket of sherds	-	-	1	59%	40%	1%	Small, worn vessels; **Silt:** some red slip; streaky cream slip; **Marl:** gray-green burnishing; **Other fabrics:** a possible Canaanite sherd.
F	36	1	Small basket of sherds	2	-	-	50%	50%	-	**Silt:** red slip traces; **Marl:** much gray-green slip; cream-white slip and burnishing.
F	46	1	Medium-full basket of sherds	8	1	2	40%	60%	-	**Silt:** some red-slips; an early–mid-Dynasty 18, black-rimmed bowl sherd; **Marl:** much gray-green slip and burnishing.
Total	-	-	**688+body sherds**	387	139	162	**52%**	**47%**	**1%**	**Note:** The silt and marl percentages represent averages from the columns.

grinder, elsewhere noted from Unit F, Locus 43), flint tools and debitage (three flakes; flint) (pl. 3:6 no.7, TBO 0102, a chert/graywacke pebble polisher?), 17 lumps of copper alloy, copper alloy tools and fittings (a staple? a nail? two needles? two blades? a rolled-up sheet) (pl. 3:5 no. 5, TBO 0083, this fragmentary point from Unit C, Locus 1, basket 4 probably came from Field II, Area 1; pl. 3:5 no. 7, TBO 0007; pl. 3:5 no. 13, TBO 0014; pl. 3:5 no. 15, TBO 0420; pl. 3:5 no. 20, TBO 0045, cylindrical handle?), jewelry (a copper alloy bead; faience beads) (pl. 3.4 no.1: TBO 0038, faience and carnelian bead; pl. 3.4 no.6: TBO 0028, circular, blue faience bead), a faience tile fragment

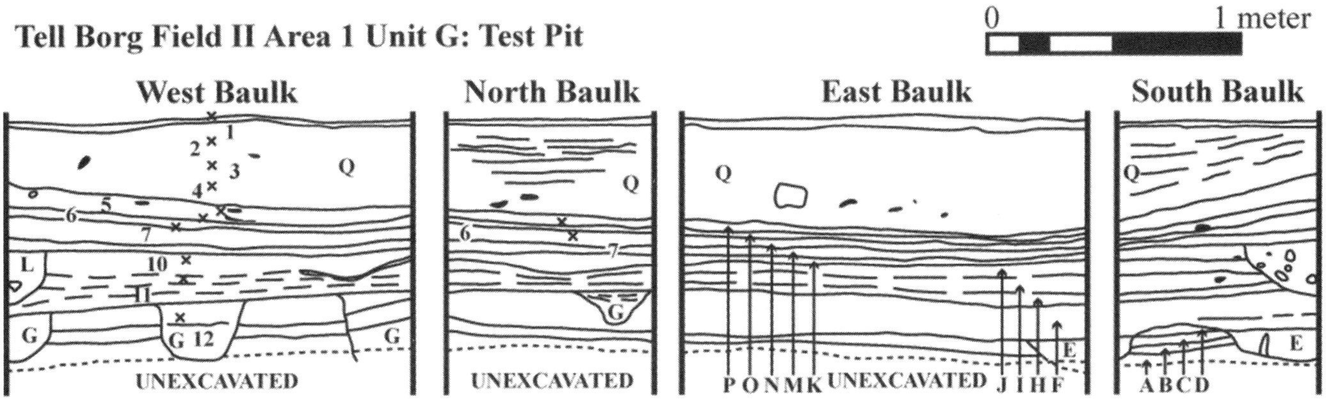

Fig. 3.24. All four baulks of Unit G test pit in Field II, Area 1 (drawn by G. Mumford; digitized by Joshua Olsen).

(pl. 3:4 no.12, TBO 0035), two or more ostrich eggshell fragments (pl. 3.2 nos. 1–2: TBO 0040 and 0023, large and medium fragments), 688 diagnostic sherds of Egyptian pottery (99%), including jar handles with stamp seal impressions (pl. 3.3 no. 3: TBO 0008/TBP 270), and foreign pottery (1%: Canaanite, Cypriot, and Mycenaean sherds). Aside from the six successive, lime-plastered surfaces, the debris below and between the lime-plastered layers appears to reflect the deposition of refuse and the collapse of parts of the stone-lined well. The percentage of foreign wares (1%) within the refuse pit is comparable to most other portions of Tell el-Borg and other Egyptian sites.

3.2.4. Field II, Area 1, Unit G (see figs. 3.1, 3.2.b, 3.18; 16 m East of Units C–F Well)
Excavator: G. Mumford.

G. Mumford excavated a test-pit, called Unit G, during the 2001 season at Tell el-Borg (see detail map in fig. 3.3). This unit lies 16 m east of the stone-lined well (Units C, D, E, and F) and 26 m southwest of Unit I (Area 1/2). Unit G represents a 1 × 2 m test pit. It was placed in the low ground, to the east of the stone-lined well, in order to investigate the nature of the occupation in this area. Excavation continued to a depth of 1.20 m, revealing occupation debris throughout 18 phases of deposited layers and pitting (fig. 3.24). However, this test pit did not reach the basal sand.

3.2.4.1. Phase 1: (Unit G) (fig. 3.24)

The lowest excavated layer in Unit G consists of fine- to medium-grained, gray sand (10 YR 6/1) with some charcoal flecks and several potsherds. The arbitrary Locus 12 in Unit G encompassed phases 1–6. A stone slab and stone chunk lay at the base of this phase. The occupation debris continued to extend below this part of Unit G but remains unexcavated.

3.2.4.2. Phase 2: (Unit G) (fig. 3.24)

Phase 1 was overlain by the phase 2 layer, which contained fine- to coarse-grained, yellow and white mottled sand (10YR 8/2; 10YR 7/6; 5Y 2.5/1) with brown and black clay nodules, pebble- and gravel-sized stones, and charcoal flecks.

3.2.4.3. Phases 3–4: (Unit G) (fig. 3.24)

The phase 2 layer was overlain by two white sand lenses, which were included in the excavation of Locus 12.

3.2.4.4. Phase 5: (Unit G) (fig. 3.24)

In phase 5, two small pits cut into the surface and the underlying layers of phases 1–4; these pits were backfilled with sand by the end of phase 5 (Locus 12).

3.2.4.5. Phase 6: (Unit G) (fig. 3.24)

Phase 6 represented the deposition of a very hard-packed, fine- to medium-grained sand layer (10YR 6/2; 10YR 7/2), with lime fragments and clay nodules, above the two phase 5 pits and tops of the layers of phases 2 and 4. This phase lay at the top of Locus 12.

3.2.4.6. Phase 7: (Unit G) (fig. 3.24)

In phase 7, another pit appears to have cut into the southwest corner of Unit G, cutting through phase 6 and into one of the earlier pits, severing the stratigraphic connections between the southern and eastern baulks (only the lower part of the phase 7 pit was traced, but this explains the otherwise discontinuous layer from the southern to western baulk face). In addition to the southwest pit, three further pits cut into this layer. All four pits were filled, ending phase 7. An arbitrary Locus 11 encompassed phases 6–12.

3.2.4.7. Phase 8: (Unit G) (fig. 3.24)

In phase 8 (see Locus 11), a fine-grained, yellow-gray sand layer (10YR 5/2) with some medium- to coarse-grained sand, charcoal flecks, fragments of bone, clay nodules, and potsherds overlay phase 7. As in the previous phase, it appears that the pits in the southwest corner of Unit G have caused some difficulty in tracing and matching the phase 8 layer from the southern to western baulks.

3.2.4.8. Phase 9: (Unit G) (fig. 3.24)

In phase 9 (Locus 11), a fine-grained, yellow-gray sand layer (10YR 5/2) with some medium- to coarse-grained sand, charcoal flecks, fragments of bone, clay nodules, and potsherds succeeded phase 8.

3.2.4.9. Phase 10: (Unit G) (fig. 3.24)

In-turn, a fine-grained, yellow-gray sand layer (10YR 5/2) with some medium- to coarse-grained sand, charcoal flecks, fragments of bone, clay nodules, and potsherds, also overlay phase 9. This layer spans phase 10 and was excavated as part of Locus 11.

3.2.4.10. Phase 11: (Unit G) (fig. 3.24)

In phase 11 (Locus 11), phase 10 was also overlain by a fine- to medium-grained yellow-brown soil (10YR 4/4) with charcoal flecks and potsherds.

3.2.4.11. Phase 12: (Unit G) (fig. 3.24)

In phase 12, a pit was cut through phases 7–11 but was soon backfilled with other debris. This phase lay at the top of Locus 11, which spanned phases 6–12.

3.2.4.12. Phase 13: (Unit G) (fig. 3.24)

Phases 11 and 12 (pit) were overlain in phase 13 by a firmly packed, fine- to medium-grained, yellow-brown soil (10YR 4/4) with potsherds. Arbitrary Loci 7 and 9 in Unit G covered phase 12 (fill layer in a pit) and phases 13–16.

3.2.4.13. Phase 14 : (Unit G) (fig. 3.24)

In phase 14, a fine-grained, gray-yellow sand (10YR 4/3; 10YR 5/6) with charcoal flecks overlay the layer of phase 13. Arbitrary Loci 6 and 8 in Unit G included phases 13–17.

3.2.4.14. Phase 15: (Unit G) (fig. 3.24)

In phase 15, a gray to gray-yellow, sandy clay (10YR 5/1; 10YR 6/4) with charcoal flecks, fragments of bone, and clay brick debris overlay the layer in phase 14. Arbitrary Locus 5 in Unit G also encompassed parts of phases 14–17.

3.2.4.15. Phase 16: (Unit G) (fig. 3.24)

A layer of relatively harder-packed, mottled yellow sand (10YR 5/1; 10YR 6/4; 5YR 2/5), with brown clay nodules, white clay lumps, charcoal flecks, and potsherds, succeeded the phase 15 layer. Arbitrary Loci 3 and 4 in Unit G spanned portions of phases 15–17.

3.2.4.16. Phase 17: (Unit G) (fig. 3.24)

The penultimate sub-surface layer in phase 17 consisted of poorly sorted multiple layers of soft, fine- to coarse-grained yellow sand (10YR 6/4) with mud-brick debris, charcoal flecks, tiny fragments of bone, shell, gypsum nodules, some pebble- and cobble-sized stones, salt encrustations, and potsherds (including some burned sherds). Arbitrary Locus 2 in Unit G covered phase 17.

3.2.4.17. Phase 18: (Unit G) (fig. 3.24)

The final phase (phase 18) represents a thin surface layer consisting of wind- and water-laid fine white sand (10YR 7/2). Arbitrary Locus 1 in Unit G included phases 17–18.

3.2.4.18. Discussion of Phases 1–18 (Unit G) (fig. 3.24)

Unit G yielded a variety of New Kingdom Egyptian forms and fabrics, including 63% Nile silts and 36% desert marls. The remaining fabrics consisted of a Canaanite store-jar, which represented less than 1% of the pottery assemblage (table 3.8). The remaining material culture debris included sporadic mud-brick debris (phases 15 and 17), a limestone slab, and a nearby fragment of limestone (phase 12 basket 2; table 3.7). This implies the erosion and redispersal of elements from a nearby mud brick building and possibly even a stone structure at some point during the New Kingdom.

Table 3.7. Summary of Small Finds from Unit G, Loci 1–12

Unit	*Locus*	*Basket or level*	*Unit Book no.*	*Object type*	*Material*	*Color and Surface Treatment*	*Dimensions (cm)*	*Comments: Mumford notes for Unit G*
G	1–11	1	-	-	-	-	-	No small finds
G	12	1	(a)	Stone slab Fragment	Limestone	White	38 x 34 x 10+? cm	Broken limestone slab

3.2.5. Field II, Area 1, Unit H: (see figs. 3.3; 22 m East of Units C–F Well)
Excavator: J. Cheek

Unit H (test pit) is located 22 meters east of the stone-lined well (Units C, D, E, and F) and 12 m south of Unit I. Unit H encompasses a 1 × 2 m test pit located in the low ground to the northeast of the stone-lined well. The goal of opening this unit also was to detect occupation debris in this area. Jeremy Cheek excavated the Unit H test pit to 0.70 m in depth but halted excavations

Table 3.8. Summary of Pottery from Unit G, Loci 1–12 (basket totals differ per locus)

Unit	*Locus*	*Basket/ level*	*Pottery basket*	*Rims*	*Handles*	*Bases*	*Nile silts*	*Desert marls*	*Other wares*	*Comments: Hummel pottery labels*
G	1	1	-	-	-	-	-	-	-	**No pottery from Locus 1**
G	2	2	Scanty basket of sherds	1	1	1	75%	25%	-	**Silt:** red-slipped bowl; **Marl:** amphora base and handle; Theban area marls.
G	3	1	Scanty basket of sherds	-	-	-	75%	25%	-	Small, salt-encrusted body sherds; **Silt:** jar fragment; **Marl:** cream slip.
G	4	1	Small basket of sherds	4	1	-	50%	50%	-	Small, salt-encrusted body sherds; **Silt:** red-slipped bowls; **Marl:** amphora handle.
G	5	1	Small basket of sherds	3	-	-	50%(?)	50%(?)	-	**Silt:** red slip with some burnishing; **Marl:** gray-green slip; **Other fabrics:** burnished orange slip on brown ware.
G	6	1	Small basket of sherds	3	1	-	75%	25%	-	**Silt:** red-slipped, simple bowls; **Marl:** cream slips; an amphora handle.
G	7	1	Small basket of sherds	1	1	1	60%	40%	-	Very worn surfaces. **Marl:** gray-green slips.
G	8	1	9 sherds in total	-	-	-	100%	-	-	**Silt:** red-slipped, simple bowls.
G	9	1	Scanty basket of sherds	1	-	-	75%	20%	5%	**Silt:** red slip traces; **Marl:** gray-green slips; **Other fabrics:** a Canaanite jar rim.
G	9	2	Small basket of sherds	1	1	-	50%	50%	-	**Marl:** amphorae sherds; peach slip with burnishing; peach and gray-green slips.
G	10	1	Scanty basket of sherds	2	-	-	70%	30%	-	**Silt:** red-slipped and burnished simple bowl; red-slipped bowls **Marl:** cream slip with burnishing; peach slipped amphora.
G	11	1	Scanty basket of sherds	4	2	2	50%	50%	-	**Silt:** red-slipped and burnished bowl; **Marl:** strap-handle and basket-handle from small vessels.
G	12	1	4 sherds in total	-	-	-	25%	75%	-	**Marl:** 3 Theban marl sherds. **Silt**: 1 silt sherd
G	12	2	3 sherds in total	-	-	-	67%	33%(?)	-	**Another fabric(?):** possibly marl. **Silt**: 2 silt sherds.
Total	-	-	**31+ body sherds**	20	7	4	**63%**	**36%**	**0.4%**	**Note:** The silt and marl percentages represent averages from the columns.

Table 3.9. Summary of Small Finds from Unit H, Loci 1–12.

Unit	*Locus*	*Basket or level*	*Unit Book no.*	*TBO no.*	*Object type*	*Material*	*Color and Surface Treatment*	*Dimensions (cm)*	*Comments: J. Cheek's notes for Unit H*
H	1	1	(a)	No	Lump	Copper alloy	Green (corroded)	No details (small)	Small lump of copper alloy.
H	2–6	1	-	-	-	-	-	-	No small finds
H	7	1	(a)	No	Container? <ostrich?> eggshell	<Ostrich?> eggshell	Gray?	Probably smaller than 1 × 1 cm	J. Cheek's reference to "eggshell" is interpreted as ostrich

when work shifted to Units I, J, and K. In general, this test pit yielded results similar to Unit G, revealing multiple sand layers with clay brick debris (Locus 3), limestone and sandstone chips (Loci 1–7), flecks of charcoal (Loci 1–6), fragments of bone (Locus 6), shells (Loci 6–7), copper alloy lumps (Locus 1), and potsherds (Loci 1–7; including a burned sherd in Locus 5).

This excavation unit produced a variety of New Kingdom pottery forms and fabrics, including mostly Egyptian fabrics (99%). As in most other contexts at Tell el-Borg, the only imported fabric amounted to less than 2%—namely, a sherd from a Canaanite store-jar (table 3.10, Locus 6). This test pit also contained a lump of copper alloy at the surface and an ostrich(?) eggshell (probably exploited for food; possibly reused as a container) (table 3.9).

Table 3.10. Summary of Pottery from Unit H, Loci 1–7

Unit	*Locus*	*Basket/ level*	*Pottery basket*	*Rims*	*Handles*	*Bases*	*Nile silts*	*Desert marls*	*Other wares*	*Comments: Hummel pottery labels.*
H	1	1	Scanty basket of sherds	3	1	-	80%	20%	-	Small, very worn body sherds; **Silt:** red slip traces; **Marl:** peach and cream slips; gray-green slip with burnishing.
H	2	1	11 sherds in total (including 1 rim)	1	-	-	80%	20%	-	Salt-encrusted body sherds; **Silt:** red slip; **Marl:** cream slip.
H	3	1	3 sherds in total	-	-	-	67%	33%	-	**Silt:** red-slipped sherds; **Marl:** cream-slipped Marl D2 sherd.
H	4	1	Scanty basket of sherds. ("3 sherds" noted under "other" fabrics, possibly in error).	1	-	-	50%	50%	(?)	**Marl:** 2 body sherds from cream-slipped and peach-slipped vessels; **Silt:** a rim from a red-slipped and burnished Nile silt bowl.
H	5	1	10 sherds in total (including 4 diagnostic sherds)	2	1	1	90%	10%	-	**Silt:** a red-slipped bowl base; rims from large bowls; **Marl:** gray-green slip.
H	6	1	Scanty basket of sherds	1	1	-	80%	10%	10%	**Silt:** highly burnished, red-slipped bowl; **Marl:** Marl D and Marl A sherds; **Other fabrics:** a possible Canaanite amphora sherd.
H	7	1	(?)	-	-	-	-	-	-	No pottery label.
Total	-	-	**12 + body sherds**	8	3	1	**72%**	**27%**	**2%**	**Note:** The silt and marl percentages represent averages from the columns.

3.3. Field II, Areas 1 and 2: Courtyard Area and Its Environs (Unit I and Units J–K):

(Figs. 3.1–3, 3.25–27)

Excavators: Gregory Mumford and Aaron Burke

The Trinity International University expedition excavated Units I, J, and K in 2001 (see OCHRE pls. 63–68). Units I–K lie 26 m northeast of the stone-lined well (Units C, D, E, and F), 26 m north-northeast of Unit G, 12 m north of Unit H, 16 m southwest of Unit A (East), and immediately south of the broad area explored by Unit A. Aaron Burke excavated Unit I at the border of Area 1, while Gregory Mumford worked in neighboring Units J–K in Area 1/2 (the dividing line between Areas 1 and 2 lay between Units J–K and I). This series of excavation units represent an expansion of a small test pit (Unit I) in order to delineate the extent of a hard-packed, multi-layered white floor. (This floor lay between a wall system and a structure in Unit A to the north and a stone-lined well in Units C–F to the southwest.) This multi-layered white floor was 5–8 cm

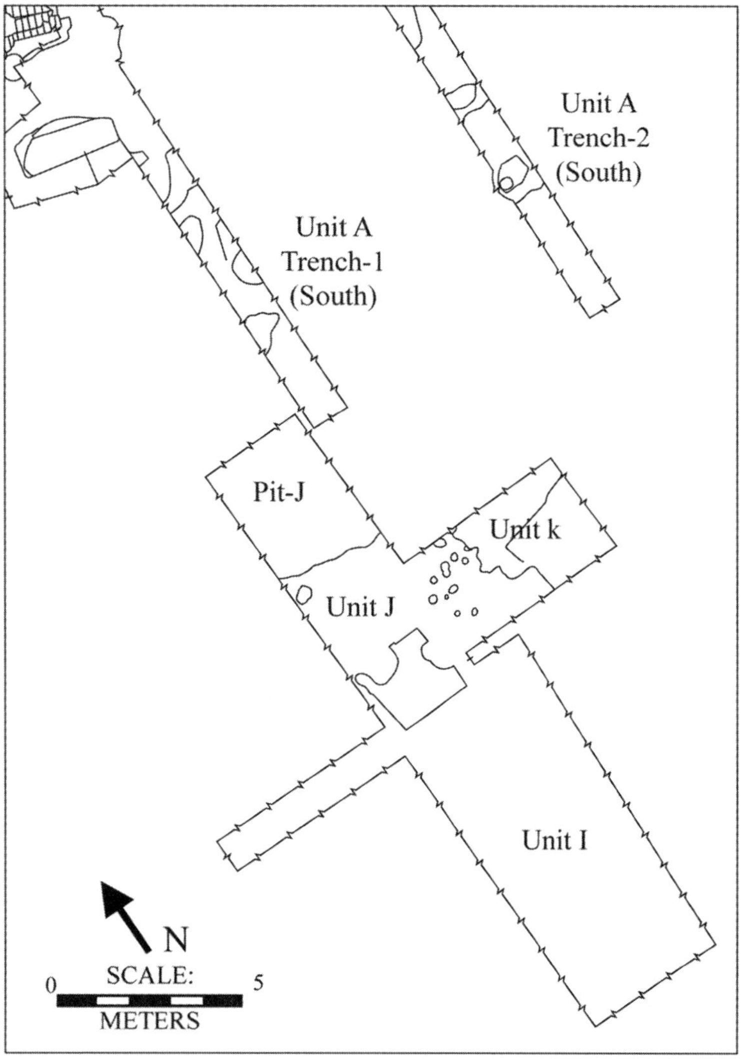

Fig. 3.25. Field II, Area 1: Unit A Trenches 1–2 (South); Units I–K (2001 season) (drawn by James Knudstad; digitized by Joshua Olsen).

thick in the southern part of this area. It overlay a sand occupation layer, which in turn capped the sterile, basal sand. The white floor was overlain in succession by a thin layer of wind-blown yellow sand, two phases of mud-brick installations, a layer of gray-yellow sand, and a modern mottled layer of gray, black, and yellow sand and clay debris. A large pit (Pit J) cut through the New Kingdom occupation layers but was covered by a more recent sub-surface layer and loose surface sand.

3.3.1. Phase 0: Basal Sand Layer (Unit I, Locus 7)

The basal sand lay close to the modern surface in Units I, J, and K, lying 52 cm below the surface of Unit J at the edge of a large pit. The basal sand was also detected in the northeast corner of Unit I (fig. 3.26). The basal sand layer consisted of a light yellow-white layer of sand underlying the occupation debris at Tell el-Borg. The excavation into this layer is reflected by the assignment of Locus I7 basket 1 to the 30-cm probe into the basal sand in the northeast corner of Unit I (this layer lacked pottery and small finds).

3.3.2. Phase 1: Early–mid-Dynasty 18 Occupation Layer (Unit I, Locus 6): (OCHRE pl. 68)

An 18-cm-deep, hard-packed, yellow-brown layer of sand and silt overlay the basal sand in Areas 1–2. It was traced along the pit edge in Unit J, the western extension of Unit I, and the northeast corner of Unit I, where this layer was excavated as Loci I6. In the east half of Unit K, part of a mud-brick wall and an adjacent sand layer was traced beyond and below the eastern edge of the multi-layered white surface. This wall has a different orientation than the later mud-brick installation above the white surface, and it represents the earliest phase of construction between the basal sand and the courtyard floor.

This layer was excavated as Locus I6 (basket 1) and produced some potsherds at the top of the layer, immediately below the materials composing the courtyard floor. The pottery sample was quite small, yielding mostly Egyptian forms and fabrics (90%) and one Canaanite amphora sherd (10%) (table 3.11). This layer cannot pre-date early Dynasty 18 owing to the presence of well-sealed pottery dating to this period. The locus lacked small finds.

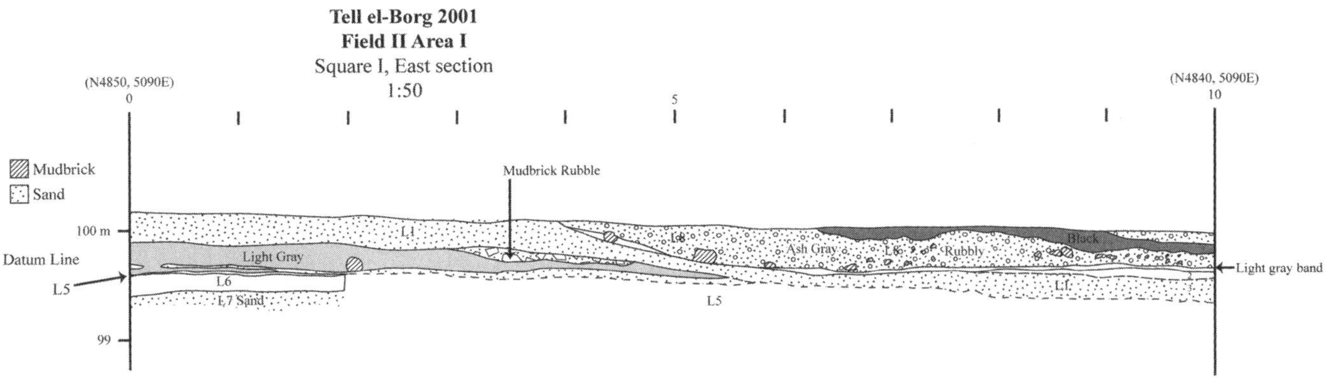

Fig. 3.26. West section of Unit I, Field II, Area 1 (drawn by Aaron Burke; digitized by Joshua Olsen).

3.3.3. Phase 2: Mid-Dynasty 18+? Courtyard Floor (Unit I, Loci 5 and 12): (OCHRE pl. 67)

A large, floored courtyard was detected in Units I–K (Areas 1–2), 16 m south of the interior corner of the zigzagging enclosure wall. Excavation in Unit J (Area 1) and Unit I (Area 2) revealed that a 5–8 cm thick sandstone-like surface composed the courtyard floor spanning Areas 1–2. In Unit I, portions of this surface were excavated as Loci I5 and I12. The flooring appeared to represent an accumulation of multiple horizontal layers of fine yellow-white sand. It was devoid of potsherds and other inclusions. Locus I12 represents the center and southern half of Unit I, where this floor had been broken and eroded. A post-hole or pit lay near the west baulk, 2 m from the south end of Unit I. Only a few isolated sherds appeared within this floor surface; otherwise, the floor was devoid of potsherds (table 3.12) and lacked small finds.

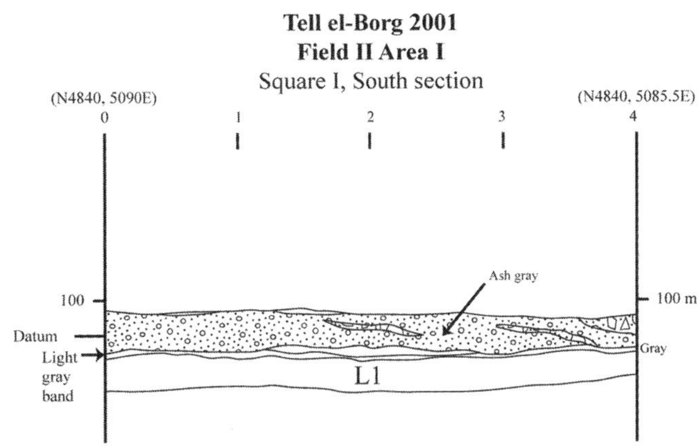

Fig. 3.27. South section of Unit I, Field II, Area 1 (drawn by Aaron Burke; digitized by Joshua Olsen).

To the north, the courtyard floor had been cut by a large ovoid pit (Units J, Ja, Jb, Jc, and Jd). This edge interrupted the court's flooring, which continued in the northern edge of the pit 11.50 m farther to the north. Hence, this flooring is preserved for at least 25.50 m north–south, beginning at least 14 m to the south of Pit J, at the southern baulk of Unit I, where the floor is badly eroded, and continuing north to the vicinity of the granite block. In Unit K (an east extension of Unit J), a west extension of Unit I, and part of Unit Jc, this floor was traced for 7–10 m east–west, before disappearing. The occurrence of early–mid Dynasty 18 pottery below the courtyard floor suggests that the floor was constructed at some point during or toward the end of this period, possibly extending into late Dynasty 18.

3.3.4. Phase 3: Mid-Dynasty 18+? Initial Mud-Brick Construction (Unit J, Locus 10a)

There is evidence for some mud-brick construction immediately above the white surface of the courtyard (OCHRE pl. 66). The exact nature of this construction was disguised by a later mud-brick expansion above it, but it is possible that it represented a small square installation (less than 2 × 2 m) that was succeeded by a larger square installation (2.10 × 2.10 m) in mud brick. This mud-brick installation was assigned Loci I10 and J10. It remained unexcavated (i.e., it was

Table 3.11. Summary of Pottery from Unit I, Locus 6, Basket 1

Unit	*Locus*	*Basket/ level*	*Pottery basket*	*Rims*	*Handles*	*Bases*	*Nile silts*	*Desert marls*	*Other Wares*	*Comments: Hummel pottery labels*
I	6	1 (P1)	Small basket of sherds	2	-	2	-	90%	10%	**Silt:** an early–mid-Dynasty 18, black-rimmed bowl. **Other fabrics:** a Canaanite store-jar base and a Cypriot white slip sherd.
Total	-	-	4+ body sherds	2	-	2	-	90%	10%	**Note:** The silt and marl percentages represent averages from the columns.

Table 3.12. Summary of Pottery from Unit I, Loci 5 and 12, Basket 1

Unit	*Locus*	*Basket/ level*	*Pottery basket*	*Rims*	*Handles*	*Bases*	*Nile silts*	*Desert marls*	*Other wares*	*Comments: Hummel pottery labels*
I	5 and 12	1 (P2)	Sherds	-	-	-	-	-	-	Only a few sherds found within floor matrix. No details.

not removed), but seemed to lack both potsherds and small finds. Like the suggestion regarding the date of construction for the courtyard's flooring, it is likely that the mud-brick installation appeared at some point in the middle of Dynasty 18.

3.3.5. Phase 4: Mid–Late Dynasty 18(?) Small Pits in White Floor (Units I–K)

The northeast corner of the courtyard's floor exhibited a cluster of twelve randomly placed circular holes cutting through the flooring (OCHRE pl. 67). The broader context and function of these holes remains unclear: they may represent cache pits or perhaps post-holes with varying diameters (13–14 cm; 15–16 cm; 17–18 cm; 21–22 cm; 26–27 cm). They may have been used for one or more later structure(s) or for scaffolding poles associated with the construction, or destruction, of a building in or near the courtyard. Eleven of these pits lay below Locus K4, while one pit lay under Locus J9 (basket 1). They each contained a sterile sand filling. A small pit ("post-hole") also was cut into the courtyard flooring in the southwest corner of Unit I. This phase of pitting post-dates the initial construction of the floor and may date to some time near the end of Dynasty 18 (or perhaps even later?). Every pit lacked pottery and small finds.

3.3.6. Phase 5: Wind-Blown, Yellow Sand Layer above Floor (Unit I, Loci 4 and 11, Unit J, Loci 9, 11, and Unit K, Loci 4–5): (OCHRE pl. 66)

A shallow sand deposit several centimeters in depth accumulated over the white floor in Units I, J, and K. This layer consisted of medium- to coarse-grained soft yellow sand, with a clam shell fragment, a copper alloy tube/bead (pl. 3:5 no. 21, TBO 299), a copper alloy hook(?) (J9 basket 4, sf.15), and medium to large potsherds (mostly flat-lying). It was excavated as Locus J9 basket 1 (north of mud-brick installation), Locus J9 basket 2 (west of mud-brick installation), Locus J9 basket 4 (east of mud-brick installation), Locus J11 (east side of mud-brick installation; below later expansion of this installation), Locus K5 basket 1 (east of Loci J11 basket 1 and J9 basket 4), Locus K4 basket 1, and Loci I4, I5, and I11.

The courtyard surface in Unit I was overlain by a thin layer of soft wind-blown, yellow sand (Loci I4 basket 1 and I11 baskets 1–2). This wind-blown sand layer was excavated as Loci I4, I11, J9, and K4, and produced a high proportion of Egyptian forms and fabrics (91%) but also exhibited a significant amount (9%) of imported Cypriot and Canaanite pottery (table 3.14).

Table 3.13. Summary of Small Finds from Units I–K, Loci 4, 5, 9, and 11

Unit	*Locus*	*Basket or level*	*Unit Book no.*	*TBO no.*	*Object type*	*Material*	*Color & Surface Treatment:*	*Dimensions (cm)*	*Comments: Mumford J–K notes; Burke Unit I notes*
I	4	1 (P5)	-	-	-	-	-	-	No small finds
I	4	Basket no.1(?)	(?)	TBO 0299	Tube-shaped bead	Copper alloy	Green (corroded)	0.08.5 cm diameter	SF register: Cited in SF index cards
I	11	1–2 (P5)	-	-	-	-	-	-	No small finds
J	9	1 (P5)	-	-	-	-	-	-	No small finds
J	9	2 (P5)	-	-	-	-	-	-	No small finds
J	9	4 (P5)	Sf.14	TBO 0203	Hook or staple fragment	Copper alloy	Green (corroded)	2.1 × 1.2 × 0.3 cm	A hook-shaped copper wire
J	11	1 (P5)	-	-	-	-	-	-	No small finds
K	4	1 (P5)	-	-	-	-	-	-	No small finds
K	5	1 (P5)	(a)	No	Fragment	Granite	Pink and black	(small piece)	No details

Table 3.14. Summary of Pottery from Unit I Loci 4 Basket 1 and 11 Baskets 1–2, Unit K, Locus 4 Basket 1, and Unit J, Locus 9 Baskets 1–4.

Unit	*Locus*	*Basket/ level*	*Pottery basket*	*Rims*	*Handles*	*Bases*	*Nile silts*	*Desert marls*	*Other wares*	*Comments: Hummel pottery labels*
I	4	1 (P5)	Scanty basket of sherds	1	1	-	60%	20%	20%	**Marl:** gray-green cream on Marl D; **Other fabrics:** a Cypriot Base Ring handle and body sherd; a Canaanite sherd.
I	11	1 (P5)	Scanty sherds	-	-	1	70%	30%		**Silt:** flat base from bowl; red slip traces; **Marl:** cream slip on a variety of marls.
I	11	2 (P5)	5 sherds	2	-	1	60%	20%	20%	**Silt:** red-rimmed bowl; **Marl:** jar rim; **Other fabrics:** a Cypriot White Slip sherd.
K	4	1 (P5)	Scanty basket of sherds	-	-	-	80%	20%	-	Small, worn body sherds; **Marl:** cream slips.
J	9	1 (P5)	Scanty basket of sherds	-	-	-	60%	40%	-	Small, very worn, body sherds; **Marl:** gritty green fabric; gray-green slip.
J	9	2 (P5)	6 sherds in total	-	-	-	60%	40%	-	**Marl:** green slip and burnishing.
J	9	3 (P5)	1 sherd in total (Pot no.3)	-	-	-	-	100%	-	**Marl:** a neck and shoulder piece from a jar with cream slip.
J	9	4 (P5)	3 sherds in total (including 1 rim sherd)	1	-	-	33%	33%	33%	**Silt:** body sherd. **Marl:** cream-slipped jar rim; **Other fabrics:** a possible Canaanite sherd with peach slip.
Total	-	-	**7 + body sherds**	4	1	2	**53%**	**38%**	**9%**	**Note:** The silt and marl percentages represent averages from the columns.

3.3.7. Phase 6: Mid-Late(?) Dynasty 18 Mud-Brick Installation (Units I–J, Locus 10)

The remnants of a 2.10 × 2.10 m mud-brick installation (Unit J, Locus 10 basket 1; Unit I, Locus 10 basket 1) lay over a smaller mud-brick installation and surrounding thin sand layer that lay on the courtyard's floor (OCHRE pl. 67). Although the limited preservation and context associated with this much-eroded installation makes any interpretation difficult, it is possible that it represents the base of a large "altar," or part of a later wall system laid over the thin sand layer covering the courtyard's floor. This mud-brick installation was partly excavated as Locus I10 (basket 1). The northern end of Locus I3 yielded traces of the southern portion of this eroded, mud-brick installation, which was assigned Locus I10, extending the application of Locus 10 to the same installation in Unit J. In Unit I, this mud-brick area lay above Locus I4 (wind-blown sand above the courtyard's floor), beside Locus I3 (hard-packed debris layer), and below Locus I1 (yellow-gray sand layer). A period of abandonment and winter rains eroded the mud-brick installations, spreading a layer of mud-brick debris over the surface of the underlying wind-blown sand layer surrounding this area.

The suggestion that the expanded mud-brick installation dates around mid–late Dynasty 18 takes into consideration the passage of time between (1) the initial occupation (early–mid Dynasty 18 pottery) of this part of Tell el-Borg, (2) the construction of a courtyard floor, (3) the installation of brickwork, (4–5) the accumulation of windblown sand and pitting, and (6) the second phase of mud-brick construction. The mud-brick installation lacked both pottery and small finds.

3.3.8. Phase 7: Late Dynasty 18 Mud-Brick Debris (Units K Locus 3 and I Locus 3)

A 2–5-cm-thick layer of eroded brown sandy clay debris spread out around the vicinity of this eroded mud-brick installation. This layer was excavated as Locus J9 basket 3 (see above), Locus K3 (basket 2/level 2: gray brick debris), and Locus I3 (OCHRE pl. 65). In Unit K, this layer contained a few intact mud bricks, which may represent the remnants of a wall heading eastward. A hard-packed layer of sand, silt, and mud-brick debris lay above the wind-blown sand layer (Locus I4). This layer was excavated as Locus I3 and K3 and contained several potsherds, which included a copper alloy bead (TBO.299) and mostly Egyptian pottery forms and wares (93%) and some (7%+) possible foreign fabrics (table 3.15).

3.3.9. Phase 8: Dynasty 19(?) Yellow-Gray Sand Layer(s) (Units I Loci 1–2, Unit J Loci 3 [south] and 5, and Unit K, Loci 3–2 [west]): (OCHRE pls. 63–64)

The surface layer in the northern side of Unit I, throughout Unit J, and in the western part of Unit K, contained a hard-packed, medium- to coarse-grained yellow-brown to gray layer of sand and silt. This layer was excavated as Loci J5 (baskets 1, 2, and 3), the southern part of J3, the western parts of K3, and K2, I1 (baskets 1–6), and I2 (baskets 1–2). This layer and loci contained some pebble- and cobble-sized limestone chips (J3; I1–2), red quartzite chips (J3), quartzite pebbles (J5), calcite fragments (J3), a sandstone fragment (J3), pieces of granite (K2), fragments of bone (J3; K2; I1–2), shells (J3; I1–2), and some mud-brick debris (J5). A pile of loose mud bricks lay in the northwest corner of Locus K5 basket 3. Other material culture debris from these loci consist of a blue faience cylindrical bead (J3 sf.3), four copper alloy lumps (J3 sf.4a–c; I1–2), a copper nail(?) (J3 sf.2) (pl. 3:5 no.9, TBO 117, awl?), a copper hook (K2 sf.2), a copper sheet (J3 sf.4), and 21 fragments from the rims and bodies of at least three copper alloy vessels (J3 sf.8a–v) (table 3.15). A chert flake of conflicting provenance may also come from this area and period (pl. 3:6 no.10, TBO 110, elsewhere assigned to Locus 8, basket 1 in Unit I) (see also OCHRE pls. 89–90).

The pottery from this layer included 99% Egyptian pottery forms and fabrics (marl and silt) and 1% foreign fabrics (a Cypriot sherd and a Canaanite sherd). The pottery dates to the New Kingdom in general, while the presence of Blue Painted pottery indicates that this layer cannot pre-date the reign of Amenhotep III, and probably dates around early Dynasty 19 (according to the relative stratigraphy).

3.3.10. Phases 1–8: New Kingdom Layers Pre-Dating Pit J in Units JA, JB, and JC

In 2007, Units Ja, Jb, and Jc were laid out as 1.50 × 8 m trenches to the east, north, and west of the northern end of Unit J, respectively, with the objective of tracing the limits of Pit J (OCHRE pls. 76–88). This goal was realized within 2–4 m of the beginning of each trench extension, revealing an ovoid-shaped pit measuring 6 m wide by around 10.5 m in length. Unit Jd

Table 3.15. Summary of Small Finds from Unit I, Loci 1–2, Unit J Loci 3 (South) and 5, and Unit K, Loci 2–3 (West)

Unit	*Locus*	*Basket or level*	*Unit Book no.*	*TBO no.*	*Object type*	*Material*	*Color and Surface Treatment*	*Dimensions (cm)*	*Comments: Mumford J–K and Burke Unit I notes*
I(?)	1	-	(?)	TBO II 50	An awl or a similar item	Copper alloy	Green (corroded)	No details	**SF register:** Cites Area II/1 Unit I(?)
I	1(?)	(?)	(?)	TBO 0110	Scraper	Chert	No details	No details	**SF register:** cites Area II/1 Unit I without a locus
I	1	1 (P10)	(a-b)	No	2+? Lumps	Copper alloy	Green (corroded)	No details	No details
I	1	2 (P10)	(c)	No	Lump	Copper alloy	Green (corroded)	No details	No details
I	1	? (P10)	(d)	No	3+ chunks	Granite	Pink and black	No details	No details
I	1	1–6 (P10)	-	-	-	-	-	-	No small finds
I	2	1–2 (P10)		-	-	-	-	-	No small finds
J	3 (S)	1 (P10)	Sf.3	(?)	Cylindrical bead frag.	Faience	Blue	0.3 cm long × 0.2 cm dia.; 0.8 mm hole	Broken, blue faience cylindrical bead
J	3 (S)	1 (P10)	Sf.4	TBO 0547	Fragmentary platter(?) with a slight lip	Copper alloy	Green (corroded)	3.3 × 2.8 × 0.6 cm	Flat sheet with a raised lip
J	3 (S)	1 (P10)	Sf.8a	TBO	Bowl rim (2 pieces join)	Copper alloy	Green (corroded)	12 cm rim dia.; 5 × 2.7 × 0.4 cm	2 rim pieces from a small copper bowl
J	3 (S)	1 (P10)	Sf.8b	TBO 0116	Bowl rim (slight bulge)	Copper alloy	Green (corroded)	20? cm dia.; 3.2 × 2.9 × 0.4 cm	1 rim piece from a large? bowl or Sf.8a?
J	3 (S)	1 (P10)	Sf.8c	TBO 0116	Jar rim (perhaps connected with Sf.8t)	Copper alloy	Green (corroded)	2.5 × 1.4 × 0.4–0.6 cm	Jar diameter a few cm with a splayed rim and grooved neck
J	3 (S)	1 (P10)	Sf.8d	TBO 0116	Body fragment from vessel	Copper alloy	Green (corroded)	1.3 × 1.1 cm surface; 0.4? cm thick	Piece from a copper bowl or jar
J	3 (S)	1 (P10)	Sf.8e	TBO 0116	Body fragment from vessel	Copper alloy	Green (corroded)	1.8 × 0.9 xm surface; 0.4? cm thick	Piece from a copper bowl or jar
J	3 (S)	1 (P10)	Sf.8f	TBO 0116	Body fragment from vessel	Copper alloy	Green (corroded)	1.4 × 1.2 cm surface; 0.4? cm thick	Piece from a copper bowl or jar
J	3 (S)	1 (P10)	Sf.8g	TBO 0116	Body fragment from vessel	Copper alloy	Green (corroded)	3 × 2.4 cm surface; 0.4? cm thick	Piece from a copper bowl or jar
J	3 (S)	1 (P10)	Sf.8h	TBO 0116	Body fragment from vessel	Copper alloy	Green (corroded)	2 × 1.6 cm surface; 0.4? cm thick	Piece from a copper bowl or jar
J	3 (S)	1 (P10)	Sf.8i	TBO 0116	Body fragment from vessel	Copper alloy	Green (corroded)	1.7 × 0.8 cm surface; 0.4? cm thick	Piece from a copper bowl or jar
J	3 (S)	1 (P10)	Sf.8j	TBO 0116	Body fragment from vessel	Copper alloy	Green (corroded)	1.8 × 0.8 cm surface; 0.4? cm thick	Piece from a copper bowl or jar
J	3 (S)	1 (P10)	Sf.8k	TBO 0116	Body fragment from vessel	Copper alloy	Green (corroded)	1.9 × 1.6 cm surface; 0.4? cm thick	Piece from a copper bowl or jar
J	3 (S)	1 (P10)	Sf.8l	TBO 0116	Body fragment from vessel	Copper alloy	Green (corroded)	2.2 × 1.7 cm surface; 0.4? cm thick	Piece from a copper bowl or jar
J	3 (S)	1 (P10)	Sf.8m	TBO 0116	Body fragment from vessel	Copper alloy	Green (corroded)	2.3 × 1.7 cm surface; 0.4? cm thick	Piece from a copper bowl or jar
J	3 (S)	1 (P10)	Sf.8n	TBO 0116	Body fragment from vessel	Copper alloy	Green (corroded)	3.5 × 2.7 cm surface; 0.4? cm thick	Piece from a copper bowl or jar
J	3 (S)	1 (P10)	Sf.8o	TBO 0116	Body fragment from vessel	Copper alloy	Green (corroded)	2.4 × 2 cm surface; 0.4? cm thick	Piece from a copper bowl or jar
J	3 (S)	1 (P10)	Sf.8p	TBO 0116	Body fragment from vessel	Copper alloy	Green (corroded)	2.5 × 1.8 cm surface; 0.4? cm thick	Piece from a copper bowl or jar
J	3 (S)	1 (P10)	Sf.8q	TBO 0116	Body fragment from vessel	Copper alloy	Green (corroded)	2 × 1.6 cm surface; 0.4? cm thick	Piece from a copper bowl or jar
J	3 (S)	1 (P10)	Sf.8r	TBO 0116	Body fragment from vessel	Copper alloy	Green (corroded)	3.3 × 2.6 cm surface; 0.4? cm thick	Piece from a copper bowl or jar
J	3 (S)	1 (P10)	Sf.8s	TBO 0116	Body fragment from vessel	Copper alloy	Green (corroded)	3.1 × 2.5 cm surface; 0.4? cm thick	Piece from a copper bowl or jar
J	3 (S)	1 (P10)	Sf.8t	TBO 0116	Shoulder from jar	Copper alloy	Green (corroded)	4.2 × 3.6 cm surface; 0.4? cm thick	Piece from a copper jar (maybe Sf.8c?)

Table 3.15. Summary of Small Finds from Unit I, Loci 1–2, Unit J Loci 3 (South) and 5, and Unit K, Loci 2–3 (West)

Unit	*Locus*	*Basket or level*	*Unit Book no.*	*TBO no.*	*Object type*	*Material*	*Color and Surface Treatment*	*Dimensions (cm)*	*Comments: Mumford J–K and Burke Unit I notes*
J	3 (S)	1 (P10)	Sf.8u	TBO 0116	Body fragment from vessel	Copper alloy	Green (corroded)	3.8 × 2.8 cm surface; 0.4? cm thick	Piece from a copper bowl or jar
J	5	1–3 (P10)	-	-	-	-	-	-	No small finds
K	2 (W)	1 (P10)	Sf.2	TBO 0205	Hook-shaped fragment	Copper alloy	Green (corroded)	3.1 × 1.9 cm; 0.7 cm dia.	A hook? or bent nail
K	2 (W)	1 (P10)	(a)	No	Lump(?)	Copper alloy	Green (corroded)	No details	No details
K	2 (W)	1 (P10)	(b)	TBO 0206	3+ fragments	Granite	Pink and black	Small to large chunks	No details
K	3 (W)	1 (P10)	(c)	-	-	-	-	-	No small finds

Table 3.16. Summary of Pottery from Units I, J, and K, Loci 1, 2, and 5

Unit	*Locus*	*Basket/ level*	*Pottery basket*	*Rims*	*Handles*	*Bases*	*Nile silts*	*Desert marls*	*Other wares*	*Comments: Hummel pottery labels*
I	1	1 (P10)	No pottery in basket 1	?	?	?	?	?	?	Pottery label absent.
I	1	2 (P10)	Small basket of sherds	1	1	2	50%	50%	-	**Silt:** Blue Painted rim; red-slipped bowl base; **Marl:** various marls with peach and gray-green slips.
I	1	3 (P10)	Small basket of sherds	2	1	-	80%	20%	-	Small, very worn sherds; **Marl:** gritty green Theban area marl; peach slip on very hard wares; gray-green slip.
I	1	4 (P10)	Small basket of sherds	6	3	3	50%	49%	1%	**Silt:** cream slip on hard silts; **Marl:** gray-green slips on Marl D; **Other fabrics:** Cypriot Base Ring neck fragment.
I	1	5 (P10)	Scanty basket of sherds	1	1	-	90%	10%	-	Very tiny, worn sherds; **Marl:** white slip on Marl F; peach slip on marl.
I	1	6 (P10)	Small basket of sherds	2	1	-	60%	40%	-	Worn surfaces. **Marl:** variety of marls; cream slip and burnishing.
I	2	1 (P10)	Scanty basket of sherds	2	-	1	50%	40%	10%	**Silt:** red slip on thick, fine silt. **Marl:** cream slip on Marl D. **Other fabrics:** a Canaanite amphora base.
I	2	2 (P10)	Small basket of sherds	2	1	-	90%	10%	-	Salt-encrusted sherds; **Silt:** red slip traces; some hard silts with orange slip.
J	5	1 (P10)	3 sherds in total	-	-	-	100%	-	-	**Silt:** red slip.
J	5	2 (P10)	?	?	?	?	?	?	?	Pottery label absent.
J	5	3 (P10)	Scanty basket of sherds	2	1	-	60%	40%	-	**Silt:** red slip traces; **Marl:** cream slip on mral D; cream slip with burnishing on hard wares; **Other fabrics:** gray-green slip on black ware.
K	2	1 (P10)	Small basket of sherds	7	3	1	60%	40%	-	**Silt:** peach slipped silt/marl sherds; Blue Painted sherd; **Marl:** gritty green; peach slipped hard marl/silts.
K	2	2 (P10)	Small basket of sherds	2	3	-	50%	50%	-	Small, very worn body sherds; **Silt:** peach slip; **Marl:** cream slip; amphora handles.
K	3	1 (P10)	Scanty basket of sherds	2	1	-	80%	20%	-	Salt-encrusted body sherds; **Silt:** cream slip; **Marl:** cream slip.
Total	-	-	**51 + body sherds**	29	15	7	**68%**	**31%**	**1%**	**Note:** The silt and marl percentages represent averages from the columns.

Table 3.17. Summary of Pottery from Unit I, Locus 3 Basket 1, Unit K, Locus 3 Basket 1

Unit	*Locus*	*Basket/ level*	*Pottery basket*	*Rims*	*Handles*	*Bases*	*Nile silts*	*Desert marls*	*Other wares*	*Comments: Hummel pottery labels*
I	3	1 (P7)	5 sherds in total (including rims)	2	-	-	60%	20%	20%	**Silt:** simple bowls; **Other fabrics:** black ware sherd with large chunks of limestone inclusions.
K	3	2 (P7)	Medium-full basket of sherds	13	2	-	75%	25%	-	Small, worn sherds; many tiny, discarded bowl rims. **Marl:** Marl D with peach slip and burnishing; gray-green slip.
Total	-	-	**5 + body sherds**	15	2	-	**70%**	**23%**	**7–10%**	**Note:** The silt and marl percentages represent averages from the columns.

was placed in each quadrant between trenches J, Ja, Jb, and Jc to trace the perimeter of Pit J. This was realized in the southwest, southeast, and northeast quadrants but remains more ambiguous in the northwest sector where the ground level rises and remains mostly unexcavated.

The less complex strata in Units Ja, Jb, and Jc reveal four phases of activity between the basal sand level and the overlying modern sand surface, which equate with phases 1–8 in Units I, J, and K to the south. In layer-1, an 18 cm thick gray-brown and white layer of sand (10YR 7/2) accumulated above the basal sand and below an overlying and mostly continuous thin white occupation surface: the courtyard flooring. The exposed edges of Pit J reveal several New Kingdom potsherds. The southern baulk at the western end of Unit Jc has a 7 cm thick gray ash lense within this layer but lacks any trace of the overlying white surface that appears to have petered out in this area. Regarding layer-2, the white surface is 1 cm thick and multi-layered, sealing much of the underlying phase and characterizing the main New Kingdom occupation in Units I, J, and K. It was traced along the pit edge and interiors of trenches J, Ja, Jb, and most of Jd. Layer-3 represents a yellow to gray-brown sand layer (10YR 5/2) that overlies the white flooring in Units J, Ja, and Jb. It contained gray clay nodules, shells, some limestone pieces, and potsherds of varying sizes. This layer is found in Unit Jc, but lacks both the underlying thin white layer (in Units J, Ja, and Jb) and the overlying gray-brown layer (visible in Unit Jb). The last layer (no. 4) yielded gray-brown sub-surface sand (10YR 6/4) and is the layer from which Pit J is cut. This places Pit J stratigraphically at some point at the end of the New Kingdom occupation and possibly, albeit less likely in the excavator's opinion, later into more recent times (Roman period?). This vestigial layer is evident mainly in Unit Jb, but the occurrence of a small pit at the interface between Pit J's upper edge and this layer creates some ambiguity on whether Pit J was dug from the bottom or top of layer-4. An examination of the strata from other sections, however, suggests that Pit J was likely cut from layer-4's base.

The New Kingdom layers pre-dating Pit J contained several artifacts (see table 3.18): some copper alloy pieces (Jc2 sf.1), stone tools (Jc2), and potsherds. Several other artifacts, however, remained less well-stratified, and may have come from either the fill layers in Pit J or the pre-pit occupation layer adjacent to the upper edge of Pit J: Ja3 (sf.2–3; calcite fragment; lithics) and Jb2 (sf.1; calcite piece; slag/pumice).

3.3.11. Phase 8/9: Dynasty 19(?) Large Pit (Unit J) (figs. 3.25 and 3.28)

In Unit J, a large pit cutting through the courtyard's floor measures about 6 × 10.50 m in area by 1.26 m in depth (fig. 3.28; see OCHRE pls. 76–77). The excavation of the fill layers in the pit and exposure of the underlying strata along the pit's sides reveal that the courtyard's multi-layered 1 cm to 9–10 cm thick flooring lay above a 17 cm thick sand layer, which in turn overlay the basal sand layer.

Table 3.18. Summary of Small Finds from Units J, JA, JB, and JC (Pre-Pit Layers)

Unit	*Locus*	*Basket*	*Unit Book no.*	*TBO no.*	*Object type*	*Material*	*Color and Surface Treatment*	*Dimensions (cm):*	*Comments: Mumford J–K notes; Burke unit I notes*
JA	3	no.1	Possible Small finds	-	**Note:** JA3 artifacts equated with pit-J (but may be pre-pit)	-	-	-	**Note:** Locus JB2 spans the pit-top and the upper pre-pit layer.
JB	2	no.1	Possible Small finds	-	**Note:** JB2 artifacts equated with pit-J (but may be pre-pit)	-	-	-	**Note:** Locus JB2 spans the pit-top and the upper pre-pit layer.
JC	1–2	no.1 Pre-Pit	Sf.1 a	(?)	Fragment from a fitting(?)	Copper alloy	Green (corroded)	0.7 × 1 × 1.2 cm	Square plate with an L-shaped edge (drawn in note book)
JC	1–2	no.1 Pre-Pit	Sf.1b	(?)	Sheet/side from a vessel(?)	Copper alloy	Green (corroded)	0.2 × 0.5 × 0.7 cm	Triangular shaped (drawn in note book)
JC	1–2	no.1 Pre-Pit	Sf.1c	(?)	Lump	Copper alloy	Green (corroded)	0.2 × 0.4 × 0.6 cm	Roughly rectilinear (drawn in note book)
JC	2	no.1 Pre-Pit	Sample	No	Stone tools (lithics)	Stone	No details	Small	No details

Table 3.19. Summary of Pottery from Units J, JA, JB, JC, and JD (Pre-Pit Layer)

Unit	*Locus*	*Basket/ level*	*Pottery basket*	*Rims*	*Handles*	*Bases*	*Nile silts*	*Desert marls*	*Other wares*	*Comments: Hummel pottery labels*
JC	2	Basket no.2 (Pre-pit)	Scanty (20 sherds)	2	-	1	Count: 14 sherds	Count: 4 sherds	Count: 2 Pal. sherds	Note: 18th–19th Dynasty wares and forms; red burnished, carinated bowl; marl A2 flask body.
JC	3	Basket no.2 (pre-pit)	Scanty (15 sherds)	2	1	1	Count: 6 sherds	Count: 6 sherds	Count: 3 sherds	Note: An assortment of New Kingdom marls; 1 Palestinian amphora handle; 3 bowl fragments.
Total	-	-	**35+ body sherds**	4	1	2	**20 57%**	**10 29%**	**5 14%**	**Note:** The silt and marl percentages represent averages from the columns.

I personally excavated the pit and suggest that it had several functions: (1) it may originally have represented part of a large foundation for a late Dynasty 18 stone installation (perhaps the massive, ex situ granite block to the north). The subsequent postulated robbing of this foundation may have left limestone chunks and pulverized decorated wall blocks in the pit and the adjacent ground surface. If the large pit represents a foundation pit/trench, the backfill would represent a later period of stone robbing and backfilling. (2) The ovoid pit may have been excavated to create another ovoid-like stone-lined well, similar to the abandoned structure to the south. It is possible that this structure was completely robbed of its stone lining in the Ramesside period, which began to reuse limestone in the moats placed on two sides of the Ramesside fort built in Fields V–VI. This latter suggestion seems the most likely, with several possible variants, such as the aborted construction of a stone-lined well. In general, there appears to be a west-to-east shift in occupation at Tell el-Borg with the abandonment of the Second Intermediate Period to early Dynasty 18 reed huts (Field VI), the construction of a Dynasty 18 fort, and the abandonment and placement of a Ramesside fort above and to the east of the earlier fort. Hence, Pit J, which required not insignificant labor to dig it, was soon filled in with much New Kingdom debris, including extensively broken and pulverized architectural pieces, decorated and inscribed blocks, and other items and materials. The abandonment of this feature may date to the same period as the initial construction and subsequent halt on the moats placed on two sides of the Ramesside fort.

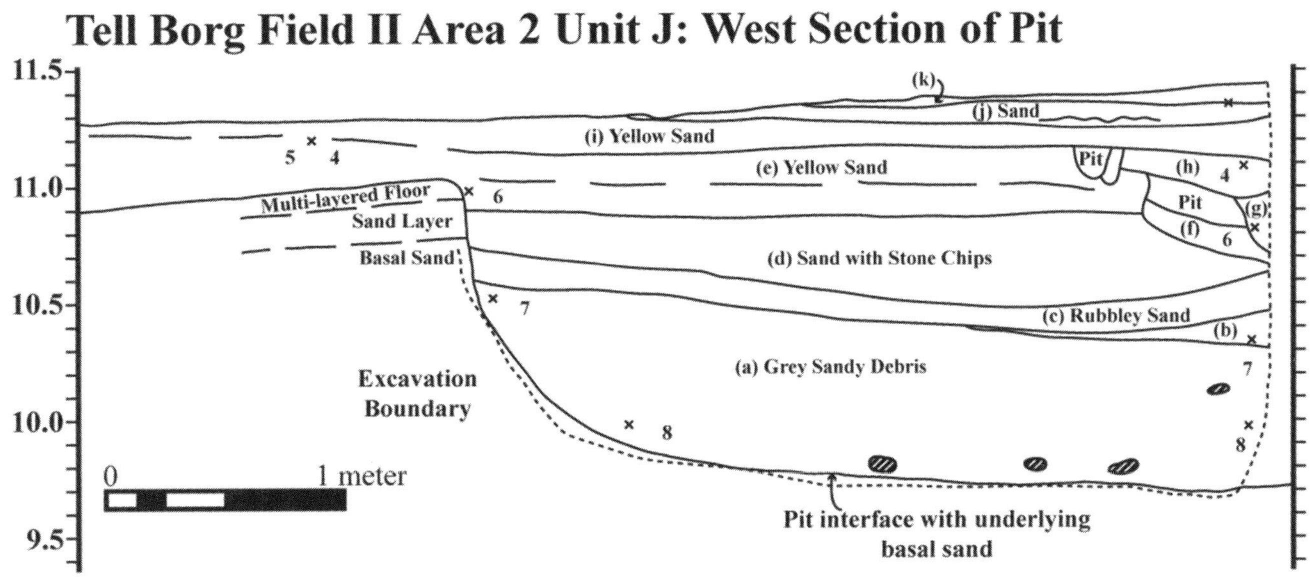

Fig. 3.28. West baulk of Unit J and Pit J in Field II, Area 1–2 (drawn by G. Mumford; digitized by Joshua Olsen).

Regardless of the pit's function, the relative stratigraphy in this area demonstrates that the ancient excavation and filling of this pit did not pre-date late Dynasty 18 and may extend into early Dynasty 19. The debris filling the pit includes Blue Painted pottery, which suggests that the pit could not have been back-filled prior to the reign of Amenhotep III, during whose reign this pottery first appears (if not a little sooner). If the fragments from a destroyed limestone structure date to mid-late Dynasty 18, as is suggested here, the destruction and filling of the pit would probably have occurred during early Dynasty 19. Unfortunately, there is no continuous stratigraphic section between the northern boundary of this pit and the Dynasty 19 wall and "shrine" to the north and northeast. However, the impression provided by these areas is that Pit J post-dates the initial construction of the zigzagging wall and associated buildings.

3.3.12. Phase 9: Dynasty 19(?) Back-Fill in Pit J (Units J, Ja, Jb, Jc, and Jd) (fig. 3.28)

A series of ten layers filled the large pit. The lower layers in this back-fill produced many small fragments from painted architectural pieces, indicating that this pit had remained open sufficiently for New Kingdom destruction debris to become incorporated in its initial backfilling. However, the upper layers contained the majority of the limestone debris, confirming that this pit served as a continuous repository for such debris from one or more destroyed temples.

3.3.12.1. Phase 9a: Basal Sand Layer (Pre-Pit) (fig. 3.28)

The basal sand layer, into which Pit J cut, consists of white sand with striations in red and black (see Units Ja, Jb). The red and black striations appear to be the remnants of ancient plant materials(?), reflecting an earlier, more moist environment.

3.3.12.2. Phase 9b: Pit Base Mud Smear (Base of Loci J8, Ja6, Jb6, and Jc6) (fig. 3.28)

At some point, probably not long after the cutting of the pit, a thin, 1–3-cm-thick layer of mud covered the flat base of the pit, which might suggest a mud-lined water reservoir (such as the one suggested, albeit now contested, at Deir el-Balah). Unit Ja revealed a layer of dirty gray-

Table 3.20. Summary of Pottery from Unit Loci J8, JA6, JB6, and JC6

Unit	*Locus*	*Basket/ level*	*Pottery basket*	*Rims*	*Handles*	*Bases*	*Nile silts*	*Desert marls*	*Other wares*	*Comments: Hummel pottery labels*
J	8	1 (P9)	Small basket of sherds	5	-	-	60%	40%	-	**Silt:** much red slip with some burnishing; **Marl:** cream-green slip and burnishing; burnished cream slip with black stripes.
J	8	2 (P9)	Small basket of sherds	8	1	-	90%	10%	-	**Silt:** many red slipped and burnished bowls; **Marl:** amphora with a possible foreign ware.
J	8	3 (P9)	Scanty basket of sherds	2	1	2	60%	40%	-	**Silt:** red slip traces on bowls; **Marl:** cream slip with burnishing; amphora handle.
JA	6	Basket no.1	Small (47 sherds)	3	-	1	Count: 41 sherds 87%	Count: 5 sherds 11%	Count: 1 sherd 2%	**Note:** Variety of New Kingdom wares (nothing in late 19th Dynasty)
JB	6	Basket no.1	Scanty (1 sherd)	-	-	1	Count: 1 sherd 100%	-	-	**Note:** 1 large body and base of a jar (very accreted [salt encrustation])
JB	6	Basket no.1/2?	Small (61 sherds)	4	-	-	Count: 48 sherds 78%	Count: 12 sherds 20%	Count: 1 sherd 2%	**Note:** 1 black-rimmed bowl; New Kingdom simple bowls.
JC	6	Basket no.1	Medium	6	2	2	70%	28%	2%	**Note:** Two Palestinian amphora handles; amphora fragments; a variety of wares: Nile B2, marl D, Nile E, and G6-type. Various slips: peach, cream, and red slip.
Total	-	-	**+ body sherds**				**78%**	**21%**	**1%**	**Note:** The silt and marl percentages represent averages from the columns.

white sand with brown sand and clay (at the base of Locus Ja6). Unit Jb contained some traces of water and wind-laid sand, including a thin deposit of dirty white sand (10YR 8/2), gray sandy clay, and some gray mud-brick lumps (7.5YR 4/1). This thin layer was less distinct on the western side of the pit (Unit Jc). Hence, there is some evidence for a brief passage of time after the cutting of this pit to enable the accumulation of wind- and water-laid materials, but presumably less than a year passed before the deposition of other materials. The accumulation of wind-blown sand suggests that the pit had not reached a sufficient depth to supply water and thereby argues against it ever having functioned as a well.

3.3.12.3. Phase 9c: Pit Base, Hard Sand Layer (Loci J8, JA6, JB6, and JC6) (fig. 3.28)

After this brief period of mud accumulation, albeit in a discontinuous fashion, across the pit's base, the pit appears to have become a refuse dump. It was next filled with about 58–69 cm of fine- to medium-grained red and white basal sand that had been mixed with coarse gray sand (2.5Y 8/1; 10R 4/8), many gray clay nodules and lumps, charcoal flecks, and many limestone chips. The dense red stains lay at all angles and appear to be redeposited basal sand. However, unlike the undisturbed basal sand layer, this layer became progressively compacted, especially at its downward-sloping sides and base, where the lower 20 cm merges into a distinct extremely hard layer that is otherwise mostly indistinguishable from its looser upper part. This layer was at first easy to excavate when freshly exposed and still damp, but it hardened quickly into a cement-like consistency in the sun (in contrast, the underlying basal sand remained easy to excavate after exposure). The following discussion will maintain the subdivision between the lower, harder portion and the upper, softer part of this debris layer.

Table 3.21. Summary of Small Finds and Debris from Unit Loci J8, JA6, JB5, and JC5

Unit	*Locus*	*Basket or level*	*Unit Book no.*	*TBO no.*	*Object type*	*Material*	*Color and Surface Treatment*	*Dimensions (cm)*	*Comments: Mumford notes for Unit J*
J	8	1 (P9)	Sf.14	(?)	Disk bead	Faience	Blue	0.5 diameter × 0.2 cm height; 0.15 cm hole	Simple disk bead with rounded edge.
J	8	1 (P9)	Sample (a)	No	Lump	Copper alloy	Green (corroded)	No details	No details
J	8	2 (P9)	Sample (b)	No	Chunk	Calcite ("alabaster")	Yellow-white	"Large chunk"	No details
J	8	2 (P9)	Sample (c)	No	Wall block chip	Limestone	White with blue pigment	2.3 × 1.1 cm surface	No details
J	8	Basket no.1 (P9)	(?)	TBO 0093	Two scrapers (from pottery basket?)	Sandstone	Yellow	No details	**SF register:** Cites two scrapers from Unit J, Locus 8 basket no.1.
JA	6	Basket no.1	Note book	No	Chunks	Limestone	(white)	Various sizes	No details
JB	6	Basket no.1	Sf.6	TBO 0911	Stone mortar (Grinding bowl) frag.	"Basalt" (field book: "quartzite?")	Gray-black. Polished, worn interior	30 cm diameter 1.3–2.4 cm thick 6 cm high	Fragment of mortar (drawn in note book).
JB	6	Basket no.1	Sf.7	(?)	Part of a tool or amulet?	Copper alloy	Green (corroded)	0.7 × 0.8 × 1.2 cm	Details masked by corrosion (drawn in note book).
JB	6	Basket no.1	Note book	No	Chunks	Limestone	(white)	Various sizes	No details
JB	6	Basket no.1	Pot no.1	-	Beer jar	Ceramic	Red slip	-	Salt encrusted
JB	6	Basket no.1	Pot no.2	-	Amphora base	Ceramic	Cream slip	-	Salt encrusted
JC	6	Basket no.1	Sf.4	TBO 0874	Blockish chunk or fragment (burnisher?)	Copper alloy	Green (corroded)	1.8 × 1.8 × 2.6 cm	Blockish chunk of copper (drawn in note book).
JC	6	Basket no.1	Sf.<a>	TBO 0878 (a)	Statuette(?) fragment or relief frag.	Limestone	White with sculpted garment	2.7 × 3 × 7.3 cm	Sculpted garment (drawn in note book).
JC	6	Basket no.1	Sample b	No	Flake	Stone	Stone with bulb of percussion	0.9 × 3.5 × 4.7 cm	Flake with no retouch (drawn in note book).
JC	6	Basket no.1	Sf.5	(?)	Wall block fragment	Limestone	White slab with a smooth surface and three vertical incised lines (2 thin; 1 wide)	(thickness?) 15.5 × 23 cm	Decorated wall block (drawn in note book).
JC	6	Basket no.1	Sf.<6>	TBO 0907	Ceiling block fragment	Limestone	White slab with border lines and fragments of stars	No details	**SF register:** Found by the excavator during clean-up (not in field notes)

In the lowest portion of this layer, a broad range of refuse was found, including small- to medium-sized potsherds (J8; Ja6; Jb6; Jc6), two sherds of Blue Painted pottery (J8), an intact beer jar (Jb6 pot no. 1; OCHRE pl. 94), and a store-jar base (Jb6 pot no. 2). The latter two vessels bore significant salt encrustations; other domestic utensils include a quartzite grinding stone (Jb6 sf.6). Waste food is represented by small-to-large fragments of burned bones (J8; Ja6; Jb6) and a clam shell fragment (J8). Building debris consisted of yellow and gray mud-brick nodules and chunks (J8; Ja; Jb; Jc). The existence of nearby stone structures and monuments is attested by the high proportion of pulverized non-indigenous stones: a chip of calcite (J8), numerous limestone chips (J8; Jb6), many larger limestone block fragments (J8), and six fragments from limestone blocks bearing painted sunken relief (J8; J8 basket 2; Jc6 sf.). The remaining refuse contains

Table 3.22. Summary of Small Finds and Debris from Unit Loci J7, JA5, JB5, and JC5

Unit	*Locus*	*Basket or level*	*Unit Book no.*	*TBO no.*	*Object type*	*Material:*	*Color and Surface Treatment*	*Dimensions (cm)*	*Comments: Mumford notes for Unit J*
J	7	1 (P9)	Sf.13a	TBO 0237	Wall block fragment	Limestone	White	5.3 × 2.3 × 0.8 cm	Yellow-painted side with a blue-painted edge
J	7	1 (P9)	Sf.13b	(?)	Wall block fragment	Limestone	White	2.2 × 1.2 × 0.4 cm	Smooth face with a blue edge
J	7	1 (P9)	Sf.13c	(?)	Wall block fragment	Limestone	White	5.4 × 4.3 × 1.7 cm	Smooth top with one red-painted edge
J	7	1 (P9)	Sample (a-c)	No	3 chips	Calcite ("alabaster")	Yellow-white	No details	Small chip; not drawn.
J	7	1 (P9)	Sample (d)	No	Container? ostrich eggshell	Ostrich eggshell	Gray	No details; probably less than 1 × 1 cm	Small fragment; not drawn.
J	7	1 (P9)	Sample (e)	No	Lump	Copper alloy	Green (corroded)	No details	No details
J	7	2 (P9)	Sample (f-g)	No	2 chips	Diorite	Black	No details	No details
J	7	2 (P9)	Sample (h-j)	No	3 chips	Calcite ("alabaster")	Yellow-white	No details	No details
JA	5	Basket no.1	Sample	No	Chunk (fragment)	Calcite	Yellow-white	3.4 × 3.5 × 5.1 cm	Triangular shaped chunk of calcite (drawn in note book).
JB	5	Basket no.1	Sample	No	Core(?) with multi-faceted sides	Calicte	Yellow-white	1.5 × 1.8 × 3.3 cm	Possible core; may be natural like quartz (drawn in note book).
JB	5	Basket no.1	Sf.5	No	Wall block chip	Limestone	White with blue painted groove	0.9 × 2.3 × 4.1 cm	A smooth surface with a blue painted shallow groove (drawn in note book).
JC	5	Basket no.1	Sample a	No	Chunk from calcite block(nat. fracture)	Calcite	Yellow-white	3.1 × 3.9 × 9 cm	Internal chunk with cortex (drawn in note book).
JC	5	Basket no.1	Sample b	No	Chunk from calcite block (nat. fracture)	Calcite	Yellow-white	(thickness?) × 4.7 × 6.5 cm	Internal chunk with cortex (drawn in note book).
JC	5	Basket no.1	Sf.3	TBO 0906	Wall block chip/ chunk	Limestone	(white) with incised outline of a human leg	5 × 11.5 × 16.8 cm	Block face with decoration (drawn in note book).

both valuable materials, such as a blue faience disk-bead (J8 sf.14; OCHRE pl. 92) and a copper alloy lump (J8; Jc6 sf.), and non-valuable, discarded "rubbish" and other debris, such as chunks of kurkar sandstone (Jb6) and sandstone chips/scrapers(?) (pl. 3:6 nos. 17–18, TBO 0093a–b). It is the presence, at the bottom of the pit, of the discarded albeit mostly intact vessels, however, that suggests that the pit had become a repository for refuse at some point soon after its initial cutting.

3.3.12.4. Phase 9d: Pit Fill Firm Sand (Loci J7, Ja5, Jb5, and JCc) (fig. 3.28)

The upper portion of the previous layer was not as compacted and contained the same gray and reddish mottling (2.5Y 8/1; 10R 4/8). It also yielded the remains of building and domestic activity: strong gray clay bricks (J7; Ja5; Jb5; Jc5), many small- to medium-sized potsherds (J7; Ja; Jb; Jc), some chunks of kurkar sandstone (Jb5), a copper alloy lump (J7), pieces from burned bones (J7; Ja5; Jb5), a tooth (J7), an ostrich eggshell fragment (J7), and part of a clam shell (J7). The bulk of the refuse consisted of the components from demolished stone structures and monuments: numerous limestone chips (J7; Ja5; Jb5; Jc5), many larger stones of limestone (throughout J) (pl. 3.1 no.5: TBO 906, incised human leg), a limestone fragment with a blue-painted edge and yellow painted surface (J7 sf.13a; OCHRE pl. 91), two limestone pieces with smoothed surfaces and blue paint (J7 sf.13b; Jb5 sf.5; OCHRE pls. 91–92), a piece with a smoothed face and red-

Table 3.23. Summary of Pottery from Unit Loci J7, JA5, JB5, and JC5

Unit	*Locus*	*Basket/ level*	*Pottery basket*	*Rims*	*Handles*	*Bases*	*Nile silts*	*Desert marls*	*Other wares*	*Comments: Hummel pottery labels*
J	7	1 (P9)	Medium-full basket of sherds	9	2	4	39%	60%	1%	**Silt:** red slips; Blue Painted sherd; **Marl:** gray-green slipped basket handle; **Other fabrics:** a Cypriot Base Ring sherd.
J	7	2 (P9)	Small basket of sherds	11	1	4	70%	20%	10%	**Silt:** red-slipped bowls with some burnishing; two Blue Painted sherds; **Marl:** pale brown slip and cream slip with burnishing; **Other fabrics:** a Canaanite amphora sherd.
JB	5	Basket no.1	Small (68 sherds)	6	-	-	Count: 56 sherds 82%	Count: 10 sherds 15%	Count: 2 sherds 3%	**Note:** 1 black-rimmed bowl; some soot on some jars and bowls; New Kingdom wares.
JC	5	Basket no.1	Small (39 sherds)	1	-	-	Count: 33 sherds 85%	Count: 2 sherds 5%	Count: 4 sherds 10%	**Note:** 1 carinated bowl; non-diagnostic sherds.
Total	-	-	**31+ body sherds**	20	3	8	**69%**	**25%**	**6%**	**Note:** The silt and marl percentages represent averages from the columns.

painted edge (J7 sf.13c; OCHRE pl. 91), a limestone fragment with paint traces (Jc5), several small-to-large chips of calcite (J7; Ja5; Jb5; Jc5), and a fragment of diorite (J7). The limestone fragments displaying painted carving appear to represent the shattered remains of an inscribed and decorated structure that contained large incised hieroglyphs and figures.

3.3.12.5. Phase 9e: Pit Fill Firm Sand (Loci J6, Ja4, Jb4, and Jc4) (fig. 3.28)

The debris filling Pit J started to be deposited from the east in broad, sloping layers, which eventually filled the upper half of the pit in a horizontal band measuring 54 to 82 cm in depth. The first tip line (fill layer 4) consisted of fine- to coarse-grained medium-yellow sand. The next sloping debris layer (no. 5) contained fine- to medium-grained medium-yellow sand. This deposit covered layer 4 and measured about 26 cm in thickness at the eastern end of Unit J.[5] The subsequent debris layer (no. 6) consisted of a fine- to medium-grained medium-yellow sand, which measured approximately 50 cm in depth. The following layer (no. 7) contained medium-yellow sand with stone chips. It lay above the slope of layer 6, measuring about 44 cm in depth. Layer 8 yielded a 10–14 cm thick band of medium-yellow sand with stone chips. It contained more rubble than Layer 9, which extended from 18 to 42 cm in depth and consisted of medium-yellow sand with stone chips. This layer had been cut partly by a series of later small pits. The final debris layer (no. 10) ranged from 24 to 30 cm in depth and was made up of mottled yellow sand with small clay nodules, stone chips, and gypsum flecks. This layer included a series of pits that were cut and back-filled in succession at the western end of Unit J. The seven tip layers appear to have been deposited in a relatively short period and were excavated in arbitrary horizontal levels.[6]

5. Of interest, at the northern end of Locus 6, an intrusive rodent hole yielded the skeletons of four mice (two adults and two infants).

6. The northern part of Locus 3 lay above the top of the pit but has been included in the backfill owing to the concentration of fragmentary limestone chips above the pit, which contains similar debris to the pit itself. Of note, the pitting evident in the upper parts of the northwest and northeast baulks of Unit J explains the presence of a stray Roman period sherd in Locus 3, which contains other late pits (e.g., Unit J, Locus 2).

Text continues on p. 79

Table 3.24. Summary of Limestone Fragments from Units J, JA, JB, JC, and JD (Pit Fill)

Unit	*Locus*	*Basket or level*	*Unit Book no.*	*TBO no.*	*Object type*	*Material*	*Color and Surface Treatment*	*Dimensions (cm)*	*Comments: Mumford notes for Unit J*
J	6	1 (P9)	Sf.10a	(?)	Wall block fragment	Limestone	White with yellow pigment	6.4 × 5.7 × 2.5 cm	Yellow-painted sunken area
J	6	1 (P9)	Sf.10b	(?)	Wall block fragment	Limestone	White with blue pigment	4 × 2.8 × 1.1 cm	Smooth, raised band with blue painted edges
J	6	1 (P9)	Sf.10c	(?)	Wall block fragment	Limestone	White with yellow pigment	4.8 × 3.1 × 1.3 cm	Raised area with yellow-painted edges & sunken areas
J	6	1 (P9)	Sf.10d	(?)	Wall block fragment	Limestone	White with blue pigment	3.1 × 1.7 × 0.8 cm	Smooth, raised area and blue-painted edge
J	6	1 (P9)	Sf.10e	(?)	Wall block fragment	Limestone	White with yellow pigment	5.7 × 2.5 × 1.1 cm	Yellow-painted sloping face
J	6	1 (P9)	Sf.10f	(?)	Wall block fragment	Limestone	White with blue & yellow pigments	2 × 1.1 × 0.9 cm	Yellow painted raised area with blue edge
J	6	1 (P9)	Sf.10g	(?)	Wall block fragment	Limestone	White with red pigment	No details	Small chip; not drawn.
J	6	1 (P9)	Sf.10h	(?)	Wall block fragment	Limestone	White with red and yellow pigments	No details	Small chip; not drawn.
J	6	1 (P9)	Sf.10i	(?)	Wall block fragment	Limestone	White with yellow pigment	No details	Small chip; not drawn.
J	6	1 (P9)	Sf.10j	(?)	Wall block fragment	Limestone	White with red and blue pigments	No details	Small chip; not drawn.
J	6	1 (P9)	Sf.11a	(?)	Wall block fragment	Limestone	White with blue pigment	7.6 × 2.6 × 1.4 cm	Raised band blue traced on top and sides
J	6	1 (P9)	Sf.11b	(?)	Wall block fragment	Limestone	White with yellow pigment	7.6 × 4 × 1.4 cm	Raised, smooth area with a yellow edge
J	6	1 (P9)	Sf.11c	(?)	Wall block fragment	Limestone	White with red and blue pigment	5.7 × 5.2 × 1.5 cm	Smooth area with a red and blue edge
J	6	1 (P9)	Sf.11d	(?)	Wall block fragment	Limestone	White with red pigment	(?) × 1.2 × 0.5 cm (length?)	Smooth side with red edge
J	6	1 (P9)	Sf.11e	(?)	Wall block fragment	Limestone	White with red and yellow pigments	(?) × 3 × 1 cm (length?)	Smooth side with red and yellow edge
J	6	1 (P9)	Sf.11f	(?)	Wall block fragment	Limestone	White with red and yellow pigments	(?) × 2.2 × 0.7 cm (length?)	Yellow-painted side and a red –painted side
J	6	1 (P9)	Sf.11g	(?)	Wall block fragment	Limestone	White with yellow pigment	No details	Small chip; not drawn.
J	6	1 (P9)	Sf.11h	(?)	Wall block fragment	Limestone	White with blue pigment	No details	Small chip; not drawn.
J	6	1 (P9)	Sf.11i	(?)	Wall block fragment	Limestone	White with black pigment	No details	Small chip; not drawn.
J	3 (N)	1 (P9)	Sf.1	TBO 0178	Wall block Fragment	Limestone	White chip with yellow pigment on sunken bands	15 × 10.5 × 2.6 cm	Surface has two parallel, sunken bands (yellow)
J	3 (N)	1 (P9)	Sf.1a	(?)	Wall block Fragment	Limestone	White chip with blue pigment in groove	4.7 × 4.6 cm surface area	Small chip with blue-painted groove
J	3 (N)	1 (P9)	Sf.1b	(?)	Wall block Fragment	Limestone	White chip with blue pigment in groove	3.8 × 2.8 cm surface area	Small chip with blue-painted groove
J	3 (N)	1 (P9)	Sf.1c	(?)	Wall block Fragment	Limestone	White chip with blue pigment on surface	2.5 × 2.1 cm surface area	White chip with blue-painted surface
J	3 (N)	1 (P9)	Sf.1d	(?)	Wall block Fragment	Limestone	White chip with blue pigment in groove	3.2 × 2.8 cm surface area	Small chip with blue-painted groove
J	3 (N)	1 (P9)	Sf.9	TBO 0100	Wall block fragment	Limestone	White chip with smoothed side & red pigment	7.3 × 3 × 1.5 cm	2 smoothed faces with 1 red-painted edge
J	4	1 (P9)	Sf.5	TBO 0099	Wall block fragment	Limestone	White with yellow, blue and red pigments	9 × 3 × 1.9 cm	Raised, curved band with yellow top and red and blue edges
J	4	1 (P9)	Sf.6a	TBO 0099	Wall block fragment	Limestone	White with yellow, red, and blue pigments	3.5 × 3.5 × 1.1 cm	Yellow top with red and blue edges
J	4	1 (P9)	Sf.6b	TBO 0099	Wall block fragment	Limestone	White with yellow, red, and blue pigments	3.2 × 2.6 × 0.6 cm	Yellow top with blue and red edges
J	4	1 (P9)	Sf.6c	TBO 0099	Wall block fragment	Limestone	White with yellow, red, blue, & black? pigments	2.1 × 1.6 × 0.8 cm	Yellow top with blue, red, and black edges

Table 3.24. Summary of Limestone Fragments from Units J, JA, JB, JC, and JD (Pit Fill)

Unit	Locus	Basket or level	Unit Book no.	TBO no.	Object type	Material	Color and Surface Treatment	Dimensions (cm)	Comments: Mumford notes for Unit J
JB	3	Basket no.1	Sf.3.a	(?)	Wall block fragment	Limestone	White with a yellow painted incised line	2.1 × 3.5 × 4.1 cm	A smooth surface with a curving incised line (drawn in note book).
JB	3	Basket no.1	Sf.3.b	(?)	Wall block fragment	Limestone	White with a blue painted incised line	0.6 × 2.5 × 3.8 cm	A smooth surface with a straight incised line (drawn in note book).
JB	3	Basket no.1	Sf.3.c	(?)	Wall block fragment	Limestone	White with a red painted incised line	1.7 × 1.9 × 3 cm	A smooth surface with a deep incised line (drawn in note book).
JB	3	Basket no.1	Sf.3.d	(?)	Wall block fragment	Limestone	White with a red painted incised line (cut deeply)	0.8 × 3.4 × 4.1 cm	A smooth surface with a straight incised line (drawn in note book).
JB	3	Basket no.1	Sf.3.e	(?)	Wall block fragment	Limestone	White with a red painted incised line (cut deeply)	1.2 × 0.6 × 3.1 cm	A smooth surface with a deep incised line (drawn in note book).
JB	3	Basket no.1	Sf.3.f	(?)	Wall block fragment	Limestone	White with a blue painted incised line	1 × 1.6 × 3.7 cm	A smooth surface with a straight incised line (drawn in note book).
JB	3	Basket no.1	Sf.3.g	(?)	Wall block fragment	Limestone	White with a red painted incised line and a blue painted incised line	0.7 × 2.1 × 3.9 cm	A smooth surface between two parallel incised lines (drawn in note book).
JB	3	Basket no.1	Sf.3.h	(?)	Wall block fragment	Limestone	White with a yellow painted surface	0.3 × 1.3 × 2.1 cm	A small chip with a smooth yellow surface (drawn in note book).
JB	3	Basket no.1	Sf.3.i	(?)	Wall block fragment	Limestone	White with a red painted smooth surface and red painted incised line	0.8 × 2.8 × 3.1 cm	A smooth surface with a straight incised line (drawn in note book).
JB	3	Basket no.1	Sf.3.j	(?)	Wall block fragment	Limestone	White with a yellow painted smooth surface and yellow painted incised line	0.6 × 1.2 × 2.5 cm	A smooth surface with a straight incised line (drawn in note book).
JB	3	Basket no.1	Sf.3.k	(?)	Wall block fragment	Limestone	White with a blue painted incised line	1.1 × 2.4 × 4.6 cm	A worn/rough surface with a straight incised line (drawn in note book).
JB	3	Basket no.1	Sf.3.l	(?)	Wall block fragment	Limestone	White with a black-painted shallow incised line	0.9 × 3.7 × 3.8 cm	A worn surface with a straight incised line (drawn in note book).
JB	3	Basket no.1	Sf.3.m	(?)	Wall block fragment	Limestone	White with a yellow painted surface	(thickness?) × 1.7 × 2.5 surf.	A worn surface (drawn in note book).
JB	3	Basket no.1	Sf.3.n	(?)	Wall block fragment	Limestone	White with a yellow painted surface and yellow painted groove	0.5 × 0.7 × 1.9 cm	A smooth surface and part of an incised line (drawn in note book).
JB	3	Basket no.1	Sf.3.o	(?)	Wall block fragment	Limestone	White with a yellow painted smooth surface	(thickness?) × 1.1 × 1.7 cm	A smooth surface (drawn in note book).
JB	3	Basket no.1	Sf.3.p	(?)	Wall block fragment	Limestone	White with a yellow painted surface and a red painted incised line	0.8 × 1.9 × 2.2 cm	A smooth surface with an incised line (drawn in note book).
JB	3	Basket no.1	Sf.3.q	(?)	Wall block fragment	Limestone	White with red paint in a wide and shallow concave groove	1.7 (thick) × 1 × 2.5 cm	A shallow groove in a rough chip (drawn in note book).
JB	3	Basket no.1	Sf.3.r	(?)	Wall block fragment	Limestone	A smooth surface with a blue painted groove	0.8 × 3.6 × 3.7 cm	A straight groove in a smooth surface (drawn in note book).
JB	3	Basket no.1	Sf.3.s	(?)	Wall block fragment	Limestone	An irregular (sculpted?) white surface with red, black, and blue paint	0.4 × 2 × 2.9 cm	A small chip, possibly from a sculpted figure (drawn in note book)
JB	3	Basket no.1	Sf.3.t	(?)	Wall block fragment	Limestone	White surface with a red painted groove	0.9 × 2.1 × 3.3 cm	A rough surface with part of a smooth groove (drawn in note book)
JB	3	Basket no.1	Sf.3.u	(?)	Wall block fragment	Limestone	White fragment with part of a blue painted groove	1.5 × 2.1 × 3.5 cm	A fragment with part of a deep groove (drawn in note book)
JB	3	Basket no.1	Sf.3.v	(?)	Wall block fragment	Limestone	White chip with a yellow painted surface	(thickness?) × 1 × 1.2 cm	A small chip (drawn in note book)

Table 3.24. Summary of Limestone Fragments from Units J, JA, JB, JC, and JD (Pit Fill)

Unit	*Locus*	*Basket or level*	*Unit Book no.*	*TBO no.*	*Object type*	*Material*	*Color and Surface Treatment*	*Dimensions (cm)*	*Comments: Mumford notes for Unit J*
JB	3	Basket no.1	Sf.3.w	(?)	Wall block fragment	Limestone	White chip with a red painted area	(thickness?) × 0.9 × 1.3 cm	A small chip (drawn in note book)
JB	3	Basket no.1	Sf.3.x	(?)	Wall block fragment	Limestone	White chip with yellow painted surface and a red painted groove	0.6 × 0.6 × 1.7 cm	A smooth surface and a straight groove (drawn in note book)
JB	3	Basket no.1	Sf.3.y	(?)	Wall block fragment	Limestone	White chip with a yellow painted smooth surface	1.2 × 1.3 × 2.8 cm	A smooth surface with worn areas (drawn in note book)
JB	3	Basket no.1	Sf.3.z	(?)	Wall block fragment	Limestone	White with a smooth surface and part of a blue painted groove	0.7 × 2.1 × 2.9 cm	Part of a surface and an incised groove (drawn in note book)
JB	3	Basket no.1	Sf.3.aa	(?)	Wall block fragment	Limestone	White chip with a black painted surface	0.5 × 2.6 × 2.6 cm	A chip with part of a smooth surface (drawn in note book)
JB	3	Basket no.1	Sf.3.bb	(?)	Wall block fragment	Limestone	White chip with part of a red painted groove?	(thick?) × 1.1 x 1.9 cm	Tiny chip (drawn in note book)
JB	3	Basket no.1	Sf.3.cc	(?)	Wall block fragment	Limestone	White chip with part of a blue painted groove?	(thick?) × 1.1 x 1.2 cm	Tiny chip (drawn in note book)
JB	3	Basket no.1	Sf.3.dd	(?)	Wall block fragment	Limestone	White chip with red painted surface	(thick?) × 1.6 x 1.6 cm	Tiny chip (drawn in note book)
JB	3	Basket no.1	Sf.3.ee	(?)	Wall block fragment	Limestone	White chip with red painted surface	(thick?) × 1.2 x 1.3 cm	Tiny chip (drawn in note book)
JB	3	Basket no.1	Sf.3.ff	(?)	Wall block fragment	Limestone	White chip with yellow painted surface and red painted groove	0.8 × 1 x 2 cm	A smooth surface with part of an incised line (drawn in note book)
JB	4	Basket no.1	Sf.5a	TBO 0878	Wall block fragment	Limestone	Large white fragment with an upper blue painted incised line, a portion of an incised glyph (r?), and part of an incised vertical blue painted glyph. Block surface is mostly rough.	3.3 cm thick fragment 11.3 cm high fragment 6 cm wide fragment	The best preserved limestone block face with hieroglyphs from the pit (drawn in note book)
JB	4	Basket no.1	Sf.5b	(?)	Wall block fragment	Limestone	A large white fragment with a curved incised band	5 cm thick 9.2 × 9.7 cm Surface area	Smooth surface with an incised and curved band; (drawn in note book)
JB	4	Basket no.1	Sf.5c	(?)	Wall block fragment	Limestone	White chip with a red painted incised line	1 × 2.9 × 4.1 cm	(drawn in note book)
JB	4	Basket no.1	Sf.5d	(?)	Wall block fragment	Limestone	White chip with a red painted area	(thickness?) 1.5 × 1.7 cm	(drawn in note book)
JB	4	Basket no.1	Sf.5e	(?)	Wall block fragment	Limestone	White chip with a yellow painted surface(?) and a red painted incised line(?)	1.4 × 0.7 × 2.8 cm	Deeply incised line (drawn in note book)
JB	4	Basket no.1	Sf.5f	(?)	Wall block fragment	Limestone	White chip with a smoothed surface (no paint)	1.4 × 3.5 × 3.7 cm	(drawn in note book)
JB	4	Basket no.1	Sf.5g	(?)	Wall block fragment	Limestone	White fragment with a red painted area	(thickness?) 4.2 × 5.1 cm	(drawn in note book)
JB	4	Basket no.1	Sf.5h	(?)	Wall block fragment	Limestone	White chip with a smooth surface and red painted groove	0.6 × 2.4 × 2.4 cm	(drawn in note book)
JC	4	Basket no.1	Sample	(?)	Wall block fragment	Limestone	Badly worn decorated piece (not drawn; discarded)	Small	Badly preserved decorated piece.
JC	4	Basket no.1	Sf.3a	(?)	Wall block fragment	Limestone	White flake with smooth surface and a curved incised line: upper side of cartouche?	2.1 × 8 × 11 cm	Cartouche frag.(?) (drawn in note book)
JC	4	Basket no.1	Sf.3b	(?)	Wall block fragment	Limestone	White chip with a smooth panel flanked by a blue painted incised straight line	2.3 × 4.4 × 7.3 cm	Border panel(?)(drawn in note book)
JC	4	Basket no.1	Sf.3c	(?)	Wall block fragment	Limestone	White chip with a smooth surface and a blue painted incised straight line	1.2 × 3.8 × 6 cm	Border panel(?)(drawn in note book)

Table 3.24. Summary of Limestone Fragments from Units J, JA, JB, JC, and JD (Pit Fill)

Unit	*Locus*	*Basket or level*	*Unit Book no.*	*TBO no.*	*Object type*	*Material*	*Color and Surface Treatment*	*Dimensions (cm)*	*Comments: Mumford notes for Unit J*
JC	4	Basket no.1	Sf.3d	(?)	Wall block fragment	Limestone	White chip with a smooth surface and a blue painted incised straight line	1.2 5.9 × 6.4 cm	Border panel(?)(drawn in note book)
JC	4	Basket no.1	Sf.3e	(?)	Wall block fragment	Limestone	Slightly curved, smooth yellow painted surface	1.2 × 5.1 × 6.4 cm	Border panel(?)(drawn in note book)
JD	2	Basket no.1	Sf.1	0901	Wall block fragment	Limestone	Carved decoration	No details	No details
JD	2	Basket no.1	Sample	(?)	Wall block fragments	Limestone	No details	Small	**Note:** Very fragmented (discarded)

The most common finds included limestone chips, potsherds, and gray mud-brick debris. According to their find-spot distribution, the decorated fragments appear throughout all the layers in the pit. However, the densest concentration of limestone chips and decorated limestone pieces appear in the upper layers 4–10 in Units J (Loci 3[North], 4, 6), JA (Locus 4), JB (Loci 3–4), JC (Loci 2–4), and JD (Locus 2). Out of the hundreds of limestone chips of varying sizes, more than 30 diagnostic fragments bore portions of smooth surfaces, incised lines and parts of figures, painted borders, glyphs, and backgrounds (see pl. 3:6 no. 23, TBO 0901, Unit JD Locus 2 basket 1), and a limited range of colors: yellow, red, blue, and black (pl. 3.1 no. 1: TBO 0178). The other stone types were less common but included seven pieces of calcite, some chert lithics, a few granite chunks, three pieces of quartzite, and a well-polished graywacke fragment (which may have originated from a whetstone [unlikely to represent part of a statuette's scepter]: J6 sf.12; OCHRE pl. 92; pl. 3:6 no.16, TBO 0106). The remainder of finds from the pit's upper layers included fragments of burned bones (J3–4; J6; JA4), shells (J3), and copper alloy lumps (J4; J6).

3.3.12.6. Phase 10: Surface Layer Overlying Pit and Environs (Units JA; JB; JC) (fig. 3.28)

Locus JA2 lay in the eastern third of Unit JA and represents a sloping layer of mottled sand with white, yellow, gray, brown, and black sand, soil, organic, and other remains. It contained some potsherds and lithic debris. Thomas Davis examined the white powder from this layer and determined that it came from modern explosives, suggesting that old military ordinance had been collected and set off in this area during the recent clearance of such materials across North Sinai. Three bronze lumps (JA2 sf.1a-c) and a chert flake (sample) lay at the interface between this modern layer and the loose, wind-blown surface sand.

A loose, yellow-white sand layer covered Units JA, JB, JC, and JD. It was designated Locus 1 in each of these units and yielded some modern vegetation (camel thorn bushes) and contained some limestone chips (JA; JB; JC), a few granite chunks (JA; JB; JC), some pieces of copper alloy (JA; JS sf.1a–c), and many potsherds (JA; JB; JC). This layer partly overlay Locus 2 (i.e., the modern ordinance layer) (see OCHRE pls. 89–90).

3.3.13. Phase 11: Dynasty 19/20(?) Mottled Debris Layer (Units I and K)

A hard-packed, mottled band of three debris layers of yellow, gray, and black sand, silt, and clay lay in the southeast corner of Unit K and dominated the majority of Unit I, aside from the northern quarter of this Unit. This debris layer contained rubble and chunks from mud brick (I8), shells (I8), limestone chips (I8), a limestone slab (K2), granite fragments (I8), a piece of calcite (I8), a quartzite flake/awl(?) (pl. 3:6 no.14, TBO 0222, Unit I, Locus 8), pockets of dark gray ash

Text continues on p. 83

Table 3.25. Summary of Calcite Fragments from Units J, JA, JB, JC, and JD (Pit Fill)

Unit	Locus	Basket or level	Unit Book no.	TBO no.	Object type	Material	Color &Surface Treatment	Dimensions (cm)	Comments: Mumford notes for Unit J
J	6	1 (P9)	(b)	(?)	Fragment	Calcite ("alabaster")	Yellow-white	No details	One smoothed face and a hammered part
J	6	1 (P9)	(c)	(?)	Fragment	Calcite ("alabaster")	Yellow-white	No details	A core with a hammered part
J	3 (N)	1 (P9)	(d–f)	(?)	Fragments	Calcite ("alabaster")	Yellow-white	No details	3+ fragments of calcite
J	4	1 (P9)	(b)	(?)	Core fragment	Calcite	Yellow-white	No details; small chip	Hammered piece
J	4	1 (P9)	(c)	(?)	Chip	Calcite	Yellow-white	No details; Small chip	Hammered piece
J	4	1 (P9)	(d)	(?)	Core fragment	Calcite	Yellow-white	No details; small chip	Hammered piece
JB	2	Basket no.1	Sample	(?)	Slag(?) or pumice(?)	Slag(?) Pumice(?)	Green-gray	1.4 × 2 × 3.1 cm	Light weight, which may argue it is pumice (drawn in note book).
JB	2	Basket no.1	Sample	(?)	Fragment	Calcite	Yellow-white	1.3 × 1.9 × 3.5 cm	Core or natural fracturing in calcite (drawn in note book).
JB	3	Basket no.1	Sample a–d	(?)	4 fragments	Calcite	Yellow-white	a. 1.1 × 2.2 × 4.1 b. 0.9 × 3.7 cm c. 1.4 × 4.1 cm d. 0.8 × 1.6 cm	All four irregularly shaped chunks (drawn in note book).
JB	2	Basket no.1	Sf.1a	(?)	Side sheet/part from a vessel?	Copper alloy	Green (corroded)	0.2 × 1.1 × 1.6 cm	Vessel(?) fragment (drawn in note book).
JB	2	Basket no.1	Sf.1b	(?)	Side sheet/part from a vessel?	Copper alloy	Green (corroded)	0.2 × 1.3 × 1.3 cm	Vessel(?) fragment (drawn in note book).
JB	2	Basket no.1	Sf.1c	(?)	Rim and side from a vessel	Copper alloy	Green (corroded)	0.2 × 0.9 × 1.3 cm; rim = approx. 13 cm in dia	Bowl rim (drawn in note book).
JB	2	Basket no.1	Sf.1d	(?)	Side sheet/part from a vessel?	Copper alloy	Green (corroded)	0.5 × 1.1 × 1.3 cm	Vessel(?) fragment (drawn in note book).
JB	2	Basket no.1	Sf.1e	(?)	Lump	Copper alloy	Green (corroded)	0.4 × 0.7 × 0.8 cm	Vessel(?) fragment (drawn in note book).
JB	2	Basket no.1	Sf.1f	(?)	Side sheet/part from a vessel?	Copper alloy	Green (corroded)	0.1 × 0.5 × 1.4 cm	Vessel(?) fragment (drawn in note book).
JB	2	Basket no.1	Sf.1g	(?)	Ball, or droplet	Copper alloy	Green (corroded)	4 cm dia ball-shaped item	Ball/droplet (drawn in note book)
JC	3	Basket no.1	Sample a	(?)	Chunk from calcite block (nat. fracture)	Calcite	Yellow-white	1.3 × 1.7 × 4.4 cm	Basket 1 = pit-J (drawn in note book)
JC	3	Basket no.1	Sample b	(?)	Chunk from calcite block (nat. fracture)	Calcite	Yellow-white	1.5 × 2.1 × 4.1 cm	Basket 1 = pit-J (drawn in note book)
JC	3	Basket no.1	Sample c	(?)	Chunk from calcite block (nat. fracture)	Calcite	Yellow-white	1.2 × 2 × 3.6 cm	Basket 1 = pit-J (drawn in note book)
JC	3	Basket no.1	Sample d	(?)	Chunk from calcite block (nat. fracture)	Calcite	Yellow-white	0.9 × 1.2 × 4 cm	Basket 1 = pit-J (drawn in note book)
JC	3	Basket no.1	Sample e	(?)	Chunk from calcite block (nat. fracture)	Calcite	Yellow-white	1.2 × 2.6 × 4.2 cm	Basket 1 = pit-J (drawn in note book)
JC	3	Basket no.1	Sample f	(?)	Chunk from calcite block (nat. fracture)	Calcite	Yellow-white	(thickness?) × 1 × 2.1 cm	Basket 1 = pit-J (drawn in note book)
JC	3	Basket no.1	Sample g	(?)	Chunk from calcite block (nat. fracture)	Calcite	Yellow-white	0.8 × 1.4 × 2.8 cm	Basket 1 = pit-J (drawn in note book)
JC	3	Basket no.1	Sample h	(?)	Chunk from calcite block (nat. fracture)	Calcite	Yellow-white	1 × 1.2 × 3 cm	Basket 1 = pit-J (drawn in note book)
JC	4	Basket no.1	Sample a	(?)	Chunk from calcite block	Calcite	Yellow-white	3.9 × 4.7 × 9 cm	Natural fracture (drawn in note book)
JC	4	Basket no.1	Sample b	(?)	Chunk from calcite block	Calcite	Yellow-white	2.8 × 3.6 × 3.9 cm	Natural fracture (drawn in note book)
JC	4	Basket no.1	Sample c	(?)	Chunk from calcite block	Calcite	Yellow-white	0.9 × 1.2 × 4 cm	Natural fracture (drawn in note book)
JC	4	Basket no.1	Sample d	(?)	Chunk from calcite block	Calcite	Yellow-white	1 × 1.2 × 4.7 cm	Natural fracture (drawn in note book)
JC	4	Basket no.1	Sample e	(?)	Chunk from calcite block	Calcite	Yellow-white	1.2 × 1.8 × 5.8 cm	Natural fracture (drawn in note book)

Table 3.26. Summary of Other Stone Pieces from Units J, JA, JB, JC, and JD (Pit Fill)

Unit	*Locus*	*Basket or level*	*Unit Book no.*	*TBO no.*	*Object type*	*Material*	*Color and Surface Treatment*	*Dimensions (cm)*	*Comments: Mumford notes for Unit J*
J	6	1 (P9)	Sf.12	TBO 0106	Statue(?) scepter fragment; whetstone	Graywacke fine-grained ("basalt")	Black with high polished surface	13.2 × 4 × 2.4 cm	Longitudinal half of a shaft originally with an octagonal section
J	6	1 (P9)	(d)	(?)	3+ chips	Granite	Pink and black	No details	No details
J	6	1 (P9)	(e)	(?)	2+ chips	Quartzite	No details	No details	No details
J	3 (N)	1 (P9)	(g)	(?)	Stone tool	Chert(?) (fine, igneous stone)	Red flint	No details	Flaked tool (re-touched; blade?)
J	3 (N)	1 (P9)	(h)	(?)	Chip	Quartzite	Red	No details	No details
J	4	1 (P9)	(a)	(?)	Chip	Quartzite	Yellow	No details	No details
J	3 (N)	1 (P9)	Sf.7	(?)	Fragment	Sandstone	Yellow with red banding	Small ("chip")	Small chip; not drawn.
JA	3 Mix?	Basket no.1	Sample	(?)	Flake with retouch(?)	Stone	Not noted (dark gray?)	1.5 × 1.8 × 2.7 cm	**Note:** Locus 3 spanned pit fill and pit edge (mixed?) (drawn in note book)
JA	3 Mix?	Basket no.1	Sf.2a	(?)	Sheet from a vessel(?)	Copper alloy	Green (Corroded)	0.1 × 0.5 × 0.5 cm	**Note:** Locus 3 spanned pit fill and pit edge (mixed?) (drawn in note book)
JA	3 Mix?	Basket no.1	Sf.2b	(?)	Sheet from a vessel(?)	Copper alloy	Green (Corroded)	0.2 × 0.4 × 0.7 cm	**Note:** Locus 3 spanned pit fill and pit edge (mixed?) (drawn in note book)
JA	3 Mix?	Basket no.1	Sf.2c	(?)	Lump	Copper alloy	Green (Corroded)	0.2 × 0.3 × 0.5 cm	**Note:** Locus 3 spanned pit fill and pit edge (mixed?) (drawn in note book)
JA	3 Mix?	Basket no.1	Sf.3	TBO 0913	Ring(?) fragment	Chalcedony	Semi-translucent red	0.2 × 0.2 × 0.6 cm	**Note:** Locus 3 spanned pit fill and pit edge (mixed?) (drawn in note book)
JA	3 Mix?	Basket no.1	Sample	(?)	Fragment (core?)	Calcite	Yellow-white	1.5 × 2.6 × 2.7 cm	**Note:** Locus 3 spanned pit fill and pit edge (mixed?) (drawn in note book)
JA	4	Basket no.1	Sample	(?)	Flake	Lithic	Color(?)	0.6 × 2.3 × 2.9 cm	Simple flake with no signs of retouching. (drawn in note book)

Table 3.27. Summary of Copper Alloy Pieces from Units J, JA, JB, JC, and JD (Pit Fill)

Unit	*Locus*	*Basket or level*	*Unit Book no.*	*TBO no.*	*Object type*	*Material*	*Color and Surface Treatment*	*Dimensions (cm)*	*Comments: Mumford notes for Unit J*
J	6	2 (P9)	(a)	(?)	Lump	Copper alloy	Green (corroded)	0.7 × 0.6 × 0.4 cm	Ovoid lump
J	3 (N)	1 (P9)	Sf.2	(?)	Nail(?)	Copper alloy	Green (corroded)	3.4 cm long by 0.7 cm diameter	Cylindrical length with one rounded end
J	3 (N)	1 (P9)	(a)	(?)	Lump	Copper alloy	Green (corroded)	1.7 × 0.8 × 0.5 cm	Cylindrical item with circular section and rounded end
J	3 (N)	1 (P9)	(b)	(?)	Lump	Copper alloy	Green (corroded)	1.7 × 1 × 0.5 cm	Ovoid lump
J	3 (N)	1 (P9)	(c)	(?)	Lump	Copper alloy	Green (corroded)	1.6 × 0.8 × 0.4 cm	Irregularly shaped lump
J	4	1 (P9)	(e)	(?)	Lump	Copper alloy	Green (corroded)	1.1 × 0.7 × 0.4 cm	Ovoid-shaped lump
JB	3	Basket no.1	Sf.2	(?)	Lump	Copper alloy	Green (corroded)	0.08.5 × 1.9 × 2.1 cm	Small irregular-shaped piece with a concave side. (drawn in note book)
JB	4	Basket no.1	Sf.4	(?)	Plate (from vessel?)	Copper alloy	Green (corroded)	0.2 × 1.3 × 1.3 cm	A small sheet of copper alloy (drawn in note book)
JC	3	Basket no.1	Sf.2	(?)	Cylindrical rod	Copper alloy	Green (corroded)	1.8 cm long 0.2 cm diameter	Possibly a small nail or a pin (drawn in note book)

Table 3.28. Summary of Other Items from Units J, JA, JB, JC, and JD (Pit Fill)

Unit	*Locus*	*Basket or level*	*Unit Book no.*	*TBO no.*	*Object type:*	*Material:*	*Color and Surface Treatment:*	*Dimensions (cm):*	*Comments: Mumford notes for Unit J*
JC	3	Basket no.1	Sample	(?)	Lump	Slag	Gray	No details	-

Table 3.29. Summary of Pottery from Units J, JA, JB, JC, and JD (Pit Fill)

Unit	*Locus*	*Basket/ level*	*Pottery basket*	*Rims*	*Handles*	*Bases*	*Nile Silts*	*Desert marls*	*Other wares*	*Comments: Hummel pottery labels*
J	6	1 (P9)	Small basket of sherds	2	1	-	80%	20%	-	**Silt:** much red slip; **Marl:** gritty green marl; gray-green slip with burnishing.
J	6	2 (P9)	Large basket of sherds	17	3	5	50%	50%	-	**Silt:** Blue Painted potsherds; **Marl:** a small basket-handle; pale green slip with burnishing.
J	3	1 (P9)	Medium-full basket of sherds	14	-	4	50%(?)	49(?)	1%(?)	**Silt:** an early–mid-Dynasty 18, black-rimmed bowl; red slipped sherds with some burnishing; **Marl:** cream-green slip; **Other fabrics:** a Cypriot Base Ring sherd; **Note:** this locus yielded a possible Roman period, ridged sherd.
J	3	2 (P9)	Scanty basket of sherds	5	2	-	80%	20%	-	Very small, worn body sherds; **Silt:** traces of red slip; **Marls:** gray-green slip; peach-colored marl sherd.
J	4	1 (P9)	Small basket of sherds	10	-	-	50%	50%	-	**Silt:** early-mid, Dynasty 18, red-slipped, black-rimmed bowls; much red slip with some burnishing; Blue Painted potsherds; **Marl:** gray-green and peach slips.
JA	3	Basket no.1	Small basket (93 sherds)	7	3	1	Count: 69 sherds 74%	Count: 16 sherds 17%	Count: 8 sherds 9%	**Note:** A mix of 18th and 19th Dynasty forms and wares; Theban marls; Palestinian fabric; 1 black-rimmed bowl; amphora sherds.
JA	4	Basket no.1	Small basket (127 sherds)	12	2	-	Count: 102 sherds 80%	Count: 24 sherds 19%	Count: 1 sherd 1%	**Note:** Two Blue Painted body sherds; tiny bowl rim fragments; an assortment of New Kingdom wares.
JB	2	Basket no.1 MIX	Small basket (36 sherds)	1	-	2	Count: 23 sherds 64%	Count: 12 sherds 33%	Count: 1 sherd 3%	**Note:** This locus spans the pit and pre-pit upper layer (= mixed). **Note:** 1 Blue Painted sherd; 1 Palestinian flask body with concentric circles; many G6-type vessel sherds (see R. Hummel chapter on pottery).
JC	2	Basket no.1 (= pit)	Small (72 sherds)	10	-	-	Count: 59 sherds 82%	Count: 5 sherds 7%	Count: 8 Pal. Sherds 11%	**Note:** 2 black-rimmed bowls; a mix of Egyptian 18th–19th Dynasty wares; many red-slipped bowls.
JC	3	Basket no.1 (= pit)	Small (77 sherds)	10	1	-	Count: 55 sherds 71%	Count: 13 sherds 17%	Count: 9 sherds 12%	**Note:** 1 Cypriot milk bowl handle; 1 blue painted sherd; 1 Palestinian flask sherd; a variety of New Kingdom wares.
JC	4	Basket no.1	Small (51 sherds)	4	1	1	Count: 41 sherds 80%	Count: 5 sherds 10%	Count: 5 sherds 10%	**Note:** 1 Mycenaean body sherd; 1 oasis ware sherd; 1 sherd with red bands on cream slip on a marl D sherd; a variety of New Kingdom wares.
JD	2	Basket no.1	Small (105 sherds)	11	1	4	Count: 74 sherds 70%	Count: 23 sherds 22%	Count: 8 sherds 8%	**Note:** 1 Cypriot Base Ring sherd; 1 Palestinian TBP 828; 1 possible neck of a Roman amphora.
Total	-	-	**624+ body sherds**	103	14	17	**69%**	**26%**	**6%**	**Note:** The silt and marl percentages represent averages from the columns.

Table 3.30. Summary of Items from the Surface of Units JA, JB, JC, and JD

Unit	*Locus*	*Basket or level*	*Unit Book no.*	*TBO no.*	*Object type*	*Material*	*Color and Surface Treatment*	*Dimensions (cm)*	*Comments: Mumford notes for Unit JA, JB, JC, and JD*
JA	1	Basket no. 1	Notebook	(?)	Irregularly shaped chunks	Granite	Pink & black	Small-medium	Non-diagnostic (no details)
JA	1	Basket no. 1	Notebook	(?)	Irregularly shaped chunks	Limestone	White	Small-medium	Non-diagnostic (no details)
JB	1	Basket no. 1	Notebook	(?)	Irregularly shaped chunks	Granite	Pink & black	Small-medium	Non-diagnostic (no details)
JB	1	Basket no. 1	Notebook	(?)	Irregularly shaped chunks	Limestone	White	Small-medium	Non-diagnostic (no details)
JC	1	Basket no. 1	Notebook	(?)	Irregularly shaped chunks	Granite	Pink & black	Small-medium	Non-diagnostic (no details)
JC	1	Basket no. 1	Notebook	(?)	Irregularly shaped chunks	Limestone	White	Small-medium	Non-diagnostic (no details)
JA	2 Surf.	Basket no. 1/2	Sf.1a	(?)	Cylindrical lump	Copper alloy	Green (corroded)	1.6 cm long by 0.5 cm diameter	A cylindrical piece, possibly a nail(?); (drawn in note book)
JA	2 Surf.	Basket no. 1/2	Sf.1b	(?)	Triangular piece/ frag.	Copper alloy	Green (corroded)	0.1 × 0.4 × 0.9 cm	Copper sheet fragment (drawn in note book)
JA	2 Surf.	Basket no. 1/2	Sf.1c	(?)	Cylindrical piece	Copper alloy	Green (corroded)	0.5–0.3 cm diameter at opposite ends; 1.6 cm length	Folded over sheet (drawn in note book)
JA	2 Surf.	Basket no. 2	Sample	(?)	Flake (no retouch)	Stone (chert?)	Brown	0.4 × 1.5 × 2.2 cm	Flake with no sign of retouching (drawn in note book)

Table 3.31. Summary of Pottery from the Surface of Units JA, JB, JC, and JD

Unit	*Locus*	*Basket/ level*	*Pottery basket*	*Rims*	*Handles*	*Bases*	*Nile silts*	*Desert marls*	*Other wares*	*Comments: Hummel pottery labels*
JA	1	Basket no. 1	Tiny (8 sherds)	-	-	-	Count: 5 sherds	Count: 3 sherds	-	**Note:** All marls are late New Kingdom; mixed clays from amphoras.
JB	1	Basket no. 1	Tiny (15 sherds)	-	1	-	Count: 5 sherds	Count: 9 sherds	Count: 1 Cypriot	**Note:** Very hard mixed clay sherds: 19th Dynasty; 1 Palestinian sherd.
JC	1	Basket no. 1	Tiny (11 sherds)	1	1	-	Count: 5 sherds	Count: 3 sherds	Count: 1 sherd	**Note:** 1 marl D amphora handle; 1 mixed clay large bowl rim.
JA	2	Basket no. 1	Tiny (13 sherds)	1	1	-	Count: 9 sherds	Count: 4 sherds	-	**Note:** Upper debris layer. **Note:** 1 jar rim with a black band on the shoulder; 1 mixed clay amphora handle.
Total	-	-	**43+ body sherds**	2	3	-	**24 56%**	**19 44%**	**2 5%**	**Note:** The silt and marl percentages represent averages from the columns.

(K2; I8–9), patches of darker soil (K2), fragments of bone (I8), a piece of glass (I8), a copper alloy lump (I8), three copper alloy, cylindrical wire/needle fragments (K2 sf.3), and potsherds (I8) (tables 3.32–33). This layer lay directly above the gray-yellow sand layer but had been cut by the modern surface currently overlying it. In Unit K, the mottled debris layer extended as deeply as 16 cm to 21 cm along the eastern side of this excavation area. At least three pits cut into this mottled debris layer.

The pottery from baskets 1–4 of Locus I8 included body sherds, 14 rim pieces, 12 handles, 10 bases, 65% Nile silts, 35% desert marls, and 0.5% foreign wares (a Cypriot and a Canaanite sherd). Locus I9 was assigned to the thin, gray layer lining the depression ("pit") containing the dark gray mottled debris; Locus I9 lacked pottery (table 3.33).

Table 3.32. Summary of Small Finds from Units I Loci 8–9 and Unit K, Locus 2 (East)

Unit	*Locus*	*Basket or level*	*Unit Book no.*	*TBO no.*	*Object type*	*Material*	*Color & Surface Treatment*	*Dimensions (cm)*	*Comments: Mumford Unit K, Burke Unit I notes*
1	8	1 (P11)	-	-	Fragment	Granite	Pink and black	No details	No details
I	8	1 (P11)	(?)	TBO 0222	Stone sample	Quartzite	No details	No details	**SF register:** Determined not to be an artifact (discarded)
I	8	2 (P11)	(a)	-	Lump	Copper alloy	Green (corroded)	No details	No details
I	8	3 (P11)	(b)	-	Fragment	Calcite ("alabaster")	Yellow-white	No details	No details
I	8	3 (P11)	(c)	-	Fragment	Glass	-	No details	No details
I	8	4 (P11)	-	-	-	-	-	-	No small finds
I	9	1 (P11)	-	-	-	-	-	-	No small finds
K	2 (E)	1 (P11)	Sf.3a	-	Wire/needle fragment	Copper alloy	Green (corroded)	0.8 cm long × 0.25 cm dia.	Cylindrical fragment
K	2 (E)	1 (P11)	Sf.3b	-	Wire/needle fragment	Copper alloy	Green (corroded)	1.2 cm long × 0.25 cm dia.	Cylindrical fragment with slight curve
K	2 (E)	1 (P11)	Sf.3c	-	Wire/needle fragment	Copper alloy	Green (corroded)	0.7 cm long × 0.3 cm dia.	Cylindrical fragment

Table 3.33. Summary of Pottery from Unit I, Locus 8, Baskets 1–4 and Locus 9

Unit	*Locus*	*Basket/ level*	*Pottery basket*	*Rims*	*Handles*	*Bases*	*Nile silts*	*Desert marls*	*Other wares*	*Comments: Hummel pottery labels*
I	8	1 (P11)	Small basket of sherds	6	3	1	50%	50%	-	**Silt:** Blue Painted sherd; **Marl:** cream slip on Marl D1 flask; peach and gray-green slips on marl.
I	8	2 (P11)	1 sherd	-	1	-	100%	-	-	**Silt:** probable hard silt handle with rust-peach slip.
I	8	3 (P11)	Large basket of sherds	5	7	7	50%	48%	2%	Sherds from fine table vessels; **Marl:** a Theban area marl ring base; **Other fabrics:** a Cypriot Base Ring fragment; a possible Canaanite amphora sherd.
I	8	4 (P11)	Scanty basket of sherds	3	1	2	60%	40%	-	Worn sherds; **Marl:** variety of marls; orange slip hard wares; amphorae.
I	9	1 (P11)	-	-	-	-	-	-	-	No pottery recorded.
Total	-	-	**36 + body sherds**	14	12	10	**65%**	**35%**	**0.5%**	**Note:** The silt and marl percentages represent averages from the columns.

3.3.14. Phase 12: Pitting into Mottled Debris Layer (Units I and K)

The mottled debris layer had been cut by at least three pits in Unit K. One pit (no. 1) in Unit K extended 22 cm deep, while its fill (Locus K2a) yielded no potsherds. The remaining pits (nos. 2–3) were visible as small, shallow, debris-filled depressions in the east baulk but had not been discerned during the excavation of the eastern portion of Locus 2 in Unit K.

3.3.15. Phase 13: Sub-Surface and Surface Layers Above the Gray-Yellow Sand Layer (Units I, J, and K)

In the northwest areas of Units I and K, the gray-yellow layer was overlain by sub-surface and surface layers of sand. These layers lay to the northwest of the black, gray, and yellow mottled debris layer, which overlay the gray-yellow sand layer in the southeast third of Unit K and in

Table 3.34. Summary of Small Finds from Unit J, Locus 1 and Unit K, Locus 1 (West)

Unit	*Locus*	*Basket or level*	*Unit Book no.*	*TBO no.*	*Object type*	*Material*	*Color and Surface Treatment*	*Dimensions (cm)*	*Comments: Mumford units J–K notes*
J	1	1 (P13)	(a)	(?)	Fragments	Quartzite	"Dark"	Small	No further details
J	1	1 (P13)	(b)	(?)	Fragment	Granite	Pink & black	Small	No further details
J	1	1 (P13)	(c)	(?)	Lump	Copper alloy	Green (corroded)	1 × 1.1 × 0.3 cm	Irregularly shaped disk-like lump (J1 south side)
J	1	1 (P13)	(d)	(?)	Textile fragment	Cloth	-	-	No details (modern debris from surface)
K	1 (W)	1 (P13)	Sf.1	TBO 0104	Block edge fragment	Granite	Pink & black	6.1 × 5 × 4 cm	Edge piece with smoothed sides
K	1 (W)	1 (P13)	(a)	-	Lump	Copper alloy	Green (corroded)	No details	No details

Table 3.35. Summary of Pottery from Units J, Loci 1–2, Baskets 1–3 and K Locus 1

Unit	*Locus*	*Basket/ level*	*Pottery basket*	*Rims*	*Handles*	*Bases*	*Nile silts*	*Desert marls*	*Other wares*	*Comments: Hummel pottery labels.*
J	1	1 (P13)	Small basket of sherds	4	4	-	80%	20%	-	Very worn body sherds; **Silts:** many Dynasty 19 hard wares; some cream and gray-green slip; **Marl:** peach, cream and gray-green slips.
J	1	2/3 (P13)	Scanty basket of sherds	3	-	-	80%	20%	-	Very worn body sherds; **Silt:** red slips; **Marl:** gray-green cream slips.
J	2	1 (P13)	Scanty basket of sherds	2	-	-	80%	15%	5%	Very worn body sherds; **Marl:** gray-green slip; **Other fabrics:** a possible foreign amphora handle.
K	1	1	Scanty basket of sherds	2	-	-	60%	40%	-	**Marl:** Gray-green on Marl D; cream slip on Marl D. Some hard marl/silt wares.
Total	-	-	**15 + body sherds**	11	4	-	**75%**	**24%**	1%	**Note:** The silt and marl percentages represent averages from the columns.

the majority of Unit I (excepting its northwest corner). In Unit J, the sub-surface and surface layers were excavated as Loci J1 and J2. In Unit I, Locus I1 contained part of these layers in the northwest portion of this excavation unit. In Unit K, the western portion of Locus 1 represented these layers.

The upper sand layers consisted of a medium to light yellow sand, which contained poorly sorted fine- to coarse-grained wind-blown sand. These layers also yielded roots from surface vegetation (J1), pebbles (J1; K1), burned limestone chips (J1), sandstone chips (J1), dark quartzite chunks (J1), a pink granite piece (J1), many shells (J1), fragments of burned bones (J1), many gypsum inclusions (J2), two copper alloy lumps (J1; K1), pieces from cloth (J1), a smoothed, edge fragment from a granite block/statuette(?) (K1 sf.1; pl. 3.1 no. 2: TBO 104), and potsherds (J1, J2) (tables 3.34–3.35). The pottery from this layer consisted of 99% Egyptian forms and wares and 1% foreign and other fabrics (table 3.35). Many of the sherds dated to Dynasty 19, suggesting that the underlying mud-brick structure either predated this period or existed into part of Dynasty 19.

3.3.16. Phase 14: Roman Period(?) Pitting in Sub-Surface Layers (Unit J).

The sub-surface layer in Unit J had been partly disturbed by a later pit (pit no. 1; Locus J2 basket 1) that cut 34 cm deep into this and the lower sand layers. This pit had been filled successively by a thick layer of water-laid white sand, a thinner wind-laid yellow sand layer, a thin water-laid layer of gray mud and sand, a deeper deposit of wind-laid yellow sand, a thin water-laid layer of gray mud and sand, a thin wind-laid layer of sand, and a thicker water-laid layer of gray mud and sand. In turn, this pit had been sealed by two thin layers of wind-blown sand. In essence, a rainstorm, three floods, and four to five windstorms had contributed to the filling and covering this pit, which only yielded a few potsherds.

Locus 2 did yield a fragment of a stone disk (weight?) that likely represents a New Kingdom piece of debris redeposited in the backfill of this pit (table 3.36). Of note, the Roman-period sherd from Unit J, Locus 3 (above) was likely introduced into a lower layer by one of the various shallow pits cutting into Locus J3. Based on the occurrence of some Roman pottery in other pits at Tell el-Borg, it is likely that this and other pits reflect some sort of Roman period activity at Borg, probably mainly robbing stone for reuse at Pelusium or other neighboring Roman settlements in North Sinai.

Table 3.36. Summary of Small Finds from Unit J, Locus 1 and Unit K, Locus 1 (West)

Unit	*Locus*	*Basket or level*	*Unit Book no.*	*TBO no.*	*Object type*	*Material*	*Color and Surface Treatment*	*Dimensions (cm)*	*Comments: Mumford Unit J notes*
J	2	1 (P14)	Sf.16	-	Weight(?)	Fine-grained, conglomerate	Black with white mottling	Originally 5.9 cm dia by 1.1 cm high.	Quarter piece left of a convex-topped disk

3.3.17. Discussion of Phases 1–14 (Units I–K) (figs. 3.19–22)

Areas 1–2 in Field II have yielded several interesting features indicative of large-scale, state-sanctioned construction. The installation of a well-laid, expansive floor (at least 10 × 25 m) is suggestive of a significant courtyard area. Taken in context, with the proximity of many fragments of broken-up painted hieroglyphs, border trim, and scenes from limestone wall blocks, and the occurrence of inscribed granite pieces, it is quite possible that a small temple or some elite, formal structure originally lay in or near this area. However, no foundation trenches turned up in the magnetometer survey or excavations in this area, suggesting that if such a structure existed, it was not substantial enough to require deep foundations. The discovery of a Ramesside (or later?) large, 1.26-m-deep and 6 × 10 m ovoid pit, which contained many of the fragmentary limestone pieces, may indicate several functions: a robbed-out foundation for a large stone structure, a dismantled stone-lined well, an aborted shallow well, or some other feature of undetermined function. As elsewhere at Tell el-Borg, the foreign pottery (Canaanite and Cypriot sherds) ranged from 0.5%, to 1%, 2%, 9%, and 10% within the various occupation phases in Units I–K, while the small finds (see OCHRE pls. 89–93) included pieces of calcite, basalt, quartzite, diorite, and granite (possibly from structures, statuary, and vessels), a stone weight(?) fragment, copper alloy lumps, fragments from two or three copper alloy vessels (a jar; 1–2 bowls), tools and fittings of copper alloy (a hook? a nail? three wires/needles?), jewelry (a faience bead), and ostrich eggshell fragments. The nature and richness of these finds, such as the architectural and statuary(?) fragments and copper vessels, suggest the remnants of cultic structures, decoration, and offerings, bolstering arguments for the presence of a temple within this area at Tell el-Borg.

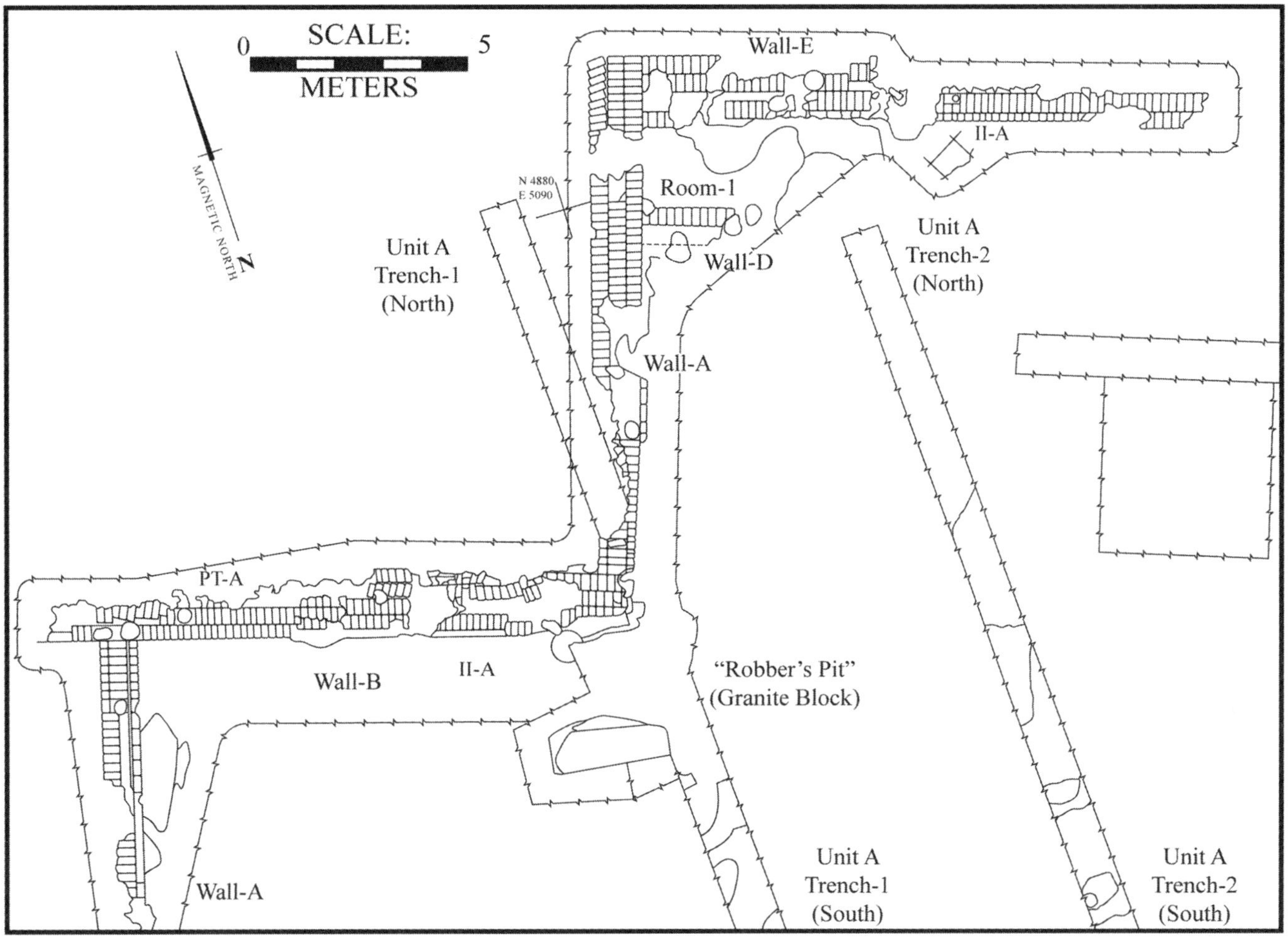

Fig. 3.29. Field II, Area 1: Unit A zigzagging walls A–E; Unit A Trenches 1–2 (drawing: Knudstad; digitized by Joshua Olsen).

3.4. Field II, Area 2

Area 2 covers a broad area along the northeast portion of Field II (see figs. 3.3 and 3.29) and has revealed traces of substantial structures near the ancient river channel. Area 2 is subdivided into excavation Units A, B, C, D, E, F, G, H, and I and investigated a river channel and its bank, a probable "shrine" (or another structure), a zigzagging enclosure wall, and granite blocks inside this portion of Tell el-Borg. Thomas Davis excavated Units D–I in Area 2, with some assistance from Scott Haddow, Ashraf Melika, and architectural planning by James Knudstad.

3.4.1. Granite Block and Its Environs (Unit A, Trench 1):
Excavators: Rosa Frey and Linda Wilding

Test Trench 1 (Unit A) extended 23 m north–south and measured 1 meter in width, straddling a large granite block (figs. 3.3 and 3.29), which measures approximately 2.75 × 1.30 × 1.16 m, a "robber's pit" on the northeast side of the block, a sand surface layer yielding numerous narrow to wide circular and irregular pitted depressions, with part of the zigzagging wall to the north. Several phases of occupation appear in this area: an initial Ramesside occupation and debris layer; the re-deposition of the granite block; an accumulation of wind-blown sand around the block; a series of "robber pits"; and a light layer of wind-blown sands and modern debris covering the surface and filling the modern robber pits.

3.4.1.1. Basal Sand (Unit A, Trench 1)

The basal sand pre-habitation layer was detected along the length of Unit A Trench 1, lying relatively close to the modern ground surface (fig. 3.29). It was overlain by Ramesside occupation debris to the north and south of the granite block, while in other areas pitting and erosion had removed the early occupation surface and associated debris.

3.4.1.2. Ramesside Debris Layers (Unit A, Trench 1: Loci 3 and 5)

The overlying Ramesside occupation layers (Locus 3) appeared 2 m south of the robber's pit and granite block, beginning as a mud smear that continued for 3.50 m further to the south. The southern mud smear represented a thin layer of sandy soil and mud, with ash deposits concentrated in a 20-cm-deep lens. It contained charcoal flecks, a 7-cm-thick rectilinear patch of lime or deteriorated limestone (possibly a basin?) extending 50 cm in width by 110 cm in length, many potsherds, some granite chunks, and copper alloy fragments. This layer continued to the north of the granite block and pits in a 20–40 cm deep, compact deposit of sandy soils (Locus 5) with distinct horizontal layering and an upper ash lense (Locus 3). The northern area yielded an intrusive ash-filled pit, a mass of eroded clay, and some potsherds. The northern extension of Trench 1 yielded part of a New Kingdom wall immediately below the surface sand and 3 m to the north of the granite block. The wall has two rows of gray-black mud-brick headers, in which each brick measures 10 × 19 × 30–40 cm and is defined by a sandy yellow mortar. Several sandy brown bricks lay beside this wall, resting directly on the basal sand layer, which extended under the adjacent walling system. The initial Ramesside occupation layer was overlain by Loci 3 and 2 in the northern portion of Trench 1, while the wind-blown surface sand covered it in the southern part.

3.4.1.3. Granite Block and Stone Debris (Unit A, Trench 1: Locus 2)

The massive granite block is roughly smoothed, measures approximately 2.75 × 1.30 × 1.16 m, and lies 2 m south of the interior corner of a zigzagging wall (figs. 3.3, 3.29–3.30a–b). The great size and weight of this block suggests that it probably had not been moved far from its original position inside the enclosure wall, while its rougher shape indicates that it either formed part of a foundation platform to stabilize a heavy, above-ground feature, such as a large stela or statue or that it represented part of a more complex unfinished (or destroyed?) installation. The discovery of other granite and limestone blocks from this area (see figs. 3.32–3.33) dating to the reign of Ramesses II and the Ramesside period in general indicate that a temple may have lain originally within or near this area during Dynasty 19 (see table 3.37).

The excavation of this area produced an immense mass of small to large fragments of limestone and many granite chips, which the excavator suggested indicated the breaking up of blocks in this area, perhaps from the dismantling of a stone building. The "level 2" disturbed and redeposited Ramesside debris continues to the south of the granite block and robber's pit and consisted of a mixed layer of brown soil, clay, sand streaks, numerous limestone chips, and some granite chunks. The mud lumps and other debris display some horizontal layering. The upper

Fig. 3.30a–b. Granite block lying southeast of "zigzag" Wall E (Photo: NSAP).

20–30 cm portion of this layer contained a noticeable concentration of ash. This layer was cut by the recent pitting beside the massive granite block (perhaps an earlier archaeological test pit).

3.4.1.4. Modern Pitting and Surface Debris (Unit A, Trench 1: Loci 0, 1, and 4)

Recent activities are responsible for the cutting of pits around and beside the granite block and the dispersal of earlier debris across the modern wind-laid sand. Successive deposits of wind-laid sand appear to underlie, fill, and cover the recent cuttings and subsequent debris deposits in and beside these modern pits.

The excavators designated this redistributed debris and subsequent wind-blown sand deposits as Locus 1, including the pits around and beside the granite block. Locus 1 contains numerous lumps and chunks of mud, brown sandy soil, small chips of limestone, some copper alloy lumps (pl. 3:5 no. 16, TBO 0069), and some granite chunks. This locus lay above a layer of fine, wind-blown sand, capped the wind-blown sand filling the "robber's pit," and was partly covered by subsequent deposits of wind-laid sand.

The excavator's section drawing and notes concerning the large granite block indicate that a piece of plastic was found about 1 m below the ground surface, lying in the wind-blown sand (Locus 4) filling the pit beside the granite block. This item confirms that both the cutting and filling took place in recent years, since this pit and the other nearby, relatively shallow pits would have been filled within a year of their cutting. The main pit's back-fill was also loosely compacted and contained sand lenses, ash lenses, sandy brown soil, layers, charcoal flecks, small fragments of limestone and granite, and a few large granite chunks. The modern "robber" pit continued to basal sand in parts, revealing no preserved ancient strata immediately below the granite block, thereby having removed all stratigraphic associations between the granite block and pre-modern layers. Several loose mud bricks, which measured 10 × 19 × 40 cm, appeared at the southern end of Locus 1, near the "robber's pit." The excavators suggested that this pit may have displaced these bricks from their original New Kingdom context.

3.4.2. Zigzagging Wall System (Unit A, Wall and Chamber: Loci 6, 8, 9, 10, and 11): Excavator: Rosa Frey

The foundations and lower portion of a large enclosure wall lay to the west of the "shrine" (next section) and retained three courses of brickwork in the southwestern area, one to two

Table 3.37. Summary of Small Finds from the Surface of Unit A Trench 1 (Field II)

Unit	*Locus*	*Basket or level*	*Unit Book no.*	*TBO no.*	*Object type*	*Material*	*Color and Surface Treatment*	*Dimensions*	*Comments*
A	Locus 3	-	001	TBO II 1	Fragments: Oblong pieces, maybe beads(?)	Copper alloy	Green (corroded)	Largest piece is 1.5 cm	**SF register:** Cites Trench 1 south, Locus 3
A	Locus 0 Surface?	-	002	TBO II 2	Unknown (Bead?)	Stone (Carnelian?)	Red	0.5 × 0.5 × 0.1 cm	No details
A	Locus 0 Surface?	East of peg 7	003	TBO II 3	5 small fragments	Copper alloy	Green (corroded)	Largest piece = 0.5 × 0.5 × 1.9 cm	Presumably near robber's pit (near granite block)
A	Locus 0 Surface?	-	004	TBO II 4	Shell fragment	Ostrich egg shell	(gray)	1.5 × 2.5 × 0.2 cm	No details
A	Locus 0 Surface?	-	005	TBO II 5	Small fragment	Glass	Turquoise green color	1.5 × 2.5 × 0.2 cm	Possibly Roman(?)
A	Locus 4	-	006	TBO II 6	Ovoid- shaped fragment	Copper alloy	Green (corroded)	0.5 × 1.5 × 0.5 cm	**SF register:** Cites Trench 1 west, Locus 4
Á	Locus 0 Surface?	-	007	TBO II 7	Block fragment reused as a knife sharpener	Gabbro ("black granite")	Cut and smoothed on one side; plaster in deep cut	-	Northeast end of trench
Á	Locus 0 Surface?	-	008	TBO II 8	Sculpture/statue fragment	Black granite fragment	Smoothed on one side	-	**SF register:** Described as granite
Á	Locus 0 Surface	-	009	TBO II 9	Block/relief fragment	Limestone	Traces of yellow paint	-	Relief fragment
A	Locus 0 Surface	East of peg 7	010	TBO II 10	Burnisher tool	Soapstone	Ground stone	-	From robber's pit near granite block.
A	Locus 5 Pit ext.	-	011	TBO II 11	Block fragment	Limestone	White with traces of yellow paint **Notes:** Relief scene fragment with yellow pigment	-	**SF register:** Cites Trench 1 west, Locus 4
A	Locus 5 Pit ext.	-	012	TBO II 12	Block fragment	Limestone	White relief scene fragment with red, black and yellow pigment	-	**SF register:** Cites Trench 1 west, Locus 4
A	Locus 0 Surface	-	013	TBO II 13	Slag	Slag	-	-	Manufacturing residue
A	Locus 0 Surface	-	014	TBO II 14	Fragment of relief or statue?	Pink granite	Carved	-	Travertine pit (i.e. zigzag wall)
A	Locus 0 Surface	-	015	TBO II 15	3 fragments (unknown items)	Copper alloy	Flat fragments	2 × 2 × 0.2 cm, 2.5 × 2 × 0.2 cm, 2 × 1.5 × 0.2 cm.	Travertine pit (i.e. zigzag wall)
A	Locus 0 Surface	-	016	TBO II 16	8 fragments (1 = conical shaped: a weight?)	Copper alloy	Green (Corroded)	Conical-shaped item (weight?): 2 × 1.3 × 1 cm	Travertine pit (i.e. zigzag wall)
A	Locus 0 Surface	-	017	TBO II 17	Vessel fragment (very abraded)	Faience	No decoration	-	Travertine pit (i.e. zigzag wall)
A	Locus 0 Surface	-	018	TBO II 18	Block/relief fragment	Limestone	White fragment with traces of red and yellow paint	-	No details
A	Locus 0 Surface	-	019	TBO II 19	Block/relief fragment	Limestone	White with no traces of pigment	-	No details
A	Locus 0 Surface	-	020	TBO II 20	Block/relief fragment	Limestone	White; possibly two legs with traces of red pigment	-	No details
A	Locus 0 Surface	-	021	TBO II 21	Block/relief fragment	Granite	Incised fragment ("inscription")	-	No details
A	Locus 0 Surface	-	022	TBO II 22	Possible statue or sculpture fragment	Granite	One side incised or worked	-	No details
A	Locus 0 Surface	1	-	No s.f. number	Block; possibly the base of a naos or another monument	Pink granite	-	2.75 × 1.30 × 1.16 meters	Roughly hewn (not square)

Table 3.37. Summary of Small Finds from the Surface of Unit A Trench 1 (Field II)

Unit	*Locus*	*Basket or level*	*Unit Book no.*	*TBO no.*	*Object type*	*Material*	*Color and Surface Treatment*	*Dimensions*	*Comments*
A	Locus 0 Surface	(X.B1)	004	TBOX 31	Block/relief fragment	Pink granite	Smooth face with a line in sunken relief (ridge)	-	**SF register:** Southwest of Trench, Unit A
A	Locus 0 Surface	NE of Unit A Trench 1	001	TBOX 34	Monument fragment ("block")	Pink granite	**Kitchen note:** statue of Re or group statue of Re & Ramesses II	Inscription dimensions = 22.5 x 7 cm	**Small find reg.:** Northeast of Unit A, Trench 2
A	Locus 0 Surface Location: N48.48.91 E50.20.40	General Surface (noted in Field II)	X.B4	TBOX 43	Monument fragment	Pink granite	Pink and black with inscribed prenomen cartouche of Ramesses II(?)	-	**Field book:** Possibly the prenomen of Ramesses II
A	Locus 0 surface	Surface survey	-	TBOX 7	Pounder	Pink granite	-	-	No details
A	Locus 0 Surface	Surface survey	-	TBOX 8	Pounder	Basalt	-	-	No details
A	Locus 0 Surface	Surface survey	-	TBOX 25	Pounder	Granite	Pink and black	No details	**SF register:** Just north of inscribed granite block
A	Locus 0 Surface	Surface survey	-	TBOX 26	Rim of vessel	Basalt	Black	Too small to get a diameter	**SF register:** Beside TBO.25 Near test trench

courses along the northern part, and several courses to the northeast. The preserved walling system ranged from at least 1.20 to 1.50 meters in width and extended in a zigzag pattern that strengthened the wall and adapted it to the topography of the gentle slope, up which it ascended. The wall lies about 7.70 m to the west of a "shrine" and extended 14.50 m to the northwest, turned southwest for 12 m, and headed northwest again for 12 m before disappearing. The remains of a narrower, 90-cm-wide interior wall headed southwest for 7.50 m from the westernmost portion of this enclosure wall. Another 90-cm-wide interior wall lay beside the northeasternmost corner, heading 2.15 m to the northeast before it disappeared. The fragmentary architectural remains suggest a few interior chambers or spaces of varying sizes.

The excavators uncovered this subsurface zigzag wall and proceeded from south to north, assigning Loci 9, 10, and 11 to the matrix associated with the southern east–west, central north–south, and northern east–west portions of the wall (figs. 3.29 and 3.31). The remnants

Fig. 3.31. Walls A–B, looking east along Wall B toward the large granite block (Photo: NSAP).

Table 3.38. Summary of Pottery from Surface in Unit A, Trench 1, and Environs

Unit	*Locus*	*Basket /level*	*Pottery basket*	*Rims*	*Handles*	*Bases*	*Nile Silts*	*Desert marls*	*Other wares*	*Comments: Hummel pottery labels.*
A	Locus 0 Surface	Full basket	Basket no.1<a>	16	3	3	60%	40%	-	**Note:** Variety of slips and wares. Thick crude tubs, amphoras, simple bowls. Peach and gray green slip.
A	Locus 0 Surface near test trench	Full basket	Basket no.1<b> (vicinity of test trench)	8	1	3	98%	2%	-	**Note:** Variety of slips: green, peach, red. New Kingdom red bowl. 1 possible New Kindom amphora.
A	Locus 0 Surface of test trench	25% full	Basket no.2	3	-	2	99%	1%	-	**Note:** Variety of wares and slips; red, peach and green slips; some late New Kingdom, mostly amphoras.
A	Locus 0 Surface of test trench	Small	Basket no.3	4	-	1	100%	-	-	**Note:** Variety or wares; possible New Kingdom red slipped bowl; thick cream slip on jars.
A	Locus 0 Surface of trench 1 extension (3 x 5 m)	Small	Basket no.4	4	-	2	100%	-	-	**Note:** Variety of wares and slips; possible New Kingdom amphora; New Kingdom red slipped bowl; possible Roman ridged sherd.
A	Locus 0 Surface	Scanty	Basket no.5	4	1	1	60%	40%	-	**Note:** Variety of wares; New Kingdom red sips; green and cream slips.
A	Locus 0 Surface of wall east of "travertine" piece	Large	Basket no.6	20	9	4	79%	20%	1%	**Note:** Three black on green decorated sherds; one Palestinian bowl sherd joining a bowl found in 1999 survey; New Kingdom types; many amphoras.
A	Locus 0 Surface near "travertine piece"	Small	Basket no.7	6	7	-	90%	10%	-	**Note:** Variety of wares and slips. New Kingdom red, peach, and green slips; many New Kingdom style amphoras.
A	Locus 1 (Trench 1: South side)	Small	Basket no.1	9	1	4	100%	-	-	**Note:** Variety of wares and slips; peach slip and New Kingdom red-slipped bowls; sherds small and worn; no obvious foreign wares.
A	Locus 1 (Trench 1: North extension)	Tiny	Basket no.1	1	3	-	100% (?)	-	-	**Note:** Very worn and abraded sherds; green slip on two sherds; evidence for amphoras
A	Locus 2	Small	Basket no.1	4	-	1	99%	1%	-	**Note:** Some cream and peach slips; small worn sherds; possible Roman sherd; non-descriptive sherds.
A	Locus 3	Medium	Basket no.1	2	-	-	98%	2%	-	**Note:** Hard and soft silt sherds with blackening; thick green slip on hard silt sherds; pottery appears to be domestic in nature.
A	Locus 3	Tiny	Basket no.2	2	-	-	80%	20%	-	**Note:** Very worn and encrusted sherds with peach, cream, and gray-green slips; New Kingdom rim sherds.
A	Locus 4	Full(?) basket	Basket no.1	3	3	-	99%	1%	-	**Note:** A wide variety of wares with green slip on amphoras, peach slip on different wares; a New Kingdom bowl with red slip.
A	Locus 4(?) Robber's pit	Small	Basket no.2	8	1	1	90%	10%	-	**Note:** A variety of wares and slips: peach, cream, green, and New Kingdom red slips; one storage jar has a pot mark; some New Kingdom sherds.
Total	-	-	145+ body sherds	94	29	22	**89%**	**10%**	**0.1%**	**Note:** The silt and marl percentages represent averages from the columns.

of a small partly enclosed area (designated here as Room 1) lay along the interior, southern side of the northern part of the walling system and was subdivided into Loci 6 (west) and 8 (east). The southern east–west wall (Locus 9) was traced 13.60 m to the east from the interior corner of

Fig. 3.32a–b. Looking east along Wall E, with a travertine block to the south (Photo: NSAP).

the north–south wall. This northwestern extension is composed of lighter sandy mud bricks but disappears in the adjacent area, which contains a subterranean bunker and debris from bulldozer activity dating to the 1960s through early 1980s. An affiliated 90-cm-wide side wall was also found, heading southwest for 2.80 m, but also disappeared in an area speckled with numerous pits (ranging from 30 to 110 cm in diameter). Like the main wall, the side wall yielded bricks measuring 10 × 20 × 40 cm. Elsewhere in the main wall, the partly eroded bricks also range from 15–17 cm in width by 33–34 cm in length.

The main gray-black brick wall contained an outer lining of sandy, light brown bricks placed on edge in a row of headers (10 × 20 × 40 cm) along the western side of the walling system. This lining measured 85–90 cm in width, contained a double row of headers, and extended only one course in depth. It lay adjacent to the uppermost preserved brick course in the main wall, revealing the probable ancient ground level and suggests an anti-erosional feature found on various ancient and modern buildings to guard against undercutting by both wind and water abrasion. The excavator noted, however, that this double row of bricks on edge (rollock-style) extended only 1.50 m along the interior wall face and may represent a doorsill. This suggestion is bolstered by the discovery of fragmentary limestone doorsill pieces 3.50 m to the south. A pair of brickwork projections may also represent the emplacement for a pair of doorjambs.

The northern partly defined chamber (Room 1) yielded a 2 × 1.80-m hard-packed sandy mud surface (Locus 6), which forms a surface ("floor") associated with the neighboring northern, western, and southern walls. A pit to the east defines and separates Locus 6 from Locus 8, which represents an extension of this hard-packed surface. Locus 8 also included the clearance of sand above the adjacent wall to the north and is bounded on the east by a pit containing a travertine block (figs. 3.32a–b).

3.4.3. Area to the East of the Granite Block (Unit A, Trench 2: Locus 7): Excavator: Rosa Frey

The detection of a distinct mass of hard-packed mud in the base of a modern pit initiated the placement of another trench (Unit A Trench 2) 6.85 m to the east of and parallel to Trench 1. This trench began as a 4.70-m-long test trench, straddling another granite block smaller than the massive piece noted in Trench 1. This block measured about 0.92 × 0.70 m and lay 12 m

Table 3.39. Summary of Small Finds from the Surface of Unit A Trench 1 (Field II)

Unit	*Locus*	*Basket or level*	*Unit Book no.*	*TBO no.*	*Object type*	*Material*	*Color and Surface Treatment*	*Dimensions*	*Comments*
A	Locus 6 Rm-1	Basket no.1	023	TBO II 23	Raw material	Blue mineral	Raw material	-	No details
A	Locus 6 Rm-1	Basket no.1	024	TBO II 24	Blade broken into two pieces	Copper alloy	Green (corroded) Two pieces	9.5 x 3 x 0.2 cm	No details
A	Locus 6 Rm-1	Basket no.1	025	TBO II 25	Fragmentary pin	Copper alloy	Green (corroded) Several pieces	-	No details
A	Locus 6 Rm-1	Basket no.1	026	TBO II 26	Blade fragment	Copper alloy	Green (corroded) Broken into five pieces	-	No details
A	Locus 6 Rm-1	Basket no.1	028	TBO II 28	16 fragments of a blade	Copper alloy	Green (corroded) 16 pieces	-	No details

Fig. 3.33. An *ex-situ* limestone block (from an unidentified, and presumably local, pharaonic structure), lying on the modern surface in Field II (Photo: NSAP).

to the southeast of the interior corner of the zigzag wall and 10 m to the southeast of the massive granite block in Trench 1. Like the massive block, it is possible that this piece formed a foundation block or component in a cultic installation (table 3.40). In addition, the excavator found an inscribed granite fragment beside one of two pits situated in or near Area A.

Trench 2 extended across many pits and a sand layer that were excavated as Locus 7. The pitting exhibited multiple phases, with successive pits cutting into earlier ones. This locus held numerous small chips of limestone, most of which were devoid of finished faces or decoration, with the exception of two pieces with smoothed sides. Locus 7 in Trench 2, and its environs, produced a black granite/"basalt" mortar fragment (pl. 3:6 no. 22, TBO 0029 / II.27 / TBO 0027), and a limestone fragment bearing relief (TBO 0029).

3.4.4. Excavation Units B–C (Area 2, Unit B)

After the 2000 season at Tell el-Borg, the subdivision of Field II into Areas 1–3 removed excavation Units B–E from Area 2, which received a new series of excavation units beginning with D (see below).

3.4.5. Temple Area, Enclosure Wall, and River Bank (Area 2, Units D–I)
Excavator: Thomas Davis (with some assistance by Scott Haddow)

The remaining portion of Field II contains a Dynasty 18 occupation layer, an overlying Dynasty 19 mud-brick structure (badly destroyed "shrine"), traces of a later gray brick wall that extended over the mud-brick structure, and a series of refuse pits and a possible tomb that post-date the building activity (fig. 3.34). The postulated "shrine" fits such an interpretation architecturally, based upon its foundations for three rear rooms (sanctuaries?), a broad mud-brick paved hall, and

Table 3.40. Summary of Small Finds from the Surface of Unit A Trench 2 (Field II)

Unit	Locus	Basket or level	Unit Book no.	TBO no.	Object type	Material	Color and Surface Treatment	Dimensions	Comments
A	Locus 0 Surface	1	001	-	Slab: threshold? with socket	Limestone	White with a hole near one end	99 x 55 x 13 cm	Found near granite block
A	Locus 0 Surface	1	002	-	Slab	Limestone	White	106 x 41 x 17 cm	Found near granite block
A	Locus 0 Surface	1	003	-	Slab	Limestone	White	79 x 41 x 13 cm	Found near granite block
A	Locus 0 Surface	1	004	-	Slab: threshold? with socket	Limestone	White with a hole near one end	56 x 41 x 13 cm	Found near granite block
A	Locus 7	Basket no.1	27	TBO II 27	Fragment from a bowl(?)	Granite ("basalt")	Described as either a tool or statue fragment (perhaps a bowl)	-	Registered as both TBO II 27 and TBO 0029 A, trench 2, loc.7
A	Locus 7	Basket no.1	29	TBO II 29	Block fragment	Limestone	Relief decoration	-	No details A, trench 2, loc.7
A	Locus 7	Basket no.1	-	-	Block fragment	Pink granite	-	0.92 x 0.70 meters	-

part of an outer court. In addition, the rich nature of the associated, albeit scattered and mostly *ex-situ*, small finds and royal statuettes also fit well in a cultic context (see below).

3.4.5.1. Phase 0: Basal Sand Layer (Pre-Occupation) (Area 2, Units D–I)

A sterile band of yellow-white sand underlies the initial occupation layers in Area 2, marking the pre-occupation basal sand phase at Tell el-Borg. This sterile band lay at varying depths below the modern surface across the site, but it tends to be closer to the modern surface in Area 2 in comparison to Area 1 in Field II. This layer lacked material culture.

3.4.5.2. Phases 1–9: Ancient River Bank and Geology Test-Pit (Area 2, Unit D, Locus 7)

The river bank and channel lay about 17.00 to 21.70 m beyond a mud-brick structure ("shrine") in Units D–F (see figs. 3.34–35 and 3.37). Thomas Davis and Stephen Moshier investigated this area (*Tell el-Borg I*, 74–81), which lies at the southeast end of a 40 × 1 m trench that forms the backbone of the eastern section of Area 2 in Field II. The ancient river channel separated the Dynasty 18 fort to the southeast (Fields IV and VIII) from the shrine and other features to the northwest (Field II). A geological test pit was placed in the eastern, 5-m segment of Unit D. This pit yielded separate major mud deposits below the modern ground surface, reflecting fluctuating periods of water-laid silt deposits along the banks of a tributary leading into the Eastern Lagoon (Paleolagoon).

The surface sand layers surrounding the geological test pit consisted of wind-blown sand devoid of artifacts in a radius of 10 m around the test pit. The geological sounding contained six levels, starting from a 0-datum point at the modern ground surface at the southeast corner of Unit D: Level 1 (0 to –0.80/–1.50 m; D7 basket 1), Level 2 (–0.80/–1.50 to –2.00 m; D7 basket 2: 1.50–2.00 m), Level 3 (–2.00 to –2.20 m; D7 basket 3), Level 4 (–2.20 to –2.80 m; D7 basket 4), Level 5 (–2.80 to –3.20 m), and Level 6 (–3.20 to –3.45 m; basal sand). The modern water table lay 3.45 m below the modern surface in this area. Only one sherd came from the surface layer (Level-1: D7 basket 1), while significant amounts of pottery appear in mud layers at Level-2 (–1.50 m; D7 basket 2), Level-3 (–2.00 to –2.20 m; D7 basket 3), and Level-4 (–2.80 to –3.00 m; D7 basket?).

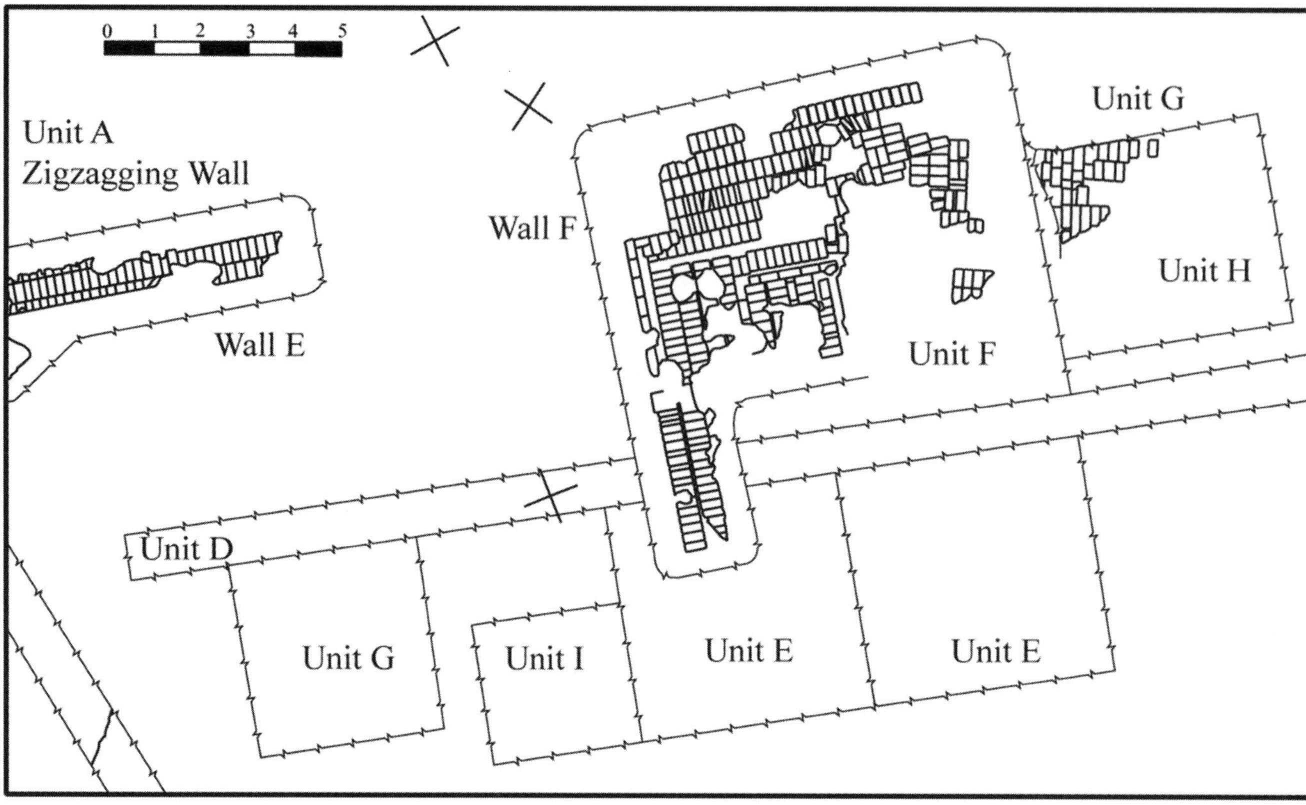

Fig. 3.34. Eastern end of Wall E in relation to a "shrine" (late phase) and environs in Units D–I (drawing: Knudstad; digitized by Joshua Olsen).

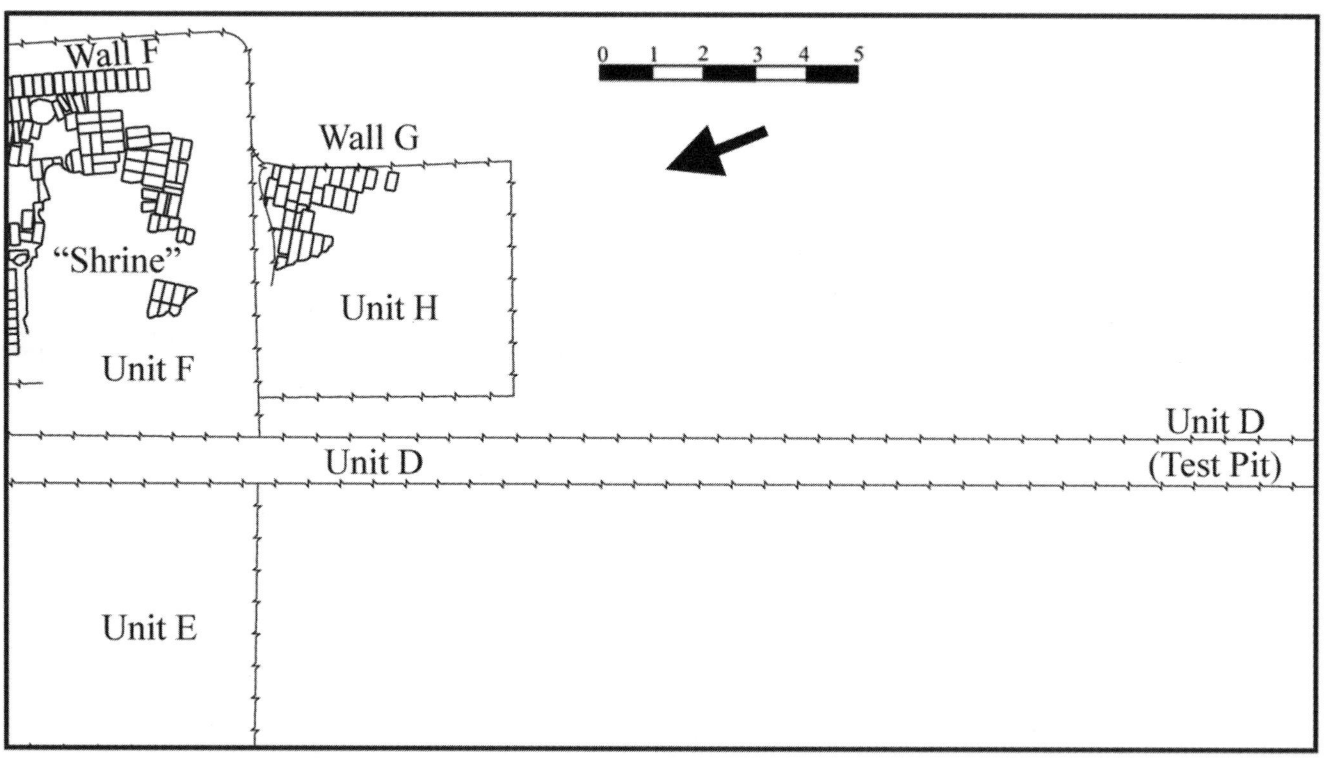

Fig. 3.35. The excavation trench extending from the "shrine" to the test pit in Unit D, beside the ancient river channel (drawing: Knudstad; digitized by Joshua Olsen).

Table 3.41. Summary of Pottery from Unit D, Locus 7, Levels 0 to –3.45 m

Unit	*Locus*	*Basket/ level*	*Pottery basket*	*Rims*	*Handles*	*Bases*	*Nile Silts*	*Desert marls*	*Other wares*	*Comments: Hummel pottery labels*
D	7 (P8–9)	**L-1** 0.00 m to 0.80 m	-	-	-	-	-	-	-	**No pottery**
D	7 (P6–7)	**L-2** -0.80/-1.50 m to 2.00 m	Scanty basket of sherds	-	-	1	50%	50%	-	**Silt:** crude base from a large bowl; **Marl:** assortment of marl wares.
D	7 (P4–5)	**L-3** -2.00 m to -2.20 m	Scanty basket of sherds -2.10 m	5	1	-	50%(?)	50%(?)	-	Extremely weathered and salt-encrusted body sherds**;** **Silt:** white-slipped; **Marl:** cream slip traces.
D	7 (P2–3)	**L-3** -2.20 m	2 sherds in total	1	-	-	100%	-	-	**Silt:** a fine, silt jar with a cream-slipped surface, dating to late Dynasty 18.
D	7 (P2–3)	**L-4** -2.10 m to -2.80 m	Small to medium basket of sherds	15	2	3	70%	30%	-	Small, salt-encrusted body sherds**;** **Marl:** cream slip traces.
D	7 (P1)	**L-4** -2.50 m	9 sherds in total (with 1 rim)	1	-	-	60%	40%	-	**Silt:** cream-tan slip; fine rust-orange ware; **Marl:** gray-green slip.
D	7 (P1)	**L-5** -2.80 m to -3.15 m	Small basket of sherds	15	1	3	50%	30%	20%	**Silt:** including an early–mid-Dynasty 18, black-rimmed bowl; **Marl:** a Dynasty 18, carinated, marl D bowl.
D	7 (P0)	**L-6** -3.15 m to 3.45+ m Basal	1 sherd in total	-	-	-	-	100%	-	**Marl:** a dark brown, marl body sherd with an exterior buff slip and white limestone inclusions. (sherd found immediately above the basal sand).
Total	-	-	**48 + body sherds**	37	4	7	**54%**	**43%**	**3%**	**Note:** The silt and marl percentages represent averages from the columns.

The layers of silt deposited in the river bed and on its adjacent northwest bank date from early–mid-Dynasty 18 (pottery from level-5) to late Dynasty 18 (pottery from level-4). This translates into a span of at least 250 years (Dynasty 18: ca. 1550–1300 B.C.) for a silt deposition measuring 1.15 m in depth (Levels 4–5: –2.00 to –3.15 m). Hence, one might expect that the overlying 2 m of silt deposits date from at least 1300–1070 B.C., incorporating the end of the New Kingdom (ca. 1550–1070 B.C.) into the silting up of the river course. This area yielded mostly Egyptian pottery (97%–98%; marl and silt fabrics), with a sherd from a foreign vessel (2–3%) (table 3.41). Other than pottery, these layers did not produce any small finds, but some granite chunks were noted in pottery basket D7 level 2 (1.50–2.00 m).

3.4.5.3. Phase 1: Early–Mid-Dynasty 18 Occupation Layer (Units D–F, Loci 5, 11, 18)

A sand and clay occupation layer lay above the basal sand layer and underlay the foundation sand and mud-brick platform of a "shrine" in Units D–F. This pre-foundation layer has been partly traced and excavated in Loci F11 (basket 1) and F18 (baskets 1–2). These loci contained a hard layer of brown sand, some chunks of mud (possibly mud-brick debris), chipped stones, and a few potsherds.

An identical or similar layer is represented by Locus 5 in Units D, E, and G, separated spatially from the layer excavated below the mud-brick "shrine." This layer consists of a sterile, yellow-brown sand layer, which has been excavated in Unit D as Locus 5, basket 1 (D), basket 2 (100–102 m), basket 3 (110?–115 m), basket 4 (110–15 m), and basket 5 (110–15 m), in Unit E as Locus 5 basket 6 (E), and in Unit G as Locus 5 basket 7.

Table 3.42. Summary of Small Finds from Units D–F, Locus 5, b.1–7, Unit F, Locus 18, b.1–2.

Unit	*Locus*	*Basket or level*	*Unit Book no.*	*TBO no.*	*Object type*	*Material*	*Color and Surface Treatment*	*Dimensions (cm)*	*Comments: Davis Units D–I notes*
D	5	Basket no.2 (P1)	(?)	TBO 0043	Earring with loop	Glass (vitreous material)	White	Small	**SF register:** Cites Unit D, Locus 5.
D	5	Basket no.2 (P1)	(?)	TBO 0049	Fish hook	Copper alloy	Green (corroded)	No details	**SF register:** Cites Unit D, Locus 5.
E	5	Basket no.2 (P1)	Statue (see below)	TBO 0005	Fragment fitting the statuette (TBO 0006 and TBO 0026)	Limestone	No details	No details	**SF register:** Cites Unit E, Locus 5; See Locus E15 in Phase 6
E(?)	5	Basket no.2 (P1)	(?)	TBO 0019	Cast metal pendant with a loop (grapes?; heart?; pomegranate?)	Copper alloy	Green (corroded)	No details	**SF register:** Cites Trench 3 Locus 5 pottery basket no.2
E(?)	5	Basket no.2 (P1)	(?)	TBO 0020	Blade or projectile point ("spearhead")	Flint	No details	No details	**SF register:** Cites Locus 5 pottery basket no.2
F	11	Basket no.1 (P1)	(?)	TBO 0015	Fragments of copper alloy (types unknown)	Copper alloy	Green (corroded)	No details	**SF register:** Cites Unit F, Locus 11
G	5(?)	Basket no.? (P1)	(?)	TBO 0054	Plaster sealing from a container	Plaster (or mud?)	No details	No details	**SF register:** Cites Unit G, Locus 005 (= Locus 5)

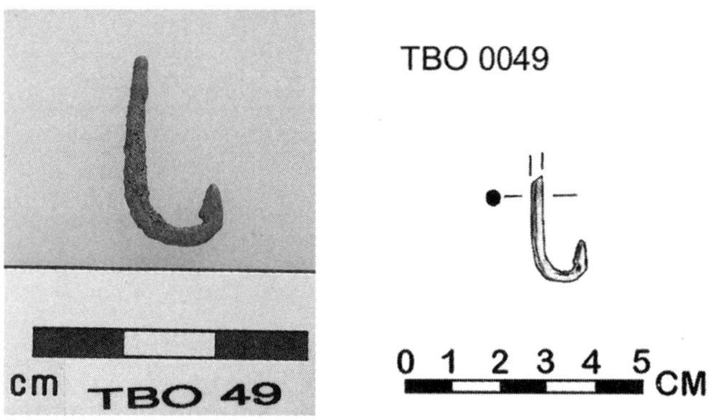

Fig. 3.36a–b. Photograph and drawing Copper alloy fish hook from Locus 5 in Unit D (Photo: NSAP; drawn by Lyla Pinch-Brock).

This layer dates to the early–mid-Dynasty 18, as is evidenced by many black-rimmed bowls from Loci D5 (basket 2), G5 (basket 7), and F18 (baskets 1–2). The majority of the pottery represents Egyptian forms and fabrics (marl and silt; 98%–99%), while 1% reflects a Canaanite krater fragment (table 3.43). This phase yielded various artifacts: a fragment of the statuette found mostly in later loci (pl. 3.1 no. 6: TBO 0005, 0006, 0026, *nemes* headdress, face, wig), a fishhook (fig. 3.36a–b; pl. 3:5 no. 2, TBO 0049), part of an earring (pl. 3:4 no. 9, TBO 0043, a vitreous loop earring), a copper alloy earring/pendant with a loop and grape cluster (pl. 3:5 no. 14, TBO 0019), a chert flake with a pointed end (pl. 3:6 no. 4, TBO 0020), and a plaster sealing fragment from a container (pl. 3.2 no. 3: TBO 0054) (table 3.42).

3.4.5.4. Phase 2: Foundation Base for a "Shrine" (Unit F, Loci 10, 12, 14)

The foundation trench for the "shrine" contained a 20–25 cm thick layer of medium- to fine-grained yellow-brown (10YR 5/4) sand. Loci 10, 12, and 14 represent the sand fill within and below the chambers of the tower/shrine's foundation platform. Loci 10, 12, and 14 will be discussed below in conjunction with the mud-brick platform.

3.4.5.5. Phase 3: Early Dynasty 19 "Shrine" and Its Environs (Units D–F Loci 2, 10, 12, 14, 19)

Thomas Davis excavated the foundations of a small mud-brick structure (figs. 3.34–35 and 3.37) to the northwest of the ancient riverbank. This structure measured 7.60 m east–west by at least 6.75 m north–south, having three completed wall faces along its eastern, northern, and

Table 3.43. Summary of Pottery from Units D–F, Locus 5, b.1–7, Unit F, Locus 18, b.1–2.

Unit	*Locus*	*Basket/ level*	*Pottery basket*	*Rims*	*Handles*	*Bases*	*Nile Silts*	*Desert marls*	*Other wares*	*Comments: Hummel pottery labels.*
D	5	1 (P1)	Scanty basket of sherds	3	-	-	80%	20%	-	Many simple bowls.
D	5	2 (P1)	Scanty basket of sherds	6	-	1	80%	19%	1%	**Silt:** an early–mid-Dynasty 18, black-rimmed bowl; **Other fabrics:** a possible Canaanite krater sherd.
D	5	4 (P1)	Scanty basket of sherds	3	-	-	90%	10%	-	Tiny, worn body sherds; many simple bowls; **Silt:** red slips; **Marl:** green marl sherd
E	5	5 (P1)	Scanty basket of sherds	-	-	-	80%	20%	-	Some body sherds; **Silt:** red slips; some very hard silts.
F	5	5a (P1)	Small basket of sherds	-	1	2	50%	50%	-	Salt-encrusted body sherds; One stamp-impressed handle.
E	5	6 (P1)	Scanty basket of sherds	1	-	-	60%	40%	-	**Silt:** including a simple bowl. **Marl:** gritty green; cream-green slip; peach, cream, and white slips.
G	5	7 (P1)	Medium-full basket of sherds	11	1	5	60%	40%	-	**Silt:** an early–mid-Dynasty 18, black-rimmed bowl; red slips; many simple bowl; **Marl:** gray-green, white, and cream slips.
F	11	1 (P1)	?	?	?	?	?	?	?	Pottery label absent.
F	18	1 (P1)	Small basket of sherds	12	2	1	80%	20%	-	Very tiny, worn body sherds; **Silt:** much red slip; two early–mid-Dynasty 18, black-rimmed bowls; a jar with red slip and black stripes.
F	18	2 (P1)	Scanty basket of sherds	2	-	1	90%	10%	-	Small, worn body sherds; **Silt:** ring-based, simple bowl; an early–mid-Dynasty 18, black-rimmed bowl; red slipped sherd with black painted decoration.
Total	-	-	**52+ body sherds**	38	4	10	**74%**	**25%**	**2%**	**Note:** The silt and marl percentages represent averages from the columns.

western sides. Three foundational casemate chambers are enclosed by the base platform and include a "northwest" chamber (0.80 × 1.80 m), a central chamber (0.98 × 1.57 m), and a "southeast" chamber (1.25 × 2.15 m). The west chamber yielded a yellow-brown (10YR 5/4) sand layer of foundation fill (Locus 12 [012] baskets 1–2) and an intrusive pit in the northwest corner of the chamber. The center chamber lacked traces of robber pits; the foundation fill in the center chamber was excavated as Locus F10 (010), while the underlying pre-foundation fill was excavated as Locus F11 (011) (fig. 3.39). Locus F10 baskets 1–2 contained a layer of sand with a few mid-Dynasty 18 potsherds (salt-encrusted) and a Mycenaean sherd. The east chamber enclosed a yellow-brown (10YR 5/4) layer of foundation sand (excavated as Locus F14, baskets 1–3). The east chamber had been disturbed by several shallow pits, which were excavated first before defining the chamber's fill (Locus F14). Basket 2 of Locus F14 yielded copper alloy pieces, gold foil, a green faience amulet fragment with a black-painted stripe (part of an *ankh*?) (pl. 3:4 no. 10, TBO 0017),[7] an ovoid seal ("scarab") with a wadjet-eye top and inscribed base (TBO 0048; fig. 3.43; pl. 3:4 no. 13), and a bead (pl. 3.4 no. 5: TBO 0032, ivory/bone cylinder bead) (table 3.44). The west chamber had

7. The curved faience fragment with a black painted line has a square section and is best paralleled by a New Kingdom *ankh*-amulet or inlay glyph (see W. C. Hayes, *The Scepter of Egypt: A Background for the Study of the Egyptian Antiquities in the Metropolitan Museum of Art*, Part II: *The Hyksos Period and the New Kingdom (1675–1080 B.C.)* (rev. ed.; New York: Abrams, 1990), 149, fig. 82.).

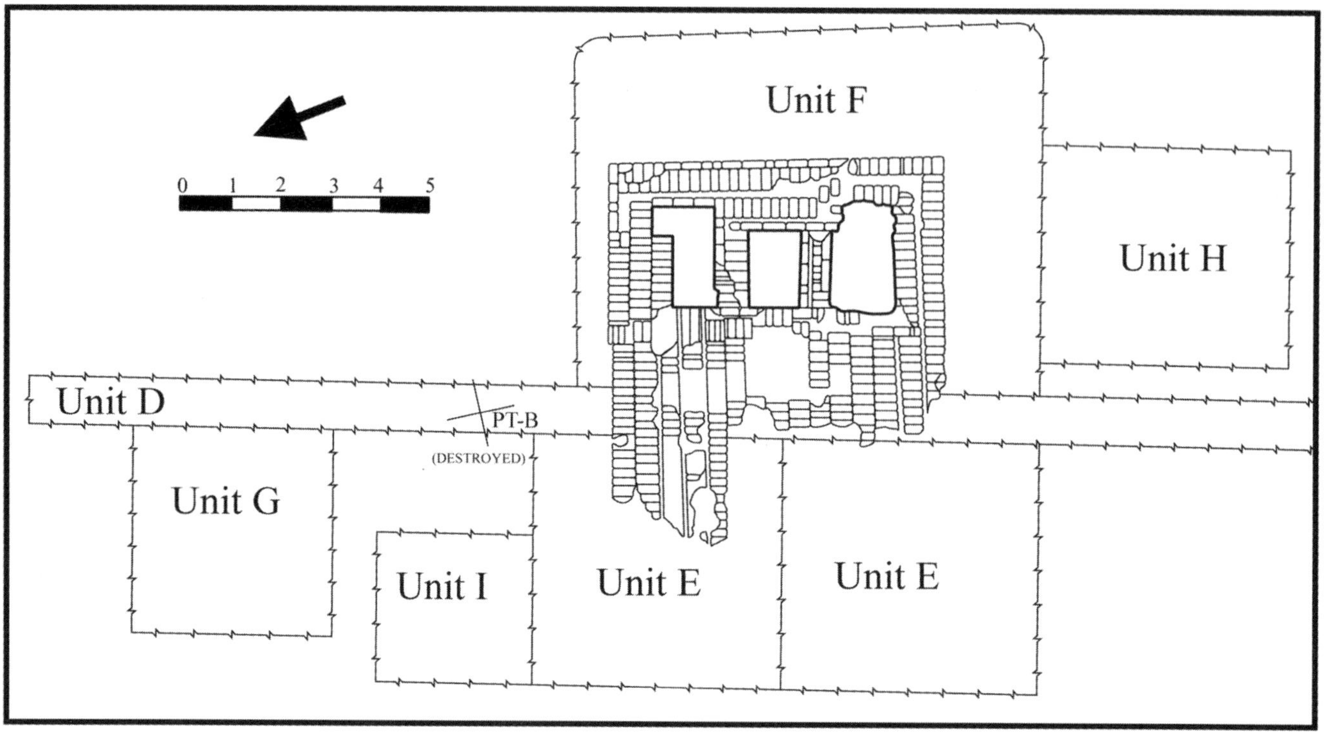

Fig. 3.37. The "shrine" (early phase) and environs in Units D–I, Field II, Area 1 (drawing: James Knudstad; digitized by Joshua Olsen).

Fig. 3.38. Looking south at Locus 2 (mud-brick walls) and extant "Shrine," including its three chambers (Unit F) and truncated southern walls crossing Trench D into Unit E (Photo: NSAP).

been sealed by a mud-brick floor, while a portion of the center chamber also yielded remains of flooring in the southeast corner. It is probable that the eastern portion of the platform had been eroded sufficiently, destroying the original flooring. Other finds from outside this structure include a cylindrical ceramic bead (pl. 3.3 no. 4: TBO 079), a faience circular bead (pl. 3:4 no. 8, TBO 055), and a chert scraper(?) with a serrated edge (pl. 3:6 no. 8, TBO 0073, from Unit I, Locus 19 basket 1), among other finds.

The sand and debris deposit filling the exterior western foundation trench was excavated as Locus F19 (basket 1). Locus F19 contained very few sherds. Only the foundation trench, sand foundation base, and mud-brick foundations and platform survived sufficiently to assess the structure's function. The rectilinear platform probably supported narrower upper walls, creating three rear chambers, a paved hall, and a lower(?)open courtyard to the south. An alternate reconstruction might be a tower gateway with two chambers on either side of an entryway. The mud bricks are a light yellow sandy clay and have an average length of 37 cm, width of 12–15 cm, and height of 8–10 cm. A 5–7 cm thick layer of mortar covers the platform's exterior.

Profile #4 Field II/Area 2
Locus 020, E. Wall

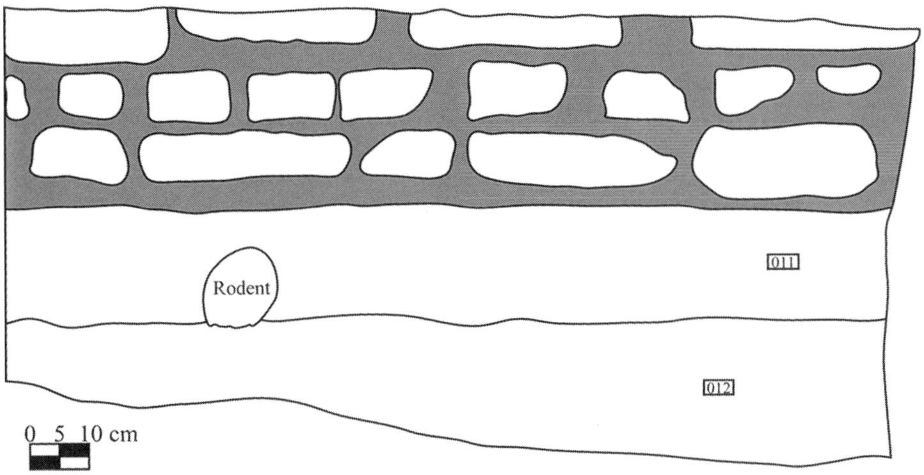

Fig. 3.39. Profile-4: Eastern foundation wall courses and lower layers in the central chamber of the "Shrine" in Unit F (drawing by Thomas Davis; digitized by Joshua Olsen).

Profile #7
S Profile in Trench E at 97.60
from 108.5-110

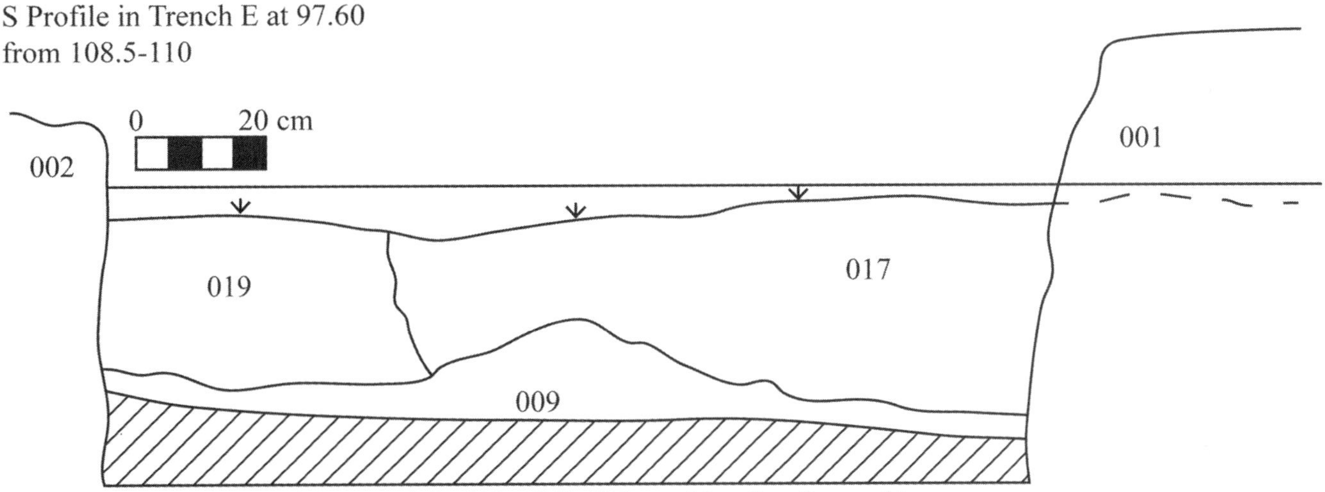

Locus 019 = foundation trench for 002. 10YR 6/8 brownish yellow fine sand loose compaction
Locus 005 = general fill 10 YR 5/4 brownish yellow mudbrick compaction, shell and mudbrick detritus Locus 019= Loci 010,012,014
Locus 009 = basal 10 YR 7/6 yellow sterile sand
Locus 017 = Pit cut into 005; cuts 002

Fig. 3.40. South profile-7: Foundation trench (Locus 19) for the "Shrine" (wall Locus 2) and earlier layers (Loci 17, 9) (drawing by Thomas Davis; digitized by digitized by Joshua Olsen).

The foundation platform is slightly wider on its eastern side, extending a further 6 cm, while the overlying mud-brick wall base is inset 6 cm. The platform's foundations contain one-and-a-half courses of brick on its western side and four courses of bricks on its eastern side. Thomas Davis traced the foundation trench for this platform, which was labeled Locus E19 (fig. 3.39). The platform lay above a sand base. The profile drawings reveal mud-brick debris in a few layers to the east of the "Shrine" (fig. 3.41).

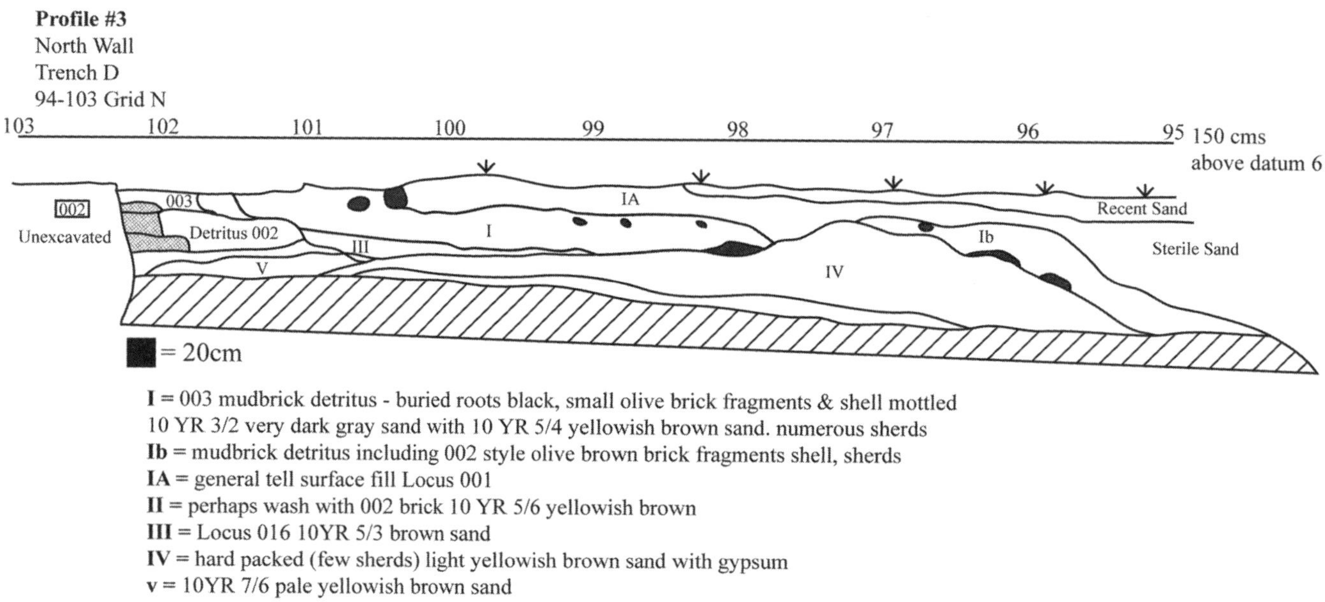

Fig. 3.41. North profile-3: The "Shrine" wall (unexcavated Locus 2) and adjacent debris layers Ib–II (Loci 2–3) to the east (drawing by Thomas Davis; digitized by Joshua Olsen).

Much of the pottery from the foundation casemate chambers date to early–mid-Dynasty 18 (e.g., Loci F10 basket 1, F12 baskets 1–2, F14 basket 2–3, and F19 basket 1). However, Locus 19 basket 1, which forms part of the exterior foundation trench of the structure, has yielded a potsherd dating to Dynasty 19, thereby placing the construction of the mud-brick structure at some point in Dynasty 19. The foundational debris has yielded a significantly lower proportion of Egyptian pottery (90%) in contrast to the presence of Cypriot and Canaanite vessel fragments (10%) (table 3.45). This peak in foreign pottery, and other rich findings, is not wholly unexpected, considering the probable elite and cultic nature of this structure during late Dynasty 18 and Dynasty 19.

The excavator (Davis) suggested that the building may have contained a statue placed on a plinth set in each chamber.[8] He noted that one foundation chamber contained some valuable items (above), while fragments from a statue had been discarded in a nearby pit (pl. 3.1 nos. 6–7: TBO 0047 and 0058, face area, wig/garment?). Although the suggestion of a (royal) statue plinth installation has much merit, Hoffmeier's hypothesis is equally plausible, suggesting that the structure's foundations reflect the remnants of a small temple.[9] If so, this structure would represent only a small shrine, containing exterior walls no wider than 1 m in the foundation courses (and presumably a bit narrower surface walls), two interior walls (no wider than 0.50 m and separating

8. See further J. Hoffmeier and M. Abdel Maksoud, "A New Military Site on the 'Ways of Horus'—Tell el-Borg 1999–2001: A Preliminary Report," *JEA* 89 (2003) 183.

9. The suggestion by T. Davis and Hoffmeier ("A New Military Site on the 'Ways of Horus'," 183–84) is very enticing, but it should also be stated that the presence of several valuable items in the foundation debris of one chamber can also be explained through the incorporation of earlier debris into the backfill of the foundations. The redistribution of such artifacts as unnoticed refuse into foundations does occur elsewhere in ancient Egypt (e.g., Tell Tebilla) and is equally possible in this situation since the pre-Dynasty 18 layers around the mud-brick "shrine"/tower(?) also appear to have represented a cultic area. A more formal foundation deposit composed of specific items, attested elsewhere in ancient Egypt (Dieter Arnold, *The Encyclopaedia of Ancient Egyptian Architecture* [London: Tauris, 2003], 93), would provide a stronger case for a ritual deposit below the chamber's flooring.

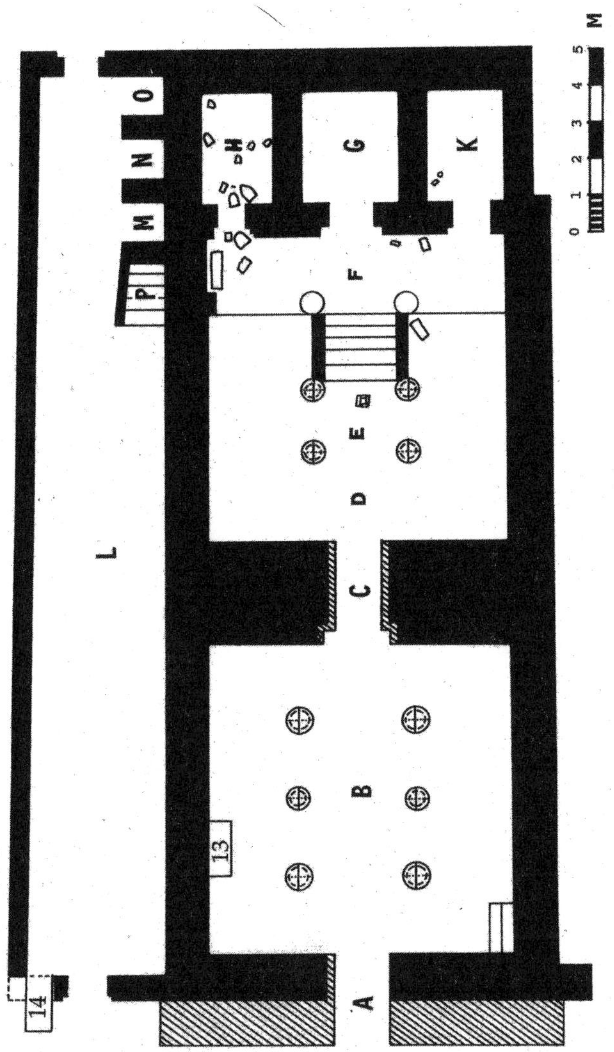

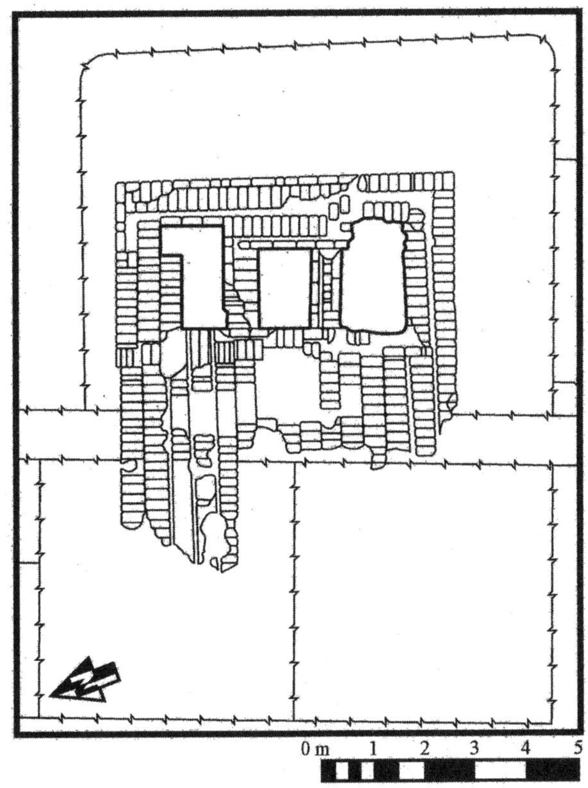

Fig. 3.42a (left). Dynasty 18 temple at Gurob with a 10-m-wide back wall (adapted from Loat 1904: pl. xiv).

Fig. 3.42b (above). Suggested New Kingdom shrine at Tell el-Borg with a 6.75-m-wide back wall (drawn by James Knudstad).

the three northern sanctuaries), two side-sanctuaries (measuring at least 1.20 × 2.20 m), and a central sanctuary (covering at least 1.00 × 1.50 m). The wide mud-brick platform to the south of the three chambers might reflect the paving for a transverse hall, while the "wall" extending to the southwest might simply be the remnants of a wall enclosing a small, partly paved and open court (or a roofed outer hall). If this is the case, the Tell el-Borg structure, which is only 6.70 m wide, would rank alongside the small New Kingdom Hathor shrine (7.5 × 7.5 m) at Gebel Zeit, Ramesses II's Horus and Seth shrine (7.00 × 10.00 m) at Wadi Sannur, a Ramesside shrine in the fort at Zawiyet Umm el-Rakham (8 × 11 m [i.e., the innermost structure]), another small temple in the fort at Kom Firin (14.5 × 29 m), the Ramesside Hathor shrine (9.00 × 10.30 m) at Timna (southern Negev), the New Kingdom chapels at Tell el-Amarna and Deir el-Medina, and a shrine of Thutmose III at Gurob (figs. 3.42a–b).[10]

10. For the Wadi Sannur shrine, see G. Brunton, "Ramesside Stelae from the Eastern Desert," *ASAE* 36 (1936) 201. For the Timna Hathor shrine, see B. Rothenberg, *The Egyptian Mining Temple at Timnah: Researches in the Arabah 1959–1984* (London: Institute for Archaeo-Metallurgical Studies Institute of Archaeology, University College London, 1988) 1:201; for the chapels at Deir el-Medineh and Tell el-Amarna,

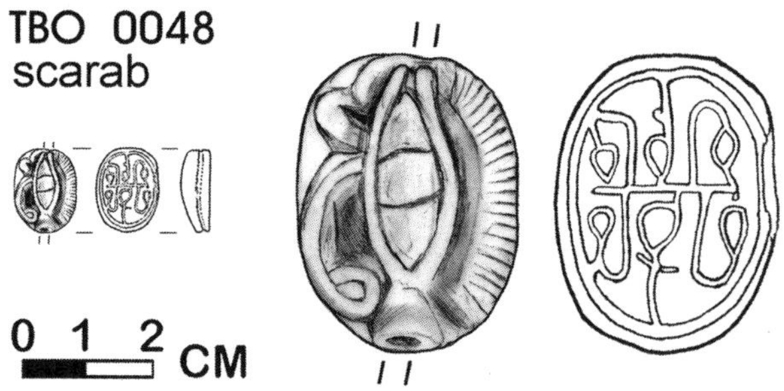

Fig. 3.43. A faience scarab from the eastern chamber debris in the "shrine," registered from Locus 14 in Unit F (drawn by Lyla Pinch-Brock).

It is also pertinent to mention another architectural possibility—namely, that the structure could also represent the foundations for a riverside bastion/tower[11] having a 2.30-m-wide wall extending to the southwest, parallel to the river course, and a zigzag wall system a few meters away to the northwest. If it served as a tower at the northeast corner of an irregularly shaped enclosure, this building may have formed part of a docking facility and traffic control point fronting the river channel. A 2.25-m-wide wall extended 2–3 m to the southwest, from the southwest corner of the structure. In addition, the foundations of a zigzagging, 50-m-long by 1.70-m-wide wall system lay to the west and probably spanned a 7-m-gap (or gateway? or possibly merely a destroyed/missing wall segment) to join the northwest corner of the three-chambered structure. Hence, this structure appears to lie at the corner of two wall systems, which may support the interpretation of the structure as a tower/bastion.

In the overall balance, however, the concentration and richness of the material culture assemblage from this area, including the suggestive architectural form of the structure, seems most indicative of a small "shrine"/"temple." Unfortunately, the poor state of preservation precludes any conclusive determination regarding the structure's function, and all of the above suggestions still remain possible.

---

see A. H. Bomann, *The Private Chapel in Ancient Egypt: A Study of the Chapels in the Workmen's Village at El-Amarna with Special Reference to Deir el-Medina and Other Sites* (London: Kegan Paul, 1991); for the Gurob shrine of Thutmose III, see L. Loat, *Gurob*, Egyptian Research Account 10 (London: Bernard Quaritch (published as part-volume with M. Murray, *Saqqara Mastabas, Part 1*) xiv; for plans and discussion of the Zawiyet Umm el-Rakham fort shrine, see S. Snape and P. Wilson, *Zawiyet Umm el-Rakham I: The Temple and Chapels* (Bolton: Rutherford, 2007) 32 fig. 2.33, 94 fig. 5.1); Kom Firin's temple is reassessed by N. Spencer, *Kom Firin I: The Ramesside Temple and the Site Survey*, The British Museum Research Publication no. 170 (London: British Museum, 2008) 36–55, fig. 2; N. Spencer et al., *Kom Firin II: The Urban Fabric and Landscape*, The British Museum Research Publication no. 192 (London: British Museum, 2014) 7 fig. 5); for reference to the Gebel Zeit shrine, see G. Castel, *Gebel El-Zeit I: Les Mines de Galene (Egypte, II emillenaire av. J.-C.)*; Fouilles de l'Institut Francais d'Archeologie Orientale 35 (Cairo: Institut Francais d'Archeologie Orientale, 1989). Other Dynasty 19 small temples, including some fort shrines, are known from Aksha, Amara West, Buhen North Temple, Wadjmose Chapel (Thebes), El Kab, and Deir el-Medina (see Snape and Wilson, *Zawiyet Umm el-Rakham I*, 9–32; 7 fig. 1.3; 71 fig. 4.1; 74 fig. 4.2; 77 fig. 4.3; 85–86 fig. 4.5; 88 fig. 4.6; 89 fig. 4.7).

11. Casemate chambers are known in the foundations of many types of ancient Egyptian buildings, including New Kingdom bastions/towers, such as at the New Kingdom fort of Haruba in North Sinai (see E. Oren, "Sinai: Northern Sinai," *The New Encyclopedia of Archaeological Excavations in the Holy Land* [Jerusalem: The Israel Exploration Society, 1993] 4:1390, plan of fort). The structure at Tell el-Borg uses a construction technique common in ancient Egyptian architecture—namely, founding weight-bearing walls on deeper foundations and filling casemate chambers with debris to support a mud-brick paving, a surface of beaten plaster, or firm earth. For example, the brick platform of the Hyksos palace at Tell el-Dabʿa, an early New Kingdom palace platform at Deir el-Ballas, and a Dynasty 26 fort-tower platform at Tell Defenna (Defenneh) contain a grid-work of foundation walls surrounding earth-filled spaces within the building's foundations (Arnold, *The Encyclopaedia of Ancient Egyptian Architecture*, 50, 66, 169–70, and 240).

Table 3.44. Summary of Small Finds from Unit F, Locus 14

Unit	*Locus*	*Basket or level*	*Unit Book no.*	*TBO no.*	*Object type*	*Material*	*Color and Surface Treatment*	*Dimensions (cm)*	*Comments: Davis Units D–I notes*
D	14	Basket no.6/2?	(?)	TBO 0055	Bead	Faience	Striated vertically	Small	**SF register:** Cites Unit D, Locus 14 (versus Unit F).
E	19	Basket no.2 (P3)	(?)	TBO 0082	Barrel bead	Ceramic	Brown silt; perforated longi-tudinally	Large bead	**SF register:** Cites Unit E, Locus 19
F	12	Basket no.? (P3)	(?)	TBO 0017	Fragment of large amulet or inlay piece (part of an ankh?)	Blue faience	Blue-green faience with a black painted stripe	-	**SF register:** Cites Unit F, Locus 12 (Probably pit no.2)
F	12	Basket no.? (P3)	(?)	TBO 0032	Fragment of a bead	Bone (or ivory)	White	-	**SF register:** Cites Unit F, Locus 12 (Notes pit no.2)
F	14	2 (P3)	-	-	Lumps	Copper alloy	Green (corroded)	-	-
F	14	2 (P3)	-	TBO 0092a	Foil	Gold	Gold	-	**SF register:** Cites Unit F, Locus 14
F	14	2 (P3)	-	TBO 0048	Scarab	Faience	-	-	**SF register:** Cites Unit F, Locus 14
F	14	2 (P3)	-	-	Bead	-	-	-	-
F	14	Basket no.? (P3)	(?)	TBO 0002	Large flat piece of copper (broken into four pieces)	Copper alloy	Green (corroded)	-	**SF register:** Cites Unit F, Locus 14
I	19	Basket no.1 (P3)	(?)	TBO 0058	Fragment of a statuette wig (associated with TBO 0026, 0 047, 0600)	Limestone	White	No details	**SF register:** Cites Unit I, Locus 19
I	19	Basket no.1 (P3)	(?)	TBO 0073	Scraper with a serrated edge	Chert	Large with a serrated edge	No details	**SF register:** Cites Unit I, Locus 19

3.4.5.6. Phase 4: Late Dynasty 19 Gray Wall (Unit F, Locus 13)

After the abandonment of the yellow brick "shrine," a gray brick wall was built, partly cutting(?) and crossing the corner of the tower at a slightly different angle than the earlier structure. This later brick wall (Locus F13) contained dark gray bricks with many shells and a different type of mortar between the bricks. The brickwork of Locus 13 did not yield any pottery or small finds. This gray wall probably dates either to late Dynasty 19 or possibly early Dynasty 20, prior to the decline and abandonment of the last fort at Tell el-Borg.

3.4.5.7. Phase 5: Dynasty 19/20 Initial Pitting (Units D, E, I, Loci 16–17)

Several pits appear in succession in the southern part of Area 2 after the abandonment of both the yellow brick "shrine" and the subsequent gray brick wall. These pits were excavated as Locus 17 in Units E and I (labeled here Pit I/E17) and as Locus 16 in Units D and E (designated here as Pit D–E16). The relative stratigraphy suggests a date in late Dynasty 19, and possibly into the advent of Dynasty 20.

3.4.5.7.1. Phase 5: Pit I/E17 (Units D–E, Locus 17)

Pit I/E17 lies to the west of the "shrine" and had cut into some of the bricks on the southwest side of this structure (Pit I/E17 is also later cut into by Pit I/E15). The matrix filling Pit I/E17 consists of a firm orange-brown layer of sand and silt. It was excavated as Locus 17 baskets 1–3, 4, and 5 in Units E and I, and as Locus 17 basket 4 in Unit I. This pit produced a stone vessel frag-

Table 3.45. Summary of Pottery from Unit F, Locus 10 Basket 1, Unit F, Locus 12, Baskets 1–2, Units F, Locus14, Baskets 1–3, and Units E and I, Locus 19, Baskets 1–2

Unit	*Locus*	*Basket/ level*	*Pottery basket*	*Rims*	*Handles*	*Bases*	*Nile silts*	*Desert marls*	*Other wares*	*Comments: Hummel pottery labels*
D–F	2 (= Wall)	1 (P3)	-	-	-	-	-	-	-	No pottery from brickwork
F	10	1 (P3)	Small basket of sherds	9	-	4	60%	35%?	5%?	**Silt:** three early–mid-Dynasty 18, black-rimmed bowls; red-slipped sherd with a black stripe; many red-slipped bowls; **Other fabrics:** three Cypriot Base Ring sherds.
F	10(?)	(?) (P3)	Small basket of sherds	18	-	4	70%	30%	-	Tiny, worn, salt-encrusted body sherds; **Silt:** early–mid-Dynasty 18, black-rimmed bowls with red slip; red slip and burnishing; black-painted stripes on red slip.
F	10(?)	Robber pit (P3)	1 handle in basket	-	1	-	-	-	100%	Handle from an amphora of dark gray ware (foreign?) with sand inclusions, black and white grit, and an exterior coating of thick, cream slip.
F	12	1 (P3)	Scanty basket of sherds	9	1	-	50%(?)	50%(?)	-	Very tiny, worn body sherds; **Silt:** red-slipped bowl; **Marl:** peach and cream slip and burnishing; a Marl B handle (popular in southern Egypt from Dynasties 17 to early 18).
F	12	2 (P3)	Small basket of sherds	14	-	4	80%	20%	-	**Silt:** a virtually intact "flower" pot; an early–mid-Dynasty 18, black-rimmed bowl; much red slip on simple bowls; **Marl:** Marl A and D.
F	14	1 (P3)	Scanty basket of sherds	3	1	1	75%	24%	1%	Very small, worn body sherds; **Silt:** red slip; **Marl:** Marl D; **Other fabrics:** a possible Canaanite amphora.
F	14	2 (P3)	Scanty basket of sherds	22	-	6	50%	50%	-	Very tiny, worn body sherds; **Silt:** bowl with a black-painted design; an early–mid-Dynasty 18, black-rimmed bowl; **Marl:** cream slip with black stripes.
F	14	3 (P3)	Scanty basket of sherds	2	-	-	50%	50%	-	**Silt:** red slip; early–mid-Dynasty 18, black-rimmed bowl; **Marl:** gray-green slip.
I	19	1 (P3)	Large basket of sherds	16	6	2	50%	50%	-	**Silt:** many red-slipped bowls; **Marl:** much peach and gray-green slip; some peach slip with burnishing; sherds dating to Dynasties 19–20?
I	19	1a (P3)	Scanty basket of sherds	4	-	1	75%	25%	-	Mostly simple bowls; **Silt:** an early–mid-Dynasty 18, red-slipped, black-rimmed bowl; red and cream slips.
E	19	2 (P3)	Scanty basket of sherds	4	-	-	80%	20%	-	Small, worn body sherds; **Silt:** red-slipped sherds; **Marl:** gray-green slip.
Total	-	-	**132+ body sherds**	101	9	22	**58%**	**32%**	**10%**	**Note:** The silt and marl percentages represent averages from the columns.

ment with red ochre (Unit E, Locus 17 basket 1). Although both Pits I/E17 and I/E16 post-date the "shrine," the exact temporal relationship between the two pits remains uncertain. A large pit (I/E15) cut into Pit I/E17 to the west of the tower/shrine(?). The pottery from this pit contained 100% Egyptian pottery forms and fabrics (table 3.47).

3.4.5.7.2. Phase 5: Pit D–E16 (Units D–E, Locus 16)

Pit D–E16 lies to the east of the "shrine," appearing in the northern and southern baulks of Unit D. The fill in Pit D–E16 contains a firm brown sandy silt layer with ash; it was excavated as

Table 3.46. Summary of Pottery from Unit E, Locus 17, Baskets 1–4

Unit	*Locus*	*Basket/ level*	*Pottery basket*	*Rims*	*Handles*	*Bases*	*Nile silts*	*Desert marls*	*Other wares*	*Comments: Hummel pottery labels.*
E	17	1 (P5)	Small basket of sherds	2	-	1	60%	40%	-	Very small, worn body sherds; **Silt:** red slip; **Marl:** cream-green slip on Marl D and other marls.
E	17	2 (P5)	-	-	-	-	-	-	-	Pottery label absent
E	17	3 (P5)	Medium-full basket of sherds	5	4	-	40%	60%	-	**Silt:** one red-slipped sherd; **Marl:** much white and peach slips; various marl wares.
E	17	4 (P5)	Medium-full basket of sherds	7	2	1	50%	50%	-	**Silt:** red slip; sherd with a potter's mark; **Marl:** gray-green slip and burnishing; peach and cream slips.
Total	-	-	**22+ body sherds**	14	6	2	**50%**	**50%**	-	**Note:** The silt and marl percentages represent averages from the columns.

Table 3.47. Summary of Small Finds From Units D and F, Locus 16, Baskets 1–3

Unit	*Locus*	*Basket or level*	*Unit Book no.*	*TBO no.*	*Object type*	*Material*	*Color and Surface Treatment*	*Dimensions (cm)*	*Comments: Davis Units D–I notes*
D	16	Basket no.2	(?)	TBO 0009	Scraper with one serrated edge	Chert	Yellow	No details	**SF register:** Cited in register.
D	16	Basket no.2	(?)	TBO 0010	Two beads	Faience	No details	No details	**SF register:** Cited in register.

Table 3.48. Summary of Pottery from Units D and F, Locus 16, Baskets 1–3

Unit	*Loc.*	*Basket/ level*	*Pottery basket*	*Rims*	*Handles*	*Bases*	*Nile silts*	*Desert marls*	*Other wares*	*Comments: Hummel pottery labels*
D	16	1 (P5)	Scanty basket of sherds	1	-	-	100%	-	-	Very small, worn body sherds; **Silt:** early–mid-Dynasty 18, black-rimmed bowl.
F	16	2 (P5)	Medium-full basket of sherds	11	4	5	60%	40%	-	Salt-encrusted body sherds; **Marl:** cream and peach slips.
D	16	3 (P5)	Small basket of sherds	5	1	-	50%	50%	-	**Marl:** white slip on Marl D; peach and white slips on vessel rims.
Total	-	-	**27 + body sherds**	17	5	5	**70%**	**30%**	-	**Note:** The silt and marl percentages represent averages from the columns.

Locus 16 baskets 1–3. (The temporal relationship between Pits D–E16 and D–E17 remains uncertain). Another pit, Pit D–E3, subsequently cut into Pit D–E16. The pottery from this pit dates at least to early–mid-Dynasty 18 and contains 100% Egyptian pottery forms and fabrics (table 3.48). Since the Dynasty 19 foundation trench of the adjacent "shrine" predates Pit D–E16, this pit must date to some point later in Dynasties 19/20. Two faience disk beads are registered from Locus 16, basket 2, of Unit D near the "shrine" (pl. 3.4 no. 2: TBO 0010).

3.4.5.8. Phase 6: Early–Late? Dynasty 20 and Roman-Period Pitting (Units D, E, I, Loci 3 and 15)

Pits I/E15 and D–E3 later cut into the aforementioned pits I/E17 and D–E16. These pits represent the last surviving ancient activity in this part of Tell el-Borg. The relative stratigraphy

Table 3.49. Summary of Small Finds from Units E and I, Locus 15, Baskets 1–9

Unit	*Locus*	*Basket or level*	*Unit Book no.*	*TBO no.*	*Object type*	*Material*	*Color and Surface Treatment*	*Dimensions (cm)*	*Comments: Davis Units D–I notes*
E	15	5 (P6)	Statue (above)	TBO 0050	Shoulder from a statuette	Limestone	White stone, sculpted	-	**SF register:** Cites Unit I, loc.15, B.5
E	15	1 (P6)	Statue	TBO 0050	Arm from a statuette	Limestone	White stone, sculpted	-	**SF register:** Cites Unit I, loc.15, B.5
E	15	2 (P6)	Statue (above)	TBO 0026	Ear fragment from a statuette (matches TBO0600 and 0005)	Limestone	White stone, sculpted	-	**SF register:** Cites Unit E, loc.15, B.2; See Unit E, Locus 5 in phase 1
E	15	5 (P6)	Statue (above)	TBO 0047	Forehead from a statuette	Limestone	White stone, sculpted	-	**SF register:** Cites Unit I, loc.15, B.5
E	15	5 (P6)	Statue (above)	TBO 0600	Face of small statuette (matches TBO0026 and 0005)	Limestone	White stone, sculpted	-	**SF register:** Cites Unit E, loc.15, B.2; See Unit E, Locus 5 in phase 1
E	15	2 (P6)	(?)	TBO 0004	Fragment	Ivory and gold	White ivory Yellow gold	-	**SF register:** Cites Unit E, loc.15, B.2
E	15	Basket no.2 (P6)	(?)	TBO 0016	Bead	Faience	No details	No details	**SF register:** Cites Unit E, loc.15, B.2
E	15	Basket no.2 (P6)	(?)	TBO 0112	Vessel body fragment (with ochre)	Calcite	Yellow-white (yellow ochre stain)	No details	**SF register:** Cites Unit E, loc.15, B.2
E	15	Basket no.7 (P6)	(?)	TBO 0061	Spool-shaped gaming piece (Senet counter)	Faience	No details	No details	**SF register:** Cites Unit E, loc.15, B.7
I	15	Basket no.? (P6)	(?)	TBO 0059	Round bead with vertical striations	Gold	Vertical striations	No details	**SF register:** Cites Unit I, loc.15
I	15	Basket no.5 (P6)	(?)	TBO 0090A	Vessel stopper	Calcite	Yellow-white	No details	**SF register:** Cites Unit I, loc.15, basket no.5
I	15	Basket no.6 (P6)	(?)	TBO 0070	Scraper	Chert	No details	No details	**SF register:** Cites Unit I, loc.15, basket no.6

in this area suggests a phase of pitting no earlier than Dynasty 20 and possibly into the Roman period (see below).

3.4.5.8.1. Phase 6: Pit I/E15 (Units E and I, Locus 15)

At some point after the abandonment of the nearby "shrine," a large pit (Locus I/E15) was located to the west, cutting through Locus I/E17 (earlier pit), part of Locus D–E19 ("foundation trench") and probably Locus D–F2, which represents the westward projecting wall from the "shrine." The location and nature of Pit I/E15 argues that it had to have cut through the western wall projection, unless the wall had never extended farther west, ending instead in an irregular edge. The fill in this pit was removed as Locus 15 (baskets 1–3, 7, and 9; 4, 5a–c, 6, and 8). This fill consisted of compact dark brown sand with silt, ash, charcoal, mud-brick debris, bones from a large mammal, human bones, limestone statue fragments, and a concentration of potsherds (including large sherds).

The pottery dates to the New Kingdom and consisted mainly of Egyptian forms and wares (99.7%), whereas a single Cypriot sherd represented only 0.3% of the pottery assemblage (table 3.50). In contrast, Locus 15 yielded gold foil covering an ivory backing(?) (pl. 3:5 no. 1, TBO 0004), a fragmentary, circular gold bead (pl. 3:5 no. 6, TBO 0059), a faience gaming piece(?) (pl. 3.3 no. 3: TBO 0061), a faience disk bead (pl. 3.4 no. 3: TBO 0016, Locus 15 basket 2 in Unit E), a chert blade with retouched edges (pl. 3:6 no. 9, TBO 0070), a calcite stopper/plug(?) (pl. 3:6 no. 13, TBO 0090a, Unit I, Locus 15 basket 5), a calcite flask base(?) (pl. 3:6 no. 20, TBO 0112), and pieces from at least one limestone royal statue that had been broken up and discarded in the pit. These statue

Table 3.50. Summary of Pottery from Units E and I, Locus 15, Baskets 1–9

Unit	*Locus*	*Basket/ level*	*Pottery basket*	*Rims*	*Handles*	*Bases*	*Nile silts*	*Desert marls*	*Other wares*	*Comments: Hummel pottery labels*
E	15	1 (P6)	Medium-full basket of sherds	8	4	1	25%	75%	-	**Silt:** red-slip; **Marl:** various types of marl; two cream-slipped sherds with black stripes.
E	15	2 (P6)	?	?	?	?	?	?	?	Pottery label absent.
E	15	3 (P6)	?	?	?	?	?	?	?	Pottery label absent.
I	15	4 (P6)	Large basket of sherds	36	2	3	60%	40%	-	Very small, worn body sherds; **Silt:** much red slip; an early–mid-Dynasty 18, black-rimmed bowl; **Marl:** cream-slip with black painted decoration; cream-slip with red stripes; gray-green and peach slips.
I	15	5 (P6)	Large basket of sherds	11	13	3	40%	60%	-	**Silt:** some red slips; **Marl:** cream slip with burnishing
I	15	5a (P6)	Very large basket of sherds	39	19	7	50%	50%	-	**Silt:** cream-slip with red stripes; red slips; **Marl:** various types of marls; peach slips; cream slip with red-brown stripes; gray-green slips with some burnishing.
I	15	6 (P6)	Large basket of sherds	31	9	4	50%	50%	-	Many small body sherds; **Silt:** many red-slipped bowls; **Marl:** much cream and peach slip; gray-green slip.
E	15	7 (P6)	Large basket of sherds	25	1	4	50%	49%	1%	**Silt:** red-slipped and burnished bowls; **Marl:** much peach and cream slip on various marl wares; **Other fabrics:** a Cypriot Base Ring sherd.
I	15	8 (P6)	Large basket of sherds	25	13	13	40%	60%	-	**Silt:** much red slip; **Marl:** much peach and gray-green slip with some burnishing; cream-green slipped base with a potter's mark; Marl D sherd with ridging.
E	15	9 (P6)	Large basket of sherds	19	11	4	40%	60%	-	Small body sherds; **Silt:** Blue painted sherd; **Marl:** much peach and cream slip.
Total	-	-	**304 + body sherds**	194	72	39	**44%**	**56%**	**0.3%**	**Note:** The silt and marl percentages represent averages from the columns.

pieces included an arm fragment, part of an ear, a portion from a forehead, and a shoulder(?) fragment (pl. 3.1 no. 6: TBO 050, shoulder and upper arm fragment) (table 3.49).

3.4.5.8.2. Phase 6: Pit D–E3 (Units D and E, Locus 3)

Pit D–E3 represents a large pit cutting into Pit D–E17 to the southwest of the "shrine." This pit contained mud-brick debris, debris from a conflagration, burned red brick, and numerous sherds (fig. 3.44). Pit D–E3 was excavated as baskets 1–2 of Locus 3 in Units D and E and as basket 3 in Unit D (95 m), basket 4 in Unit D (95–100 m), and basket 5 in Unit E (06? m).

Most of the pottery forms and fabrics originate from Egypt (99%), with less than 1% representing an imported Cypriot Base Ring sherd (table 3.52). The pottery dates to the New Kingdom, with several sherds dating to Dynasties 19–20 (Locus D3 basket 2 and E3 basket 5), while one sherd probably dates to the Roman period (D3 basket 2). Hence, this phase of pitting has been dated no earlier than Dynasties 19–20 and may extend as late as the Roman period (unless the Roman sherd was introduced by a missed pit). This phase yielded a few artifacts, including a lead clamp/net weight, calcite jar fragment, a ceramic disk, and a piece of copper alloy.

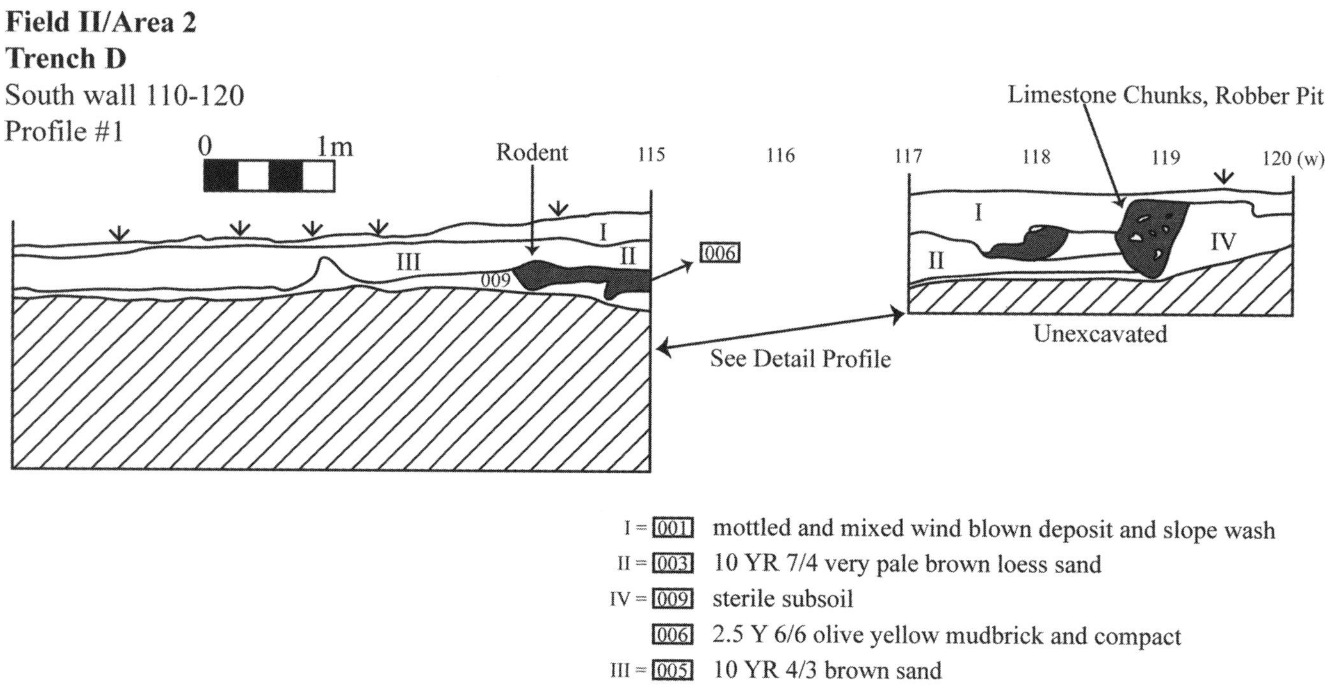

Fig. 3.44. Profile-1: South section of Trench D, with an eastern mud-brick debris layer (Locus 6) and western robber pit (drawing by Thomas Davis; digitized by Joshua Olsen).

Table 3.51. Summary of Small Finds from Units D, E, and F, Locus 3, Baskets 1–6

Unit	*Locus*	*Basket or level*	*Unit Book no.*	*TBO no.*	*Object type*	*Material*	*Color and Surface Treatment*	*Dimensions (cm)*	*Comments: Davis Units D–I notes*
D	3	Basket no.1 (P6)	(?)	TBO 0034	U-shaped clamp or weight	Lead	Gray	No details	**SF register:** Cites Unit D, Locus 3
D	3	Basket no.? (P6)	(?)	TBO II 53	Jar fragment	Calcite	Yellow-white	No details	**SF register:** Cites Unit D, Locus 3
D	3	Basket no.? (P6)	(?)	TBO II 54	Gaming piece	Ceramic	No details	No details	**SF register:** Cites Unit D, Locus 3
D	3	Basket no.? (P6)	(?)	TBO II 55	Non-diagnostic piece	Copper alloy	Green (corroded)	No details	**SF register:** Cites Unit D, Locus 3
E	3	Basket no.? (P6)	(?)	TBO 0419	Large block-shaped fragment tapering to one end	Copper alloy	Green (corroded)	No details	**SF register:** Cites Unit E, Locus 3

3.4.5.9. Phase 7: Possible Dynasty 19/20(?) Tomb (Units D and G, Loci 4, 6, 8)

The remnants of a possible tomb lie to the northwest of the "shrine." This "tomb" is represented by a course of mud bricks (Locus 6) lining one edge of the burial pit and some debris (Locus 8) filling the tomb chamber/shaft. The western edge of the tomb is lined by a robber's trench, while Locus 4 lies over the mud-brick wall and its adjacent layer.

The pit and its fill, which have been interpreted as a possible burial shaft, were excavated as Locus 8 baskets 1–2. This locus contained a compact, pale brown (10YR 7/3) sand fill that yielded a beer jar and a few potsherds (see fig. 3.45). This locus extends along part of the northwest side of Unit D and was overlain by Locus D4 (baskets 1–3), which in turn was overlain by a darker

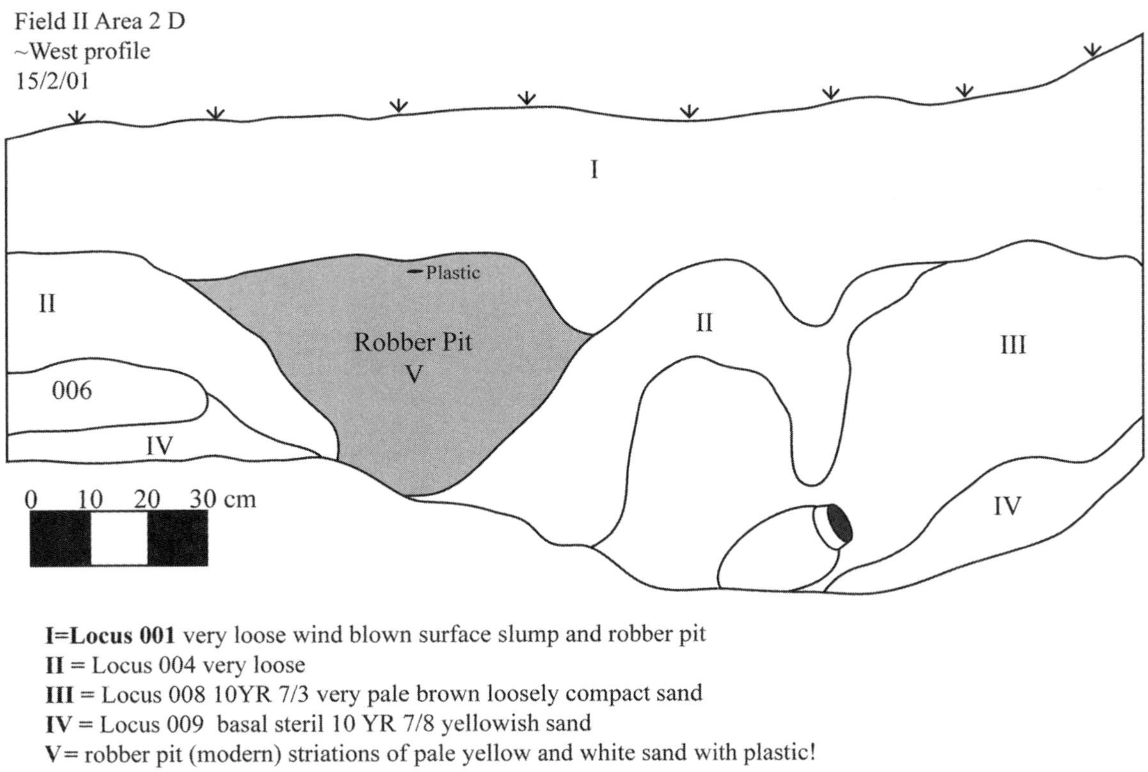

Fig. 3.45. West Profile in Unit D, featuring a modern robber's pit (with plastic) and a pottery jar in an underlying layer (drawing by Thomas Davis; digitized by Joshua Olsen).

Table 3.52. Summary of Pottery from Units D, E, and F, Locus 3, Baskets 1–6

Unit	*Locus*	*Basket/ level*	*Pottery basket*	*Rims*	*Handles*	*Bases*	*Nile silts*	*Desert marls*	*Other wares*	*Comments: Hummel pottery labels*
D	3	1 (P6)	Large basket of sherds	13	2	2	70%	30%	-	Small, worn body sherds; New Kingdom vessels
D	3	2 (P6)	Medium-full basket of sherds	8	2	1	55%	45%	-	Tiny, worn body sherds mostly dating to Dynasties 19–20; **Silt:** red slips; **Note:** one sharply ridged sherd may date to the Roman period.
D	3	3 (P6)	Probably large basket of sherds	22	6	-	60%	39%	1%	Tiny, worn body sherds; **Other fabrics:** a Cypriot Base Ring sherd
F	3	4 (P6)	Large basket of sherds	34	4	3	60%	40%	-	Tiny, worn body sherds; **Silt:** red and cream slips; Blue Painted sherd; **Marl:** peach slip.
E	3	5 (P6)	Large basket of sherds	17	7	6	60%	40%	-	Small, salt-encrusted body sherds, mostly jars. **Silt:** streaky peach slip; Dynasty 19–style sherds; **Marl:** white and cream-green slip
E	3	6 (P6)	Large basket of sherds	18	7	5	50%	50%	-	Salt-encrusted body sherds; **Silt:** some red slip; Blue Painted sherd; **Marl:** cream-slipped vessel with black stripes; much peach slip.
Total	-	-	**157+ body sherds**	112	28	17	**59%**	**41%**	**0.6%**	**Note:** The silt and marl percentages represent averages from the columns.

Table 3.53. Summary of Small Finds from Unit D, Locus 4, Baskets 1–4, Unit D, Locus 6, Basket 1, and Unit D, Locus 8, Baskets 1–1a

Unit	Locus	Basket or level	Unit Book no.	TBO no.	Object type	Material	Color and Surface Treatmen	Dimensions (cm)	Comments: Davis Units D–I notes
D	4	Basket no.1 (P7)	(?)	TBO 0037	Scraper	Chert	No details	No details	**SF register:** Cites Unit D, Locus 4
G	4	Basket no.? (P7)	(?)	TBO 0060	Barrel bead with vertical striations	Bone	White	No details	**SF register:** Cites Unit G, Locus 4

Table 3.54. Summary of Pottery from Unit D, Locus 4, Baskets 1–4, Unit D, Locus 6, Basket 1, and Unit D, Locus 8, Baskets 1–1a

Unit	Locus	Basket/ level	Pottery basket	Rims	Handles	Bases	Nile silts	Desert marls	Other wares	Comments: Hummel pottery labels.
D	4	1 (P7)	?	?	?	?	?	?	?	Pottery label absent
D	4	2 (P7)	Scanty basket of sherds	-	-	1	75%	25%	-	**Silt:** red-slipped sherd.
D	4	3 (P7)	?	?	?	?	?	?	?	Pottery label absent
G	4	4 (P7)	Medium-full basket of sherds	24	1	3	60%	39%	1%	**Silt:** early–mid-Dynasty 18, black-rimmed bowls; many red-slipped bowls; **Marl:** white slip with black paint; **Other fabrics:** a Cypriot sherd.
D	6	1(?)(P7)	19 sherds in total (including 1 rim)	1	-	-	100%	-	-	**Silt:** simple bowls.
D	8	1 (P7)	5 sherds in total	-	-	-	20%	60%	20%	**Silt:** a fine, silt bottle neck; **Other fabrics:** possible foreign amphora sherd.
D	8	1a (P7)	Scanty basket of sherds	2	-	1	50%	50%	-	Salt-encrusted body sherds; **Marl:** including a sherd with two black lines; amphora base.
Total	-	-	**33 + body sherds**	27	1	5	**61%**	**35%**	**4%**	**Note:** The silt and marl percentages represent averages from the columns.

layer (Locus D3 baskets 3–4). The layer capping the burial shaft (Locus D8) is represented by Locus D4 (baskets 1–3), which extends into Unit G (Locus G4 basket 4). This layer consists of a soft, pale brown (10YR 7/4) layer of fine-grained sand and is overlain by Locus D3 (baskets 3–4). The registration records indicate that a bone barrel bead with vertical striations came from Locus 4 in Unit G to the west of the "shrine" (pl. 3:4 no. 7, TBO 0060), while Locus 4 in Unit D produced a chert flake/scraper(?) (pl. 3:6 no. 6, TBO 0037).

A mud-brick wall (Locus D6) lay to the southeast of Loci 4 and 8, spanning the 1 m width of Unit D. This wall contained light brown (2.5Y 6/6) mud bricks and some mud-brick debris, while the average brick size measured 22 cm long, 14 cm wide, and 7 cm high. Only one course of this wall survived and it was assigned Locus 6 basket 1. (Of note, Locus 5 lay to the southeast of wall D6, spanning a 1 m × 4.70 m area of Unit D and extending into part of Unit E (see fig. 3.46); Locus 9 lay to the northwest of pit D8, and a robber pit, probably cutting into the earlier robber pit, which in turn had cut into the "tomb"(?) shaft).

Although Egyptian pottery (96%) dominates the ceramic assemblage from this structure, a significant amount of pottery is represented by Cypriot and other foreign wares (4%; table 3.54). The pottery dates to early–mid-Dynasty 18 and the New Kingdom in general but likely post-dates the adjacent Dynasty 19 structures (the "shrine" and gray wall) to the southeast. No small finds were found in this phase.

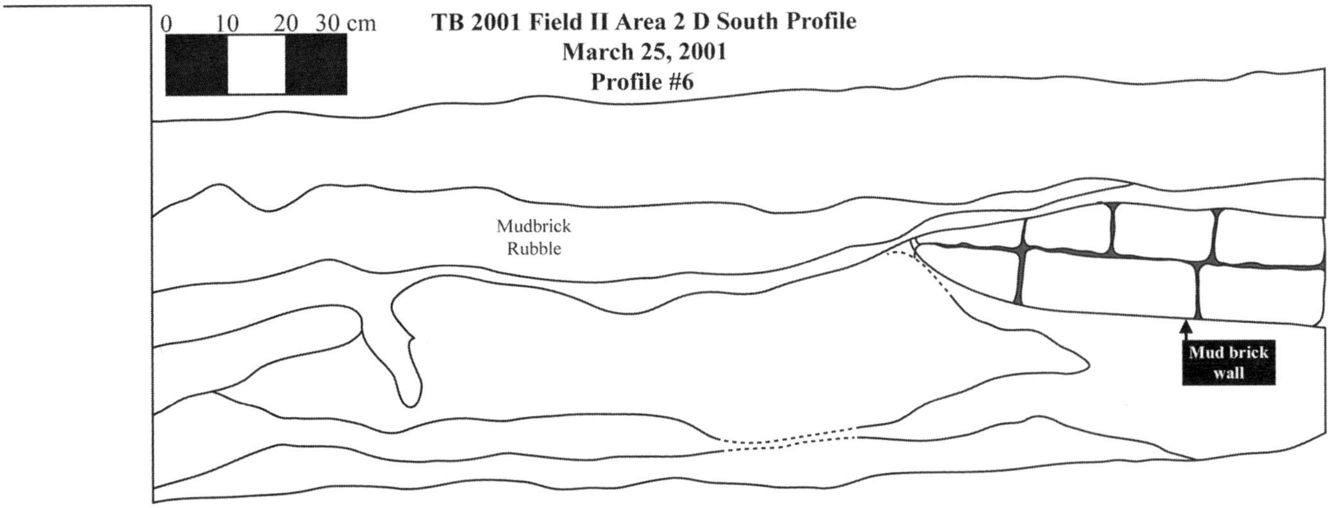

Fig. 3.46. Profile-6: South section in Unit D, to the south of the "shrine" and adjacent to and transecting a mud-brick wall (drawing by Thomas Davis; digitized by Joshua Olsen).

3.4.5.10. Phase 8: Late Dynasty 20(?) Sterile Sand Layer (Unit D, Locus 9)

The northwest end of Unit D contained a sterile yellow sand layer (Locus 9), which fills a pit that had cut through an earlier robber pit. This earlier robber pit had cut through the northwest side of what the excavator thought might have been part of a tomb (Locus D8). This phase of disturbance may date as late as the end of the Ramesside period. Locus 9 was devoid of pottery and small finds.

3.4.5.11. Phase 9: Modern Surface (Units D–I, Locus 1, Baskets 1–21)

The surface layer covering the "shrine" and its environs (Units D–I) consisted of a soft layer of wind-blown, mottled, yellow sand with some silt, chipped stones, and mud-brick debris. This layer had been disturbed by several modern military and robber trenches, while the erosion of debris caused by recent bulldozer and other activities had washed down into this area, mixing with the wind-blown sand.

The surface area in Units D, E, F, G, H, and I was excavated as Locus 1, which contained numbered basket subdivisions to distinguish spatially separated areas. Within this surface layer, Trench D measured 40 m long by 1 meter wide and contained 5-m-long arbitrary subdivisions from 80 m north to 120 m north. The basket boundaries lay at set locations along the northern site grid coordinates, bounded between the 100- and 101-m east grid line. Field II, Area 2, Unit D, Locus 1 is subdivided into baskets 1 (115–120 m north), 2 (110–115 m north), basket 3 (105–110 m north), basket 4 (100–105 m north), basket 5 (110–120 m north), basket 10 (95–100 m north), and basket 13 (90–95 m north). Locus 1 in Unit E encompasses baskets 6 (100–105 m north), 7 (105–110 m north), 11 (sweeping Unit E), 12 (minimal excavation), 14 (90 m, 100 m). Locus 1 in Unit F contains baskets 8–9. Locus 1 in Unit G consists of baskets 18, 20, and 21. Locus 1 in Unit H comprised baskets 15–16. Locus 1 in Unit I is represented by basket 17. The general clean-up of Locus 1 in Units D, E, and F consisted of basket 19.

The material culture found in the surface layers consisted of New Kingdom pottery in general (e.g., store-jars, beer jars, and bowls), with many examples dating to Dynasty 18 and a few forms being restricted to Dynasty 19. The pottery collected from Locus 1, baskets 1–21, in Units D, E, F,

Table 3.55. Summary of Small Finds from Units D–I, Locus 1, Baskets 1–21

Unit	*Locus*	*Basket or level*	*Unit Book no.*	*TBO no.*	*Object type*	*Material*	*Color and Surface Treatment*	*Dimensions (cm)*	*Comments: Davis Units D–I notes*
F	1	(P9)	TBO 0011	TBO 0011	Grape cluster amulet	Faience	Mould-made model grape cluster	-	-
F	1	(P9)	(?)	TBO 0001	Two large fragments (function?)	Copper alloy	Green (corroded)	No details	**SF register:** Cites Unit F, Locus 1.
F	1	(P9)	(?)	TBO 0021	Four fragments of copper alloy	Copper alloy	Green (corroded)	No details	**SF register:** Found in vicinity of the grape pendant/amulet.
F	1	(P9)	(?)	TBO II.62	Disk-shaped bead	Faience	Dark blue (lapis paste)	Diameter= 1.8 cm; perforation = 0.2 cm	**SF register:** Cites Unit F, Locus 1
F	1	Basket no.8 (P9)	(?)	TBO 0003	Fragment of a rectilinear tile	Faience	-	-	**SF register:** Cites Unit F, Locus 1
F	1(?)	Basket no.1 (P9)	(?)	TBO 0053	Wall block fragment	Limestone	White fragment with worn relief	No details	**SF register:** Noted as being found on the surface of Unit F
E	1	(P9)	(?)	TBO II 52B	5 fragments of copper alloy item (possibly an awl)	Copper alloy	Green (corroded)	-	**SF register:** Cites Unit E, Locus 1
E	1	Basket no.2 (P9)	(?)	TBO 0424	Cylindrical item with a point at one end (an awl/nail?)	Copper alloy	Green (corroded)	No details	**SF register:** Cites Unit E, Locus 1
E	1	Basket no.3 (P9)	(?)	TBO 0036	An iron fragment, possibly a handle	Iron	Reddish-brown metal	-	**SF register:** Cites Unit E, Locus 1
E	1	Basket no.3 (P9)	(?)	TBO 0033	Scraper	Chert	No details	No details	**SF register:** Cites Unit E, Locus 1
E	1	Basket no.3 (P9)	(?)	TBO 0423	Triangular shaped tip (an arrowhead?)	Copper alloy	Green (corroded)	No details	**SF register:** Cites Unit E, Locus 1
D–I	1	(P9)	TBO II.52A	TBO II 52	Grape cluster amulet	Faience	-	-	-
D–I	1	(P9)	-	-	Lumps	Copper alloy	Green (corroded)	-	-
D	I	(P9)	(?)	TBO 0031	Vessel stopper or plug(?)	Calcite	Yellow-white	No details	**SF register:** Noted in SF register card
D(?)	1	Basket no.6 (P9)	Sf.8(?)	TBO 0085	Awl or similar implement	Copper alloy	Green (corroded)	No details	**SF register:** Noted in SF register card
D(?)	1	Basket no.1 (P9)	(?)	TBO II 56	Possible handle(?) or curved fragment of copper	Copper alloy	Green (corroded)	No details	**SF register:** Noted in SF register card
H	1	Basket no.1 (P9)	(?)	TBO 0057	Scraper	Chert	No details	No details	**SF register:** Noted in SF register card as being found in pottery basket

G, H, and I (from Area 2 of Field II), amounted to 198 diagnostic sherds (99 rims; 54 handles; 45 bases) and at least 10 times as many body sherds (see table 3.56). Of these 198 diagnostic pieces, 99% represent Egyptian fabrics (silt: 56%; marl: 43%), while two sherds (1%) consist of foreign wares: a Canaanite sherd and a Mycenaean sherd (table 3.56). Other discoveries included a wall block fragment (pl. 3.1 no. 9: TBO 0053 with a sun-disk and uraeus), copper alloy lumps (pl. 3:5 no. 10, TBO 0021, nail? and other pieces), part of a green faience tile (pl. 3:4 no. 11, TBO 0003), a chert flake/scraper(?) (pl. 3:6 no. 5, TBO 0033), another chert scraper(?) (pl. 3:6 no. 11, TBO 0057, Unit H, Locus 1), and artifact fragments, such as two grape cluster pendants/earrings (F1) (pl. 3:4 no. 14, TBO 0011; pl. 3:5 no. 14, TBO 0019), a calcite stopper/plug fragment (pl. 3:6 no. 12, TBO 0031, Unit D), and an iron bar (pl. 3:5 no. 18, TBO 0036, Unit E, Locus 1, basket 3), which lay near and above the "shrine" (table 3.55).

Table 3.56. Summary of Pottery from Units D–I, Locus 1, Baskets 1–21

Unit	*Locus*	*Basket/ level*	*Pottery basket*	*Rims*	*Handles*	*Bases*	*Nile silts*	*Desert marls*	*Other wares*	*Comments: Hummel pottery labels.*
D	1	1 (P9)	Small basket of sherds	4	1	2	80%	20%	-	New Kingdom vessels; **Marl:** amphora handle.
D	1	2 (P9)	Tiny basket of sherds	-	-	1	70%	30%	-	Small, worn body sherds; **Silt:** red-slipped simple bowl base.
D	1	3 (P9)	?	?	?	?	?	?	?	Pottery label absent.
D	1	4 (P9)	5 sherds in total (including 1 handle)	-	1	-	(?)	(?)	-	Includes peach slip.
D	1	5 (P9)	Small basket of sherds	5	1	4	60%	40%	-	Small, worn body sherds; Dynasty 19 sherd; **Silt:** red slips.
D	1	5a (P9)	Small basket of sherds	3	1	3	90%	10%	-	**Marl:** Peach marl with black paint on red slip.
E	1	6 (P9)	Scanty basket of sherds	1	1	-	25%	75%	-	Dynasty 19 jar rim; **Marl:** amphora with cream slip
E	1	7 (P9)	9 sherds in total	3	-	1	50%	50%	-	Jars and bowls; **Marl:** cream slip
F	1	8 (P9)	Small basket of sherds	4	-	3	40%	60%	-	**Silt:** peach slip and burnishing with black and red paint; red slip; **Marl:** gray-green slip
F	1	9 (P9)	Tiny basket of sherds	10	1	2	(?)	(?)	2%	**Silt:** black-rimmed bowls; red slip; **Marl:** gray-green marl; **Other:** bichrome-decorated Canaanite sherd.
E	1	9a (P9)	Small basket of sherds	5	1	2	95%	5%	-	**Silt**: many red slipped bowls**;** **Marl:** cream slip with burnishing; amphora handle with cream slip
F	1	10 (P9)	2 sherds in total	-	-	-	(?)	(?)	-	**Silt:** body sherd; **Marl:** sherd with peach slip and burnishing.
D	1	10a (P9)	Small basket of sherds	2	2	-	60%	39%	1%	Small, worn body sherds; **Marl:** peach slip on an amphora; **Other fabrics:** Mycenaean sherd
E	1	11 (P9)	Small basket of sherds	3	6	2	(?)	(?)	-	Including a flask; **Silt:** red slip; **Marl:** peach and cream slips; peach slip with burnishing
E	1	12 (P9)	Large basket of sherds	13	8	10	50%	50%	-	Small, very worn body sherds; mostly amphorae.
D	1	13 (P9)	2 sherds in total	-	-	-	-	100%	-	-
D	1	13a (P9)	13 sherds in total (including 1 rim)	1	-	1	75%	25%	-	Tiny, worn body sherds; **Silt:** a beer jar base; **Marl:** a jar rim with cream slip.
D	1	14 (P9)	Small basket of sherds	7	3	1	50%	50%	-	Salt-encrusted body sherds Dating mainly to Dynasties 19–20? **Marl:** streaky peach slip; white slips
H	1	15 (P9)	Medium-full basket of sherds	8	5	2	60%	40%	-	Small, worn body sherds; **Silt:** beer jar base; **Marl:** white and peach slips.
H	1	16 (P9)	Large basket of sherds	16	13	7	55%	45%	-	Small, worn body sherds; **Silt:** red slip; Blue Painted sherd; **Marl:** gray-green and white slips; much peach slip.
I	1	17 (P9)	Large basket of sherds	6	6	1	50%	50%	-	**Silt:** Blue Painted sherd**;** **Marl:** much peach and green slips; an Oasis ware fabric colored yellow, pink, and gray
G	1	18 (P9)	Small basket of sherds	1	-	1	60%	40%	-	**Silt:** red slip and burnishing; **Marl:** gritty green; gray-green and peach slips
F	1	19 (P9)	?	?	?	?	?	?	?	Pottery label absent.
G	1	20 (P9)	Medium-full basket of sherds	7	4	2	50%	50%	-	**Silt:** some red slipped bowls; **Marl:** much peach and gray-green slip.
G	1	21 (P9)	?	?	?	?	?	?	?	Pottery label absent.
Total	-	-	**198 + body sherds**	99	54	45	**56%**	**43%**	1%	**Note:** The silt and marl percentages represent averages from the columns.

3.5. Field II, Area 1, Unit L

Excavator: Gregory Mumford

Unit L lies about 65 m northwest of the stone-lined well, immediately south of the modern earthen road that subdivides Fields II and VI (see fig. 3.2, northwest side of Field II plan). In March 2007, a magnetometer survey of this area detected a symmetrical alignment of two rows of five circular patches measuring roughly 1.5 to 2 m in diameter each. A visual observation of this area confirmed that these features most likely represented modern pits, each of which displayed a slight sand filled depression surrounded by a raised perimeter spoil heap of potsherds and other debris. However, one of the most distinct of these features was selected for excavation to ascertain its nature.

Fig. 3.47. View of Unit L in Area 1 of Field II (Photo: G. Mumford).

Unit L was laid out as a 2 × 4-m area spanning the eastern half of one of these crater-like surface depressions. The depression in Unit L measured 2 m in diameter and exhibited a scatter of potsherds in a rough ring around a sand covered slight depression (see fig. 3.47; OCHRE pl. 124). As suggested by the surface observations, the feature was indeed a modern pit, which cut through a 10–15-cm layer of soft surface sand and extended into a very hard, compact subsurface sand layer. The pit's fill was much looser and easy to trace. The upper fill layers consisted of white wind-blown sand and some clay debris; the middle fill layers contained gray sand; the lower layers yielded sand, silt, bone fragments, some stones, a baked brick fragment, and a full basket of small to large potsherds (see Unit L cross-section). The cultural material in the pit appears to have originated from the upper subsurface layer, while the hard-packed sand through which the pit cut did not reveal evidence for any habitation activity. It was concluded that the nine remaining features would yield similar results. This regular series of pits may represent earlier test pits by the Supreme Council of Antiquities, or even earlier remnants of military activity in the 1960s to 1980s.

Table 3.57. Summary of Pottery from Unit L

Unit	*Locus*	*Basket/ level*	*Pottery basket*	*Rims*	*Handles*	*Bases*	*Nile silts*	*Desert marls*	*Other wares*	*Comments: Hummel pottery labels*
L	Locus 1	Basket no.1	Basket no.1	10	1	2	Count: 73	Count: 29	Count: 2	**Note:** Two Roman period ridged sherds; a mixture of New Kingdom wares and forms.
Total	-	-	**13+ body sherds**	10	1	2	**70%**	**28%**	**1%**	**Note:** The silt and marl percentages represent averages from the columns.

3.6. Field II, Area "1" (actually in Area 2), Sondage Unit M (see OCHRE pls. 125–127)

Excavator: Gregory Mumford

Sondage Unit M is located approximately 130 m northeast of the stone-lined well at the eastern end of Field II; it lies south of Field III, and to the north of Field VIII (see fig. 3.2, northeast side of Field II plan). In the pharaonic period, Unit M straddled the northern riverbank opposite the Dynasty 18 fort, which lay directly to the south. The 2007 magnetometer survey detected an anomaly along the ancient riverbank, which displayed two distinct parallel lines or ridges. Based on a similar signature that had revealed a New Kingdom moat in Field VII, Unit M was established to determine whether a similar architectural feature existed in this part of Tell el-Borg.

Unit M measured 2 × 12 m and was placed across the clearest portion of the magnetometer signature in Field II. The sondage revealed only a series of ten successive layers and earlier shore lines for the ancient riverbank, sloping from the northwest down to the southeast. The excavation depth extended up to 1 m in the test trench along the north baulk, a sufficient depth to verify that the magnetometer reading had not detected another moat but instead had indicated what appears to be a series of ancient "beach ridges" and associated debris (see figs. 3.48–3.50; OCHRE pls. 125–27).

3.6.1. Layer-1 (Sondage Unit M: Lower Layer Unexcavated)

The earliest layer lay at the northwestern end of Unit M and remained unexcavated. It displays a mottled coloration with yellow (2.5Y 7/4), gray-white (2.5Y 8/1), gray (2.5Y 7/1), and cream gray (2.5Y 8/2) sandy soil. This layer included flecks of charcoal and some potsherds.

3.6.2. Layer-2 (Sondage Unit M: Locus 10 [Test Trench])

The next layer is characterized by a darker gray sandy soil matrix (2.5Y 6/3) with dense gray powdery ash, charcoal flecks, shells, and potsherds. A 50-cm-wide test trench was placed along the northern side of Unit M to assist in detecting the interfaces between each successive northeastward-sloping layer. Locus 10 basket 1 in this test trench revealed layers 2–5 (see north section) and produced more than a hundred potsherds. Layer 2 was partly excavated by Locus 10 basket 2, which was extended southward at the western end of Unit M. This small portion of layer 2 yielded more than two hundred potsherds in a half full basket of pottery.

3.6.3. Layer-3 (Sondage Unit M: Locus 10 [Test Trench])

Layer 3 contains charcoal flecks, shells, and potsherds in a lighter gray sandy soil (2.5Y 7/2). This layer remained mostly unexcavated, aside from Locus 10 in a 50-cm-wide test trench that incorporated several layers within it.

3.6.4. Layer-4 (Sondage Unit M: Loci 2 [Base] and 10 [Test Trench])

This layer also has charcoal flecks, shells, and potsherds but is composed of a darker gray sandy soil (2.5Y 6/3). This layer remained largely unexplored, excepting Locus 10 in a 50-cm-wide test trench that contained several layers.

3.6.5. Layer-5 (Unit M: Loci 2 [Base] and 10 [Test Trench])

The fifth layer displays a lighter gray color (2.5Y 7/2) and yields flecks of charcoal, shells, and potsherds. The lower part of Locus 2 defines the upper portion of layer 5 and contains a couple of small intrusive pits that range from 21 to 30 cm in diameter and from 22 to 23 cm in depth. This layer is also characterized by soft sand. The base of Locus 2 produced some large pieces of bone, a couple of bivalve shells, an ostrich eggshell piece, and a stone fragment (lithic?). Layer 5 is partly represented in Loci 6 and 10 in the test trench along the northern baulk.

3.6.6. Layer-6 (Unit M: Loci 5 [Base] and 9)

Layer 6 is composed primarily of gray-white sand (2.5Y 6/2) with a gray-brown mottling (2.5Y 4/2). It yielded charcoal flecks, shells, some isolated lenses of gray-brown sand, and potsherds. The lower part of Locus 5 encompasses the top of layer 6, which is a hard-packed sand layer with some clay, very few potsherds, and some shells. It merges slowly into the overlying layers 7–8. Locus 6, which was assigned to the southwestern two-thirds of Unit M, formed the upper part of the 50-cm-wide test trench and included part of layer 6. This locus yielded a couple of copper alloy fragments, which may have originated in layer 6. Locus 9, which was excavated stratigraphically using the test trench, combined layers 6 and 7 and recovered several pieces of bone and more than 100 potsherds. Locus 5 formed the upper part of layer 6 and yielded several pieces of bone and a few potsherds (25+).

3.6.7. Layer-7 (Unit M: Locus 9)

The next deposit consists of a thin layer of light olive-gray sandy soil (5Y 6/2), which contained flecks of charcoal, shells, and potsherds. This thin layer was excavated with layer 6 as part of Locus 9 (see above).

3.6.8. Layer-8 (Unit M: Loci 3 [Base], 7, and 8)

The eighth layer is light gray in color (5Y 7/2) but is actually two layers that are partly subdivided by an increasingly dark-brown to black lense of organic material at the eastern end. It contained shells and potsherds, with the vestiges of intrusive roots from recent vegetation. The base of Locus 3 defines the upper part of layer 8 and contains a couple of mud bricks, small lumps from mud bricks, and sand. Loci 7 and 8 represent a stratigraphic peel-back from a smaller north–south sondage trench along the north baulk. Locus 8 lay below the distinct black organic layer that becomes thicker toward the east and foot of the riverbank slope, while Locus 7 lay above this organic layer.

Locus 8 consists of a soft to firm layer of damp sand (5Y 7/2) with some stones, several bone fragments, and 26 sherds (baskets 1–2). Locus 8 basket 1 represents a 50-cm-wide sondage area beside the north baulk, while basket 2 is the main part of Locus 8, which was peeled back stratigraphically toward the south. Locus 8 has a blurred interface with the overlying Locus 7, which becomes more distinct toward the northeast, down-slope end of Unit M.

Locus 7 represents the dark-brown to black soil that gradually becomes increasingly denser and darker toward the northeast end of Unit M and the base of Locus 7. It contained some sandy and organic soil, charcoal flecks, stones, an immense amount of fish bones, and some animal bones. Locus 7 basket 1 lay in the 50-cm-wide sondage along the northern baulk, while basket 2 covers the rest of this locus. The layer began at 2–3 cm thickness at the top of the riverbank and expanded to 18 cm in depth at the northeastern end of the excavation unit. The layer was fully sieved, yielding two full bags of fish bones, the volume measuring 3 × 5 × 20 cm (basket 1) and 6 × 8 × 27 cm (basket 2). This area also produced more than 75 potsherds.

The base of Locus 3 produced some shells, a few potsherds, and a sandstone chunk. It appears to represent the top and last phase of the adjacent riverbank, after which it was covered in sand after the river ceased flowing, or retreated, beyond this area.

Table 3.58. Summary of Pottery from Unit M

Unit	*Locus*	*Basket/ level*	*Pottery basket*	*Rims*	*Handles*	*Bases*	*Nile silts*	*Desert marls*	*Other wares*	*Comments: Hummel pottery labels*
M	1	Basket no.1	Extra large	21	6	10	55%	40%	5%	**Note:** Very abraded (wind blasted); traces of red slip; 1 Roman body fine Egyptian A ware sherd with red slip and burnishing; 1 stamped amphora body sherd with an impressed hetep-sign; traces of red slip on silt; white and peach slips on marl.
M	2	Basket no.1	Extra large	31	2	5	60%	34%	5%	**Note:** 5% Cypriot; 1% Roman. Mostly bowls and amphora fragments; two Roman A ware sherds; 1 Roman terra sigilatta; 1 blue painted sherd; 1 early Dynasty 18 decorated sherd; 1 marl D token.
M	3	Basket no.1	Extra small (10 sherds)	-	-	-	Count: 7 70%	Count: 3 30%	Count: -	**Note:** Very abraded sherds; non-diagnostic; some "late" G6-type amphora sherds; white and peach slips on marl.
M	4	Basket no.1	Extra small	-	-	-	Count: 11 73%	Count: 2 13%	Count: 2 13%	**Note:** Two pieces of very hard gray ware (unknown ware) from amphoras; evidence of burning; very abraded non-diagnostic sherds; some white slips on marl.
M	5	Basket no.1	Small	1	1	-	Count: 11 41%	Count: 16 59%	Count: -	**Note:** Very abraded, sand-blasted sherds; a variety of marls: marl D, type G6 vessels, marl B. Bowl rim type G6a with cream slip; marl D amphora handle with cream slip.
M	7	Basket no.1	Small	2	-	-	Count: 2 100%	Count: -	Count: -	**Note:** Very abraded; a variety of marls: marl D and type G6 vessel; marl A; two bowl rims of Nile B2 ware.
M	7	Basket no.2	Extra small	1	2	1	Count: 32 58%	Count: 16 29%	Count: 7 13%	**Note:** One silt bowl rim; one strange pedestal base; New Kingdom wares.
M	8	Basket no.2	Small	1	1	-	Count: 18 51%	Count: 12 34%	Count: 5 14%	**Note:** 1 Levantine and 4 other ware types; very abraded sherds, non-diagnostic; 1 silt sherd with peach slip; several dark gray sherds of unknown ware; 1 Nile B2 jar and 1 Levantine handle with cream slip.
M	9	Basket no.1	Large	4	2	0	100% (?)	-	-	**Note:** One type G6 meat jar; Nile silt bowls; New Kingdom wares.
M	10	Basket no.2	Small	20	4	9	Count: 97 63%	Count: 40 26%	Count: 18 12%	**Note:** Two black-rimmed bowls; one blue painted sherd; one possible Greek sherd; a variety of early and late New Kingdom sherds.
Total	-	-	**43 + Body sherds**	25	8	10	**67%**	**27%**	**6%**	**Note:** The silt and marl percentages represent averages from the columns.

3.6.9. Layer-9 (Unit M: Loci 2, 3, 4, and 5)

Layer 9 is also light gray in color (5Y 7/2) and has shells and potsherds. This layer was mostly excavated as Locus 2 (in the southwestern third of the trench), Loci 5 and 3 (straddling the center of the trench), and Locus 4 (in the northeastern third of the trench). The southwestern end of Unit M contained the upper 19–20 cm of a distinct gray ash layer that continued beneath Loci 3–5. In essence, the lower levels of Loci 2–5 represented the upper portions of four successive layers (nos. 4, 5, 6, and 8) that slope down from the northwest to the southeast end of Unit M (excavated as Loci 2, 5, 3 and 4). The northeastern locus (4) represents the accumulation of wind-blown sand over the last active phase of the ancient river bank (see layer 8 and Locus 7 above) and descends gently toward the ancient river bed. Its base and further underlying layers are marked by increasingly darker brown to black soils and greater densities of fish bones. Locus 4 contained a handful of potsherds (15+) and numerous fishbones.

Fig. 3.48. Looking northwest at upper slope of an ancient river bank detected by magnetometer in Unit M in 2007; many fish bones concentrated along the riverbank's slope (Photo: G. Mumford).

Fig. 3.49. View looking south at modern pit, detected by magnetometer, and ancient sloping riverbank edge in Unit L (Photo: G. Mumford).

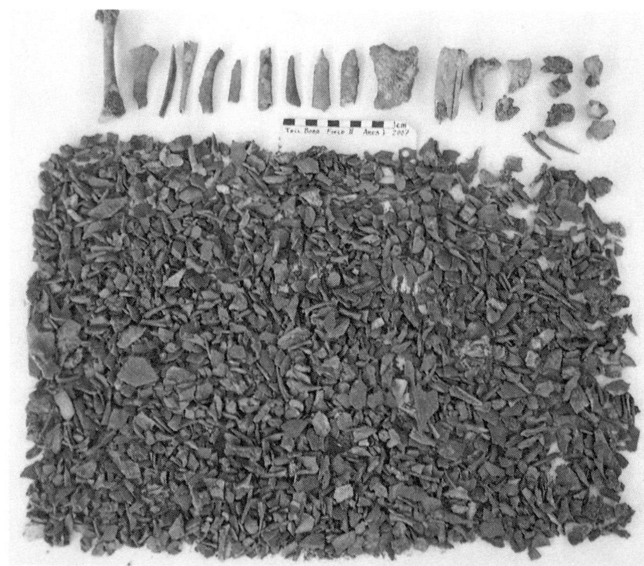

Fig. 3.50 (right). Fish and other bones from Locus 7 (ancient river bank slope) in Unit M (Photo: G. Mumford).

3.6.10. Layer-10 (Unit M)

The tenth layer represents the loose, light white-gray surface sand (5Y 7/2). This layer was excavated as Locus 1 and contained some stones, numerous fragments of bone, part of an ostrich eggshell, two stone flakes, a full basket of potsherds, and two copper alloy lumps.

3.7. Field II, Area 3, Unit A

Excavator: Thomas Davis

Unit A in Area 3 lies about 95 m to the southwest of the stone installation in Area 1 of Field II (fig. 3.1). Unit A measured 5 × 5 m and was placed in Area 3 to investigate an anomaly discovered by Stephen Moshier's magnetometer survey in this area. This unit contained Loci A1, A2, and A3. The surface layer, Locus A1 (baskets 1–2), consisted of a soft, mottled gray-white and yellow sand layer. Locus A2 (basket 1) lay below the surface layer and represented a firmer sand layer. The underlying Locus A3 (baskets 1–2) consists of a small pit filled with darker sand.

The potsherds from these loci included a variety of Egyptian Nile silt vessel sherds (50%), some Egyptian sherds of marl fabrics (23%), a Cypriot Base Ring ware sherd (13.5%), and a Canaanite sherd (13.5%) (table 3.60). This abnormally high proportion of foreign wares is influenced mainly by the tiny amount of pottery recovered from this area. However, despite this limited sample, this relatively high proportion of foreign potsherds may indicate that this area was a more affluent part of the New Kingdom settlement at Tell el-Borg. The layers did not yield any small finds, but the surface in Area 3 did yield a stone flake with some retouch along one edge (pl. 3:6 no. 2, TBO 0236) (table 3.59).

Table 3.59. Summary of Small Finds from Field II, Area 3

Unit	*Locus*	*Basket or level*	*Unit Book no.*	*TBO no.*	*Object type*	*Material*	*Color and Surface Treatment*	*Dimensions (cm)*	*Comments: Davis Units D–I notes*
Area 3	1 Surface	Basket no.1	(?)	TBO 0236	Lithic	Stone	No details	No details	SF register: Cites surface find from Field II, Area 3

Table 3.60. Summary of Pottery from Unit A Loci 1–3 in Field II, Area 3

Unit	*Locus*	*Basket/ level*	*Pottery basket*	*Rims*	*Handles*	*Bases*	*Nile silts*	*Desert marls*	*Other wares*	*Comments: Hummel pottery labels*
A	1	1	Sherds	-	-	-		70% ?	30%	**Marl:** Variety of marl wares; **Other fabrics:** 1 Cypriot Base Ring sherd.
A	1	2	Sherds	-	-	-	50%	-	50%	**Silt:** Two tiny silt sherds. **Other fabrics:** a Canaanite sherd.
A	2	1	?	?	?	?	?	?	?	Pottery label absent.
A	3	1	Sherds	-	-	-	100%	-	-	**Silt:** very worn, tiny silt sherds.
Total	-	-	**Body Sherds**	-	-	-	**50%**	**23%**	**27%**	**Note:** The silt and marl percentages represent averages from the columns.

3.8. Field II, Areas 1–3

A variety of items have been noted and collected from the surface of Areas 1–3 in Field II but lack an exact provenance. These include a limestone block bearing some inscribed decoration, a travertine vessel base fragment (pl. 3:6 no. 21, TBO 0379), a gold bead (pl. 3:5 no. 17, TBO 0081, surface of test pit), faience beads (pl. 3.4 no. 4: TBO 0022, bead fragment), copper alloy utensils and fragments (pl. 3:5 no. 3, TBO 0025, sheet fragment; pl. 3:5 no. 19, TBO 0024, two pieces), and perforated limestone plaques (net or loom weights) (pl. 3.3 no. 2: TBO 0082/0079, perforated limestone item).

Table 3.61. Summary of Small Finds from the Surface of Field II, Area 2

Unit	*Locus*	*Basket or level*	*TBO no.*	*Object type*	*Material*	*Color and Surface Treatment*	*Dimensions (cm)*	*Comments: Davis Units D–I notes*
Field II Area 2	Locus 1	Basket No.1 Surface	TBO 0022	Bead fragment	Faience (vitreous material)	No details	No details	**SF register:** Bead found on surface in Field II, Area 2 (probably near "shrine")
Field II Area 2	Locus 1	Basket no.1 Surface	TBO 0024	Two diagnostic fragments	Copper alloy	Green (corroded)	No details	**SF register:** Fragments found on surface in Field II, Area 2 (probably near "shrine")
Field II Area 2	Locus 1	Basket no.1 Surface	TBO 0025	A fragment of copper alloy	Copper alloy	Green (corroded)	No details	**SF register:** Fragment found on surface in Field II, Area 2 (probably near "shrine")
Field II Area 1	Locus 1	Basket no.1 Surface	TBO 0079	A tablet-shaped item with a perforation at one end (possible net or loom weight?)	Limestone	White slab with a perforation	No details	**SF register:** Fragment found on surface in Field II, Area 1 (probably near "well")
Field II	Locus 1	Basket no.1 Surface	TBO 0379	A fragment from a shallow vessel (bowl?)	Travertine	No details	No details	**SF register:** Fragment found on surface in Field II
Field II	Locus 1	Basket no.1 Surface	TBO 0438	A fragment with a pointed end and square shaft	Copper alloy	Green (corroded)	No details	**SF register:** Fragment found on surface in Field II
Field II	Locus 1	Basket no.1 Surface	TBO 0461	A fragment with a pointed end and square shaft (possibly a nail? Or awl?)	Copper alloy	Green (corroded)	No details	**SF register:** Fragment found on surface in Field II
Field II	Locus 1	Basket no.1 Surface	TBOX 48	A worn wall block with traces of relief decoration	Limestone	White slab with traces of decoration	24 × 20 × 11 cm	**SF register:** Fragment found 6 meters west of large pit; found west of Field II at N30.92510 and E32.41014
Field II Area 1	Test Pit Locus 1	Basket no.1 Surface	TBO 0080	Fragmentary bead (pomegranate)	Faience	No details	No details	**SF register:** Fragment found on surface in Field II (test pit in Mumford "well" area)
Field II	Test Pit Locus 1	Basket no.1 Surface	TBO 0081	Floral inlay piece from a necklace(?)	Gold	No details	No details	**SF register:** Fragment found on surface in Field II ("test pit")

3.9. DISCUSSION OF OVERALL RESULTS FROM FIELD II, AREAS 1–3

The 2000–2001 seasons have uncovered a broad range of stratified occupation and debris layers, mud-brick structures, stone features, material culture, and activities across Areas 1–3 in Field II. The following sections place these different periods and areas in context in this part of Tell el-Borg and in relationship to the neighboring Fields I and III–VIII.

3.9.1. The Material Culture Assemblage from Field II (Areas 1–3)

The material culture assemblage from Field II is diverse and consists of fragments of decorated and inscribed stone-built structures (limestone, granite, and other stones), royal and cult statues (limestone; granite), evidence for copper smelting (numerous lumps and some droplets of copper alloy), various tools and fittings (copper alloy needles, nails, a chisel, a knife blade, a saw? blade, a staple, and a hook; a ceramic palette; hammer-stones; hand grinders; a mortar; a flint knife blade, tools, and debitage; a loom weight), utilitarian containers (Egyptian household pottery; Canaanite wine jars), luxury containers (blue painted vessels; Cypriot and Mycenaean vessels; ostrich eggshells; faience bowl and jar; a piece of glass; copper alloy jar and bowls), jewelry (gold beads; a copper alloy fastening pin, beads, and a lotus-shaped pendant; a faience bead; a piece of carnelian or agate; scarab), weaponry (copper alloy arrowheads), faience grape clusters, gold foil, game pieces(?) (ceramic tokens), and a weight(?) (in copper alloy and stone). The stone pieces included 13 large stone fragments (red granite; diorite; gabbro; limestone: e.g., TBO II 1, II 4), an incised limestone fragment; a ceiling fragment with blue- and yellow-painted stars in high relief, TBO II 33; pl. 3.1 no. 10: TBO 0033, reused as a jamb), a limestone block with a perforation ("tethering post"; TBO II 35), two limestone blocks with perforations (TBO II 1; II 4), a granite block bearing the name of Ramesses II (TBOX 34; pl. 3.1 no. 8, Unit A surface), and a granite block with the prenomen of Ramesses II (TBOX 43) (see tables 3.2–3.61; see also the photographs and drawings on OCHRE plates).

3.9.2. The Pottery from Field II (Areas 1–3)

The pottery retrieved from Field II contains some early Dynasty 18 pottery but dates primarily from late Dynasty 18 through Dynasty 19 (Hummel 2004b: 1, 10, figs. 1–15). The pottery contains a broad range of fabrics and forms that originate from Northwest Sinai, Egypt, the Levant, and the Aegean. The Egyptian fabrics (Sandy Nile Silt; Nile Silts B–C; Marls A–B and D; Mixed Clay) include various forms, such as simple bowls, thick-walled bowls, carinated bowls, lentoid flasks, store-jars (amphorae), jars of various sizes and forms (e.g., beer jar), bread moulds ("flower pots"), a jar fragment bearing a possible Bes-figure headdress, and vessels bearing decoration (e.g., monochrome and bichrome painted vessels; Blue-Painted pottery; red slips; cream-colored slips; vessels with cartouches, seal impressions, and pot-marks). The imported fabrics consist of Cypriot, Mycenaean, and Canaanite forms, which include 20–22 Cypriot vessels (14 Base Ring I–II vessels; two White Shaved dipper juglets; four White Slip "milk bowls"), six Mycenaean vessels (stirrup jars and vessel sherds; Mycenaean IIIA2), and at least 18 Canaanite vessels (mainly wine jars) (see tables 3.2–3.42).[12] The pottery labels from the 2001–2002 seasons in Field II (tables 3.2–3.42) record a minimum of 2,153 diagnostic sherds from this part of Tell el-Borg, revealing that Egyptian pottery amounted to 98% in comparison to Cypriot vessels (1%), Canaanite store-jars (0.8%), and Mycenaean pottery (0.3%).

3.9.3. The Fauna from Field II (Areas 1–3)

In a preliminary assessment of the 2002 season, Field II yielded 296 identifiable diagnostic bones and shells from various fauna.[13] This fauna consisted of 81 cattle bones (27%), 71 pig bones (24%), 59 fish bones (Nile Catfish; Nile Perch; Tilapia) (20%), 56 marine(?) shells (19%), 13 sheep/goat bones (4%), 6 *Aves* bones (geese; ducks; indeterminate others) (2%), six ostrich eggshell pieces (2%), two donkey bones (1%), and two horse bones (1%).[14]

In contrast to the Field III cemetery and the Field IV fort, where fish bones form the highest percentages (53% and 32%, respectively), the "shrine" area in Field II yielded the greatest proportions of cattle bones (27%), pig bones (24%), and marine(?) shells (19%) across the site.[15] Of note, the remains of dogs were restricted to the cemetery (III) and fort (IV) areas, while the remains of water-dwelling crocodiles and turtles appeared only from or near the environs of the fort and

12. The pottery from Field II was studied and illustrated in a report by R. Hummel (2004b: 1–21, figs. 1–15), whose chapter in the current volume represents a revision of her original manuscript. For more details on the forms and fabrics found at Tell el-Borg in general, see R. Hummel in *Tell el-Borg I*, 365–69.

13. See *Tell el-Borg* I, chapter 13.

14. See Michelle Loyet's analysis in this volume, chapter 12.

15. See this volume, chapter 12.

moat.[16] The 94 pieces of ostrich eggshells represent a rather high percentage (22%) in the fort area (IV) but may reflect remnants of more exotic food and luxury products.

The discrepancy in the distribution of faunal types from the fort (IV), cemetery (III), and primarily "cultic" (II) areas may be explained largely by the different functions of these three areas. Although the nature and function of Field II changes somewhat through time and its multiple occupation strata, its primarily "cultic" nature may explain the dominance of cattle and pig bones within this area. The dominance of fish and sheep/goats in the fort and cemetery areas may simply reflect the dietary and funerary offering preferences in these living and mortuary locations.[17] However, in the 2008 study season, immediately prior to the submission of this chapter, Louise Bertini completed the identification and analysis of faunal material from Tell el-Borg, which may alter many of the initial findings (see chapter 14).

Of interest, the surface of Field II has produced several human bones representing at least one individual.[18] Scott Haddow noted the presence of a rib fragment and several pedal and manual phalangeal pieces from the surface in Field II. He did not observe any pathological lesions. The absence of graves in Field II argues that these bones originated from an isolated burial, possibly post-dating the occupation in Field II or representing secondary deposition from a neighboring New Kingdom cemetery.

3.10. CONCLUSION

Although little remains in situ of a cultic stone-built installation at Tell el-Borg (excepting possibly the robbed foundations of a limestone gateway of Ramesses II in Field V), Field II has produced the most likely candidate for a Dynasty 19 shrine servicing the garrison. It contains multiple elements and features that are well-associated with temples and elite areas elsewhere: the remains of an adjacent mud-brick enclosure wall, a triple-chambered "shrine" (with the classic Theban New Kingdom three back rooms, a broad hall, and part of an outer forecourt), a nearby expansive and well-floored courtyard (at least 10 x 25 m), a stone-lined well (reusing many temple blocks), large granite blocks (indicating some major local construction work), many fragmentary limestone wall and ceiling blocks (with traces of cultic inscriptions and scenes), pieces from broken-up royal and non-royal votive statuary, and the remnants of many luxury items: e.g., fragments from gold and faience jewelry, stone and copper alloy vessels, and imported Cypriot, Mycenaean, and Canaanite pottery. In addition, this area lay beside a water channel, a feature that is also often associated with Egyptian temples.[19]

A limestone built and inscribed Ramesside gateway appears to have lain 300 m to the southwest in Field V. This gateway is represented mostly by its robbed-out foundation trenches from a destroyed superstructure set into a mud-brick wall. The block fragments bear the cartouches of Ramesses II, Merenptah, and possibly Ramesses III, and display the remains of diverse cultic scenes and architectural elements (*Tell el-Borg I*, 297–313). Similarly, in Field I, the modern exca-

16. Observations based upon chapter 12.

17. Although I (Mumford) made assessments based on Loyet's unpublished preliminary faunal report for Field II and Tell el-Borg (see chapter 12).

18. Based upon information from an unpublished preliminary report by S. Haddow, "Tell el-Borg 2000 Human Osteology Report," Tell el-Borg 2001 Manual and Preliminary Reports from the 2000 Season (ed. J. Hoffmeier, unpublished reports available on OCHRE) 1–7, table 1.

19. For discussions and overviews on Ancient Egyptian temples and shrines, and their components, see n. 11 above (p. 25).

vation of an irrigation canal had exposed several inscribed limestone blocks, which had originated from a temple, whether in Field II or Field V, or elsewhere.

In contrast, the remaining areas at Tell el-Borg contained a housing area (Fields VI–VII), a cemetery (Field III), a Dynasty 18 baked-brick moat and part of an associated building (Fields IV and VIII), and a Dynasty 19 fortress and stone gateway (Fields IV–V) (see OCHRE pl. 128). While the stone-lined well in Field II and the Ramesside fort's limestone gateway in Field V offer the best candidates for the origin of many of the dismantled and dispersed limestone blocks found across the site, both the nature of the small mud-brick "shrine" in Field II (see above) and the concentration of cultic and related debris and architectural components in Field II remain a strong argument for the existence of a late Dynasty 18–19 cultic installation in this portion of the site.

Plate 3:1. Selected Statuary and Architectural Fragments from Field II.

1. TBO 0178: II/1 Unit J loc.3 (b.1)	Limestone sculpture fragment with yellow pigment
2. TBO 0104: II/2 Unit K loc.1 (b.1)	Granite statuette(?) fragment
3. TBO 0056: II/1 Unit F loc.32	Quartzite statuette(?) fragment: knee(?)
4. TBO 0027: II/1 Unit F loc.11	Limestone "stele"(?) fragment (or part of a column?)
5. TBO 0906: II/1 Unit JC loc.5 (b.1)	Limestone block fragment bearing an incised human leg
6. TBO 0005: II/2 Unit E loc.5 (b.2)	Limestone statuette fragment: royal nemes headdress
0006: II/2 Unit E loc.15 (b.2)	Limestone statuette fragment: Face area
0026: II/2 Unit E loc.15 (b.2)	Limestone statuette fragment: wig area
0047: II/2 Unit I loc.15 (b.5)	Limestone statuette fragment: Face area
0050: II/2 Unit I loc.15 (b.5)	Limestone statuette fragment: Shoulder and upper arm
7. TBO 0058: II/2 Unit I loc.19 (b.1)	Limestone statuette(?) fragment: wig(?)/garment(?)
8. TBOX 0034: II/2 Unit A surface	Granite block fragment with several hieroglyphs
9. TBO 00053: II/2 Unit F surface	Limestone block fragment bearing a sun-disk and uraeus
10. TBO II.33: II/1 Unit Ca loc.1	Limestone ceiling block with six stars (reused as a jamb)

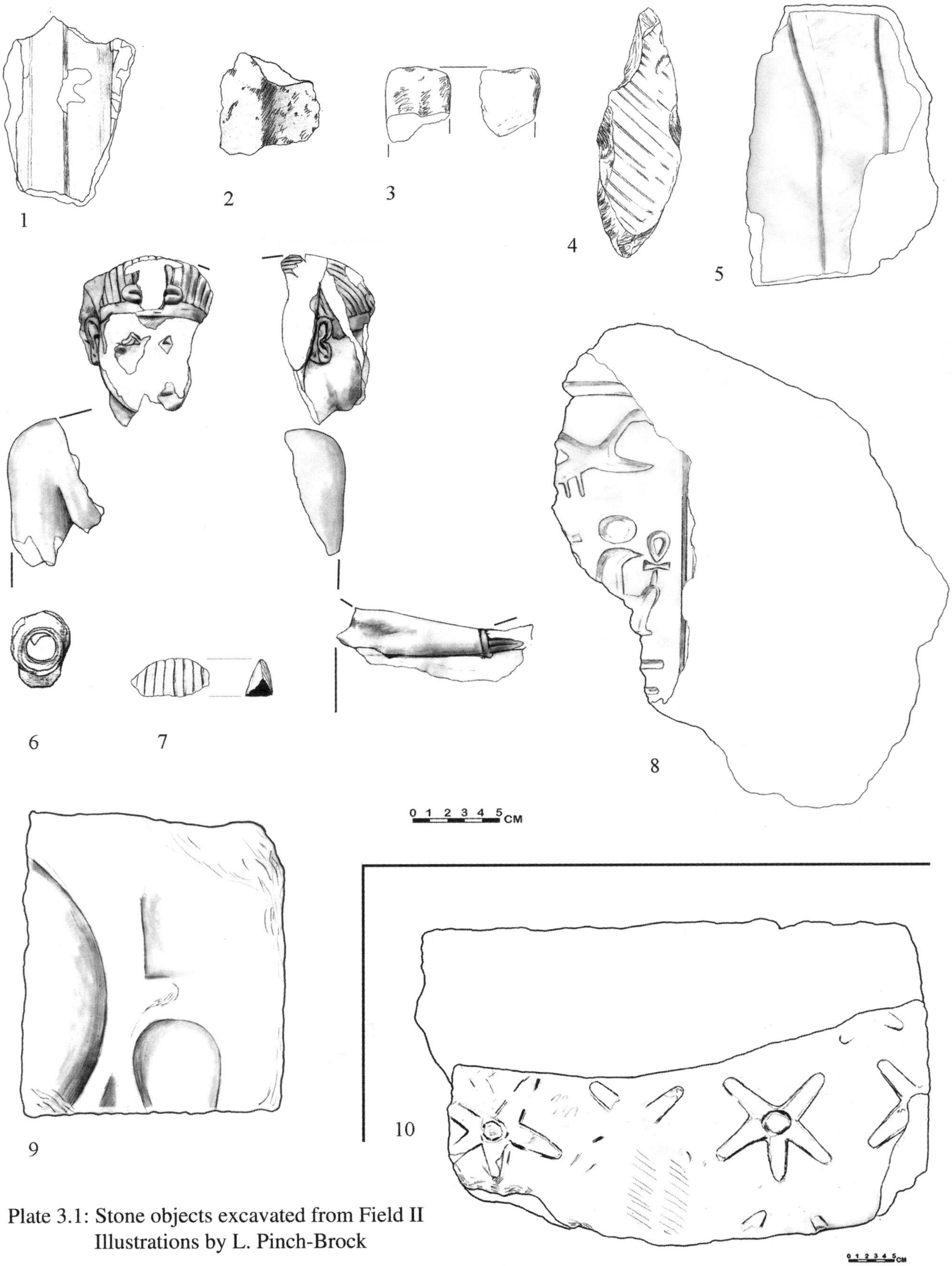

Plate 3.1: Stone objects excavated from Field II
Illustrations by L. Pinch-Brock

Plate 3:2. Miscellaneous Items from Field II

1. TBO 0040: II/1 Unit F loc.7	Large ostrich eggshell fragment (plain; not decorated)
2. TBO 0023: II/1 Unit F loc.11	Medium ostrich eggshell fragment (plain; not decorated)
3. TBO 0054: II/2 Unit G (no locus)	Plaster "sealing" fragment from a pottery jar/other container

Plate 3:3. Selected Ceramic and Other Materials Excavated from Field II

1. TBO 0008: II/1 Unit F loc.11 (b.2)	Ceramic jar handle with stamp impression
TBP 0270:	Alternate designation for pottery with fabric descriptions
2. TBO 0082: II/1(?) surface	Limestone rectilinear slab with hole (net weight?; pendant?)
3. TBO 0061: II/2 Unit E loc.15 (b.7)	Faience gaming piece
4. TBO 0079: II/2 Unit E loc.19 (b.2)	Ceramic cylindrical bead with longitudinal perforation
5. TBO 0088: II/1 Unit F loc.12	Ceramic crucible with copper inside and burnt exterior
6. TBO 0042: II/1 Unit F loc.25	Ceramic disk (token; counter; gaming piece?)
7. TBP 0223: II/1 Unit D loc.2	A marl D amphora with a stamp-impressed handle

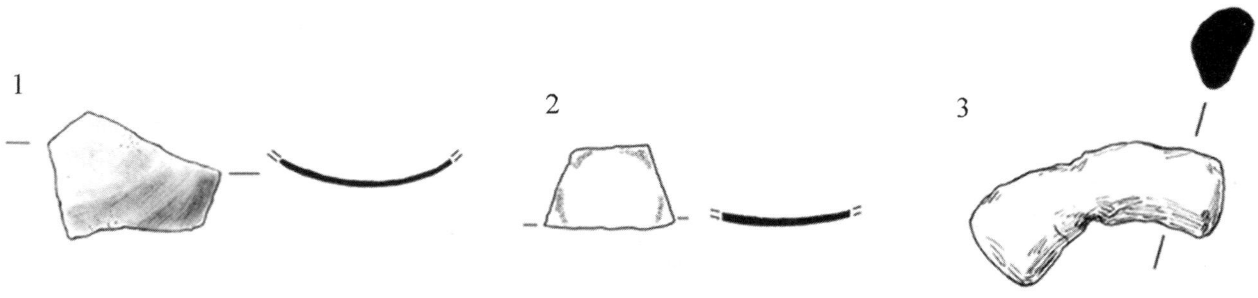

Plate 3.2: Miscellaneous objects excavated from Field II

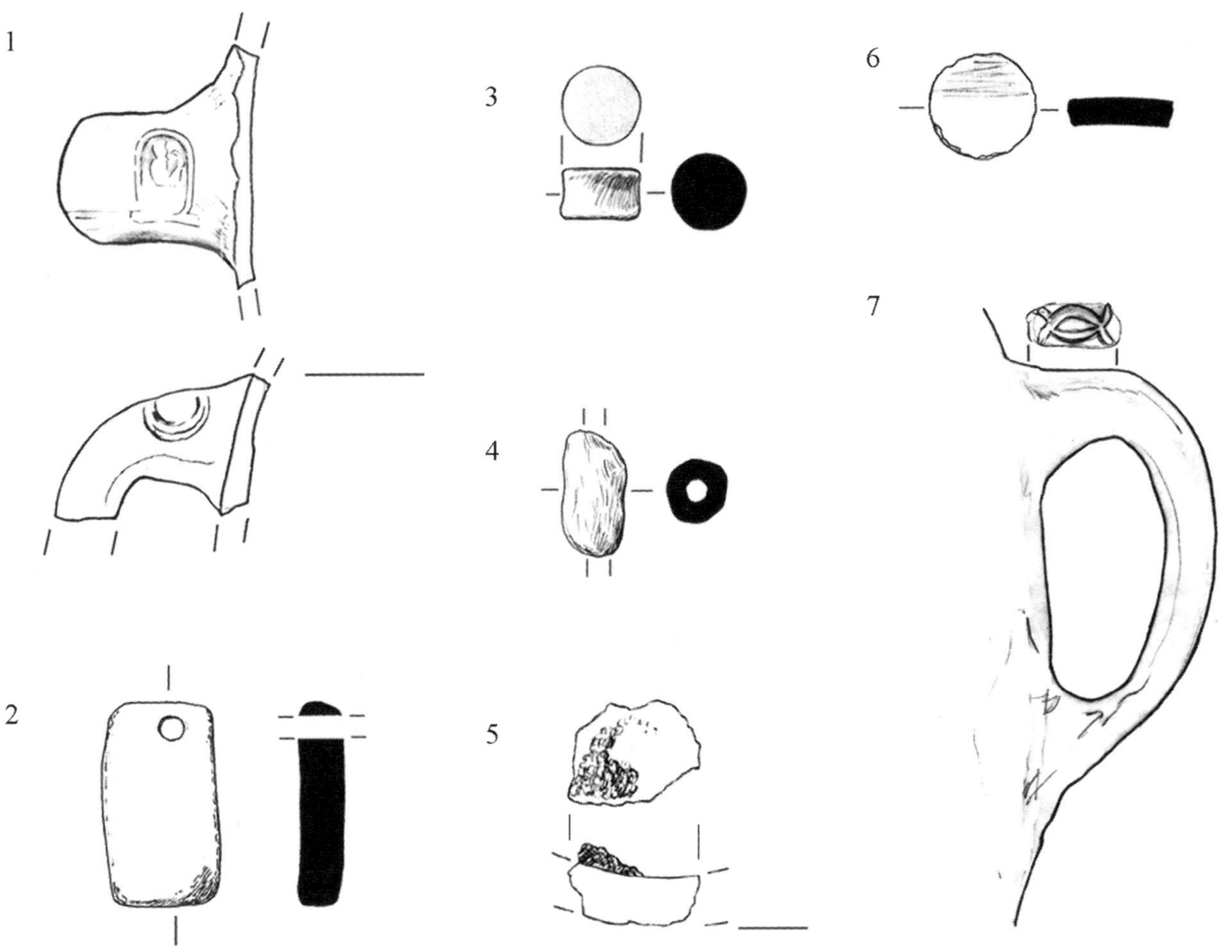

Plate 3.3: Ceramic material excavated from Field II
Illustrations by L. Pinch-Brock

Plate 3:4. Selected Faience, Glass, and Ivory/Bone Objects Excavated from Field II

1. TBO 0038: II/1 Unit D loc.5	A faience multiple bead and a carnelian disk bead
2. TBO 0010: II/2 Unit D loc.16 (b2)	Two faience disk beads
3. TBO 0016: II/2 Unit E loc.15 (b2)	Faience disk bead
4. TBO 0022: II/2 Surface	Fragment of faience bead
5. TBO 0032: II/2 Unit F loc.12	Fragment of an ivory/bone? cylindrical bead with striations
6. TBO 0028: II/1 Unit F loc.8	Blue faience circular bead with vertical striations
7. TBO 0060: II/2 Unit G loc.4	Bone barrel bead with vertical striations
8. TBO 0055: II/2 Unit D loc.14	Faience circular bead with vertical striations
9. TBO 0043: II/2 Unit D loc.5 (b.2)	A white vitreous (glass/faience?) loop-earring
10. TBO 0017: II/2 Unit F loc.12	Green faience curved fragment (ankh?): black-painted stripe
11. TBO 0003: II/2 Unit F loc.1 (b.8)	Light green faience tile with a broken edge
12. TBO 0035: II/1 Unit D loc.9	Fragment of a green faience tile
13. TBO 0048: II/2 Unit F loc.14	Faience ovoid seal with a wadjet-eye top and inscribed base
14. TBO 0011: II/2 Unit F loc.1	Mould-made faience imitation grape cluster amulet/earring

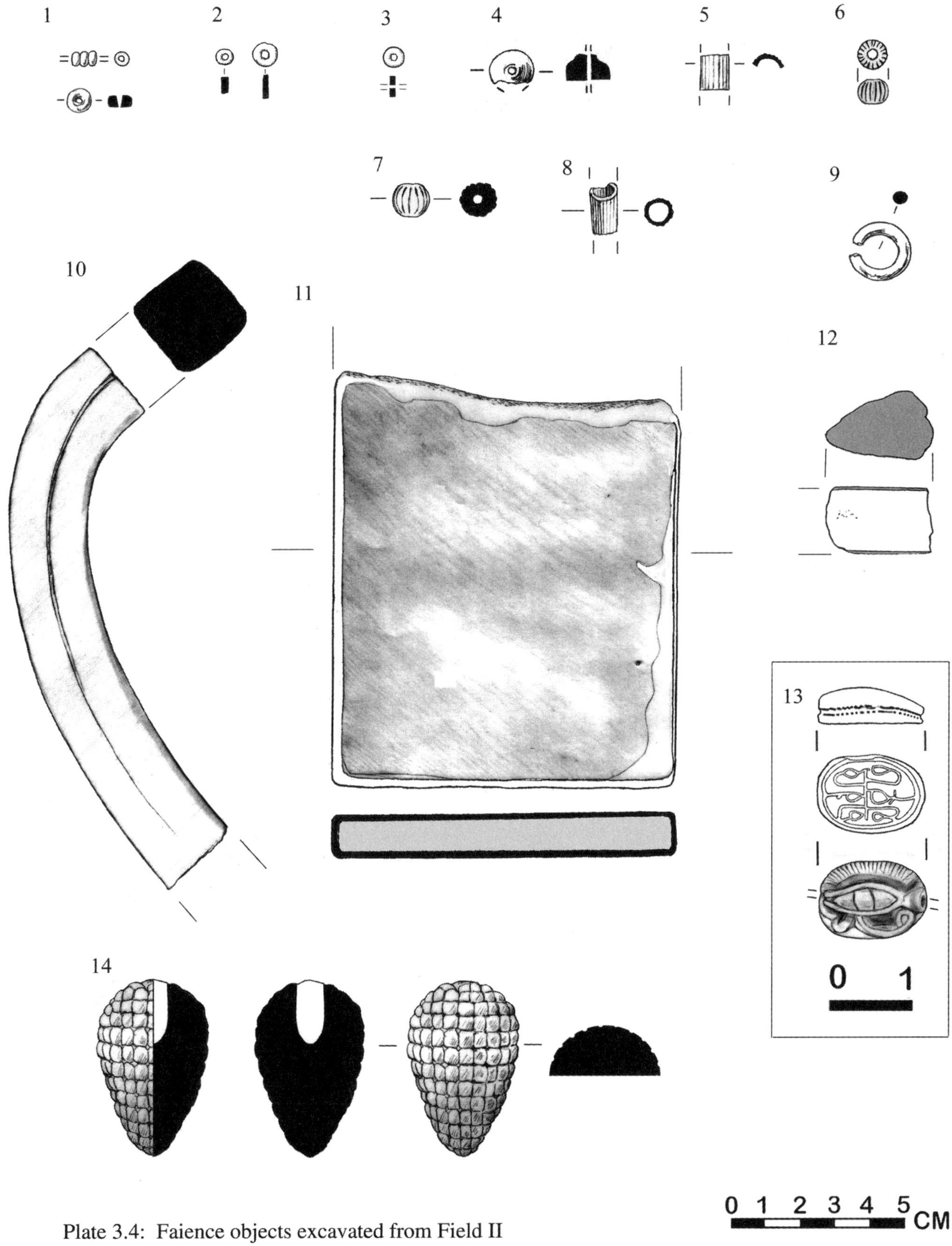

Plate 3.4: Faience objects excavated from Field II
Illustrations by L. Pinch-Brock

Plate 3:5. Selected Metal Objects Excavated from Field II

1. TBO 0004: II/2 Unit E loc.15 (b2)	Gold foil on ivory backing (vertically ribbed appearance)
2. TBO 0049: II/2 Unit D loc.5 (b.2)	Copper alloy fish-hook with a barbed end
3. TBO 0025: II/2 surface	Copper alloy sheet fragment
4. TBO 0041: II/1 Unit F loc.6	Copper alloy arrowhead
5. TBO 0083: II/2 Unit C loc.1 (b.4)	Copper alloy item with a pointed end; broken-off base
6. TBO 0059: II/2 Unit I loc.15	Gold circular bead frag. with vertical striations and collar
7. TBO 0007: II/2 Unit F loc.5 (b.3)	Copper alloy cylindrical shaft (possibly a nail)
8. TBO 0046: II/1 Unit F loc.19	Copper alloy awl(?) broken into three pieces
9. TBO 0117: II/2 Unit J loc.3 (b.1)	Copper alloy awl(?) with a circular and square section
10. TBO 0021: II/2 Unit F loc.1	A copper alloy nail(?) found with three other fragments
11. TBO 0208: II/1 Unit F loc.25 (b1)	Small copper alloy piece with a pointed end
12. TBO 0044: II/1 Unit F loc.19	Large copper alloy projectile point (arrow/spear? head)
13. TBO 0014: II/1 Unit F loc.6	Copper alloy fitting with a flat strip wrapped over a bar
14. TBO 0019: II/2 Unit E loc.5 (b.2)	Copper alloy earring/pendant with a loop and grape-cluster?
15. TBO 0420: II/1 Unit F loc.6 (b.7)	Copper alloy item with a circular section and a point
16. TBO 0069: II/1 Unit A loc.4 (b.3)	Copper alloy item with a circular section and groove (nail?)
17. TBO 0081: II surface test pit	Gold piece from a necklace(?) with a floral motif
18. TBO 0036: II/1 Unit E loc.1 (b.3)	Iron bar with a circular section: suggested to be a handle(?)
19. TBO 0024: II/2 surface	Two pieces of copper alloy: a pointed cylinder and a loop
20. TBO 0045: II/1 Unit F loc.7 (b.3)	A cylindrical copper alloy handle(?) tapering to a flat strip
21. TBO 0299: II/1 Unit I loc.4	A copper alloy sheet folded into a cylindrical bead(?)

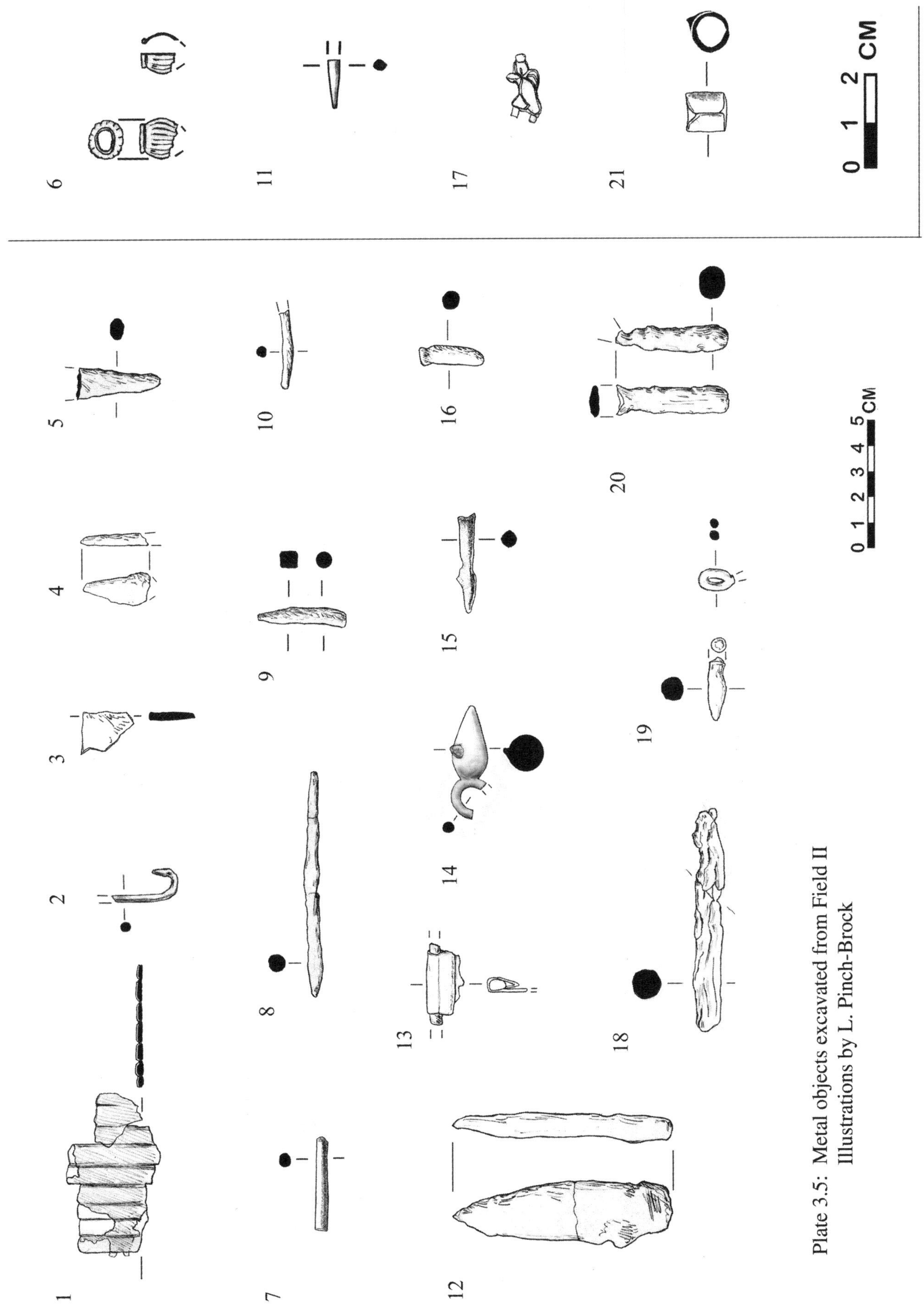

Plate 3.5: Metal objects excavated from Field II
Illustrations by L. Pinch-Brock

Plate 3:6. Selected Stone Tools and Vessels Excavated from Field II

1. TBO 0098: II/2 Unit C loc.3 (b.4)	Chert utensil with a slightly pointed end: awl(?)
2. TBO 0236: II/3 surface	Stone flake with some retouch along one edge: blade(?)
3. TBO 0030: II/1 Unit F loc.25	Chert blade with much retouching along three edges
4. TBO 0020: II/2 Unit E loc.5 (b.2)	Chert flake with a pointed and raised end: blade/point(?)
5. TBO 0033: II/2 Unit E loc.1 (b.3)	Slightly curved chert flake with retouched edge: scraper(?)
6. TBO 0037: II/2 Unit D loc.4 (b.1)	Chert flake with a retouched edge: scraper(?)
7. TBO 0102: II/1 Unit F loc.19	A chert/graywacke flake, very worn: pebble polisher(?)
8. TBO 0073: II/2 Unit I loc.19 (b.1)	A chert flake with much retouch along one edge: scraper(?)
9. TBO 0070: II/2 Unit I loc.15 (b.6)	A chert flake fragment with retouching on two edges: blade
10. TBO 0110: II/1 Unit I loc.8 (b.1)	A chert flake with traces of a flake extracted from it: blade?
11. TBO 0057: II/2 Unit H loc.1	A chert flake with retouch along one or two ends: scraper(?)
12. TBO 0031: II/2 Unit D locus(?)	A circular calcite piece with a smoothed top: stopper/plug
13. TBO 0090a:II/2 Unit I loc.15 (b.5)	A calcite stopper/plug(?) for a vessel (vs. natural fracturing)
14. TBO 0222: II/2 Unit I loc.8	A quartzite flake with a pointed end and a flat end: awl(?)
15. TBO 0018: II/1 Unit F loc.43	A chipped quartzite pounder/grinder with a smooth side
16. TBO 0106: II/2 Unit J loc.6 (b.2)	A broken, three-sided, smooth graywacke piece: whetstone?
17. TBO 0093a: II/2 Unit J loc.8 (b1)	A sandstone fragment: possible "scraper"; probably a chip
18. TBO 0093b: II/2 Unit J loc.8 (b1)	A sandstone fragment with traces of blue paint: a scraper?
19. TBO 0120: II/1 Unit E loc.107	A calcite(?) vessel piece with a short, false-spout
20. TBO 0112: II/2 Unit E loc.15 (b.2)	A calcite vessel (flask base?) fragment with traces of ochre
21. TBO 0379: II surface	A travertine vessel base
22. TBO 0029: II/2 Unit A Tr.2 loc.7	A rim fragment from a basalt bowl/mortar (TBO II.27)
23. TBO 0901: II/2 Unit Jd Locus 2 b1	A limestone block: incised disks and a sunken upper border

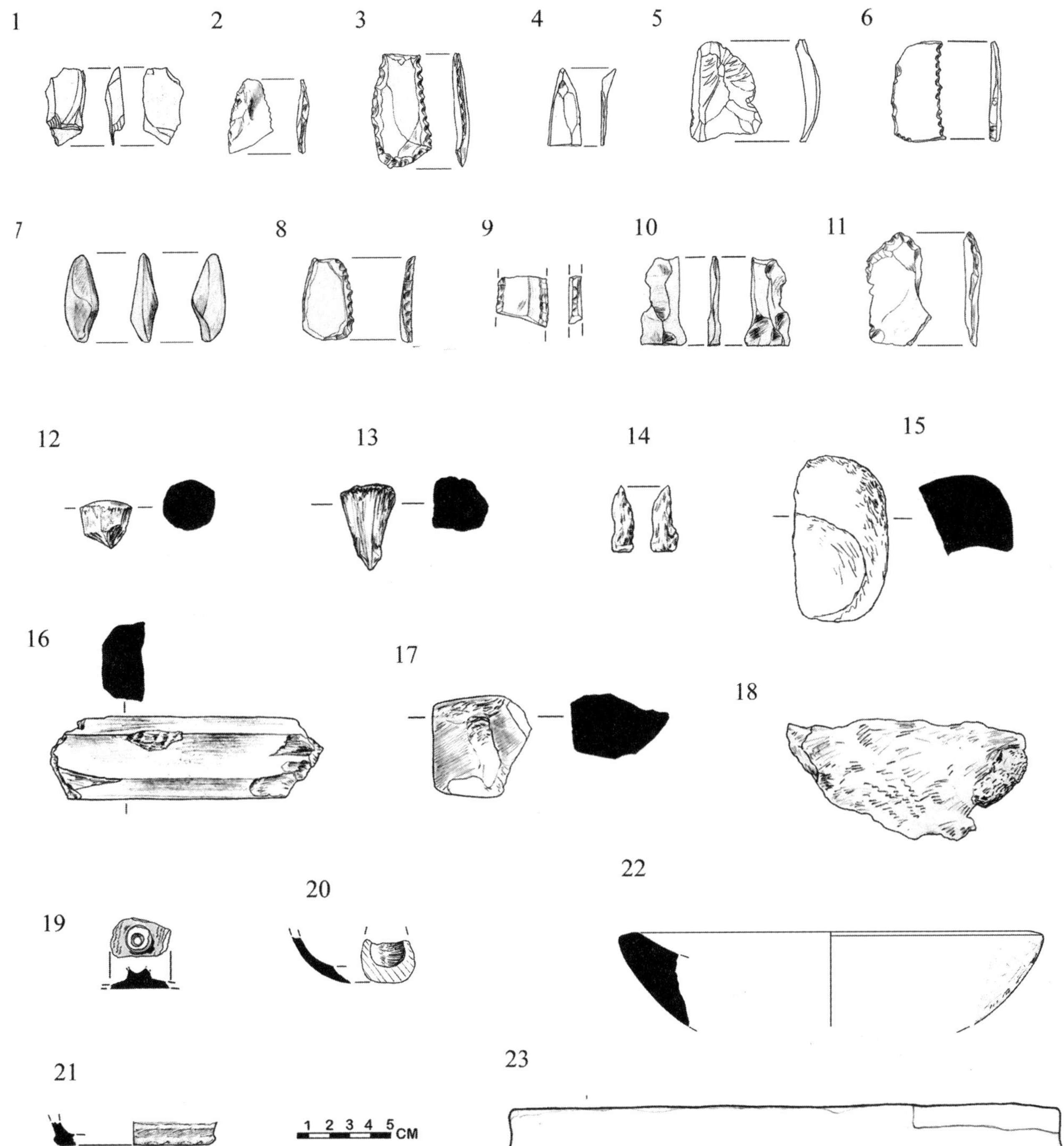

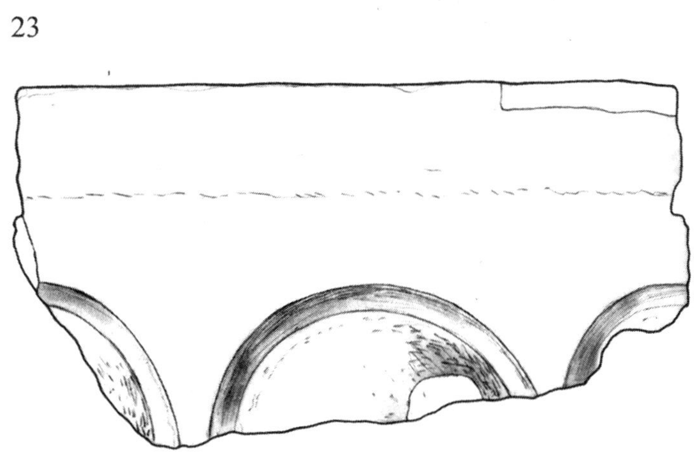

Plate 3.6: Field II: stone tools and vessels
Illustrations by L. Pinch-Brock

EXCURSUS I: CERAMIC REPORT FROM FIELD II AT TELL EL-BORG[20]

Rexine Hummel
ROYAL ONTARIO MUSEUM

The pottery in this study comes exclusively from Tell el-Borg Field II, which is located between the New Kingdom fortress area (Field IV) to the south and the New Kingdom cemetery (Field III) to the north (fig. 3.1a–b). Field II was divided in 2001 into two areas comprising: Area 1, which contains multiple occupation layers into which was dug a deep pit for the construction of a stone installation with a descending staircase, and Area 2, which includes mud-brick foundations for several structures, a pit, and a scatter of large granite, alabaster, and limestone blocks.[21] After three seasons of excavation in both of these areas, an extensive corpus of pottery has been recorded and drawn. The bulk of this pottery can be dated to the late 18th and 19th Dynasties, the evidence for which comes from pottery forms characteristic of the New Kingdom, a large number of stamped amphora handles of late 18th Dynasty kings, as well as from the imported ceramics. In addition, a much smaller corpus of ceramic forms dating to the early to mid-18th Dynasty reflects the existence of earlier activity at Tell el-Borg. It is hoped that by studying this pottery the locations of this early occupation can be pinpointed.

Field II was robbed and damaged extensively in antiquity only to suffer more devastation in recent decades from modern military activities. It is therefore not surprising that the condition of the pottery coming from this area is poor and fragmentary. Only a handful of small vessels were retrieved intact, and few were felt to be mendable.

The ceramic material is presented in two main divisions.

Part I. General Pottery from Fields II.1 and II.2
- Imports from Cyprus, Greece and Palestine
- Egyptian Decorated Pottery: blue-painted, black, or black and red-painted
- Stamped Jar Handles
- General Pot-Marks

Part II. Sherds from Selected Loci in both Fields II:1 and II:2
- Sherds from Field II, Area 1
- Sherds from Field II, Area 2

General Pottery from Fields II.1 and II.2

Imported Pottery

Cypriot Pottery[22]

Abundant evidence exists to support the existence of commercial trade between Cyprus, Egypt, and the Levant during the Late Bronze Age. Although trade had already begun sporadi-

---

20. The author wishes to thank Lyla Pinch-Brock for her computerized illustrations, Greg Mumford for his advice on the archaeology of the site, and Linda Wilding for her help in editing this report.

21. For further information concerning the archaeology of Field II, see the main portion of chapter 3 here, by Gregory Mumford.

22. For an analysis of all Cypriote ceramic materials from the site, see Stuart Swiny, *Tell el-Borg I*, chapter 10.

cally in the Middle Bronze period, imports reached their zenith during the Amarna Age in Egypt and LB IIA in Palestine. Barry Gittlin in his study of Cypriot imports[23] found that 59% of the Late Cypriot pottery from secure contexts in Palestine had been deposited in LB IIA levels and in fact began to decline during LB IIB (during the reigns of Seti I and Ramesses II). His study also revealed that the corpus of Cypriot imports during this time was dominated at the beginning by Base Ring I juglets and replaced later by Base Ring II juglets. The importation of White Slip II pottery and White Shaved pottery also peaked during LB IIA.[24] More study of Egyptian pottery in secure contexts is needed before we can assume that the same trend was paralleled in Egypt and the Sinai.

Cypriot Base Ring (see Pottery Plate 3.1)

Cypriot Base Ring ware in the form of hand-made flasks, juglets, and fragments thereof formed the largest corpus of foreign exports at Tell el-Borg. Fourteen fragments of Cypriot Base Ring vessels were found in Field II, consisting predominately of a popular form of juglet with trumpet base. Both the flasks and juglets were ideal forms for transporting precious oils. Base Ring wares begin to appear in Egypt in the early 18th Dynasty and reach their greatest frequency during the Amarna Period.

Ware

Base Ring I[25] appears in the archaeological record slightly earlier than Base Ring II, but the ware of both types is typically very thin, well levigated, and well-fired. In the Tell el-Borg examples, the clay fires to steel gray, with no visible core, and is tempered with very fine grits. In a few examples, a thin red-brown streak is visible beneath the slip, while the rest of the section is gray. The surface is covered with a thick black slip, sometimes polished or left with a matte finish. BR I is decorated with plastic decoration applied to the surface while BR II is painted with white stripes or white crossed bands. BR II seems to predominate in Field II at Tell el-Borg. Often, the preserved fragment comes from an undecorated part of the vessel, and therefore it is impossible to distinguish BR I from BR II. The label BR alone is then applicable. The addition of incised decoration is less common.

Pottery Plate 3.1

1:1 Handle of juglet, TBP[26] 0364, Locus II.1, I-8.3.[27] Ware: BR. Surface: Black slip. Incised lines decorate the handle. *Parallel:* Kromholz, pl. 39:1 and pp. 17, 18. Incised handles are not common but a similar handle with two rows of incisions was found at Tel Mevorakh in Israel.

1:2 Wall of flask, TBP 0407, Locus II.1, D-11. Ware: BR II. Surface: Black slip with white bands.

1:3 Wall of flask, TBP 0175, Locus II.1, D-11. Ware: BR II. Surface: Black slip with white bands. *Parallel:* Merrillees, pl. XXV:1 from Sidmant, and 2 from Amarna. Flask type IVB. Amiran, pl. 54:13 from Lachish.

1:4 Handle of juglet, TBP 0414, Locus II.1, I-4.1. Ware: BR. Surface: Black slip. A single line is incised along the length of the handle.

23. Barry M. Gittlen, "The Cultural and Chronological Implications of the Cypro-Palestinian Trade during the Late Bronze Age," *BASOR* 241 (1981) 51.

24. Ibid.

25. Hereafter, Base Ring I and II will be abbreviated to BR I and BR II.

26. TBP is the abbreviated form of Tell el-Borg Pot and refers to whole vessels or important fragments that have been registered.

27. This label represents Field II, Area 1, Unit I, Locus 8, Basket 3. Hereafter, only the abbreviations will appear.

1:5 Neck of juglet, TBP 0413, Locus II.1, D-10. Ware: BR. Surface: Black slip. A lump of clay has been added to the interior of the juglet to reinforce the carination of the wall.
1:6 Body sherd from juglet, TBP 0263, Locus II.1, F-8. Ware: BR II. Surface: Black slip with white bands.
1:7 Rim of bowl, TBP 0276, Locus II.1, F-10. Ware: BR. Surface: Polished black slip. Vessel has very fine thin walls. *Parallel:* Åström, fig. XLVII: 9 and 10; fig. LII:2, 3, and 4.
1:8 Base of juglet, TBP 0258, Locus II.1, D-3. Ware: BR. Surface: Black slip.
1:9 Base of juglet, TBP 0303, Locus II.1, C-100.1. Ware: BR. Surface: Black burnished slip.
1:10 Base of juglet, TBP 0262, Locus II.1, F-8. 2. Ware: BR. Surface: Black slip.
1:11 Base of round-bottomed juglet, TBP 0277, Locus II.2, F-10. Ware: BR. Surface: Black slip. *Parallel:* Åström, see fig. XLVIII; vessel is BR I

Not Illustrated

- Body sherd from juglet, TBP 0239, Locus II.1, C-2. Ware: BR II. Surface: Black slip with white bands.
- Base of juglet, TBP 0435, Locus II.1, I-8. Ware: BR. Surface: Black slip.
- Vessel fragment, TBP 0281, Field II.2, D-3.3. Ware: BR. Surface: Black slip. Obscure fragment.

Cypriot White Shaved Vessels (see Pottery Plate 3.2)

White Shaved dipper juglets from Cyprus appear frequently in excavations in Palestine and in the North Sinai during LB IIA and B (late 18th and early 19th Dynasties) but are rare among imports to Egypt.[28] The juglets, which are the most common form in the ware, are hand-made and shaved vertically with a knife. They also exhibit the characteristic Cypriot handle that is attached to the body by inserting a dowel-like piece of clay to cement the join. White Shaved Ware is represented at Tell el-Borg by five sherds, with only three coming from Field II.

Ware

White Shaved ware exhibits a medium-soft fabric, fairly dense, and fires to a pale brown matte finish (Munsell 7.5YR 7/4). No core is visible and inclusions include fine sand, as well as some black and red grits.

Pottery Plate 3.2

2:1 Body of juglet, TBP 0279, Locus II.1, F -12. Ware: Cypriot White Shaved. Surface: Finger prints are seen on the inside while the exterior exhibits vertical shaving. *Parallel:* Åström, fig. LVIII:2-8. Amiran, pl. 55:1
2:2 Handle of juglet, TBP 0256, Field II.1, F-3. Ware: Cypriot White Shaved. The clay dowel used to attach the handle to the body is clearly visible.

Cypriot White Slipped Vessels (see Pottery Plate 3.2)

Fragments of four White Slipped bowls were found in Field II. These hemispherical bowls with wishbone-shaped handles are often called "milk bowls" in the literature. The more finely made White Slip I bowls were gradually replaced by a degenerate and less carefully decorated White Slip II bowl that flooded the market from Late Cypriot IIA1 to IIB (approximately 1425–1320 B.C.). Despite the fragmentary nature of the Tell el-Borg examples, they each exhibit one or more of the characteristics of White slip II, as set out in the article "White Slip Ware" by Popham.[29]

28. Celia J. Bergoffen, "Overland Trade in Northern Sinai: The Evidence of the Late Cypriot Pottery," *BASOR* 284 (1991) fig. 3.

29. Mervyn R. Popham, "White Slip Ware," in *The Swedish Cyprus Expedition, Vol. IV, Part 1C: The Late Cypriote Bronze Age Architecture and Pottery*, by Paul Åstrom (Lund: The Swedish Cyprus Expedition, 1972) 446–47, 454–56.

Ware

Cypriot White Slip[30] is a finely levigated clay, tempered with fine black and gray grits. The clay fires to a red-orange color (Munsell 2.5YR 5/8) with a slate gray core, which often dominates the section. The surface is covered inside and out with a thick white to light-gray slip with decoration, usually a ladder motif, on the exterior in black and brown paint. The bowls have very thin, brittle walls that may account for their fragmentary condition.

2:3 Bowl fragment, TBP 0057a, Locus II.2, A surface. Ware: WS. Surface: Brown- painted ladder decoration on white slip.
2:4 Rim of bowl, TBP 0269, Locus II.1, F -1. Ware: WSII Surface: Brown-painted ladder decoration on white slip. Row of brown dots along rim.
2:5 Bowl fragment, TBP 0275, Locus II.1, F-9. Ware: WS. Surface: Black-painted decoration on grayish-white slip. *Parallel:* Åström fig LXXXVI:2 described as late White Slip II.
2:6 Bowl fragment, TBP 0058a, Locus II.2, A surface. Ware: WS. Surface: Ladder decoration painted in black on white slip.

Mycenaean Vessels (see Pottery Plate 3.3)

Mycenaean pottery is easily recognized by its fine craftsmanship. These wheel-made, beautifully decorated vessels filled the demand for luxury items both for their valuable contents of scented oils and herbs as well as for their artistic merit. The great expansion of Mycenaean trade in the eastern Mediterranean coincided with the Amarna period in Egypt. At least 2000 Mycenaean sherds have been found at Amarna,[31] and these along with the whole Mycenaean IIIA vessels discovered there, have become one of the pegs upon which the Mycenaean and Palestinian chronology are based. Six Mycenaean fragments have been found at Tell el-Borg, so far only in Area 1 of Field II (for the entire corpus, see *Tell el-Borg I*, 495–501). Their fragmentary nature makes a meaningful discussion of their decoration impossible. The types of vessels represented by the fragments were all popular imports in Mycenaean IIIA (Late Bronze IIA in Palestine and Amarna Period in Egypt).[32]

Ware

The cream-colored ware (Munsell 10YR 8/4) is very fine, dense, hard, and well fired. No core is visible, and only under magnification can very fine grits be seen. The lustrous painted decoration, usually black and dark red-brown on a cream background, is applied with great technical skill.

Pottery Plate 3.3

3:1 Body of vessel, TBP 0260, Locus II.1, F-9. Ware: Mycenaean. Surface: Finely burnished, black and brown bands on a cream-slipped background.
3:2 Body of vessel, TBP 0259, Locus II.1, F-8/7.1. Restored from two joining sherds Ware: Mycenaean. Surface: Black bands on a burnished and cream-slipped background.
3:3 Body of vessel, TBP 0236, Locus II.1, F-1. Ware: Mycenaean. Surface: Black and brown horizontal bands on a burnished cream-slipped background. The linear decoration of rust brown

30. Hereafter White Slip will be abbreviated WS.

31. J. D. Bourriau, *Umm El-Ga'ab: Pottery from the Nile Valley before the Arab Conquest: Catalogue for the Exhibition Organized by the Fitzwilliam Museum* (Cambridge: Cambridge University Press, 1981) 124.

32. See P. A. Mountjoy, *Mycenaean Pottery: An Introduction* (Oxford: Oxford University Committee for Archaeology, 1993) chapter 2, for a user-friendly guide to Mycenaean vessel types that are categorized chronologically.

lines between two wider black bands is characteristic of Mycenaean III A 2, and is especially popular on stirrup jars.[33] *Parallels*: Mountjoy, pp. 77, 167–69

3:4 Neck and shoulder fragment from stirrup jar, TBP 0242, Locus II.1, C-2. Ware: Mycenaean. Surface: Black paint on a cream slipped background.

3:5 Base of vessel, TBP 0165, Locus II.1, Ca-1. Ware: Mycenaean. Surface: Horizontal black bands on a cream background.

Palestinian Vessels (see Pottery Plate 3.4)

The Sinai during the New Kingdom was a crossroads between Palestine and Egypt, so it is not surprising to find Palestinian domestic pottery at Tell el-Borg. The wares of these vessels are discussed individually.

Pottery Plate 3.4

4:1 Carinated bowl, TBP 0008, Locus II.1, A Surface. Rim: 15 cm. Ware: The dull brown (Munsell 5YR 5/3) fabric is medium coarse and soft with a thin black core. The fresh break is full of small and large angular white chunks along with abundant sand and black and red grits. Surface: Interior and exterior are covered with a thick, greenish yellow (Munsell 2.5YR 8/4) slip with faint traces of a white wavy line design on the exterior. Sand and pebbles appear through the slip. *Parallels*: Amiran, pl. 39:10, p. 129. During LB II A the sharp carination on the bowl that was popular in the preceding period, degenerates to form a ridge. These new Palestinian bowls also have concave disc bases. The Tell el-Borg example has both these characteristics.

4:2 Fragment of vessel, TBP 0273, Locus II.1, F-1. Ware: A hard, rust-colored paste (Munsell 2.5 YR 5/6) with no core. Inclusions consist of abundant angular, black grits visible even on the inside surface. Some fine sand is also present. Surface: Narrow red and black vertical lines painted on a cream-slipped background.

4:3 Carinated bowl, TBP 0278, Locus Field II.2 surface. Rim missing. Ware: The rust colored fabric (Munsell 2.5 YR 5/6) with a light brown core is very dense, medium hard and tempered with fine sand and black and white particles. Surface: Interior and exterior are coated with a light orange slip. The exterior is decorated with a "band and zigzag" design in black paint.

4:4 Rim and handles of flask, TBP 0249, Locus II.1, Ca-2. Rim: 4 cm. Ware: Pale brown gritty paste (Munsell 5 R 7/6) with a gray core and tempered with abundant sand. Surface: Greenish-gray slip. *Parallel:* Amiran, Photo 167, p. 166. A clay petal-like formation at the base of the Flask handle is characteristic of the Late Bronze IIA period in Palestine.

4:5 Rim of juglet, TBP 0060, Locus II.1, A-4. Rim: 2 cm. Ware: The paste although resembling a rust-colored silt (Munsell 5YR 5/6) is tempered with fine sand and black and white rock particles. Surface: Two bands of white paint on top of red slip decorate the rim. The one-handled juglet is a popular Palestinian form.[34]

4:6 Rim of amphora, TBP 0253, Locus II.1, C-2. Rim: 11 cm. Ware: The fabric is a medium hard, dull rust color (Munsell 5YR 6/6) with a brown core. Inclusions are abundant, angular, black particles. Surface: Coated with a thick layer of dull orange slip. Dated by William Dever[35] to the Pre-Amarna Period.

4:7 Amphora handle and body wall, TBP 0267, Locus II.1, F-4.3. Ware: A pale brown (Munsell 2.5YR 6/6), badly mixed paste with a gray-brown core. Inclusions consist of abundant sand, and large black and white particles. Surface: Self-slipped.

4:8 Amphora base, TBP 0148, Locus II.1, Ca-2. Ware: A red-brown dense fabric (Munsell 2.5 R 5/6) with a gray core. The clay has been well-levigated and tempered with some black grits and some very large limestone chunks. Surface: Coating of thick, light gray, slip. The wheel marks visible on the inside show that the vessel has been thrown from the bottom.

---

33. Mountjoy, *Mycenaean Pottery*, 72.

34. Ruth Amiran, *Ancient Pottery of the Holy Land. From its Beginnings in the Neolithic Period to the End of the Iron Age* (Jerusalem: Massada Press Ltd, 1969) 146.

35. Professor William Dever visited Tell el-Borg in 2002 and graciously shared his knowledge concerning Palestinian pottery with us.

Egyptian-Made Pottery

Nile Silt Wares

Nile B2

The most common ware found at Tell el-Borg is a Nile Silt clay that fires to a color that ranges from a cinnamon brown (Munsell 7.5YR 6/4) to a rusty orange (Munsell 2.5YR 6/8). The freshly chipped sections usually exhibit a black or red-black-red core. This ware, which is defined in the Vienna System[36] as Nile B2, is characterized by the presence of fine-to-medium mineral inclusions and a considerable amount of fine chaff, which is often visible on the surface.

Nile E

A sandy Nile Silt variant containing abundant large rounded sand grains and no obvious plant material occurs occasionally and is considered to be a local Sinai product.[37]

Nile B1

Less frequently found is Nile B1, a very fine silt, which is well-levigated and tempered with fine grits. This clay is used for thin-walled vessels.

Nile C

Nile C is a coarser version of Nile silt that is characterized by the dominance of straw both in the section and on the surface. Sand is also present but in lesser quantities. Surface treatments on all these silt wares often include red slip, occasionally cream slip, polishing, or burnishing. A few selected vessels are decorated with black, blue, white or red paint.

Marl A

Marl A is a clay imported from the area of Thebes in the south. It is often divided into A2, which is a very dense, homogeneous, pale red fabric (Munsell 5YR 5/6), and A4, which is a much coarser version. Both are tempered with fine sand and limestone particles. Examples of both these wares are infrequent at Tell el-Borg.

Marl B

Marl B is characterized in the "Vienna System" by its very gritty, gray-white to green surface. The fabric is very dense and contains abundant angular sand. It was used to manufacture medium- to large-sized vessels and occurred in the Second Intermediate Period and the 18th Dynasty in Upper Egypt. It occurs rarely in the north in 18th Dynasty contexts, where it is considered an import.[38]

Marl D

A small number of vessels in the corpus were manufactured of Marl D. The "Vienna System"[39] describes this ware as: a dense, hard fabric with abundant fine-to-medium particles of limestone

36. Hans-Åke Nordström and J. D. Bourriau, "Ceramic Technology: Clays and Fabrics," in Fascicle 2 of *An Introduction to Ancient Egyptian Pottery* (ed. D. Arnold and J. D. Bourriau; Mainz: von Zabern, 1993) 171.

37. David Aston, *Die Keramik des Grabungsplatzes, Q I. Teil 1: Corpus of Fabrics, Wares and Shapes* (Mainz: von Zabern.1998) 63, describes a similar silt, which predominates at Qantir. He calls it Nile E.

38. Nordström and Bourriau, "Ceramic Technology: Clays and Fabrics," 179

39. Ibid., 181.

added as temper to the clay. There can also be present fine-to-coarse sand grains and some dark rock material in the clay. The clay fires to grayish-brown to red-brown, often with no core. The ware is usually coated with a thick cream slip. The clay source or sources of Marl D may be in the Delta or Memphite region, where vessels found in this fabric are very common during the 18th and 19th Dynasties.[40]

Mixed Clay

The "Mixed Clay" fabrics have recently been recognized and described in the literature.[41] A few sherds of this ware have been found at Tell el-Borg. Macroscopic analysis of the fabric has revealed it to be Nile Silt with sand used as a filler, then coated with a thick Marl slip. The ware is distinguished by its hardness and density tempered by fine sand and few organic remains. The section reveals a wide distinct black core with narrow red-brown outer zones. A common variant is distinguished by abundant fine limestone inclusions. The surface of this ware is coated with a thick cream or peach slip. Some vessels show brush strokes applied in streaks, often in random directions. Mixed Clay fabric is important for ceramicists and archaeologists, since its chronological range at Memphis begins first in 19th Dynasty contexts and continues into the Third Intermediate Period. It is generally used for particular amphorae and eventually replaces the Marl D amphorae.

Blue-Painted Vessels (see Pottery Plate 3.5)

Blue-painted pottery is widely recognized as a marker of the Amarna period in Egyptian history. A surprisingly large body of sherds decorated with blue paint has been found at Tell el-Borg, most of which was found in Field IV, the area of the two fosses. Most of the examples found in Field II exhibit a design of horizontal bands of blue separated by black or red lines on a cream- or peach-slipped background. Foliage is represented by a band of pendant petals outlined in black. This characteristic design reached its zenith in the 19th Dynasty, and these luxury vessels at Tell el-Borg may have been imported from the Ramessides' royal residence at Pi-Ramesses in the Eastern Delta.

Pottery Plate 3.5

5:1 Rim of small bowl, TBP 0318, Locus II.2, E-5.9. Rim: 15 cm. Ware: Nile B1. Surface: This fine thin-walled vessel is coated both inside and out with a burnished red slip. A layer of blue paint has been added to the rim, a narrow line on the exterior and a wider line on the interior.

5:2 Body fragment of jar, TBP 0266, Locus II.1, F-11. Ware: Nile B2. Surface: The decoration features the popular motif of a band of pendant petals outlined in black within a register of black and red bands on a pale peach background. The bottom fragment was found on the surface in 2000 while the top sherd was found in a secure locus in the foundation trench of Unit F. This highlights the amount of destruction and disturbance in this area in the past.

5:3 Jar, TBP 0246, Locus II.2 surface. Rim: 16 cm. Ware: Nile B2. Surface: A frieze of pendant petals encircles the shoulder of the jar with the panels above and below, separated by black bands and empty of decoration. The blue paint has been applied over a background of peach slip. Jars like this example, with a medium-tall neck and wide mouth are typical of the late 18th and 19th Dynasty blue-painted vessels.

5:4 Rim of small jar, TBP 0118, Locus II.1, A-6. Rim: 7 cm. Ware: Nile B1. Surface: The very thin-walled neck and rim of this fine vessel is slightly ridged on the exterior and painted blue with a

40. J. D. Bourriau and P. T. Nicholson, "Marl Clay Pottery Fabrics of the New Kingdom from Memphis, Saqqara and Amarna," *JEA* 78 (1992) 37.

41. J. D. Bourriau, L. M. V. Smith, and P. T. Nicholson, *New Kingdom Pottery Fabrics: Nile Clay and Mixed Nile/Marl Fabrics from Memphis and Amarna* (London: Egypt Exploration Society, 2000) 19.

red band where the neck joins the body.

5:5 Fragment of Bes Jar, TBP 0286, Locus II.2 surface. Rim: Missing. Ware: The ware is unusual.[42] The section is a very dense dark gray (Munsell 2.5 Y 4/1) with a dark brown blended core. The fabric is unusually hard and heavy, gritty to the touch and tempered with numerous very fine grits. This obscure fragment perhaps comes from the neck of a Bes Jar judging from the appearance of feather plumes. The clay has been modeled by hand or made in a mould. Surface: Coating of a pale brown slip that has worn off in many places. Traces of blue paint are visible on top of the slip.

5:6 Body fragment of jar, TBP 0203, Locus II.2, A Surface. Ware: Nile B2. Surface: Peach-slipped background. Blue panels divided by black straight and zigzag register lines.

Egyptian Decorated Pottery (see Pottery Plate 3.6)

From the early- to mid-18th Dynasty, Egyptian potters decorated their pots with linear patterns in black, brown, or reddish-brown paint influenced by the styles in nearby Palestine. By the time of Thutmose III ceramics decorated with painted spot and band patterns and red and black horizontal bands became very popular. This was all to change with the introduction of the blue-painted pottery of the Amarna Period. Although Tell el-Borg has produced considerable amounts of blue-painted pottery, a few decorated sherds were found that reflect the earlier years of the 18th Dynasty. Most of these fragments came originally from fine marl vessels dating from the first half of the 18th Dynasty.

Pottery Plate 3.6

6:1 Neck and rim of jar, TBP 0283, Locus II.2, E-15.1. Rim: 15 cm. Ware: Marl B. Surface: The surface fires a pale, gritty gray-green on which is painted a reddish-brown band between two black bands.

6:2 Body of jar, TBP 0335, Locus II 1, F-40.1 (pre-stone installation). Rim missing. Ware: Marl A2. Surface: Thick red slip on which is painted wide and narrow horizontal black bands.

6:3 Shoulder(?) fragment of jar, TBP 0274, Locus II 1, F-13. Rim missing. Ware: Marl D. Surface: Cream slip, decorated with descending groups of black and red bands alternating with vertical spot and band motif.

6:4 Body fragment of jar, TBP 0100, Locus II 1, A Surface. Ware: Marl A. Surface: Cream-slipped background decorated with a wide horizontal black band and traces of black cross- hatching. *Parallel* Nordström, Plate 31 IIIP/5D/e–f, three examples.

6:5 Body of lentoid flask, TBP 0252, Locus II 2, D Surface. Ware: Marl D. Surface: Cream slip with black-painted concentric circles. Traces of light black lines continue the decoration.

6:6 Neck and rim of jar, TBP 0285, Locus II 1, F-12.3 (foundation trench). Rim: 16 cm. Ware: Marl D. Surface: Thick cream slip. Three black, horizontal bands encircle the neck. Black tics are painted on the rim. This motif was a popular decoration at the time of Thutmose III.

Stamped Amphorae (see Pottery Plate 3.7)

Field II produced a considerable amount of ceramic material, including six of the total nine stamped vessels that were found in three seasons of excavation at Tell el-Borg. Five of the six came from the ancient debris from within the pit in Field II, Area 1. The stamped cartouches, naming a variety of Amarna kings have previously been published.[43] (See further in Excursus II

42. J. D. Bourriau, "A Double Vase," in *Egypt's Golden Age: The Art of Living in the New Kingdom 1558–1085 B.C.* (ed. E. Brovarski, S. K. Doll, and R. E. Freed; Boston: Museum of Fine Arts, 1982) 101, 102. In her description of Figure Vases, Bourriau mentions an unusual, dense and hard clay that is neither Nile Silt nor one of the well-known foreign clays that are imported to Egypt. She suggests that it might come from a specialized workshop.

43. James K. Hoffmeier and Jacobus Van Dijk, "New Light on the Amarna Period from North Sinai," *JEA* 96 (2010) 191–205.

below.) All the stamped amphorae were manufactured from Marl D. This ware was very common in the Memphite area and the Eastern Delta during the late 18th and 19th Dynasties. The shape of these Amphorae fall into Colin Hope's[44] category 1a, which remained popular from the reign of Amenhotep III into the Ramesside Period. It is apparent that the elites of Tell el-Borg enjoyed high quality wines imported from the capital at Memphis and later from Pi-Ramesses.`

Pottery Plate 3.7

7:1 Stamped amphora handle, TBP 0301, Locus II.2, D-5.5. Ware: Marl D. A very, damaged cartouche is stamped on the upper handle of the amphorae.

7:2 Stamped amphora handle, TBP 0270, Locus II.1, F-11.2. Ware: Marl D. A damaged cartouche with only a seated figure visible is stamped sideways on the upper handle of this amphora.

7:3 Stamped amphora handle, TBP 0222, Locus II.1, C-2. Ware: Marl D. The *ʿnḫ ḫprw rʿ wʿ-n-rʿ* (Ankh-kheperu-ra wa-en-ra) is stamped on the upper handle. Another stamp impression of this ephemeral king was found in Field IV (TBO 0077 in *Tell el-Borg I*, 137–42).

7:4 Stamped Amphora Base, TBP 0248, Locus II.1, Ca-2. Ware: Marl D. The prenomen of King Tutankhamun, (Neb-kheperu-ra) is stamped on the base of the amphora. See Excursus II in this volume for discussion.

7:5 Stamped Amphora Handle, TBP 0221, Locus II.1, C-2. Ware: Marl D. Thin-walled. The prenomen of king Tutankhamun (*nb ḫprw rʿ* — Neb-kheperu-ra) is stamped on the upper handle.

7:6 Stamped Amphora Handle, TBP 0223, II.1, D-2. Ware: Marl D. The stamp on the upper handle forms two opposing bow-shaped lines that intersect each other. This stamp impression resembles the symbol of the "two bows" associated with the goddess Neith (R-24 in Gardiner's sign list).[45] It could also be a weaving tool since Neith is also associated with that trade. It can stand for the letter "*n*" in Late Egyptian and has also been found used as the letter "*m*." The symbol may have been used as a monogram on a late New Kingdom jar handle. If so, the date is entirely appropriate.

Pot-Marks (see Pottery Plate 3.8)

A total of 16 sherds with incised potters' marks were found at Tell el-Borg, 7 of which were uncovered in Field II. All 7 were fragments of amphorae or storage jars and were manufactured from a Marl D clay that was a popular ware in the Delta in the 18th and 19th Dynasties.[46] These enigmatic marks have aroused the curiosity of ceramicists for many years. They have been interpreted as marks identifying particular workshops or potters or as indicators of certain products or their quantity. A recent study of late 18th Dynasty pot-marks from Malkata and North Karnak by Colin Hope found that the infrequent practice of incising marks on vessels before firing encompassed many types of vessels but in particular two types of large silt storage jars. These two types were also marked with a specific range of signs, perhaps indicating a special purpose.[47] At Tell el-Borg we are beginning to classify all the pot-marks in order to compare them with each

44. Colin A. Hope, *Pottery of the New Kingdom: Three Studies*. Victoria College, Archaeology Research Unit, Occasional Paper No. 2. (Burwood: Victoria College Press, 1989) fig. 2

45. I am grateful to Steven Shubert of the University of Toronto for his comments on this stamp impression.

46. Nordström and Bourriau, "Ceramic Technology: Clays and Fabrics," 181. Amphorae manufactured from Marl D ware are very common in the Faiyum and Memphis area and may only occur in the Sinai as an import from that area.

47. Colin A. Hope, "Some Remarks on Potmarks of the late Eighteenth Dynasty," in *Studies on Ancient Egypt in Honour of H. S. Smith* (ed. Anthony Leahy and John Tait; London: Egypt Exploration Society, 1999) 139. Hope presents a credible argument that the Malkata jars held beer destined for consumption in the palace.

other and with those found at other sites. Hope's study with its extensive catalogue of pot-marks greatly advances our understanding of this subject and points out the importance of publishing these poorly understood marks.

Pottery Plate 3.8

8:1 Pot-Mark on the Base of an Amphora Handle, TBP 0319, Locus II:1, F-4. Ware: Marl D. Surface: Coated with a thick gray-green slip. The potter created the pot-mark of three circles by jabbing a stick or tool into the unfired clay.

8:2 Pot-Mark on Amphora Body, TPB 0078, Locus II.2, A surface. Ware: Marl D. Surface: Thick cream slip. A hook-like mark accompanied by some obscure lines was incised into the unfired clay.

8:3 Pot-Mark on base of Amphora Handle, TBP 0271, Locus II.1, D-6. Ware: Marl D. Surface: Thick gray green slip. The pot-mark of two vertical lines has been incised before firing at the base of the handle. Three similar examples were found at Tell el-Borg.[48] *Parallel:* Hope, 1999, p. 141: C14.

8:4 Pot-Mark on Amphora Body, TPB 0255, Locus II.1, C 2. Ware: Marl D. Surface: Cream slip. A cross-shaped pot-mark was incised into the body of the vessel. *Parallel:* Hope, 1999, p. 141: C255A.[49]

8:5 Pot-Mark near Base of Jar, TBP 0344, Locus II.2, I-15. Ware: Marl D. Surface: Cream slip. The pot-mark shaped like a vertical zigzag with an accompanying dot is incised through the slip into the unfired body of the vessel. *Parallel*: Aston, 1998, p. 499, jar 1956. The Ramesside amphora from Qantir is manufactured from Marl D and has been incised with a similar pot mark on its base.

8:6 Pot-Mark on Amphora Handle, TBP 0292, Locus II.2, E-15. Ware: Marl D. Surface: Thick, cream slip. (Munsell 10YR 7/3). The pot-mark of one vertical line crossed by two horizontal lines has been incised on the top of the handle before firing. *Parallel:* Hope, 1999, p. 142: C62A.[50]

8:7 Pot-Mark on Amphora Handle, TPB 0254, Locus II.1, C-2. Ware: Marl D. Surface: Thick cream slip. Two vertical lines are incised pre-firing, at the base of the handle.

Pottery from Selected Loci (Pottery Plates 3.9–3.15)

Field II, Area 1

Pottery from stone-lined well (see pp. 28–59):

- abundant fragments of simple bowls (at least half of which were red-slipped);
- many large thick-walled bowls;
- amphora fragments (both Egyptian Marl D and Palestinian wares); the vessels stamped with the cartouches of the Amarna Kings come from Area 1;
- silt jars (many red-slipped);
- a small number of marl bowls and flasks;
- a small number of fragments of imported Cypriot White Slip, Base Ring juglets and Mycenaean jars that date to the late 18th to early 19th Dynasties (see Pottery Plates 3.1, 3.2, and 3.3);
- fragments of blue-painted jars popular in the late 18th and 19th Dynasties (see Pottery Plate 3.5).

48. This particular sign appeared four times on Hope's popular storejar type #20 but did not occur on any marl amphorae.

49. This cross-shaped mark appears 107 times on Hope's silt Jar type #20 and 17 other times on various vessels, none of which was a marl amphora.

50. This pot-mark appears three times on Hope's silt jar type #20.

The earliest sherds in the fill were small red-slipped bowls with distinctive black-painted rims dating to the early- to mid-18th Dynasty. The latest sherds comprise a group of jars manufactured from a mixed marl/silt clay. This particular ware became popular in the late 19th and 20th Dynasties, replacing the widely used Marl D. Therefore, it appears that the pit was still being filled at least in the late 19th Dynasty.

Sherds from Sealed Loci in Field II, Area 2, Unit F

Sherds from the multiple occupation layers that predate the excavation of the subterranean stone installation were separated from the corpus for examination. These sherds were studied as a group with the hope of extracting more relevant information concerning their date.

Marl and Foreign Jars (see Pottery Plate 3.9)

Pottery Plate 3.9

9:1 Rim of Jar, Locus F-9.4. Rim: 10 cm. Ware: Marl A4.
9:2 Rim of Jar, Locus F-4.1. Rim: 10 cm. Ware: Marl D. Surface: Thick cream slip.
9:3 Rim of Amphora, Locus F-12.6. Rim: 10 cm. Ware: Palestinian.
9:4 Rim of Jar(one of two), Locus F-25.2. Rim: 10 cm. Ware: Marl D with cream slip. This rim belongs to a well known long-necked table amphora with two horizontal handles that appears in the Amarna repertoire of the late 18th dynasty. *Parallels:* Peet and Woolley, Plate LIII: pot LXXVI/228.
9:5 Rim of Jar, Locus F-25.1. Rim: 11 cm. Ware: Marl D with peach slip.
9:6 Rim of Jar, Locus F-25.1. Rim: 11 cm. Ware: Marl D with peach slip.
9:7 Body of Jar, Locus F-30.1. Rim: 12 cm. Ware: Marl A
9:8 Rim of Jar, Locus F-41.1. Rim: 16 cm. Ware: Marl D. Surface: Cream slip.
9:9 Rim of 'Meat Jar', Locus F-5. Rim: 17 cm. Ware: Mixed Clay. Surface: Cream slip. This vessel form appears first in the late 18th Dynasty and continues in popularity until the beginning of the 21st Dynasty. It was manufactured from various marl wares, especially Marl D in the north, and was gradually replaced by the mixed clay fabric during the 19th Dynasty. By the 21st Dynasty, most of these vessels were manufactured from the mixed clay fabric.

Silt Jars (see Pottery Plate 3.10)

Pottery Plate 10

10:1 Rim of Jar, Locus F-43. Rim: 10 cm. Ware: Nile B2. (no obvious sand temper).
10:2 Rim of Jar, Locus F-9.4. Rim: 10 cm. Ware: Nile B2. Surface: Abraded.
10:3 Rim of Jar, Locus F-25.2. Rim: 10 cm. Ware: Coarse Nile B2
10:4 Rim of Jar, Locus F-14.1. Rim: 10 cm. Ware: Nile B2. Surface: Soot on rim.
10:5 Rim of Jar, Locus F-25.2. Rim: 10 cm. Ware: Nile B2. Surface: Thick red slip.
10:6 Rim of Jar, Locus F-30.1. Rim: 11 cm. Ware: Fine Nile B2.
10:7 Rim of Jar. Locus F-5. Rim 11 cm. Ware: Fine Nile B2. Surface: Red slip.
10:8 Rim of Jar, Locus F-9.4. Rim: 12 cm. Ware: Nile B2.
10:9 Rim of Jar, Locus F-25.1. Rim: 12 cm. Ware: Fine Nile B2.
10:10 Rim of Jar, Locus F-40.1. Rim 15 cm. Ware: Nile B2. Surface: blackened with soot.
10:11 Rim of Jar, Locus F-14.1. Rim: 20 cm. Ware: Nile B2.

Silt Bowls (see Pottery Plate 3.11)

Pottery Plate 3.11

11:1 Small Bowl/Jar, Locus F-40.1. Rim: 6 cm. Ware: Nile B2.
11:2 Carinated Bowl, TBP 029,. Locus F-25.1. Rim: 15 cm. Ware : Nile B2. The top of the rim has been impressed with a tool creating a series of small indents.
11:3 Carinated Bowl, Locus F-25.2. Rim: 15 cm. Ware Nile B2. Surface: Thick red slip in and out with a black painted rim. This type of bowl is characteristic of the early to mid-18th Dynasty.
11:4 Bowl (one of eight), Locus F-25.2. Rim: 20 cm. Ware: Nile B2. Surface: Six of the examples had a thick red slip in and out. Red-slipped bowls were very common in the 19th Dynasty.
11:5 Bowl (one of two), Locus F-25.2. Rim: 20 cm. Ware: Nile B2. Surface: Abraded.
11:6 Carinated Bowl, Locus F-5. Rim: 20 cm. Ware: Nile B2. Surface: Red slip.
11:7 Bowl, Locus F-10.2. Rim: 20 cm. Ware: Nile B2.
11:8 Bowl (one of two), Locus F-25.2. Rim: 25 cm. Ware: Nile B2. Surface: Red- slipped in and out.

Large Silt Bowls (see Pottery Plate 3.12)

Pottery Plate 3.12

12:1 Bowl (one of seven), Locus F-25.2. Rim: 25 cm. Ware: Nile B2. Surface: Five of the examples are coated with red slip in and out.
12:2 Carinated Bowl, Locus F-30.1. Rim: 27 cm. Ware: Nile B2. Surface: Thick red slip in and out.
12:3 Bowl (one of three), Locus F-25.1 Rim 31 cm. Ware: Nile B2. Surface: One of the examples was coated with a thick red- slip in and out.
12:4 Thick-walled Bowl (one of two), Locus F-10.2. Rim: 34 cm. Ware: Nile B2
12:5 Carinated Bowl, Locus F-44.1. Rim: 36 cm. Ware: Nile B2. Surface: Red- slipped in and out.
12:6 Bowl, Locus F-41.1. Rim: 40 cm. Ware: Nile B2. Surface: Red-slipped in and out.

Foreign Imports

See description for sherds in Pottery Plates 3.1, 3.2, and 3.3

3.1:6 Body sherd from BR II Juglet.
3.1:10 Base of BR Juglet.
3.2:5 Bowl, WS, ladder decoration
3.3:1 Body sherd of Vessel, Mycenaean.
3.3:2 Body of Vessel, Mycenaean.

Egyptian Vessels

3.6:2 Body of Jar. Ware: Marl. Surface: Red-slipped and decorated with black horizontal bands.

Not illustrated:

- Bases – total 2
- Decorated sherds, black bands on cream slip – total 2
- Carinated Bowl, Marl – total 1

This corpus of ceramic material provides evidence for the date of the area before the stone installation was dug. The latest material in this corpus, the mixed clay "meat jar," dates at least into the 19th Dynasty, only marginally earlier than the fill of the pit, and must have been deposited only years or decades before the large pit was dug. The presence of the Cypriot and Mycenaean fragments reflect a late 18th/early 19th Dynasty date as well. The early 19th Dynasty, therefore, provides a plausible *terminus ad quem* for the construction of the stone installation.

The presence of the earlier material in this corpus reflects residual sherds that have been removed from their original deposit due to pitting, earth-moving, and leveling activities. Even in antiquity, sherds were being moved about the site. It is important, therefore, to locate some of these original early deposits before modern disturbances can eliminate them forever.

Field II, Area 2

Sherds from Selected Loci in Field II, Area 2, Unit F

Field II, Area 2 contained a broad mud-brick foundation for a large structure. Within this foundation lay three square pits. Fortunately for us, the pits at their lowest level contained pottery sherds dating to the early- to mid-18th Dynasties. These sherds may have been lying in situ on or under an earlier surface predating the building of the structure.

Loci 10, 12, and 14 represent the three loci located immediately above the earliest levels, and despite their small sizes and worn condition, every sherd was scrutinized. Black-rimmed bowls are a ceramic marker for the early- to mid-18th Dynasty,[51] and we were delighted to find ten tiny fragments[52] of rim sherds from simple bowls exhibiting black-painted rims on red-slipped Nile silt. Typical mid-18th Dynasty decoration consisting of black-painted horizontal stripes on red-slipped silt vessels were in these loci, as well as black painted designs on marl. Also present were fragments from a single red-rimmed bowl and from numerous bowls with red-slipped surfaces. Unlike the black rims, these red decorative elements remained popular into the late 18th and 19th Dynasties.

The lowest and earliest loci, 18[53] and 11, also contained seven tiny fragments of simple bowls with black rims on red-slipped silt bowls along with red sherds decorated with black horizontal stripes. Fragments of simple silt bowls covered with red slip were ubiquitous here. All the sherds from these two early loci are presented here.

Sherds from Loci F-11 and F-18

Marl and Silt Jars (see Pottery Plate 3.13)

Pottery Plate 3.13

13:1 Rim of Jar, Locus F-11. Rim: 10 cm. Ware: Marl A.
13:2 Rim of Jar, Locus F-18.1. Rim: 12 cm. Ware: Marl A2.
13:3 Rim of Jar, Locus F-18.1. Rim: 13 cm. Ware: Marl D. Surface: Cream slip.
13:4 Rim of Jar, Locus F-18.2. Rim: 17.5 cm. Ware: Marl A4.
13:5 Rim of Jar, Locus F-11. Rim: 11 cm. Ware: Nile B2. Surface: Red slip. Black bands.

Silt Bowls (see Pottery Plates 3.14–3.15)

Pottery Plate 3.14

14:1 Base of Bowl, Locus F-18.2. Base: 4 cm. Ware: Nile B2. Surface: Red- slipped in and out.
14:2 Bowl, Locus F-18.1. Rim: 12 cm. Ware: Nile B2. Surface: Red-slipped in and out. Black rim.
14:3 Bowl, Locus F- 18.1. Rim: 12 cm. Ware: Nile B2. Surface: Red-slipped in and out. Black rim.
14:4 Bowl, Locus F-18.2. Rim: 15 cm. Ware: Nile B2. Surface: Red-slipped in and out. Black rim.
14:5 Bowl, Locus F-11. Rim: 16 cm. Ware: Nile B2.

51. Bourriau, *Umm El-Ga'ab*, 72.

52. The fragments were very tiny, and much effort was spent trying to match the various sherds in order to represent the true number of bowls.

53. Locus 11 is located below Locus 10; Locus 18 is located below Locus 14.

14:6 Bowl, Locus F-11. Rim: 17 cm. Ware: Nile B2.
14:7 Bowl, Locus F-11. Rim: 17 cm. Ware: Nile B2. Surface: Red-slipped in and out. Black rim.
14:8 Bowl, Locus F-11. Rim: 17.5 cm. Ware: Nile B2.
14:9 Bowl, Locus F-18.1. Rim: 18 cm. Ware: Fine Nile B2.
14:10 Bowl, Locus F-11. Rim: 20 cm. Ware: Nile B2.
14:11 Bowl, Locus F-11. Rim: 20 cm. Ware: Nile B2.

Pottery Plate 3.15

15:1 Bowl, Locus F-11. Rim: 20 cm. Ware Nile B2
15:2 Bowl, Locus F-11. Rim: 20 cm. Ware: Nile B2. Surface: Red-slipped in and out. Black rim.
15:3 Bowl, Locus F-18.1. Rim: 21 cm. Ware: Nile B2. Surface: Red-slipped in and out. Black rim.
15:4 Body Fragment of Vessel, Locus F-18. Body: 21 cm. Ware: Nile B2. Surface: Uncoated. Black-painted band .
15:5 Bowl, Locus F-11. Rim: 22 cm. Ware: Nile B2.
15:6 Bowl, Locus F-11. Rim: 24 cm. Ware: Nile B2.
15:7 Bowl, Locus F-11. Rim: 25 cm. Ware: Nile B2.
15:8 Bowl, Locus F-11. Rim: 25 cm. Ware: Nile B2. Surface: Red- slipped in and out. Black rim.
15:9 Bowl, Locus F-11. Rim: 30 cm. Ware: Nile B2.
15:10 Bowl, Locus F-18.1. Rim: 30 cm. Ware: Nile B2 with large particles of limestone.

Summary

Several black-rimmed bowl fragments, which are markers for the early- to mid-18th Dynasty dates, have appeared throughout the site in the various mixes and fills, and it is gratifying to finally have an early sealed context in which their appearance is entirely appropriate. The presence of jars made from Theban Marls, which were popular in the pre-Amarna years, as well as the red-slipped jars decorated with horizontal black bands, also point to an early date. We can now justify rolling back the date of the occupation at the site to the early- to mid-18th Dynasty, with the area around Locus F-11 and F-18 in Field II.2 being one of the proven locations for early activity at Tell el-Borg. This is a time in Tell el-Borg's history when the bulk of imports came from the Nile Valley and from as far south as Thebes. The advent of the Amarna Period launched the era of blue-painted pottery and a yearning for luxurious imports that gave new importance to the Northern Sinai and to Tell el-Borg as an important transit center for the importation of luxury ceramics from abroad.

The pottery in this report is a representative sample of the ceramic material found in Field II. It is abundantly clear that the majority of ceramics belong to the Amarna Period and later Ramesside Period. The ubiquitous fragments of red-slipped bowls, the vessels with Amarna blue-painted decoration, the jar sealings naming Amarna Kings, in addition to the wealth of fine imports from Cyprus and Greece reflect the richness of the site in antiquity as well as help corroborate the late-18th and 19th Dynasty date. With the addition of the earlier material, however, we can now suggest that Tell el-Borg was inhabited at least from the beginning of the 18th to the end of the 19th Dynasties.

Works Cited in Excursus I

Amiran, Ruth
1969 *Ancient Pottery of the Holy Land, from its Beginnings in the Neolithic Period to the End of the Iron Age.* Jerusalem: Massada.

Aston, David

1998 *Die Keramik des Grabungsplatzes. Q I. Teil 1, Corpus of Fabrics, Wares and Shapes.* Mainz: von Zabern.

Åström, Paul

1972 *The Swedish Cyprus Expedition, Vol. IV, Part 1C: The Late Cypriote Bronze Age Architecture and Pottery*. With a contribution by M. R. Popham. Lund: The Swedish Cyprus Expedition.

Bergoffen, Celia J.

1991 "Overland Trade in Northern Sinai: The Evidence of the Late Cypriot Pottery." *BASOR* 284: 59–79.

Bourriau, J. D.

1981 *Umm El-Ga'ab: Pottery from the Nile Valley before the Arab Conquest: Catalogue for the Exhibition organized by the Fitzwilliam Museum.* Cambridge: Cambridge University Press.

1982 "A Double Vase." Pp. 83-84 in *Egypt's Golden Age: The Art of Living in the New Kingdom 1558–1085 B.C.*, ed. E. Brovarski, S. K. Doll, and R. E. Freed. Boston: Museum of Fine Arts.

Bourriau, J. D., and Nicholson, P. T.

1992 "Marl Clay Pottery Fabrics of the New Kingdom from Memphis, Saqqara and Amarna." *JEA* 78: 29–91.

Bourriau, J. D., Smith, L. M. V., and P. T. Nicholson.

2000 *New Kingdom Pottery Fabrics: Nile Clay and Mixed Nile/Marl Fabrics from Memphis and Amarna.* London: Egypt Exploration Fund.

Gittlen, Barry M.

1981 "The Cultural and Chronological Implications of the Cypro-Palestinian Trade during the Late Bronze Age." *BASOR* 241: 49–81.

Hoffmeier, James K., and Van Dijk, Jacobus

2010 "New Light on the Amarna Period from North Sinai." *JEA* 96: 191–205.

Hope, Colin A.

1989 *Pottery of the New Kingdom: Three Studies.* Victoria College, Archaeology Research Unit, Occasional Paper No. 2. Burwood: Victoria College Press.

1999 "Some Remarks on Potmarks of the late Eighteenth Dynasty." Pp. 121–46 in *Studies on Ancient Egypt in Honour of H. S. Smith,* ed. Anthony Leahy and John Tait. London: Egypt Exploration Fund.

Kromholz, Alfred H.

1984 "Imported Cypriot Pottery." Pp. 16–20 in *Excavations at Tel Mevorakh (1973–1976)*, ed. Ephraim Stern. Qedem: Monographs of the Institute of Archaeology, The Hebrew University of Jerusalem 18. Jerusalem: The Hebrew University.

Merrillees, R. S.

1968 *The Cypriote Bronze Age Pottery Found in Egypt*. Studies in Mediterranean Archaeology 18. Lund: P. Åström.

Mountjoy, P. A.

1993 *Mycenaean Pottery: An Introduction*. Oxford University Committee for Archaeology Monograph No. 36. Oxford: Oxford University Committee for Archaeology.

Nordström, Hans-Åke

1977 "A Classification of the Wheel-Made Wares" Pp. 60–67 in *New Kingdom Pharaonic Sites: The Pottery*, by Rostislav Holthoer. The Scandinavian Joint Expedition to Sudanese Nubia 5:1. Lund: Berlings.

Nordström, Hans-Åke, and Bourriau, J. D.

1993 Ceramic Technology: Clays and Fabrics. Pp. 147–90 in Fascicle 2 of *An Introduction to Ancient Egyptian Pottery*, ed. D. Arnold and J. D. Bourriau. Mainz: von Zabern.

Peet, T. Eric, and Woolley, C. Leonard

1923 *The City of Akhenaten Part I: Excavations of 1921 and 1922 at El-Amarneh.* Oxford: Egypt Exploration Fund; reprinted 1984.

Popham, Mervyn R.

1972 "White Slip Ware." Pp. 431–71 in *The Swedish Cyprus Expedition, Vol. IV, Part 1C: The Late Cypriote Bronze Age Architecture and Pottery*, by Paul Åstrom. Lund: The Swedish Cyprus Expedition.

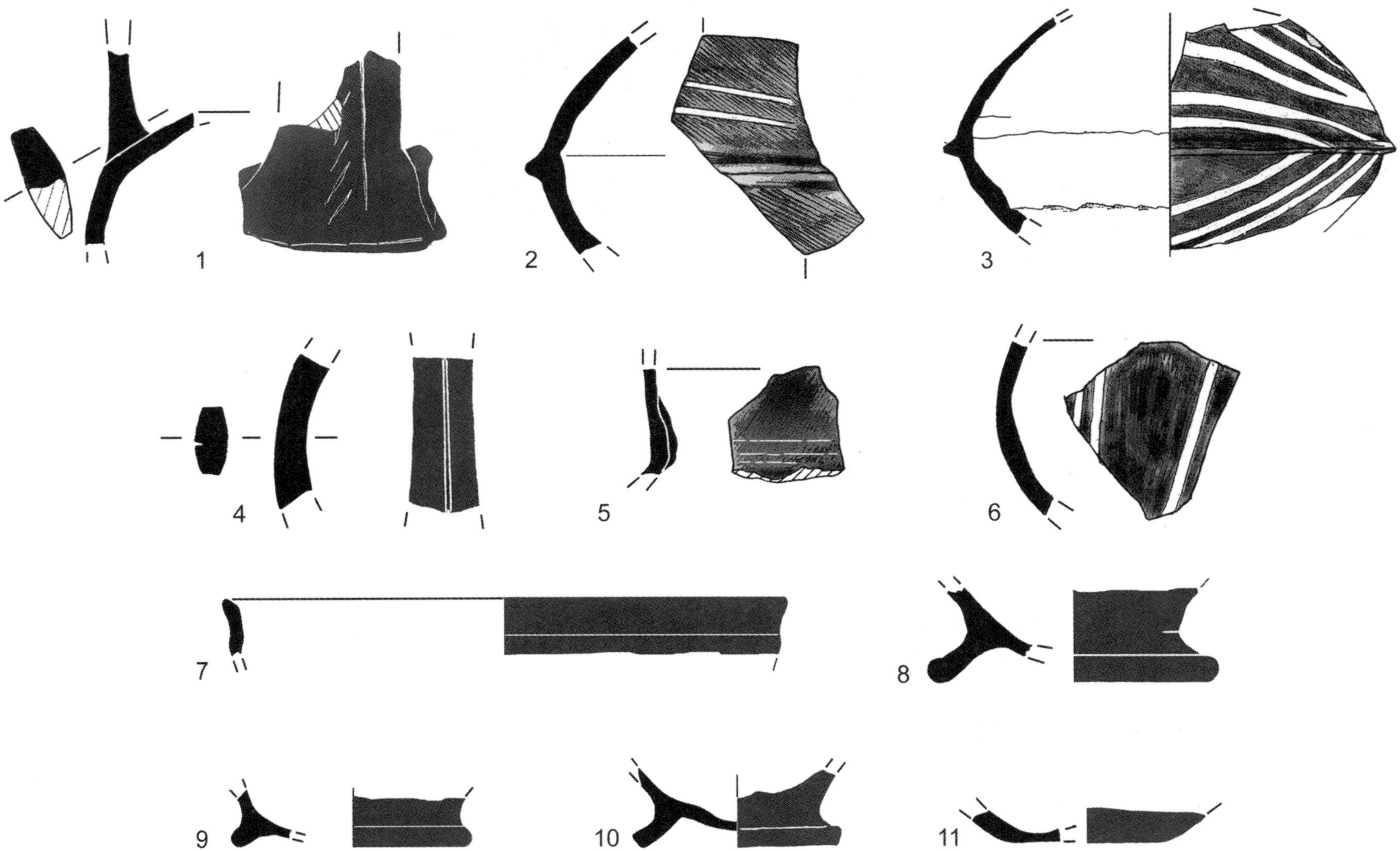

Pottery Plate 3.1: Cypriot Base Ring Ware

(Computerized by L. Pinch-Brock)

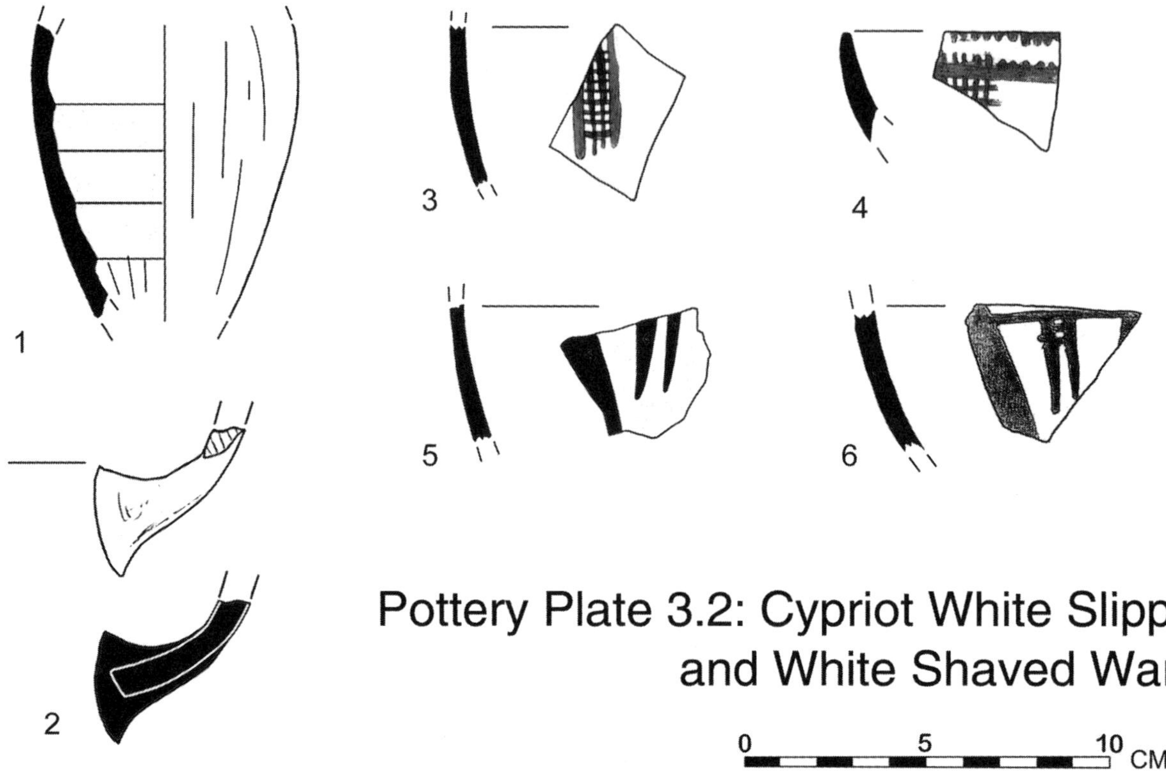

Pottery Plate 3.2: Cypriot White Slipped and White Shaved Wares

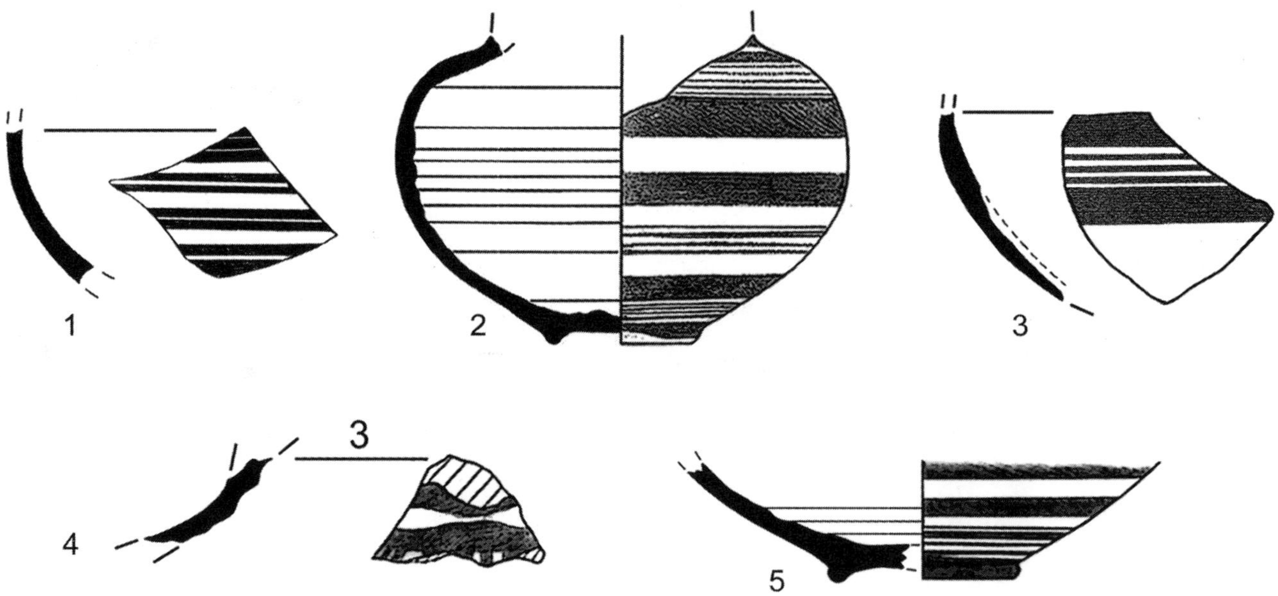

Pottery Plate 3.3: Mycenean Vessels

(Computerized by L. Pinch-Brock)

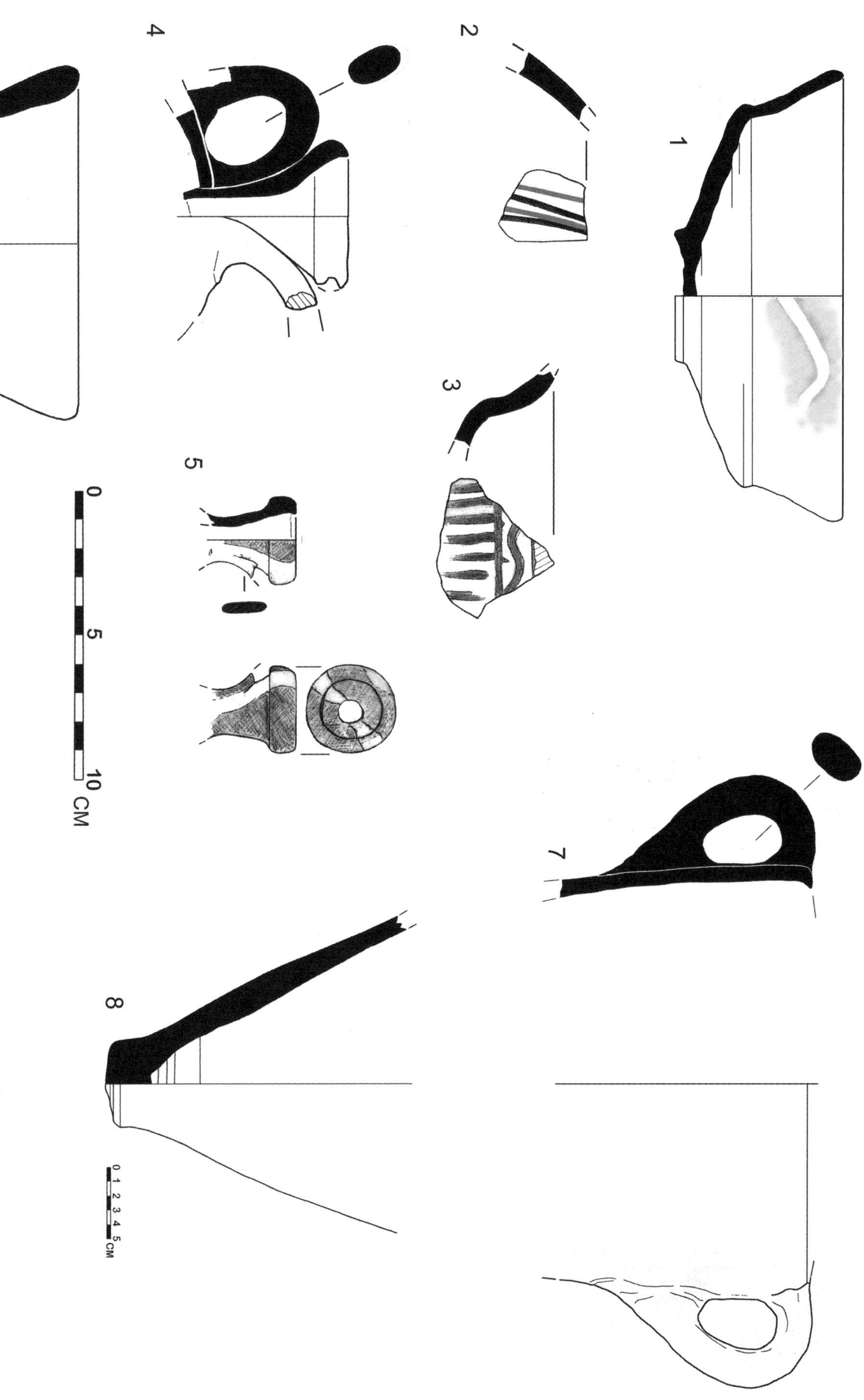

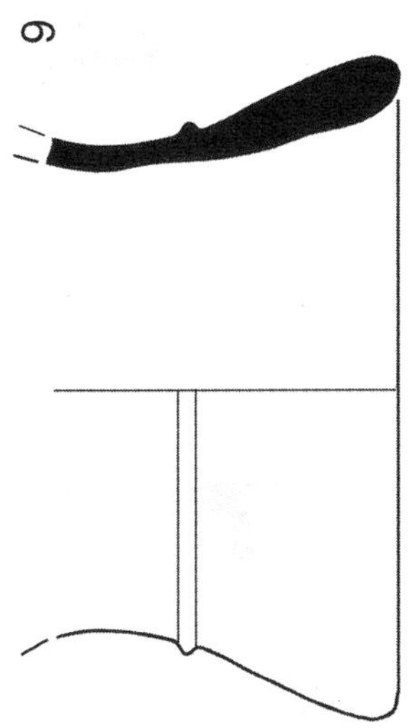

Pottery Plate 3.4: Palestinian Vessels

(Computerized by L. Pinch-Brock)

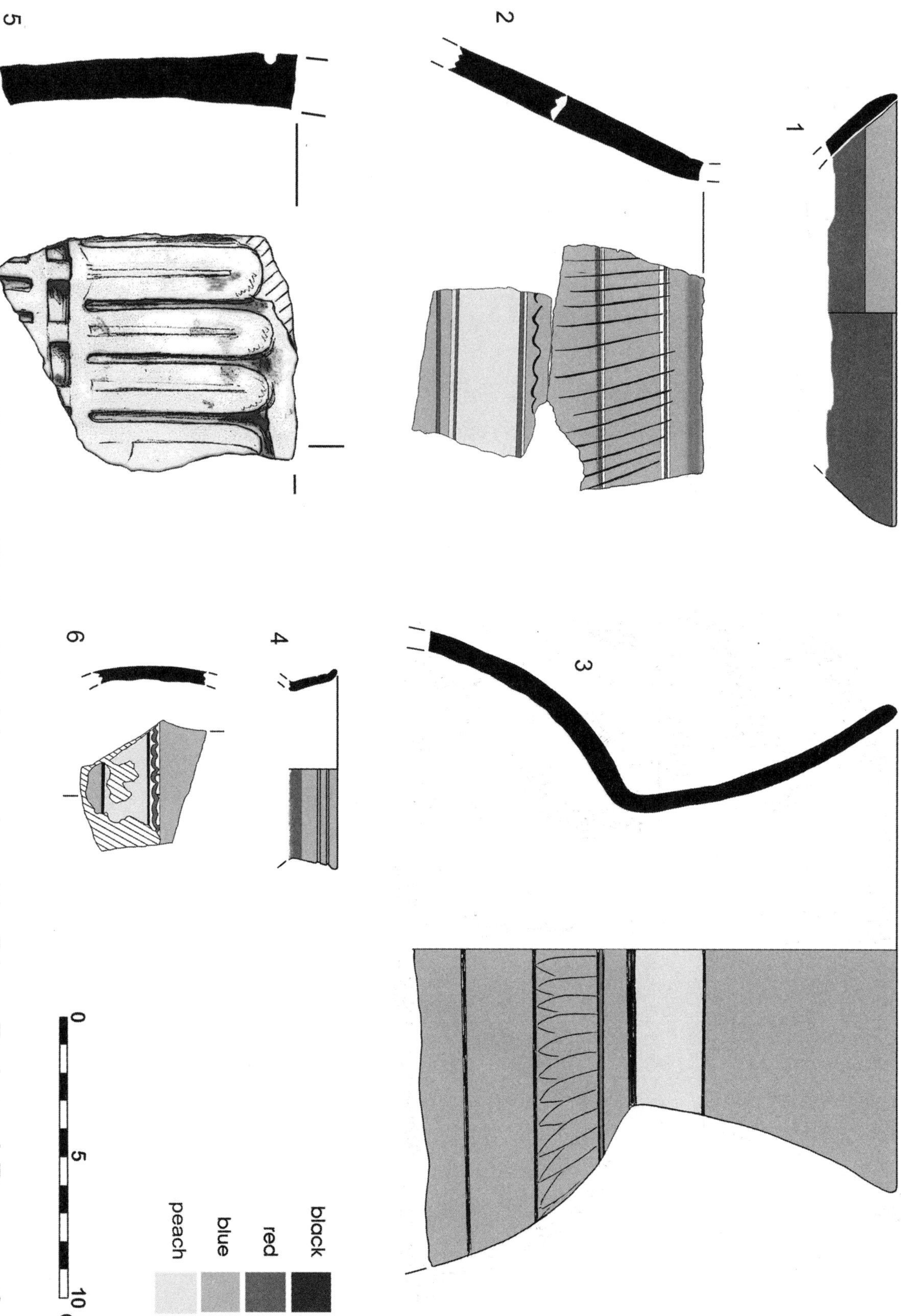

Pottery Plate 3.5: Vessels with Blue Painted Decoration

Computerized by L. Pinch-Brock)

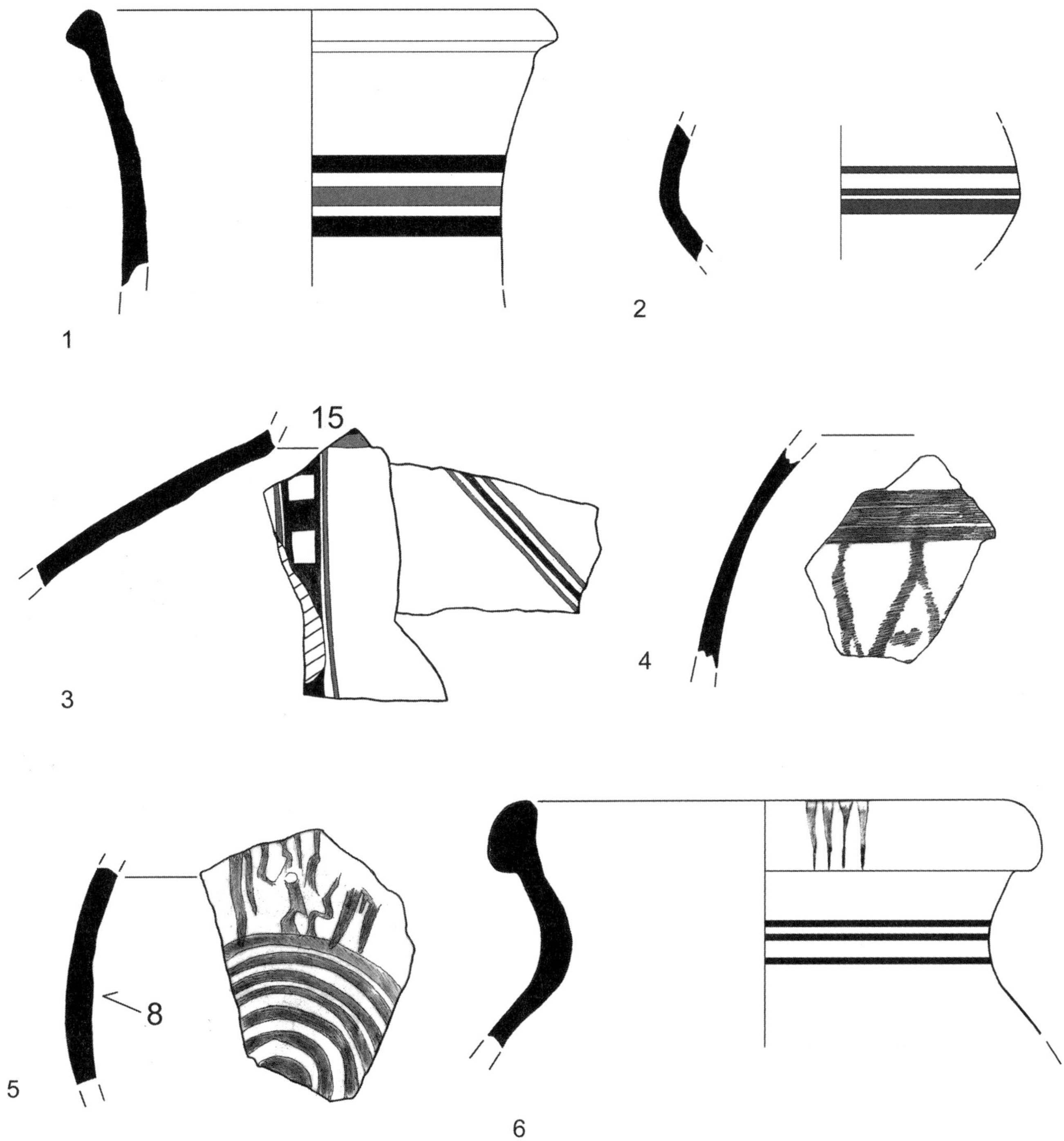

Plate 3.6: Egyptian Decorated Vessels

(Computerized by L. Pinch-Brock)

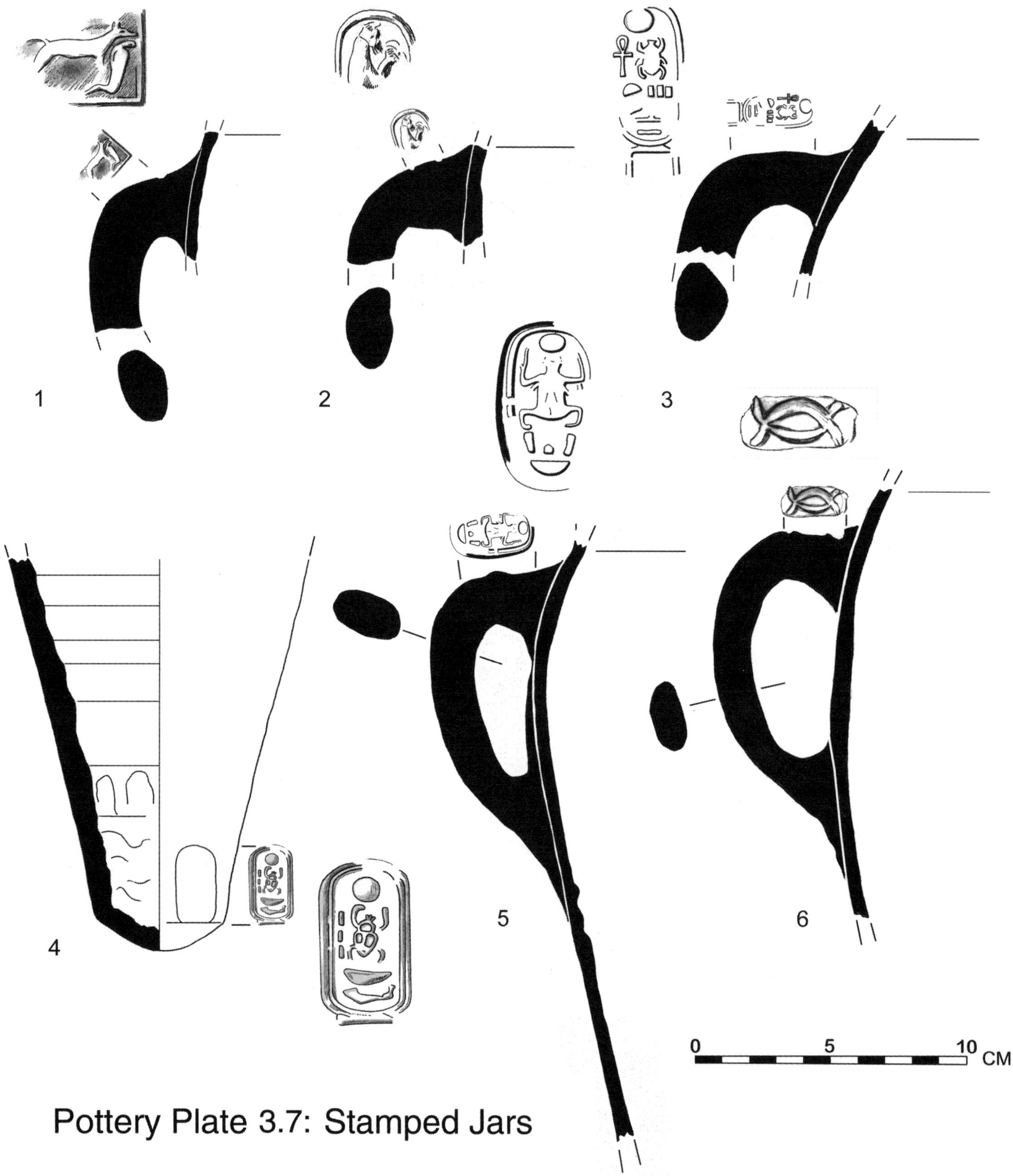

Pottery Plate 3.7: Stamped Jars

(Computerized by L. Pinch-Brock)

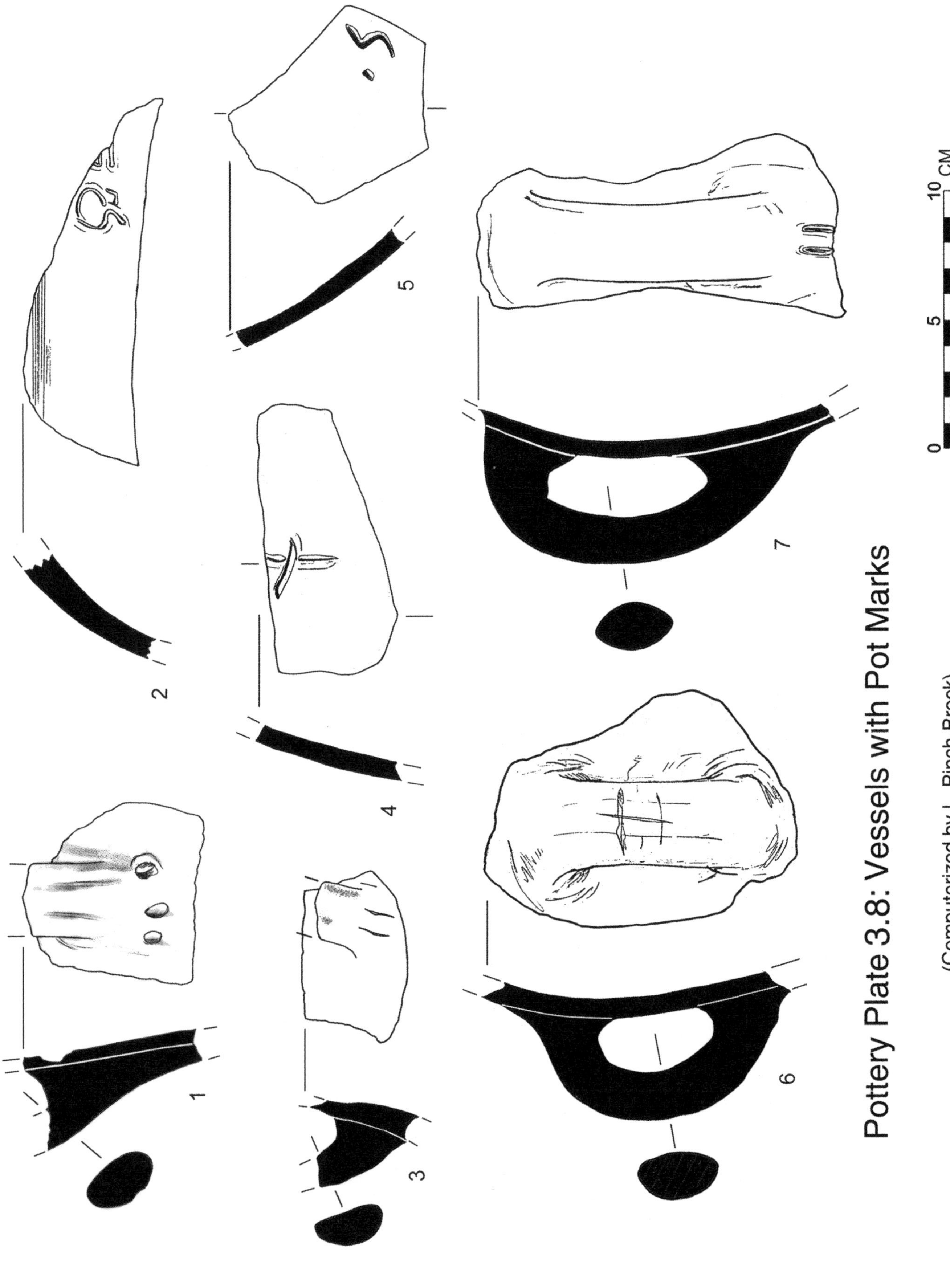

Pottery Plate 3.8: Vessels with Pot Marks

(Computerized by L. Pinch-Brock)

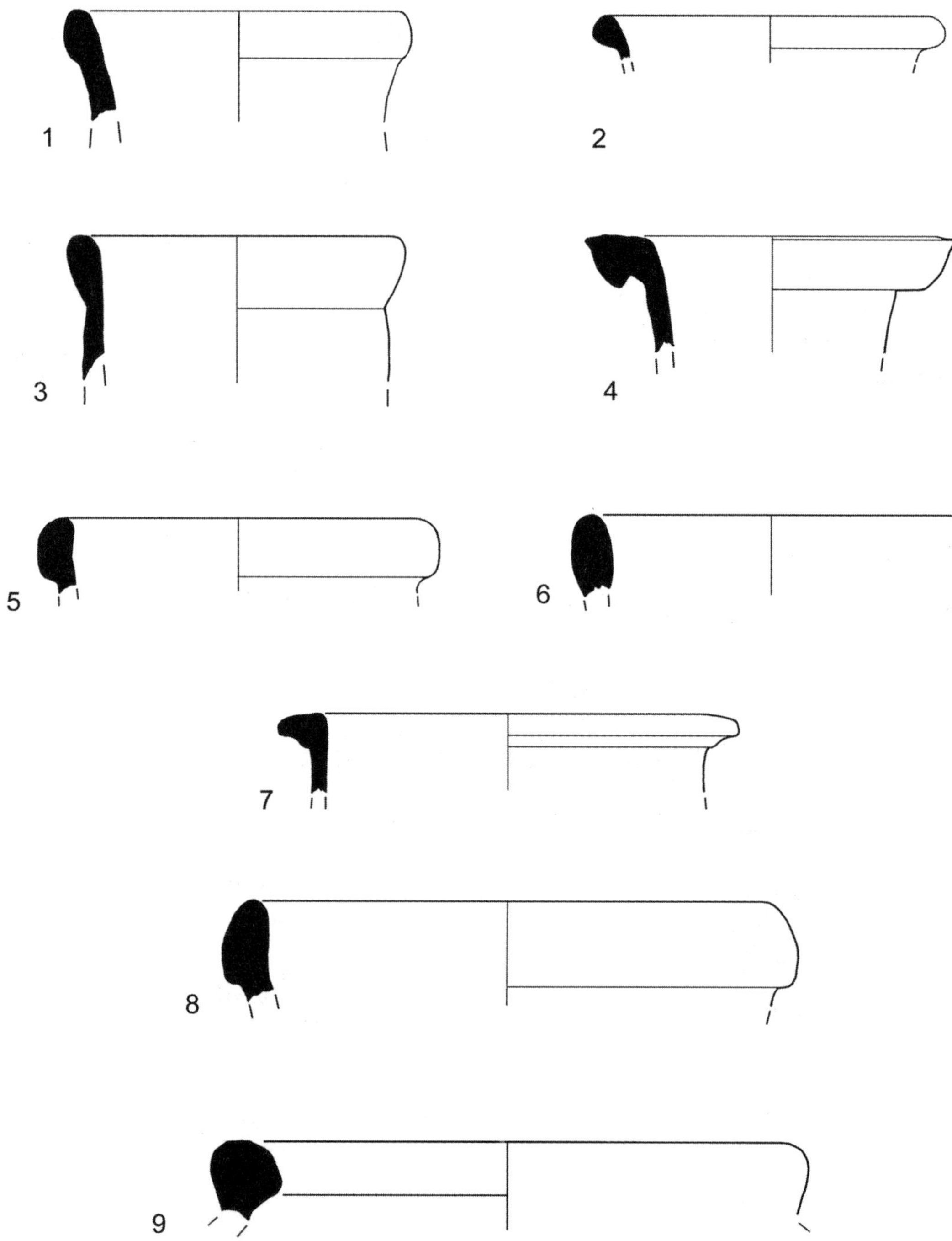

Pottery Plate 3.9: Marl Jars from Field II.1 F

(Computerized by L. Pinch-Brock)

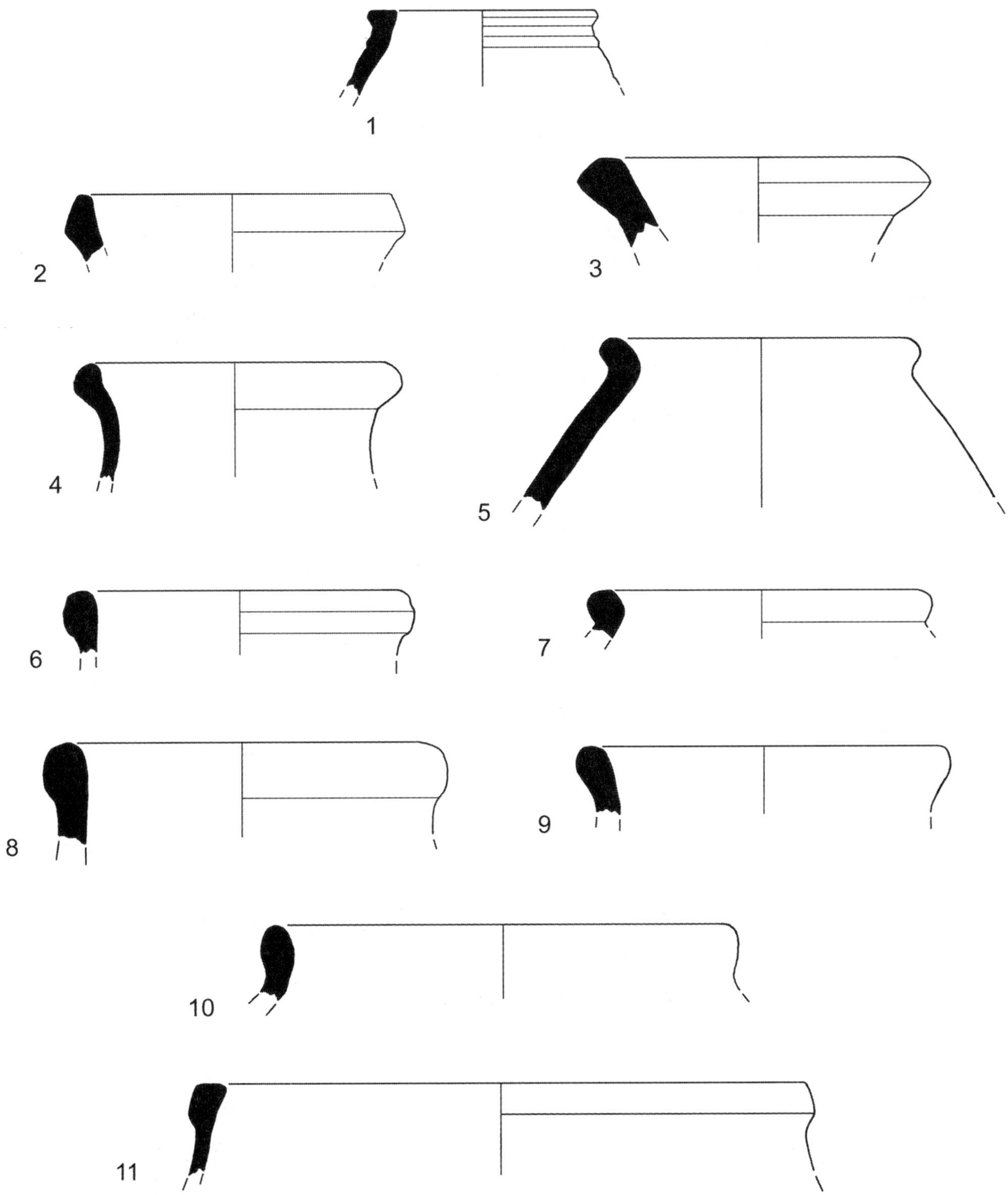

Pottery Plate 3.10: Silt Jars from Field II.1 F

Computerized by L. Pinch-Brock)

0 5 10 CM

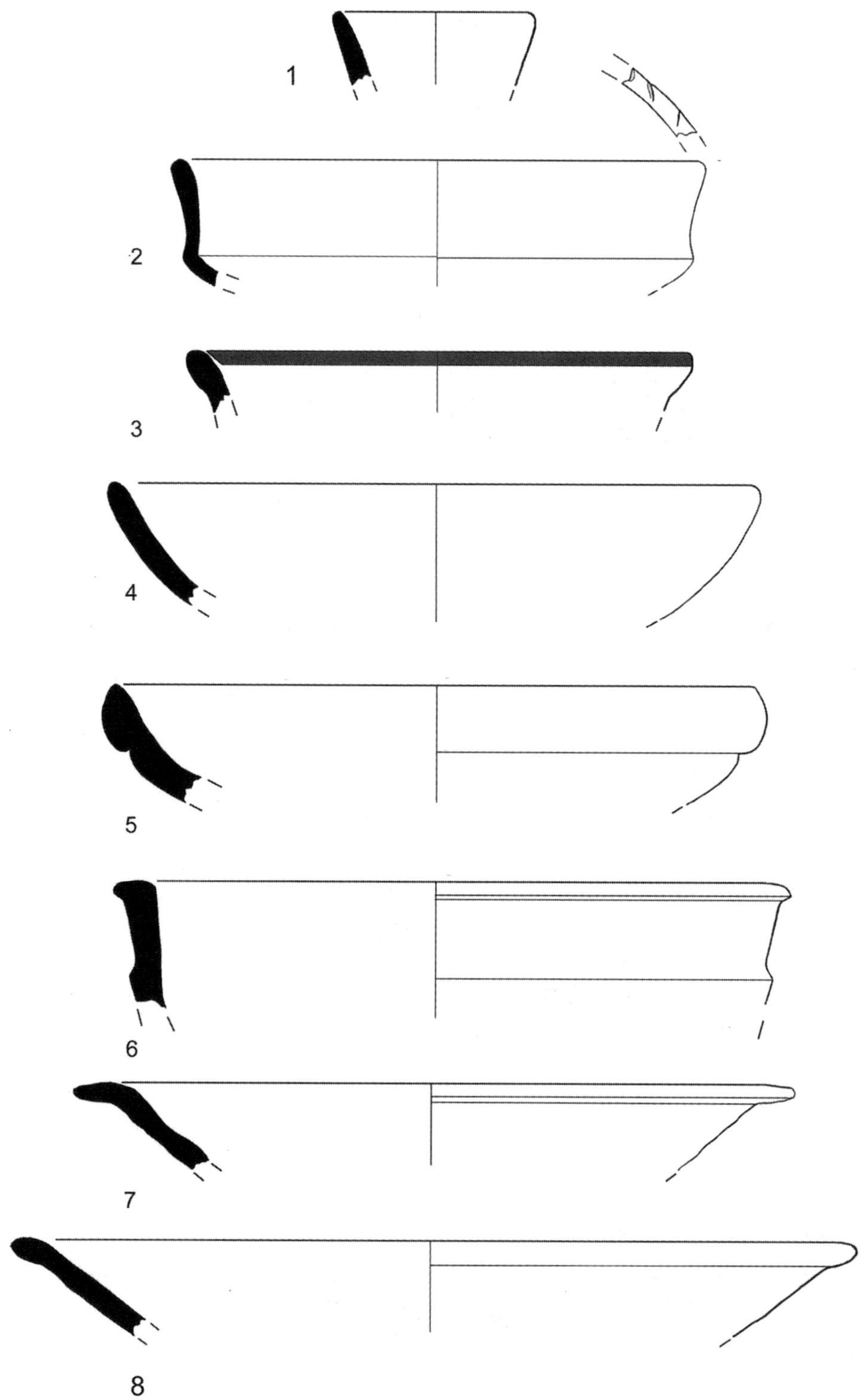

Pottery Plate 3.11: Silt Bowls from Field II.1 F

(Computerized by L. Pinch-Brock)

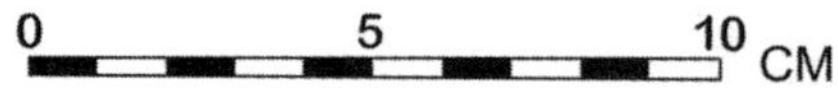

Pottery Plate 3.12: Large Silt Bowls from Field II.1 F

(Computerized by L. Pinch-Brock)

1
2
3
4
5

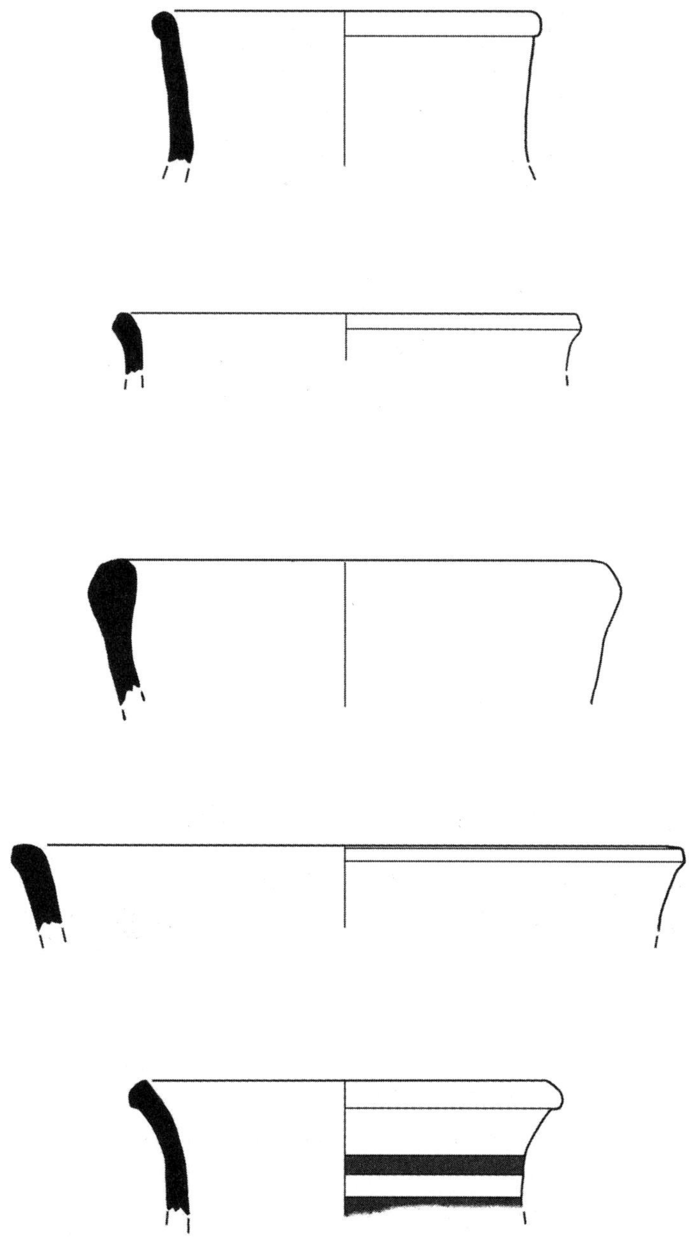

Pottery Plate 3.13: Marl and Silt Jars from Field II.2
Loci 11 and 18

(Computerized by L. Pinch-Brock)

1
2
3
4
5
6
7
8
9
10
11

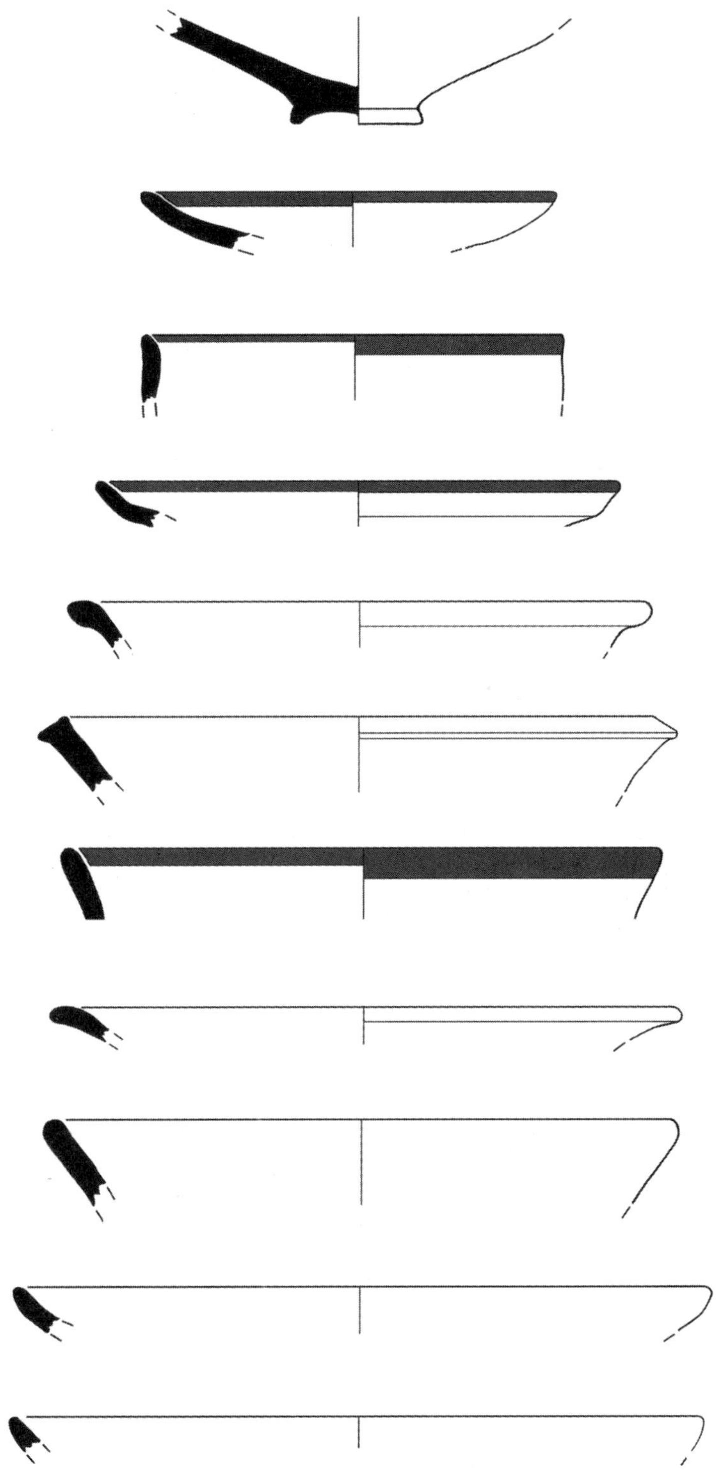

Pottery Plate 3.14: Silt Bowls from Field II.2 Loci 11 and 18

(Computerized by L. Pinch-Brock)

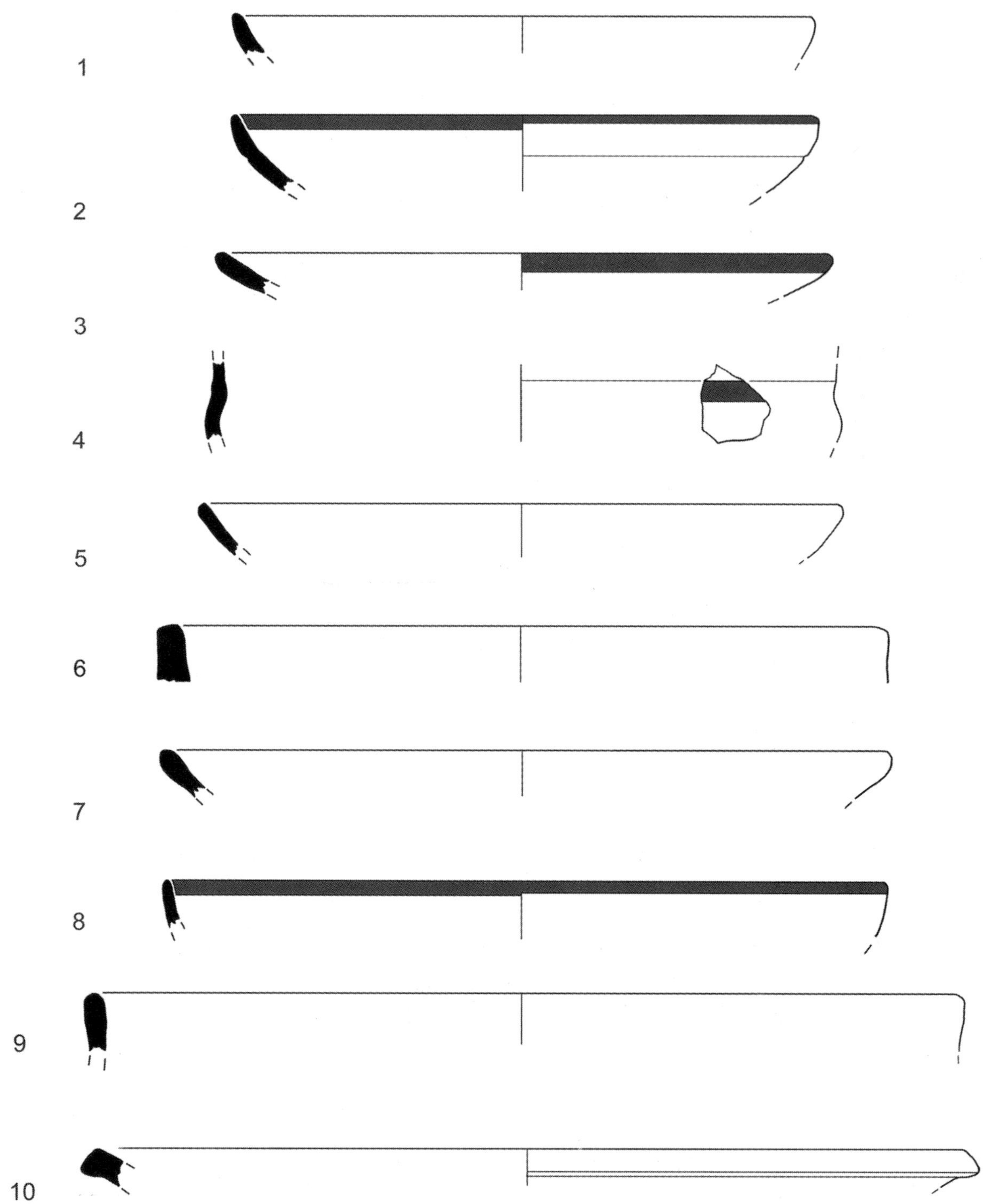

Pottery Plate 3.15: Silt Bowls from Field II.2 Loci 11 and 18

(Computerized by L. Pinch-Brock)

0 5 10 CM

Excursus II: The Stamped Jar Handles

James K. Hoffmeier
Trinity International University

A total of ten legible royal stamped seal impressions were documented at Tell el-Borg, three of which came from the Field II water installation. They all date to the late 18th Dynasty, specifically from the Amarna period. Jacobus Van Dijk and I published these inscribed objects in "New Light on the Amarna Period," *JEA* 96 (2010) 191–205. Indeed, the entire sequence of Amarna period royalty occur: Akhenaten (TBO 0309 – *Tell el-Borg I*, 139); Nefernefruaten (Nefertiti) (TBO 0565; see chapter 6); two of Anhkheperure (TBO II 37 and TBO 0077 [*Tell el-Borg I*, 137–39), one of which was found in the Field II stone water installation; two of Tutankhamun, which were also found in the same well (TBO II 0036 & TBO II 0061 = figs. 3.8, 3.9); Aye (TBO 0778); and two of Horemheb (for the last two, see chapter 8 in this volume). These impressions demonstrate that, throughout the Amarna period, military activity at Tell el-Borg was robust, sponsored by the crown.

In a recent study of seal impressions on vessels with the name of Menmaatre (Seti I) from north-central (Bîr el-ʿAbd) and northeastern (Haruba) Sinai, Orly Goldwasser and Eliezer Oren showed that beneath the royal name a boat determinative was written, signaling that the seal is associated with the royal navy.[54] The authors also pointed out that our reading of the final sign in the cartouche in TBO II 0061, which we thought was a deformed *pr*-sign for "House of Domain of *Nb-xpr-rʿ*" is really a boat.[55] After examining several different images of TBO II 0061, it is clear that Goldwasser's reading is correct. This new reading means that this seal impression of Tutankhamun from the stone-lined well is like the maritime-related seals found at Bir el-Abd and Haruba. It must be recalled that on the south side of Field II lies the Nile distributary discovered early in our work at Tell el-Borg (*Tell el-Borg I*, 63–66).

54. Orly Goldwasser and Eliezer Oren, "Marine Units on the 'Ways of Horus' in the Days of Seti I," *JAEI* 7 (2015) 31–33.

55. Ibid., 35 n. 38. See *JEA* 96, 202.

CHAPTER 4

The Funerary Area: Field III, The "Eastern Cemetery"

Scott D. Haddow and James K. Hoffmeier
UNIVERSITY OF BORDEAUX and TRINITY INTERNATIONAL UNIVERSITY

Prior to the survey seasons of May 1999 and January 2000, a north–south drainage canal, running through the east end of the site, had already been excavated by the canal engineers (fig. 3.1a). It had cut a swath about 40 m wide (including service roads, leveled and covered with crushed stone, on either side of the channel). Heaps of excavated debris had been piled parallel to both sides of the canal (fig. 4.1). These elongated mounds varied in height, ranging from 3–5 m. Walking over these debris dumps during the survey visits revealed scores of sherds, bone fragments, and mud bricks and fragments. One such area was the debris piles next to what became Field III. The presence of these archaeological objects in the excavated sands demonstrated that the canal work had disturbed a culturally rich location. Farther to the south, a number of inscribed blocks and fragments were recovered from the debris heaps, and this area became Field I (on the latter, see *Tell el-Borg I*, 16–17 and chapter 4 there).

When we returned to commence excavations in March 2000, a stretch of the mound on the west side of the canal had been hauled away, leaving only a small part of the original pile on the east side of the once massive pile. Worse yet, it was evident that the front-end loaders used to clear the debris pile, hauling it away to fill low-lying areas to create farmland, had dug well below the debris and into the occupation levels, causing further loss of cultural materials (fig. 4.2). The disturbed area was approximately 110 m long and 30 m wide, and on the west side, a baulk of sorts was created, revealing the stratigraphy of this area. Even though this "baulk" was collapsing and wind-blown sand had piled up, some mud-brick walls were visible.

This exposure prompted us to begin a salvage operation to see what of the visible material could be investigated and preserved. Thus, Field III was established, and the area between the canal on the east and a crushed-stone road just to the east of the new cut was designated Area 1, while the area west of the western edge of the road became Area 2 (fig. 4.3). This burial zone was dubbed the "eastern cemetery" to distinguish it from the "western cemetery" on the western side of the site, about 350–400 m[1] west-southwest of Field III. This area was the focus of the work of subsequent seasons. The first task, however, was to clear the slumped sections in order to see what else was present (fig. 4.4). In addition to the widespread damage done by the excavation of the canal and the subsequent removal of the debris mounds, the area was rife with small and large sand-filled circular pits from recent robbing (some of the scars in the tombs that were exposed had circular shovel holes gouging them).

1. It is difficult to know precisely where the west end of "eastern cemetery" is located and, similarly, where the "western cemetery" begins—hence this approximate range between the two burial grounds.

Fig. 4.1. Drainage canal, view from east side debris mound. Looking southwest toward Field III.

Fig. 4.2. Field III: area where west-side debris pile had been removed. Looking north.

From the salvage operation in Field III Area 1, Tombs 1, 2, 2a, and 3 were uncovered and are described in detail below. The most intriguing discovery in Area A was a large oval pit filled with a large cache of pottery, located about 20 m north of Tomb 1 and about 10 m south of Tomb 2. The pit measures 3.2 m north–south and 3.8 m east–west, with a maximumm depth of 2.3 m. It

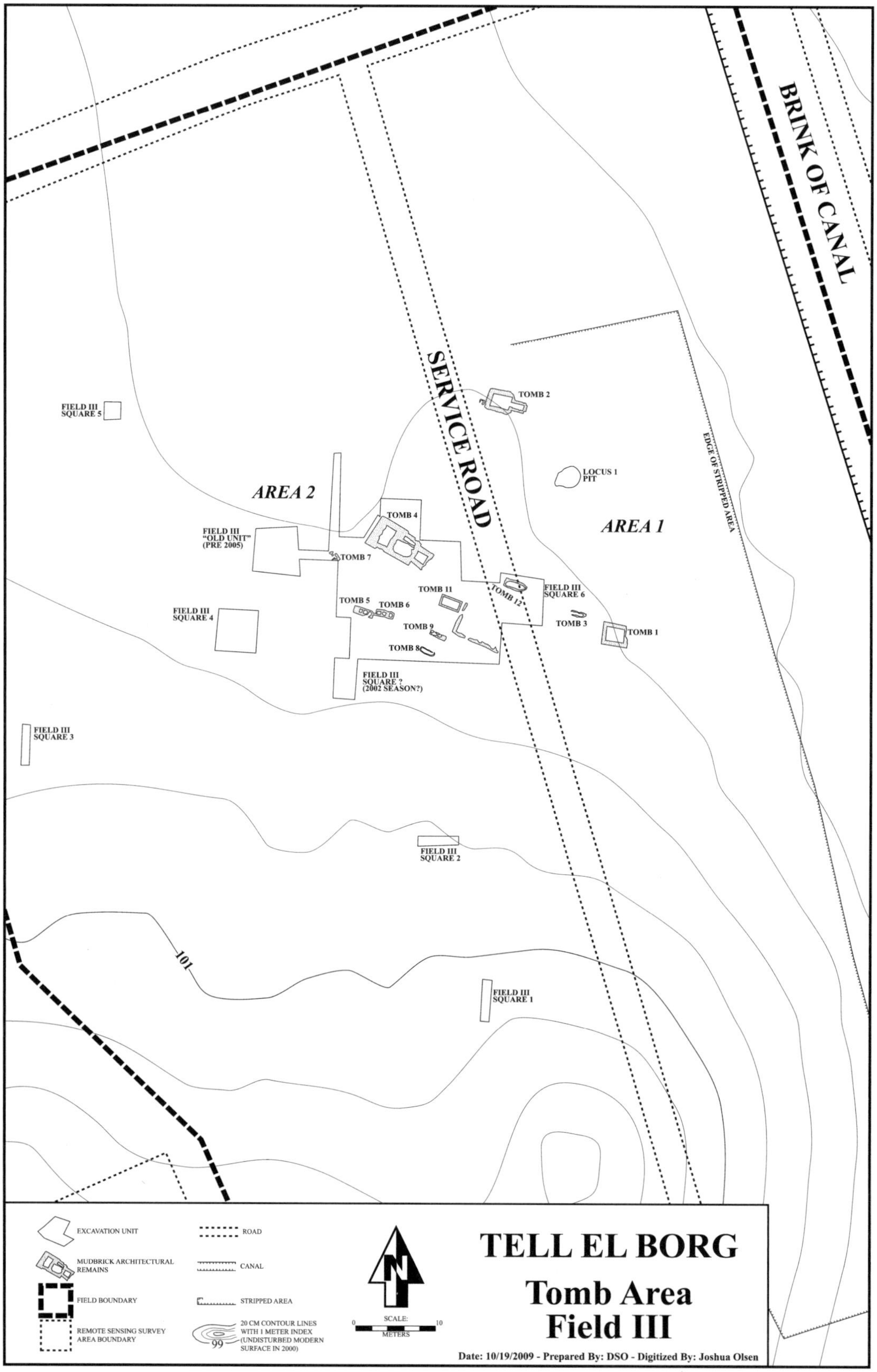

Fig. 4.3. Field III site plan.

Fig. 4.4. Setting up an excavation unit in Field III, with edge of loader cut in the background.

Fig. 4.5. Top of surviving walls of Tomb 4.

contained more than 90 mostly large vessels and has been briefly described (*Tell el-Borg I*, 272). For a detailed treatment of the pottery and the possible function of this assemblage, see Excursus I at the end of this chapter.

The 2001 excavations in Field III were begun as a result of magnetometer testing in Area 2 by Stephen Moshier. It revealed several large anomalies, just west of Tombs 1 and 2, that had been exposed in the previous year, one of which turned out to be Tomb 4, the largest exposed in the cemeteries. A 5 × 5 m excavation unit (Unit A) was initially laid out to intercept one of the more promising anomalies. Shortly after beginning excavations, what appeared to be the top of a mud-brick structure began to emerge (fig. 4.5). Later, three additional 5 × 5 m units were laid out (Units B, C, and D; Unit B was *not* excavated, because Tomb 4 did not cross into that square) in order to expose completely the top of the structure of Tomb 4 and other surrounding tombs.

Excavation Strategy

Except for the first season of excavation, which focused on recording the mud-brick tombs exposed by the removal of canal debris mounds, excavations in Field III are based on a 5 × 5 m grid system oriented to magnetic north. The 5 × 5 m excavation units are given sequential alphabetic designations (i.e., Unit A, Unit B, etc.) and carry over from the previous field season. As features such as tombs are uncovered, a new unit is opened on the grid system in order to expose the entire structure. Test trenches measuring 1 × 5 m are extended out from excavated grid squares in order to intersect new features. If a feature is discovered, the test trench is expanded to incorporate a new 5 × 5 m unit. A total of 22 5 × 5 m squares were opened in Field III Area 2 (although some squares were not excavated entirely), representing an area of approximately 400 m^2 (fig. 4.6). The units' alphabetic sequence reflects the order in which they were excavated, as is the case with the numeric order of the tombs. Features and stratigraphic layers are assigned individual locus numbers. Unfortunately, extensive looting and other human activities, combined with local wind patterns, have resulted in mixing of the surface and upper stratigraphic layers throughout Area 2. This makes it exceedingly difficult to distinguish and delineate smaller strata such as ash

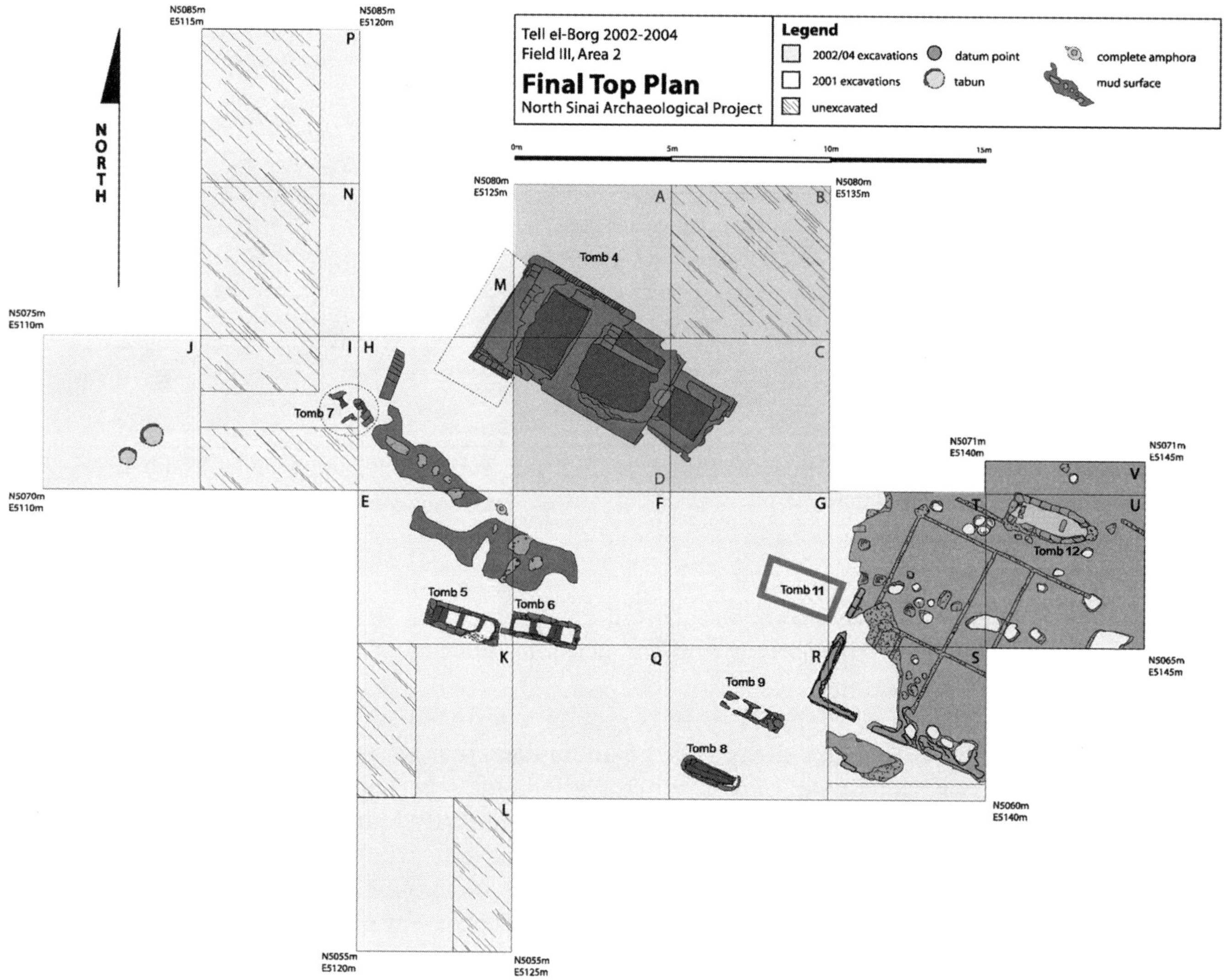

Fig. 4.6. Field III plan by Scott Haddow; digitized by Scott Haddow, enhanced by Joshua Olsen.

lenses or short-lived occupational horizons. For this reason, these disturbed upper strata have been combined under a single locus, which is referred to as the surface layer, but in fact has an average depth below surface of approximately one meter.

In addition, several test trenches were excavated at random locations throughout Field III in order to determine the extent of the cemetery and to search for further evidence of domestic activity. Unfortunately, no further traces of burials or domestic occupation were found by shovel probes or geophysical survey in the north end of Field III, Area 2 (= Area 4, A of Tomasz Herbich's geophysical survey with a Fluxgate-type grandiometers by Geoscan Research; cf. *Tell el-Borg I*, 351–56). The geophysical survey of the area south of the burial complex (i.e., including Tombs 4–13; Herbich's Area 4, C: cf. *Tell el-Borg I*, 351–53) showed no anomalies to investigate, except the shoreline of the Nile distributary. The presence of this feature no doubt explains why no burials were nearby.

In order to determine how far east of the canal the Field III cemetery continued, the area between the road and the 4–5-m-high canal debris heap (it was not removed from this area!) was surveyed. It was a narrow strip on the east bank of the canal, 180 m long by 15–30 m wide (Herbich's survey Area 4 B: cf. *Tell el-Borg I*, 347, 355–56). Some minor anomalies did appear, possibly small clusters of mud brick. Due to the leveling that occurred to make the road, it appears that there may have been some smaller tombs in this area, but they were severely disturbed. It was decided not to investigate this area further, because the road was active and no feature large enough to warrant excavation was apparent. Exploring the canal debris mound adjacent to Area 4 B revealed sherds and pieces of bone and mud brick, indicating that the excavation of the canal had demolished tombs. East of the mound, a surface survey was conducted, but the area was devoid of the hallmark signs of robbing and no pot or coffin sherds were documented. Consequently, it appears that the cemetery's eastern limit must have been somewhere under the north–south debris mound, but it is difficult to determine this with certainty.

Fig. 4.7. **a** (left): knee cap with trace of linen (top view); **b** (right): knee cap (side view).

New Kingdom Mortuary Practices

Due to the disturbed nature of the cemetery region, evidence for mummification at *Tell el-Borg I*s negligible. It is expected, however, that the deceased of Tell el-Borg would originally have been mummified, because the practice is common in the New Kingdom.[2] The only direct evidence for mummification at the site appeared during the analysis of the disturbed skeletal material recovered from Tomb 4, where a single human adult patella (kneecap) was found to retain fragments of red and white painted plaster on its anterior surface, overlaying a thin layer of linen and resin (fig. 4.7a–b). Additionally, the posterior surface of an adult scapula (shoulder blade) retained traces of linen overlaid by blue-painted plaster. Indeed, a large proportion of the painted plaster recovered from Tomb 4 retained textile impressions and traces of resin on their underside. Thus, it would appear that at least one of the occupants of Tomb 4, in addition to being mummified, had plaster and paint applied to their outer wrappings. This is a rather surprising discovery, however, given that these practices are virtually unknown in the New Kingdom. No further traces of textile were found in the cemetery area, although some may appear on the wall of the burial niche (see below).

Numerous fragments of terracotta sarcophagi were also recovered from the cemetery region and are of several types. The project's conservator, Noel Siver, was able to reconstruct two of them, however (figs. 4.8–4.9). (For full treatment of these clay coffins, see chapter 5).

General Description of Tombs in Field III

The grave architecture of the cemetery region at Tell el-Borg consists of mud-brick structures of various sizes and complexity. The tomb structures are similar to those at the New Kingdom

2. Salima Ikram, *Death and Burial in Ancient Egypt* (Cairo: AUC Press, 2015) 47–76. A. J. Spencer, *Death in Ancient Egypt* (New York: Penguin, 1982) 112–38.

Fig. 4.8. Noël Siver matching clay coffin sherds.

Fig. 4.9. Noël Siver and Scott Haddow with restored coffin, TBO 0065.

site of Hebua IV, located 5 km northwest of Tell el-Borg.[3] It was likely one of the cemeteries that served the military community residing in and around the fortresses at Tjaru (i.e., Hebua I and II).[4]

The tombs were constructed as subterranean features built into the basal (sterile) sands. The smaller single-occupant graves (i.e., Tombs 3, 5, 6, 7, 8, 9) were constructed by cutting a rectangular pit into the sand and lining the sides with four to five courses of mud brick—enough to contain a body or, in some cases, a terracotta sarcophagus. These small graves were likely capped with a layer of mud brick, but due to the damage caused by the extensive looting at the site, the tops of the tombs are lost. Tomb 3, a small single-occupant burial, has a small trace of the roofing at the east end (see below). Tomb 2 also had a small section of the roofing intact on the northwest corner. After a couple of days of exposure, it collapsed. The largest of the tombs, nos. 1, 2, and 4 (and

3. Josef Dorner, "Vorbericht über Grabungskampagnen 1993/94 auf Tell Hebwa IV/Süd am Nordsinai," *ÄuL* VI (1996) 167–77.

4. Mohamed Abd el-Maksoud, "Une nouvelle fortresse sur la route d'Horus Tell Heboua 1986 (Nord Sinaï)," *CRIPEL* 9 (1987) 13–16; M. Abd el-Maksoud and D. Valbelle, "Tell Héboua-Tjarou l'apport de l'épigraphie," *Rd'É* 56 (2005) 7–8, 18–21. Regarding Hebua II, see Mohamed Abd el-Maksoud and Dominique Valbelle, "Tell Héboua II: Rapport Préliminaire sur le décor el l'épigraphie des elements architectoniques découverts au cours des campagnes 2008–2009 dans la zone centrale du Khétem de Tjarou," *Rd'É* 62 (2011) 1–39; Mohamed Abd el-Maksoud, *Tell Heboua (1981–1991): Enquête archéologique sur la Deuxième Périod Intermédiaire et le Nouvel Empire à l'extrémité orientale du Delta* (Paris: Éditions Recherche sur les Civilisations, 1998) 30–31.

Fig. 4.11 (above). Tomb 8 with large portion of clay coffin in situ, TBO 0160.

Fig. 4.10 (left). Tomb 4 shaft with stone blocking entrance.

likely 13), were family crypts and would have contained multiple burials deposited over a period of years, a supposition confirmed when the osteological remains were analyzed (see below). Tomb 4, the largest tomb uncovered in the eastern cemetery, probably could only have been built by a higher-ranking official or military officer. A vertical entrance shaft, placed at the eastern side of the tombs, was employed in order to facilitate reentry to the burial chamber. In the case of Tombs 2 and 4, the entrance from the shaft was blocked after the interment. In Tomb 4, a large flat stone was found in situ, separating the shaft from the entrance (fig. 4.10), while in Tomb 2, mud plugs the opening.

The orientation of the tombs is generally east–west, ranging from 105° to 120° off due north. Since the surviving entrance shafts (Tombs 2 and 4) are on the east side, the back of the tomb faces west. Tomb 8 had a significant portion of a cylindrically shaped clay coffin (TBO 0160), and the head of that coffin is at the west end (fig. 4.11). This placement suggests that the deceased in the other tombs were buried with their heads to the west.

Very few small finds were actually discovered within the tombs themselves, owing to ancient robbing when contents from the tombs were tossed around and discarded. Complete vessels were rarely encountered, except in Tombs 1 and 2. The surface finds and those from the collapsing and wind-blown slump along the western side could have come from anywhere in the immediate area but were likely originally from robbed and destroyed tombs. Most of the objects are of the mundane variety (i.e., reused sherds), while some were utilitarian (e.g., misc. implements, pounder), and jewelry (beads). Two variegated glass juglet or vase fragments represent the only truly elite objects (TBO III 4 and 15; figs. 4.15 and 4.16a–b). The find-spot of TBO III 15 (TBO III D) is near Tomb 1, and because this is one of the largest tombs in the eastern cemetery, it is not

Table 4.1. Finds from Surface of Field III
(no further information on find-spot unless stated)

TBO	*Field*	*Object Type*	*Material*	*Measurements*
III 20	III	weaving/loom or net weight	limestone	5.5 × 3 × 2 cm
III 26	III	4-sided tapering instrument	limestone (?)	5.5 × 1 × 1 cm
III 27	III	triangular-shaped metal fragment	c/ca	1.5 × 1 × .1 cm
III 42	III	bead	faience	0.3 × 0.3 × 0.1 cm
III 54	III	circular token or game piece	reused clay sherd	2.2. × 2.2. × 0.5 cm

Table 4.2. Small Finds from Field III Area 1:
Units Along the Western Cut Created by Canal Excavation

TBO	*Field/Locus*	*Object type*	*Material*	*Measurements*
III 4	III A	variegated jar or vase	glass	0.5 × 0.7 × 0.3 cm
III 12	III A	chipped stone fragment	carnelian	2 × 1 × 0.5 cm
III 13	III A	metal nail	c/ca	2.5 × 0.3 cm
III 24	III A	fragment of mortar (?)	amygdaloidal basalt	6 × 6.6 × 3.5 cm
III 25a	III A	circular token or game piece	reused potsherd	2 × 2.5 × 0.8 cm
III 25b	III A	circular token or game piece	reused potsherd	1.5 x.1.5 × 0.5 cm
III 30	III A	collection of 11 beads	faience	n/a
III 31	III A	2 pieces of a tool (awl?)	c/ca	1 × 0.4 × 0.2 cm 7.5 × 0.3 cm
III 31b	III A	flat piece of metal	c/ca	4.5 × 2 × .2 cm
III 35	III A	fragment of shell	shell	1.7 × 1 × .1 cm
III 43	III A 4	curved pin, jewelry?	c/ca	2.5 × .3 cm
III 47	III A 4	pounder	granodiorite	5.5 × 5 × 4.5 cm
III 91	III Ab 1	disc-shaped, game piece (?)	fishbone	0.4 × 1.3 dia cm
III 92	III Ab 1	cylindrical fragment of metal	c/ca	1.2 × 0.2 dia cm
III 95	III Ab 2	notched arrowhead	chert	1.9 × 1.4
III 94	III B 1	stone weight (?)	limestone	6 × 5.5 cm
0427	III B 1	tool or wire (?)	c/ca	10.5 × 0.7 dia cm
III 9	III C	bead	faience	.4 × .4 × .1 cm
III 22	III C	2 pieces of metal, one possibly a nail	c/ca	1.5 × 1.2 × 0.2cm 2 × 0.4 cm
III 15	III D	variegated jar or vase	glass	2.5 × 1.3 × 0.3 cm
III 32	III G	circular token or game piece	reused potsherd	1.5 × 1.5 × 0.7cm
III 33	III G	2 pieces of a curved hollow tube	c/ca	1 × .4 and 1 × 0.5 cm
III 39	III G	round sherd w. hole, whorl? weight?	reused potsherd	7 × 7 × 2 cm
III 38	III H	broken circular token or game piece	reused potsherd	2.5 × 1.5 × 1 cm

inconceivable that the elegant vessel originated in this tomb. This type of glass jarlet is known from the period of Amenhotep III and into the 19th Dynasty.[5] TBO III 91 is a small game-piece or disc of some sort that was shaped by reworking a large fish vertebra (fig. 4.19a). TBO III 94 (fig. 4.20a–b) is a limestone piece, with grooves as if they were formed by cords, suggestive of a weight from a fishing net.

5. P. T. Nicholson and J. Henderson, "Glass," in *Ancient Egyptian Materials and Technologies* (ed. P. T. Nicholson and I. Shaw; Cambridge: Cambridge University Press, 2000) 195–225. See also Y. Israeli, Dan Barag, and Naʿama Brosh, *Ancient Glass in the Israel Museum* (Jerusalem: The Israel Museum, 2003) 27–42.

Fig. 4.12. Limestone weight, TBO III 20.

Fig. 4.13. Unknown limestone implement, TBO III 26.

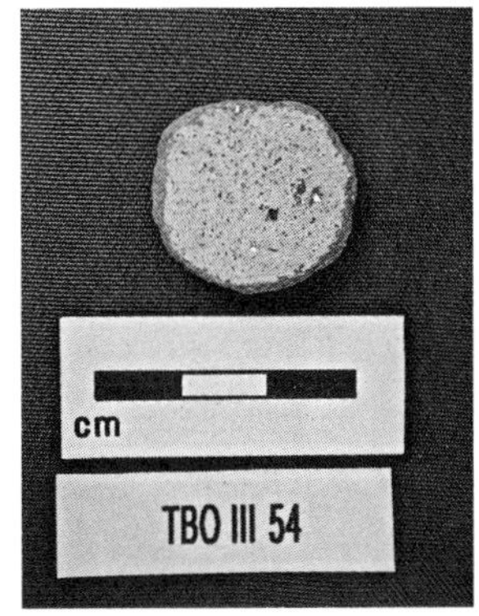

Fig. 4.14. Circular token or game piece, TBO III 54.

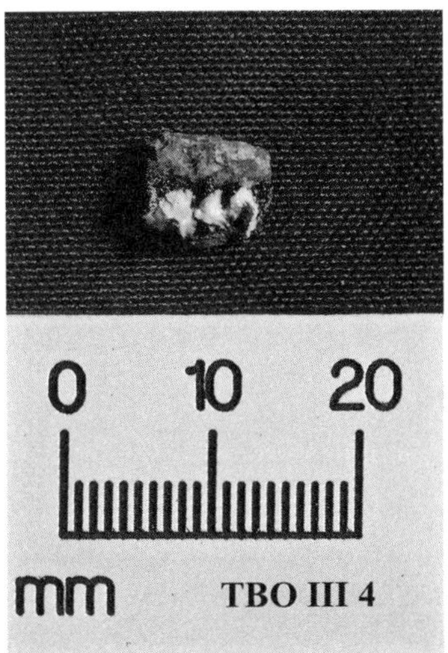

Fig. 4.15. Variegated glass jar or vase fragment, TBO III 4.

Fig. 4.16. **a** (left): Photo, variegated glass jar or vase fragment, TBO III 15; **b** (right): drawing by Lyla Pinch-Brock.

Fig. 4.17. 2 tokens or game pieces made of rounded potsherd, TBO III 25.

Fig. 4.18. Basalt fragment of a quern or mortar, TBO III 24.

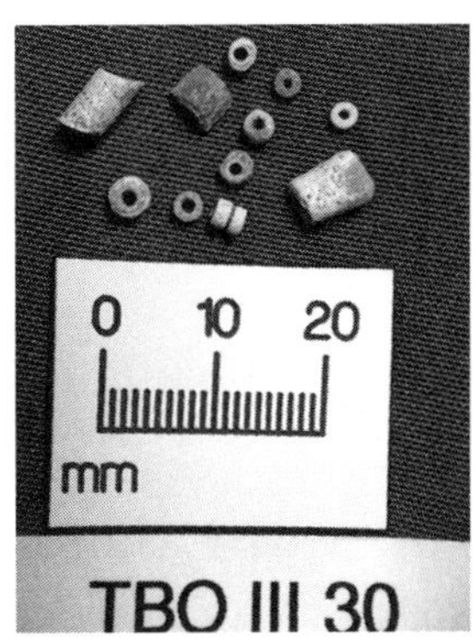

Fig. 4.19a. Collection of 11 faience beads, TBO III 30.

Fig. 4.19b. Fish vertebra shaped as gamepiece(?), TBO III 91.

Fig. 4.20. **a** (left): Limestone weight, top view(?), TBO III 94; **b** (middle): Limestone weight, end view(?), TBO III 94; **c** (right): Chert arrowhead, TBO III 95.

Fig. 4.21. Tomb 1, looking west.

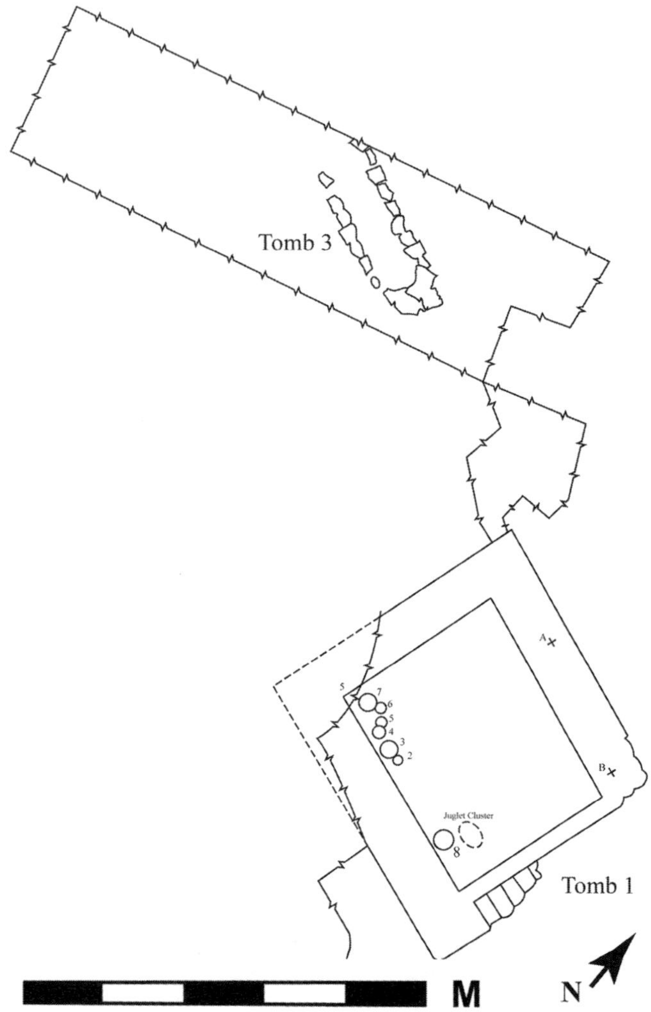

Fig. 4.22. Top plan of Tombs 1 and 3 (drawing by J. E. Knudstad, digitized by J. Olson).

The Tombs of Field III Area 1

Tomb 1

Provenance: Field III, Area 1, Units G and H
Dimensions: 3.96 m × 3.27 m
Maximal preserved height: 14 courses on north side, 16 on south side
Brick size: 34 × 18 × 8–9 cm
Orientation of long axis: 120° off north
Excavator: James Knudstad, Linda Wilding and Ashraf Melika

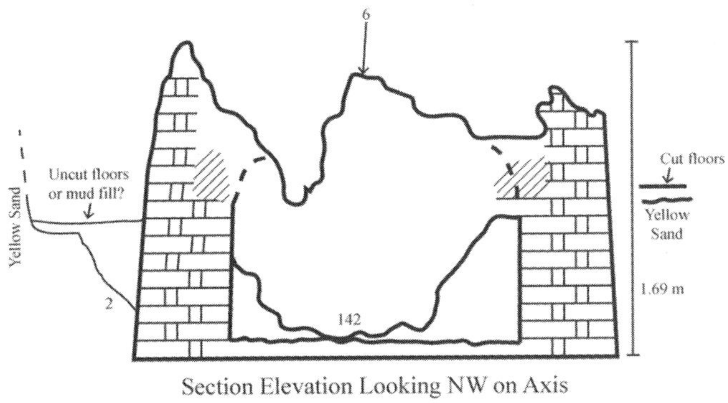

Fig. 4.23. Tomb 1 elevation (drawing by J. E. Knudstad, digitized by J. Olson).

Fig. 4.24. Tomb 1, southwest section.

Fig. 4.25. Tomb 1 with group of juglets, looking west.

Fig. 4.26. Tomb 1, close-up of juglets.

Tomb 1 is a large rectangular mud-brick structure that was partially exposed and largely destroyed by a front-end loader during the clearance of the canal debris piles described above. Indeed, the impression left by the teeth-marks of the loader are visible in the eastmost section of the floor, where the entry to the chamber would have been (figs. 4.21, 4.22). Given the size of the surviving burial chamber (interior dimensions = 2.85 m × 2.05 m) — comparable to that of nearby Tomb 2 — it appears that it would have had a burial shaft, which was entirely obliterated by the excavations of the As-Salam canal project.

The mud bricks were of uniform size, measuring 34 × 18 × 8–9 cm, and the walls varied slightly in thickness from 58 to 63 cm. The east–west wall on the south side rose to 1.69 m, indicating a slight curve inward towards the top of what was surely an arched roof (fig. 4.23). The preservation of the north side wall at the back end of the tomb was 1.50 m (fig. 4.24). With so much lost, it is fortuitous that a cache of smaller vessels along the southern inside wall eluded the loader's

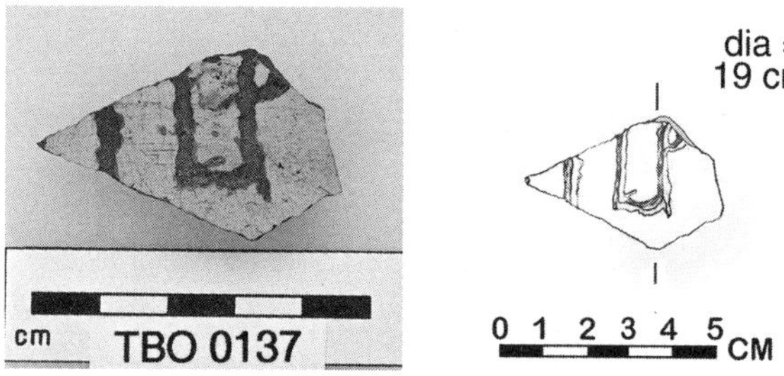

Fig. 4.27. **a** (left): TBO 0137, inscribed sherd;
b (right): TBO 0137, drawing by Lyla Pinch-Brock.

Fig. 4.28. Tomb 2, initial exposure.

blade (figs. 4.25, 4.26). In all, nine nearly complete vessels were documented and were studied as a group in *Tell el-Borg I*, 370–71 and pl. 1. The Cypriote ceramics in this group were studied by Stuart Swiny (*Tell el-Borg I*, 482–83, figs. 557–58). Two Base Ring lentoid flasks and a "spindle bottle" of Cypriote origin were included. The presence of these elite Late Cypriote II wares point to a date from the mid-18th to early 19th Dynasty.[6] No other small finds were uncovered in the tomb. One noteworthy surface find discovered near Tomb 1 was a body sherd (4.5 × 3 × 0.6 cm) with either hieroglyphs or an image of some sort etched through the wash, exposing the orange-colored fabric below (figs. 4.27a–b).

No human remains were retrieved from Tomb I. There is no doubt that, between ancient pillaging and the near demolition of the tomb by the canal construction, the bones would have been scattered in the area or lost altogether.

Tomb 2

Provenance: Field III, Area 1, Units D and D1
Dimensions: 5.80 × 3.30 m
Maximal preserved height: 1.44 m
Brick size: 37–38 × 18 × 8–9 cm.
Orientation of long axis: 120° off north
Excavator: Scott Haddow

Tomb 2 is a large mud-brick structure about 34 m north of Tomb 1. About two-thirds of the tomb was revealed in Unit D (5 × 8 m). In the rear baulk, the outline of a pit was clearly visible, revealing where the tomb had been penetrated by the ancient robbers and then how over time it filled in (fig. 4.28). The lowest stratum consists of mud-brick rubble, sharing the color of the brick (10 YR 5/3), suggesting that this debris is from the collapsed roof. In order to reach the rear part

6. On Cypriote pottery in Egypt, see R. S. Merrillees, *The Cypriote Bronze Age Pottery Found in Egypt* (Studies in Mediterranean Archaeology 18; Lund: P. Åstrom, 1968); Celia Berghoffen, "Overland Trade in Northern Sinai: The Evidence of Late Cypriote Pottery," *BASOR* 284 (1991) 59–76.

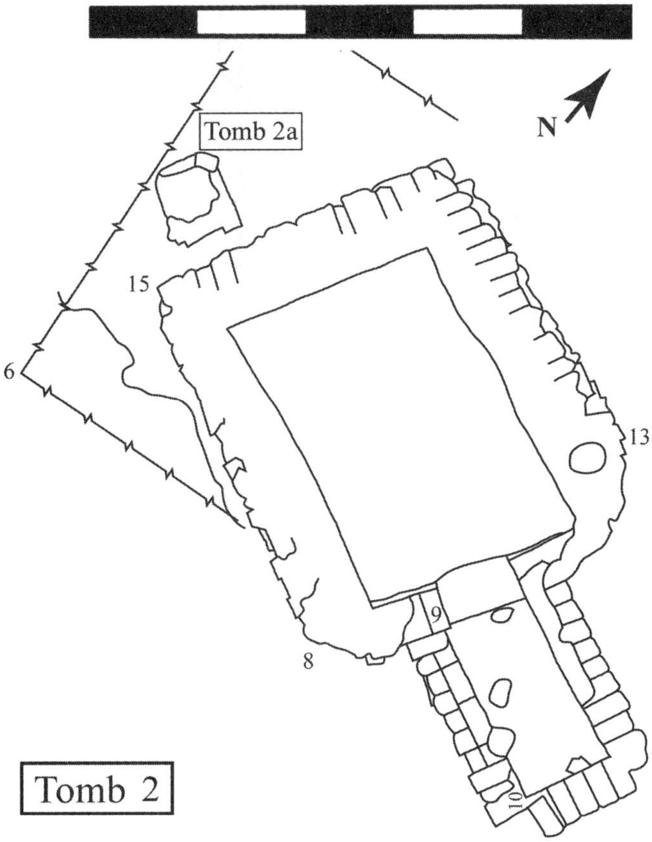

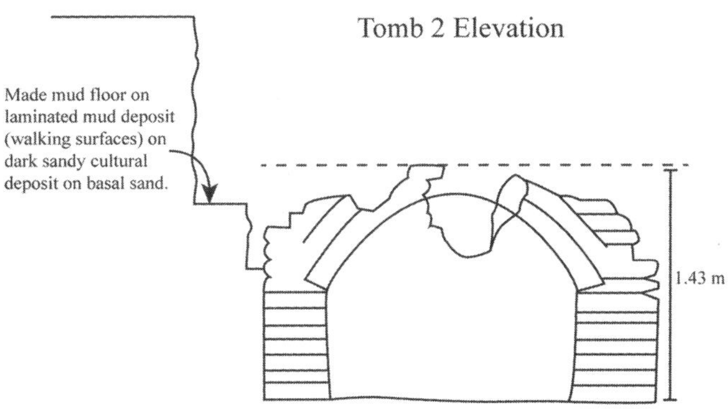

Fig. 4.29. **a** (above): Tomb 2, fully excavated; **b** (above, left): Tomb 2 plan (drawing by J. E. Knudstad, digitized by J. Olson); **c** (left): Tomb 2 elevation (drawing by J. E. Knudstad, digitized by J. Olson).

of the tomb, Unit D was extended westward by 3 m, with the extension made 4 m wide; the extension of Unit D was named D1. Remnants of a mud-brick vaulted roof were preserved on the north (back) side of the tomb chamber (figs. 4.29, 4.30). It was actually supported by some of the collapsed roof. The tops of the walls are riddled with pick and shovel holes made by modern robbers.

An entrance shaft (2.0 × 1.6 m; interior dimensions are 1.75 × 0.85) at the east side of the structure allows for access to the main chamber from the surface. The entrance to the burial chamber was blocked by a 38-cm-thick mud wall, which was largely intact. The burial chamber itself was 3.10 × 1.95 m, and the side walls were 60 cm thick, while the rear wall was 70 cm thick. The bricks were similar in size to those from Tomb 1 but slightly longer: 37–38 × 18 × 8–9 cm.

At the back of the tomb, a collection of 12 pottery vessels was discovered, consisting of funnel-necked jars (5), beakers (3) (figs. 4.31, 4.32, 4.33), conical lids (2), a bowl, and an elegant blue painted "tea" cup (fig. 4.34a–c). This assemblage was analyzed in *Tell el-Borg I*, 371–72,

Fig. 4.30. Tomb 2 and Tomb 2a, looking east.

Fig. 4.31. Tomb 2, west (back) end of tomb with vessels in situ.

Fig. 4.32 (right). Tomb 2, close up of vessels in situ.

and pl. 2. There Rexine Hummel showed that the vessels in Tomb 2 closely compare to ones found in the tomb chapels of Paser and Raʾia at Saqqara dating to the reign of Horemheb (1323–1295 B.C.).[7]

7. Throughout this volume, Kitchen's chronology for the New Kingdom is being followed (Kenneth A. Kitchen, "Regnal and Genealogical Data of Ancient Egypt (Absolute Chronology I): The Historical Chronology of Ancient Egypt, A Current Assessment," in *The Synchronisation of Civilisations in the Eastern Mediterranean in the Second Millennium B.C.* (ed. M. Bietak; Vienna: The Austrian Academy of Sciences, 2000) 49. The 27–28 year reign of Horemheb is now questioned in the light of the recent discovery of wine dockets from the tomb of Horemheb in the Valley of the Kings that date to "year 14," with no year-dates higher, suggesting a

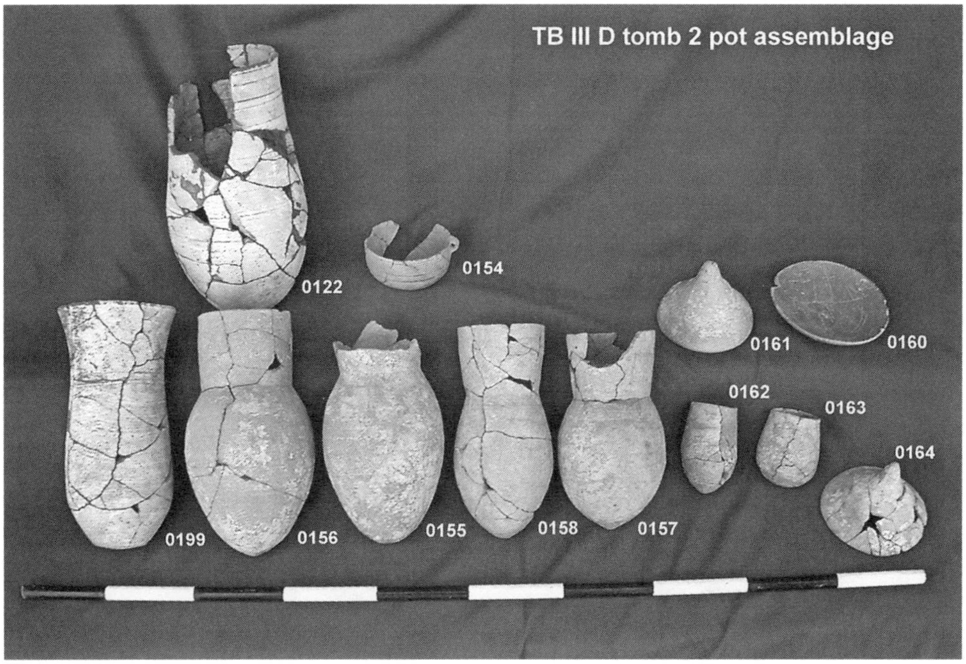

Fig. 4.33. Collection of vessels from Tomb 2.

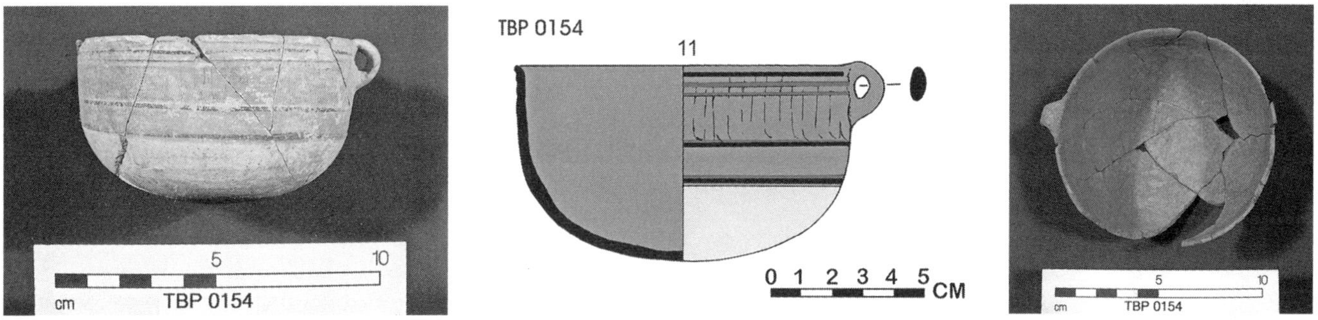

Fig. 4.34. a. "Tea cup," TBP 0154; b. drawing by Lyla Pinch-Brock; c. inside of cup.

Small Finds from Unit D

Small finds within the tomb were limited indeed; more were found outside of Tomb 2, although it is impossible to know if these originated in this tomb or were from adjacent, now demolished tombs. Smaller tombs in Field III tend to be built on higher ground, whereas the larger burials were sunk deeper into the basal sand. As a consequence, smaller graves in Area 1 were likely destroyed without a trace during the canal construction operations. Some of the pieces of brick, sherds, and small objects scattered over the new surfaces of the area are likely the only hint of these burials.

---

shorter reign (see Jacobus van Dijk, "New Evidence for the Length of the Reign of Horemheb," *JARCE* 44 (2008) 193–200. Nevertheless, for our purpose, the date ca. 1300 plus or minus several decades is sufficient for dating this tomb. Two bullae and a ring were discovered with Horemheb's cartouche on them in Field VI (see chapter 8 below and James K. Hoffmeier and Jacobus van Dijk, "New Light on the Amarna Period from North Sinai," *JEA* 96 [2010] 191–201).

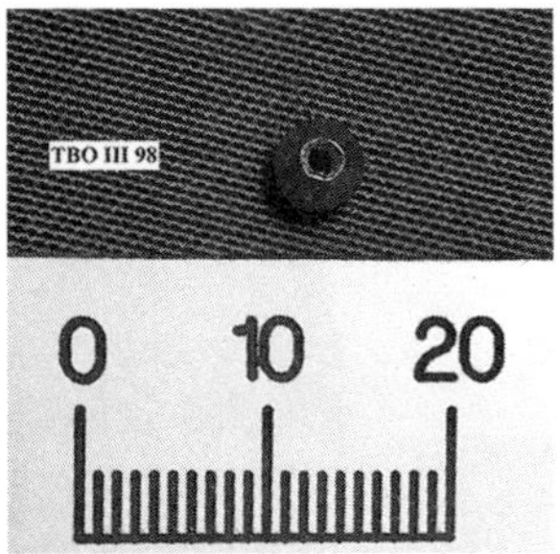

Fig. 4.35. Carnelian bead, TBO III 98.

Fig. 4.36. C/ca nail, TBO III 100.

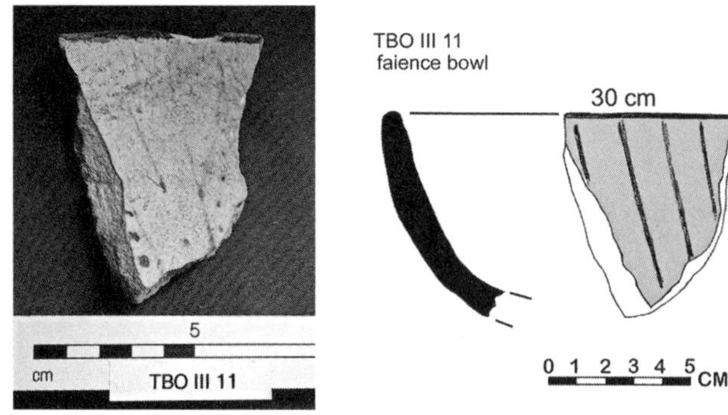

Fig. 4.37. **a**: Faience bowl, TBI III 11; **b**: drawing by Lyla Pinch-Brock.

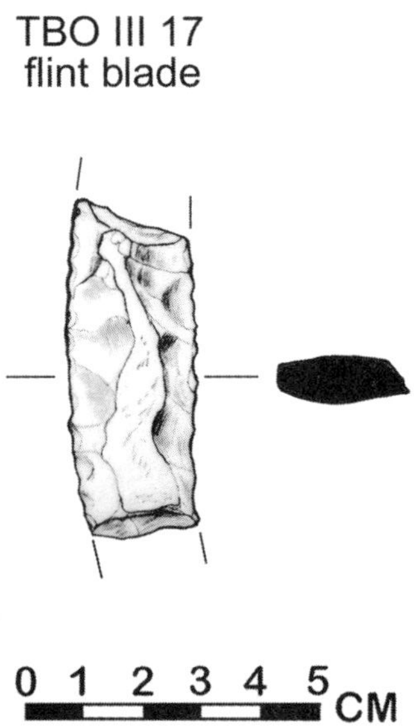

Fig. 4.38. Flint serrated sickle blade, TBO III 17 b (drawing by Lyla Pinch-Brock).

Fig. 4.39. Peridotite(?) bowl or cup rim fragment, TBO III 18.

Fig. 4.40. Clay loom device or token with incision around outer edge, TBO III 28.

Fig. 4.41. Chert pounder or pestle, TBO III 45.

Fig. 4.42. **a** (top): Sandstone conglomerate quern, TBO III 52, top view; **b** (bottom): side view.

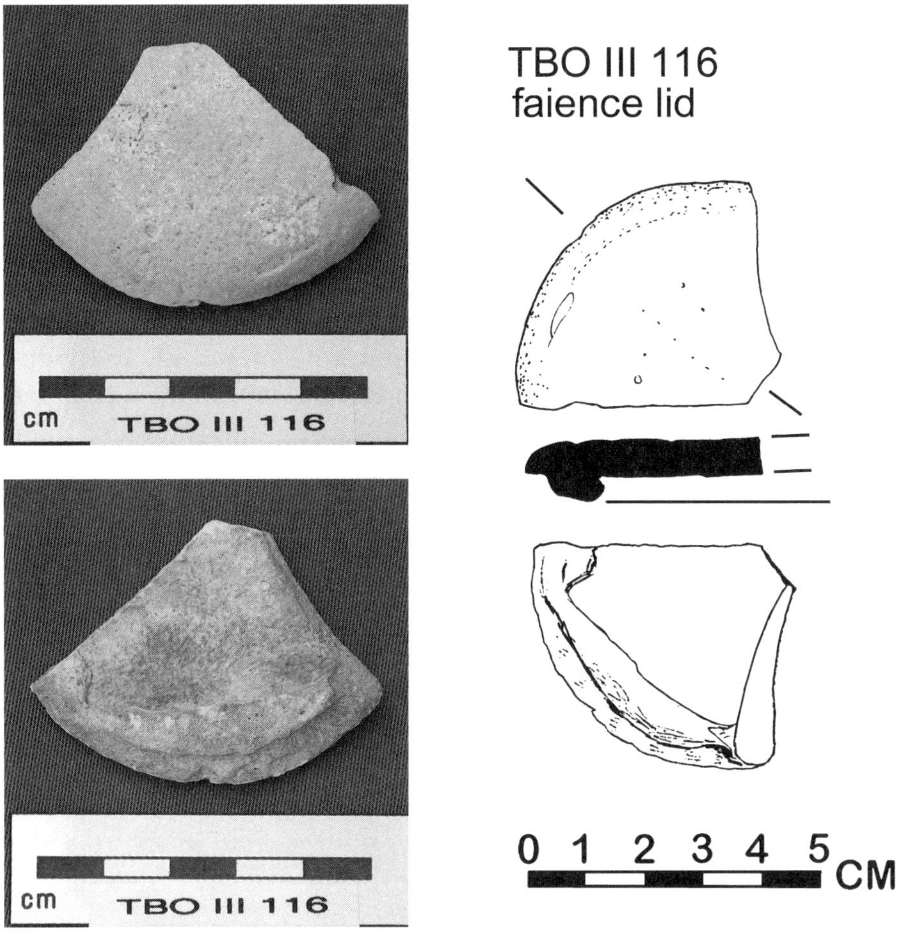

Fig. 4.43.
a–b (top, left; bottom left): Faience lid, TBO III 116;
c (right): drawing by Lyla Pinch-Brock.

Table 4.3. Small Finds from Unit D.

TBO	*Locus*	*Object Type*	*Material*	*Measurements*
III 97	in Tomb 2, loc. 4	metal tool	c/ca	2 cm × 0.5 dia cm
III 98	in Tomb 2, loc. 4	bead	carnelian	0.3 cm × 0.4 dia cm
III 100	in Tomb 2, loc. 4	nail	c/ca	7.3 × 1.5 dia head cm
III 11	III Area 1, Unit D	frag of a 30 cm dia bowl	faience	8 × 6 × 1 cm
III 16	III Area 1, Unit D	flint blade	gray chert	3 × 1.5 × 0.5 cm
III 17	III Area 1, Unit D	sickle blade	chert	5.5 × 2 × 0.5 cm
III 18	III Area 1, Unit D	rim fragment of bowl (?)	periodotite	1.5 × 2 × 0.3 cm
III 28	III Area 1, Unit D	loom device? token?	clay	3 × 3 × 0.5 cm
III 29	III Area 1, Unit D	flint blade	chert	4 × 2.5 × 0.3 cm
III 37	III Area 1, Unit D	token or game piece	reused potsherd	2 × 2 × 0.5 cm
III 40	III Area 1, Unit D	flint flake	chert	2.3 × 1.5 × 0.4 cm
III 45	III Area 1, Unit D	pounder, pestle	chert (?)	3.5 × 12 × 5 cm
III 52	III Area 1, Unit Da	quern	sandstone	23 × 22 × 3 cm
III 58	III Area 1, Unit Da	bead	uncertain	0.6 dia × 0.2 cm
III 116	III Area 1 surface	jar lid	faience	4.7 dia × 1.4 cm

The finds in and around Tomb 2 are a combination of mundane objects associated with food preparation (quern, pestle, and flint blades). There are, however, some more elite objects, such as the faience bowl, an obsidian utensil, and a carnelian bead which may have come from Tomb 2.

Fig. 4.44. Tomb 2a.

Osteological Remains from Tomb 2

The partial remains of one individual were discovered in Tomb 2. Due to robbing activity, both recent and ancient, however, the skeleton was disarticulated and incomplete (< 25%). The skeletal material consists of fragmented cranial, dental, vertebral, and appendicular elements, yielding an MNI (minimum number of individuals) of one. Each of these elements are less than 25% complete, although their condition is good. The age of this individual falls into the mature adult range (35–50 years old), based on ectocranial suture closure and dental wear. Based on measurement of the diameter of the femoral head as described by Bass,[8] the sex of this individual falls into the indeterminate range (43.5–44.5 mm), although it very nearly approaches the "probably female" range (41.5–43.5 mm). Because of the lack of pelvic material, this method was the only one available for determining the individual's sex. One corroborating piece of evidence for the assessment of female in this case, however, comes in the observation of severe osteoarthritic changes in the articular facets of the cervical vertebrae, and in the relative absence of such changes in the lumbar vertebrae. Such a scenario is often associated with females, who, in ancient times, tended to carry heavy items on their heads, eventually leading to arthritic changes in the vertebrae of the neck. Conversely, osteoarthritis of the lumbar vertebrae is more commonly observed in males, who tended to do more heavy lifting with their lower backs. One hesitates, however, to assign sex merely on the basis of pathological conditions. In addition to these pathological changes observable in the individual from Tomb 2, ossification of the posterior ligament attachments of several thoracic vertebrae can also be observed, as well as a well-healed fracture of the right second metatarsal. While the occlusal surfaces of the dentition are well worn, no pathological lesions are observable.

Tomb 2a

Provenance: Field III, Area 1, Unit D1
Dimensions: 80 × 60 cm
Maximal preserved height: 4 course, 0.36 m
Orientation of long axis: 120° off north
Excavator: Scott Haddow

Immediately behind Tomb 2, a tiny mud-brick tomb of an infant was uncovered, Tomb 2a. When ancient excavations occurred for the construction of this burial, the tomb-makers dug into the rear wall of Tomb 2 (figs. 4.29a–b, 4.44). This factor demonstrates that the infant's tomb was made after Tomb 2. Assuming an east–west orientation of the little tomb (it certainly aligns well

8. W. Bass, *Human Osteology: A Laboratory and Field Manual*, 3rd edition (Missouri: Missouri Archaeological Society, 1987) 21.

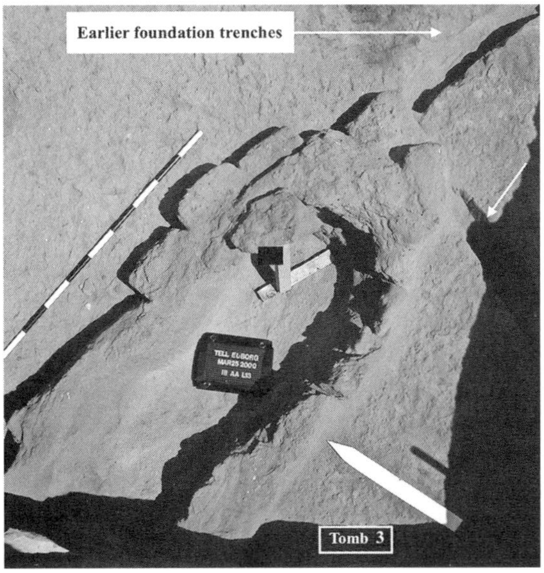

Fig. 4.45. Tomb 3.

Fig. 4.46. Tomb 3, looking south.

with Tomb 2), the roof is entirely missing; only the end walls were standing. No small finds were found, nor evidence for a burial pot in which the infant's remains might have been interred.

Tomb 3

Provenance: Field III, Area 1, Units Aa and Ab
Dimensions: 2.32 × 0.75 m
Maximal preserved height: 5 course, 0.45 m
Orientation of long axis: 120° off north
Excavator: Ronald Bull

Based on its size, Tomb 3 was made for a single adult occupant; it is located 2.75 m west of the northwestern corner of Tomb 1 (figs. 4.45–4.46). Tomb 1 and Tomb 3 share the same orientation and thus were possibly made in the same general period (fig. 4.22). Thoroughly robbed in antiquity, only a small section of the arched roof remained at the foot, or east end, of the tomb. No clay coffin sherds were documented, and a lone small find was documented (TBO III 36 = fig. 4.47), a piece of a copper/copper alloy implement. A small clump of cloth (linen?) (TBO III 74 = fig. 4.48), which could have been used in mummification, was found just outside the tomb in Unit Ab.

This piece of cloth was recently studied by Alistair Dickey,[9] who made the following observations concerning this fragment: it is of "tabby ('plain') weave with multiple layers, highly desiccated. The fiber is unidentified but possibly flax and has a golden-brown color. The color suggests flax but fiber identification can only be confirmed by microscopic analysis at high magnification. Yarn count per cm, yarn spin direction (Z, S, or I) and the thread count cannot be determined due to the preservation condition of the sample. This fragment was found in a disturbed context and appears to show high desiccation levels, which is evident by its color and state of preservation.

9. Alistair Dickey was a member of the Tell el-Borg staff for several seasons and currently is working on his Ph.D. at the University of Liverpool, where he is studying Egyptian textiles. His observations here are based solely on examining images of TBO III 74 and not the linen itself. Unfortunately, since the revolution in Egypt, we have not been able to return to north Sinai to access our small finds for further study.

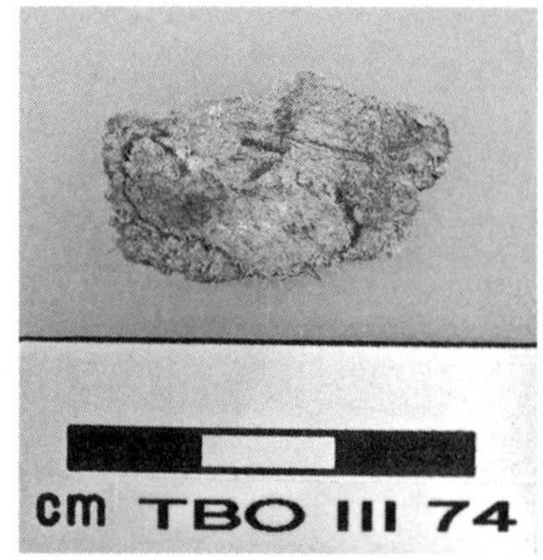

Fig. 4.47 (left). Copper/copper alloy implement, TBO III 36.

Fig. 4.48 (right). Piece of linen, TBO III 74.

Fig. 4.49. **a** (left): Fragment of faience vessel (side view), TBO III 44; **b** (right): Fragment of faience vessel (front view), TBO III 44.

Fig. 4.50. Chert fragment, TBO III 64.

Fig. 4.51. Sandstone pounder, TBO III 46.

There are possibly bone fragments attached (orange circles), indicating possible association with a burial context."

The tomb itself is constructed on and into a hard-packed mud layer (2.5y 5/6), with basal sand appearing at the bottom of the tomb. In the space on the south side of the tomb were remnants of a possible network of mud walls that were approximately 10 cm wide and 3–6 cm high. At the east end of Tomb 3 are two sets of 6–10 cm grooves or channels (6–10 cm deep) that meet to form a corner under the east end of the tomb. This combination of mini-trenches and traces of walls indicates that earlier domestic structures had occupied this area before it became a cemetery. About 15 m west of this mud floor in Field III Area 2, a similar, even larger section of hard-packed mud with channels was documented, surrounded by Tombs 9, 10(?), 11, and 12 (see below).

Due to the fact that Tomb 3 was completely looted and, no doubt, the contents scattered about, and because there is a pre-cemetery occupation phase in Units Aa and Ab, there is no way to distinguish whether the small finds in Units Aa and Ab were from the tomb or the earlier settlement. A few infant bone fragments were documented within the tomb. Given the adult size of the tomb, it seems unlikely that the tomb was intended for an infant alone.

The important loci associated with Tomb 3 in Units Aa and Ab are: (1) man-made surface fill (2.5Y 4/3), (2) hard-packed sand with charred specks and small sherds (2.5Y 6/3), (3) hard-packed mud floor around tomb (2.5Y 5/6), (4) mud-brick of tomb (2.5Y 6/13), (5) fill inside the tomb, largely post robbing, (7) fill in a robber hole, (8) hard-packed sand (2.5Y 6/3) under Locus 5, and 13 in Aa corresponds to locus 5 in Ab; both are inside the tomb.

Most of the small finds were from locus 1, 25 of which originated in Unit Ab, meaning that these objects could have come from various nearby locations, because the upper level of this area

Fig. 4.52. Copper/copper alloy blade, TBO III 55.

Fig. 4.53. Pumice sander, TBO III 57.

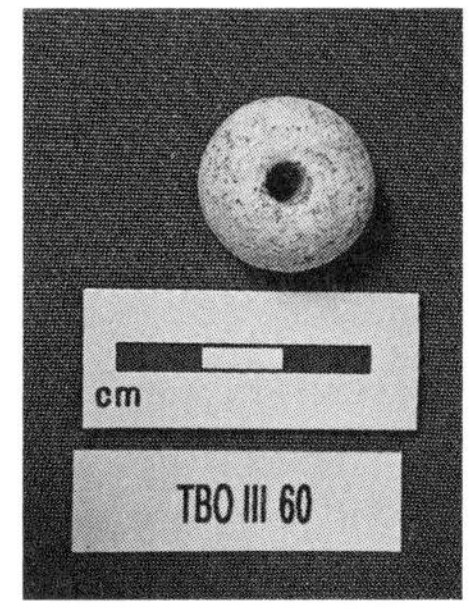

Fig. 4.54. Large white bead, TBO III 60.

Fig. 4.55. Carnelian pebble, TBO III 61

Table 4.4. Small Finds from Units Aa and Ab

TBO	*Field/Locus*	*Object type*	*Material*	*Measurements*
III 51	III Aa loc. 4	cylindrical metal object	c/ca	1.8 × .3 cm
III 36	III Aa loc. 5	cylindrical metal object[2]	c/ca	4 × .3 cm
III 49	III Aa loc. 7	unworked flint chip	chert	2 × 1 × .5 cm
III 50	III Aa loc. 7	small clump of metal	c/ca	0.7 × 0.6 × 0.4 cm
III 44	III Aa loc. 8	fragment of a vessel	faience	1 × 0.8 × 1 cm
III 64	II Aa loc. 13	flint fragment	chert	7 × 5 × 0.3 cm
III 56	III Ab surface	round stone pounder	uncertain	5 × 5 × 5 cm
III 111	III Ab surface	squared grinder or pounder	granite	5 × 5 × 5 cm
III 46	III Ab loc. 1	pounder	sandstone	7.5 × 6.5 × 4.5 cm
III 55	III Ab loc. 1	2 joining pieces of metal blade	c/ca	3.7 × 1.8 × 03 cm
III 57	III Ab loc. 1	sander	pumice	8.0 × 4.5 × 5 cm
III 59	III Ab loc. 1	metal nail	c/ca	3.5 × 0.3 cm
III 60	III Ab loc. 1	white bead	faience (?)	1.7 dia × 1 cm
III 61	III Ab loc. 1	polished pebble	carnelian?	1.8 × 1.3 × 0.5 cm
III 62	III Ab loc. 1	black polished stone	uncertain	3 × 2 × 1.3 cm
III 66	III Ab loc. 1	flat circular bead	faience	0.5 dia × 0.1 cm
III 68	III Ab loc. 1	lid or stopper for an amphora (?)	sandstone	10.5 × 8.5 × 1.5 cm
III 69[3]	III Ab loc. 1	2 beads	faience	1.5 × dia × 0.3 cm
III 70	III Ab loc. 1	1 bead	faience	0.7 dia × 0.3 cm
III 71	III Ab loc. 1	1 bead	faience	1 dia × 0.2 cm
III 72	III Ab loc. 1	2 beads	faience	0.4 × 0.2 cm
III 73	III Ab loc. 1	flint blade	chert	5 × 2.5 × 0.5 cm
III 74	III Ab loc. 1	cloth, mummy wrapping (?)	linen	1.5 × 2.5 cm
III 76	III Ab loc. 1	arrowhead	c/ca	5 × 1 × 0.2 cm
III 78	III Ab loc. 1	2 pieces of yellow and white vessel	faience	1 × 1.3; 0.8x 0.7 cm
III 79	III Ab loc. 1	chert flake	chert	1 × 1.5 × 0.3 cm
III 80	III Ab loc. 1	uncertain	bone or ivory	1.5 × 1.4 × 0.4 cm
III 81a	III Ab loc. 1	2 pieces of metal[4]	c/ca	3.5 × 0.8 × 0.3
III 81b	III Ab loc. 1	circular piece of metal	c/ca	1 × 1.5 cm
III 82	III Ab loc. 1	piece of slag	copper slag	2.2 × 2.1 × 1.2 cm
III 114	III Ab loc. 1	fragment of stone bowl or quern	amygdaloidal basalt	9 × 3.35 × 5 cm

Fig. 4.56. Polished stone, TBO III 62.

Fig. 4.57. Sandstone stopper, TBO III 68.

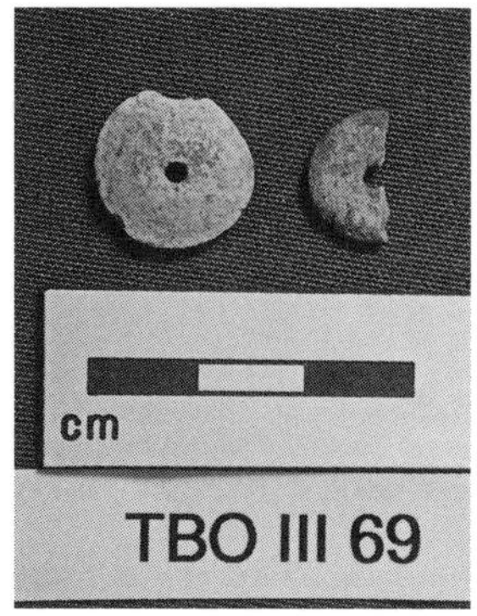

Fig. 4.58. Two beads, TBO III 69.

Fig. 4.59. Faience bead, TBO III 70.

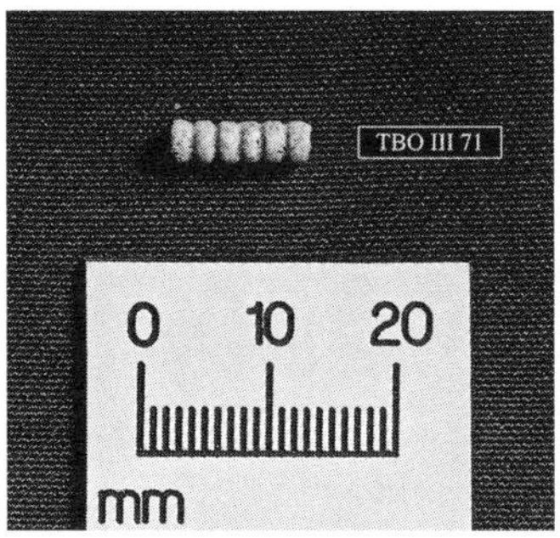

Fig. 4.60. Tube faience bead, TBO III 71.

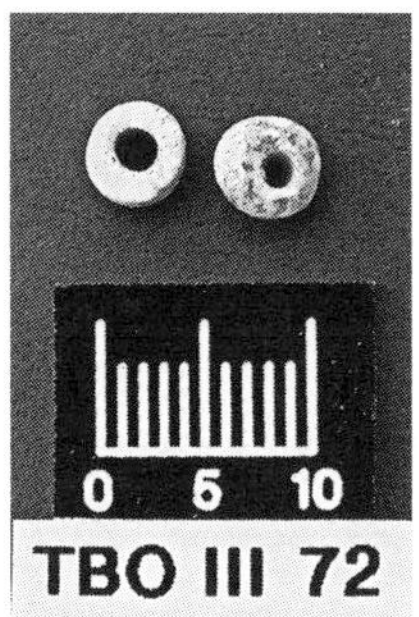

Fig. 4.61. Two white faience beads, TBO III 72.

Fig. 4.62. Flint blade, TBO III 73.

Fig. 4.63. Copper/copper alloy arrowhead, TBO III 76.

Fig. 4.64. Two fragments of faience dish or tile, TBO III 78.

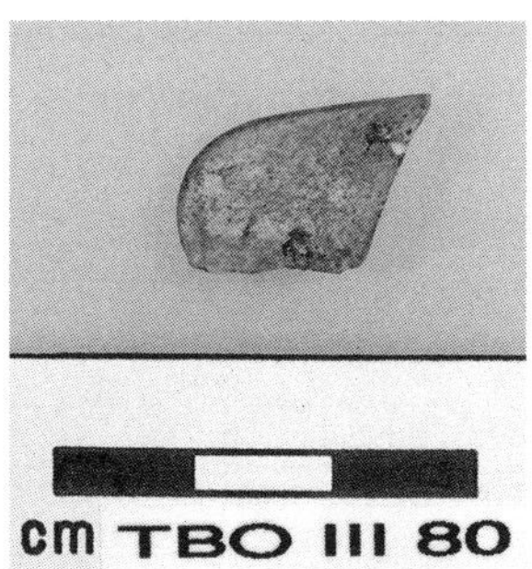

Fig. 4.65. Ivory tool, TBO III 80.

Fig. 4.66. Copper/copper alloy implement, TBO III 81.

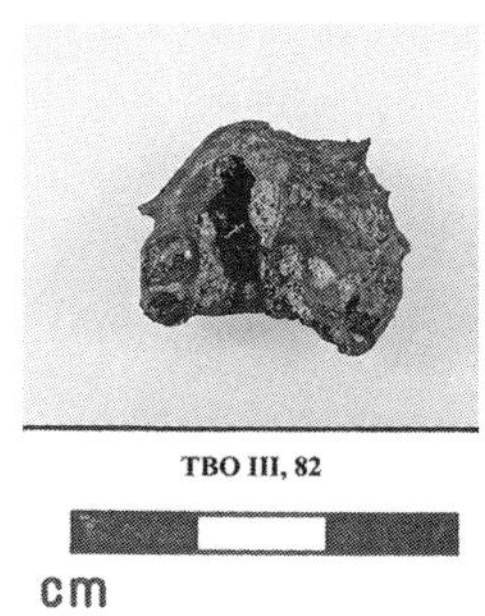

Fig. 4.67. Lump of copper slag, TBO III 82.

was disturbed by modern activity. Tomb 3 was very small, and apart from smaller objects, it seems doubtful that larger finds such as querns and pounders would have originated inside the grave.

Discussion of Small Finds from Units Aa and Ab

A piece of pumice (TBO III 57 = TBO 4.53) was discovered, but not within the tomb as was the case with most of the small finds in Aa and Ab. In all, three pieces of pumice were found in

Fig. 4.68–4.69. Basalt bowl or quern fragment: top view (left); side view (right); TBO III 114.

our excavations. The other two pieces (TBO 0659 and 0660) were recovered from "Well D," the Ramesside period feature built on the fired-brick moat wall of the 18th Dynasty fort (*Tell el-Borg I*, 267–69). So, like the sample from Field III, the provenance of the pumice gives no indication of original age or usage. Analysis of other samples of north Sinai pumice by the University of Vienna suggest that Thera/Santorini is the source of this material.[10]

Coppper/copper alloy fragments and objects abound at Tell el-Borg, but slag is rare. Hence the discovery of a small lump (2.2 × 2.1 × 1.2 cm) of slag (TBO III 82 = fig. 4.67) is indeed significant. The prevailing evidence is that smelting operations occurred closer to the mines, be they Sinai or Cyprus, and ingots were transported for use elsewhere.[11]

Other Osteological Remains from Field III Area 1

Due to the disturbed nature of Field III, ancient looting, canal construction related excavations, and modern-day robbing, most of the human remains discovered in Area 1 were not in tombs but scattered in different loci and on the surface. Consequently, we are dealing with mainly isolated, fragmentary elements found in debris contexts. Of the sixteen individuals recovered from these contexts, eight are adults, two are juveniles, two are children (9–11 years old, and 2–4 years old) and one is an infant (birth–3 years). Three individuals cannot be assigned an age due to the incomplete and fragmentary nature of the skeletal material. Several of the teeth in this assemblage are extremely worn, including the lower left first and second molars of one adult individual, and the upper right first and second premolars of a second adult individual. This second adult also has moderate to heavy calculus deposits on the buccal surface of the upper second premolar and on the buccal and lingual surfaces of the lower right canine. Lastly, two occlusal carious lesions penetrating to the root of the upper left first molar, and two occlusal carious lesions on the upper right first molar are observable in a third adult. Carabelli's cusps are observable on two of seven upper first molars recovered from Field III.

10. G. Steinhausen et al., "Provenancing Archaeological Pumice Finds from North Sinai," *Naturwissenshaft* 97 (2010) 403–10.

11. Decades ago, Peet and Gardiner reported that "at Serabit el-Khadim there are no traces of ancient copper working" (A. H. Gardiner, T. E. Peet, and J. Cerny, *The Inscriptions of Sinai* [London: EES, 1955], 5), but this is likely because turquoise was the focus of mining in that area, whereas at nearby Wadi Maghara and elsewhere in south Sinai the evidence for smelting operations has been document; see ibid. 5–7. Petrie reported large quantities of slag in the Markha Plain (ibid., 5). Now the fort associated with this operation has been discovered at Ras Budran (G. Mumford, "Tell Ras Budran (Site 345): Defining Egypt's Eastern Frontier and Mining Operations in South Sinai during the Late Old Kingdom (Early EB IV/MB I)," *BASOR* 342 (May 2006) 13–67; see also G. Mumford and S. Parcak, "Pharaonic Ventures into South Sinai: el-Markha Plain Site 346," *JEA* 89 (2003) 83–116. Further on copper production in Sinai, see Itzak Beit Arieh, *Archaeology of Sinai: The Ophir Expedition* (Tel Aviv: Tel Aviv University, 2003) 96–208

Fig. 4.70. Tomb 4, looking west.

Field III Area 2

Tomb 4

Provenance: Field III Area 2, Units A, C, D, H, and M
Dimensions: 7.70 × 3.30 m (3.6 m rear section)
Maximal preserved height: 21 courses
Brick size: 35 × 18 × 8 cm
Orientation of long axis: 120° off north
Excavator: Scott Haddow, assisted by Stephen Olsen

Field III Area 2 is situated immediately west of Area 1 (figs. 4.3; 4.70). The two were demarcated by a recently laid road on the very western edge of Area 1. Tomb 4 is located approximately 17 m south-southwest of Tomb 2 and was excavated in 2001 and 2002. Like Tombs 1–3, the long axis of this structure is approximately 120° off magnetic north (i.e., northwest–southeast). The tomb is made of mud brick (size: 35 × 18 × 8 cm; color: 10YR 4/2), rectangular in shape and comprised of three chambers: an entrance shaft (facing east-southeast), a large main chamber accessed through the entrance shaft, and a smaller rear chamber, which does not appear to communicate with the main chamber (figs. 4.71, 4.72, and 4.73). The ceiling of the tomb would most likely have been vaulted, then topped with a flat roof. However, nothing of the roof remains to give an indication of the construction techniques employed. Due to time constraints, only the northeast face of the tomb structure was completely excavated to the foundation level (1.69 m below datum). However, in 2005, the rear southwest corner of Tomb 4 was exposed, revealing 21 courses of brick (fig. 4.74). Scores of sherds from a number of shattered clay coffins were discovered in the three parts of the tomb and beyond its wall. Two were largely restored (TBO 0065 and 0078) and are discussed and depicted in detail in chapter 5.

Entrance Shaft

The entrance shaft is roughly square in shape (external dimensions ~2.10 m × 1.90 m; internal dimensions 1.4 × 1.2 m) and 19 courses of mud brick are preserved, largely situated in Unit C. The depth below datum of the floor of the shaft is 201 cm. A large, roughly hewn limestone block, 1.08 m in height, seals the entrance to the main chamber (fig. 4.10). The block appears to have been reused: much of its surface is well-polished (perhaps it was once used as a paving stone). Robbers appear to have avoided the trouble of removing the block by digging through the mud brick immediately above it. A large amount of human bone, pottery fragments, and ceramic sarcophagus fragments were recovered from the entrance shaft and immediately around it (loc. 6). Several of the sarcophagus fragments have molded anthropomorphic features (i.e., arms, hands, hair, etc.).

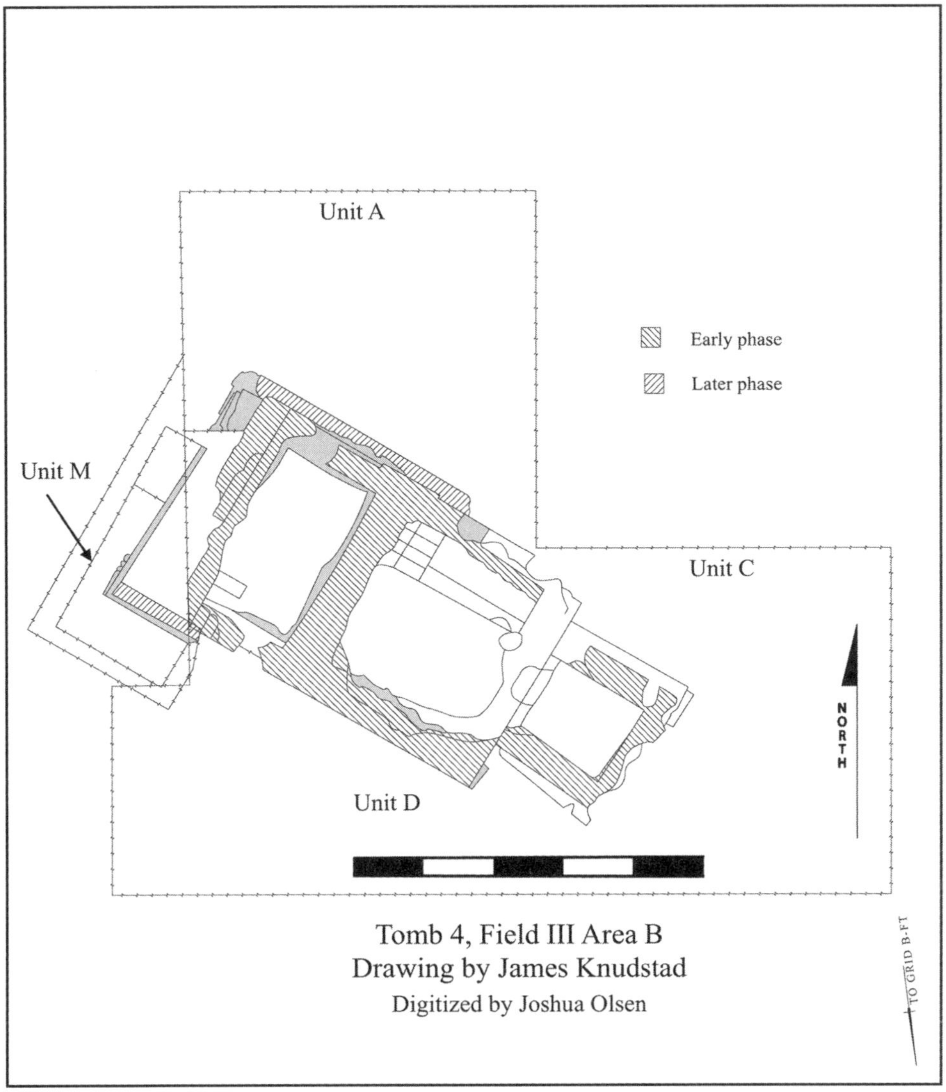

Fig. 4.71. Tomb 4, top plan.

Fig. 4.72. Tomb 4, looking north.

Fig. 4.73. Tomb 4, from end of tomb, looking south.

Fig. 4.74. Tomb 4, western back corner.

Fig. 4.75. Limestone slabs from Tomb 4.

Fig. 4.76 Limestone architectural pieces from the main chamber of Tomb 4.

Fig. 4.77. Fragments of painted plaster, TBO 0066.

Main Chamber

The main chamber of Tomb 4 is roughly square in shape (2.5 × 2.4 m) and contains a single burial niche built into the northeast wall. No human remains were found in the niche, however. Evidence for a phase of reconstruction or reuse of the tomb can be seen in the use of two types of mud brick along the northeast face of the chamber. A lighter, sandier type of brick appears to have been used to patch up or seal a large breach in the wall. In addition, the large limestone block sealing the main chamber from the entrance shaft has been largely bricked up (i.e., sealed) from the inside, as if the entrance shaft no longer served as the point of access to the tomb. There appears to be no way of accessing the rear chamber from the main chamber.

Two large rectangular limestone blocks were recovered from the fill within the main chamber (fig. 4.75). Their purpose remains unclear in the context of the tomb; however, the larger of the two blocks (1.02 × 0.40 m) had originally served as a doorsill. Smaller pieces were also found. Perhaps they had been reused as paving stones for the floor of the chamber. Several modern artifacts (i.e., plastic, iron fragments) were recovered from the lowest levels of both chambers, evidence of recent looting. Additionally, ancient domestic items not usually associated with burials at Tell el-Borg were recovered (i.e., stone querns and mortar fragments).

During excavation of the main chamber, a large amount of loose painted and unpainted plaster was recovered. The painted plaster fragments (blue, red, yellow, white) were extremely thin and fragile. The unpainted plaster fragments were pale yellow in color and generally thicker than the painted plaster fragments. In some cases, these unpainted fragments appeared to be molded and may have been part of decorative elements applied to the inner walls of the chamber (figs. 4.76, 4.77). Unfortunately, none of this type of plaster was found in situ. However, in the northeast corner, above the burial niche (fig. 4.78), remnants of painted plaster (red and blue on white) still adhere to the wall surface (fig. 4. 79a–b). It is likely that much of the painted plaster recovered from the main chamber derived from the wall surfaces. Though a tiny amount, this colored plaster indicates that this chamber was plastered and decorated. This may well have been the case with other large tombs like Tomb 1 and 2.

Furthermore, lodged into the eastern end of the niche is a sherd from this clay coffin (fig. 4.80). This sherd likely was wedged into this position when the coffin was shattered by the ancient robbers. A black resinous substance adheres to the inside wall of the crypt. In addition to large amounts of pottery sherds and plaster fragments, several stone and glass beads of varying size and color were found, including several small ones of carnelian, and a larger yellow and black

Fig. 4.78. Burial niche in Tomb 4.

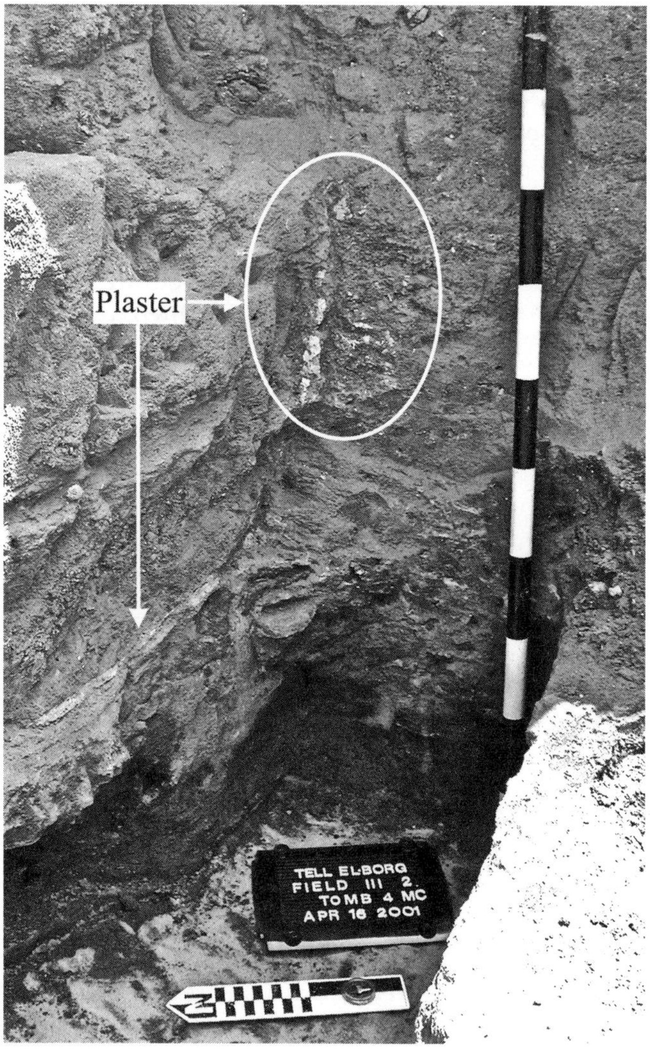

Fig. 4.79**a** (left)–**b** (right). Plaster intact over burial niche.

Fig. 4.80. Plaster, resin, and coffin fragment adhering to wall of niche.

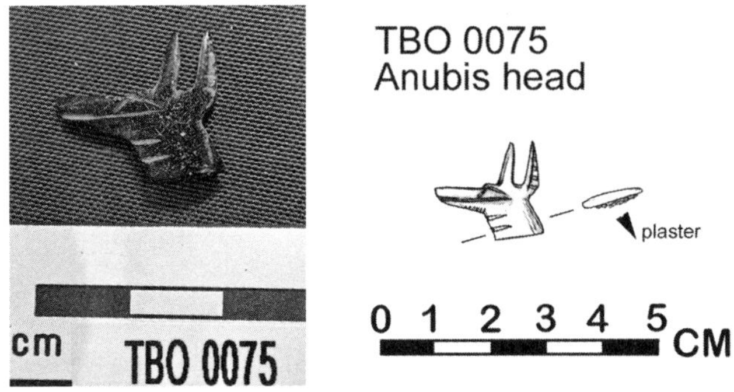

Fig. 4.81. **a** (left): Photo: figure of Anubis, TBO 0075; **b** (right): Drawing of figure of Anubis, TBO 0075 (Lyla Pinch-Brock).

striped glass bead (see below). Last, a small two-dimensional (i.e., flat) Anubis head (steatite?) was also recovered (TBO 0075 = fig. 4.81a–b). Some plaster was noted under the neck of the jackal, suggesting that the figure was glued onto a piece of funerary furniture.

Rear Chamber

The rear chamber of Tomb 4 is rectangular in shape and approximately half the size of the main chamber, (2.4 × 1.4 m). As mentioned above, the rear chamber does not appear to communicate with the main chamber. It may be that access to the rear chamber was gained through another portal, or that it was sealed off completely after the first use. Unfortunately, time constraints did not allow for the complete exposure of the outer (west) face of the rear part of Tomb 4, but there were no signs on the inner wall to suggest that this chamber was accessed from the back side. Robbing activity is responsible for a very large hole dug into the rear wall of this chamber, which allowed us to observe its unusual thickness when compared to its counterparts (figs. 4.72, 4.73). Two small rectangular limestone blocks (one broken) were recovered in the fill of the rear chamber, while a third was found lying flat and in situ, at approximately floor level. This suggests that these blocks, like their larger counterparts found in the main chamber, were perhaps used as paving stones for the floor of the tomb. Indeed, the first block found in the fill (51 cm × 24 cm × 10 cm) had mud brick adhering to both surfaces.

Material recovered from the rear chamber is similar to that recovered from the main chamber and included large amounts of pottery, human bone, and a few beads. The highest concentrations of plaster (both painted and unpainted) appear to derive from the main chamber, although a small amount was recovered from the rear chamber as well (figs. 4.76, 4.77). Modern artifacts were also recovered from the rear chamber, including iron fragments possibly relating to the recent military activities at Tell el-Borg and elsewhere. Finally, a single stamped potsherd containing the cartouche of Amenhotep II was recovered from Locus 1 immediately above the rear chamber (fig. 4.82a–b) in Unit D, but it is unclear whether or not the sherd originally derived from Tomb 4 or had been removed from another location and subsequently become part of the surface debris scattered throughout Field III. It was noted previously that the design of the impression on the sherd appears to be a combination of the 𓉴-sign with the cartouche above it, making it look like

Fig. 4.82**a** (left). Photo, sherd with prenomen of Amenhotep II (TBO 0071).
Fig. 4.82**b** (right). Drawing, sherd with prenomen of Amenhotep II (by Lyla Pinch-Brock).

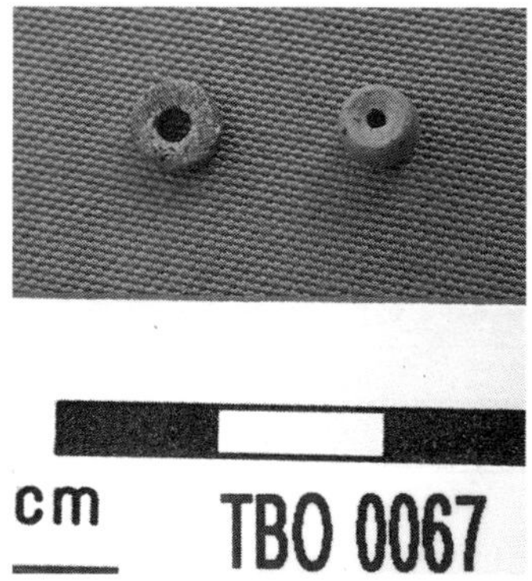

Fig. 4.83. TBO 0067 Faience beads.

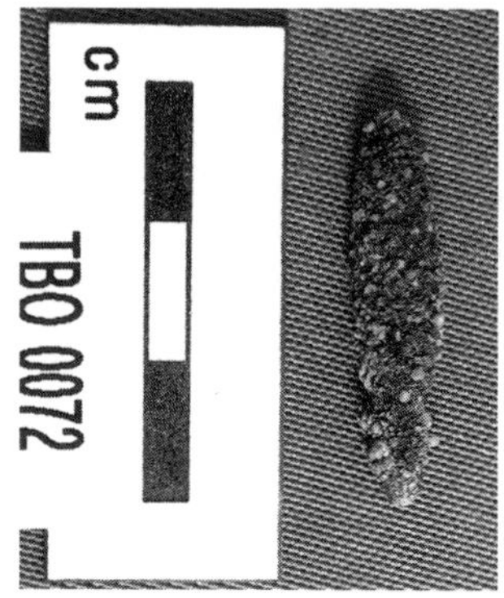

Fig. 4.84. TBO 0072 Copper/copper alloy tool.

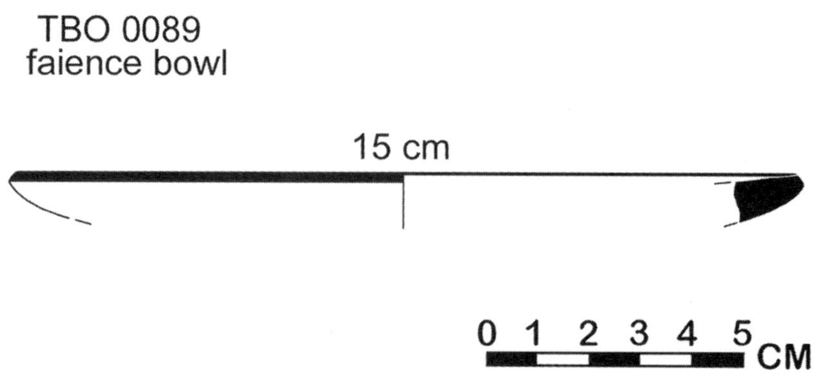

Fig. 4.85**a** (left). Photo, TBO 0089 faience bowl fragment.
Fig. 4.85**b** (right). Drawing of TBO 0089 faience bowl fragment (by Lyla Pinch-Brock).

an ☥-sign with the name *ꜥꜣ ḫprw rꜥ* in the loop. This gives the playful writing, "Ankh-kheperu-ra gives life."[12]

The cartouche is, in fact, somewhat early when compared with the rest of the pottery found in and immediately around the tomb. It ranges from the later 18th Dynasty and into the 19th Dynasty (see *Tell el-Borg I*, 372–73). Commenting on the construction of Tomb 4, both James Knudstad and Manfred Bietak (who visited during the 2001 season) have suggested that it had been rebuilt and/or reused at least once. At least two building phases are evident. Whether the earliest phase of the tomb dates as early as the end of the 15th century B.C., when Amenhotep II reigned, remains a possibility.

12. James K. Hoffmeier and Mohamed Abd el-Maksoud, "A New Military Site on 'the Ways of Horus' — Tell el-Borg 1999–2001: A Preliminary Report," *JEA* 89 (2003) 188.

Table 4.5. Small Finds from/or Associated with Tomb 4

TBO	*Unit/loc*	*Object type*	*Material*	*Measurements*
0067	III 2 A	2 beads	faience	n/a
0068	III 2 A	point of blade	c/ca	2.7 × 1.1 × 0.4 cm
0069	III 2 A	nail or cylindrical tool fragment	c/ca	1.9 × 0.5 dia cm
0072	III 2 A	metal implement/tool	c/ca	3.2 × .65 dia cm
0089	III 2 A	rim fragment of bowl	faience	15 dia cm
0109	III 2 A	rim of stone bowl	travertine	14 dia cm
0114	III 2 A	barrel-shaped bead	clay	2.2 × 1.4 dia cm
0115	III 2 A	point of tool (?)	c/ca	2.1 × 0.5 dia cm
0066	III 2 C	pieces of plaster, some with paint	gypsum	n/a
0084	III 2 C	small vessel fragment	glass	1.4 × 1.1 × 0.4 cm
0098	III 2 C	chipped stone tool, awl (?)	rhyolite or dacite porphyry	3.6 × 1.9 × 0.8
0159	III 2 C	flint tool	chert	4 × 3.9 × 0.62 cm
0181	III 2 C	rim of vessel	c/ca	1.8 × 0.9 × 0.7 cm
0190	III 2 C	5 beads of various sizes	carnelian	n/a
0196	III 2 C	4 pieces of broken tool	c/ca	n/a
0065	III 2 C	sherds from coffin	clay	n/a
0429	III 2 C L1	round token	Nile B2 clay	4.5 dia × 1.0 cm
0071	III 2 D	sherd with cartouche of *ʿ3 ḫprw rʿ*	Marl D	8.2 × 5.4 × 0.6 cm
0074	III 2 D	game piece	clay	2.3 × 2.3 × 1.1 cm
0095	III 2 D	7 white beads	faience	n/a
0096	III 2 D	piece of jewelry	sardonyx	3.5 × 1.1 × 0.2 cm
0165	III 2 D	distal flake	chert	2.2 × 3.3 × .45 cm
0180	III 2 D	painted plaster fragment	gypsum	4.5 × 2.1 × 1.3 cm
0183	III 2 D L3	bead	carnelian	0.4 × 0.3 dia cm
0184	III 2 D L3	ring fragment	c/ca	0.6 × 0.3 dia cm
0185	III 2 D L3	flat gray scalloped bead	faience	0.1 × 0.6 dia cm
0078	III 2 Tb 4	sherds from coffin	clay	n/a
0179	III 2 Tb 4 L3	bead	carnelian	0.4 × 0.3 dia cm
0169	III 2 Tb 4 L9	bead	carnelian	0.4 × 0.4 dia cm
0170	III 2 Tb 4 L9	dark blue tube bead (4 sections)	faience	0.9 × .15 dia cm
0171	III 2 Tb 4 L9	finial (?) or jewelry piece	faience	1.5 × 1.5 dia cm
0543	III 2 Tb 4 L9	neck of stone jar	travertine	3.5 × 1.7 × 1.0 cm
0108	III Tb 4 L9	white bead	faience	0.5 × .0.5 dia cm
0103	III Tb 4 L11	piece of a statue base(?), reused polisher	ferruginous sandstone	4.6 × 5.0 × 4.0 cm

Discussion of Small Finds from and Around Tomb 4

This large tomb, the use of which spanned several generations, was rich in finds despite the intensive plundering. Discussion of the two most important finds were treated above—that is, the sherd with the prenomen of Amenhotep II and the Anubis amulet. Various types of faience beads dominate the list of small finds, and carnelian examples are also attested (TBO 169, 179, 183, and 0190). Travertine (TBO 0109 and 543) and a faience jar fragment (TBO 0089) represent more elite objects associated with Tomb 4.

Architectural Comparanda for Tombs 1, 2 and 4

Tombs 2 and 4, and likely Tomb 1, originally had two main architectural features: (1) a vertical shaft by which the tombs were accessed, and (2) a vaulted burial chamber, or as in the case of

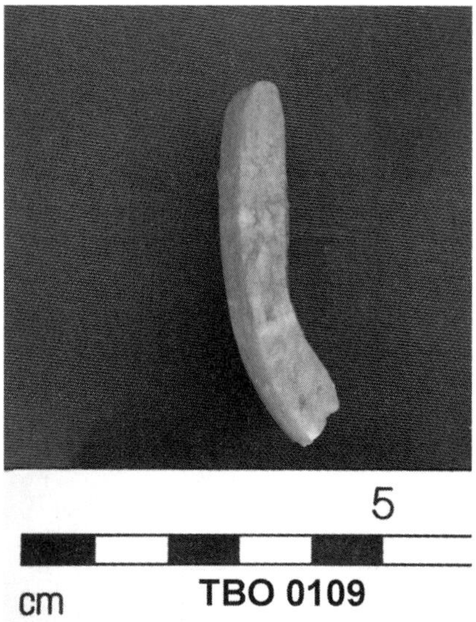

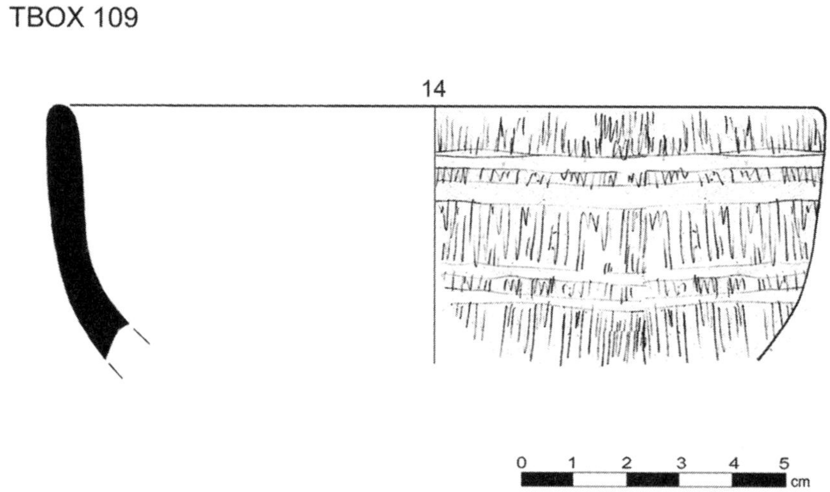

Fig. 4.86**a** (left): Photo, TBO 0109 rim of travertine bowl.
Fig. 4.86**b** (right): Drawing, TBO 0109 rim of travertine bowl (by Lyla Pinch-Brock).

Fig. 4.87. TBO 0114 clay barrel bead.

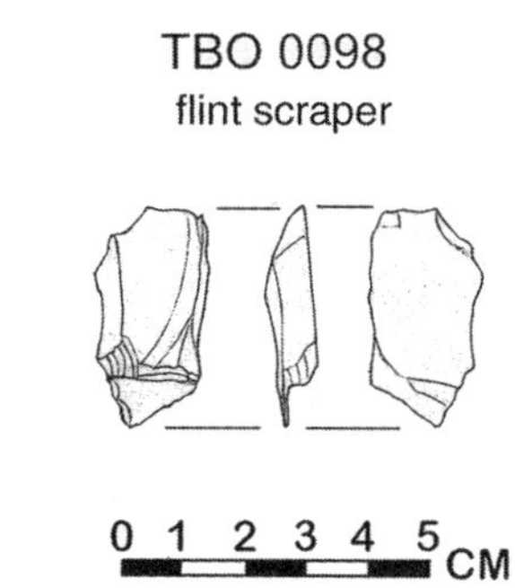

Fig. 4.88**a** (left): Photo, TBO 0098 chipped stone tool. **b** (right): Drawing, chipped stone tool (by Lyla Pinch-Brock).

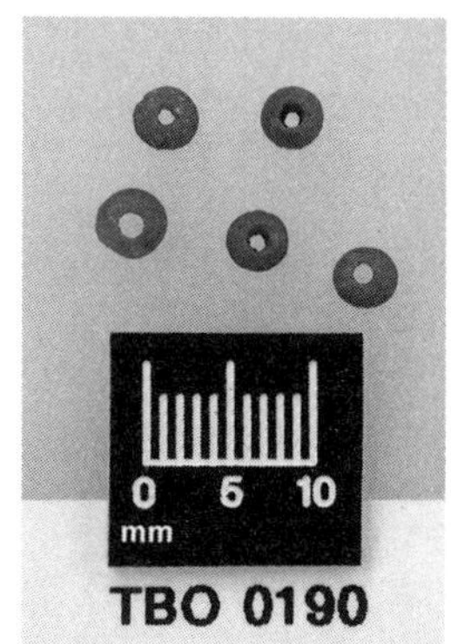

Fig. 4.89. TBO 0190 five carnelian beads.

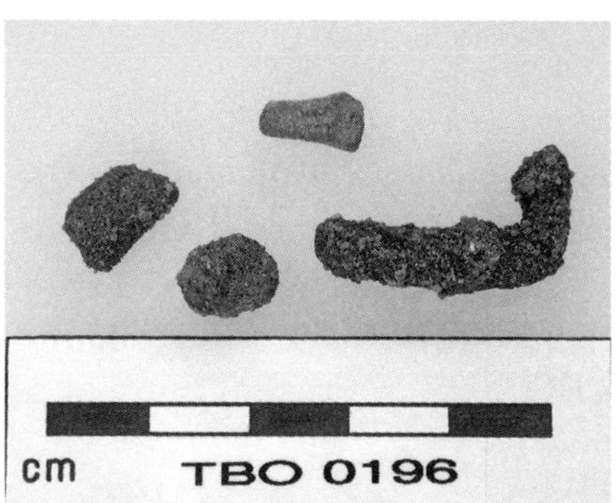

Fig. 4.90. TBO 0196 Pieces of a metal tool.

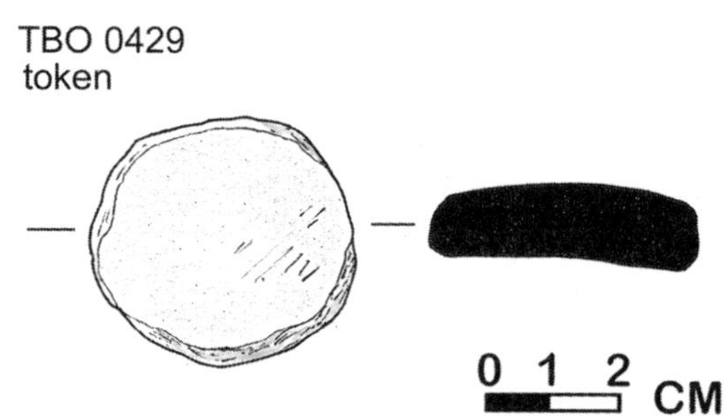

Fig. 4.91**a** (left): Photo, TBO 0429 Clay token.
b (right): Drawing, TBO 0429 Clay token (by Lyla Pinch-Brock).

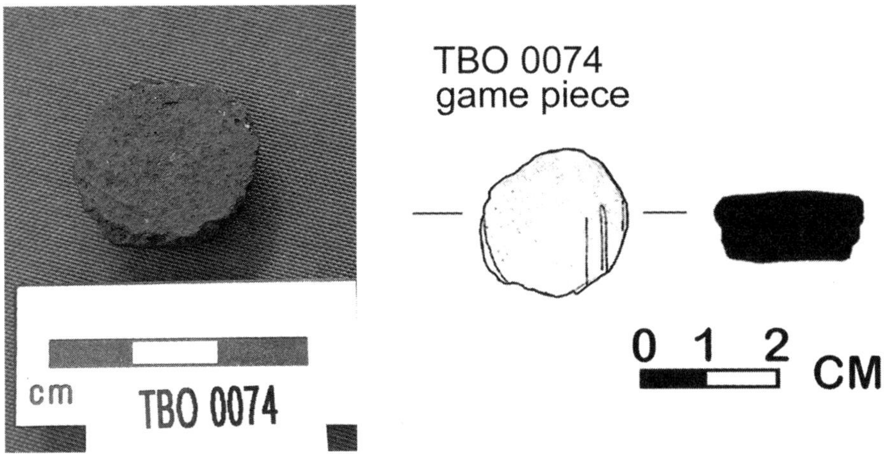

Fig. 4.92. **a** (left): Photo, TBO 0074 Clay game piece. **b** (right): Drawing, TBO 0074 Clay game piece (by Lyla Pinch-Brock).

Fig. 4.93. TBO 0095 Collection of faience beads.

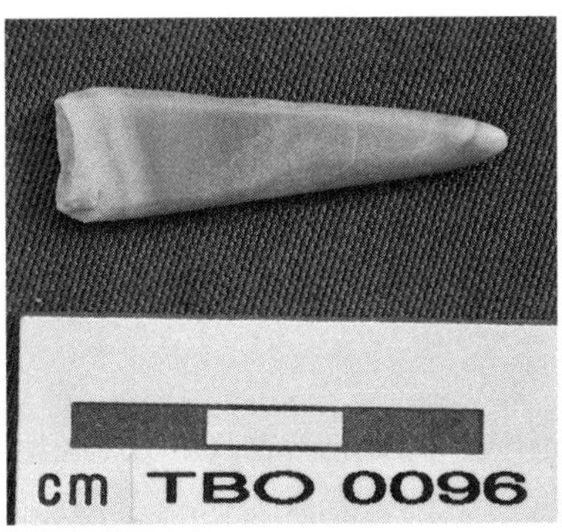

Fig. 4.94. TBO 0096 Sardonyx jewelry piece (?).

Fig. 4.95. TBO 0165 Chert blade

Fig. 4.96. TBO 0180 Piece of painted plaster.

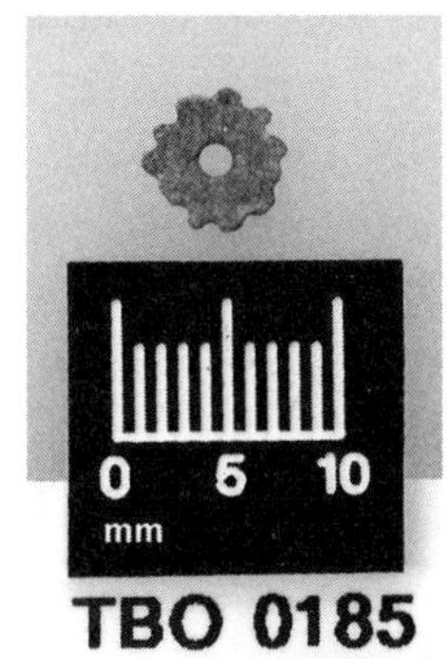

Fig. 4.97. TBO 0185 Faience scalloped bead.

Tomb 4, a second burial chamber (that seems to have been added subsequently). Access from the entry shaft to the burial area was blocked. The blocking used in Tomb 2 was a thick layer of mud (0.38 m), whereas a stone served the purpose in Tomb 4. These mud-brick graves find a parallel at Tell Hebua IV, about 5 km west-northwest of Tell el-Borg. Hebua IV has a necropolis of the frontier town Tjaru/Sile. While only briefly excavated in 1993–1994 by an Austrian team led by Josef Dorner, a number of New Kingdom burials were uncovered and a preliminary report published.[13] The largest tomb uncovered at Hebua IV, r/2 Nr. 1, is typologically the same as the largest tombs in Field III at Tell el-Borg. Though bigger (9.15 x 4.06 m) than Tomb 4 (7.70 x 3.30 m), the plan is the same. Its state of preservation is better than any of the Borg tombs, revealing the construction of the vaulted roof, even though large sections of it were lost (see fig. 101).[14] The

13. Dorner, "Vorbericht über Grabungskampagnen 1993/94 auf Tell Hebwas IV/Süd am Nordsinai," 167–77.

14. The images in fig. 101a–c were originally published in Dorner, "Vorbericht über Grabungskampagnen 1993/94 auf Tell Hebwa IV/Süd am Nordsinai," 167–77. Permission to reprint these images was graciously given by Manfred Bietak and Ernst Czerny. Special thanks to Dr. Czerny for providing the images used here, including fig. 4.173.

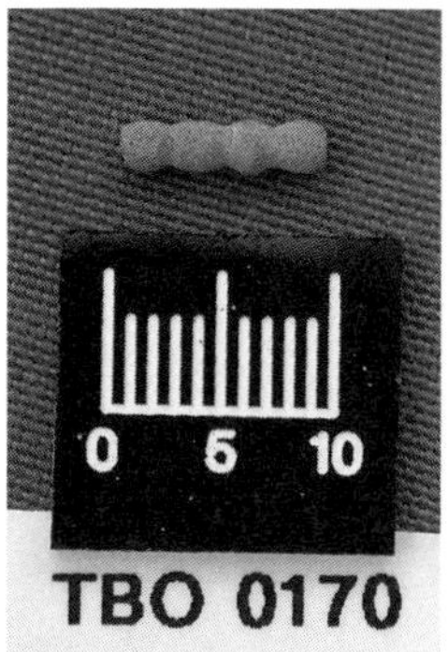

Fig. 4.98. TBO 0170 Faience tube bead.

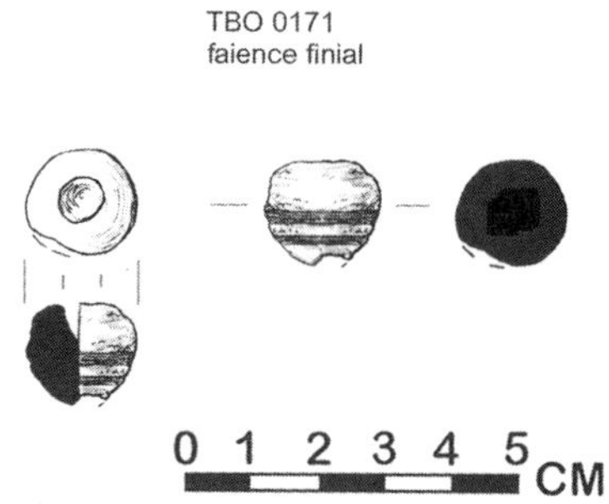

Fig. 4.99. **a** (left): Photo, TBO 0171 Faience finial or jewelry piece; **b** (right): Drawing, TBO 0171 Faience finial or jewelry piece (by Lyla Pinch-Brock).

Fig. 4.100. TBO 0103 Sandstone polisher (?).

passage between the entrance shaft and the burial chamber was separated by the stone that was held in place by slotted stone doorjambs and threshold, where a slab of stone was slid into place (fig. 101b–c). Dorner concludes that this style of tomb dates to the middle of the 18th Dynasty.[15] A preliminary report by David Aston on the pottery from this tomb group supports this dating. The burials in Field III at Tell el-Borg, based on the architecture and ceramic evidence, certainly date to the same general period.

Osteological Remains in and Around Tomb 4

Because of the high levels of disturbance in Field III, it is difficult to ascertain the precise origin of much of the disarticulated human bone recovered. The loci from Field III Area 2 that contain human bone are 1, 3, 4, 6, 8, and 9. Of these, only Loci 3 and 9 came from within the tomb structure itself. It is likely, however, that the human bone from Locus 6, found immediately outside the entrance shaft of the tomb, also originated from Tomb 4. For this reason, human skeletal remains from Tomb 4-derived loci (3, 6, 9) will be discussed separately from the human bone recovered from the remaining external loci (1, 4, 8).

Tomb 4 Loci (3, 6, 9)

Locus 3 comprises the uppermost layer of fill within the rear and main chambers, while comprising the entire fill component within the entrance shaft. Locus 6 consists of a localized sandy layer surrounding the entrance shaft and consisting of human bone, mud-brick debris, and anthropomorphic sarcophagus and ceramic fragments. Locus 9 comprises the intermediate fill layers within the rear and main chambers only. No human bone was recovered from the lower loci within the main and rear chambers. While human remains were recovered from all three tomb compartments, the majority of human bones were recovered from the main chamber, followed by the rear chamber and entrance shaft.

Locus 6

The MNI recovered from locus 6 is two: both adults. The skeletal material consists of cranial, vertebral, and lower long-bone fragments, hand and foot elements, and teeth. The condition of

15. Dorner, "Vorbericht über Grabungskampagnen 1993/94 auf Tell Hebwa IV/Süd am Nordsinai," 168.

Fig. 101. Tell Hebua, Tomb 1.

the bone is good, although individual elements—with the exception of the teeth and the hand and foot bones—are highly fragmented and incomplete. Assignation of sex and finer age-grades for the skeletal material cannot be made due to the fragmentary nature of the remains, and the lack of diagnostic skeletal elements. Of five permanent anterior teeth recovered from Locus 6, three of four contiguous mandibular teeth from a single individual display interproximal carious lesions at the cemento-enamel junction (CEJ). The teeth of this individual are also well worn.

Entrance Shaft

The MNI recovered from the entrance shaft of Tomb 4 is five: one subadult and four adults. The subadult skeletal material consists of teeth and vertebral fragments, while the adult skeletal material consists mainly of teeth, cranial and long-bone fragments, as well as hand and foot elements. The condition of the bone is good, although individual elements, especially the cranial and long bones, are highly fragmentary and incomplete. Because of the highly fragmentary nature of the skeletal material and the lack of diagnostic elements, assignation of sex and finer age-grades for the adult bone is not possible. Based on the development of the subadult bone, a general age designation of "child" (3–12 years) can be made. While the anterior surface of an adult patella shows pronounced enthesophyte formation (ossification of muscle insertions), it is unclear if this is the result of bony reaction to mechanical stress on the knee joint (enthesopathy) or, rather, a non-pathological condition observed in certain individuals who tend to be exuberant "bone-formers." Of 22 permanent teeth recovered from the entrance shaft, no carious lesions are observable. Eight of 15 anterior teeth (53%), however, show small deposits of calculus, mainly on the labial surface.

Main Chamber

The MNI recovered from the main chamber of Tomb 4 is six: two subadults and four adults. The subadult skeletal material consists mainly of lower long-bone fragments, teeth, and foot elements. The adult material consists mainly of cranial and long-bone fragments, teeth, and hand and foot elements. The condition of the bone is good, although, except for the dentition and hand and foot elements, individual bones are highly fragmented and incomplete. Because of the fragmented nature of the skeletal material and the lack of diagnostic elements, assignation of finer age-grades for the adult bone is not possible. In addition, only an extremely general age designation of "child" (3–12 years) or "adolescent" (13–20 years) can be made for the subadult bone. However, arachnoid or pacchionian depressions on the endocranial surface of one skull vault fragment indicate an individual of advanced age. Based on the maximum femoral head diameter of one individual (32.5 mm), an assessment of female can be made. In addition, measurements of the midshaft diameter of two femur fragments yield figures in the male range for the first (93 mm), and figures in the female range for the second (75 mm). Of 50 permanent teeth recovered from the main chamber, one carious lesion on an upper 3rd molar and another large carious lesion (penetrating to the root cavity) on a lower 2nd molar are observable; both lesions occur at the interproximal CEJ. Small amounts of calculus can be seen on the labial aspect of ten of 29 anterior teeth (34%). In addition, the mandibular molars of one individual display extreme occlusal wear, indicative of an individual of advanced age. Apart from the dentition, no other pathological conditions are observable in the skeletal material recovered from the main chamber.

Rear Chamber

The MNI recovered from the rear chamber of Tomb 4 is five: three adults and two subadults. The subadult skeletal material consists mainly of teeth, long-bone and vertebral fragments, while the adult material consists mainly of cranial and long-bone fragments, teeth, and hand and foot elements. The condition of the bone is good although, except for the dentition and hand and foot elements, the material is highly fragmented and incomplete. Because of the fragmented nature of the skeletal material and the lack of diagnostic elements, assignation of sex and finer age grades for the adult bone is not possible. Based on the development of the bone and dentition, a general age designation of "child" (3–12 years) can be made for the subadult material. Measurement of the midshaft circumference of one adult femur (81 mm) yields an assessment of sex that is indeterminate. Of fifteen permanent and three deciduous teeth recovered, one permanent mandibular incisor displayed small deposits of calculus on the labial aspect. No carious lesions were observed. One permanent maxillary left molar shows signs of extreme occlusal wear. Apart from the dentition, no other pathological conditions are observable in the skeletal material recovered from the rear chamber.

External Loci (1, 4, 8)

Locus 1 represents the modern surface layer that overlays all other loci in Field III. In addition to human and nonhuman bone, it contains both ancient and modern cultural material. Because of the high level of disturbance of the site, it is difficult to determine the precise origin of materials recovered from this locus. For this reason, the human bone is described separately.

The MNI recovered from Locus 1 is four: two subadults and two adults. The subadult skeletal material consists of upper long-bone fragments and teeth, while the adult skeletal material is comprised mainly of cranial, vertebral and long-bone fragments, hand and foot elements, and teeth. The condition of the bone is good, although, except for the dentition and hand and foot elements, the material is highly fragmented and incomplete. Because of the fragmented nature of the skeletal material and the lack of diagnostic elements, assignation of sex and finer age-grades for the adult bone is, for the most part, not possible. For the same reason, only a very general age designation of "child" (3–12 years) can be made for the subadult material. Measurement of the midshaft diameter of an adult femur (83 mm) yields a figure barely within the male range, an assessment that must be made with a large degree of uncertainty. Of ten teeth recovered (nine permanent; one deciduous), none show signs of calculus deposition or carious lesions. Moderate arthritic lipping can be seen in an adult cervical vertebral body. In addition, abnormal thickening of the diplöe of an adult cranial fragment can be observed. This condition is known as porotic hyperostosis, and is most often associated with anemias.

Locus 4

Locus 4 represents the sandy, largely sterile basal layer into which Tomb 4 was built. Very few artifacts or bone were recovered from this locus. The MNI recovered from Locus 4 is one. The skeletal material consists of cranial and rib fragments, one permanent tooth, and foot elements. The condition of the bone is good, although the cranial and rib fragments are incomplete. Based on the development of the dentition and bone, the skeletal material most likely derives from an adolescent (12–20 years). Assessment of sex is precluded due to the lack of diagnostic elements. No pathological lesions are observable.

Fig. 4.102. Tombs 5 and 6.

Locus 8

Locus 8 represents robbing activity above and alongside a second mud-brick tomb (Locus 7; unexcavated) found south of Tomb 4. It is likely that the human skeletal remains recovered from this locus originally derived from this second tomb. The MNI recovered from 8 is three: one subadult and two adults. The subadult is represented by long-bone fragments, foot elements, and a single deciduous molar. The adult material consists mainly of cranial, and long-bone fragments, and hand and foot elements. The condition of the bone is good although, except for the dentition and hand and foot elements, the material is highly fragmented and incomplete. Because of the fragmented nature of the skeletal material and the lack of diagnostic elements, assignation of sex and finer age grades for the adult bone is not possible. For the same reason, only a very general age designation of "child" (3–12 years) can be made for the subadult material. Pathological observations are restricted to an abnormal thickening of the diplöe of an adult cranial vault fragment similar to that observed in the cranial fragment from locus 1 (described above).

Summary and Conclusions

Because there is no duplication of skeletal elements between Tomb 4 loci (3, 6, 9) and the external loci (1, 4, 8), the MNI recovered from Field III Area 2 is six: two subadults and four adults. Because of the fragmented and incomplete nature of the skeletal material, the most that can be said about the subadult material is that they derive from either children (3–12 years) or adolescents (12–20 years). The adult material consists of at least four individuals, one of whom appears to be of advanced age. Femoral head and mid-shaft measurements indicate at least two females and one male. The most commonly observed pathological conditions are seen in the dentition and take the form of interproximal caries and small deposits of calculus on the anterior teeth. Several permanent molars also display extreme wear. The lack of carious lesions on the occlusal surface of the dentition is consistent with observations of the dentition in other parts of Egypt, where

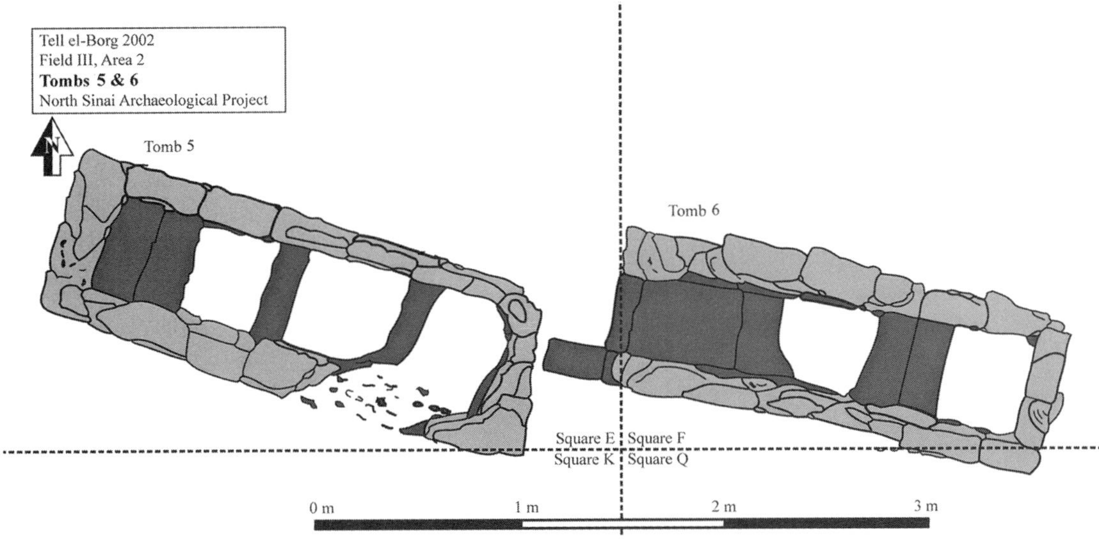

Fig. 4.103. Tombs 5 and 6 top plan (drawing and digitizing by S. Haddow, enhanced by J. Olsen).

gritty diets tend to wear down the occlusal surface before carious lesions can form. In addition, a single arthritic cervical vertebra and two cranial vault fragments displaying lesions consistent with anemia-related illnesses were also recovered. No evidence of trauma or infectious disease could be observed.

Due to the high degree of disturbance that has occurred and continues to occur at the site, the majority of the skeletal material recovered is highly fragmentary and incomplete. This makes it quite difficult accurately to determine age and sex and prevents the researcher from addressing wider concerns, such as individual and populational health patterns. Given the amount of looting that has occurred, both ancient and recent, the chances of finding many intact burials at Tell el-Borg are slim.

Tomb 5

Provenance: Field III, Area 2, Units E (locus 3) and K
Dimensions: 2.34 × .86 m
Maximum preserved height: 5 courses
Brick size: 40 × 20 × 10 cm
Orientation of long axis: 110° off north
Excavator: Scott Haddow

Tomb 5 is a rectangular mud-brick grave made for a single occupant. Located about 7 m south of Tomb 4, the foot end of Tomb 5 nearly abuts the head end of Tomb 6 in Unit F immediately to its east (figs. 4.6, 4.102–103). Fragments of a rectangular ceramic anthropomorphic sarcophagus were found in situ on the floor of the tomb (fig. 4.104). Although the face on the lid was smashed, enough of it was preserved to know that it had molded hair and hands crossing its chest. This coffin, TBO 0122, was beautifully restored by the project conservator, Noël Siver, and is studied and illustrated in detail in Chapter 5.

No human remains were found in situ. However, fragments of human bone found in the disturbed fill of the tomb indicate a single young adolescent. Potsherds and amorphous bronze fragments were also recovered from the tomb fill (Locus 2). The floor of the tomb was constructed

Fig. 4.104 (above). Tomb 5, with coffin fragments.

Fig. 4.105 (right). Tomb 5, with beer jar under head end

Fig. 4.106. Tomb 5, side view, with beer jar in situ.

by placing three sets of mud bricks end to end across the width of the floor of the tomb in order to create an elevated surface upon which to place the sarcophagus (fig. 4.105). The space between the brick rows was filled with sand. The same building technique used in the floor of Tomb 5 occurs in Tombs 6, 8, and 9. These perpendicular brick supports for the coffin are reminiscent of the placing of boards under wood and stone coffins.[16]

A broken but largely complete New Kingdom beer jar was also found underneath the lowest course of mud brick at the northern corner of the tomb (TBP 0403 = figs. 4.106 and 107a–c). The number of "beer jars" from *Tell el-Borg I*s quite small (10 jars plus 109 sherds out of more than 12,000 recorded), and the majority were recovered in the cemetery area (see Appendix I below). The Borg beer jars typically date to the later 18th Dynasty (see *Tell el-Borg I*, 400).

The find-spot of TBP 0403, just under the head end of the grave, is not insignificant. Due to the small size of Tombs 5, 6, 7, 8, and 9, and especially if a ceramic coffin was used (as is clearly the case with Tombs 5 and 8), there was simply no space for pottery vessels within the burial. This factor may explain the placement of this beer jar; vessels used in connection with the burial rites may have been placed outside the tomb as was the case of the amphora (TBP 402) discovered about 4 m north of Tomb 5 in Unit E (see discussion below).

Despite the limited sherds found in and around Tombs 5 and 6, some diagnostic sherds were studied by our ceramicists: 2 blue-painted jar body sherds, 1 Cypriot Base-Ring handle of juglet (TBP 445), 1 marl D amphora rim that dates late 18th to early 19th Dynasties, 1 straight-walled simple bowl rim, 1 thick-walled red-slipped bowl, 1 ring-base of bowl with streaky red slip inside (mid 18th Dynasty), 1 carinated bowl with black rim tics (TBP 420) (mid-to-late 18th Dynasty), 1 black-rimmed bowl with ledge under rim (parallel at Qantir: Ramesside), large carinated bowl

16. For examples of this, see William C. Hays, *The Scepter of Egypt: From Earliest Times to the End of the Middle Kingdom* (Cambridge: Harvard University Press, 1953) 315–17.

Table 4.6. Small finds in and around Tomb 5 (Field III, Area 2 Units E, K, and L)

TBO	*Unit / Locus*	*Object type*	*Material*	*Measurements*
0144	E 2, in tomb 5	piece of a vessel?	copper/copper alloy	2.5 × 1.3 × .95 cm
0152	E 2, in tomb 5	bead	faience	0.5 × 0.12 cm
0153	E 2, in tomb 5	bead	carnelian	0.3 × .0.1 cm
0154	E 2, in tomb 5	amulet	steatite	0.8 × 0.4 × 0.2 cm
0105	E 1	sherd with ☥-like mark	clay	9.1 × 4.4 × 0.6 cm
0122	E 1	sherds from coffin	clay	n/a
0136	E 1	pounder	granite or rhyolite porphyry	5.5 × 5 × 3.2 cm
0138	E 1	jar lid	travertine	5 × 1.8 × 4.4 cm
0141	E 1	piece of a vessel(?)	c/ca	3.8 × 2.6 × 0.1 cm
0163	E 1	game piece	clay	1.6 × 1.6 × 1.3 cm
0166	E 1	bead	faience	1.2 × 1.05 dia cm
0176	E 1	javelin blade	c/ca	6.2 × 1.2 × 0.75 cm
0194	E 1	bead	faience	0.4 × 0.9 dia cm
0200	E 1	4 pieces of an awl (?)	c/ca	9.8 × 0.7 dia cm
0217	E 1	3 pieces of an awl (?)	c/ca	3.4 × 0.5 dia cm
0304	E 1	3 beads	faience	0.5 × 1.25 dia cm
0242	E 2	part of earring	carnelian	1.6 × 0.5 cm
0248	K 1	not identified	limestone	2.9 × 2.7 × 1.2 cm
0305	K 1	tool (?)	hippo ivory	5.6 × 2.8 × 1.5 cm
0389	K 1	reworked sherd game piece (?)	B2 Nile clay	0.9 × 2.4 dia cm
0434	K 1	needle or wire	c/ca	10.6 × 0.4 cm
0238	L 1	bifacial blade	chert	6.1 × 2.1 × 1.1 cm
0243	L 1	bead(?), weight (?)	limestone	3.5 × 2.2 × 2.0 cm
0258	L 1	rim of jar	travertine	1.4 × 2.9 dia cm
0259	L 1	stone fragment	travertine	5.4 × 1.1 × 1.0 cm
0260	L 1	stone fragment	travertine	4.6 × 1.25 × 0.75 cm
0266	L 1	bead	faience	0.2 × 0.6 dia cm

Fig. 4.107. **a** (left): Tomb 5, with beer in situ jar under head end; **b** (middle): Photo of restored beer jar from Tomb 5, TBP 0403; **c** (right): Drawing of TBP 0403 by Lyla Pinch-Brock).

Fig. 4.108. TBO 0105 Sherd with ☥-like potter's mark.

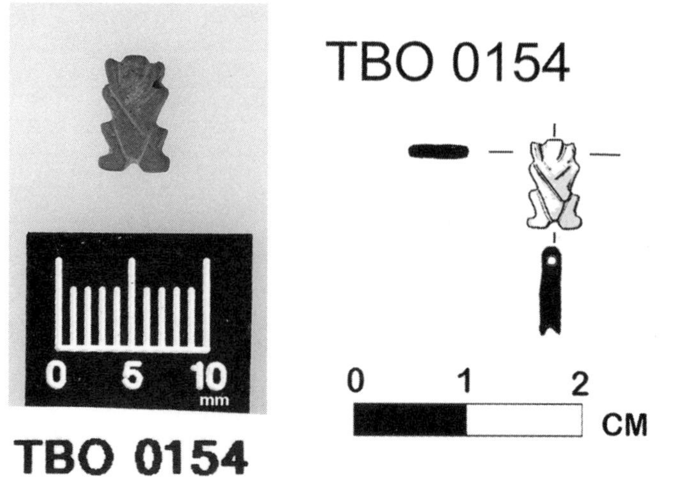

Fig. 4.109. TBO 0154. **a** (left). Bes-amulet photo. **b** (right). Drawing by Lyla Pinch Brock.

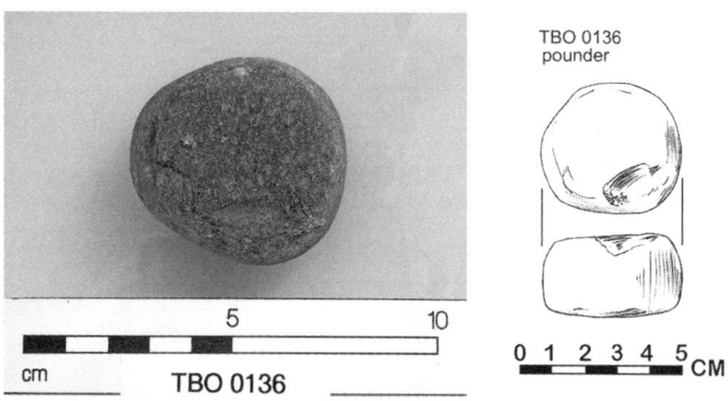

Fig. 4.110. TBO 0136. **a** (left). Photo of Pounder; **b** (right). Drawing by Lyla Pinch-Brock.

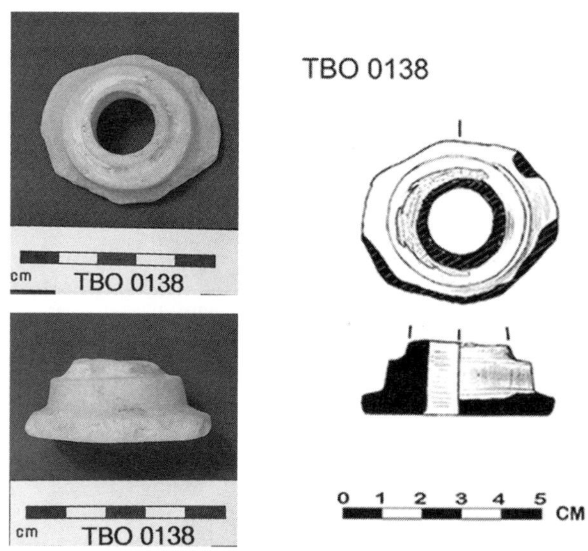

Fig. 4.111. TBO 0138. **a–b** (right, top and bottom). Photo of chipped stone tool; **c** (far right). Drawing by Lyla Pinch-Brock.

Fig. 4.112. TBO 0200. Copper/copper alloy awl.

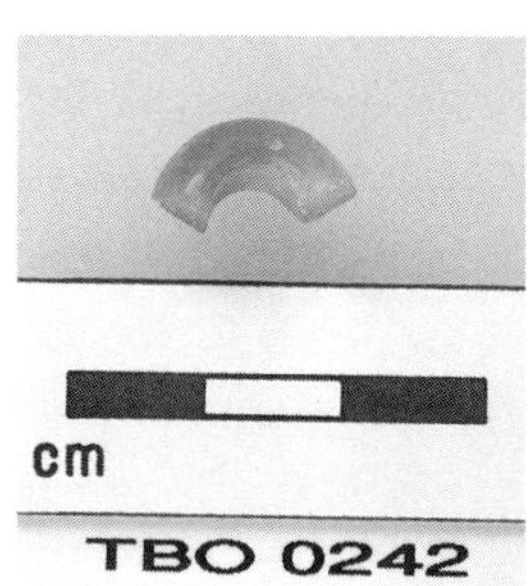

Fig. 4.113. TBO 0242. Carnelian earring.

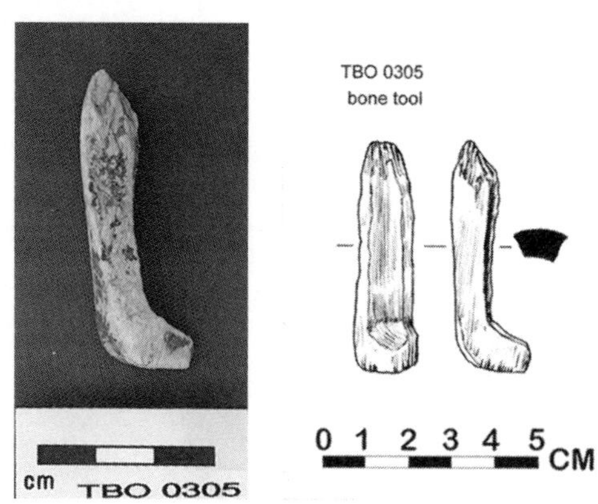

Fig. 4.114. TBO 0305. Hippo-ivory tool. **a** (left): Photo; **b** (right): Drawing by Lyla Pinch-Brock.

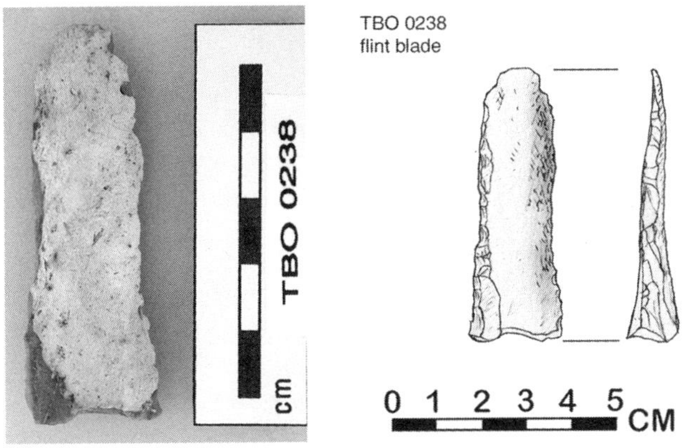

Fig. 4.115. TBO 0238. Bifacial chert blade. **a** (left): Photo; **b** (right): Drawing by Lyla Pinch-Brock.

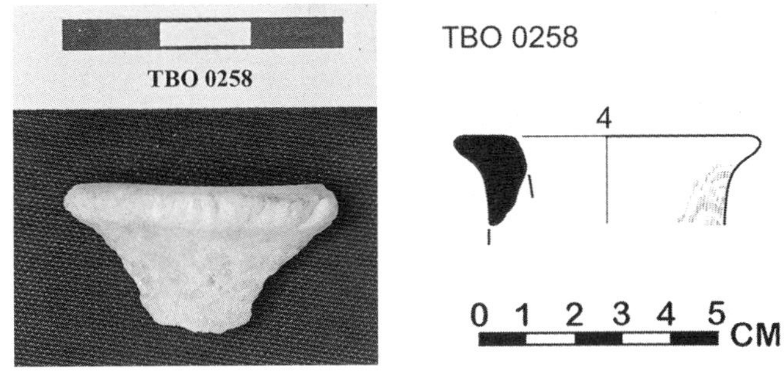

Fig. 4.116. TBO 0258. Travertine jar rim. **a** (left): Photo; **b** (right): Drawing by Lyla Pinch-Brock.

Fig. 4.117. TBO 0259. Fragment of travertine.

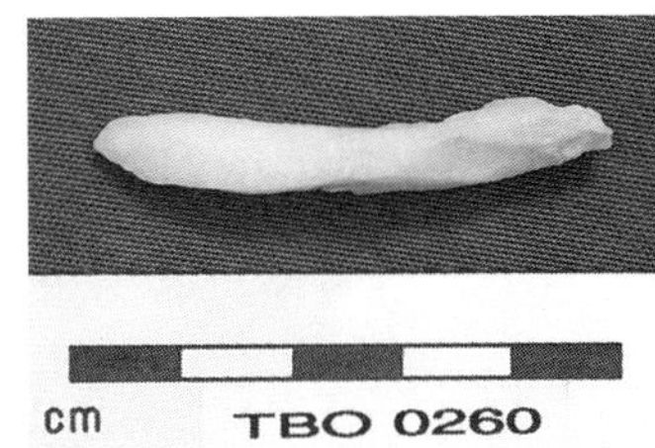

Fig. 4.118. TBO 0260. Fragment of travertine.

and 2 jar rims, both uncoated. Thus, according to Rexine Hummel, a dating spanning from mid-18th Dynasty to the 19th Dynasty is represented in this area. This range indicates how disturbed this area is. Nearby Tomb 4 may be the source of the mid-18th Dynasty sherds.

Discussion of Small Finds

The small finds treated here were discovered in Unit E, at the southeast corner of which lies Tomb 5. Due to the location of the nearly identical Tomb 6, which slightly crosses into Unit E, it is possible that grave goods from this tomb mingled with those from Tomb 5 when the tombs were looted. Unit K is immediately to the south of Tomb 5 and may well contain objects that originated in the tomb, but only three registered finds were documented (see fig. 4.6). The entire square, however, was not cleared. Several more objects were recovered in Unit L, directly south of K. This unit is 5 m away from Tomb 5, so it is less likely that they came from this burial. Since no other feature around Unit L was uncovered or detected by the geophysical survey, the small finds from Unit L are included here.

The repertoire of small finds found in and around Tomb 5 are similar to those found in and around Tombs 1–4. These include jewelry, mostly faience beads with the occasional one made of carnelian (TBO 0153) and a carnelian earring (TBO 0242 = fig. 4.113); a number of travertine fragments (TBO 0259 = fig. 4.117 and TBO 0260 = fig. 4.118) and a jar rim and lid (TBO 0138 = fig. 111a–c and TBO 0258 = fig. 116a–b) were among the more elite objects found. Unique among the finds at *Tell el-Borg I*s the hippo-ivory tool (TBO 0305 = fig. 114a–b), the purpose of which remains unclear. A tiny Bes-amulet (TBO 0154 = fig. 109a–b) was actually found in the fill of the tomb. A pin-sized hole in the neck of the Bes figurine indicates that the amulet was placed on a string and worn around the neck or wrist. This particular amulet is a close match to Petrie's no. 188 in his study of amulets, which he dates to the 18th Dynasty.[17] For a discussion of this and the other two Bes-amulets discovered at Tell el-Borg, see the previous study by Hoffmeier.[18]

17. W. M. F. Petrie, *Amulets* (London, 1914) 40.

18. James K. Hoffmeier, "Deities of the Eastern Frontier," in *Scribe of Justice: Egyptological Studies in Honour of Shafik Allam* (ed. Z. A. Hawass, Kh. A. Daoud, and R. B. Hussein; Cairo: Supplement aux Annales du Service des Antiquités de l'Egypte, Cahier 42, 2011) 197–216.

Fig. 4.119. Tomb 6.

Tomb 6

Provenance: Field III, Area 2, Units E (Locus 5) and Q
Dimensions: 2.42 × 0.91 m
Maximum preserved height: 5 courses
Brick size: 40 × 20 × 10 cm
Orientation of long axis: 105° off north
Excavator: Scott Haddow

Tomb 6 is another rectangular mud-brick grave, similar in size and construction to Tomb 5. It lies mostly within Unit F, but a length of one brick crosses west into Unit E, almost touching Tomb 5 (figs. 4.6, 4.102–103, 4.119). The southeast corner of Tomb 6 crosses into Unit Q. The partial remains of human lower limb bones were found in situ on the floor of the tomb, which leads to the conclusion that a sarcophagus was not used in this instance. Based on the orientation of the bones, the head of the individual was oriented to the west. As with Tomb 5, the floor of Tomb 6 was constructed using only three mud bricks placed at regular intervals. The human bones recovered from the tomb fill (Locus 4) indicate an adult individual.

Discussion of Small Finds

A couple of unique small finds merit discussion from in and around this tomb. A limestone life-size frog figurine (TBO 0124 = fig. 4.120a–b) seems to have been an amulet of some sort, although it is too large to have been worn. Like the Bes amulet, the frog, representing Hekat, falls into the class of personal or domestic deities.[19] A goddess associated with fertility and childbirth,[20] Hekat is present in the famous birthing story in Pap. Westcar, as well as the royal birthing scenes of Hatshepsut at Deir el-Bahri and Amenhotep III at the Luxor temple.[21]

19. Hoffmeier, "Deities of the Eastern Frontier," 202–3.

20. Carol Andrews, *Amulets of Ancient Egypt* (London: British Museum, 1994), 10, 63.

21. For details, see Hoffmeier, "Deities of the Eastern Frontier," 202–4. For the Hatshepsut scenes, see Edouard Naville, *The Temple of Deir el Bahri II* (London: EEF, 1897) pl. 48.

Table 4.7. Small Finds in and Around Tomb 6 in Field III, Area 2, Units F and Q

TBO	*Unit/Locus*	*Object Type*	*Material*	*Measurements*
012	F 1	frog figurine	limestone	7.5 x 6.5 x 3.5 cm
0140	F 1	pestle or pounder	limestone	5.9 x 4.0 x 3.8 cm
0146	F 1	cylindrical metal tool	copper/copper alloy	4.2 x 0.4 dia cm
0150	F 1	23 beads	faience	n/a
0155	F 1	bead	faience	0.3 x 1.5 dia cm
0156	F 1	fragments of a knife blade	copper/copper alloy	6 x 2.4 x 0.4 cm
0157	F 1	fragment of stone vessel	travertine	1.8 x 1.9 x 0.8 cm
0167	F 1	uncertain	faience	6 x 2.9 x 0.8 cm
0193	F 1	fish hook, 3 fragments	copper/copper alloy	n/a
0198	F 1	bead	faience	1 x 1.4 cm
0199	F 1	cylindrical bead (broken)	faience	1.7 x 0.6 dia cm
0215	F 1 (surface)	hand amulet	carnelian	1.2 x 0.6 x 0.3 cm
0223	F 1	chipped stone blade	chert	3.4 x 2.2 x 0.6 cm

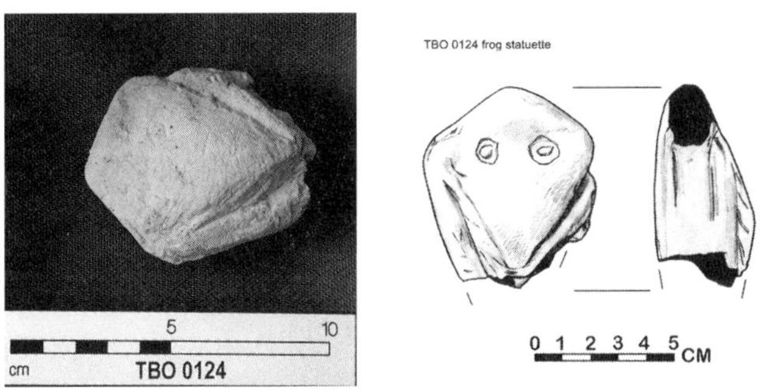

Fig. 120. TBO 0124. Frog figurine. **a** (left): Photo; **b** (right): Drawing by Lyla Pinch-Brock.

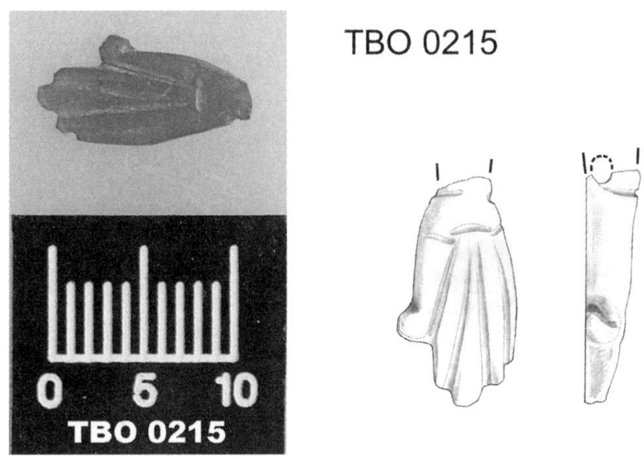

Fig. 121. TBO 0124. Hand figurine. **a** (left): Photo; **b** (right): Drawing by Lyla Pinch-Brock.

The small carnelian amulet is a carefully carved hand (TBO 0215 = fig. 4.121a–b), although it looks like it could be a lotus flower. Its identification as a hand is clinched by the way in which the thumb curls out, which is consistent with the design of hand amulets where the thumb curves out slightly, precisely as witnessed in TBO 0215.[22] Like TBO 0215, carnelian is one of the favorite materials for this type of amulet,[23] perhaps because it represents the color of human skin.

Osteological Remains from Other Features in Units E and F

Between Tomb 4 in Units H and D and Tombs 5 and 6 in Units E and F is a large dark area (about 12 m long) with some hardened mud patches. Another such feature is found in Unit H, north of E (fig. 4.6). It is unclear whether this hardened mud layer came from decomposed bricks from tombs or was an earlier walking surface like that found 10 m east in Units S, T, U, and V (see further on this feature below). Since the general orientation of these patches is similar to nearby

22. Petrie, *Amulets*, pl. 1, no. 11a, c, and d.
23. Petrie, *Amulets*, 11; Andrews, *Amulets of Ancient Egypt*, fig. 67.

Fig. 4.122. TBO 0140. Limestone pestle. **a** (left): Photo; **b** (right): Drawing by Lyla Pinch-Brock.

Fig. 4.123. Canaanite amphora TBP 0402 in situ.

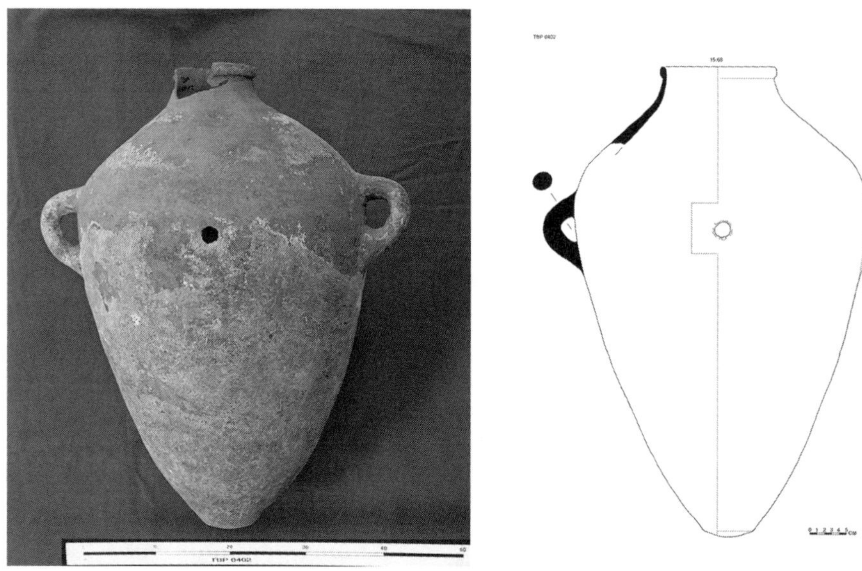

Fig. 4.124. TBO 0402. Canaanite amphora. **a** (left): Photo; **b** (right): Drawing by Lyla Pinch-Brock.

Tombs 4, 5, and 6, it seems more likely that these mud patches are the disintegrated remains of tombs.

In the northeastern corner of Unit E, between the mud patches, an amphora was uncovered, standing vertical in the sand (fig. 4.123), not seemingly connected to a particular tomb. TBP 0402 is a Canaanite-type amphora of the 18th Dynasty and was published by Catherine Duff in *Tell el-Borg I* (pl. 5, pp. 458–59). This amphora likely dates to the LB IIa–b period (ca. 1400–1200 B.C.). It has a hole intentionally made in the upper half of the amphora, close to the shoulder (fig. 4.124a–b). A hole of this type in a vessel has been called a "killing hole," believed to have been used for pouring libations, especially in funerary rituals (see Excursus I at the end of this chapter). The provenance of this amphora, between several tombs, might indicate that it had been used ritually for more than one tomb in the area.

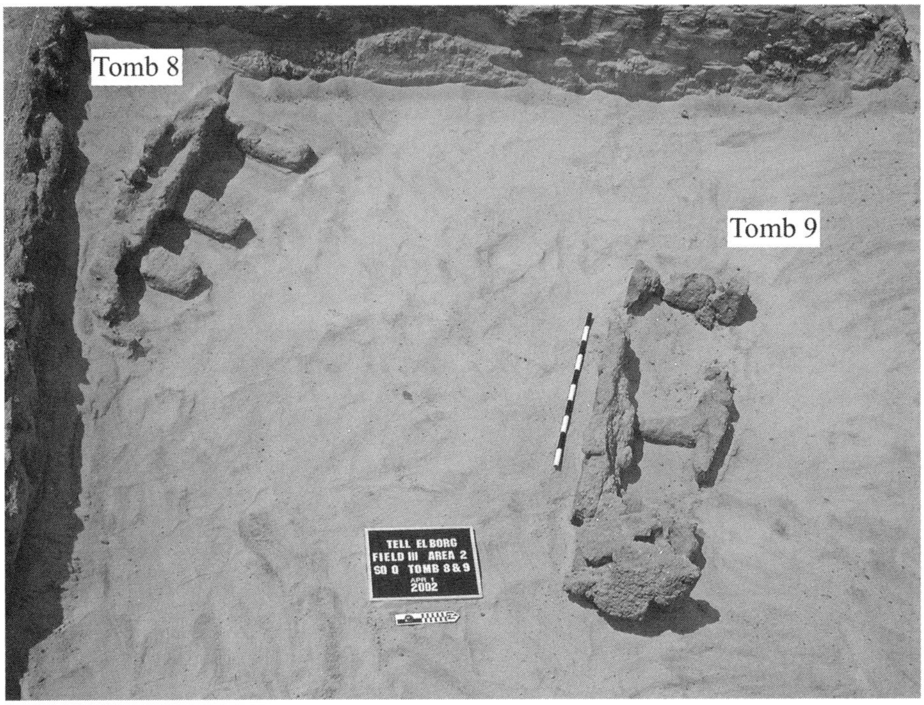

Fig. 4.125. Tombs 8 and 9.

Tomb 7

Provenance: Field III, Area 2, Units H and I
Dimensions: approximately 81 × 142 cm
Maximum preserved height: possibly 2 bricks
Orientation of long axis: unclear
Excavator: Scott Haddow

A small pile of mud bricks is all that remains of what is believed to be Tomb 7. It was most likely built as a simple pit grave, lined and covered with mud bricks (fig. 4.22). Under and around it were recovered several human bones belonging to an infant of less than six months.

Tomb 8 (Locus 15)

Provenance: Field III, Area 2, Unit R
Dimensions: 80 × 204 cm
Maximum preserved height: 1 course
Brick size: 40 × 20 × 10 cm
Orientation of long axis: 105°
Excavator: Scott Haddow

Tomb 8 is a crude rectangular mud-brick grave. The remains of a small tubular sarcophagus (top portion broken away) were found in situ (figs. 4.11, 4.125–126). This sarcophagus, TBO 0160, was never restored, but appears to have been similar in shape and design as TBO 0122 from Tomb 5. The head of the sarcophagus was oriented west. As with Tomb 5 and 6, the sarcophagus was placed on a set of three mud bricks. Unlike Tombs 5 and 6, however, the architecture of Tomb 8 suggests that it was built by lining the walls of a pit dug into the sand with one or two courses of brick sufficient enough to enclose the sarcophagus.

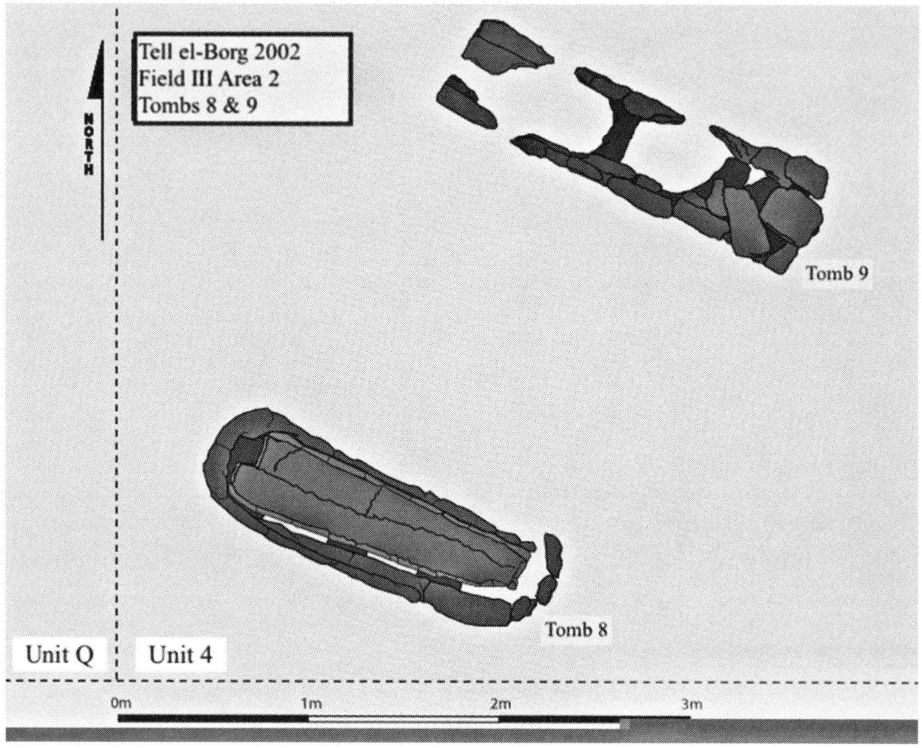

Fig. 4.126. Top plan of Tombs 8 and 9. Drawing and digitizing by Scott Haddow.

Osteological Remains from Tomb 9

No skeletal remains were found in situ but the fill within the tomb (Locus 1) contained cranial, vertebral, and long bone fragments, as well as ribs, foot elements, and three moderately worn permanent teeth. The condition of the bone is good, although individual elements (with the exception of the teeth and the foot bones) are highly fragmented and incomplete. These elements represent a minimum of one individual. Based on the wear of the dentition and the overall size of the bones themselves, a general age estimate of an adult is given. No pathological conditions are observable.

A fine faience ring inscribed with the cartouche of Queen Tiye was also found nearby (TBO 0252; fig. 4.127a–b). It is not certain, however, if this item originally derived from Tomb 8.

Tomb 9 (Locus 16)

Provenance: Field III, Area 2, Unit R
Dimensions: 64 × 221 cm
Maximum preserved height: 1 course
Brick size: 40 × 20 × 10 cm
Orientation of long axis: 105°
Excavator: Scott Haddow

Tomb 9 is a crude rectangular mud-brick grave similar in construction to nearby Tomb 8, although no traces of a sarcophagus were observed (fig. 4.128). No human remains were found in situ, although skeletal fragments recovered from the tomb fill (Locus 17) indicate at least one individual in the young adolescent age range. Tombs 5, 6, 8, and 9 all share the same brick size (40 × 20 × 10 cm), whereas the bricks in Tombs 1, 2, and 4 are smaller. The size consistency of the bricks in Tombs 5, 6, 8, and 9, as well as their proximity, suggests that they date to the same

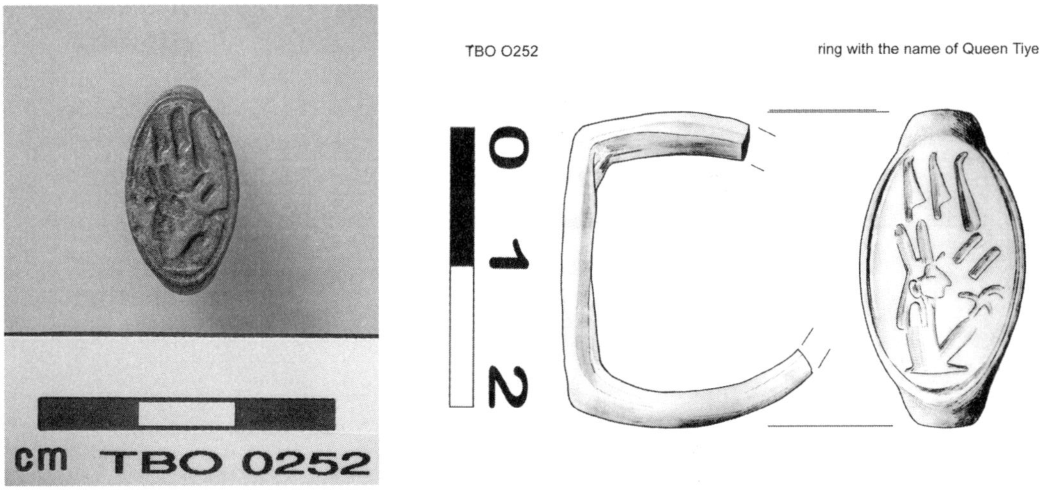

Fig. 4.127. **a** (left): TBO 0252, ring of Queen Tiye, photo; **b** (right): Drawing by Lyla Pinch-Brock.

Fig. 4.128. Tomb 9 (front) and 8 (behind).

period. Dating these tombs is difficult, given the disturbed nature of the graves and the fact that the sherds are scattered. The only complete vessel in this cluster of tombs is the beer jar buried under the western end of Tomb 5, and it dates to the late 18th Dynasty (see above).

Discussion of Small Finds

Locus 1 in Unit R represents the surface layer in Area 2 that is largely made up of the disturbed fill left in the aftermath of the looting. Beneath this yellow-brown fill (10YR 6/4) surrounding the tombs is the basal sand into which the tombs were constructed. The limestone fragment (TBO 0162, likely reused from earlier architectural structure) may have been a piece of flooring from a tomb in the area, like those pieces found in Tomb 4 (see fig. 4.76). Numerous thin tubular copper/copper alloy fragments of tools were uncovered in the cemetery area and elsewhere; they appear to be needles. In TBO 0172b, however, the corroded and mineralized eye of the tool is visible 1.8 cm from the end. The cache of beads (TBO 0411) was the largest found at Tell el-Borg. Included in this mini-hoard were 62 blue, 16 yellow/brown, 8 dark brown, and 3 miscellaneous

Table 4.8. Small Finds in Field III, Area 2, Unit R around Tombs 8 and 9

TBO	*Unit/Locus*	*Object Type*	*Material*	*Measurements*
0162	R 1	reused architectural fragment	limestone	10.8 × 11.9 × 4.6 cm
0172a	R 1	metal tool, possibly a needle	copper/copper alloy	4.2 × 0.4 dia cm
0172b	R 1	metal tool, possibly a needle	copper/copper alloy	6.1 × 0.7 dia cm
0267	R 1	flat white bead	faience	0.2 × 0.5 dia cm
0280	R 1	large bead of small weight	clay	3.5 × 2.4 dia cm
0281	R 1	bead	carnelian	0.3 × 0.4 dia cm
0403	R 1	game piece (?)	Nile B2 clay	1.0 × 2.0 dia cm
0411	R 1	collection of beads	mostly faience	n/a
0418	R 1	worked stone fragment	sandstone	7 × 5 × 1.6 cm

Fig. 4.129. Reused limestone architectural fragment (TBO 0162).

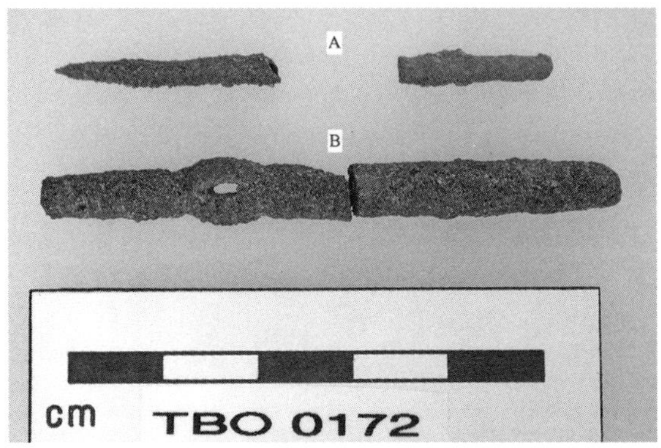

Fig. 4.130. Copper/copper alloy needles(?) TBO 0172a–b.

Fig. 4.131. Clay bead or small line weight (TBO 0280).

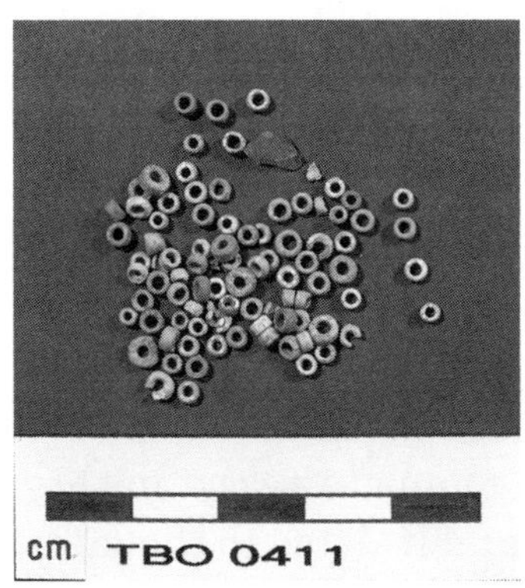

Fig. 4.132 (left). Collection of beads (TBO 0411)

Fig. 4.133 (right). Carved sandstone fragment (TBO 0418).

beads, for a total of 89, and a piece of carnelian. A small sandstone fragment (TBO 0418) contains markings that might reflect its use as a whetstone.

Tomb 10 = The Locus 18 and 22 Structures

Provenance: Field III, Area 2, Units S, R and T (Locus 18)
Courses of brick: 4
Brick size: not clear
Orientation of long axis: 110°
Excavator: Scott Haddow

Fig. 4.134. "Tomb 10" = Locus 18 Structure, looking north.

Fig. 4.135. "Tomb 10" = Locus 18 Structure, looking west.

This mud-brick structure (Locus 18) turns out not to be a tomb at all. Believing initially that it was a tomb, when the corner of the mud-brick wall was cleared (Unit R and S), it was assigned a tomb number. The structure's orientation (110°) was the same as the previously discovered nine tombs, which supported the expectation that it was a grave. The length of the two walls, as well as how narrow they were, led us quickly to abandon interpreting the structure as a tomb. Unlike the other mud-brick tombs in Field III, erosion patterns observable on the lowest course of bricks suggest that the structure may have originally been built above-ground and exposed to the elements for a period of time before it fell out of use (figs. 4.134, 135, 136). The wall that runs northeast is

Fig. 4.136. "Tomb 10" = Locus 18 Structure, looking west; Tomb 12 is in the foreground and Locus 22 foundations are in between.

3.5 m long (running from Unit R, crossing the northwest corner of Unit S and in T), followed by a break in the wall of about 0.60 m, three more bricks were extant where this narrow (1 brick) Locus 18 wall ends. The total length, then, is 4 m. The break in the wall was caused when Tomb 11 was constructed. The eastern end of this tomb is evident, protruding from the section in Unit T (see figs. 4.134, 135).

The southeastern wall is but one brick thick and runs for 6.2 m in Units R and S. It may have continued into the next area, but it was not excavated. About 1.60 m from the corner of the Locus 18 structure (in Unit R) there is an opening of about 0.60 m that could have been a doorway. The north side wall of this structure has not survived. This area (Units S, T, and U) was badly looted in modern times, as the circular pits resulting from the use of hand shovels attests (figs. 4.134–136).

The orientation of the structure is the same as the tombs themselves, perhaps indicating that it was built during the same general period and was architecturally aligned with the tombs in Field III (or the tombs aligned with this structure). No human remains or sarcophagus fragments were found within the structure itself, however. It is possible that this structure served a cemetery-related function, perhaps serving as a mortuary chapel or a place to prepare the burials.

Another important feature found within and northeast of the walled structure is a network of narrow mini trenches (10–15 cm wide and 5–10 cm deep) that were cut into the hard-packed grayish-brown (10YR 5/2) mud floor (Locus 22), which covers much of Units S and T and all of Unit U (see figs. 4.134–135). The trenches cut into the layer below Locus 22—that is, Locus 23, a hard-packed gray, ashy layer (10YR 5/1) with bits of charcoal in the matrix. Below Locus 23, which ranges from 5 to 10 cm deep, is the basal sand that covers the site.

The various trenches are labeled as Ta–Ti on the top plan (fig. 4.137). They run in straight lines, some parallel to each other, and meet at right angles to form the outline of a building subdivided into smaller rooms. It might be suggested that these lines gouged into the hard surface were foundation trenches for a reed structure.

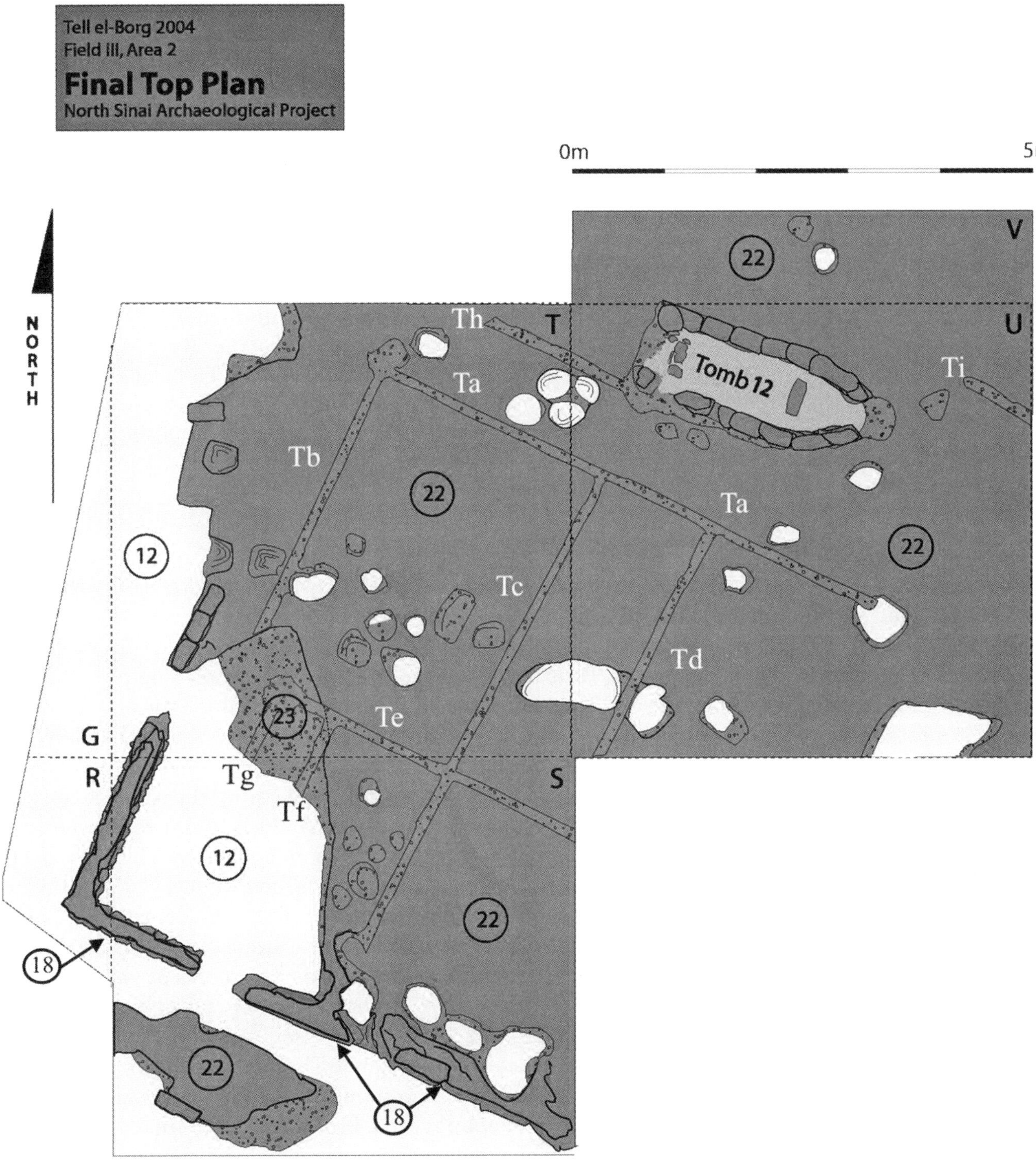

Fig. 4.137. Plan of Locus 18 and 22 Structures. Drawing and digitizing by S. Haddow.

In Field VI, the burned-out remains of a group of reed huts were uncovered (see chapter 7 below) and recently a published analysis of these structures appeared.[24] These residential huts

24. J. K. Hoffmeier, T. W. Davis and R. Hummel, "New Archaeological Evidence for Ancient Bedouin (Shasu) on Egypt's Eastern Frontier at Tell el-Borg," *Ägypten und Levante* 26 (2016) 185–311.

were constructed in sand, not on the hard-packed mud surface found in Field III, Area 2, Units S, T, U, and V. Because the Field VI huts had been burned in ancient times, traces of the ash of the reeds filled the channels into which the reeds had been set. Had these huts not been burned, it is unlikely they would have been visible when the area was excavated. In Field III, however, there was no sign of burning in Locus 22, meaning that the reeds might have been intentionally removed or simply deteriorated over time in the moist environment of north Sinai. Whatever the circumstances of the termination of the original reed structure and construction of the new (replacement?) structure made of mud brick, it is clear that there was no hiatus between them. No layer of wind-blown sand or accumulation of debris that would account for a period of abandonment between the two structures was found. Consequently, it might be that the reed structure was systematically removed and replaced by the secondary mud-brick building.

Based on the extant foundation trenches, it is evident that the reed structure was quite substantial. Ta is 6 m long and appears to be the outer (northeast) wall. Ta and Tb meet to form the northern corner of the feature. Tb is 3.40 m long, and its southwest section was severed when the hard-packed surface (Locus 22) was removed (or eroded?), revealing Locus 23, a gray, ashy layer (10YR 5/1). It may itself have been removed, possibly when the mud-brick wall building was built subsequently. Tb runs parallel to the northeastern mud-brick wall, but about 0.50 m to its east. Tc is 5.70 m long and would have supported the longest internal wall. Te crosses Tc, forming at least two rooms on the south side of the structure. Ta and Te are parallel to each other, but a third parallel trench to the south that would have marked the entrance side of the structure has not survived. It could be that the southeast mud-brick wall covered that trench when it (the new replacement?) building was constructed. Assuming this scenario, the reed structure would at least have been 6 × 6 m, a total of 36^2 m. Ta is severed by a modern robber hole about 0.70 m in diameter, but no sign of Ta occurs beyond that intrusion. If indeed Ta continued for just another 24 cm for a total of 6.24 m, that would have made the wall 12 cubits (0.52 m = 1 cubit) long, thus encompassing an area of 144 square cubits.

Parallel trenches Tg and Tf, both less than a meter in length, were cut by the same construction operation that terminated Tb. They are only about 0.50 m apart. And the distance between Tg and Tb was even narrower. This configuration may mean that the room formed by Tb, Tc, and Te had smaller compartments in it. The chamber at the norther corner (formed by Ta, Tb, Tc, and Te measures about 2.5 × 4.60m. In the southern sector of the structure, the room formed by Tc and Te (the other two walls are missing) appears to have been around the same size as its northern counterpart. This structure, then, was about 36^2 m and had as many as five rooms of varying size.

To the northeast of Ta, the outside wall of the Locus 22 structure, and running parallel to it, is Th. Approximately 0.90 m separates Ta and Th. The latter was subsequently overlaid by Tomb 12. Near the midway point of Tomb 12, one can see the channel of Th. Here, it ends about 3.4 m from its beginning point in Unit T. A final mini-foundation is found in the northeastern corner of Unit U—namely, Ti. It is about 0.96 m long but was not pursued, because the square east of U was never opened. Th and Ti are parallel to each other and were apparently damaged and parts lost when Tomb 12 was built, apparently signaling the existence of another reed structure. Whether it functioned concurrently with the Locus 22 building or was an earlier or later installation we may never know.

The remaining question concerns the function of the reed structure. It certainly precedes the Locus 18 mud-brick structure. Given its placement in the cemetery and the fact that it is surrounded by tombs with which it shares the same alignment, it may have had a funerary function. It is well known that the *ibw*, or purification tent, attested as early as the Old Kingdom, used in

Table 4.9. Small Finds from Locus 18 and 22 Structures: Field III, Area 2, Units S, T, and U

TBO	*Unit/Locus*	*Object Type*	*Material*	*Measurements*
0303	S 1	knife blade	copper/copper alloy	3.7 × 1.6 × 0.9 cm
0307	S 1	jarlet	travertine	7.0 × 6.9 × 1 cm
0308	S 1	pounder or grindstone	dolerite	6.7 × 4.8 × 3.8 cm
0310	S 1	flat circular bead	faience	0.2 × 1.4 dia cm
0311	S 1	nail	copper/copper alloy	3.6 × 1.4 dia cm
0313	S 1	bead	faience	0.15 × 0.5 dia cm
0318	S 1	pounder or grindstone	rhyolite or dacite	2.5 × 7.5 dia cm
0324	S 1	bead	gold	0.7 dia cm; 0.1 gm weight
0326	S 1	game piece or token	reworked sherd	0.70 × 2.1 dia cm
0381	S 1	tube bead (9 sections)	faience	2.1 × .45 dia cm
0408	S 1	flat circular bead	faience	0.1 × 0.6 dia cm
0409	S 1	tube bead	faience	1.3 × .35 dia cm
0433	S 1	metal tool, awl (?)	copper/copper alloy	4.9 × .06 × .06 cm
0452	S 1	metal tool, needle (?)	copper/copper alloy	5.6 × 0.3 dia cm
0406	S 19	bead	glass	0.7 × .05 dia cm
0407	S 19	2 disc-shaped beads	faience	.45x.15 dia; 0.4x1.5 dia cm
0312	T 1	cylindrical bead	clay	2 × 1.8 dia cm
0312	T 1	grindstone or pounder	sandstone	4 × 3 × 3.5 cm
0361	T 22	metal tool, needle (?)	metal tool	3 × 0.4 dia cm
0358	U 1	rim of stone jar	travertine	3.4 × 2.7 × 1.3 cm
0359	U 1	metal tool (awl?)	copper/copper alloy	7.5 × 0.6 × .04 cm
0364	U 1	sherd with cartouche stamped	Marl B	6.8 × 4.5 1.1 cm
0365	U 1	disc-shaped bead	faience	0.1 × 0.6 dia cm
0366	U 1	stone tool	granite	7.7 × 2.2 × 0.7 cm
0368	U 1	grindstone or pounder	granite	7.4 × 7.4 × 7.7 cm
0384	U 1	cylindrical bead	clay	2.6 × 1.2 dia cm
0416	U 1	worked stone scraper or blade	chert	3.2 × 2 × 0.7 cm
0385	U 1 in Tomb 12 (fill)	reworked sherd, game piece (?)	clay	0.7 × 1.9 dia cm
0367	III, 2 surface	statue of falcon-headed deity	copper/copper alloy	4.1 × 0.7 × 1.1 cm

the initial stages of the mummification process was a temporary structure erected at the edge of the necropolis and could be made of reeds or woven mats.[25] The reason for utilizing reeds in the purification tent, Hoffmeier has suggested, was to represent the Lake or Field of Reeds (*š n ỉꜣrw/ sḫt n ỉꜣrw)* in the Pyramid Texts—the Lake or Field of Reeds being the place where the king was purified and from which the sun-god rises.[26]

Discussion of Small Finds in Units S, T, and U

While the main (and largest) features in these three squares are the Locus18 mud-brick structure and the earlier Locus 22 reed building, three tombs also share these three units. The eastern end of Tomb 11 (to be discussed below) crosses into Unit T, Unit U includes Tomb 12 in

25. For a study of the funerary structures, *ỉbw* and *sḥ nṯr* and their functions and iconography, see James K. Hoffmeier, "The Possible Origins of the Tent of Purification in the Egyptian Funerary Cult," *Studien zur Altägyptischen Kulture* 9 (1981) 167–77.

26. Ibid., 174–76.

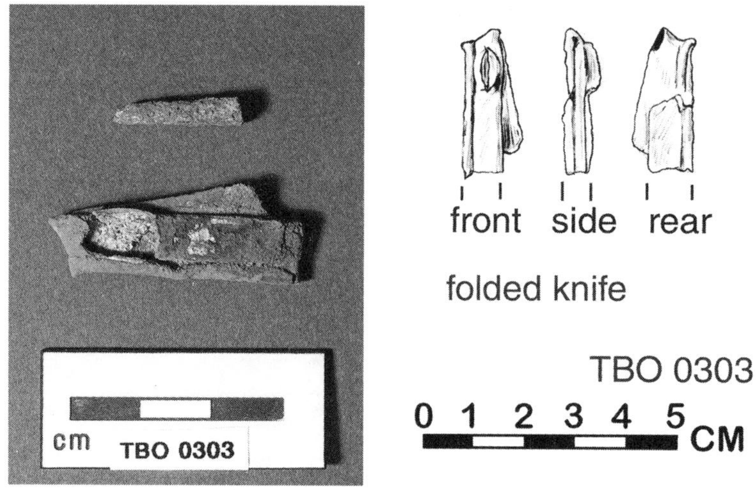

Fig. 4.138. TBO 0303, Copper/copper alloy knife. **a** (left): photo; **b** (right): drawing by Lyla Pinch-Brock.

Fig. 4.139. Travertine jarlet (TBO 0307). **a–b** (left and center): photo; **c** (right): drawing by Lyla Pinch-Brock.

Fig. 4.140. Pounder or grindstone (TBO 0308).

Fig. 4.141. Pounder or grindstone (TBO 0318).

Fig. 4.142. Faience tube bead (TBO 0381).

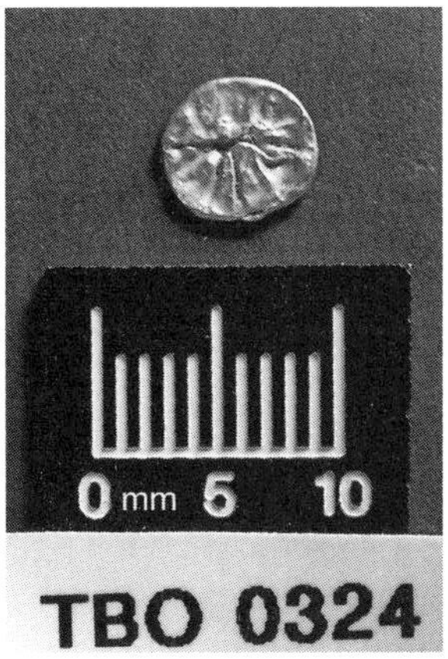

Fig. 4.143. Gold bead (TBO 0324).

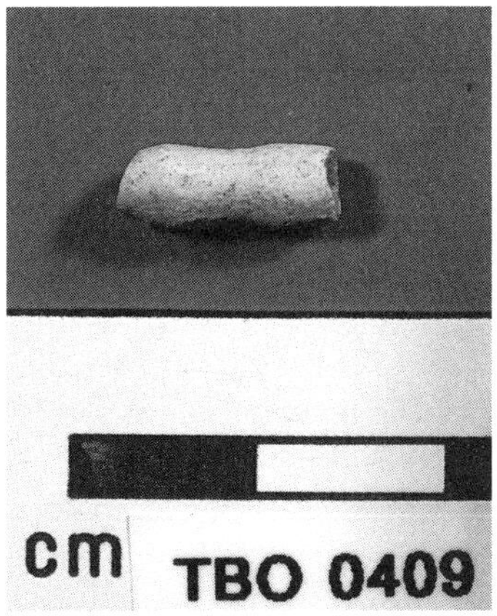

Fig. 4.144. Tube bead (TBO 0409).

Fig. 4.145. Travertine jar rim (TBO 0358). (Two photos.)

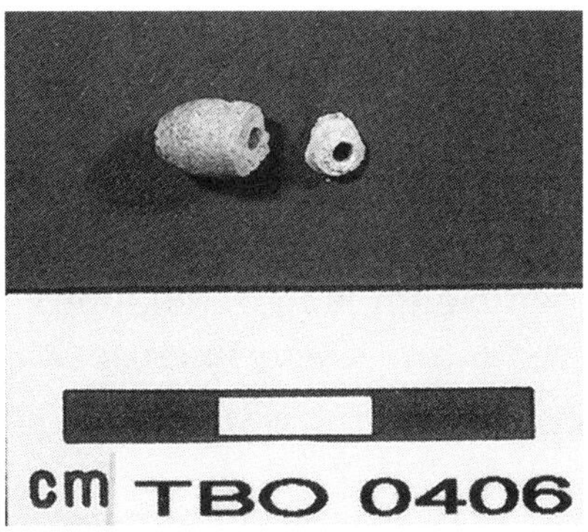

Fig. 4.146. Glass bead (TBO 0406).

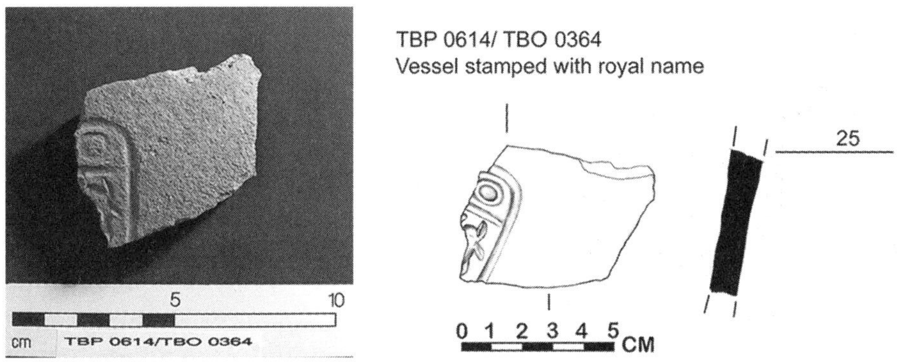

Fig. 4.147. Cartouche on body sherd (TBO 0364). **a** (left): Photo; **b** (right): drawing by Lyla Pinch-Brock).

its northern section, and the southeastern corner of Tomb 11 is a meter away from the western corner of the Locus 18 structure. In other words, three badly disturbed tombs surround these structures, making it impossible to distinguish objects coming from the tombs from those that may have originated in the two buildings. This is particularly true of finds in Tomb 1, which is immediately below the surface and is made up of this churned and robbed area.

Fig. 4.148. Stone tool (TBO 0366).

Beads are by far the best-represented finds, and as elsewhere in Field III, Areas 1 and 2, there are various domestic tools, but typically they are smaller (no querns or mortars). Although the beads are mostly faience, a gold bead (TBO 0324) stands out among the more common types. A long faience tube bead (TBO 0381 = fig. 4.142) looks like nine smaller beads joined as one. It compares with TBO 0170 (fig. 4.98) found in Tomb 4 but has only four sections, and TBO III 77 (fig. 4.60), which has six.

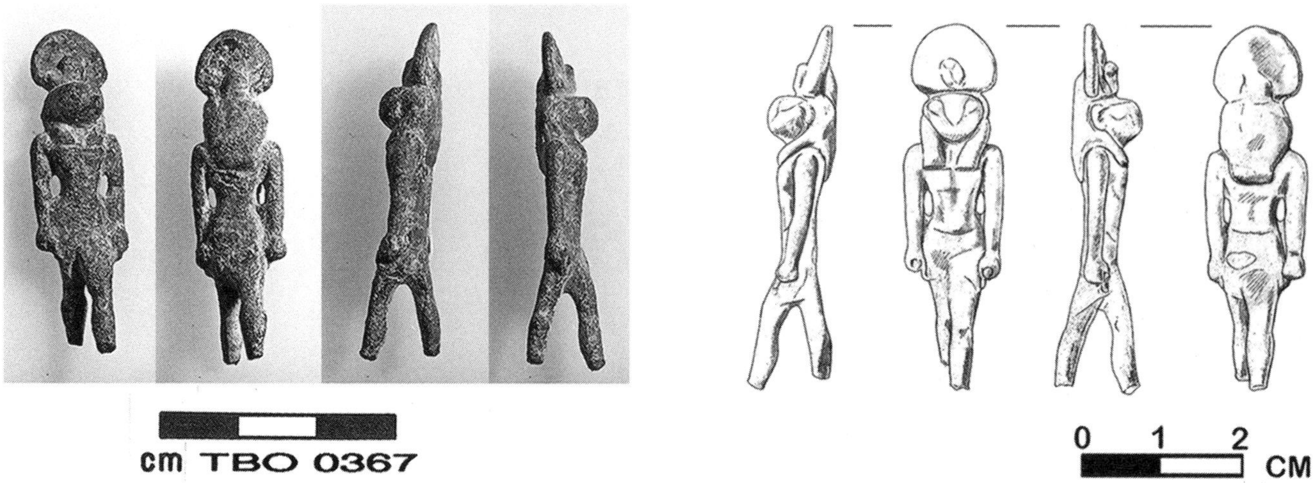

Fig. 4.149. Copper/copper alloy figurine of falcon-headed deity (TBO 0367). **a** (left, above): Photo; **b** (right): Drawing by Lyla Pinch-Brock.

The most important object for dating purposes is TBO 0364, a body sherd containing a partial cartouche (fig. 4.147a–b). The top of the cartouche is preserved, as is most of the right side, but the entirety of the bottom is lost. Three signs remain. The top is clearly the sun-disc, and the third or bottom sign is clearly the *ḫpr*-sign (𓆣). The reading of the middle sign is more challenging. The horizontal line is either 𓏠 or 𓉻. Against the former, there are no tiny dashes across the top of the sign that would represent the game-pieces on the *mn* game-board.[27] With regard to the latter, the right side of the horizontal sign does not taper as one would expect with the 𓉻 sign. Amenhotep II's nomen is attested on the aforementioned sherd discovered in this same cemetery, possibly originating in Tomb 4 (fig. 4.82 = TBO 0071). When compared to the orthography of TBO 0071, we can see that the right side of the 𓉻 sign also does not taper to a point but flares out on the left side, which is missing in TBO 0364. Consequently, the shape of the middle sign in TBO 0364 seems to correspond better to 𓉻. Thus, the cartouche probably contains the nomen of Amenhotep II, *ꜥ3-ḫprw-rꜥ*.[28] In addition to TBO 0071, door-jambs bearing Amenhotep II's name were discovered at Tell el-Borg, reused in the foundations of the early Ramesside moat in Field V and published in *Tell el-Borg I*, 245–48. These include TBO 0703, TBO 0704/0715, TBO 0705, TBO 0714, TBO 0726, and TBO 0727 (totaling two occurrences of *ꜥ3-ḫprw-rꜥ* and four of *ỉmn ḥtp*). Royal activity under Amenhotep II at this military site was significant indeed.

Consequently, we favor the reading *ꜥ3-ḫprw-rꜥ* but cannot rule out *mn-ḫprw-rꜥ*, which could point to Thutmose III or IV. Sherds dating to the 2nd Intermediate Period, the early 18th Dynasty, and specifically from the era of Thutmose III have been documented at Tell el-Borg (*Tell el-Borg I*, 376–78). Combining the two sherds with the royal name *ꜥ3-ḫprw-rꜥ*, found less than 20 m apart in the same cemetery, seemingly dates the earliest phase of this necropolis to the same period when the first fort was established (*Tell el-Borg I*, 184–97) at Tell el-Borg in the last third or quarter of the 15th century B.C.

27. If *mn* is the sign, the nomens of Thutmose III and IV could be intended. Thutmose III's name occurs on only one recarved limestone block at Tell el-Borg (see *Tell el-Borg I*, 91–92). It is impossible to say which inscribed surface was original and which was secondary. Because many limestone blocks at Tell el-Borg were reused, it is plausible that they were brought to this remote site for reuse.

28. Peter Dorman looked at a picture of this cartouche for us and concluded that the sign was likely 𓉻 and that Amenhotep II was therefore more likely.

Fig. 150. **a** (left): Tomb 11 with bones in situ (looking west); **b** (right): Tombs 8, 9, 11, and the "Tomb" 10/ Locus 18 structure (looking west).

A unique tool was found in Unit U. Although one end is broken, this stone implement remains 7.7 cm long (fig. 4.148). Rounded at one end, the stone tool then flattens out to form something like a chisel blade. It is tempting to speculate that this tool might have been an implement used in mummification or funerary rites.

A small figurine of a falcon-headed god was found on the surface of the eastern cemetery (Area 2) (fig. 4.149a–b). The figure is broken at the ankles, but the remainder of the small image is preserved and quite well executed for a small object. A sun-disc with uraeus is on the head of the falcon-head, which wears a wig, the lappets of which lay on his chest in front and which flows down the back. The figure appears to wear a *Šndyt*-kilt. The deity could be Montu, Re-Harakhty, or Horus. Given the prominent role of Horus in the region, one might be inclined to think that he is the deity portrayed.[29]

Tomb 11 (Locus 20)

Provenance: Field III, Area 2, Units G and R
Dimensions: 1.32 × 2.63 m
Maximum preserved height: 5 courses
Brick size: 40 × 20 × 10 cm
Orientation of long axis: 110°
Excavator: Scott Haddow

Tomb 11 is a medium-sized rectangular mud-brick grave (fig. 4.150a–b). The dark gray-brown bricks (10YR 4/2) are the same size as those used in the construction of Tombs 5, 6, 8, and 9. The walls of the tomb are much thicker, and it is larger than the other tombs in Area 2, except for the large family burial, Tomb 4. Robbing activities have greatly damaged the inside, thus obscuring its original appearance. When the space was excavated for the construction of Tomb 11, the tomb builders cut into and destroyed a section of the Locus 18 wall in Unit T (figs. 4.6, 4.134, 4.135,

29. Hoffmeier, "Deities of the Eastern Frontier," 197–200.

Table 4.10. Small Finds in and around Tomb 11

TBO	*Unit/Locus*	*Object Type*	*Material*	*Measurements*
0239	G 1	nail	copper/copper alloy	2.7 × 0.4 dia cm
0249	G 1	rework sherd, game piece/token	clay	1.2 × 3.4 dia cm
0255	G 1	metal fragments, ring	copper/copper alloy	n/a
0386	G 1	2 small beads	faience	0.1 × 0.3 dia cm
0397	G 1	chipped stone blade	chert	5.2 × 2.8 × 0.5 cm
0440	G 1	1 blue, 1 black bead	faience	0.4 × 0.15 × 0.45; 0.5 × 0.25 × 0.4 cm
0380	G1, inside tomb	tube bead (6 sections)	faience	1.0 × 0.3 dia cm

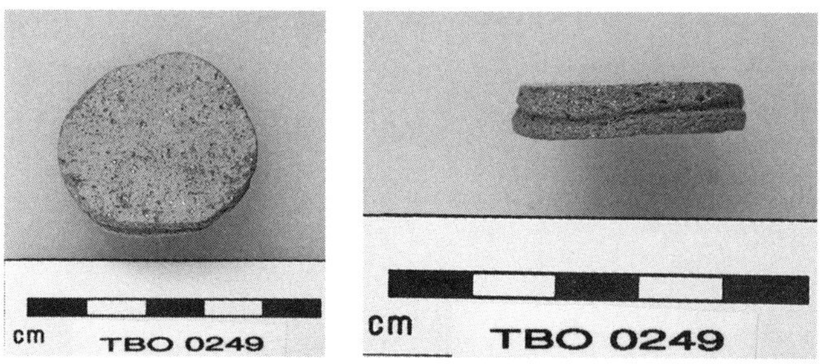

Fig. 4.151. Game piece or token (TBO 0249). **a** (left): Top view; **b** (right): Side view.

Fig. 4.152. Copper/copper alloy fragments, ring (TBO 0255). **a** (left): Photo; **b** (right): Drawing by Lyla Pinch-Brock).

4.136, and 4.150b). No trace of a sarcophagus was found, and only one small find was recovered from inside Tomb 11, while others immediately outside were likely tossed out during the robbing.

Discussion of Small Finds in and Around Tomb 11

All over the site, circular reworked potsherds were found that are variously called "tokens" or "game-pieces" by archaeologists, although their function remains uncertain. TBO 0249, like several others discovered by our staff (e.g., TBO III 54 = fig. 4.14) has a line cut into the edge around the entire circumference of the disc. It looks like a pulley, perhaps a spindle whorl, but the absence of a hole cut through the center of the disc seems to rule out such functions. The small finds associated with Tomb 11 are largely consistent with those found associated with the tombs in Area 2. One find, a copper/copper alloy ring (TBO 0255 = fig. 4.152), was badly corroded, making it uncertain whether it was an ear- or finger ring is not clear. The one side is flattened as if it had contained a decoration or text.

Osteological Remains from Tomb 11

Partial human lower limb bones were found in situ on the floor of the tomb and indicate that the head of the deceased was oriented west (fig. 4.150). Other skeletal remains found in the fill of the tomb suggest at least one adult individual, possibly of advanced age. The distal portions of a right and left tibia, along with foot bones, were found in situ (Locus 21). The condition of the bone is good. Although the tibiae are incomplete, individual pedal elements are complete. These elements represent a minimum of one individual. Based on epiphyseal union of the bones, a general age estimate of adult is given. The cortical bone of the tibial and foot remains is extremely thin, especially of the first foot phalanx, which is uncharacteristically light, the result of unusually

Fig. 4.153. Tomb 12, showing a majority of Unit U, north view.

Fig. 4.154. Tomb 12 close up, view to the north.

diaphanous trabecular bone. This occurrence may be associated with osteoporosis (a metabolic condition often linked with advanced age), or perhaps with muscle and bone atrophy subsequent to a disabling injury. Unfortunately, because of the lack of additional skeletal elements for observation, the etiology of this condition remains unclear.

Tomb 12 (Locus 24)

Provenance: Field III, Area 2, Units U
Dimensions: 1.08 × 2.62 m
Maximum preserved height: 4 courses
Brick size: 35 × 20 × 10 cm
Orientation of long axis: 110° off north

Tomb 12 is a rectangular mud-brick grave oriented roughly east–west, with the foot (east) end being rounded (figs. 4.136, 4.153, and 4.154). No artifacts or human remains were found in situ. Potsherds and amorphous bronze fragments were also recovered from the tomb fill (Locus 25). The construction of Tomb 12 is similar to previously excavated single-occupant tombs in Field III, Area 2. It is cut directly into the mud surface (Locus 22) and was built over one of the mini-channels (Th) from the earliest building phase in the necropolis. Below Locus 22 is the same ashy layer (Locus 23) that was exposed in Units S and T. This is the most direct stratigraphic evidence yet found for the sequencing of occupational activity in Field III. The brick size is shorter (35 cm) than the length of those used in the construction of Tombs 5, 6, 8, and 9 (40 cm) and seems to indicate that Tomb 12 was not built at the same time as these nearby interments. We cannot determine if it pre- or postdates them. Two bricks lay across the width of the tomb like the other single interment graves; these served to support a clay coffin, mummy case, or mummy. No remains of any kind were found within Tomb 12.

Tomb 13

Provenance: Field III, Area 1
Dimensions: 4.3 m × 2.25 m
Maximal preserved height: floor only
Orientation of long axis: 116° off north

Fig. 4.155. Scant remains of Tomb 13.

Only the floor of Tomb 13 has survived. Originally, it had been a large mud-brick tomb, approximating the size of Tomb 1. It was discovered by one of our local Egyptian workers during the 2004 season; he noticed a mud patch in the middle of the sand in Area 1. This area had been dug out by the Canal Authority when removing piles of excavation debris (see figs. 4.1–2a). Only the floor remains; no traces of the superstructure survived. No artifacts were found in situ, although several extremely fragmented and unidentifiable human bones were found pressed into the surface of the mud floor.

Tomb 14 (Field VI Area 2, Unit G)

Tomb 14 was uncovered in Field VI, about 85 m west of the exposed tombs in Field III. It was excavated by Thomas Davis and is treated in Chapter 8, which covers Field VI Areas 1–3.

Miscellaneous and Surface Osteological Remains from Field III

In addition to the skeletal material recovered from within the tombs described above, a large amount of human bone was recovered from the surface and debris layers (Locus 1) removed during the course of excavation (an area of approximately 45 m^2). This bone comprises the majority of the human skeletal remains recovered from Field III and, along with potsherds, beads, amulets, and sarcophagus fragments, represents the aftermath of many years of looting activities in the cemetery. As a result of these disturbances, it is very difficult to determine the precise origin of much of the bone recovered. In most cases, skeletal fragments found above or near looted tombs do not correspond to skeletal fragments found within the tombs themselves, suggesting that successive periods of looting have scattered tomb contents far and wide. It is also likely that some of the skeletal material originated in tombs that have yet to be discovered by the present expedition. A minimum of four individuals were recovered from Locus 1. In addition, deeper excavations of the southwest corner of Tomb 4 (Loci 12 and 14) revealed a small amount of human bone representing at least one individual.

Locus 1

The skeletal material recovered from the surface/debris layers (Locus 1) of Field III, Area 2 represents a minimum of four individuals. Several unfused vertebral fragments corresponding to an age in the late fetal to neonatal range represent the first individual. The second individual is represented by 14 unworn permanent teeth, which give an age estimate (based on tooth eruption and wear) of adolescent. The third individual is represented by jaw fragments containing twelve permanent teeth with extreme wear on the lower molars and small amounts of calculus deposition on the labial surfaces of the lower incisors, canines, and premolar, as well as the upper first molar. The lower left second premolar is missing antemortem, and there is an interproximal carious lesion on the cemento-enamel junction of an upper left molar. Based on the degree of tooth wear, this individual is given an age estimate of between 35 and 45 years.[30] Three moderately worn teeth with no pathological lesions observable represent the fourth individual, who has been given a general age estimate of adult. In addition, an assortment of cranial, vertebral, rib, scapular, pelvic, and long-bone fragments, as well as hand and foot bones, were also recovered. All observable epiphyses were completely fused, thus indicating adult status. Traces of resin indicative of mummification were found on several cranial fragments and long bones. No skeletal elements are duplicated, although bone coloration and size variation indicates at least two individuals. These do not, however, affect the MNI of four.

Loci 12 and 14

A small amount of skeletal material was also recovered outside of Tomb 4 during the excavation to fully expose its southwest corner. Locus 12, which represents the basal sand layer into which the tombs of Field III were built, yielded several cranial fragments representing at least one individual. Incomplete union of the cranial sutures indicates an individual in the adolescent or young adult age range. Locus 14, a mud layer at the base of Tomb 4, representing the foundation level, yielded a single pelvic fragment (from the acetabulum) of an individual of indeterminate age. No pathological lesions are observable on any of the bones. Taken together, the skeletal material from Loci 12 and 14 represent an MNI of one, although it is more likely that the bone derives from two individuals because of the stratigraphic relationship of the two loci.

Field III Early Domestic Space

During the 2002 excavation season, the first traces of domestic (or industrial?) activity was found in situ at Tell el-Borg. This find helped to shed light on the occupation sequence of this area. In the course of extending the excavation grid outward, a test trench (1 × 5m) was extended to the west of Unit I, primarily to expose the entirety to the badly preserved Tomb 7 (fig. 4.6). This test trench was expanded to a 5 × 5 m excavation unit and designated as Unit J. Approximately 60 cm below datum, the tops of two partially preserved ceramic lined ovens or *tabun*s were uncovered (figs. 4.156, 4.157, and 4.158).

The left (west) one of the two is smaller; its diameter is 40 cm and it is 23 cm deep. The second *tabun*, situated about 40 cm to the east has a 50 cm diameter and a depth of 43 cm. The pottery lining of the *tabun*s is thick, like the clay coffins that were used in this cemetery. Just north of this larger oven (ca. 34 cm) is a pit (ca. 40 cm dia) the identity of which was difficult to determine. Given how pitted with modern robber holes the area was, we were inclined to think that this feature was a pit (#3). However, it could be a pit associated with baking or firing activity. Alongside this pit is a yet smaller one in a very ashy matrix. This fourth pit lies at the eastern side of Unit J, at the intersection of the 1 × 5 m trench of Unit I (fig. 4.156). Like the third pit, it is unclear whether this was a fire pit or a robber hole subsequently filled with ash-filled sand.

Slightly farther east in the Unit I trench, another apparent fire pit was uncovered. At the bottom lie two halves of a jar turned concave side up, presumably to serve as a pan for a fireplace

30. Bass, *Human Osteology,* 301.

Fig. 4.156. Field III, Area 2 with Unit J in background.

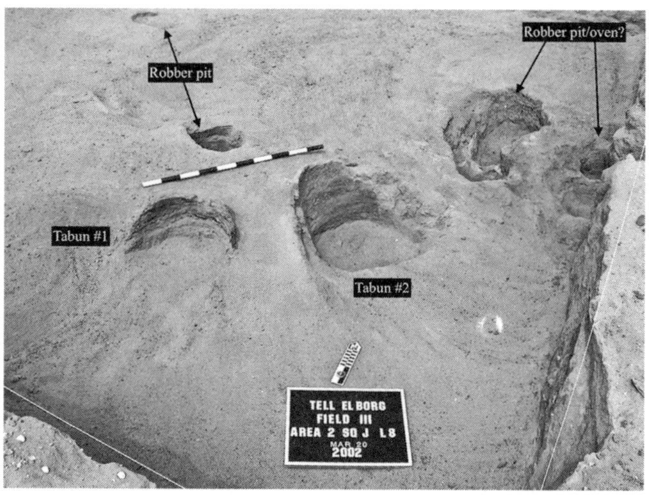

Fig. 4.157. Two *tabun*s in Unit J, and possible fire pit.

Fig. 4.158. Two *tabun*s close up.

or a container where baking (or melting materials) occurred (fig. 4.159). The jar (TBP 0422) was partially restorable, but the neck and rim, which would have helped establish a more precise date, were missing (fig. 4.160). Based on the incomplete remains, a mid-18th Dynasty is suggested by Hummel.[31] The intensity of the heat in and around this installation is evident from the hardening of the sand (as around pit #3) and the outside of the jar is blackened, even though it faced the ground below the fire.

These installations (possibly up to four) were found within a thick layer of ashy sand mixed with charcoal, burned pottery, and animal bone (Locus 13) (fig. 4.161). The thickness of the ash

31. This suggestion comes via email, after studying the piece, but she admits that the missing neck and rim preclude any certainty. She thinks it could be a rounded-bottom beer jar or some sort of offering jar.

Fig. 4.159. Fire pit with jar halves in situ.

Fig. 4.160 (right). Restored jar from fire pit, TBP 0422.

layer (approx. 35 cm) implies that this activity was intensive and/or carried out for a relatively long period of time. In the western half of Unit J, Locus 13 is cut into by a later disturbance or series of disturbances (Locus 8), most likely representing robber activity (see Square J north profile = fig. 4.162). No trace of locus 13 is found east of Unit J, although much thinner layers of ash do appear throughout Field III; for example, small ash and charcoal lenses found underneath the mud surface in Squares D, E, F, and H might derive from the same domestic context.

Initially, it was unclear whether the remains associated with the ovens and fireplaces pre- or post-dated the area's use as a cemetery. Further work in 2004, however, appears to have settled the question. This work revealed a large and intact portion of a mud surface (Locus 22, Units S, T, U, V) previously seen in other areas of Field III and directly underlain by an ash layer (Locus 23) that, although not as thick as locus 13 in Unit J, has a nearly identical composition. The mud-brick foundation of Tomb 12 is cut through Loci 22 and 23 and thus post-dates them. This earlier mud surface is also incised with long grooves, approximately 10 cm wide, cut at right angles, appearing to form compartments that may have formed the layout for constructing reed huts or animal pens. It appears, then, that Field III originally had a domestic or industrial function within Tell el-Borg and that at some point this area was abandoned in favor of its use as a place for burial. Attempting to date the occupation of both activities in Field III is exacerbated by the extent of the disturbance, both ancient and recent, in the area. The pottery sequence in Field III dates the area to the late 18th and 19th Dynasties, but due to the lack of in situ artifacts, it is presently unclear when during this period the change in use took place.

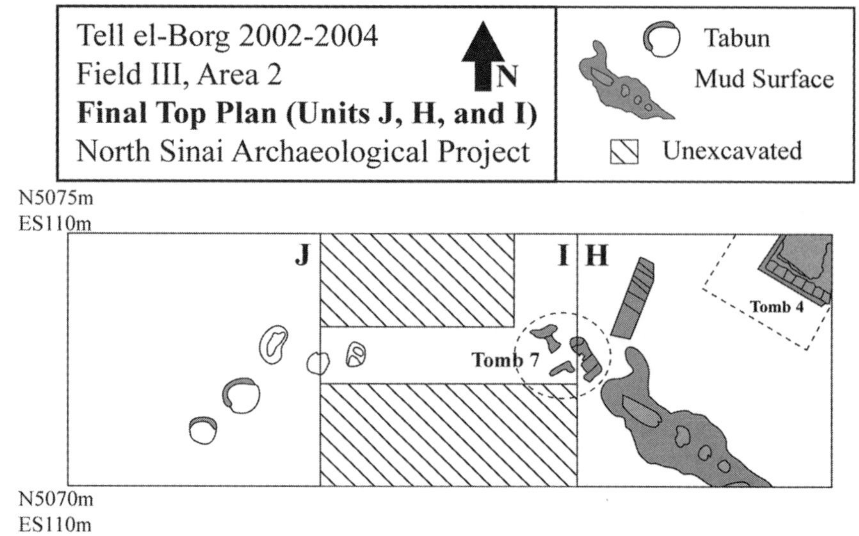

Fig. 4.161. Top Plan of Units H, I, and J.

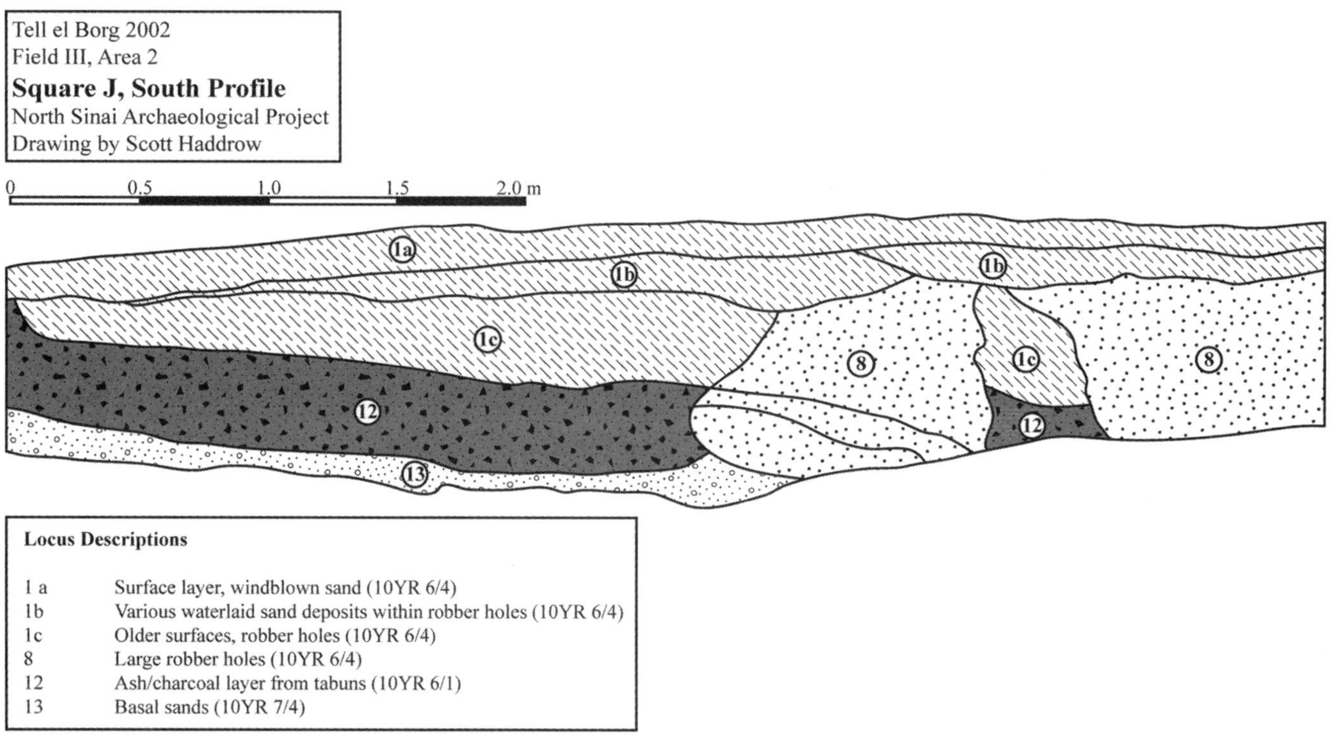

Fig. 4.162. Unit J, south section. Digitized by S. Haddow and enhanced by Joshua Olsen.

Discussion of Small Finds in Units I and J

The most significant find from this locus is a steatite object (TBO 0106). Though broken at both ends, the 13.2 cm long rectangular stone object was obviously longer than what is preserved. The front side (the one depicted in figs. 4.163, 4.164), 4.0 cm wide, is beveled on both sides, while the backside is flat. The beveling is similar to the beveling found on cubit rods. The rod from

Table 4.11. Small Finds in Units I and J (Field III, Area 2)

TBO	*Unit/Locus*	*Object Type*	*Material*	*Measurements*
0220	I loc 1	lump of metal	copper/copper alloy	1.0 × 0.7 × 0.4 cm
0216	J loc 1	1 lumps and 1 piece of metal	copper/copper alloy	n/a
0263	J loc 1	small, broken metal rod	copper/copper alloy	2.4 × 0.6 dia cm
0106	J loc 6	stone tool	steatite	13.2 × 4.0 × 2.1 cm
0230	J loc 8	disc-shaped game piece (?)	reused potsherd	2.8 × 0.5 cm
0377	J loc 9	disc-shaped game piece (?)	reused sherd, Marl A	0.7 × 1.6 dia cm

Fig. 4.163. Steatite tool, TBO 0106.

Fig. 4.165. Disc-shaped game piece (?), TBO 0230.

Fig. 4.166. Disc-shaped game piece (?), TBO 0377.

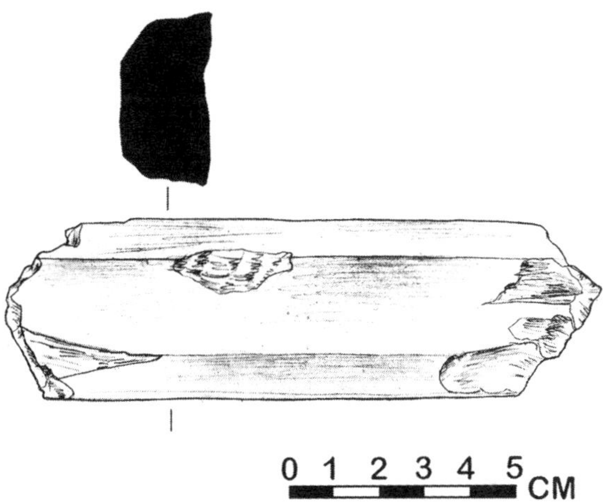

Fig. 4.164. Steatite tool, TBO 0106; drawing by Lyla Pinch-Brock.

the tomb of Kha at Deir el-Medineh is beveled on one side,[32] but the recently found steatite rod from the tomb of Aper-el at Saqqara is beveled on both sides like TBO 0106. If this steatite object is a section of a cubit rod, one might expect to see the perpendicular markings characteristic of a measuring device, but none are visible. Thus, its function remains uncertain.

Discussion of Small Finds

Although the "pottery pit" was so named because of the nearly 100 larger vessels recovered from this cache, a number of small finds were registered (see Excursus, pp. 236ff.). From this locus came the largest collection of grain-grinding implements: a mortar, querns, and grindstones, eight in all (figs. 4.167, 4.168, 4.169, and 4.170). This concentration in a single locus supports the view that the purpose of the objects found in the pit was food related: food storage, preparation, and consumption associated with funerary rites, meals and festivals.

32. For the example from the tomb of Kha, see Ernest Schiaparelli, *La Tomba intatta dell'architetto Cha: Relazione sui lavori della missione italiana in Egitto, ani 1903–1920* (Turin: Museo di Antichità), 1927) 168–73, figs. 154–56. For the classic study on Egyptian cubit rods, see Nora E. Scott, "Egyptian Cubit Rods," *Metropolitan Museum of Art Bulletin* 1 (1942) 70–75.

Table 4.12. Small Finds from "Pottery Pit"

TBO	*Unit/Locus*	*Object Type*	*Material*	*Measurements*
III 83	III B, pit	small bead	glass(?)	n/a
III 84	III B, pit	4 fragments of a bowl (?)	faience	n/a
III 85	III B, pit	toggle (?)	bone (?)	3.8 × 1.3 × 0.4 cm
III 86	III B, pit	retouched blade	chert	2.3 × 1.9 × 0.4 cm
III 87	III B, pit	awl or chisel (?)	copper/copper alloy	12.5 × 0.6–0.2 dia cm
III 88	III B, pit	body sherd w partial cartouche	ceramic	10.5 × 5.5 cm
III 89	III B, pit	blade flake	carnelian	1.0 × 1.1 cm
III 90	III B, pit	metal tool (?) fragment	copper/copper alloy	1.5 × 1.3 × 0.8 cm
III 93	III B, pit	grindstone/quern fragment	sandstone	6 × 4 × 2.4 cm
III 96	III B, pit	grindstone/quern (?) fragment	limestone	11 × 10 × 1.9 cm
III 99	III B, pit	chipped stone blade fragment	chert	2.5 × 2.4 × 0.3 cm
III 101	III B, pit	corner of stone tray/trough	limestone	33 × 21 × 21 cm
III 102	III B, pit	mortar fragment	limestone	28 × 7 cm
III 103	III B, pit	quern	sandstone	19 × 15 × 4 cm
III 104	III B, pit	grindstone	sandstone	22 × 17 × 5 cm
III 105	III B, pit	corner of stone tray/trough	limestone	48 × 42 × 10 cm
III 106	III B, pit	quern	sandstone	23 × 15 × 7 cm
III 107	III B, pit	bowl or mortar	limestone	18 × 12 × 5 cm
III 108	III B, pit	quern	sandstone	18 × 13 × 5 cm
III 109	III B, pit	fragment of stone vessel	travertine	n/a
III 112	III B, pit	flake from III 112 (?)	travertine	2.3 × 2.3 × 1.6 cm

Fig. 4.167. Sandstone quern, TBO III 93.

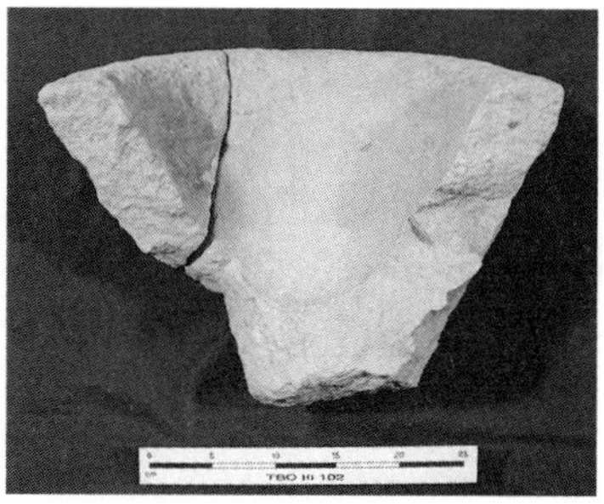

Fig. 4.168. Limestone mortar, TBO III 102.

Fig. 4.169. Sandstone quern, TBO III 104.

Fig. 4.170. Sandstone quern, TBO III 108.

Parts of two limestone rectangular trays were also uncovered (TBO III 101 and 105 = figs. 4.171a–b and 4.172). The function of these trays remains uncertain. A significant number of fragments or complete limestone objects of this kind were found in association with the fortress in Fields IV and V, but typically they are among reused blocks (see *Tell el-Borg I*, 95, 241–43). One tray was discovered in a tomb at Hebua IV (fig. 4.173). No examples of these limestone trays have been uncovered in a tomb at Tell el-Borg.

There were several small finds from the pit that are seemingly unrelated to the food function of the majority of the objects and ceramics recorded. These objects reflect a more elite class of finds. They include fragments of a faience vessel (a dish or platter? TBO III 84 = fig. 4.174), a bone (or possibly ivory) toggle (TBO III 85 = fig. 4.175), and a flake of carnelian (TBO III 89). The

Fig. 4.171. Limestone tray, TBO III 101. **a**: side; **b**: top.

Fig. 4.172. Limestone tray, TBO III 105.

Fig. 4.173. Limestone tray in a tomb at Hebua IV (N5 Tomb 1).

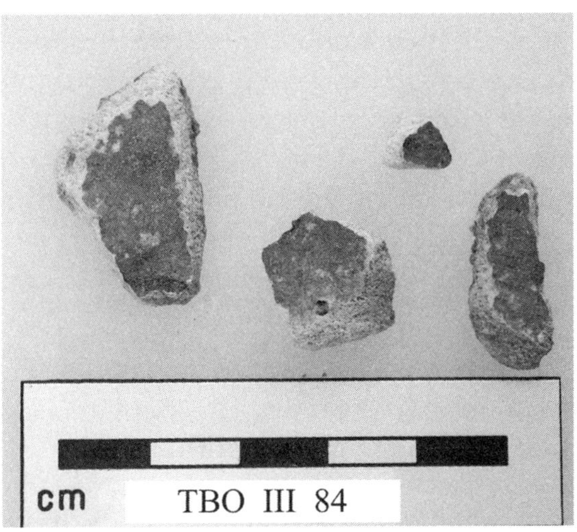

Fig. 4.174. Faience bowl fragments, TBO III 84.

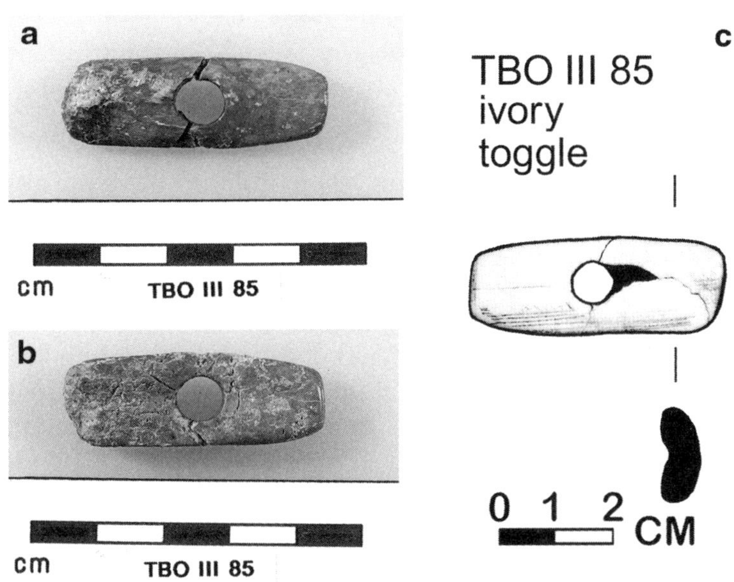

Fig. 4.175 (right). Bone toggle, TBO III 85 **a**: front; **b**: back; **c**: Drawing by Lyla Pinch Brock.

toggle has no parallel at the site and its function is unclear. The flake of carnelian could either be from making a blade (e.g., TBO 0165 = fig. 4.95), or making beads (e.g., TBO 0190 = fig. 4.89) or jewelry (e.g., TBO 0242 = fig. 4.112) or amulets (TBO 0215 = fig. 4.120a).

EXCURSUS: A DEPOSIT OF RESTORABLE POTTERY RETRIEVED FROM A CEMETERY PIT

Rexine Hummel
ROYAL ONTARIO MUSEUM

Description of Pit

An oblong pit measuring approximately 3.8 × 2.7 m and 2.3 m deep was uncovered in Field III (Unit B) between Tombs 1 and 2 (figs. 4.3, 4.176–179). The darker sand within the pit marked it off from the surrounding basal sand (fig. 4.176). As the excavations proceeded, a large cache of pottery was uncovered (fig. 4.177). On the western side of the pit, three stone blocks were placed at descending depths, resembling a crude staircase. In addition to pottery, some animal bones, ash, and charcoal were documented by the excavator. The objects from the pit consisted of stone materials, including three limestone bowls, four sandstone querns, one limestone tray, and three chert blades (see below for review of the small finds).[33] Thanks to a dedicated team of conservators, profiles of nearly 100 of the vessels were fully or partially restored and then registered. Because of the pit's proximity to the cemetery (between Tomb 1 and 2) and its many robbed graves, it was tentatively labeled a robber's pit. However, in line with recent studies that emphasize the function of ceramic deposits, it seems appropriate to revisit this assemblage in order to extract more information from the pottery it contained.

Pottery deposits or caches are often found close to temples, shrines, tombs, or cemeteries and, when found in sealed contexts, present the ceramicist with an opportunity to study a group of vessels that were deposited around the same time for a special purpose or occasion. Such hoards include embalming caches, foundation deposits, cultic deposits, burial pottery, and remains of funerary meals. In this light, the Tell el-Borg pit appears to have many of the elements present in both a deposit for the remnants of funeral meals and a depository for cultic offerings.

A more detailed study of the Borg assemblage reveals the following interesting facts.

1. The vessels in the pit were broken but restorable. In many cases, most of the pieces of each pot were present; hence, they were likely broken in this area.
2. The curious stone staircase seems out of place in a robbers' pit or dump. The stone blocks that form the staircase are not local but were imported from the valley and thus were placed in the pit intentionally.
3. A few of the pots reveal definite "killing holes." Other pots may have had possible "killing holes" but were too damaged to clearly identify such holes.
4. The types of vessels in the pit are not as random as they would be in a dump but are limited mainly to five specific categories of vessels.

33. The stone fragments were very small and random and therefore are not considered to be part of the ceramic deposit. For discussion and illustrations, see the previous section.

Fig. 4.176. Early phase of discovery of pit.

Fig. 4.177. Pottery exposed with stone steps on right side.

Out of a total of 184 vessels and diagnostic sherds that were processed, 146 could be properly identified and assigned a type that fit into one of the five categories; it is this group that was used to calculate their percentage in the distribution list below. The remaining sherds fall into two groups: (1) painted, special, unusual sherds, or foreign imports that do not connect with the restored vessels, and (2) tiny rims and bases that cannot be with any certainty assigned to a specific type of vessel.

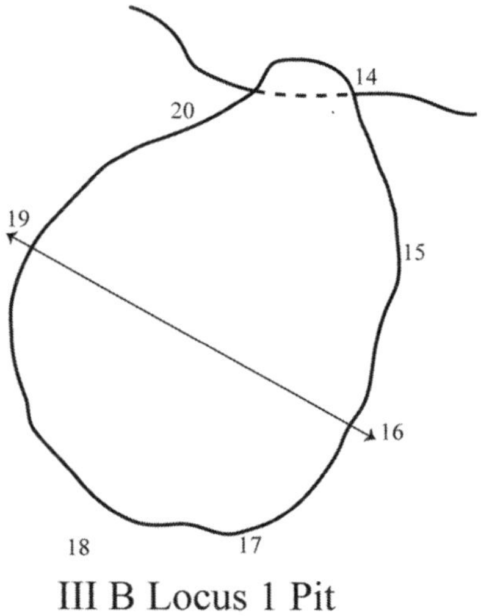

Fig. 4.178. Top plan of pit; drawing by J. Knudstad; digitized by Joshua Olsen.

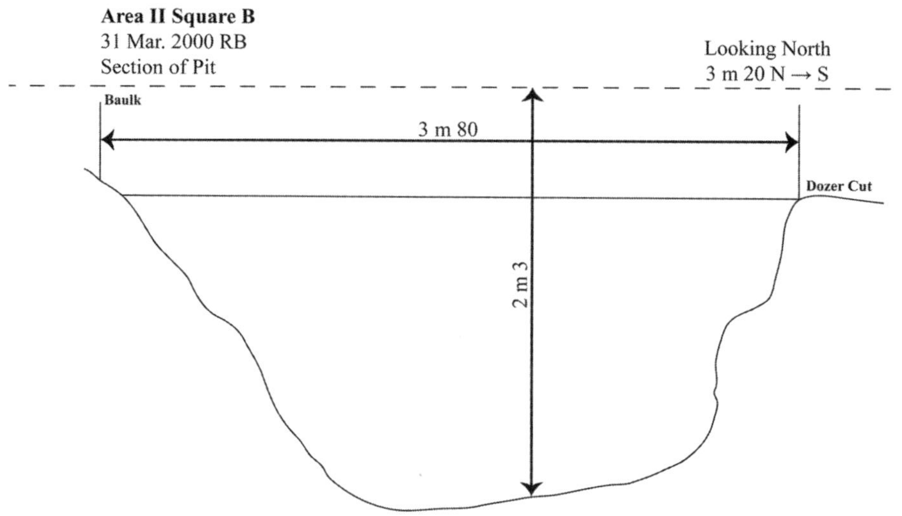

Fig. 4.179. Elevation of pit; drawing by J. Knudstad; digitized by Joshua Olsen.

Frequency Distribution of Vessels Forms

Total numbers: 146 (99%)
Offering vessels: 30 beer jars, 3 offering stands = 33 (23%)
Large containers: 26 amphorae, 4 zirs, 13 store-jar bases = 43 (29%)
Medium-sized jars: 21 (14%)
Large bowls: 21 (14%)
Small bowls: 28 (19%)

Not included in the distribution are 38 miscellaneous sherds that were also found in the pit: decorated sherds, flasks, fish plate, etc.

The largest category, at 29%, encompasses large container vessels such as amphorae, large store-jars, and zirs. Most significant are the amphorae, the majority of which were imported from the Levant. Fragments of three zirs were also found in the pit.

- Medium-sized jars are much less numerous: 14%. They appear in a variety of shapes and fabrics without any single shape dominating.
- Large bowls with rim diameters over 35 cm: 14%.
- Smaller bowls of less than 35 cm and averaging 20 cm in diameter: 19%.

The most important group for our discussion is that of the offering vessels. These crudely made jars with deep fingerprints around the base are immediately recognizable as the ubiquitous New Kingdom "beer jars." The term "beer jar" is deeply imbedded in the ceramic jargon, although there is very little evidence that these vessels ever held beer. Since they are found everywhere, but especially around temples, shrines, and cemeteries, the term "offering vessel" is more accurate; nevertheless, the term "beer jar" is still used in this chapter.

Almost all of the offering vessels in the Tell el-Borg pit (99%) had an intentional hole piercing the bottom of their bases before they had been fired. The hole must be important, but its significance is not entirely clear; perhaps it is connected with ritual libation.

Vessels Retrieved from the Pit

The description of the fabrics of the vessels in this chapter follow the Vienna System, when possible. Some fabrics are unique to the Sinai—namely, the Bir el-ᶜAbd and Haruba marl clays. The fabric labeled "Bir el-ᶜAbd Marl" comes from the archaeological site of Bir el-ᶜAbd, which is located in the northern Sinai 80 km east of Tell el-Borg. The site was excavated briefly and studied by Eliezer Oren.[34] The petrography of this Sinai marl is very similar to that of the Egyptian Marl C fabric of the Vienna System. Like Marl C, the section usually fires red, with a grayish-white surface and is characterized by the presence of abundant limestone particles, many of which are decomposed as a result of the firing process.[35] The fabric labeled "Haruba ware" comes from a site situated in the north Sinai, more than 100 km east of Bir el-ᶜAbd where some kilns were found. The local fabric is characterized by the presence of very calcareous, silty (usually greater than 10%) marl, rich in iron oxide grains and tempered by coastal, rounded sand grains. Several unfired vessels of this clay were discovered in the potters' workshop, proving that they originated at this site.[36]

Large Containers

Levantine Amphorae

Since Tell el-Borg was situated along the Mediterranean coast it is not surprising that the majority of imported amphorae found in the pit were from the Levant (see, too, *Tell el-Borg I*, Chapter 9). The precious contents would have been consumed by the elite of the fortress, leaving the empties to be recycled by the families of the soldiers and retainers. These now empty large vessels were perfect for storing water, although dry goods and meat products are also a possibility.

Most of the Levantine amphorae were thrown on the wheel and appear to be manufactured from a similar clay source: a very hard and dense fabric with a reddish or brown outer zone and a dark brown/gray inner zone. Prominent temper includes abundant sand and white limestone particles. In many cases, the surface is so heavily coated with white accretions it is almost impossible to see the true color. This description best fits fabric P30,[37] which is a popular fabric during the New Kingdom. Amphorae made from this fabric appear to have been used to carry pistachio resin.[38] The Levantine amphorae in the Tell el-Borg pit have lost their rims, but their bodies were thrown on the wheel, are oval in shape, with rounded shoulders and bases, and fall into Aston's Type 1a, which dates to the early to mid-18th Dynasty.[39] This same form continues into the late 18th Dynasty, as seen at Amarna.[40]

---

34. Y. Goren, E. D. Oren, and R. Feinstein, "The Archaeological and Ethnoarchaeological Interpretation of a Ceramological Enigma: Pottery Production in Sinai (Egypt) during the New Kingdom Period," *KVHAA Konferenser* 34 (1995) 101–9.

35. Ibid., 110. "Two main factors distinguish it from Marl C: (i) the presence of large particles in this fabric in significant quantities, and (ii) the relatively high firing temperature (900–1000 degrees), which has caused typical reshaping and melting of the shale particles."

36. Ibid., 110.

37. David Aston "Amphorae in New Kingdom Egypt," *ÄuL* 14 (2004) 175–214.

38. Margaret Serpico and Raymond White, "The Botanical Identity and Transport of Incense during the Egyptian New Kingdom," *Antiquity* 74 (2000) 891. The fabric P30 equates with Amarna fabric III.10, which was one of only two fabrics that carried pistachio resin.

39. Aston, "Amphorae in New Kingdom Egypt," 177, fig. 1.

40. Pamela Rose, *The Eighteenth Dynasty Pottery Corpus from Amarna* (London: EES, 2007) 293: 689 Type NB 1:3.

Pottery Plate 4.1 (scale 1:8)

1:1 Amphora. TBP[41] 0183. Height: 54 cm.
1:2 Amphora. TBP 298. Height: 48 cm.
1:3 Amphora. TBP 190. Height: cm. 39 cm. Surface: A cross-shaped pot-mark is engraved on the pre-fired clay below the handle.
1:4 Amphora. TBP 197. Height: 48 cm. Surface: A cross-shaped pot-mark is incised on the pre-fired clay below the handle.
1:5 Amphora. TBP 194. Height: 38 cm.
1:6 Amphora. TBP 300. Height: 46 cm.
1:7 Amphora. TBP 196. Height: 48 cm.
1:8 Amphora. TBP 299. Height: 48 cm.
1: 9 Amphora. TBP 195. Height: 32 cm.
1:10 Amphora. TBP 317. Height: 36 cm. Fabric: dense brick-red matrix. Core: none. Inclus: abundant black rock particles, gray grits, white flecks, and voids. Surface: red (Munsell 10YR 6/6) wet-smoothed.

Large Containers

Amphorae from the Western Oasis

Along with the many Canaanite amphorae, three almost completely intact Oasis Ware amphorae were found in the large pit in the cemetery. These amphorae are large and extremely heavy; therefore, to transport such vessels from the Oases to the Valley must have been a laborious and difficult physical process. Happily, transportation from the Valley to the North Sinai was much easier, requiring only river transport. At Amarna, where Oasis Ware fragments have been studied extensively, the chronological distribution shows a steady increase from the beginning of the 18th Dynasty to the Ramesside period, with the most numerous occurring in the level corresponding to the late 18th to early 19th Dynasties.[42]

Pottery Plate 4.2 (scale 1:8)

2:1 Amphora. TBP 0182. Height: 53 cm. Rim: missing. Fabric: hard and dense, orange fabric (Munsell 2.5YR 7/6). Core: none. Inclusions: abundant, medium-to-very-large chunks of white limestone, many black stains, and particles of grog. Although the surface is heavily accreted with salts, traces of red paint on the shoulder and handle may be all that remains of an original slip. The amphora appears to have been made in three sections; a mold-pressed base, a handmade section with obvious vertical finger marks on the interior, which attaches the base to the upper wheelmade region.
Parallel: Aston 1998: 537:2202
2:2 Amphora. TBP 031. Height 52 cm. Rim: missing. Fabric: hard and dense orange fabric (Munsell 10R 5/6), no core. Inclusions: abundant medium and large white limestone chunks, some large dark red particles, and some fine sand. The surface although heavily encrusted with salts appears to be uncoated. The vessel is made in three sections and the outer surface of this amphora is decorated with sharp horizontal ridges in the zone between the shoulder and base of the handle.
2:3 Amphora. TBP 0181. Height: 65 cm. Rim: missing. Fabric: a very dense and hard orange fabric (Munsell 2.5YR 6/8). Core: none. Inclusions: abundant medium-to-very-large chunks of limestone. A smaller scatter of black and yellow particles is seen as well. The surface, although heavily accreted with salts, appears to have gray areas (Munsell 7.5YR 5/1) as well as orange. Large chunks of limestone protrude from the surface. The vessel is made in three sections. The handles have an unusual tilt that actually facilitates grasping them.

41. TBP refers to Tell el-Borg Pot registration number.

42. Janine Bourriau, "Fabrics of the Oasis Amphorae in the New Kingdom from Memphis, Kom Rabiʾa," in *Egypt and Nubia: Gifts of the Desert* (ed. R. Friedman; London: British Museum, 2002) 113.

Bir el-ʿAbd Marl Amphorae

The body shapes of the Sinai-made amphorae in the Tell el-Borg pit date from the reigns of Thutmose IV and Amenhotep III.[43]

2:4 Amphora. TBP 313. Height: 38 cm. Thrown. Fabric: dark gray. Core: very hard and heavy. Inclusions: abundant, decomposing limestone, abundant pale red flakes, large white particles, many voids, has a salt and pepper appearance. Surface appears to be light gray.
Parallels: Aston 2004: fig. 18:b

2:5 Amphora. TBP 310. Height: 38 cm. Thrown. Fabric: brown, Core: very hard and heavy. Inclusions: abundant decomposing limestone, abundant pale brown particles, some large gray and white particles, many voids, and has a salt and pepper appearance. Surface appears to be light gray under a coating of white accretions.
Parallels: Aston 2004: fig. 18:a

2:6 Amphora. TBP 193. Height: 38 cm. Thrown. Fabric: brown, Core: very hard and heavy. Inclusions: abundant, decomposing limestone, some large gray and black particles, many voids, and has a salt and pepper appearance. Surface is coated with accretions.
Parallels: Aston 2004: fig. 18:b

Egyptian Amphorae

The amphorae that were manufactured from Marl D, probably in the Memphis area, fall into Aston's type B1[44] and range in date from the early 18th Dynasty to the 19th Dynasty.

Pottery Plate 4.3 (scale 1:8)

3:1 Amphora. TBP 316. Height: 54 cm. Rim dia: 10 cm. Fabric: Marl D. Surface: pale gray-green slip. Shoulder has been stamped with a cartouche, which is illegible; however, a cartouche (only a sun-disc is discernible at the top) on an identical amphora from East Karnak has been identified with Thutmose I.
Parallel: Aston 2004: 187–88, fig. 6a

3:2 Amphora rim. SC7.32. Height: 4 cm. Rim dia: 9 cm. Fabric: Marl D. Surface: cream slip.

3:3 Amphora rim. SC11.37. Height: 4 cm. Rim dia: 1 cm. Fabric: Marl D. Surface: cream slip.

3:4 Amphora. TBP 315. Height: 32 cm. Fabric: Marl D. Surface: cream slip.

3:5 Amphora. TBP 191. Height: 37 cm. Fabric: Marl D. Surface: A killing hole has been pierced through the wall beside the handle after the vessel was fired.

3:6 Amphora. TBP 291. Height: 35 cm. Fabric: Marl D.

3:7 Amphora. TBP 187. Height: 28.5 cm. Fabric: Marl D.

Storage Jar Bases

3:8 Storage jar base. TBP 332. Height: 40 cm. Fabric: Mixed clay. (Marl G6)

3:9 Storage jar base. TBP 372. Height: 30 cm. Fabric: Mixed clay. (Marl G6)

3:10 Storage jar base. TBP 288. Height: 21 cm. Fabric: Marl D.

3:11 Storage jar base. TBP 580. Height: 15 cm. Fabric: Nile B2.

Large Containers

Zirs and Large Storage Jars

Pottery Plate 4.4 (scale 1:8)

4:1 Zir. TBP 184. Height: 65 cm. Rim dia: 18 cm
Parallel: Goren et al. 1995: 15, fig. 6a. An Egyptian form but manufactured in a local Sinai fabric, either Bir el-ʿAbd or Haruba ware. The fabric was too hard to chip. Many jars of this large type were found at Haruba.

---

43. Aston, "Amphorae in New Kingdom Egypt," 205, fig.18:b.
44. Ibid., 188–89, figs. 6 and 7.

4:2 Zir. TBP 189. Height: 40 cm. Fabric: Haruba Marl. Pale buff outer zone, pale orange inner zone. Inclus: abundant fine-to-large sand, frequent black particles, and fine limestone grits. Very dense and hard.
4:3 Zir. TBP 336. Height: 13 cm. Rim dia: 23 cm. Fabric: very hard and heavy, similar to TBP 184.
4:4 Zir. TBP 325. Height: 17 cm. Rim dia: 19 cm. Fabric: very hard and heavy, similar to TBP 184.
4:5 Large jar. TBP 326. Height: 45 cm. Rim dia: 20 cm. Fabric: Haruba Marl. Pale buff outer zone, pale orange inner zone. Inclus: abundant fine-to-large sand, frequent black particles, and fine limestone grits. Very dense and hard.[45]
4:6 Large jar. TBP 499. Height: 20 cm. Fabric: Haruba Marl. Fabric same TBP 326 (IV: 5).
4:7 Zir. TBP 173. Height: 41.5 cm. Rim dia: 10 cm. Fabric: Nile B2. Surface: cream slip.
4:8 Zir. TBP 330. Height: 42 cm. rim missing. Fabric: Nile B2.

Medium-Sized Jars

Pottery Plate 4.5 (scale 1:8)

5:1 Globular Jar. TPB 188. Height: 31.5 cm. Rim dia: 10 cm. Fabric: Marl B.
5:2 Globular jar. TBP 334. Height: 21 cm. Rim dia: 10 cm. Fabric: Marl B.
5:3 Slender jar. TBP 333. Height: 28 cm. Rim missing. Fabric: Fine Nile B2. Surface: self-slipped and smoothed, two horizontal grooves incised around the neck.
Parallels: Aston 2012: 21: "these slender ovoid jars are very common in the tombs at Hebua IV dating to mid-18th Dynasty." Dorner and Aston 1997: pl. I:8, 9 and pl. II:10–12. Hebua IV/ South.
5:4 Slender jar. TBP 370. Height: 24.5 cm. Rim missing. Fabric: Nile B2.
5:5 Slender jar. TBP 371. Height: 29.5 cm. Rim missing. Fabric: Nile B2. Hole pierced in bottom of pre-fired vessel.
5:6 Slender jar base. TBP 340. Height: 9 cm. Rim missing. Hole pierced in bottom of pre-fired vessel. This is probably a beer jar/offering jar with a round base.
5:7 Globular jar. TBP 322. Height: 29 cm. Base missing. Rim dia: 11 cm. Fabric: Nile B2.
5:8 Slender jar. TBP 324. Height: 25 cm. Rim missing. Fabric: Nile B2. Surface: coated with red slip.
5:9 Jar. SC8.12.[46] Height: 8 cm. Rim dia: 17 cm. Fabric: Marl B.
5:10 Funnel jar. TBP 327. Height: 29 cm. Rim missing. Fabric: Nile B2.
5:11 Jar. TBP 351. Height: 33 cm. Rim and base missing. Fabric: Nile B2.
5:12 Jar base. TBP 350. Height: 31:5 cm. Rim and base missing. Fabric: Nile D.

Large Bowls (over 35 cm in rim diameter)

The carinated bowls with handles, often decorated with designs reminiscent of the Levant, are more prevalent at Tell el-Borg than in other parts of Egypt. In fact, the fabric is hard to identify and may come from the Levant or, more likely, from the Sinai. At Bir el-ʿAbd, it was noted that bowls, or "tableware," outnumbered the storage jars, indicating that household vessels were made locally. We suspect that some of our thick-walled carinated bowls at Tell el-Borg were manufactured from this local Sinai fabric.

The straight-sided large bowls with modeled rims are typically more Egyptian in design. Both of these types of bowls would serve as excellent platters for serving communal meals to family groups at funeral banquets or annual festival celebrations.

Pottery Plate 4.6 (scale 1:8)

6:1 Carinated bowl. TBP 139. Height: 15 cm. Rim dia: 40 cm. Fabric: Bir el-ʿAbd. Surface: black-painted decoration on a cream slip background.

45. I thank David Aston, who visited Tell el-Borg and suggested that this jar was made from Haruba clay.

46. SC8.12 refers to Sherd number in the sherd drawing database.

6:2 Carinated bowl. TBP 294. Height: 17 cm. Rim dia: 35cm. Fabric: Nile B2. Surface: uncoated.
6:3 Carinated bowl. TBP 290. Height: 12 cm. Rim dia: 39 cm. Fabric: Nile B2.
6:4 Bowl. TBP185. Height: 11.5 cm. Rim dia: 40 cm. Fabric: possibly Sinai fabric.
Parallel: Aston 2012: 47:87. Hebua.
6:5 Bowl. TBP 323. Rim dia: 39 cm. Height: 14.5 cm. Fabric: Nile B2.
6:7 Carinated bowl. TBP 356. Height: 13.5 cm. Rim dia: 38 cm. Fabric: Bir el-ʿAbd. Surface: black-painted decoration on a cream-slipped background.

Medium-Sized Bowls (rim diameters 29–31 cm)

6:8 Carinated bowl, SC12.23. Height: 5.5 cm. Rim dia: 30 cm. Fabric: Bir el-ʿAbd. Surface: black – painted decoration on a cream-slipped background.
6:9 Carinated bowl. SC10.39. Height: 11 cm. Rim dia: 31 cm. Fabric: Marl D. Surface: traces of cream slip, two horizontal rows of rope indentations.
6:10 Bowl. TBP 328. Height: 10 cm. Rim dia: 29 cm. Fabric: Nile B2.
6:11 Bowl. SC9.3. Height: 7 cm. Rim dia: 33 cm. Fabric: Nile B2. Surface: orange slip.
Parallel: Aston 2012: 44:52.

Small and Medium-Sized Bowls

The very small bowls (under 15 cm in diameter) were probably used for drinking cups or incense vessels.

Pottery Plate 4.7 (Scale: 1:4)

7:1 Bowl. SC3.16. Height: 3 cm. Rim dia: 15 cm. Fabric: Marl B.
7:2 Cup. SC5.58. Height: 3.5 cm. Rim dia: 9 cm. Fabric: Nile B2. Surface: white coating inside and out.
7:3 Cup. SC3.20. Height: 3.5 cm. Rim dia: 13 cm. Fabric: Nile B2. Surface: red slip on interior and narrow red slip on exterior.
7:4 Carinated cup. SC3.18. Height: 1.5 cm. Rim dia: 10 cm. Fabric: Nile B2. Surface: black-painted rim on red-slipped external surface.
Parallels: Aston 1998: 87:1, Qantir, early18th Dynasty; Seiler 1997: pl.1, fig. 1: ZN 94/124 early 18th Dynasty, Hebua I.
7:5 Cup. TBP 352. Height: 5.5 cm. Rim dia: 14 cm. Fabric: Nile B2. Surface: black- rimmed bowl with horizontal dots on a red line between two black bands under the exterior rim.
Parallel: Bourriau 2005: 120. Decoration is common during the reign of Thutmose III.
7:6 Carinated bowl. TBP 406. Height: 8 cm. Height: 14 cm. Base dia: 8 cm. Fabric: Nile B2. Surface: black-rimmed bowl, the surface inside and out is coated with red paint. A black band decorates the rim, and decorative flutes are incised into the exterior of the bowl below the carination.
7:7 Flower pot. TBP 358. Height: 14 cm. Rim dia: 8 cm. Fabric: Nile B2. Surface: hole pierced in bottom of pre-fired base.
Parallel: Aston 2012: 20, 48:92 Hebua (characteristic of mid-18th Dynasty).
7:8 Carinated bowl. SC7.34. Height: 4 cm. Rim dia: 15 cm. Fabric: Nile B2. Surface: exterior is coated with red slip. *Parallel*: Aston 2012: 32:173, 56:173.
7:9 Bowl. SC2.45. Height: 7 cm. Rim dia: 20 cm. Fabric: Nile B2. Surface: red slip on interior and exterior.
7:10 Bowl. TBP 373. Height: 5 cm. Rim dia: 23 cm. Fabric: Nile B2.
Parallel: Rose 2007: Amarna Type SE 11.2 (p. 217, no. 280)
7:11 Carinated bowl. SC4.47. Height: 7 cm. Rim dia: 23 cm. Fabric: Nile B2.
7:12 Bowl. SC6.1. Height: 4 cm. Fabric: Nile B2. Rim dia: 25 cm.

Miscellaneous Vessels

7:13 Small jar. SC5.57. Height: 1 cm. Rim dia: 5 cm. Fabric: Fine Nile B1. Surface: black dots decorate top of rim.
Parallel: Rose 2007: Type MG3.1, p. 286:636. Amarna.

7:14 Bottle. SC13.14. Height: 4.5 cm. Rim dia: 6 cm. Fabric: Nile B2.
Parallel: Rose 2007: Amarna Type SG5.1, p. 232 no. 364; use unknown.
7:15 Bread Tray. TBP 241. Height: 2 cm. Fabric: Marl E. Surface: deeply incised geometric pattern on interior of tray in order to decorate the bread.
7:16 Pitcher. TBP 381. Height: 10 cm. Fabric: Fine Nile B2. Surface: black lines on a pink slip, handle scar is evident. Red and black decoration on vessels developed during early to mid-18th Dynasty and is characteristic of the reign of Thutmose III.[47]
7:17 Jar. TBP 146. Height: 6 cm. Dia: 10 cm. Fabric: Nile B2. Surface: black and red decoration on a cream-slipped background.
7:18 Jar. TBP 168. Height: 6 cm. Dia: 9 cm. Fabric: Marl A. Surface: black and red painted decoration on a cream-slipped background.
7:19 Flask. SC10.40. Height: 6.5 cm. Fabric: brown, medium and dense. Core: gray. Inclus: abundant voids and decomposed limestone, some white particles. (Bir el-ʿAbd). Surface: coated with a gray green-burnished slip.

Beer Jars/Offering Vessels (Nile B2)

The beer jars from the Tell el-Borg pit fall into Holthoer's[48] beer bottle type "BB4 ordinary," which he claims are the most common and date from the beginning of the 18th Dynasty to the 19th Dynasty. They typically have a short, slightly everting neck, simple rim (8–12 cm in diameter), and a flat base finished with deep fingerprints. The bases range in diameter from 8 to 10.5 cm.

Pottery Plate 4.8 (scale 1:5)

8:1 TBP 176. Height: 26 cm. Rim dia: 11 cm. Base dia: 9 cm. Fabric: Nile B2. Comment: the only beer jar in the Tell el-Borg pit with no hole pierced in the base.
8:2 TBP 177. Height: 28 cm. Rim dia: 10.5 cm. Base dia: 10 cm. Fabric: Nile B2
8:3 TBP 186. Height: 28.5 cm. Rim dia: 8.75 cm. Base dia: 10 cm. Fabric: Nile B2
8:4 TBP 287. Height: 23.5 cm. Rim dia: 9.5 cm. Base dia: 8.5 cm. Fabric: Nile B2
8:5 TBP 198. Height: 29.5 cm. Rim dia: 9 cm. Base missing. Fabric: Nile B2
8:6 TBP 374. Height: 10 cm. Base dia: 8.6 cm. Fabric: Nile B2
8:7 SC14.43. Height: 7.5 cm. Base dia: 8 cm. Fabric: Nile B2

Beer Jars/Offering Vessels (Nile D and E)

Pottery Plate 4.9 (scale 1:5)

9:1 TBP 170. Height: 25 cm. Rim dia: 12 cm. Base dia: 8.5 cm. Fabric: Nile E
9:2 TBP 171. Height: 23 cm. Rim dia: 11.75 cm. Base dia: 8 cm. Fabric: Nile E
9:3 TBP 172. Height: 23 cm. Rim dia: 13 cm. Base dia: 9 cm. Fabric: Nile E
9:4 TBP 199. Height: 25 cm. Rim dia: 10.5 cm. Base dia: 9 cm. Fabric: Nile E.
9:5 TBP 369. Height: 25 cm. Rim dia: 12 cm. Base dia: 9 cm. Fabric: Nile E
9:6 TBP 347. Height: 15 cm. Base dia: 9.2 cm. Fabric: Nile D
9:7 TBP 346. Height: 11 cm. Base dia: 10.5 cm. Fabric: Nile D
9:8 TBP 209. Height: 10 cm. Base dia: 8 cm. Fabric: Nile E

Offering Stands

9:9 TBP 174. Height: 23 cm. Base dia: 13 cm. Fabric: Nile B2. Surface: uncoated.
Parallels: Hulin 1984: fig. 12:6, from workmen's village at Amarna.
9:10 TBP 357. Height: 24 cm. Base dia: 24 cm. Fabric: Nile B2. Surface: uncoated.

47. Colin Hope, "Innovation in the Decoration of Ceramics in the Mid-18th Dynasty," *Cahiers de la Céramique Égyptienne* 1 (Cairo: IFAO, 1987) 187.

48. Rostislav Holhoer, *New Kingdom Pharaonic Sites: The Pottery* (The Scandinavian Joint Expedition to Sudanese Nubia 5:1; Berlings: Lund, 1977) 86, pl. 18

Comparanda Within Pottery Pit

A comparison of the types of pottery found in the pit with the burial pots found in the nearby tombs at Tell el-Borg revealed some significant differences. The most significant difference is the presence in the pit of a large number of amphorae and especially the many offering jars. These vessel types are not found in the Borg tombs. Borg Tomb 1 contains precious imported juglets from Cyprus, as well as some very fine marl vessels. Borg Tomb 2 contains funnel-necked jars, some beakers, and a very fine blue-painted cup (see *Tell el-Borg I*, 370–72 and pls. 1 and 2).

Although Beer jars are found on most New Kingdom sites in the hundreds, they do not appear to be typical grave goods that accompany the body to the afterlife. In large tombs one might find them in a side room, in the corridors, or in the courtyard. On occasions when they are found in the burial chamber, they do not have holes pierced in their bases.

Aston studied the pottery (with special attention to the Cypriot vessels) from several tombs at Hebua IV,[49] a site located about 4 km from Tell el-Borg in the North Sinai. The pottery described by Aston, dating to the reigns of Thutmose III to Amenhotep III, contains many parallels to the Borg corpus. Significant for our study is the fact that beer jars were rarely found in the burial chambers at Hebua IV.[50] It is also clear that the types of vessels found in the Borg pit, with the exception of the beer jars, are the same types that are found in tombs as well as settlements.

Comparanda with Other Sites

Ceramic deposits like that found in the Borg pit are difficult to find in the archaeological record, since early excavators focused on uncovering temples and tombs.[51] Fortunately, recent excavations have realized the importance of sherds and have added many deposits to the public record. For example, at Tell el-Dabᶜa, located in the eastern Delta and the site of the ancient Hyksos capital Avaris, the Austrian archaeologists have discovered more than 150 offering deposits dating to the Second Intermediate Period and early New Kingdom. Most of these pits were found next to tombs or groups of tombs and contained vessels that had been used in cultic meals and then deliberately broken before deposition.[52] David Aston mentions a pit in a Ramesside cemetery at Ezbet Helmi containing vessels that he suggests were a communal pit for offerings for poor burials.[53] Barbara Aston[54] has published an assemblage of vessels found in loose sand in the southeast corner of the forecourt of Horemheb's tomb. The pottery dating to the first half of the 19th Dynasty originated in the cult chapels and was finally cleared out and placed in the forecourt of the tomb. Of the total of 151 vessels, 138 were beer jars, 7 of which had holes pierced in their bases.

49. David Aston, "Cypriot Pottery and Its Imitations from Hebua IV," in *All the Wisdom of the East: Studies in Near Eastern Archaeology and History in Honor of Eliezer D. Oren* (ed. Mayer Gruber et al.; Orbis Biblicus et Orientalis 255; Göttingen: Academic Press Fribourg, 2012) 13.

50. Ibid., 21.

51. Foundation deposits are an exception to this, since many of them are described in detail in publications.

52. V. Müller, "Offering Deposits at Tell el-Dabᶜa," in *Proceedings of the Seventh International Congress of Egyptologists, Cambridge 3–9 September 1995* (ed. C. J. Eyre; Orientalia Lovaniensia Analecta 82; Leuven: Peeters, 1998) 797–98.

53. David Aston, *Burial Assemblages of Dynasty 21–25: Chronology – Typology – Developments* (Denkschriften der Desamtakademie 54 = Contributions to the Chronology of the Eastern Mediterranean 21; Vienna: Österreichische Akademie der Wissenshaften, 2009) 398.

54. Barbara Aston, "The Pottery," in *The Memphite Tomb of Horemheb, Commander in Chief of Tutankhamun* (ed. M. J. Raven et al.; Turnhut: Brepols, 2011) 217–29.

Fig. 4.180. TBP 0170.

Fig. 4.181. TBP 0326.

The Tell el-Borg Pit as a Ritual Deposit

The evidence for calling the Tell el-Borg assemblage a ritual deposit consists of the following:

1. A deposit of restorable vessels in a pit in a cemetery that is very close to tombs.
2. At least three of the vessels in the Borg pit have intentionally drilled or pierced holes in their bodies after they were fired. Ritual "killing holes" have been attested elsewhere in Egypt in cultic contexts.

M. J. López Grande published a group of slender jars with intentional holes drilled in them from a 2nd Intermediate Period and early 18th Dynasty funerary deposit near the tomb of Djehuty at Draʿ Abu el-Naga in Western Thebes.[55] Also at Draʿ Abu el-Naga, Susanne Michels[56] from the German Expedition published one vessel[57] from a cultic context with a killing hole and several storage jars with holes from a burial context.[58]

55. M. J. López Grande, "Red Vases at Dra Abu el-Naga: Two Funerary Deposits," in *Functional Aspects of Egyptian Ceramics in Their Archaeological Context* (ed. B. Bader and M. F. Ownby; Orientalia Lovaniensia Analecta 217; Leuven: Peeters, 2013) 257, figs. 2 and 3, pl. 2.

56. S. Michels, "Cult and Funerary Pottery from the Tomb-Temple of K93.12 at the End of the 20th Dynasty (Draʿ Abu el-Naga/Western Thebes)," in *Vienna 2: Ancient Egyptian Ceramics in the 21st Century. Proceedings of the International Conference held at the University of Vienna, 14th–18th of May, 2012* (ed. Bettina Bader, Christian Knoblauch, and E. Christiana Köhler; Orientalia Lovaniensia Analecta 245; Leuven: Peeters, 2016) 403–21.

57. Ibid., fig. 3.5.

58. Ibid., figs.8, 9a, and 15.

Because the Tell el-Borg pit is 2 m deep, the small, crude staircase would facilitate access into the pit by persons who were trying to deposit additional vessels. The stone blocks that form the staircase are not local but were imported from the Valley and therefore were intentionally placed here.

There are a limited number of ceramic forms found in the Borg pit, of which some are not typical grave goods. The vessel forms, however, are those that would be useful in performing rituals, as well as having domestic uses.

- The numerous large container vessels made up of amphorae, zirs, and storage jars open a small window on the amount of food and liquid that was necessary to accumulate in order for families to participate in their ritual feasts. A considerable amount of water would have been essential to perform libations.
- The medium-sized jars can hold water, wine, beer, or milk or could be used to transfer water from the zirs and amphorae to the offering jars.
- The large bowls could be used for food presentation or communal meals.
- The smaller bowls could be used for individual drinking cups or, more likely, for burning incense.

I suspect that the offering jars (beer jars) with pre-fired holes in the base are specially made for outdoor ceremonies. Most likely, the offering jars with holes were used to drain liquids and to control where the libation liquids went. These jars could be lined up close to the tomb walls, their flat bottoms nestled into the sand; water or beer obtained from one of the large amphorae or zirs using a medium-sized jar could be poured into the offering jar. The liquid would drain out the bottom hole slowly and trickle through the sand down to the tomb owner, exactly where it was intended to go to nourish and to regenerate the ancestor.[59]

Summary

It was the responsibility of the ancient Egyptian family to maintain the tomb of their ancestors and to provide offerings on feast days. This custom prevails even today in Egypt, where both Muslim and Coptic families, laden down with picnic baskets, visit the graves of their relatives.

59. The manufacture of offering jars with pre-fired holes in their bases was not limited to the New Kingdom. A few beer jars with pre-fired holes were found at Saqqara dating to the Late Old Kingdom in an offering deposit. They were filled with ashes and were found together with beer jars also filled with ashes but without holes pierced in the bases. See Teodozja Rzeuska, *Saqqara II: Pottery of the Late Old Kingdom Funerary Pottery and Burial Customs* (Warsaw: Centre d'Archéologie Méditerranéenne de l'Académie Polonaise des Sciences, 2006) 469. The pierced jars seem to have disappeared during the Middle Kingdom (personal communication from Susan Allen). The idea was revived again in the 2nd Intermediate period and continued throughout the New Kingdom. It is interesting to note that the form continues into the Libyan period and onward. Julia Budka, in her study comparing pottery deposits between Thebes and Umm el Qaᶜab at Abydos, describes the main offering jar of the Libyan period as a large-sized "beer jar" with a round, almost conical base, many of which have pre-fired holes in their base. She noted that they were produced locally and for a special purpose. See Julia Budka, "The Use of Pottery in Funerary Contexts during the Libyan and Late Period: A View from Thebes and Abydos," in *Egypt in Transition: Social and Religious Development of Egypt in the First Millenium BCE. Proceedings of an International Conference, Prague, September 1–4, 2009* (ed. Ladislav Bareš, Filip Coppens, and Květa Smoláriková; Prague: Czech Institute of Egyptology, Charles University in Prague, 2010) 53, and figs. 14:4, 5, and 6. I suspect that the New Kingdom practice of pouring liquid offerings in the open courtyards of tombs of the ancestors or to worship local divinities using these special jars to direct the liquid contents into the ground continued into the 3rd Intermediate Period.

All of the vessel types in the Tell el-Borg pit could have been used to provide funerary offerings; these were "offerings that were brought to the tomb in order to support the spirit (and cult) of the deceased."[60] The food was prepared and offered to the deceased, either after the funeral or during one of the many feast days, and then it would have been shared and eaten by family members. At the conclusion of the meal, the dishes used were gathered together, intentionally broken, and then buried along with leftover bones and other remains of the meal in a pit near the tomb, in a shaft in the courtyard of the tomb, or a pit in a cemetery. A sacred location close to the beloved dead is an appropriate place to retire the vessels used in such an important religious ceremony. Obviously, the cultic market called for two types of offering vessels: (1) whole jars and (2) jars with holes in their bases. There must have been a practical reason for the holes. The shapes and uses of pottery are very slow to change, and only a technical change that had a practical application for the buyers would have prodded conservative potters into producing a new product. Tomb scenes regularly show vessels pouring out streams of liquid, without showing where the liquid goes. Some scenes, mainly found in the tombs of the elite, show basins receiving the liquids. Pouring liquid on the ground in the area on which you are probably going to sit and eat creates an unnecessary mess. How much more sensible it would have been to have purchased some offering jars with holes pierced in the bottom. The family then could enjoy their liquid refreshment along with the dearly departed, as well as sit in a dry area to participate in the feast. Families could order many whole jars to hold dry goods or fish or meat, as well as the large amphorae for the liquid that they needed, but the order would include a small number of the pierced jars with drains in order to send libations down to their ancestors. This theory cannot be proved, but it does provide a logical reason for the presence of offering jars with holes in their bases.

In conclusion, the Tell el-Borg pit ceramic assemblage is not from a robber's pit, nor is it from a dump, but rather it is a final depository for vessels used in a ritual meal or meals connected with the cult of the dead. The funeral cultic rituals at Tell el-Borg that required food and liquid offerings to the ancestors would be performed on festival days and on special anniversaries. If there were cult chapels, they were tiny, with limited space, so that the family or families would be restricted to areas near the tombs to perform their cultic duties and to enjoy partaking in the food and drink.[61]

60. Salima Ikram, "Food and Funerals, Sustaining the Dead for Eternity," *Polish Archaeology in the Mediterranean* 20 (2008) 368.

61. Ibid., 368. Ikram suggests: "the fact that many of these (funerary-cultic) deposits are (found) in the area of burial chambers and shafts and in cemeteries is strongly indicative of a funerary-cult context."

Works Cited: Excursus

Aston, Barbara

2005 "The Pottery." Pp. 99–128 in *The Tomb of Pay and Raia at Saqqara*, ed. Martin Raven et al. London: EES.

Aston, David

1998 *Die Keramik des Grabungsplatzes. Q I.* Teil 1: *Corpus of Fabrics, Wares and Shapes.* Mainz: von Zabern.

2004 "Amphorae in New Kingdom Egypt." *ÄuL* 14: 175–214.

2009 *Burial Assemblages of Dynasty 21–25: Chronology – Typology – Developments.* Denkschriften der Desamtakademie 54 = Contributions to the Chronology of the Eastern Mediterranean 21. Vienna: Österreichische Akademie der Wissenshaften.

2012 "Cypriot Pottery and Its Imitations from Hebua IV." Pp. 13–56 in *All the Wisdom of the East: Studies in Near Eastern Archaeology and History in Honor of Eliezer D. Oren*, ed. Mayer Gruber et al. Orbis Biblicus et Orientalis 255. Göttingen: Academic Press Fribourg.

Bourriau, Janine
2002 "Fabrics of the Oasis Amphorae in the New Kingdom from Memphis, Kom Rabiʾa." Pp. 113–15 in Colin Hope, "Oases Amphorae of the New Kingdom." Pp. 95–131 in *Egypt and Nubia: Gifts of the Desert,* ed. R. Friedman. London: British Museum Publications.

Budka, Julia
2010 "The Use of Pottery in Funerary Contexts during the Libyan and Late Period: A View from Thebes and Abydos." Pp. 22–72 in *Egypt in Transition: Social and Religious Development of Egypt in the First Millennium BCE. Proceedings of an International Conference, Prague, September 1–4, 2009,* ed. Ladislav Bareš, Filip Coppens, and Květa Smolárikoví. Prague: Czech Institute of Egyptology, Charles University in Prague.

Dorner, J., and Aston, David
1997 "Pottery from Hebua IV/ South." *Cahiers de la Céramique Égyptienne* 5: 41–45.

Goren, V., Oren, E. D., and Feinstein, R.
1995 "The Archaeological and Ethnoarchaeological Interpretation of a Ceramological Enigma: Pottery Production in Sinai (Egypt) during the New Kingdom Period." *KVHAA Konferenser* 34: 101–20.

Holthoer, Rostislav
1977 *New Kingdom Pharaonic Sites: The Pottery.* The Scandinavian Joint Expedition to Sudanese Nubia, Volume 5:1. Lund: Berlings.

Hope, Colin
1987 "Innovation in the Decoration of Ceramics in the Mid-18th Dynasty." *Cahiers de la Céramique Égyptienne* 1: 97–122.

Hulin, L. C.
1984 "Pottery Cult Vessels from the Workmens' Village." Pp. 165–77 in *Amarna Reports I,* ed. B. J. Kemp. EES Occasional Publications 1. London: EES.

Ikram, Salima
2008 "Food and Funerals, Sustaining the Dead for Eternity." *Polish Archaeology in the Mediterranean* 20 (2008): 361–71.

López-Grande, M. J.
2013 "Red Vases at Dra Abu el-Naga: Two Funerary Deposits." Pp. 249–72 in *Functional Aspects of Egyptian Ceramics in Their Archaeological Context*, ed. B. Bader and M. F. Ownby. Orientalia Lovaniensia Analecta 217. Leuven: Peeters.

Michels, Suzanne
2016 "Cult and Funerary Pottery from the Tomb-Temple of K93.12 at the End of the 20th Dynasty (Draʿ Abu el-Naga/Western Thebes)." Pp. 403–22 in *Vienna 2: Ancient Egyptian Ceramics in the 21st Century, Proceedings of the International Conference held at the University of Vienna, 14th–18th of May, 2012*, ed. Bettina Bader, Christian Knoblauch, and E. Christiana Köhler. Orientalia Lovaniensia Analecta 245. Leuven: Peeters.

Müller, Vera
1998 "Offering Deposits at Tell el-Dabʿa." Pp. 793–803 in *Proceedings of the Seventh International Congress of Egyptologists, Cambridge 3–9 September 1995*, ed. C. J. Eyre. Orientalia Lovaniensia Analecta 82. Leuven: Peeters.

Rose, Pamela
2007 *The Eighteenth Dynasty Pottery Corpus from Amarna*. London: EES.

Rzeuska, Teodozja
2006 *Saqqara II: Pottery of the Late Old Kingdom Funerary Pottery and Burial Customs*. Warsaw: Centre d'Archéologie Méditerranéenne de l'Académie Polonaise des Sciences.

Seiler, Anne
1997 "Hebua I: Second Intermediate Period and Early New Kingdom Pottery." *Cahiers de la Céramique Égyptienne* 5: 23–34.

Serpico, Margaret, and White, Raymond
2000 "The Botanical Identity and Transport of Incense During the Egyptian New Kingdom." *Antiquity* 74: 884–97.

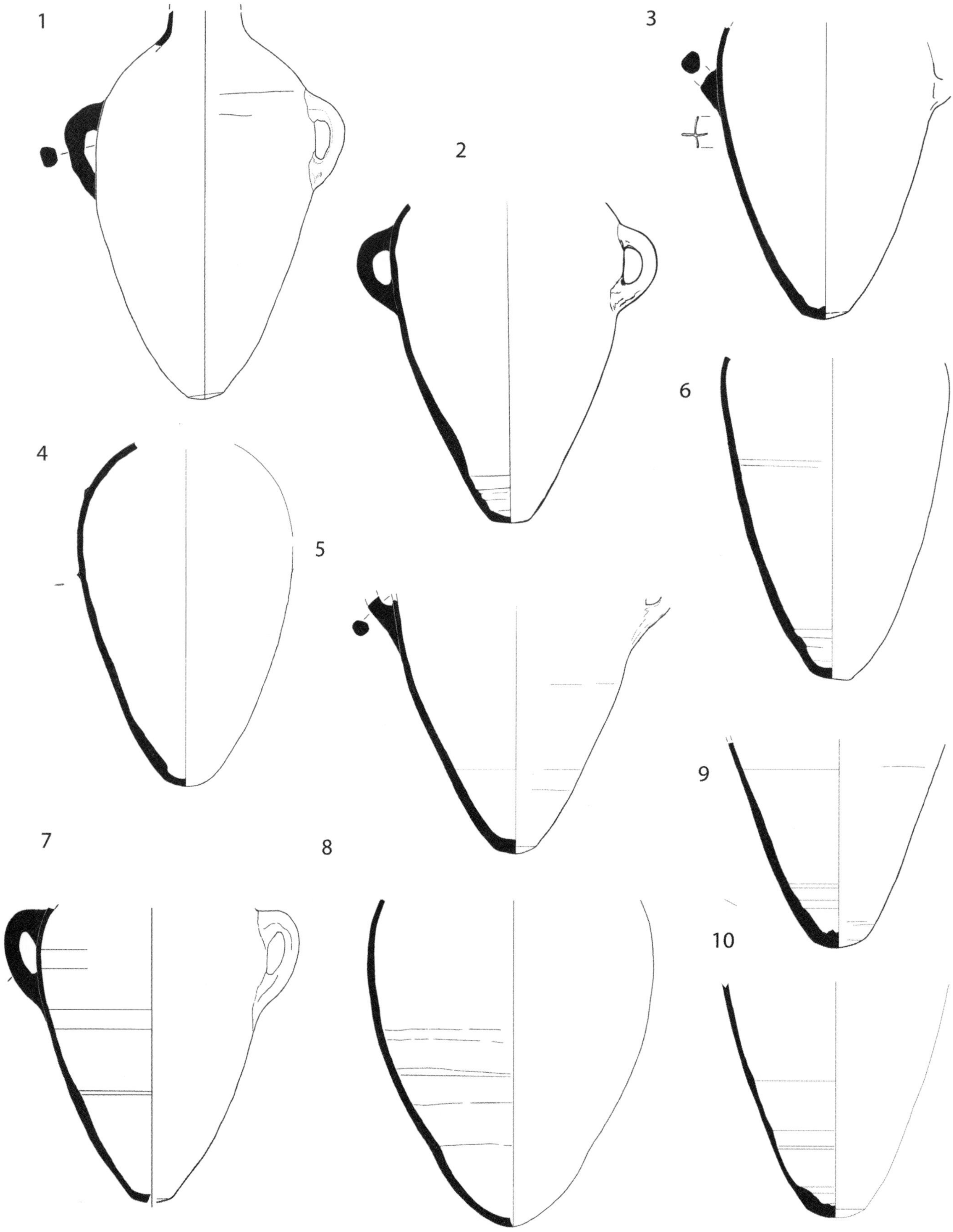

Pottery Plate 4.1 LEVANTINE AMPHORAE (Drawings by L. Pinch-Brock) SCALE 1:8

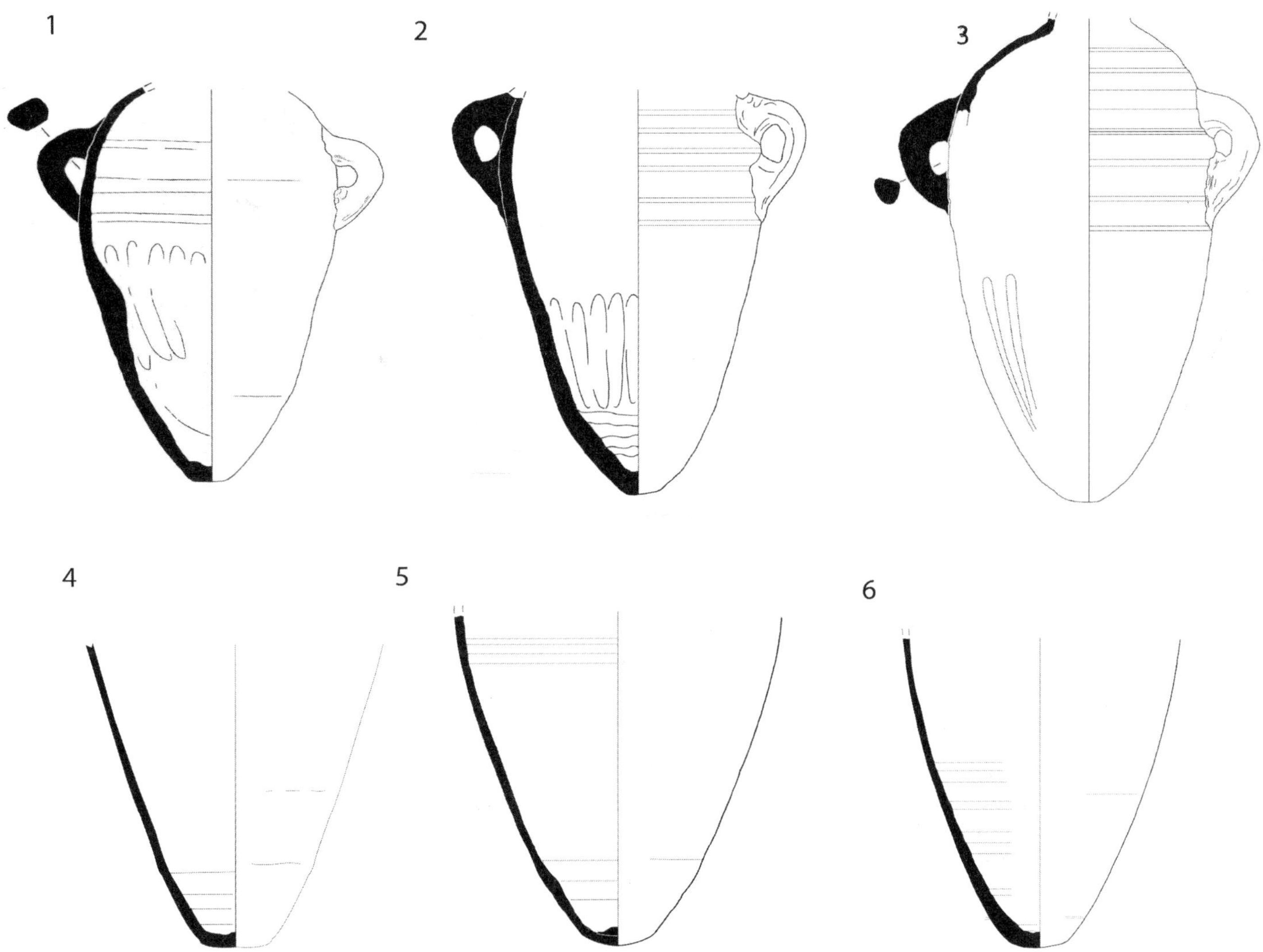

Pottery Plate 4.2 AMPHORAE FROM THE OASIS AND BIR EL-'ABD SCALE 1:8
(Drawings by L. Pinch-Brock)

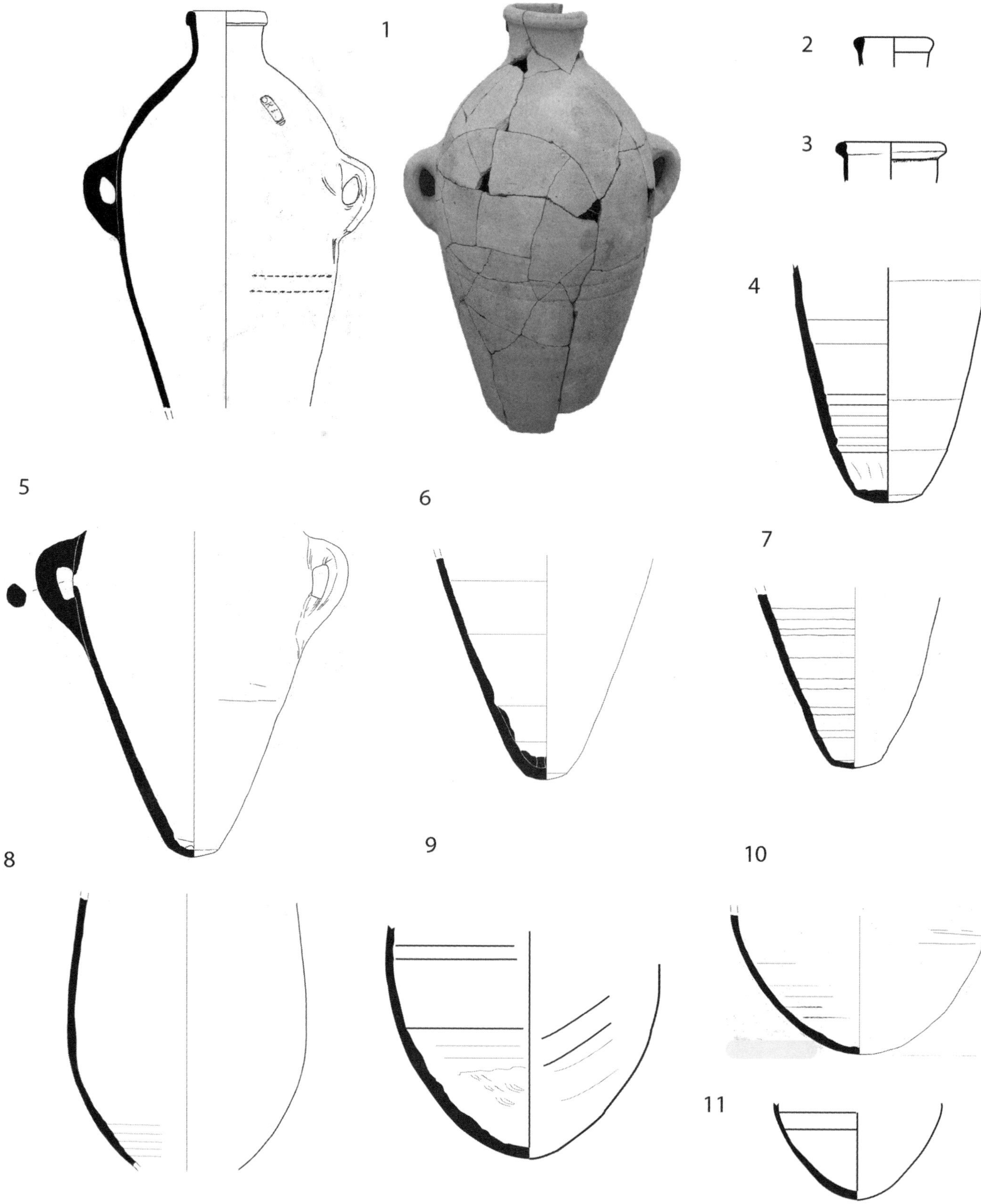

Pottery Plate 4.3 EGYPTIAN AMPHORAE AND STOREJARS SCALE 1: 8

(Drawings by L. Pinch-Brock)

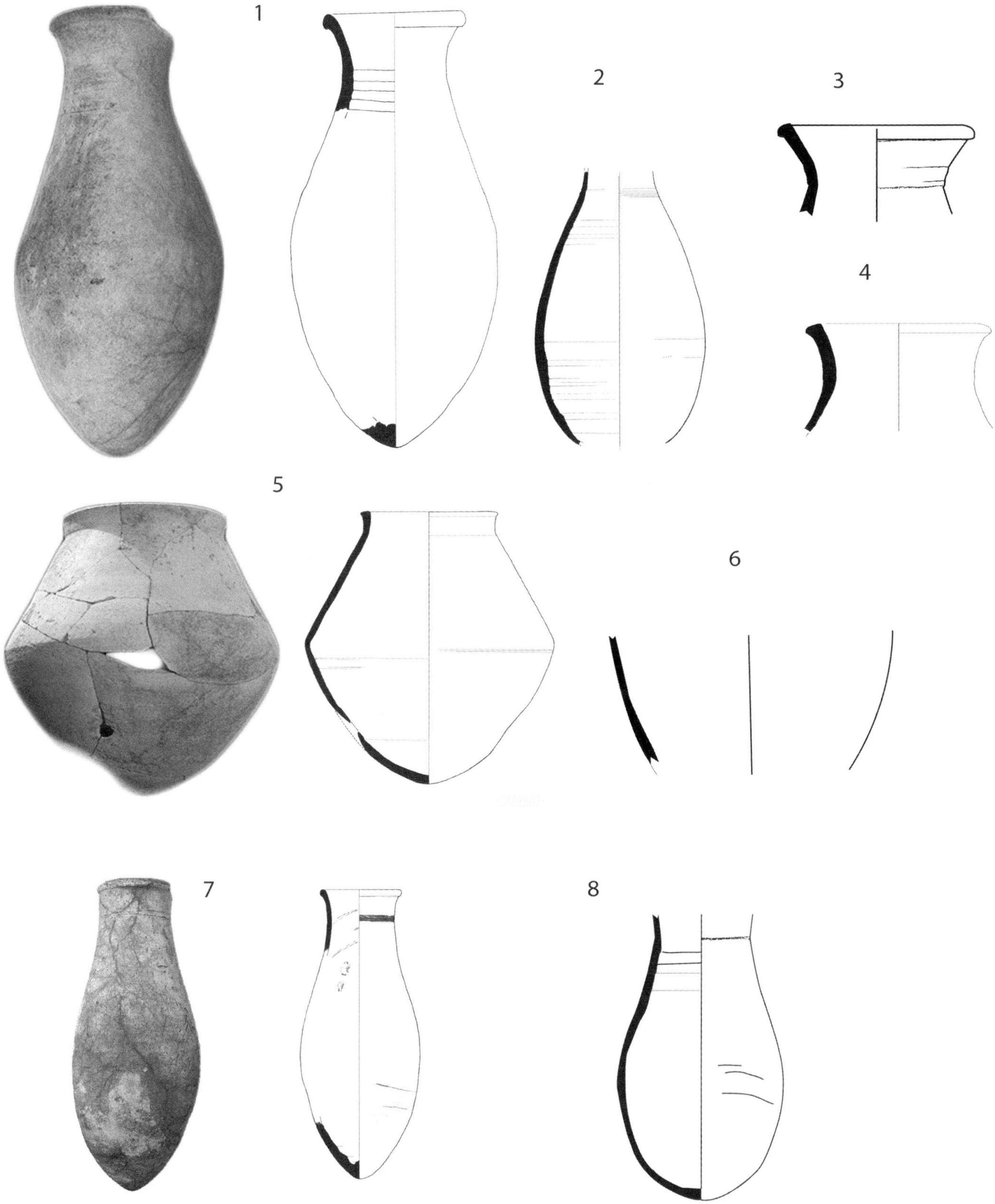

Pottery Plate 4.4 ZIRS AND LARGE JARS SCALE 1:8

(Drawings by L. Pinch-Brock)

1

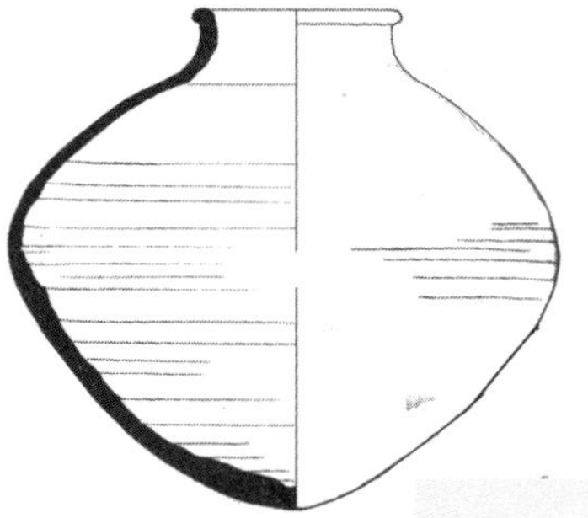

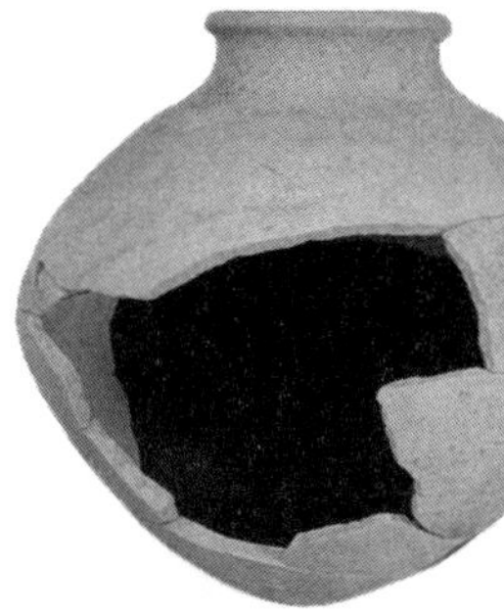

2

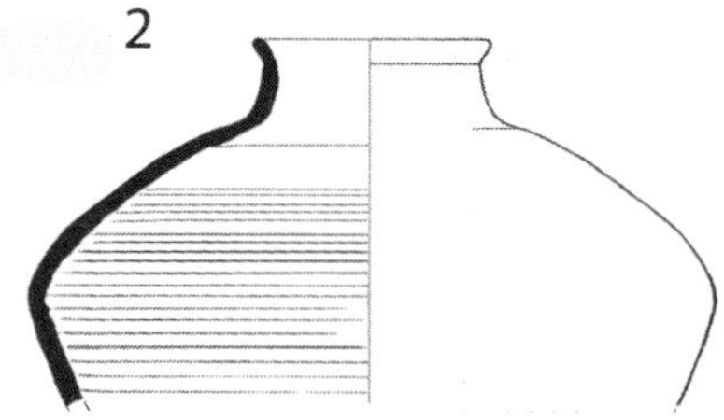

3

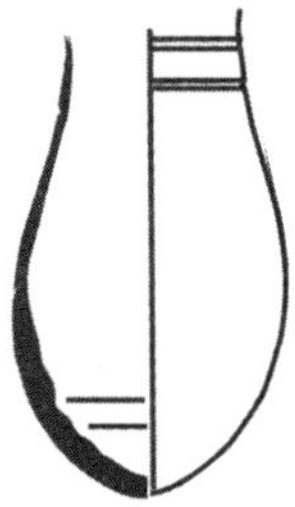

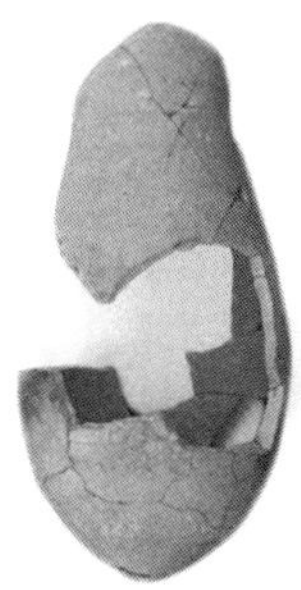

4

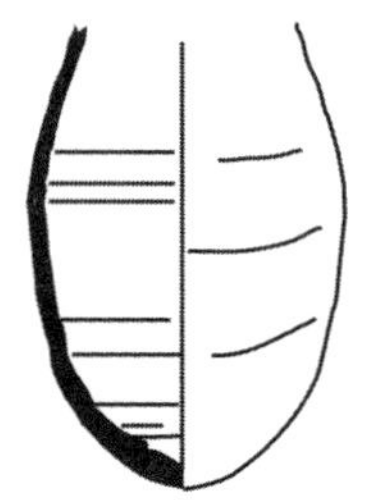

5

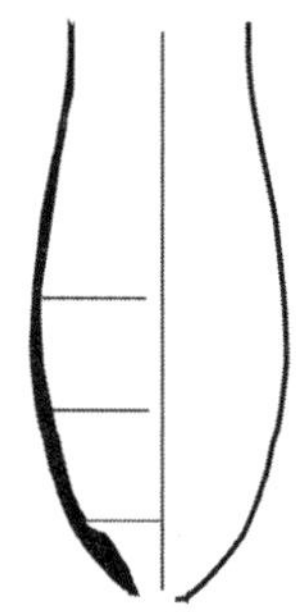

6

7

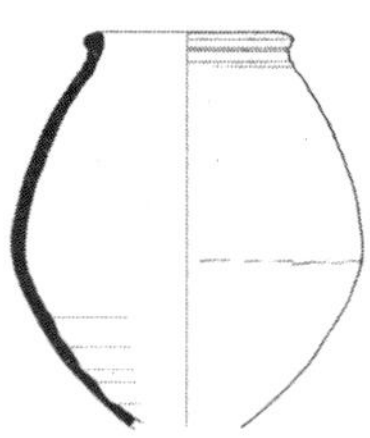

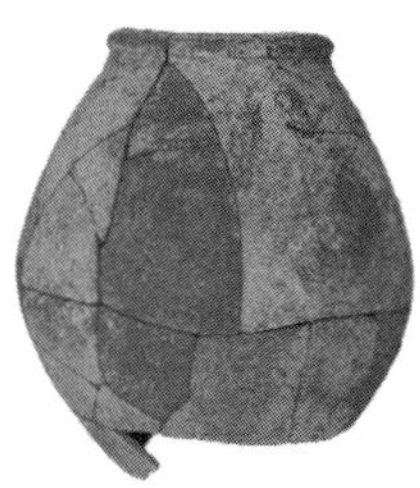

8

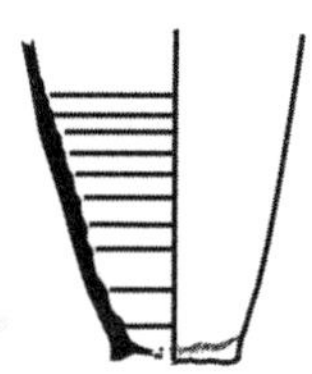

9

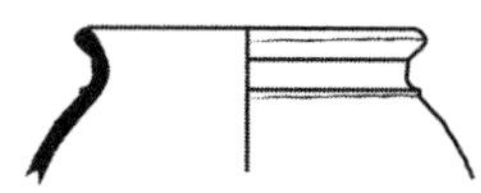

10

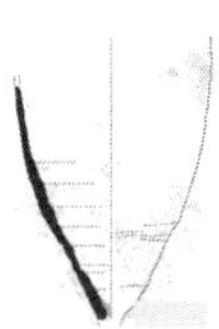

11

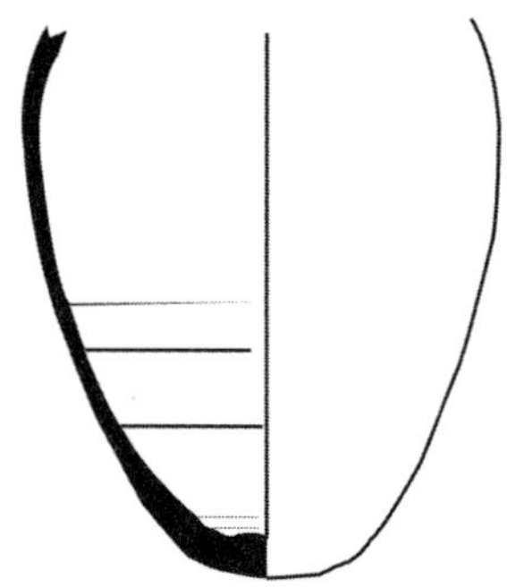

12

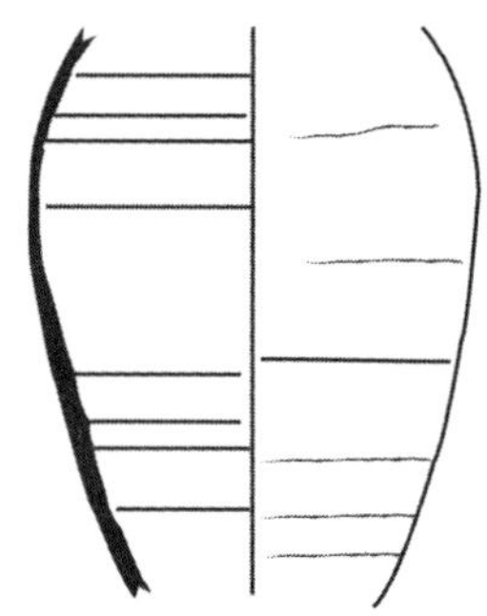

Pottery Plate 4.5 MEDIUM-SIZED JARS SCALE 1:8

(Drawings by L. Pinch-Brock)

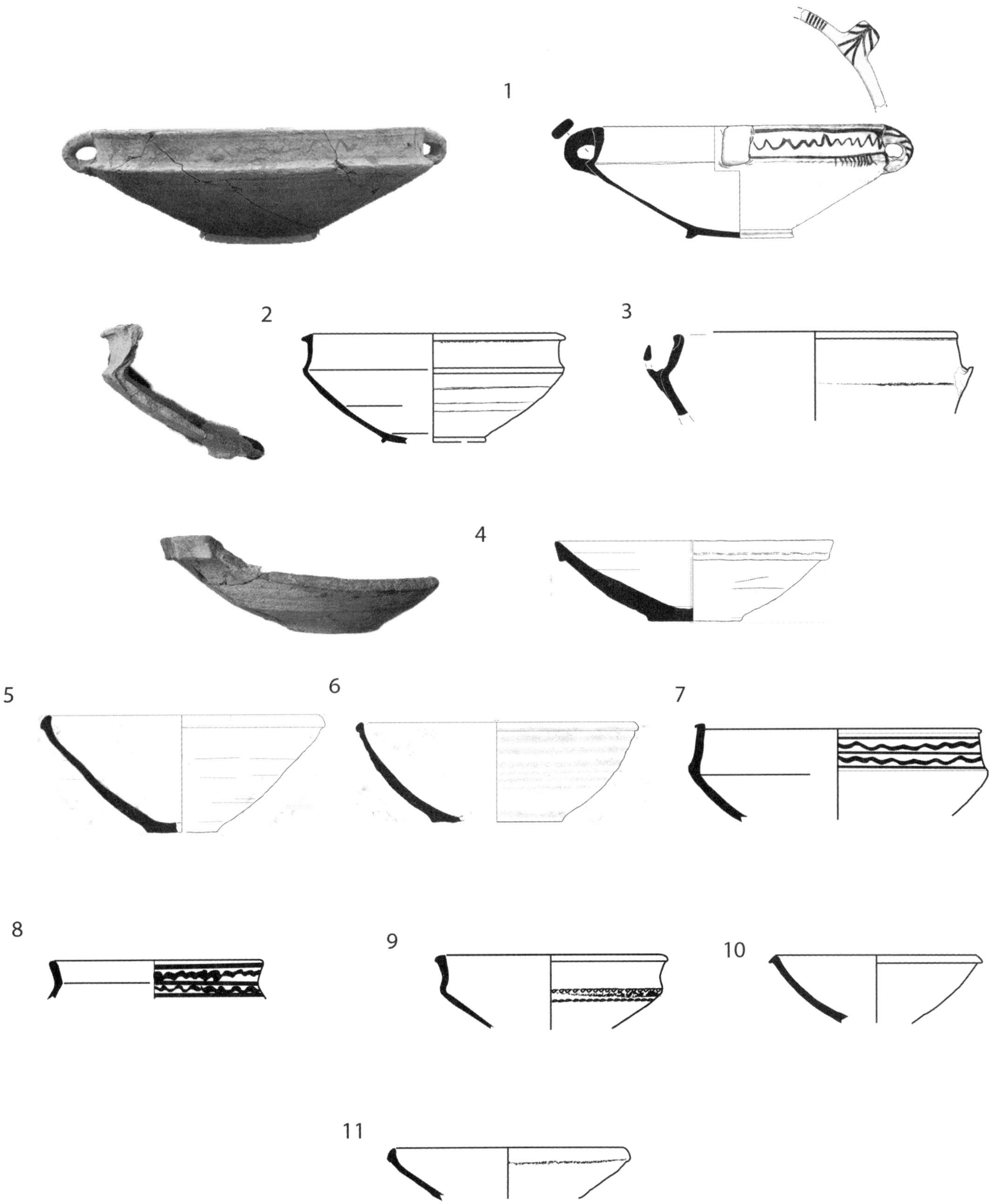

Pottery Plate 4.6 LARGE AND MEDIUM BOWLS SCALE 1:8

(Drawings by L. Pinch-Brock)

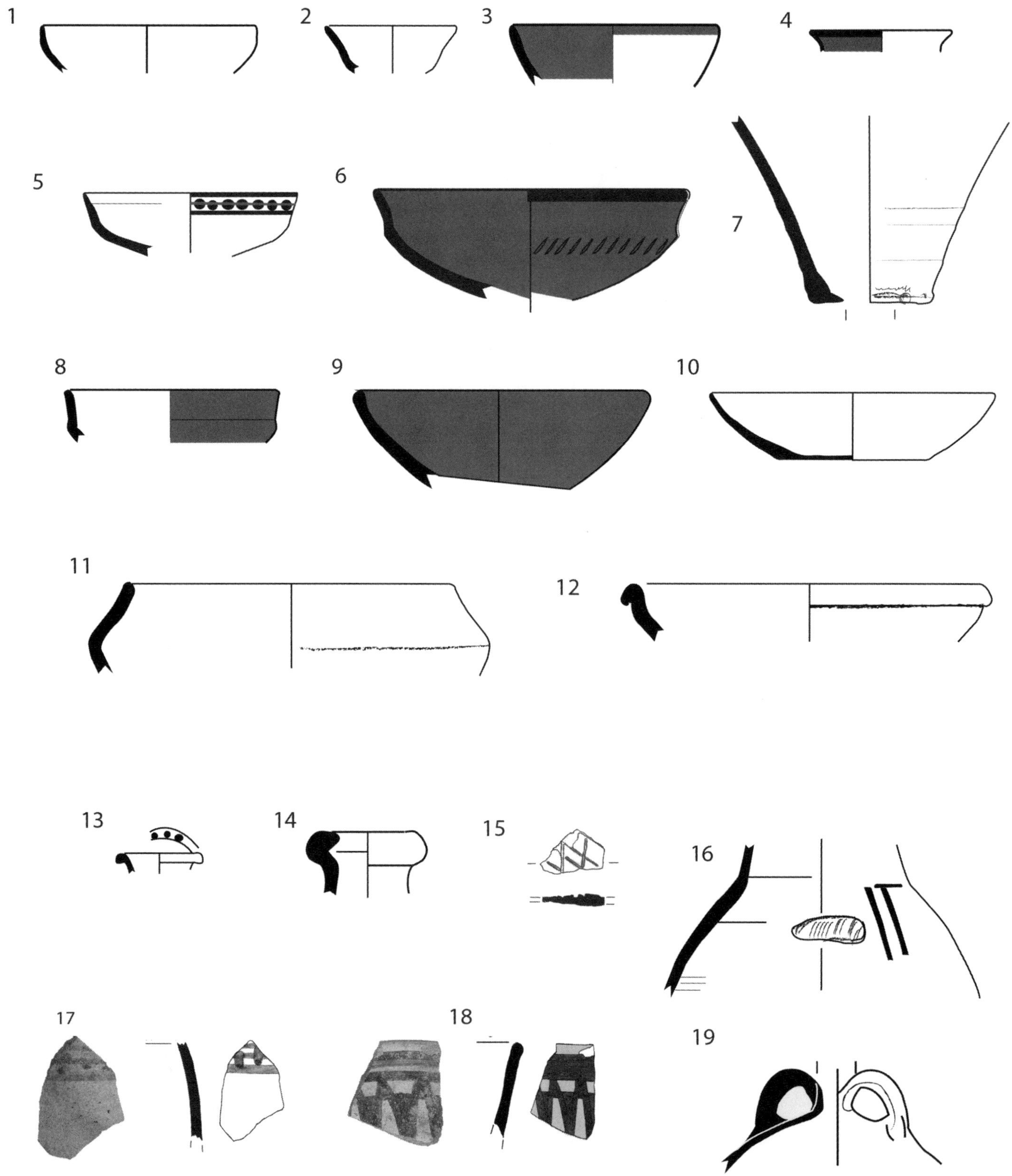

Pottery Plate 4.7 SMALL BOWLS AND MISCELLANEOUS VESSELS SCALE 1:4

(Drawings by L. Pinch-Brock)

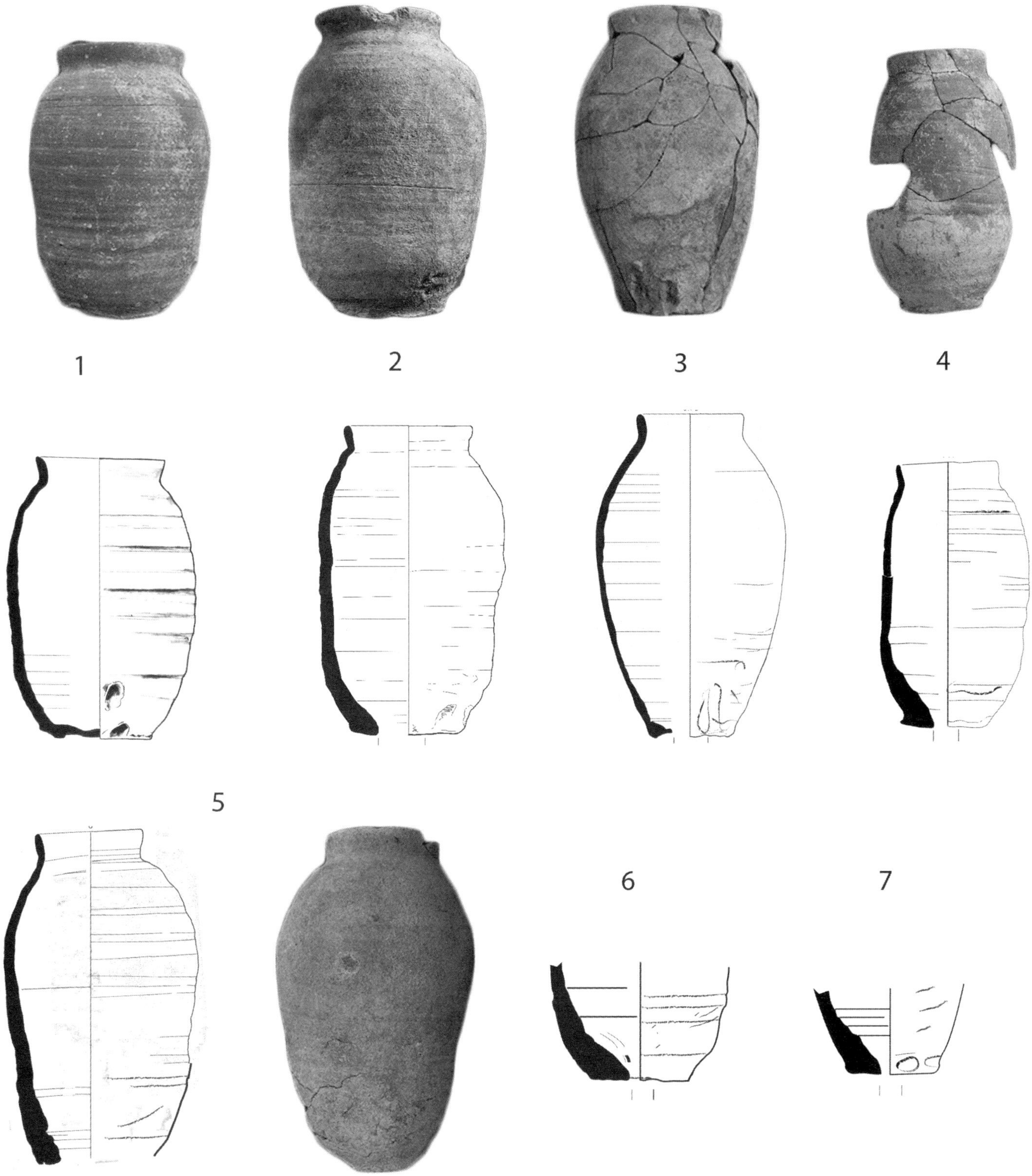

Pottery Plate 4.8 OFFERING JARS (NILE B2) SCALE 1:5

(Drawings by L. Pinch-Brock)

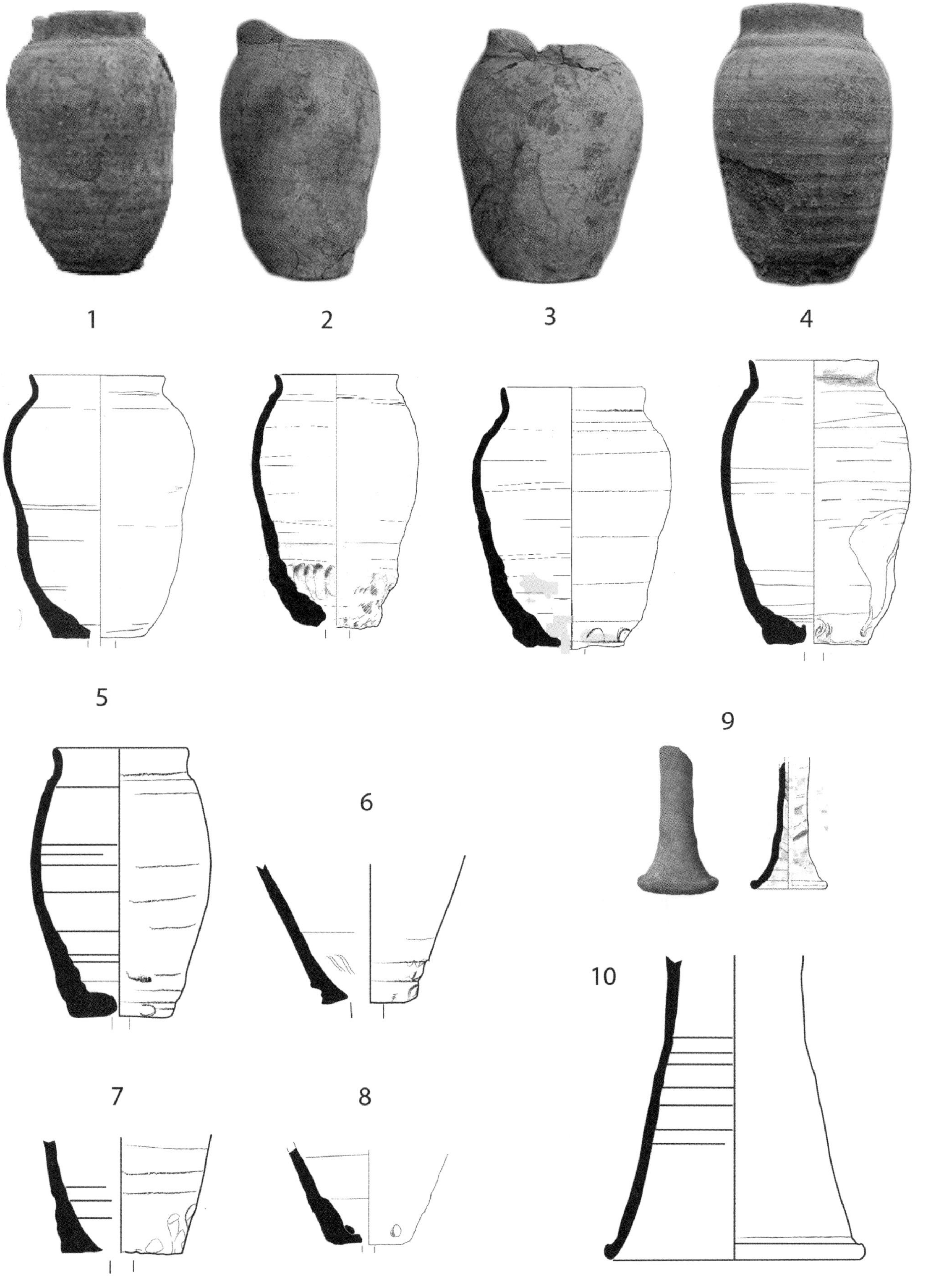

Pottery Plate 4.9 OFFERING JARS AND STANDS SCALE 1:5

(Drawings by L. Pinch-Brock)

CHAPTER 5

Clay Coffins from Tell el-Borg

Mark Janzen
SOUTHWESTERN BAPTIST THEOLOGICAL SEMINARY

TELL EL-BORG: PRELIMINARY INFORMATION

Archaeological excavations at Tell el-Borg uncovered the remains of four ceramic coffins that could be restored. Tell el-Borg is located 10 km northeast of Qantara East, in the Suez Canal region.[1] Work carried out from 1999 until 2007 revealed fortification walls from three different New Kingdom periods, leading James K. Hoffmeier to determine "that one of the forts along the so-called 'Ways of Horus' has been uncovered, but which one?"[2] The site was disturbed by military occupation in the 1970s and 1980s and threatened by the recent As-Salam irrigation project.[3] Due to these factors, it is not surprising that none of the four coffins was found intact; in fact, not a single intact tomb has been discovered.[4]

FIELD III: THE CONTEXT

All the coffin remains were found in Field III, located on the eastern part of the tell.[5] This area has been demonstrated to be a cemetery, which was robbed in ancient times and plundered in recent decades.[6] A great many potsherds, ranging from the early 18th Dynasty down to the 19th Dynasty, were found spread throughout the area, the result of ancient looting.[7] This situation, of course, makes determining from which tomb the sherds come nearly impossible. Regardless, a wide variety of foreign types were discovered: Cypriot base rings, Mycenaean, and Canaanite vessels. Egyptian wares, both Nile silt and Marl D, were found in approximately equal number; also included were Theban wares, beer jars, amphorae, and blue-painted "Amarna" wares, also

1. James K. Hoffmeier, "Tell el-Borg in North Sinai," *EA* 20 (2002) 18.
2. James K. Hoffmeier and Mohamed Abd el-Maksoud, "A New Military Site on the 'Ways of Horus'—Tell el-Borg 1999–2001: A Preliminary Report," *JEA* 89 (2003) 195.
3. James K. Hoffmeier, "The North Sinai Archaeological Projects Excavations at Tell el-Borg (Sinai): An Example of the 'New' Biblical Archaeology?" in *The Future of Biblical Archaeology: Reassessing Methodologies and Assumptions* (ed. James K. Hoffmeier and Alan R. Millard; Grand Rapids, MI: Eerdmans, 2004) 55–56.
4. See chapter 4 in this volume.
5. Hoffmeier and Abd el-Maksoud, "A New Military Site on the 'Ways of Horus,'" 184.
6. See chapter 4 in this volume.
7. See chapter 4 in this volume.

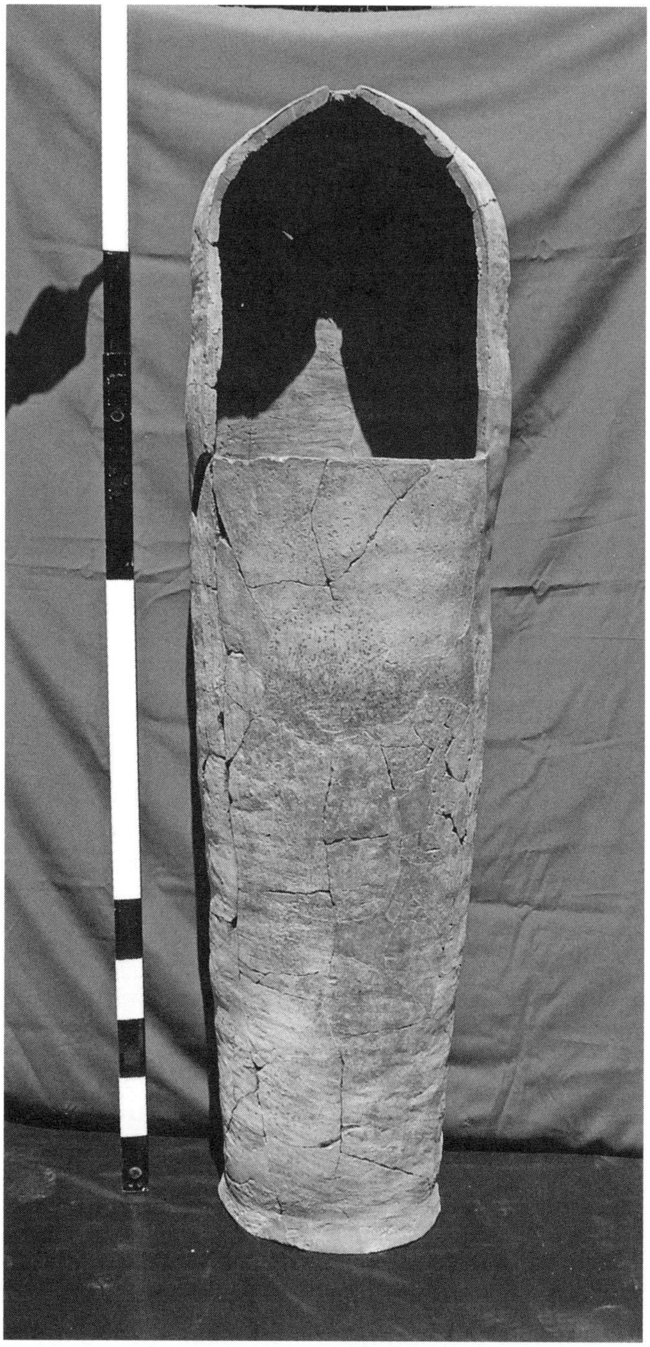
Fig. 5.1. TBO 0065 Restored Coffin.

ranging in date from the early 18th Dynasty down to the 19th Dynasty.[8] All the excavated soil was sifted, with the result being that several small objects, such as beads, were recovered. The remains of the four clay coffins discovered were designated TBO 0065, TBO 0078, TBO 0122, and TBO 0160.

TBO 0065

The remains of this clay coffin were discovered in Tomb 4 (Field III, Area 2). Much of the roof had collapsed into the tomb, making it part of the debris that was cleared.[9] The tomb has two chambers, and its overall dimensions are 7.7 m × 1.9 m.[10] Thick clay fragments were found both inside and outside of the tomb. Some of these were painted, and others were molded, leading Hoffmeier and Abd el-Maksoud to suggest that "at least two different coffins were represented."[11] The fragments have been reconstructed, as seen in fig. 5.1.

TBO 0065 is the only clay coffin that was restored to display standard (fig. 5.1). It is 1.76 m long.

At its widest point (approximately the shoulder area), its circumference is 1.46 m, which tapers down to 1.39 m in the middle of the coffin and 1.08 m at the bottom. The opening for insertion of the body measures 0.54 m × 0.40 m. Its base contains a circular hole, most likely for drainage. The coffin is decorated with black, red, and yellow paint. Its surface texture resembles wood.

The most interesting find from Tomb 4 was a red body sherd incised with a cartouche containing a prenomen of Amenhotep II (fig. 4.82a–b, p. 196). Unfortunately, due to the fact that this tomb and those adjacent to it were badly looted, its original context is uncertain. However, while a precise date is difficult to ascertain, the presence of diagnostic sherds from the late 18th and early 19th dynasties does allow for confident

8. Haddow, in chapter 4. See also Hoffmeier and Abd el-Maksoud, "A New Military Site on the 'Ways of Horus,'" 184–89.
9. Ibid., 187.
10. Ibid., 187–88.
11. Ibid., 188.

dating of a more general time period. This tomb appears to have had two building phases and thus could span from the mid-18th Dynasty down to the early 19th Dynasty.[12]

The coffin would have been constructed using a technique similar to methods employed for making large pottery vessels.[13] It was likely slab constructed: large sheets of clay are flattened out and then joined together, until the vessel's form is "true"—in this case, a symmetrical coffin. From 3500 B.C. onward, slab construction appears to have been used alongside coiling to produce radially symmetrical vessels.[14] In fact, if the coils were broad enough, they could arguably be called slabs.[15] In this regard, slab construction is often difficult to distinguish from coiling. After the coffin form held true, a window was cut in the upper part for interring the human body.[16] Presumably, the size of the body would have determined the size of the opening and, consequently, the size of the lid.

The holes in the bottom (and in other cases top or other places) could have been used for drainage purposes, to drain out the effluvia of the corpse.[17] Since it is not known whether the corpse was mummified, it is difficult to say whether or not the coffin was designed for drainage of this kind. Mummies, of course, do not need drainage. These holes could also have served a symbolic religious purpose, enabling the *Ka* to pass in and out of the coffin.[18] However, one would expect a hole for the *Ka* to be at the top of the coffin to allow the soul easier passage, not at the bottom. A third option is that the holes were made in an attempt to keep the coffin from breaking during firing.[19] This last option seems most feasible for TBO 0065, though the circumstances of its discovery and reconstruction negate the possibility of drawing a definitive conclusion.

TBO 0078

An insufficient number of fragments of the body of this Tomb 4 coffin were recovered to permit its full restoration. However, it was possible to carry out a partial reconstruction of its base (diameter 0.35 m, with central hole having an average diameter of 0.135 m; fig. 5.2); the horizontal rim of the opening for the insertion of the body (fig. 5.3); and the vertical curving rim and notch from the upper left hand side of the opening (fig. 5.4).

It was also possible to undertake a partial restoration of its lid. The lid fragments show detailed renditions of hands and hair (figs. 5.5 and 5.6). It is 0.59 m in length and 0.57 m in width. Its average thickness is 0.022 m. The lid is of the "naturalist" type (discussed below) with the arms crossed at the shoulders.

---

12. See discussion of the architectural history of Tomb 4 in chapter 4.

13. Eliezer D. Oren, *The Northern Cemetery of Beth Shan* (Leiden: Brill, 1973) 132–33.

14. Dorothea Arnold and Janine Bourriau, eds., *An Introduction to Ancient Egyptian Pottery* (Mainz: Von Zabern, 1993) 29–33. Coiling was prominent among Egyptian potters from the period of Naqada II (3500 B.C.) onward, and many Naqada I (4000–3500 B.C.) pots were probably made this way also.

15. Arnold and Bourriau, *Ancient Egyptian Pottery*, 29.

16. Oren, *The Northern Cemetery of Beth Shan*, 133.

17. A. Rowe, *The Topography and History of Beth Shan* (Philadelphia: University of Pennsylvania Museum, 1930), 39.

18. Georg Steindorff, *Aniba II* (Glückstadt: Augustin, 1937) 72.

19. Ahmed Galal and David Aston, "New Kingdom Anthropoid Pottery Coffins from Kom Abu Rady and Sedment," *JEOL* 37 (2001–2002) 127.

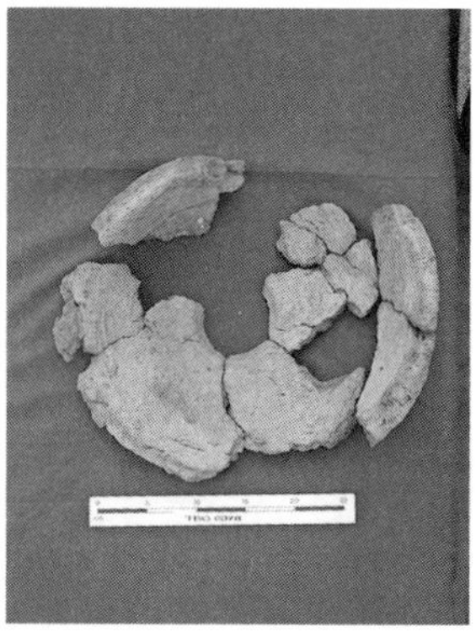

Fig. 5.2. TBO 0078 Base.

Fig. 5.3. Horizontal rim.

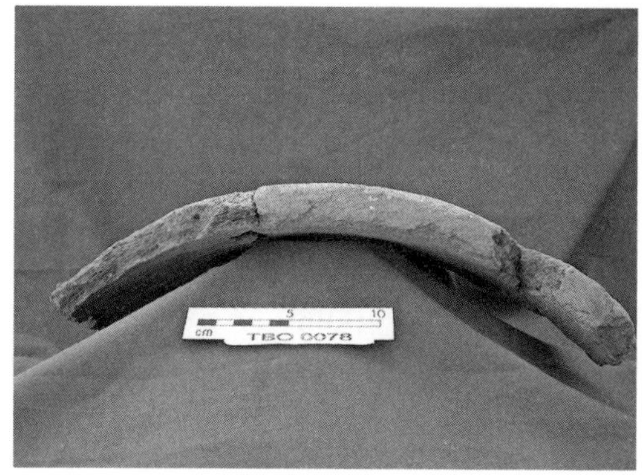

Fig. 5.4. Upper rim with notch.

Fig. 5.5 (right). TBO 0078 Coffin lid.

Fig. 5.6 (far right). Detail of hair.

TBO 0122

This anthropoid coffin was found in 2002 in Tomb 5, a small rectangular mud-brick structure (2.5 m by 0.85 m), used for a single burial.[20] The human skeletal remains are most likely from a single individual. The lack of tooth wear indicates a young adolescent.[21] The coffin's total length is 1.80 m. It can be divided into three zones: base, lower portion with four walls, and upper portion with three walls terminating in a "head" (fig. 5.7). The floor of the base has a rectangular perforation, with rounded corners. Projecting from the front wall at the level of the base there is a semicircular foot. The top surface of the foot was plastered and painted with red and yellow stripes (fig. 5.8).

The four-walled lower portion, or "box," of the coffin is trapezoidal in section. The length of the front wall from the base to the level of the horizontal rim (fig. 5.9) of the opening for insertion of the body is 1.19 m. The width of the front wall at the horizontal rim is 0.39 m. One can see the impressions from the string that cut the clay to form the edge of this rim (fig. 5.10).

The three-walled upper portion of the coffin (fig. 5.9) measures 0.61 m in length. Between the horizontal rim and the notch at the top, the upper portion narrows both in width and depth. At a point halfway between the horizontal rim and the top of the coffin, all three sides of the up-

20. Chapter 4 in this volume, pp. 205–9.

21. See chapter 4 in this volume for a full report on the human skeletal remains from various tombs (5–13) in Field III (pp. 189, 200–205, 211–12, 214, 226–27, and 228–29).

Fig. 5.7. TBO 0122, Side view of coffin.

Fig. 5.8. Foot fragment with painted plaster.

Fig. 5.9. TBO 0122 upper portion close-up.

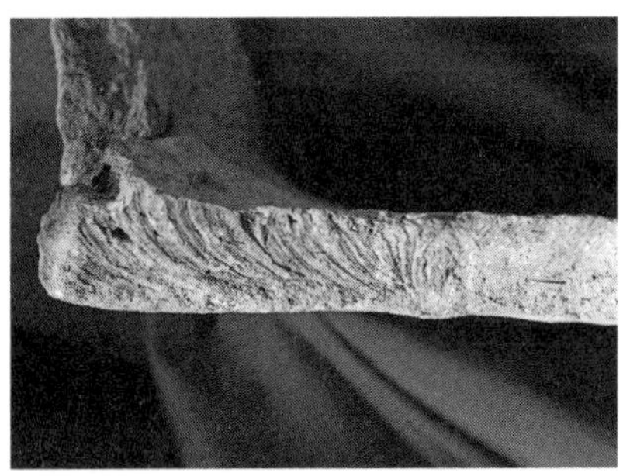

Fig. 5.10. Close-up of string-cut horizontal rim.

Fig. 5.11. View of top with notch.

permost portion are stepped in by 0.020–0.025 m to form a "head." This head portion is 0.36 m long. It is wider (0.34 m) than it is deep (0.19 m). There is a circular notch in the front side of the top of the head (fig. 5.11).

In both the left- and right-hand walls of the upper portion of the coffin, there are two perforations (one above and one below the step) for attachment of its lid (fig. 5.12). There are remains of gold-colored paint on the coffin's exterior surface. Another interesting detail is a graffito (figs. 5.13–5.14) lightly inscribed in the upper left sidewall of the upper portion of the coffin. The drawing appears to be a bouquet of plants. The foot of this coffin flared out at the bottom so as to

Fig. 5.12. Side view of lid with holes for attachment aligned with corresponding holes in body.

Fig. 5.13. Graffito on left side of TBO 0122.

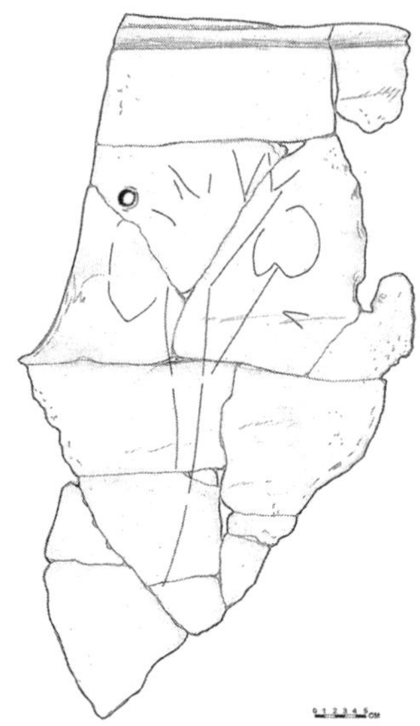

Fig. 5.14. Graffito on left side of TBO 0122 (drawing by Lyla Pinch-Brock).

allow it to stand on its own, perhaps for opening-of-the-mouth ritual as classically portrayed in contemporary illustrations in tombs and in vignettes on papyri.[22] Fragments of the decorated coffin lid were also found. They show one lappet of the wig and the arms crossed over the chest (fig. 5.16).

TBO 0160

The last of the clay sarcophagi recovered from Tell el-Borg was found in Tomb 8, a small mud-brick structure. The fact that this slipper coffin was partially found in situ makes it unique among the Tell el-Borg coffins. The tapering cylindrical coffin (fig. 4.11) was supported on three sets of mud bricks placed at regular intervals.[23]

The maximum preserved length of the coffin is 1.48 m. Its full circumference has not survived. Although they do not appear in the photograph, joining fragments of the horizontal rim of the opening for insertion of the body were also recovered. The uppermost portion was not found. Part of its base did survive and has a central circular perforation. There are remains of yellow paint on the exterior surface of the coffin.

No human skeletal remains were uncovered in situ, though a wide variety of bone fragments were found in the fill, representing at least one individual.[24] Just outside the tomb, a faience signet ring with the name of Queen Tiye (wife of Amenhotep III) was uncovered (fig. 4.127a–b).[25] As in other cases, due to looting, it is impossible to say whether or not the ring originated in the tomb.

---

22. See the Book of the Dead of Hunefer, R.O. Faulkner, *The Book of the Dead* (London: British Museum) 54.

23. For treatment of the osteological remains, see Haddow, chapter 4 above, pp. 213–14.

24. Ibid.

25. James K. Hoffmeier and Jacobus Van Dijk, "New Light on the Amarna Period from North Sinai," *JEA* 96 (2010) 198–99.

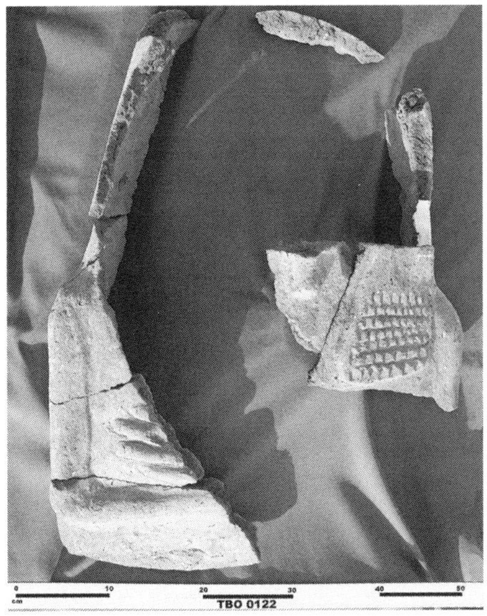

Fig. 5.15 (far left). Foot attached to coffin.

Fig. 5.16 (left). Anthropoid coffin lid, TBO 0122.

Comparative Data

Clay coffins are first attested in 18th Dynasty contexts and appear in increasing numbers down to Roman times.[26] New Kingdom ceramic coffins have been found at a number of sites, particularly in the Delta region and lower Nubia,[27] as well as Syria–Palestine.[28] Unfortunately, as excavators from Tell el-Borg can attest, such coffins are usually found badly broken and for this reason little time is devoted to their reconstruction and restoration. This problem is further complicated by the fact that many sites in the Delta region are buried beneath either the alluvium or modern occupation.[29] Thus, clay coffins are generally poorly preserved, resulting in some erroneous interpretations. These coffins were often associated with the Philistines by earlier generations of archaeologists, such as W. F. Albright.[30]

26. Lisa Kuchman, "Egyptian Clay Anthropoid Coffins," *Serapis* 4 (1977–1978) 12. For useful catalogues of clay coffins from various contexts and time periods, see also Laurence Cotelle-Michel, *Les sarcophages en terre cuite: en Egypte et en Nubie de l'é poque pré dynastique a' l'é poque romaine* (Dijon: Faton, 2004); and Lisa Sabbahy, *Anthropoid Clay Coffins: Nos. 17037–17091, 7127–7129, Catalogue General of Egyptian Antiquities in the Cairo Museum* (Cairo: Supreme Council of Antiquities Press, 2009).

27. Galal and Aston, "New Kingdom Anthropoid Coffins," 127. For Nubian sites, see Steindorff, *Aniba II*, 170; pls. 39c and 40.2. At Aniba, 20 clay coffins were found.

28. See, for example, Trude Dothan, "Deir el-Balaḥ," in *NEAHL* (ed. Ephraim Stern; New York: Simon and Schuster, 1993), 343–47; W. F. Albright, "An Anthropoid Coffin from Saḥab in Transjordan," in *AJA* 36 (1932), 295–306; and A. Rowe, *The Topography and History of Beth Shan.*

29. James M. Weinstein, "Delta" in Eric M. Myers, ed., *OEANE* 2 (New York: Oxford University Press, 1997), 141.

30. Albright, "An Anthropoid Coffin from Saḥab in Transjordan," 304. See also W. M. Flinders Petrie, *Tanis I* (EES 2: London: Trubner, 1885). But see also Ora Negbi, "Were the Sea Peoples in the Central Jordan Valley at the Transition from the Bronze Age to the Iron Age? Once Again," in *Tel Aviv* 25 (1998), 184–207; and "Were the Sea Peoples in the Central Jordan Valley at the Transition from the Bronze Age to the Iron Age?" in *Tel Aviv* 18 (1991), 205–43 for a more up-to-date examination. That the Philistines eventually adopted Egyptian burial customs is virtually certain from evidence at Deir el-Balaḥ, Beth Shan, and Tell Farah; see T. Dothan, *The Philistines and Their Material Culture* (New Haven: Yale University Press, 1982), 280–88. For genuinely unique Philistine cultural items, see Trude Dothan, "Philistine Fashion," *BAR* 29:6 (Nov/Dec 2003), 46–49.

There are two primary shapes for ceramic coffins. Group A is mummy-shaped, with the shoulders and head delineated in various proportions—hence the term "anthropoid."[31] Group B coffins do not delineate the shoulders or head (thus the label "slipper").[32] TBO 0065 belongs to this latter category, while TBO 0122 is an anthropoid coffin. The other two coffins found at Tell el-Borg are not well enough preserved to allow for definitive classification.

"Anthropoid" and "slipper" coffins have also been divided into those with "naturalistic" lids and those with "grotesque" lids.[33] As Trude Dothan notes, "The basic distinguishing feature of the "naturalistic" lids is the clearly-marked outline of the face. . . ."[34] The hair is most frequently modeled after the Egyptian style and usually frames the face,[35] as is the case with both lids from Tell el-Borg. By contrast, the "grotesque" lids follow no clearly delineated facial outline, making the face "somewhat bizarre" and giving it a "perhaps caricature-like effect."[36] This difference in lid types may be due to differences in construction, whereby the "grotesque" lids were made by adding individual pieces of clay for each facial feature before the clay was baked.[37] Thus, the features end up stretched out and exaggerated. Unfortunately, both of the face-plates recovered from Tell el-Borg are incomplete, though it seems they more readily fit into the "naturalistic" lid category.

Comparable coffins come from a number of sites in Egypt and Syria–Palestine. Excavations at the site of Kom Abu Rady from 1984 to 1987 revealed tombs in use during the 18th and 19th Dynasties. The best preserved of the coffins came from Tomb 375; it measures 1.9 m long, with a maximum width of 0.5 m and a height of 0.5 m.[38] Although this coffin contained a "grotesque" lid, it does have numerous other similarities to the coffins at Tell el-Borg. Both the lid and the body were painted with red and black on yellowish material. Facial features on the lid were painted red, and along the chest, down to the crossed arms, is a stylized *nemes* headdress in black on yellow.[39] Thus, the same coloration—red, black, and yellow—is evident, as well as the motif of crossed arms.

From nearby Sedment come two other reconstructed clay coffins. Both coffins were found in Tomb 44, room 3, both dating to the 19th Dynasty.[40] The first measures 1.94 m long by 0.4 m maximum width. Like the example above, this coffin was profusely decorated with red and black paint on a yellow surface.[41] The second coffin measures 1.92 m by 0.47 m.[42] Unlike the others, this coffin is decorated with red and yellow colors and a black background. Regardless, the same primary colors are involved.

Perhaps the coffin with the most similarities to TBO 0065 comes from Tell el-Yahudiyeh. This site lies approximately 32 km northeast of Cairo in the eastern Delta. The most important excavations at Tell el-Yahudiyeh were those conducted by Edouard Naville and Francis Llewellyn

31. Trude Dothan, "Anthropoid Clay Coffins from a Late Bronze Age Cemetery Near Deir el-Balaḥ," *IEJ* 23 (1973), 130.

32. Ibid.

33. Ibid., 130–31.

34. Ibid., 131.

35. Oren, *The Northern Cemetery of Beth Shan*, 133–34.

36. Dothan, "Anthropoid Clay Coffins," 131.

37. Kuchman, "Egyptian Clay Anthropoid Coffins," 15.

38. Galal and Aston, "New Kingdom Anthropoid Coffins," 128–29.

39. Ibid., 128.

40. Ibid., 145.

41. Ibid.

42. Ibid. Several fragments were found also, some with inscriptions, indicative of a finer quality than what has thus far been found at Tell el-Borg. See ibid., 145–66.

Griffith in 1887 and W. M. Flinders Petrie in 1906.[43] Petrie found a slipper coffin with a naturalistic style lid; early 18th Dynasty pottery was found to either side of its head.[44] Most interesting is Petrie's mention of "pottery from the age Amenhotep II,"[45] found among the grave goods. If one takes the inscribed sherd of Amenhotep II from Tomb IV at Tell el-Borg to be from the same context as TBO 0065, this could be another interesting parallel between this coffin from Tell el-Yahudiyeh and TBO 0065. As with other examples, the coffin was painted yellow, with details in yellow, black, and white. The headdress was banded with alternating colors of blue and yellow. Pictures show Isis and Nephthys standing alongside the four sons of Horus, while Anubis, as a jackal, is seen lying on a shrine. At the foot of the coffin, Isis is seen standing on a *nb*-basket. As Galal and Aston point out, "Such a decorative scheme is clearly reminiscent of early 18th Dynasty wooden coffins, on which this clay coffin is evidently modeled."[46] While the coffins from Tell el-Borg do not contain such elaborate decoration, TBO 0065 is obviously modeled after wooden coffins, as the clay was molded and treated to resemble wood.

Furthermore, the use of yellow paint might be a way to represent gold. Even more intriguing is the idea that blue paint might be a substitute for lapis lazuli. The use of these vibrant colors is echoed in "The Shipwrecked Sailor," which says of the serpent: "His body was overlaid with gold; his eyebrows were of real lapis lazuli."[47] Additionally, from Papyrus Westcar comes this description of the birth of royal children: "The child slid into her arms, a child of one cubit, strong boned, his limbs overlaid with gold, his headdress of true lapis luzuli."[48] Gold and lapis lazuli were often associated with gods and royalty, and it is not at all unlikely that the coffins of officials and other elites would use such colors in order to either emulate the deity or to function as a status symbol in the afterlife. This connection is even more obvious when one considers that the better-preserved coffins, such as the one from Tell el-Yahudiyeh, contained painted scenes of the gods as well.

At Riqqeh, near Meydum, clay coffins were also found painted in red, black, and yellow.[49] Significantly, Engelbach states that these coffins were "by no means confined to the lower classes, as some of the burials contained very good amulets and the bodies were well-mummified."[50] This is an important point, because even though clay was more readily available, and thus cheaper than stone or wood,[51] it does not mean that clay coffins are necessarily an indicator of poor socioeconomic status.

Similar clay coffins have been found in Late Bronze Age Canaan. The largest quantity of anthropoid clay coffins ever discovered was found at Deir el-Balaḥ, located 14 km southwest of Gaza. At least 40 clay coffins were found here, and as Dothan notes, these coffins "display a wider spectrum of types than any other group of pottery coffins known from Egypt—home of the anthropoid

43. James M. Weinstein, "Yahudiyeh, Tell El-" in *Oxford Encyclopedia of Archaeology in the Near East* (ed. Eric Meyers; New York: Oxford University Press, 1997) 5.368.

44. W. M. Flinders Petrie, *Hyksos and Israelite Cities* (BSAE 12: London, 1906) 16; pls. XIV, XV.

45. Petrie, *Hyksos and Israelite Cities*, 16; pl. XII. Petrie bases this comment on the fact that the incision lines around the necks of jars are unique to the time of Amenhotep II and are never found from the time of Thutmosis III or Thutmosis IV.

46. Galal and Aston, "New Kingdom Anthropoid Coffins," 167.

47. "The Shipwrecked Sailor," translated by Miriam Lichtheim in *Context of Scripture* (ed. W. W. Hallow and K. L. Younger; Leiden: Brill) 1.83.

48. Miriam Lichtheim, *Ancient Egyptian Literature* (Berkeley: University of California Press, 1973) 1.220–21.

49. R. Engelbach, *Riqqeh and Memphis* (London: British School of Archaeology in Egypt, 1915) VI:10; 18. Kuchman, "Egyptian Clay Anthropoid Coffins," 15.

50. Engelbach, *Riqqeh and Memphis*, VI:18.

51. Kuchman, "Egyptian Clay Anthropoid Coffins," 11.

burial—or Palestine."[52] These cylindrical coffins range in height from 1.6 to 2 m, with a circumference ranging from 1.7 to 2.2 m.[53] From this large site, two tombs that show strong affinities to TBO 0065 will be considered.

Tomb 114 contained an in situ anthropoid coffin, with crossed hands depicted on its lid.[54] Also found were Mycenaean and Egyptian vessels, alongside local Canaanite wares.[55] The coffin itself differs from the one at Tell el-Borg in that it is of the naturalistic body type, with the shoulders and head delineated. The coffin is slightly larger as well, measuring 1.90 m long by 0.59 m wide, with a circumference of 2.17 m.[56] It is noteworthy that the coffin's style fits well with known Egyptian prototypes.[57]

From Tomb 116 comes a cylindrical coffin in which the shoulders and head are not delineated, just as with TBO 0065; this coffin measures 1.9 m long by 0.7 m wide, while its circumference is 1.95 m.[58] The face-lid is of the naturalistic type, and it contains a misconstrued attempt at an "Osiris beard."[59] The hands are crossed like others; however, in this example, it is in a particularly crude fashion.[60]

It is worth highlighting the anthropoid coffins found at Tell el-Far'ah and Beth Shean. The former lies just 20 km southeast of Deir el-Balaḥ. The coffins are of the slipper-type; no coffins have been found there which delineate the head and shoulders.[61] The lids associated with the coffins belong to the "grotesque" variety, even including poor artistic attempts at the "Osiris beard."[62] Finally, the coffins were found alongside a large assemblage of Philistine cultural materials.[63]

At Beth Shean, approximately 50 anthropoid coffins were found, covering the thirteenth down to the eleventh centuries.[64] As with Tell el-Farʿah, all the coffins found here are of the "slipper" type, and none of the mummy-shaped coffins have been found. "Naturalistic" lids were first attested at Beth Shean from the thirteenth century down to the Iron Age, with "grotesque" lids following thereafter.[65] This fits well with Mazar's understanding of Beth Shean as a relatively small, yet important, Egyptian stronghold for 300 years, until its destruction, at which point Canaanite culture continued to thrive.[66] The Canaanites continued their practice of adopting Egyptian culture into their own, especially in the matter of anthropoid coffins.

52. Dothan, "Anthropoid Clay Coffins," 134. For more on the Egyptian presence at this site, see also I. Perlman, F. Asaro, and Trude Dothan, "Provenance of the Deir el- Balaḥ Coffins," *IEJ* 23 (1973), 166–71; and Raphael Ventura, "Four Egyptian Stelae from Deir el-Balaḥ," *IEJ* 37 (1987), 105–15.

53. Dothan, "Anthropoid Clay Coffins," 129.

54. Trude Dothan, in Y. Yadin et al., eds., *Excavations at the Cemetery of Deir el-Balaḥ* (Qedem 10; Jerusalem: Hebrew University of Jerusalem. 1978), 5.

55. Dothan, *Excavations at the Cemetery of Deir el-Balaḥ*, 5.

56. Ibid., 10.

57. See ibid., 10–11 for details.

58. Ibid., 30.

59. Ibid.

60. Ibid.

61. See Petrie and Olga Tufnell, *Beth Pelet I* (London: British School of Archaeology in Egypt, 1930), 6–9.

62. Dothan, *Excavations at the Cemetery of Deir el-Balaḥ*, 102.

63. See T. Dothan, *The Philistines and Their Material Culture*, 252–78.

64. A. Rowe, *The Topography and History of Beth Shan*, 23; see also Oren, *The Northern Cemetery of Beth Shan*, 132–39.

65. Dothan, *Excavations at the Cemetery of Deir el-Balaḥ*, 102.

66. Amihai Mazar, "Beth Shean in the Second Millennium B.C.E.: From Canaanite Town to Egyptian Stronghold," in *The Synchronisation of Civilisations in the Eastern Mediterranean in the Second Millennium B.C. II* (ed. Manfred Bietak: Vienna: Osterreichischen Akademie der Wissenschaften: 2003), 438–39.

Conclusion

Anthropoid clay coffins undoubtedly originated first in Egypt.[67] Typically, scholars have interpreted these coffins from two main points of view: (1) that such coffins are indicative of foreign populations, usually attributed to the Sea Peoples in general or the Philistines more specifically; and, (2) that these types of burials belong to those of poorer means who were unable to afford more expensive burials, such as wooden or stone sarcophagi.[68] However, regarding the first point, it as been demonstrated by Oren, Kuchman, and others that such burials were not always indicative of foreign elements. Where clay coffins have been found in Canaan, there is sufficient reason to view them as Egyptian first, then Philistine at a later time. For instance, both Beth Shean and Deir el-Balaḥ were situated at the heart of Egyptian domination in the Levant in the Late Bronze Age.[69] In the New Kingdom, as Egyptian influence spread, it is not surprising to find characteristic Egyptian cultural and religious elements present in Canaanite burials.[70] These burials could be those of Egyptian officials living in Palestine or those of native Canaanites who borrowed Egyptian cultural motifs. Additionally, the presence of early 18th Dynasty pottery in tombs containing clay coffins proves that clay coffins were in use well before the Sea Peoples invasion.

Regarding the second point, anthropoid burials are generally found poorly preserved and in tombs that have been robbed, partially leading to the erroneous belief that they represent poor burials. Many such burials might have contained artifacts indicative of wealth before being plundered. In fact, many of these coffins have been found in brick and stone-built tombs, which are indicators of wealth.[71] This is especially true of the coffins found in Tomb IV at Tell el-Borg. In fact, the poor were probably not buried in a coffin but rather in reed mats or nothing at all.[72]

Concerning the Tell el-Borg coffins then, it seems reasonable to conclude that these coffins are those of individuals associated with the 18th and 19th Dynasty forts—perhaps Egyptian officials and their families who were stationed at the fort. Small finds associated with burials rule out the possibility that the coffins come from the Sea Peoples invasion, which did not take place until the 20th Dynasty. The limited small finds found in the tombs are unquestionably Egyptian. Also, from what is known of clay coffins in other locations, such burials should not be viewed as indicative of poor economic status. As has been demonstrated, quite the opposite is true. Only the wealthy could afford clay coffins, especially coffins with elaborate decoration. Unfortunately, looting and modern construction that has taken place at Tell el-Borg make it difficult to definitively state exactly who these individuals were or in what capacity they served.

---

67. See Taylor, *Egyptian Coffins*, 2–8.
68. Galal and Aston, "New Kingdom Anthropoid Coffins," 173.
69. Dothan, *Excavations at the Cemetery of Deir el-Balaḥ*, 104. For the implications of the collapse of Egyptian rule at these sites and the resulting distinct Philistine material culture, see also Amihai Mazar, "The Emergence of the Philistine Material Culture," *IEJ* 35 (1985) 95–106.
70. Niel Asher Silberman, "Coffins in a Human Shape: A Short History of Anthropoid Sarcophagi," *BAR* 16:4 (1990) 52–54.
71. Galal and Aston, "New Kingdom Anthropoid Coffins," 175.
72. Ibid.

Chapter 6

The "Western Cemetery"

Scott D. Haddow and James K. Hoffmeier
University of Bordeaux and Trinity International University

The "Western Cemetery" — Field VII

In the initial survey of Tell el-Borg in May 1999, the western side of the site stood out for the scores of robber holes visible across the area (fig. 3.1). It looked like a large egg carton with circular holes that had filled with windblown sand (fig. 6.1). Surrounding the holes was the debris piles left by the looters, along with scatters of ceramic coffin pieces, potsherds, pieces of limestone, and bone fragments (fig. 6.2).

Large numbers of coffin sherds were found around some of the robber pits (fig. 6.3), and several examples that have molded human features were collected from the surface. Here are four such examples:

TBOX 60 (17 × 20.5 × 2 cm) has what appear to be fingers or plaits of hair from a wig (fig. 6.4). Two considerations point to the decoration as representation of hair. First, since there are five of these tube-shaped lines, one would have to be a thumb, if the molding is of a hand. While there are insufficient numbers of molded coffins recovered at Tell el-Borg to do careful comparative analysis, nevertheless, a damaged modeled anthropomorphic coffin lid from Field III (TBO 0078 = fig. 5.5) shows a figure with hair plaits and hands. The thumb is appropriately short and stubby compared to the other fingers. Second, the end of each plait on TBO 0078 (fig. 5.6) is a small, square depression, likely representing the end of the braided plait or possibly a bead woven into the hair. The same dimple is present on TBOX 60.

TBOX 65 (16 × 12.6 × 2 cm) is a triangular-shaped coffin sherd that has a small portion decorated (fig. 6.5). Because the critical areas above the modeled area are lost, determining the features represented here is problematic. However, it looks like lips, with the rounded portion below them being the chin.

TBO 0373 (14 × 16 × 2.2 cm) has a clear impression on the right side, measuring 4.9 cm long and 3.1 wide, but what it represents is uncertain (fig. 6.6). The left side of the sherd is a finished edge, suggesting that this sherd comes from the left side of the coffin lid.

TBO 0374 (23 × 16 × 1.5 cm) has what appears to be three fingers of a molded hand (fig. 6.7) Since the left side edge is finished, it likely was the left side of the coffin lid, which in turn means that the partially preserved hand is the left hand of the figure. The surface area over the top part of the hand (where the thumb would be) is lost. A cream-colored wash seems to have covered this coffin lid.

Fig. 6.1. The Western Cemetery, looking north.

Fig. 6.2. Robber pit, with fragments of clay coffin, limestone, and caliche sandstone.

Beside or in some of the robber pits were large limestone slabs that had been exposed during the robbing (figs. 6.1, 6.8a–b, 6.9–10).[1] Several of the large slabs appear to have been reused architectural blocks, although their purpose in the cemetery is not immediately evident. The other material observed on the surface were small pieces of crude, caliche sandstone (fig. 6.11). The surface finds, especially the coffin fragments, suggested to us that this area had been a cemetery, and we thus dubbed it the "Western Cemetery."

1. These blocks were not assigned small find numbers and were left in the field after examining them on site.

Fig. 6.3. A group of broken clay coffin sherds.

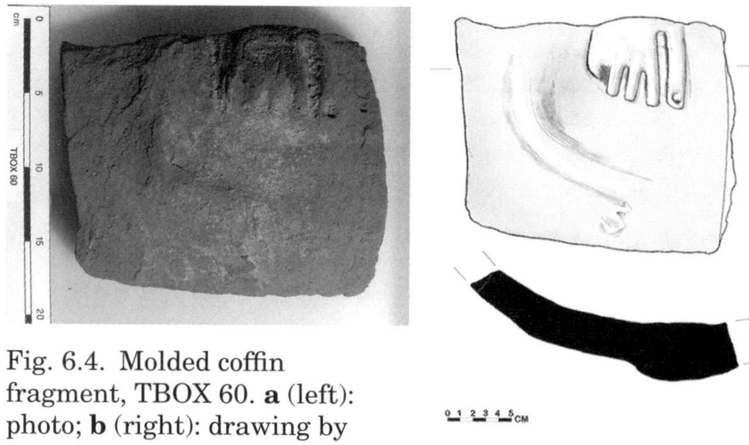

Fig. 6.4. Molded coffin fragment, TBOX 60. **a** (left): photo; **b** (right): drawing by L. Pinch-Brock.

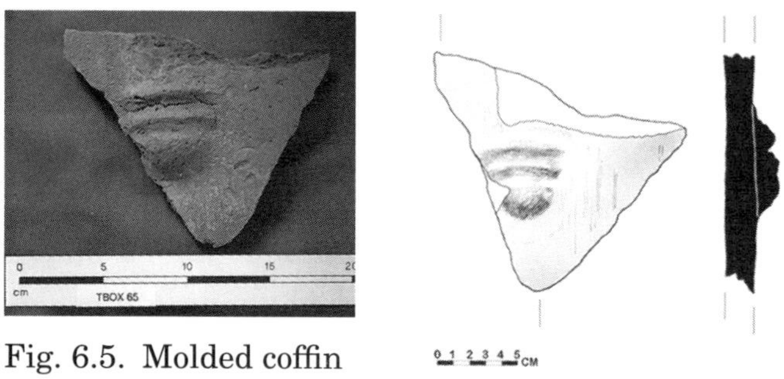

Fig. 6.5. Molded coffin sherd, TBOX 65. **a** (left): photo; **b** (right): drawing by L. Pinch-Brock.

Fig. 6.6. Molded coffin sherd, TBO 0373.

Fig. 6.7. Molded coffin sherd, TBO 0374.

Fig. 6.8a. Stone block as discovered by excavation staff.

Fig. 6.8b. Same block removed for measuring.

Fig. 6.9. Stone block in robber pit.

Because the area was so completely robbed, we thought the area would produce little intact data. Furthermore, some inspectors of the Supreme Council of Antiquities had dug eight *sondages* that were ca. 2 × 2 m in our Field VII (fig. 6.12). The work was done in 1997–1998, and verbal reports we received indicated that nothing was discovered and, for this reason, they abandoned work at the site. In the interest of determining more precisely the nature of this pilfered area, we briefly excavated three units in 2002, identifying the area as Field VII.

Fig. 6.10 (far left). Reused architectural block.

Fig. 6.11 (left). Flat stone block.

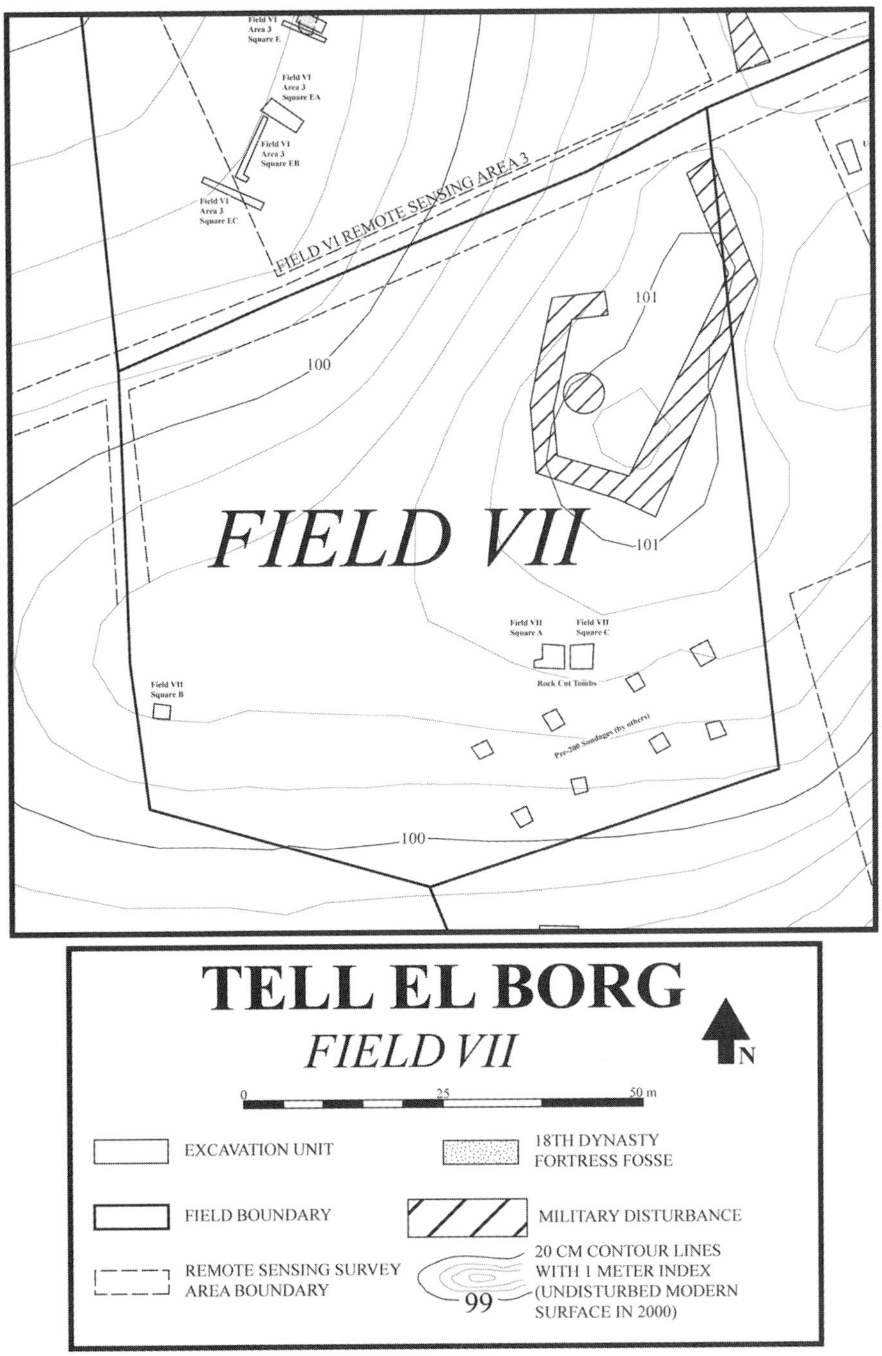

Fig. 6.12. Site map of Field VII (map by D. Olney, digitally enhanced by Joshua Olsen).

Fig. 6.13 (below). Clumps of caliche sandstone on the surface in Field VII.

Fig. 6.14. Tomb 1, cut through sandstone layer (L 4) in Unit A.

Fig. 6.15. Tomb 1, cut through sandstone layer (L 4) and possible tomb in northeast corner of Unit A.

Excavation Results from Field VII, Units A, B, and C

The abundance of the broken clay-coffin fragments strongly suggested that this area was indeed a cemetery. Three 3 × 3 m squares were excavated in Field VII, confirming this assumption but revealing something unexpected. Previously, it was noted that small clumps of caliche sandstone were among the surface finds; in some ares, the concentration of these stones could be quite heavy and the pieces were of varying size (fig. 6.13). Approximately 60 cm below the well-churned surface sand and debris (Locus 1) in Unit A, a hard surface appeared (figs. 6.14–6.15), and within that surface some quarrying had taken place to make tombs. The same crude sandstone surface was revealed in the adjacent Unit C. Project geologist Stephen Moshier described this material as "calcareous sandstone (beach rock)" that probably is a remnant of an coastal ridge older than the kurkar ridge that marks the Pelusium line on which Hebua I was built and what was the Mediterranean coastline in the 2nd and 3rd millennia (*Tell el-Borg I*, 68–69).

The discovery of this geological feature provides answers to a number of questions the site raises. Clearly, the "tell" area of Tell el-Borg was elevated by the underlying beach rock. Second, the fragments of the crude sandstone found scattered around this area were the result of excavating the tombs in this field, and this formation is the source for some larger stones found in the gate area of Field V (*Tell el-Borg I*, 285–86, fig. 427). Last, the soft sandstone layer served as a layer into which the burial pits for the tombs in parts of the "western cemetery" could be dug.

Unit A and C were located adjacent to each other, while the second square investigated was Unit B, which was located 50 m west of Unit A (fig. 6.12) to see if the kurkar formation continued; it did not. Only a few stray nondiagnostic sherds were recovered, and a pit was found that appears to be of modern origin (fig. 6.16). The absence of kurkar sandstone in Unit B indicates that it tapered off somewhere between the two exploratory squares. Consequently, a third square was opened adjacent (east) of Unit A—namely, Unit C.

Fig. 6.16. Possible modern pit in Unit A.

Fig. 6.17. Tomb 2 in Unit C.

Within Unit A, one and possibly the remains of two tombs were uncovered (fig. 6.17). Most of Tomb 1 is in the southwest corner of Unit A. The burial pit was cut into the sandstone (Locus 4), with the east or foot end being semicircular in shape. The head end was located beneath the western baulk (but not excavated); approximately 1.65 meters of the tomb was exposed, and the depth to a maximum of 52 cm (figs. 6.14–6.15). A mud-brick wall was found running along the southern baulk, set within the pit, and a small amount of brick was found on the opposite side of the pit wall, but most of it had not survived. What is not clear is whether the mud-brick walls rose to a vault over the tomb or, alternatively, the slabs of stone found in the area had been laid across the tomb. Another explanation for the mud bricks is that they came from a collapsed vault, not from walls that lined the pit.

This tomb had been thoroughly plundered and razed and, as a result, no small finds were uncovered. In the top fill layer of Unit A (Locus 1), two flat joining pieces of copper/copper alloy (3.72 × 0.03 cm), possibly from a bowl or dish (fig. 6.18), were found. The ceramic witness from around the tomb (and in Unit C) consisted of worn, abraded, and crushed sherds, but several Cypriote base-ring sherds and Marl D amphora handles were documented, assuring a 14th century B.C. date for these burials.

When the area around Tomb 1 was being cleared, a slight ovoid depression was exposed, within which were a number of chunks of sandstone (Locus 6). It may be that the depression was originally intended to be a tomb but was subsequently abandoned (wrong orientation? It pointed north!). Tomb 1 actually cuts through this earlier feature, and perhaps the rough pieces of kurkar were tossed here from the excavation of that tomb. Fig. 6.14 shows the shallow depression with the stones in situ, whereas in fig. 6.15, the sandstone pieces have been removed.

Another shallow depression (Locus 8) extends from adjacent Unit C, where it appears more rectangular in shape, with rounded edges; this depression is about 1.70 m long (fig. 6.17). This shallow feature may be the result of an attempt to create a tomb. As with Tomb 1, a second tomb (#2) was cut into the kurkar sandstone bedrock and over the Locus 8 sunken feature. Tomb 2 lies on the northeast corner of Unit A and the northwest corner of Unit C, with the central section lying beneath the baulk that separated the two squares. Scant traces of a mud-brick wall remain (Locus 9). This wall clearly was constructed on the outside of the pit, although no brick remnant was found on the west (head) end of the pit. The preserved length of Tomb 2 is 1.65 m. Small

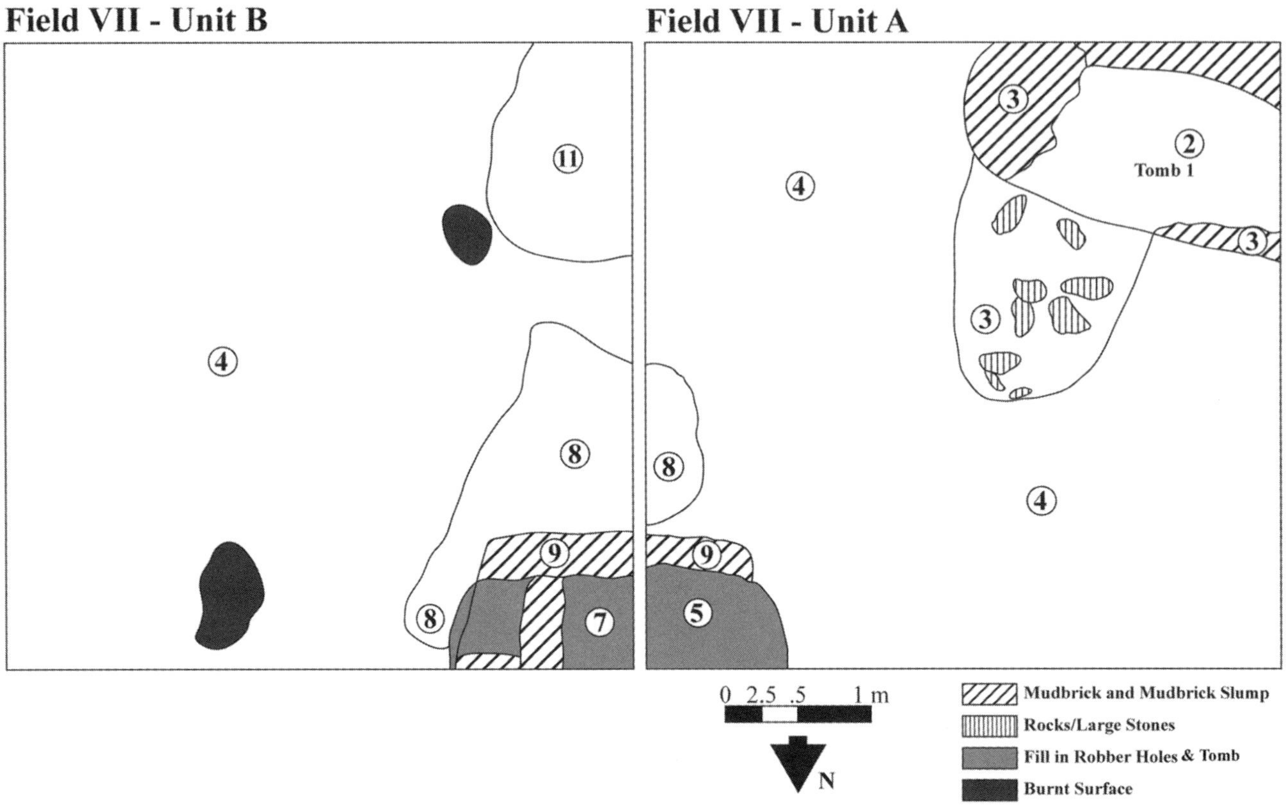

Fig. 6.18. Plan of Unit A and C (drawing by Scott Haddow, digitally enhanced by Joshua Olsen).

finds were negligible in Unit C. In the burial pit (Locus 7), a 1-cm-long piece of a copper/copper alloy nail or tool was found (TBO 0254) (fig. 6.20). A similar, but larger, fragment was found in the surface fill, Locus 1 (TBO 0253) (fig. 6.21).

Based on the limited scope of excavations in Field VII, along with the poor condition of the tombs and small amount of pottery and small finds discovered, it is impossible to say much about the status of the people buried in this cemetery. Clay coffins were used, and of the two (possibly three) burial pits exposed, each would have been for a single occupant.

Osteological Remains

Various types of bones were found scattered on the surface: mainly large mammal fragments (possibly water buffalo, donkey, or camel); highly fragmented and incomplete (< 25%) human skeletal material was also identified and recovered, including cranial, dental, and vertebral elements, as well as fragments of long bones and manual phalanges. Despite their fragmented nature, the bones are well preserved, but their well-bleached appearance suggests that they had been exposed to the elements for some time. The material was collected from several locations within the area, usually near the edge of a robber pit. Because there is no duplication of elements or representation of different ages or sexes in the assemblage, the minimum number of individuals (MNI) identified is one, but the material probably represents several individuals, disinterred during looting activity. Given their size and the closure of all observable epiphyses, the bones appear to fall into the adult age range, although no finer distinctions can be made, again due to the highly

Fig. 6.19. Copper/copper alloy fragment (TBO 0240).

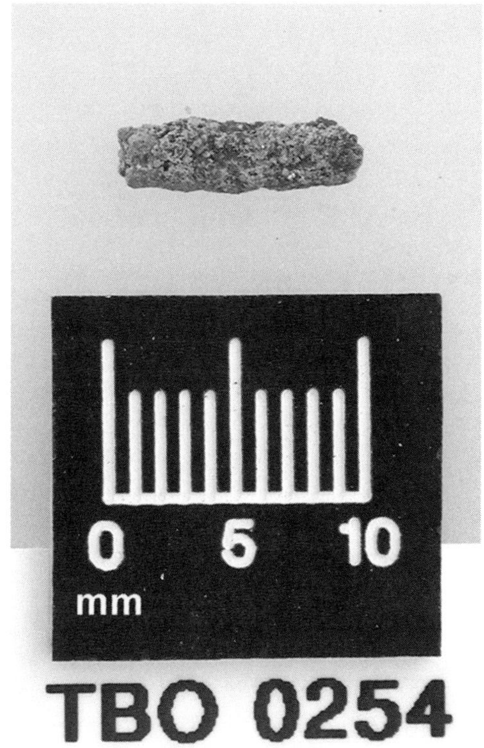

Fig. 6.20 (above). Copper/copper alloy tool (TBO 0254).

Fig. 6.21 (left). Copper/copper alloy tool (TBO 0253).

fragmented nature of the material. Sex cannot be assigned, given the lack of diagnostic skeletal elements, and no pathological lesions are evident.

CHAPTER 7

Field VI: The Domestic Space

Thomas W. Davis
SOUTHWESTERN BAPTIST THEOLOGICAL SEMINARY

with contributions by James K. Hoffmeier

Field VI designates the highest surviving areas of the site (fig. 3.1, fig 7.1). The evidence from the 2007 season clearly indicates that the site was at least 1.5 m higher during the New Kingdom occupation. The excavation field was divided into three areas, delineated as follows: Area 1 consists of an artificially flattened surface just south of the central Egyptian/Israeli defensive system (the "crater"; see *Tell el-Borg I*, figs. 16 and 18). Area 2 consists of the space inside the "crater" and included a 3-m-high mound christened the "borg." All of the survey points after the 2002 season used a rebar driven into the top of the borg as a base point. This was necessary when the original concrete and metal datum point was destroyed some time before the 2004 season. Area 3 is the area west of Area 1, separated from Area 1 by a series of modern defense trenches.

Initial inspection of Field VI revealed a deflated surface, with numerous ground-stone artifacts, domestic pottery, and white shells (*Tell el-Borg I*, fig. 16; fig. 7.2 here). Fragments of ceramic coffins indicated that looted tombs were in the vicinity. The surface was pockmarked with robber pits and military and/or squatter fire pits. Portions of the surface of Field VI had evidently been stripped mechanically and the surface sand pushed into defensive berms—the "crater." The visible evidence of disturbance led us to assign Field VI a lower priority for investigation. No work occurred in this Field in 2000 or 2001.

FIELD INVESTIGATIONS, AREA 1

This area yielded what turned out to be an ancient Bedouin (Shasu) encampment made of a group of huts and a fence that encircled the small structures. Details are given below, but the pottery from this area has been introduced in *Tell el-Borg I*, 375–78, and a more detailed study of this encampment was recently published by Davis, Hoffmeier, and Hummel.[1] See pottery plates 7.1–7.3 at the end of this chapter.

1. Thomas Davis, James Hoffmeier, and Rexine Hummel, "New Archaeological Evidence for Ancient Bedouin (Shasu) on Egypt's Eastern Frontier at Tell el-Borg," *Ägypten und Levante* 26 (2016) 285–311, including analysis of the ceramic finds by Hummel, pp. 305–9.

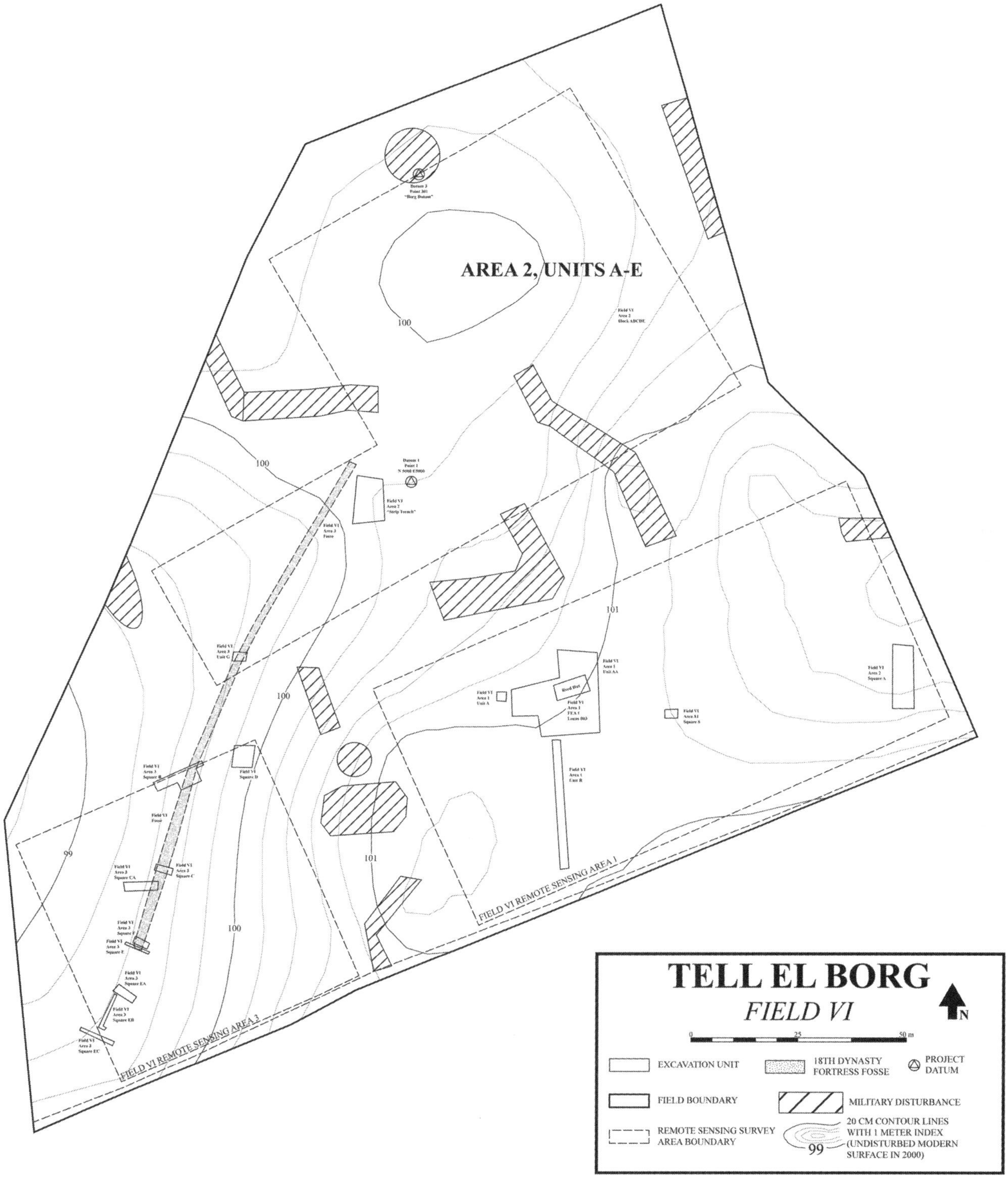

Fig. 7.1. Field VI site map, by D. Olney; digitally enhanced by Joshua Olsen.

Fig. 7.2. Initial excavations of Area 1, with part of the "crater" to the north.

The 2002 Season

In 2002, a 5 × 15 m-long trench was stripped by hand in the eastern sector of Area 1, Field VI (figs. 7.2, 7.13). Unit A is a smaller 5 × 5 m square within the large stripped unit (fig. 7.4). Sterile basal sand lay just below the surface, approximately 5 cm deep. A smaller (5 × 5 m) square was stripped on the west of the field in what would later be designated Area 3, and a 3 × 6 m block (Unit B) near the center. A series of shovel tests (35 cm diameter cuts) were also placed in the field to make sure that no buried deposits were present. All of the shovel tests encountered basal, sterile sands just beneath the surface disturbance. A straight dark (10YR 4/2) charcoal-flecked stain was identified within the central block (Locus 003). A possible fire pit (Locus 002) was identified on the surface 2 m east of the straight stain. Locus 003 was treated as a possible feature and the surface exposure widened. The fire pit was sectioned and a carbon sample removed for dating (fig. 7.5). A small carbon sample was taken from Locus 003. A small < 3 cm fragment of what appeared to be lead (TBO 0315 = fig. 7.6) was recovered from the initial cleaning of the stain. A tiny 2 mm carnelian bead was also recovered from Locus 3. The stain extended down at least 10 cm into the surrounding sands. The dark material appeared to be burned sand and carbonized

Fig. 7.3. Unit A, looking west.

Fig. 7.4. Unit B (part of Unit E at top of image). Looking east.

Fig. 7.5. Sectioned fire pit (Locus 2) in Unit B.

Fig. 7.6. Possible piece of lead, TBO 0315.

reeds. The initial interpretation was that this represented a Bedouin encampment of the recent past. Under this scenario, the sherds recovered from the feature resulted from surface sherds being pushed into the soil by the placement of the reeds. It is impossible to determine, given the bulldozing in this area, if the surface sherds and those in Locus 1 were originally from this area or were pushed there from adjacent locations. It is clear from a cursory examination of the walls of the "crater" that scores of sherds from the area were scooped up and included in the sandy matrix berm, along with fired bricks from the nearby recent Egyptian military installations.

The first signal of an early date of these habitats came from carbon dating of burned reeds:[2]

- Sample TEB 02/1 from the fire pit yielded a conventional date of 3630 ±140 BP; 2 Sigma cal. 2200–1770 B.C. (95%); 1 Sigma cal. 2450–1630 B.C. (68%).

2. The carbon samples were of non-archaeological materials collected in cooperation with members of the Geological Survey of Egypt, and testing was done at Beta Analytics.

Fig. 7.7. Granodiorite pounder, TBO 0244.

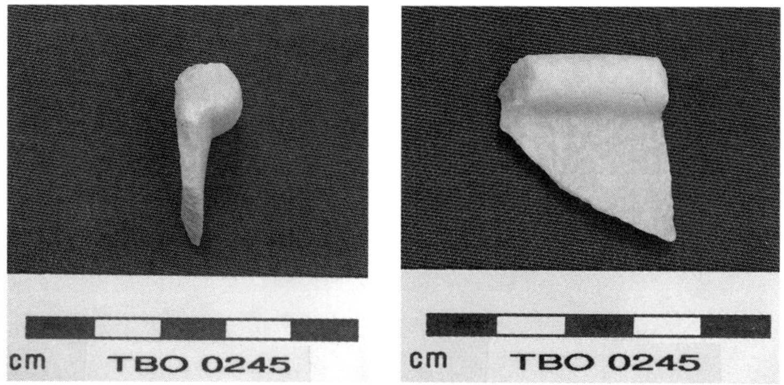

Fig. 7.8a–b. Travertine jar rim, TBO 0245.

Fig. 7.9. Granite pounder, TBO 0247.

Fig. 7.10. Copper/copper alloy tool, TBO 0235.

Fig. 7.11. Basalt quern, TBO 0229. **a** (left): photo; **b** (right): drawing by Lyla Pinch-Brock.

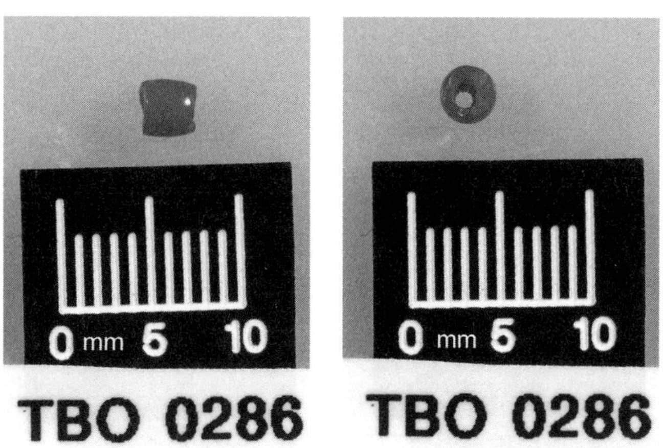

Fig. 7.12a–b. Carnelian bead, TBO 0286.

- Sample TEB 02/2 from the burned stain yielded a conventional date of 3570 ±130 BP; 2 Sigma cal. 2290–1600 B.C. (95%); 1 Sigma cal. 2120–1740 B.C. (68%).

This date range for the calibration curve is very broad and such an ancient date for the features was widely questioned by the excavation team, although a date from the early New Kingdom and as early as the 2nd Intermediate Period seems plausible, aligning with the ceramics found in Unit AA (*Tell el-Borg I*, 375–79).[3] For the ceramic remains from Field VII Area 1, see pottery plates 7.1–7.2 at the end of this chap-

3. Davis, Hoffmeier, and Hummel, "New Archaeological Evidence," 305–9.

Table 7.1. Small Finds from Field VI Area 1, 2002 Season

TBO	*Unit/Locus*	*Object Type*	*Material*	*Measurements*
0244	VI surface	pounder	granodiorite	n/a
0245	VI surface	jar rim	travertine	2.5 × 2.6 × 1.0 cm
0246	VI surface	metal blade fragment	copper/copper alloy	2.1 × 1.1 × 0.2 cm
0247	VI surface	pounder/grinder	granite	4.4 × 4.5 dia cm
0232	A Locus 1	metal tool point	copper/copper alloy	3.73 × 0.7 dia cm
0235	A Locus 1	metal tool fragments	copper/copper alloy	4.8 × 0.5 dia cm
0229	B Locus 1	quern	amygdaloidal basalt	9.5 × 9.1 × 3.9 cm
0233	C Locus 1	metal tool fragment	copper/copper alloy	1.2 × 0.5 dia cm
0234	C Locus 1	scalloped bead	faience	0.2 × 0.6 dia cm
0286	E Locus 3	tube-shaped bead	carnelian	.25 × 0.3 dia cm

Fig. 7.13. Expansion of AA to 20 × 20 m.

ter. The small finds in Locus 1 throughout Area 1, like the pottery, had been moved around, and precise context is impossible to determine.

Small Finds from Field VI Area 1, 2002 Season

While the number of small finds are limited in number, they are consistent with what might be expected in a domestic context: pounder/grinders, querns, copper/copper alloy tools and beads. The same range of objects were also in the funerary area in Field III (see chapter 4), and this is true of the small finds in Area A documented in the following sections.

2004 and 2005 Seasons

The investigations in the 2004 season were designed to expose the features to understand their nature better and to gather sufficient carbon for a suite of radiocarbon dates to settle the question of the antiquity of the features. When the season began in 2004, the straight-line feature and the fire pit could be clearly identified from the surface. A much wider area was hand-stripped surrounding the initial block. Eventually, an area measuring more than 20 × 20 m was opened

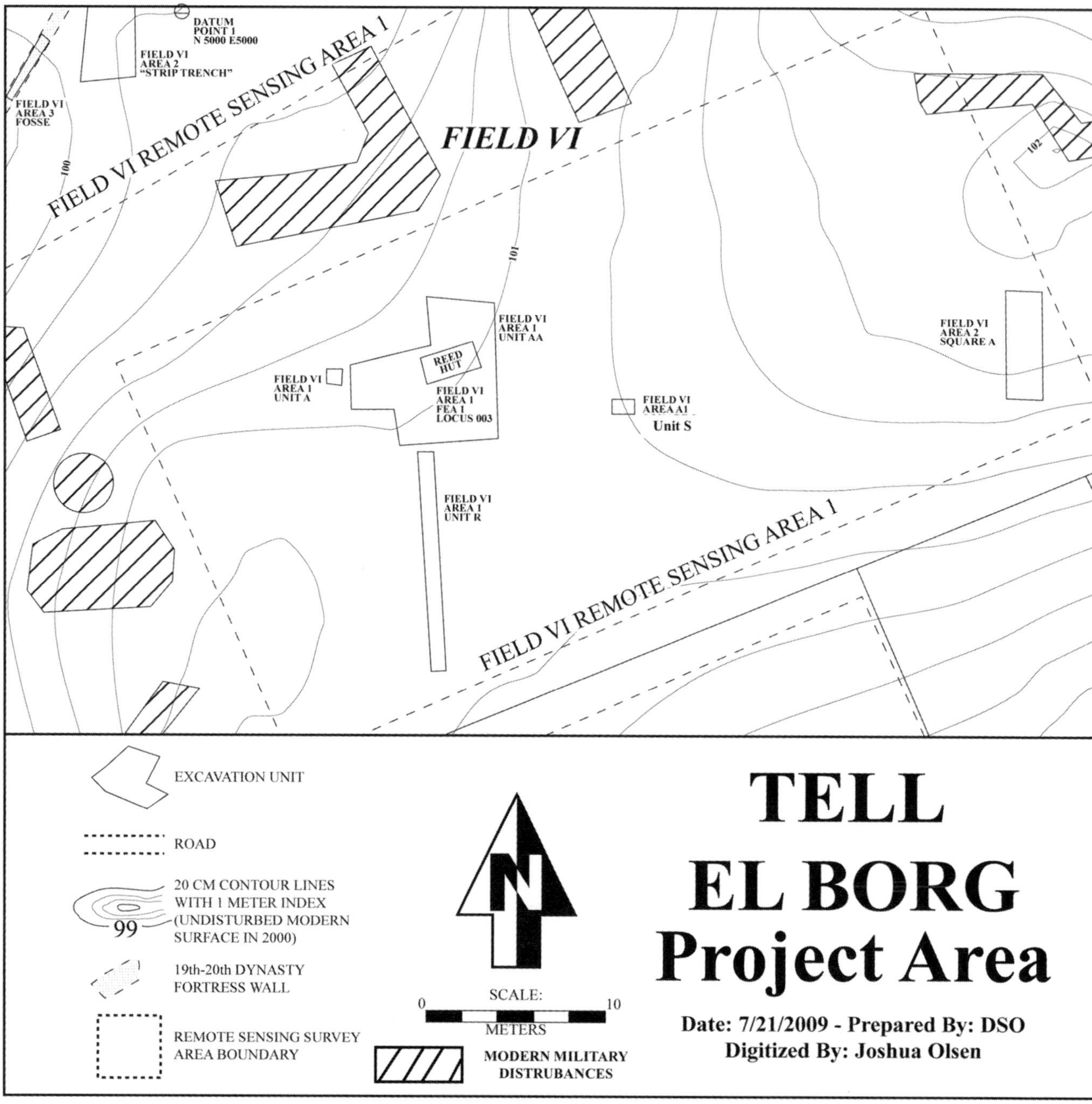

Fig. 7.14. Field VI Area 1 site plan.

(fig. 7.13); this area (Area AA) was reexamined in 2005. Work in Field VI during 2005 focused on delineating features in the southern half of the excavation block and determining if the cluster of cultural features extended into other portions of the field (fig. 7.13).

Trench R measured 2 m × 30 m and ran north–south from the south edge of Area AA, with a baulk of 1.24 m left in place (fig. 7.15). It was placed 10 m west of the eastern baulk of Area AA. The goal of this trench was to determine the presence or absence of soil stains; no suspected ancient features were excavated, although clearly modern pits and natural or modern intrusive

Fig. 7.15. Trench R.

elements were removed. Numerous stains similar to the alignments identified in the main trench were exposed at a depth of 10–15 cmbs.[4] Numerous robber pits disturbed Trench R; one robber pit extended 50 cmbs. The activity area appears to extend for at least 25 m south of the exposed block. Two 3 × 2 m test blocks were placed to the east. Trench S1 was opened up 15 m due east of the centerline of the main exposure, and Trench S2 was placed 15 m south of Trench S1 (fig. 7.15). The eastern test blocks were sterile, except for a surface find of one copper alloy bead.

One 3 × 2 m test block, Trench S3, was placed 10 m west and 5 m south of the northwest corner of Trench R. When the loose top layer of sand was removed, a tank-tread pattern was observed, as well as the edge of a pit of military origin. The pit was filled with numerous artifacts, unfortunately in a secondary depositional context. Cypriot White Slip (WS) I and II sherds were recovered, along with a stone bead, 2 bronze needles, a groundstone fragment, a rubbing stone, and a possible sling-stone. No further work was undertaken here due to the disturbance.

Numerous cultural and natural soil loci were identified just below the surface fill in the main test block. The surface sand was very disturbed and, as a guiding principle, all features and deposits were treated as potentially disturbed unless they were clearly intact beneath the upper stratum. Clearly modern features were removed. The dark stains, lacking any stone or mud-brick architecture, had to be carefully delineated through a combination of shallow (1–2 cm) shovel scraping and careful trowel work. The best method was to cut away surrounding sterile sand and leave the feature lines to emerge from the background. Once potentially intrusive material was removed, all excavated cultural deposits were screened through 0.625 sq. cm hardware cloth. Flotation samples were taken from fire pits and burned reed features. (The charred remains of reeds, grasses, and seeds were analyzed by Claire Malleson and are reported on in chapter 12 of this volume.) The dry conditions at Tell el-Borg and the strong Sinai sun quickly leached out the stains, making them more vulnerable to being swept away by the daily afternoon breeze. On more than one occasion, newly exposed elements were nearly invisible after 15 minutes.

Numerous fire pits were present, some of which were modern. In the field, the key to identifying the age of the fire pits was assumed to be the presence or absence of fish bones. Fire pits that had fish bones were likely to be ancient, since the Nile had shifted away from the site before modern times and the surrounding marshy areas dried up. Support for this argument was the observation that some of the pits that lacked fish bones contained modern glass in the matrix. On at least one occasion, a modern fire pit had intruded into an ancient one. All of the fire pits were simple holes in the ground, with no permanent features such as stones being used as a base or a hearth ring. Such fire pits are used today by Bedouin to make tea or bread (fig. 7.16). Robber holes were clearly identifiable by white sand fill. They were removed as they were identified.

4. Cmbs = centimeters below surface.

Fig. 7.16. Our Bedouin workers making bread over an open fire during breakfast break.

Field Results: Area 1

A total of 35 loci were identified within Area 1, Field VI in 2004 and 2005. (See Table 7.2). Loci 21 and 22 referred to stains that did not survive long enough to be recorded. Some of the loci appeared to form individual structures and are discussed together below. This analysis assumes that all of the stains identified as "hut" elements are contemporary, which cannot be definitively demonstrated when the stains are not physically linked together. However, the clear indications of fainter stains, overridden by darker ones, provides for a convenient method of discerning phasing. This allows for the grouping of alignments with a fair degree of probability.

Surface and Disturbed Fill (Locus 001)

The surface sands and all potentially disturbed material were designated Locus 001. A bulldozer and vehicle traffic had heavily disturbed the sand during the military occupations. In some places, the potential disturbance extended nearly 20 cm below the surface; the depth of disturbance averaged 10–15 cmbs. The surface was pockmarked with numerous robber pits and military and/or squatter refuse pits. Bulldozer cuts had obliterated any cultural features at the north edge of the block. Fill from all of these intrusive features also was designated Locus 001. Some of the reed-feature stains extended up into the overlying matrix of Locus 001, indicating that the original ground surface was higher than the surviving level. Locus 001 yielded numerous sherds, including Cypriot WS, Levantine LB, Mycenaean, and a range of Egyptian material such as black-rimmed bowls and abundant Marl B sherds. The Egyptian material suggested early to mid-18th Dynasty activity (*Tell el-Borg I*, 375–79).[5] The sherds were generally well worn and wind eroded. Very few limestone chips were recovered from Locus 001, but nearly a dozen small finds were recorded.

5. Davis, Hoffmeier, and Hummel, "New Archaeological Evidence," 305–9.

Table 7.2. Field VI Area 1 Loci

Locus No.	*Unit*	*Structural Feature*	*Sampled?*	*Identification*
L 001	All	No	Yes	Material from the surface, disturbed upper fill and disturbance features
L 002	B	No	Yes	Ancient fire pit
L 003	B, AA	Hut 1	Yes	Burned reed stain; outline of Feature 1 (=Hut 1)
L 004	B, AA	No	No	Modern fire pit
L 005	B, AA	No	No	Bulldozer cut with fill W of Feature 1
L 006	B, AA	Hut 1	Yes	East-most room of Feature 1
L 007	B, AA	No	No	Modern fire pit along S wall of Feature 1
L 008	B, AA	Hut 1	Yes	"L" shaped room in Feature 1
L 009	B, AA	Hut 1	No	Room in northwest corner of Feature 1
L 010	B, AA	No	Yes	Large ancient fire pit
L 011	BB	No	Yes	Occupational debris, perhaps courtyard, outside (S) of fence line
L 012	BB	Hut 2	No	Outline of Feature 2
L 013	BB	Hut 2	No	East-most room of Feature 2
L 014	BB	Fence line	No	Fence line including bundle stains
L 015	BB	Hut 2	Yes	Interior of squared feature in Feature 2
L 016	BB	No	Yes	Area west of 15
L 017	BB	Hut 3	No	Outline of Feature 3
L 018	BB	Hut 3	No	Interior of Feature 3
L 019	BB	No	No	Bulldozer cut
L 020	AA	No	Yes	Occupational debris between fence and huts
L 021	AA	No	No	Undefined ephemeral stain west of Feature 3
L 022	AA	No	No	Undefined ephemeral stains west of Feature 3
L 023	AA	No	Yes	Older fire pit overlaid by L 009
L 024	AA	No	Yes	Ancient trash pit W of Feature 1
L 025	AA	Hut 1	Yes	Long deep linear feature at E of end of L 006
L 026	AA	No	Yes	Large oblong ancient fire pit
L 027	BB	Unknown	No	Fence line delineating E edge of courtyard (L 001)
L 028	BB	No	Yes	Open space with staining
L 029	BB	Yes	Yes	Elongated stain comprised of occupational debris along S baulk in SE corner; fence line?
L 030	BB	Hut 2	Yes	Fire pit in L 013, interior room
L 031	BB	Hut 2	Yes	Pit cluster including fire pit and stains along S wall "T-rex" (shaped feature)
L 032	BB	Hut 2	Yes	Interior space of Hut 2B
L 033	BB	Hut 2	Yes	Stain along S wall of testing area and attached linear stains running north and northwest
L 034	BB	Unknown	Yes	East–west stain
L 035	BB	Unknown	No	East–west stain juts out from W baulk
L 036	BB	Unknown	No	Earlier phase wall
L 037	BB	Unknown	Yes	Open space
L 038	BB	Unknown	Yes	Reed posthole
L 039	Trench R	Unknown	No	"Lion head" shaped feature
L 040	Trench R	Unknown	No	Band S of lion head
L 041	Trench R	Unknown	No	Band S of L 040
L 042	Trench R	Unknown	No	½ circle S of L 40
L 043	Trench R	Unknown	No	Wall/fence system (?)
L 044	Trench R	Unknown	No	Pit

Table 7.3. Field VI Area 1 Surface and Unit A/AA

TBO	Unit/Locus	Object Type	Material	Measurements
0448	Surface/Unit A	pounder	peridotite	5.9 × 6.8 × 2.2 cm
0515	Surface/Unit A	pounder	granodiorite	7.5 cm dia × 4 cm
0516	Surface/Unit A	quern	sandstone	9.2 × 5.0 × 2.7 cm
0542	Surface/Unit A	reworked sherd	clay	1.1 × 1.4 dia cm
0600	Surface/Unit A	4 potsherd game pieces	clay	n/a
0442[a]	AA Locus 1	lithic blade	chert	2.4 × 1.7 × 0.4 cm
0443	AA Locus 1	rim fragment of a vessel	faience	2.1 × 1.7 × 0.7 cm
0444	AA Locus 1	grindstone fragment	sandstone	4.5 × 3.6 × 3.7 cm
0445	AA Locus 1	rim of large bowl	limestone	13.2 × 8.4 × 5.0 cm
0446	AA Locus 1	tube-shaped bead	faience	0.45 × 0.3 dia cm
0447	AA Locus 1	tube bead (4 sections)	faience	0.6 × 0.3 dia cm

a. TBO 0442, a chert blade was treated in Davis, Hoffmeier, and Hummel, "New Archaeological Evidence for Ancient Bedouin (Shasu) on Egypt's Eastern Frontier at Tell el-Borg," 309–10 and is analyzed by Carole McCartney in Chapter 10.

Fig. 7.17. Peridotite pounder, TBO 0448.

Fig. 7.18. Granodiorite pounder, TBO 0515.

Fig. 7.19a–b. Sandstone quern, TBO 0516.

Fig. 7.20. Four reworked sherd game pieces, TBO 0600.

Fig. 7.21. Faience rim sherd, TBO 0443.

Fig. 7.22a–b. Large limestone bowl fragment, TBO 0445.

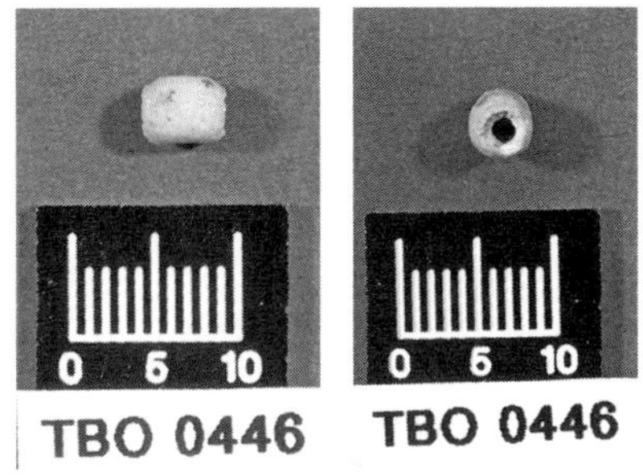

Fig. 7.23a–b. Faience tube-shaped bead, TBO 0446.

Fig. 7.25 (above). Hut 1, looking south.

Fig. 7.24 (left). Hut 1, looking west. Shown, right to left, are Dr. James Phillips, Tom Davis, and Mrs. Phillips.

Field VI Area 1 Surface and Unit A/AA

Modern Fire Pits: Loci 004, 007

Locus 007 is a modern fire pit that intruded into Locus 005, a bulldozer cut north of the feature cluster. Composed of firm very pale brown (10YR 7/3) sand and ash, the fire pit was 16 cm deep and 50 cm in diameter. It had an indistinct chromatic interface with the bulldozer debris, but the texture change was clear. Numerous woody fragments remained among the ashes. The fire pit probably was a product of the military occupation, after the initial military trenches were created. The fill from this Locus was not screened and no pottery was retained.

Locus 007 overlapped the north wall of Locus 008. This large (1.75 m × 2.00 m) modern fire pit yielded large pieces of modern drinking glasses and several very-well-preserved pieces of charcoal (> 2 cm). No fish bones were recovered from the fill, which was screened before it was determined to be modern. When it was removed, pre-modern deposits were revealed. The large size of Locus 007 suggests that it also belongs to the modern military occupation of the site.

Feature/Hut 1 (Loci 002, 003, 006, 008, 009, 025)

The first loci identified in the north of the test block were eventually designated Feature 1 or Hut 1 (figs. 7.24–7.26). Feature 1 appears to be the remains of a rectangular reed hut and associ-

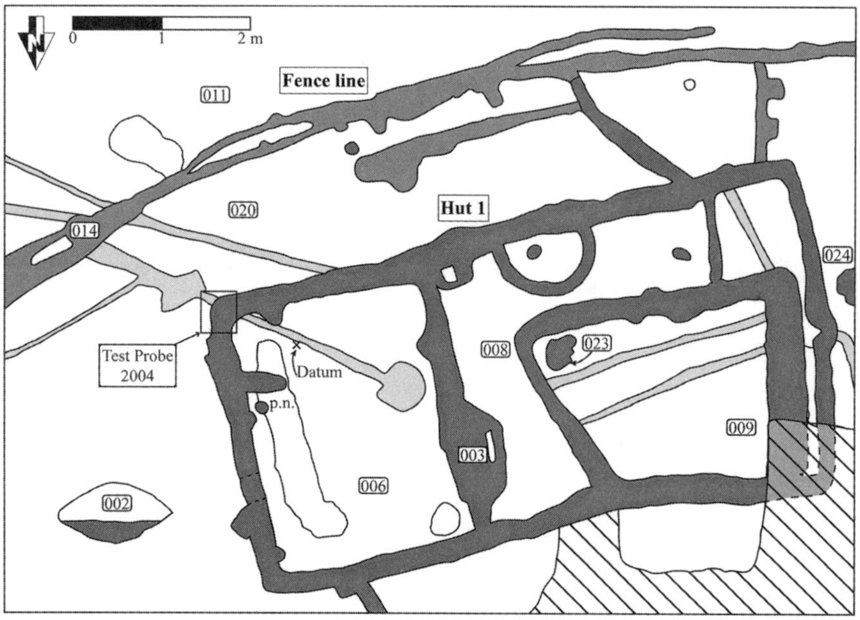

Fig. 7.27 (above). Clumps of mud daub from the hut.

Fig. 7.26 (left). Plan of Hut 1 and surrounding fence; drawing by Thomas Davis, digitized by Joshua Olsen.

Fig. 7.28. Section showing narrow V-shaped foundation trench with ash from reed structure.

Fig. 7.29. Reed bundles used to support surrounding fence.

ated pits and structures. The main structure measured 7.5 m east–west along its south edge and 3.75 m along the east edge. The dark brown (10YR 4/2) outline stain, Locus 003, was fairly wide, approximately 30 cm in width. The stain consisted of fragments of burned reed, darkened sand, and occasional small (<1 cm) clumps of burned daub. Reed impressions were preserved on at last one piece of daub (fig. 7.27). Sectioning Locus 003 along the east edge revealed a V-shaped base extending 20–25 cm below the initial surface (fig. 7.28). Locus 003 yielded some early ceramic markers, including a "Tell el-Yehudiyah" fragment and black-rimmed bowl sherds (*Tell el-Borg I*, 375).

The outline of the structure was nearly complete, except for approximately 1 m in the northwest corner, where the bulldozer had destroyed the stain. No visible doorway or entry space was identified. Periodically, semicircular stains extended beyond the wall from the inside and outside edges of Locus 003. These stains represent the remains of reed bundles, placed to strengthen

Fig. 7.30. Bundles of corn stocks for sale in market.

Fig. 7.31. West end of Hut 1, showing possible compartments and fallen roof beam (bundles).

the reed walls of the structure. The use of such bundles is most clearly seen in the wall that surrounded the huts (fig. 7.29). This type of construction is still used in Egypt today for huts, fences, and lean-tos. One can still purchase reeds or corn stalks by the bundle (fig. 7.30)

Feature 1 was divided into three areas, designated Loci 006, 008, and 009 (from east to west). Locus 006 was the largest space, with an internal measurement of 2.60 × 3.40 m or 8.84 m^2. Once the interior edges of the locus were identified, all of the burned staining within the area was treated as in situ material and screened. It is likely that the thin, nonconcentrated carbonized material represented either roofing material fallen in, remains of the side walls, or possibly floor matting (fig. 7.31). Minimal ceramic material was recovered from Locus 006. One rim sherd from an early 18th Dynasty black-rimmed bowl was recovered, along with Marl B sherds. The sherds were very small, for the most part (< 2 cm), and quite abraded. This could indicate that either the sherd material was present on the surface before the structure was built or that they were exposed to weathering after the structure burned. When the diffuse staining was removed, the yellowish-brown (10YR 6/6) basal sand contained a long, thin (30–40 cm) stain running parallel to the east wall of Locus 006, and a small 36-cm, round stain in the northwest corner, 10 cm from the north wall. The long stain was removed separately as Locus 025.

Locus 025 appears to be ashy and organic occupational debris in a deep trench. At the surface, the stain measures 45 cm wide and 33 cm deep, narrowing to a rounded bottom approximately 24 cm wide. Minimal pottery was recovered from Locus 25, and no bone fragments. This may represent a subterranean pit used for storage. It may have been covered with a reed mat that burned with the hut. Two carbon samples were taken, as was a 2-liter flotation sample. It is possible that Locus 25 had an unknown structural role; this may be indicated by a corresponding, apparently similar stain along the western edge of Hut 1 within Locus 009 (fig. 7.26). Unfortunately, the extensive disturbance along the western edge of Locus 009 prevented a determination of the nature of that possible deposit.

Locus 008 is the central space of the hut, forming an L shape, with the base along the south side. The north–south leg is from 90 cm to 1.70 m wide and 3.25 m long; the east–west space measures 1 × 4.5 m. The internal walls are slightly lighter in color. A large patch of ash bulged into the space along the eastern separation. This may be the product of a bundle leaning against the divider and that burned in place or a reinforced section of the structure. The relatively centralized

Fig. 7.32. Semicircular installation and post-hole inside Hut 1.

Fig. 7.33 (right). Ash line of fence that surrounded cluster huts on the south side.

location of the expanded segment of the divider may indicate a structural role, perhaps a double bundle of reeds or another type of thickened support. Much ash was scattered across the surface of the locus suggesting roof collapse. The walls of Locus 008 had numerous reed bundles in their construction, particularly along the north separator wall, dividing Locus 008 from Locus 009 (at least three bundles). The average bundle stain extends 10 cm out from the wall and 20–25 cm along the wall, in a rounded shape.

A semicircle of ash from burned reeds extends north from the south wall of Locus 008. In the center of the semicircle is a small post-hole. This strange feature may indicate a platform or shelf. Directly above this area was the modern fire pit, Locus 007. When it was removed, the strange semicircle was revealed (fig. 7.32).

Locus 009 is the easternmost section of the hut, 225 cm north–south and 310 cm east–west at its largest internal measurement. All of the walls of the space show internal buttressing. The western wall is very disturbed, and a long, wide stain runs parallel to it. This may be structural or it may be a similar storage pit or remains of a sleeping platform, similar to Locus 025 within Locus 006. This was greatly disturbed and lost coherency when it was cleaned. When the area was recleaned at the beginning of the 2006 season, Locus 009 appeared to be a separate square room, not directly connected to the easternmost wall of Hut 1, suggesting a separate construction or occupation phase. A modern fire pit (locus 023) was removed from the southeast corner of Locus 009. Locus 009 yielded a small number of nondiagnostic vitrified sherds and a flint blade.

Locus 008 may represent a connector space or shared familial space that links the 2 more private spaces, Loci 006 and 009. The strange ash feature and the thick accumulation of ash

Fig. 7.34. Hut 1 with surrounding fence (to the left), looking west.

Fig. 7.35. Hut 2, looking north.

along one wall suggest that this space was more crowded, not employed for personal use such as sleeping but for communal storage. Since the entire outline was only cleared but not excavated, it is possible that some of the apparent outline is not the result of reeds that were driven into the ground but may reflect burned matting that followed the wall line and collapsed across possible openings. Thus, a doorway or reed curtain, if burned in place, would produce the same surface signature as a wall that was anchored in the soil, although the cross-section would be different.

Associated Features

A double line of stains (Locus 014) delineated the exterior space to the south of the hut (figs. 7.26, 7.29, and 7.33). This feature is the remains of a reed fence line. The light brownish-gray (10YR 6/2) ashy sand lines extended from the eastern baulk for at least 15 m in a curving semicircle separating Hut 1 from Hut 2, a second hut to the south. The line extends west to the south of Hut 3, a smaller structure west of Hut 1. The feature terminates in a cluster of stains that were not excavated. These stains were probably produced by the collapse of the fence, mingled with reeds stacked against the fence.

The fence appears to have two alignments with irregularly spaced reed-bundle buttresses. The fence is shallow (< 15 cm) and lighter in color than the hut outlines; it contains less charcoal and ash. Two meters of the fence line were fully excavated, screened, and carbon and flotation samples were taken. Short alignments appear to link the fence and Hut 1 near the southwest corner of Locus 003, making the fence contemporary with the main occupation of Hut 1. One of these alignments is darker, with more charcoal and ash, and has squared buttress stains, suggesting a more substantive segment. The two linking segments form a small, enclosed space. Few sherds were recovered from Locus 014; one may have been Levantine in origin. Most of the sherds appear burned; they may have been kicked or brushed against the fence line during the occupation.

The space delineated by this fence was designated as Locus 020. A light scatter of ash and sherds covered the yellow (10YR 7/6) sand surface. This material is most likely contemporary with the occupation of Hut 1, although pale linear stains representing earlier fence lines cross the open space. Small patches of remnant ash may indicate single-use fire pits or gathered fuel/reeds. The ceramics (20 sherds) were 30% Levantine in origin and included one Cypriot milk bowl

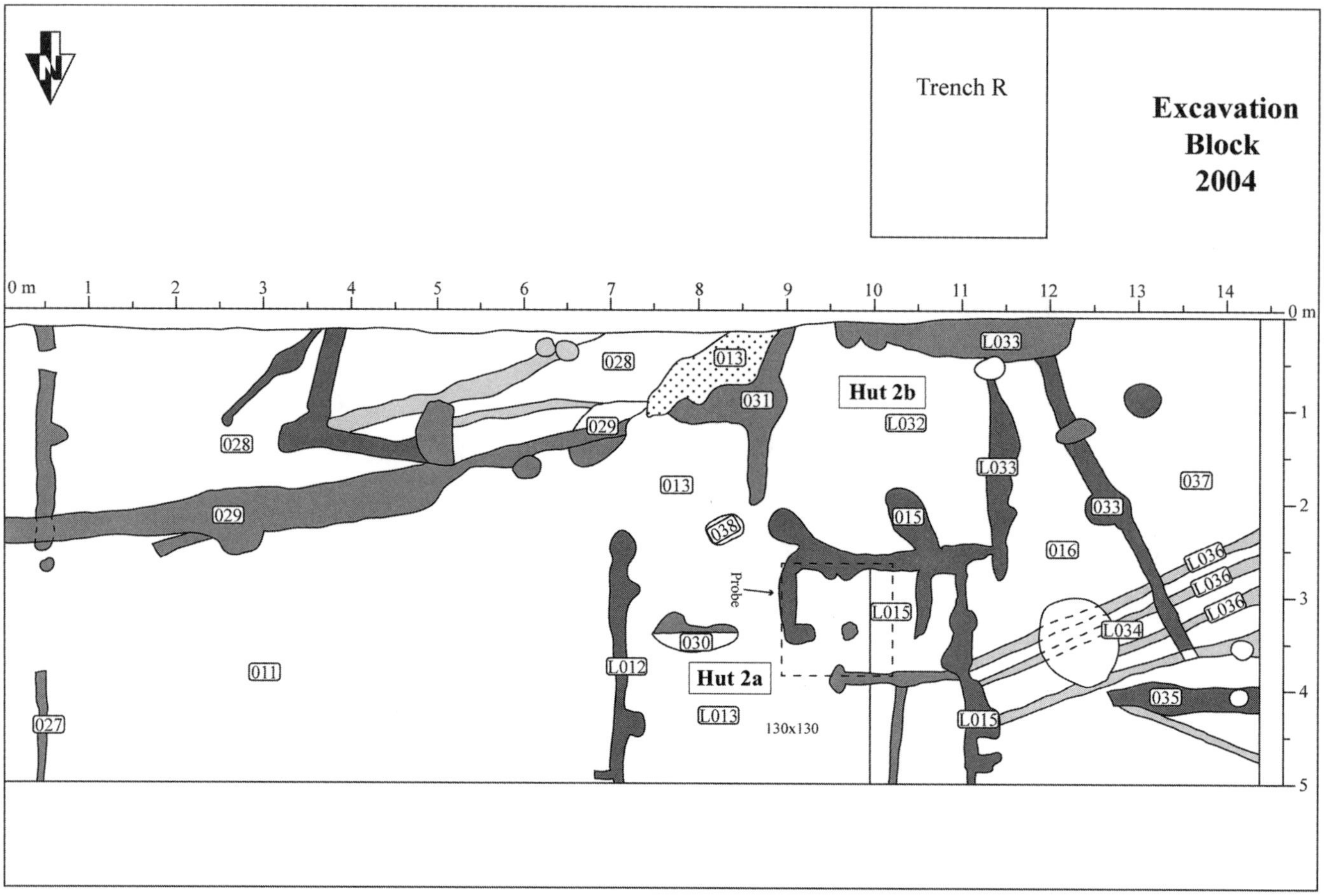

Fig. 7.36. Plan of Hut 2 and surrounding area (drawing by T. W. Davis, digitized by Joshua Olsen).

fragment and two black-rimmed bowl sherds. This early 18th Dynasty material is consistent with the material recovered from inside the hut and from the hut stain, Locus 003 (*Tell el-Borg I*, 375).

A large fire pit (Locus 002) lay within Locus 020, two m east of Locus 003 (figs. 7.26, 7.34). The stain formed an irregular oval, approximately 160 cm north–south by 200 cm east–west. Locus 002 consisted of at least 2 distinct firing episodes separated by 3–4 cm of burned sand. The radiocarbon date from 2002 came from material from the bottom layer of the fire pit. The feature contained small vitrified pottery sherds, probably present on the site when the fire pit was first used. A Levantine amphora fragment was identified among nondiagnostic New Kingdom marl sherds. Fish bones were also present.

This may have been the location of the main cooking-fire for the structure. The sand-dividing layer probably was blown over the first fire after the fire was extinguished. A second fire was then built in the same spot, suggesting that Locus 002 likely represents two closely contemporary use episodes, maybe even a daily succession of fires. The fire appears to have burned very hot: the sand is discolored and slightly vitrified. The top covering of sand appears uniform and was not burned, suggesting that the sand was blown over the fire pit after final abandonment. The fuel appears to have been dung, reeds, and small branches/roots of the local vegetation.

Feature/Hut 2 (Loci 012, 013, 015, 030, 031, 032, 033)

The Feature 2 cluster began approximately 1 m south of the main fence line, near the center of the excavation block (figs. 7.35, 7.36). The floor plan, wall construction, and most likely the function of Feature 2 were very different from Hut 1. The main structures in the Feature 2 stain cluster consisted of two squared areas adjacent to one another. The walls were uniformly thin and light in color, containing less visible charcoal and burned reed fragments. The stains evidenced the same texture as the burned lines from Hut 1. The walls do not form a continuous line, but included gaps and isolated postholes associated with the gaps. Most of the lines appeared to include reed bundles.

It is possible that the original ground surface was slightly higher in the southern portion of the Field VI, Area 1 excavation block. If so, the level at which the lines were isolated during excavation would be correspondingly deeper in relation to the original reed structure. As a result, less of the original burned lines would have been remaining when the excavation team first identified the stains. Since the reed walls narrow near the base and if the excavation surface was deeper, the remaining stains would be thinner and lighter in color, producing the feature signature that has been recorded here.

The northernmost squared structure, Hut 2A, was delineated by Locus 012 and Locus 015. The interior space measuring 3.75 m east–west by 2.75 m north–south and was designated Locus 013. Locus 012 was a relatively thin (15 cm) stain, running north–south for approximately 3.35 m. The line terminated on the north end with a west facing hook for 40 cm, which terminated in an isolated posthole approximately 12 cm in diameter and 15 cm from the end of Locus 012. The southern end of Locus 012 was a reed bundle; at least three reed bundles buttressed the line. The stain had a depth of only 7 cm. This is unlikely to be a major structure, perhaps simply a screen or flimsy animal pen.

Locus 015 was a complex sequence of reed stains that delineated the north, south, and west sides of Hut 2A. The northern side of Hut 2A was partially closed, with a short reed alignment and two separate reed posts forming the side. The placement of the reed posts suggests a designed entryway, although there is less than a meter separating the fence line from the edge of Hut 2A. It is impossible to determine if the fence line was present at the same time as Hut 2A.

The west side of Locus 015 is very uneven, showing evidence of five reed bundles. The average depth is 5–7 cm, but the reed bundles go down at least 15 cm. The southwest corner of Hut 2A contains a rectangular inner room, 1.75 m × 1.25 m. A separate post appears to screen the small 20–25 cm opening. The northern closing reed alignment appears to be only abutted to the main outline of Locus 015 and may indicate either a movable screen or a later addition, changing the function of the smaller space. The small screened space leaves a 1.50 m opening along the south side of Hut 2A. A line of 3 larger posts or supports, approximately 40 cm south of the opening in Hut 2A, makes a partial screen along the length of the south side of Locus 015. The easternmost post is isolated (Locus 038) but in line with the southern terminal post of Locus 012, suggesting a more open screened area, perhaps with the posts supporting a roof, creating a primitive portico. This post was sectioned and removed. A relatively large fire pit isolated inside of Hut 2A (Locus 030) supports the idea of a more open space. The fire pit 55 cm × 110 cm, yielded small fragments of burned bone and some fish bones but no ceramics. Locus 013 was heavily stained with nonaligned burned patches, smeared across the surface; these ashy stains may be the remains of the roofing material. Locus 013 yielded only a small number of pottery sherds, including black-rimmed bowls and Levantine sherds. Locus 013 yielded 1 red-slip bowl base used as a tool of unknown function. It was perforated and had soot marks on it.

Hut 2B, south of Hut 2A, was a more enclosed space delineated by substantive linear staining, Loci 031, 033, and the southern line of 015. The delineated interior space, Locus 032, measures 2.40 m × 2.30 m. The interior of "Hut 2B" yielded ash patches, ceramics, and bone fragments. The material was clustered along the eastern half of the space, with the western portion almost barren. Huts 2A and 2B appear to be contemporary structures as the western stain of Locus 033 joins the Hut 2A alignment at the northwest corner of Hut 2B. Unfortunately, a modern robber pit has destroyed the corner linkage along the south edge of Hut 2B. Locus 33 extended at least 10 cm into the surrounding matrix, with even burning. Reed bundles are visible to a depth of 15 cm and suggest an actual structural role. One bundle measured nearly 40 cm across.

The southern wall of Hut 2B may be something much more substantive, because it is nearly 50 cm wide and extends into the southern baulk separating the main trench from Trench R. Two reed-bundle posts mark the eastern end of this stain immediately adjacent to each other. A 50 cm gap separates them from the tail of the eastern alignment of Hut 2B (Locus 031). Locus 031 had a depth of 6–10 cm and yielded a crocodile scale. It is possible that the central space in Hut 2B was accessed from the south, although the apparent association with Hut 2A suggests a focus to the north and east.

Associated Features

There appears to be a well-delineated courtyard, marked by a thin fence line (Locus 027) running along the eastern baulk of Area 1, the main fence line (Locus 014), and a long linear feature, probably another fence-type structure, along the south edge of Area 1 (Locus 29) (fig. 7.36). Locus 011 is the material from this courtyard, south of the main fence and outside of the Hut 2 cluster of stains.

The ceramic subassemblage from Locus 011, although limited in number, comprised an unusually high percentage of Levantine wares (> 30%). Most of the sherds were tiny and abraded heavily, suggesting exposure to animal/foot traffic and wind abrasion. The subassemblage included four black-rimmed bowl fragments and other early to mid-18th Dynasty marls. The identifiable forms were small bowls and small store-jars.

Locus 027 is a very thin stain in two sections, probably a fence, which delineates the eastern edge of the open area of Locus 011. The two north–south segments are separated by a gap of 1.40 m; the gap appears to be a part of the construction, with two possible posts flanking it. A later barrier, Locus 029, overrides the southern segment. Locus 027 is too insubstantial to be a structure but may indicate a separation of activity or even of control.

Locus 029 is a major stain forming a concave line running from the east baulk toward the south, where it terminates at the eastern extension of Locus 031. It is possible that Locus 031 should actually be considered an element of the barrier line and not a hut member. Originally, the main stain was very broad and mottled, indicating a mixture of sources. Upon further excavation, it narrowed to appear to be a robust curved fence, with a visible indentation sloping toward the center of the line. It separates the open area east of Feature 2. This barrier may echo Locus 014, the double fence line delineating Hut 1. The fence overrides a small fire pit, Locus 29, near Hut 2B. This indicates a change in function, perhaps seasonally. South of the barrier, a complex series of lines running into the south baulk indicates that the *quartier* extends beyond the excavated area. Locus 028 is the nonstain areas south of the barrier line. This area yielded a few small nondiagnostic sherds and a fishbone in general clean-up, suggesting ancient use.

West of Hut 2A–B, a long (3.60 m) stain extends toward the northwest from the southern portion of Locus 033, outsider of the Hut 2B walls. This stain has three distinctive reed buttresses

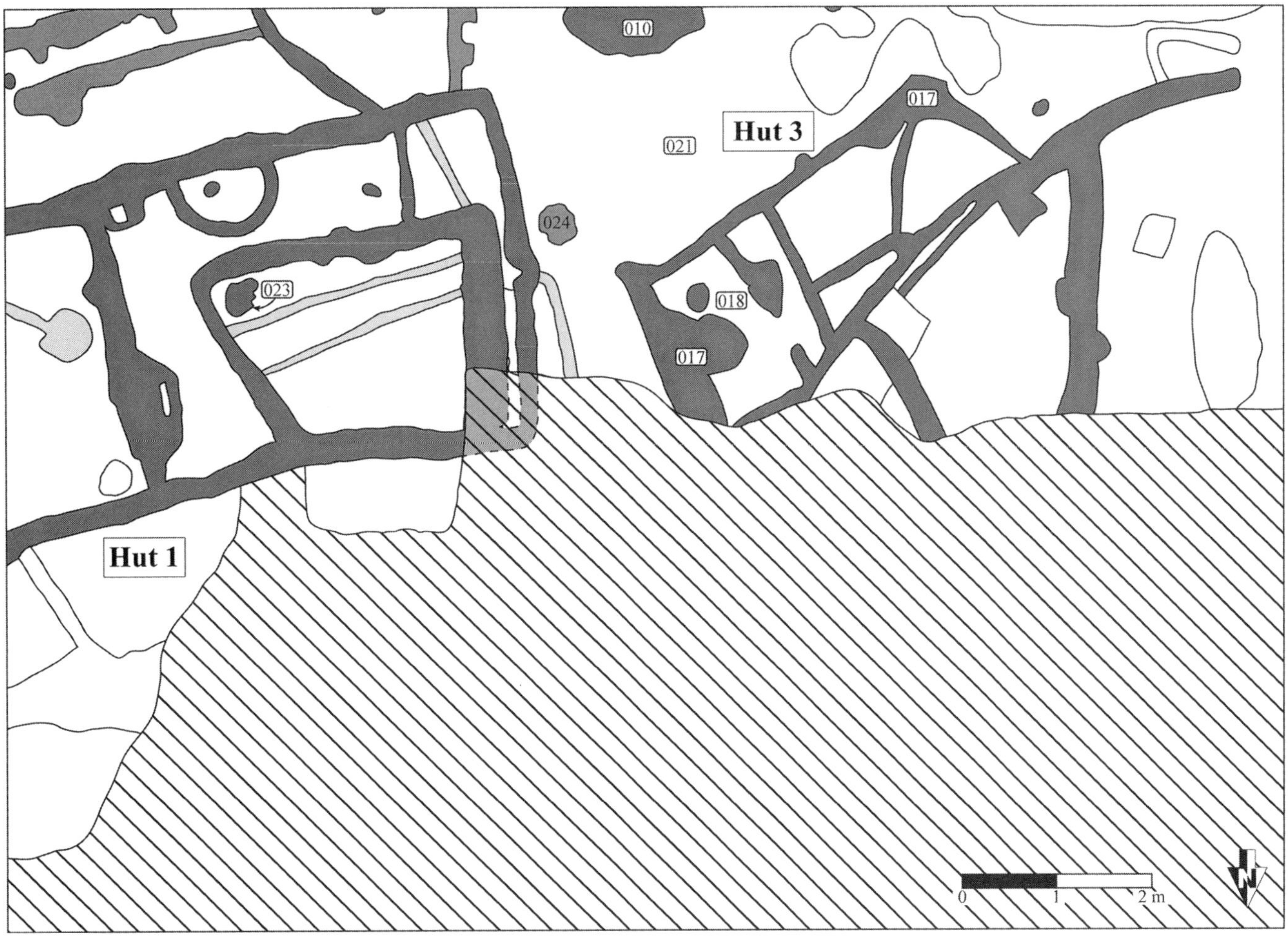

Fig. 7.37. Hut 1 (western half) and Hut 3 (Drawing by Thomas Davis, digitized by Joshua Olsen).

supporting it. The resultant triangular space isolated as Locus 016 encompasses a large (75 cm diameter) but very shallow fire pit/ashy stain designated Locus 034. The shallow staining designated Locus 034 appears to have been blown over the earlier lines beneath it and may not have been a constructed pit. This material may be associated with activity areas as yet unrecorded since Hut 2A and 2B appear to be oriented east. A deep (29 cmbs) V-shaped stain, 35 cm in width, extended approximately 1.70 m east from the western baulk. It is rather substantive and may be the remnant of another hut, located under the western baulk. This may be associated with what appears to be another open space, Locus 037, which extends into the southern and western baulks.

Feature 3 (Loci 010, 017, 018, 020, 024, 026?)

The Feature 3 stain cluster was identified approximately 1.50 m west of the west wall of Hut 1, north of Fence 014 (fig. 7.37). The lines were cleared but not excavated. The lines appear to be the outline of a large double hut, extending into the disturbed zone to the north. A rectangular closed shape, 1.25 × 3.00 m, extends almost to the fence line. This is attached to a much larger curving line, with two extensions running to the north. This may be a larger hut similar to Hut 1. Extensive disturbance west and north of these features and within them made their excavation a lower priority. A large 1.0 m × 2.0 m fire pit (Locus 026), which appears ancient, lies along the western baulk. No fish bones were identified, although flotation samples were taken. The pit yielded few sherds, which suggests that it was ancient, because the modern pits tended to include more sherds and other material from the surface.

A small storage or trash pit, 50 cm wide by 15 cm deep (Locus 024), is located near the west wall of Hut 1 within the open area between the features. The pit yielded a bronze knife, charcoal, and a minimal subassemblage of small sherds. Its ancient nature cannot be definitively proved due to the absence of fish bones. It does not appear to have a structural function.

Locus 010 is a fire pit measuring 0.85 × 1.60 m, located southeast of Feature 3 and southwest of Feature 1, within the curve of the fence line. Ovoid in shape, the pit evidenced relatively intense burning, with numerous fragments of burned reed. A fair amount of fish bones are present, so this appears to be an ancient fire pit. Carbon samples and four liters of flotation were taken. No other cultural material was recovered.

Earlier Occupation

At least two phases of activity are visible in Field VI, Area 1. When Locus 006 was cleared, a faint stain running southeast–northwest was uncovered. The stain terminated in a round post-hole/reed bundle hole near the west wall of Locus 006. The main structure wall cut the stain and clearly predated Feature 1. The earlier phase line continued beyond the southeast corner of the structure, was crossed by the main fence line (Locus 014), and continued to the east baulk of the excavation block (figs. 7.26, 7.33). This likely represents an earlier fence line, because it was much thinner at the base than the main structure outline. Previous phase lines were also visible within Loci 008 and 009, although no coherent structure could be determined. A fire pit (Locus 023) within Locus 009 may be associated with the earlier activity in Field VI. This earlier occupation may have been separated from the main phase by a very short interval. No visible charcoal was seen in the early lines, and they seem to be the product of surface sands filling in when structures were removed. No pottery could be definitively associated with the earlier lines. It is unlikely but not impossible that Locus 025 represents a structural remnant of the earlier occupation, although if so, all connections have since disappeared.

A series of thin parallel lines (Locus 036) cross the open area 016, west of Hut 2A (fig. 7.36). The lines underlay the fire pit Locus 034. They appear to be a series of small fences that terminate at the west wall of Hut 2A. Earlier phase lines are also visible south of the open area to the east of Hut 2A and under Feature 3. The lines do not form discernible structures. Except for the earlier phase lines under Hut 1, the earlier material only survives in the open courtyard(?) areas of the excavation zone.

A small 1.50 × 1.50 m probe was excavated within the square feature in Hut 2A. This probe was excavated to a depth of 1.50 m into sterile sand. No cultural material was recovered from the probe. This confirms the negative results of the 2002 shovel tests regarding the absence of any deeply buried cultural deposits in Field VI.

Excursus: Pottery from Field VI.1 AA

Rexine Hummel

Field VI.1 AA produced a large number of diagnostic sherds, all of which were drawn and registered in the database. Many of the sherds came from disturbed contexts and represent dates ranging from the late 2IP to the early 19th Dynasty.

Plate 7.1 presents a selection of sherds whose dates range mainly from the beginning of the 18th Dynasty to the end of the reign of Thutmose III. Because of the long lifetime and popularity of some ceramic forms it is possible that some examples might date as early as the 2IP and others might linger into the Amarna Period.

Pottery Plate 7.1

1:1 Rim of narrow beaker (drop pot). Prov: VI.1 AA.1 basket 4 (Surface Fill). Dia: 7 cm. (11%) Preserved height: 3 cm. Ware: Marl B. Surface: uncoated.
Parallel: Seiler 1997: pl. III, fig. 5 ZN 94/69 (Hebua I, early 18th Dynasty).

1:2 Rim of narrow beaker (drop pot). Prov: VI.1 AA.1 basket 4 (Surface Fill). Dia: 9 cm. (12.5%). Preserved height: 3.8 cm. Ware: Nile B2. Surface: wet-smoothed.
Parallel: Aston 1997: 189:12, (Hebua IV, mid-18th Dynasty).

1:3 Rim of narrow beaker. (drop pot). Prov: VI.1 AA.20 basket 2. (between fence and hut). Dia: 10 cm. (2.5%) Preserved height: 3.5 cm. Ware: Nile B2. Surface: red slip with two horizontal black bands below the rim.
Parallel: Bourriau et al 2005: 110 "black-banded decoration on red slip is popular in the early New Kingdom"

1:4 Rim of beaker (drop pot). Prov: VI.1 AA.18 basket 2 (inside feature 3). Dia: 11 cm. (12%) Preserved height: 7.5 cm. Ware: Nile B2, Surface: horizontal, incised line on neck.
Parallels: Seiler 1997: pl. II, fig. 4 ZN94/9. (Hebua I, early 18th Dynasty), Aston 1996: tafel 4:13, (dated Thutmose IV–Amenhotep), Bourriau 2010: 137:4.12.1 (Memphis, early to mid-18th Dynasty).

1:5 Rim of jar. Prov: VI.1 AA.11 basket 2 (same level as occupation). Dia: 12.5 cm. (20%) Preserved height: 3.5 cm. Ware: Nile B2. Surface: uncoated and abraded.
Parallel: Bourriau 2010: 129:10.4.3. (Memphis, early to mid-18th Dynasty).

1:6 Rim of jar. Prov: VI.1 AA.11 (occupation debris). Dia: 15cm. (11%) Preserved height: 8 cm. Ware: Nile B2. Surface: wet-smoothed.
Parallel: Bourriau 2010: 128:10.4.3. (Memphis, early to mid-18th Dynasty)

1:7 Rim of jar. Prov: VI.I AA 23 (pit in room 9 of Hut 1) Dia: 13 cm. Preserved height: 10.5 cm. Ware: Nile B2. Surface: uncoated, soot inside and out.
Parallels: Aston 1997: 189:11, (Hebwa IV, mid-18th Dynasty), Bourriau 1997: fig. 6.16: 14 and 16 (late 2IP).

Black-Rimmed Bowls

A total of 183 black-rimmed bowls were recorded at Tell el-Borg, clustering particularly in the cemetery Field III and the settlement area of Field VI. Black rims have been used by ceramicists as a chronological marker for the 2nd Intermediate Period (2IP) and early New Kingdom. Bourriau states that "a black rim on Nile Silt wares became fashionable during the late 2IP but died out early in the reign of Thutmose III."[6]

6. Bourriau 2005: 111.

1:8 Rim of bowl. Prov: VI.1 AA.11 basket 2 (same level as occupation). Dia: 20 cm. (10%). Preserved height: 3 cm. Ware: Fine Nile B2. Surface: red slip in and out, wide black rim out, and narrow black rim inside.
Parallel: Seiler 1997: pl.I, fig. 1 ZN94/125 (Hebua I, early 18th Dynasty).

1:9 Rim of bowl. Prov: VI.1AA.11 basket 2 (same level as occupation). Dia: 21 cm (25%). Preserved height: 3 cm. Ware: Nile B2. Surface: red slip in and out, wide black rim out and narrow black rim inside.
Parallel: Seiler 1997: pl. I, fig. 1 ZN94/125 (Hebua I, early 18th Dynasty).

1:10 Intact simple bowl. VI.1 AA.1 TBP 657 (surface fill). Dia: 19 cm. (11%). Preserved height: 5 cm. Ware: Nile B2. Surface: Traces of red slip on exterior and rim area of interior, tiny fragments of red slip on interior. The entire bowl may have been originally coated with red slip but the slip is mostly worn off.
Parallel: Aston 1998: 100–101, fig. 83 (Qantir, late 2IP).

1:11 Rim of carinated bowl. Prov: VI.1 AA.12 basket 2. Dia: 20 cm. (5%). Preserved height: 2.5 cm. Ware: Nile B2. Surface: red slip inside and out with black rim.
Parallels: Seiler 1997: pl. I, fig. 1 ZN94/127(Hebua I early 18th Dynasty); Aston 1998: 87:1 (Qantir, late 2IP).

1:12 Rim of bowl. Prov: VI.1 AA.11 basket 1 (occupation debris) Dia: 19 cm. (2%). Preserved height: 4 cm. Ware: Nile B2. Surface: red slip in and out with black rim.
Parallel: Seiler 1997: pl. I, fig. 1 ZN94/125 (Hebua I early 18th Dynasty).

1:13 Rim of carinated bowl. Prov: VI.1 AA.11 basket 2 (same level as occupation). Dia: 19 cm. (6%) Preserved height: 3 cm. Ware: Marl B. Surface: smoothed.
Parallels: Wodzińska 2010: 132:128 (early 18th Dynasty); Bourriau 2010: fig. 4.12.1; Bourriau 1997: fig. 6.15, 22, and 26 (Memphis, late 2IP through early 18th Dynasty).

Pottery Plate 7.2

2:1 Intact flower pot. Prov: VI.1 AA.1 TBP 658. Dia: 25 cm. Preserved height: 7 cm. Ware: Nile E. Surface: untreated. Hole pierced in base before firing.
Parallels: Bourriau 2010: 4.12.1, Bourriau 1997: fig. 6.15, 22, and 26 (Memphis, late 2IP through early 18th Dynasty); Dorner and Aston 1997: pl. I:7 (Hebua IV South, mid-18th Dynasty).

2:2 Rim of large carinated bowl. Prov: VI.1 AA 1 (surface fill). Dia: 36 cm. (10%) Preserved height: 6 cm. Ware: Surface: red slip in and out, black tics on rsim.
Parallel: Bourriau 2010: fig. 4.12.1 (Memphis, late 2IP through early 18th Dynasty).

2:3 Rim of bread tray. Prov: VI.1 AA.1 TBP 659 (surface). Dia: 34 cm. Preserved height: 6 cm. Ware: Marl E. Surface: Gritty and deeply incised with a geometric design, surface has spalled off.
Parallels: Bourriau 2010: 134, fig. 2.4.1 (Memphis, early to mid 18th Dynasty); Bourriau 1997: fig. 6.15, 22, and 26 (Memphis, late 2IP through early 18th Dynasty).

2:4 Rim of bowl. Prov: VI.I AA.1. Diam: 39 cm. Preserved height: 6.5 Ware: Nile E Surface: burned inside and out.
Parallel: Bourriau 2010: 127: fig. 4.18.3 (Memphis, early to mid 18th Dynasty)

2:5 Rim of large bowl. Prov: VI.I AA 11 basket 2 (same level as occupation). Dia: 37 cm. Preserved height: 7 cm. Ware: Nile B2/C. Surface: uncoated and abraded.
Parallels: Fuscaldo 1998: fig. 1e (late 2IP); Bourriau 2010: 130, fig. 3.10.9 (Memphis, late 2IP through early 18th Dynasty).

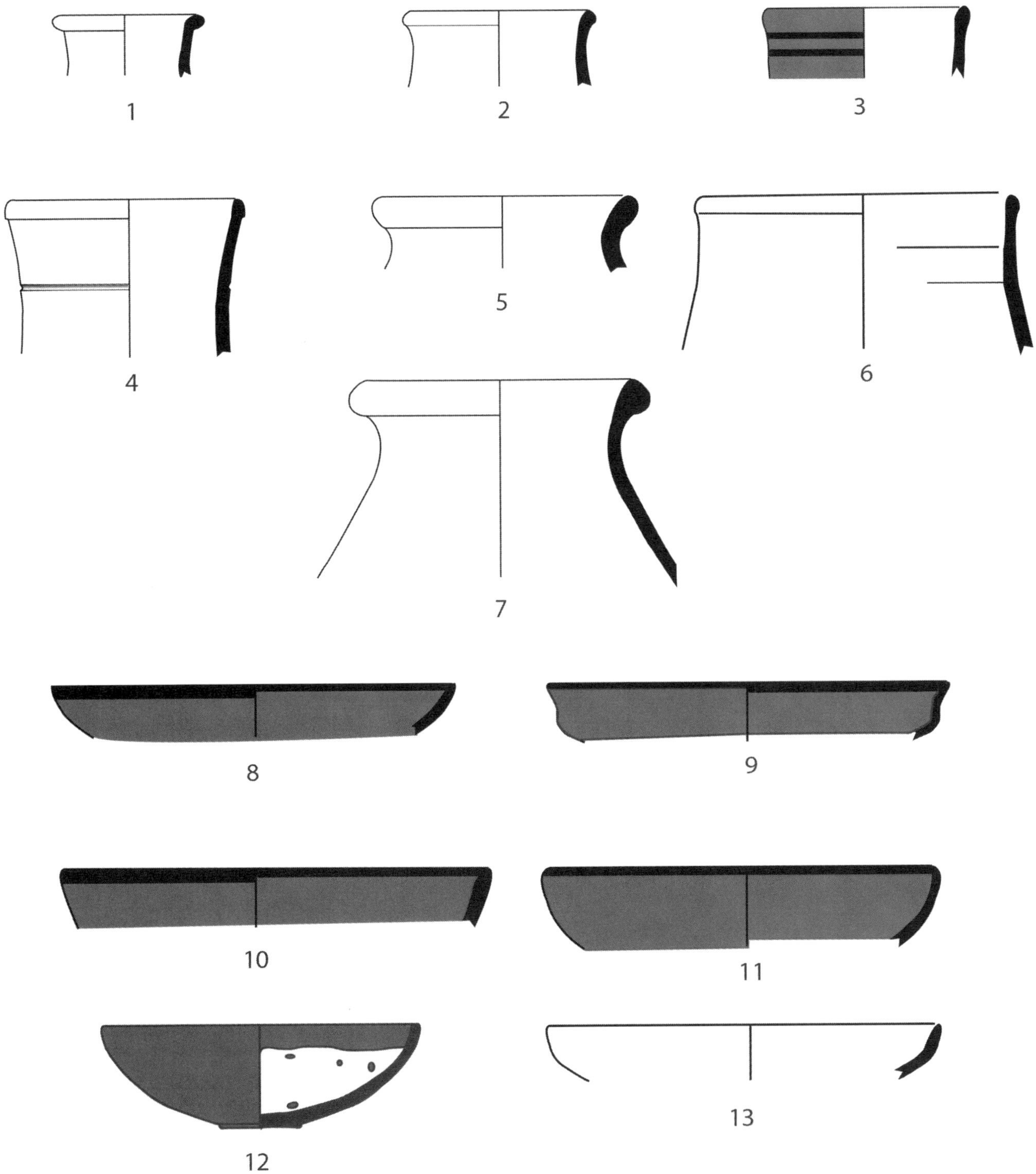

POTTERY PLATE 7.1 1:3

Computerized drawings by L. Pinch-Brock

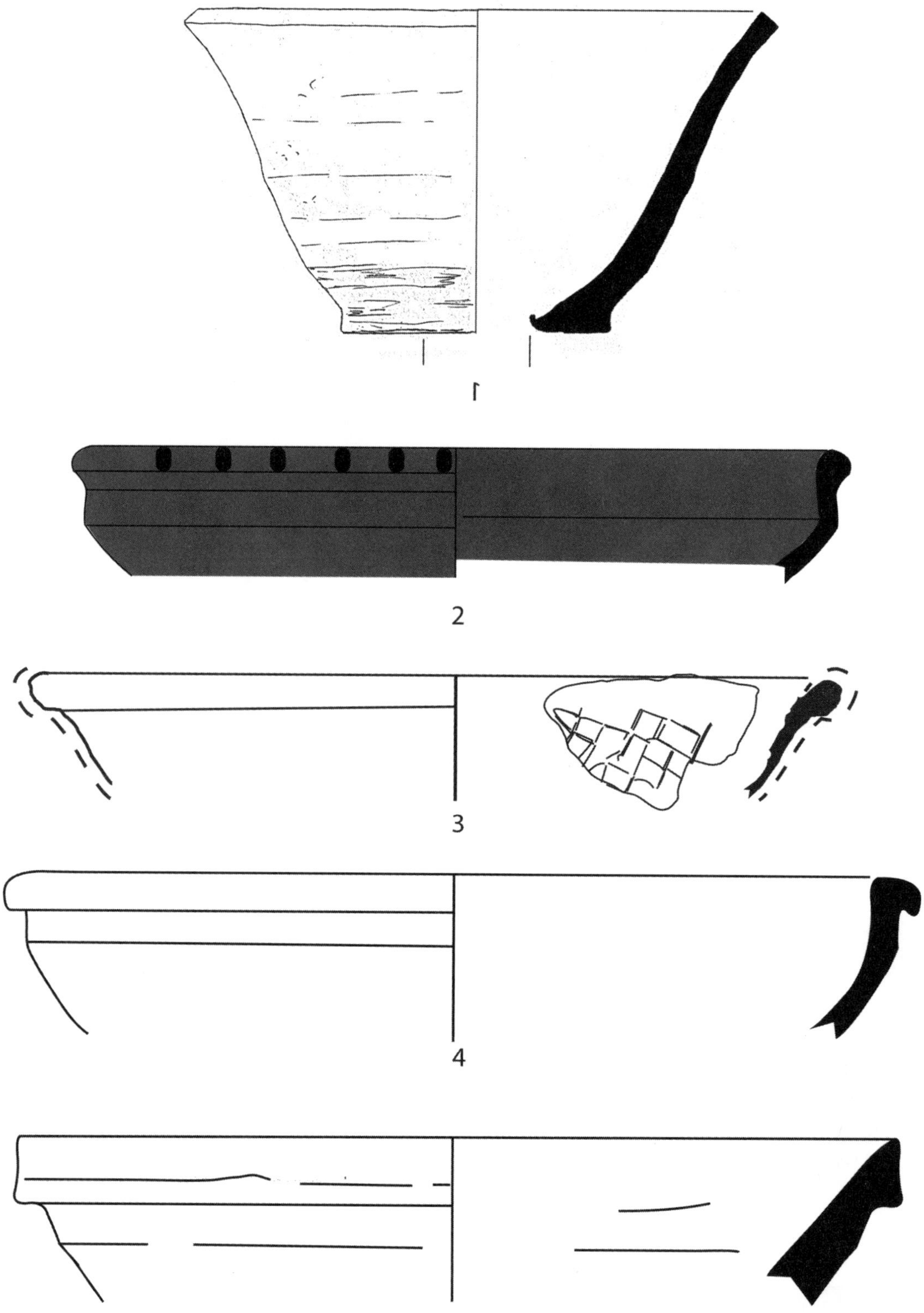

POTTERY PLATE 7.2 1:3

Computerized drawings by L. Pinch-Brock

Works Cited

Aston, David
1996 "Tell Hebwa IV Preliminary Report on the Pottery." *Ägypten und Levante* 6: 177–97.
1998 *Die Keramik des Grabungplatzes Q1, Teil 1: Corpus of Fabrics, Ware and Shapes*. Mainz.

Bourriau, Janine
1997 "Beyond Avaris: The Second Intermediate Period in Egypt Outside, The Eastern Delta." Pp. 159–182 in E. Oren (ed.) *The Hyksos: New Historical and Archaeological Perspectives, I.* University Museum Monograph 96. Philadelphia.
2010 *The Survey of Memphis IV, Kom Rabia: The New Kingdom Pottery*. Excavation Memoir 93. Egypt Exploration Society, London.

Bourriau, Janine, et al.
2005 "The Second Intermediate Period and Early New Kingdom at Deir Al-Barsha." *Ägypten und Levante* 15: 101–23.

Dorner, J., and Aston, D.
1997 "Pottery from Hebua South." Pp. 41–44 in *Cahiers de la Céramique* Égyptienne 5. Cairo.

Fuscaldo, Perla
1998 "A Preliminary Report on the pottery from the Late Hyksos Period Settlement at 'Ezbet Helmi (Area H/III, Strata D/3 and D/2)." *Ägypten und Levante* 7: 59–69.

Seiler, Anne
1997 "Hebua I, Second Intermediate Period and Early New Kingdom." Pp. 23–24 in *Cahiers de la Céramique Égyptienne* 5. Cairo.

Wodzińska Anna
2010 *A Manual of Egyptian Pottery, Volume 3: Second Intermediate Period–Late Period.* AERA Field Manual Series I, Ancient Egypt Research Associates. Boston.

Area 1 Discussion

Chronology

The original 2002 conventional carbon dating from Field VI Area 1 indicated a late Middle Kingdom/early New Kingdom date for the features. The four dates from the 2005 season, run as AMS dates, provide a more accurate picture. The dates suggest at least 2 phases of occupation on the site, a late Second Intermediate/early New Kingdom date and the main occupation in the early 18th Dynasty. A fire pit (Locus 023) overlain by Hut 1 yielded an AMS radiocarbon date of 3310±40 BP, with a 2 sigma-calibrated range of 1690–1510 B.C. The other three dates indicate a relatively tight date range for the main phase of the occupation. The 2 sigma-calibrated date ranges are: 1530–1410 B.C. from the fence line (locus 014); 1500–1380 B.C. from a fire pit (Locus 010); and 1530–1400 B.C. from Hut 1 (Locus 003). All three dates show the features are contemporaneous and date to the pre-Amarna period. The entire final complex appears to have been destroyed at the same time, because the stains from the later phase share the same characteristics in terms of color, texture, and evidence of burning. The total ceramic assemblage from Field VI supports the radiocarbon dates. The predominant black-rimmed bowls, an early to mid-18th Dynasty type, also falls into this range (pottery plates 7.1–7.3). The Cypriot imports have a use-life that overlaps with the bowls, as does the Mycenaean material. The diagnostic Levantine material also falls into the earlier half of the Late Bronze Age sequence. Taken together, this material indicates that the Field VI settlement was occupied during the early 18th Dynasty, probably contemporary with the early fosse fort. This area of the site may not have been occupied domestically during the second half of the 18th Dynasty and Ramesside period.

Spatial Organization and Activities

The floor plan of the reed features uncovered in Field VI Area 1 suggests conscious spatial organization. The major fence lines appear to separate the visible features into four major clusters: Hut 1, Hut 3, and their accompanying courtyards, Locus 020; Hut 2A, 2B, and Loci 011, 013, 016, and 037; and the area to the south of fence line (Locus 029). Both major fence lines were replaced at least once in their use life. This spatial separation suggests the delineation of nuclear family space within a larger kinship grouping.

The organization of the Hut 1/Hut 3 cluster suggests organized activity areas. Most communal tasks probably took place in the open courtyard inside the fence and outside of the hut outline. The external fire pits (Loci 002, 010, and possibly 026) indicate that cooking and food preparation occurred outside of the huts. The obvious danger of fire makes this a rational choice. This is supported by the recovery of groundstone tool fragments from either disturbed contexts above the open courtyards or from the clean-up of the courtyards. The phasing of fires in Locus 002 indicate repetitive activity, although the fires could have been lit within a very short time and do not necessarily imply abandonment and reoccupation of the hut. Cooking was probably by direct heat, using ceramic cooking vessels, because no identifiable boiling stones were found.

The floor plan of Hut 2A and 2B is not as clear as Hut 1. Hut 2B is more closed, with Hut 2A having a very open plan. Hut 2B may have been the sleeping space, with Hut 2A being a more communal space. Hut 2A is marked by the distinctive use of isolated reed bundles, which may have held up a roof, creating a portico-like effect. A small fire pit, probably contemporary with the use of Hut 2A, provides a focal point immediately in front of a small squared-off space. The small size of the fire and its location within the apparent boundaries of the space suggest that it may have fulfilled a social rather than a purely utilitarian function.

It is tempting to associate this structure with a more overtly communal role, such as a gathering place for the family or a larger kinship unit. Hut 2A has an oblique opening onto a wide courtyard area (Locus 011) measuring more than 36 m^2. Locus 011 has no fire pit or other structural indications of domestic activity. This could have been a family/clan gathering place. Perhaps the small squared-off space within Hut 2A was set aside for the use of a single high status individual or to store/display a significant artifact. The minimal size of the directly associated material assemblage precludes any definitive statements.

Another possibility is that Hut 2A and 2B are short-term animal pens reused and rebuilt during the occupation of the main huts. The flotation from Field VI identified sheep dung, indicating that domestic animals were quartered among the human occupants.

The ceramic subassemblage from the excavation in Field VI Area 1 is almost entirely domestic in character, with small black-rimmed bowls and small store-jars predominant. The amount of pottery recovered in situ is small, although it is consistent with the overlying disturbed material. This subassemblage probably represents household utilitarian wares. A relatively large amount of Levantine material was recovered, in some case nearly 40% of a locus assemblage. A few luxury items were also recovered from here, although very few luxury imports were from good contexts. The Cypriot subassemblage included sherds of White Slip I and II milk bowls, Base Ring I and II juglets, and Red-Burnished wares. Mycenaean stirrup-jar fragments and stone vessel fragments were also found. Of course, the luxury items recovered from disturbed contexts may be associated with activities dating after the burning of the huts and were intermixed by subsequent deflation and modern activity.

The variety of nonceramic material recovered from the area indicates generalized domestic life. The evident deflation of the area, combined with mechanical stripping during the modern

Table 7.4. Small Finds Discovered in 2004–2005 in Field VI Area 1, A/AA

TBO	*Unit/Locus*	*Object Type*	*Material*	*Measurements*
0602	Area 1 surface	point of tool	copper/copper alloy	1.0 × 0.2 dia cm
0636[a]	Area 1 surface	chipped stone tool	chert	.24 × .34 × 0.5 cm
0872[b]	Area 1 surface	chipped stone blade	chert	6.4 × 3.38 × 0.8 cm
0605	Area 1 Locus 001	blade fragment	copper/copper alloy	1 × 0.8 × 0.3 cm
0606	Area 1 Locus 001	bead	carnelian	0.3 × 0.4 dia cm
0609[c]	Area 1 Locus 001	spearhead	copper/copper alloy	9.1 × 2.2 × 0.3 cm
0612	Area 1 Locus 001	fragment of tool (?)	copper/copper alloy	3.7 × 0.6 dia cm
0631	Area 1 Locus 001	bead	carnelian	0.4 × 0.3 dia cm
0635[d]	Area 1 Locus 001	chipped stone blade	chert	3.2 × 2.6 × 0.9 cm
0603	Area 1 Locus 011	tool fragment	copper/copper alloy	1.4 × 0.6 dia cm
0604	A Locus 020	2 piece of cylindrical tool	copper/copper alloy	3.7 × 0.5 dia cm 2.2 × 0.8 dia cm
0544[e]	AA surface	chipped stone blade	chert	4.1 × 1.5 × .42 dia cm
0540	AA Locus 001	fragment of grindstone	sandstone	8.0 × 6.5 × 5.2 cm
0835[f]	AA Locus 003	spearhead	copper/copper alloy	7.2 × 1.9 × 0.3 cm
0538	AA/E Locus 007	game piece or token	clay	0.9 × 2.2 dia cm
0601[g]	AA Locus 011	serrated chipped stone blade	chert	3.3 × 3.0 × 0.7 cm
0610[h]	AA Locus 015	chipped stone blade	chert	3.1 × 1.6 × .47 cm
0537	AA Locus 018	bead	faience	0.1 × 0.3 dia cm
0536	AA Locus 020	large spherical bead	clay	0.4 × 2.0 cm dia
0611	AA Locus 029	bead	faience	0.4 × 0.5 cm dia
0614	AA Locus 034	flat bead	faience	0.2 × 0.9 dia cm
0615	AA Locus 034	Taweret amulet	faience	2.2 × 1.1 × 0.42 cm
0618	AA Locus 034	piece of bent metal	copper/copper alloy	2.5 × 1.0 × 0.5 cm
0637	AA Locus 038	chipped stone blade fragment	chert	1.9 × 1.5 × 0.4 cm
0539	BB Locus 011	rectangular stone fragment	sandstone	6.2 × 5.2 × 2.9 cm

a. TBO 0636 is treated in chapter 10, p. 375.
b. TBO 0872 is treated in chapter 10, p. 373.
c. TBO 0609 is treated in *Tell el-Borg I*, 518–20.
d. TBO 0635 is treated in chapter 10, p. 375.
e. TBO 0544 is treated in chapter 10, p. 375.
f. TBO 0835 is treated in *Tell el-Borg I*, 518–20.
g. TBO 0601 is treated in chapter 10, p. 370.
h. TBO 0610 is treated in chapter 10, p. 374.

Fig. 7.38. Point of copper/copper alloy tool, TBO 0602.

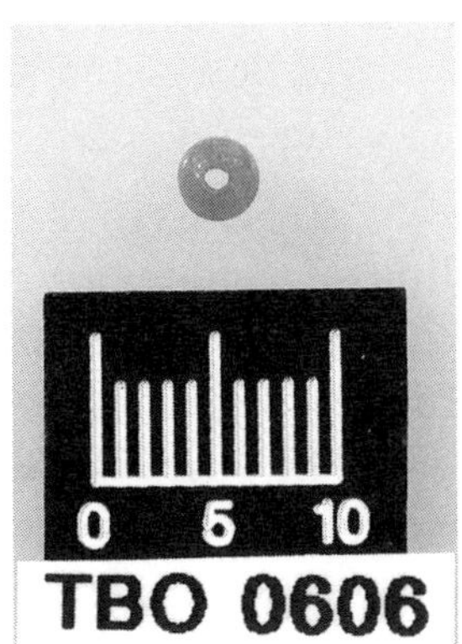

Fig. 7.39. Carnelian bead, TBO 0606.

Fig. 7.40. Fragment of copper/copper alloy tool, TBO 0612.

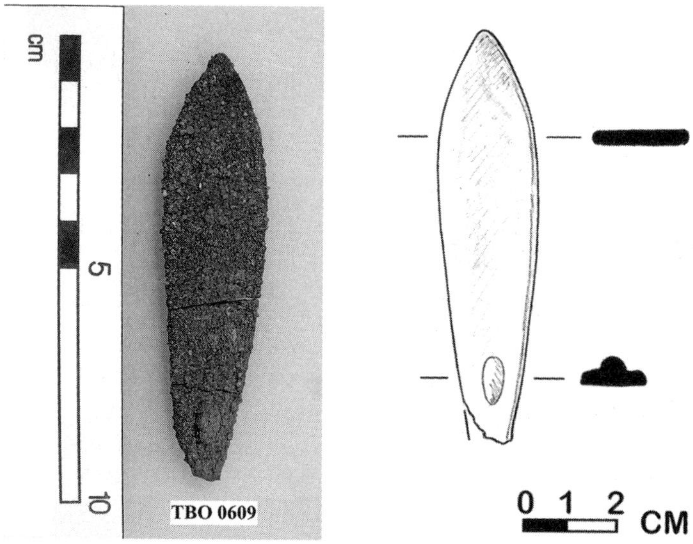

Fig. 7.41. **a** (left): Photo, TBO 0609, copper/copper alloy spearhead before conservation; **b** (right): After conservation, drawing by Lyla Pinch-Brock.

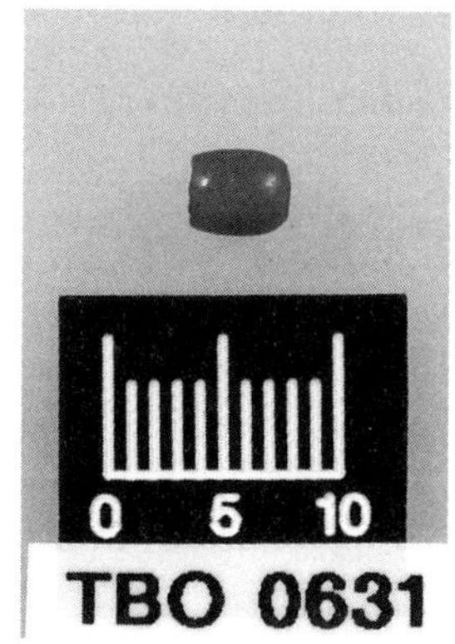

Fig. 7.42. Carnelian bead, TBO 0631.

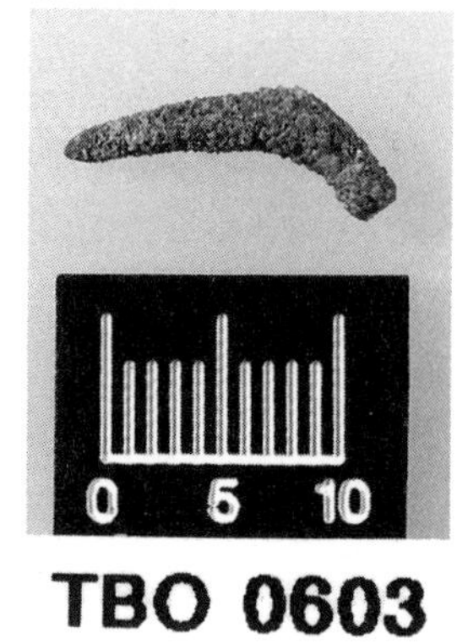

Fig. 7.43. Copper/copper alloy tool fragment, TBO 0603.

Fig. 7.44. Copper/copper alloy tool fragments, TBO 0604.

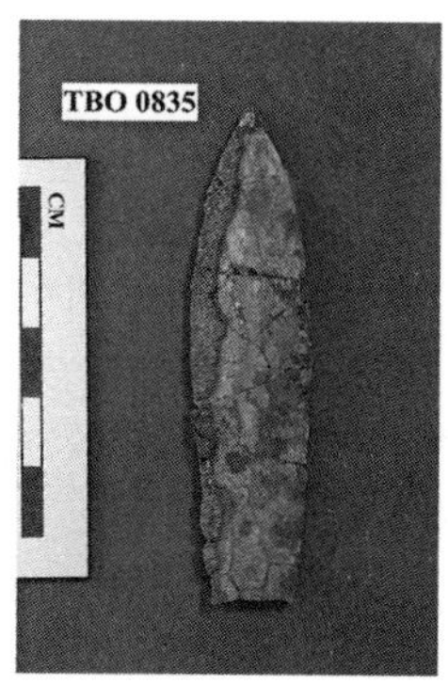

Fig. 7.45. Copper/copper spearhead, TBO 0835.

Fig. 7.46. Clay sherd token or game piece, TBO 0538.

Fig. 7.47. Large clay bead, TBO 0536.

military occupation, created a palimpsest of material, preventing the affiliation of most of the recovered finds with a distinctive occupational/chronological episode. The copper alloy knife recovered from the small storage/refuse pit (TBO 0494) was broken in antiquity; this knife was not a weapon but a tool. Other copper alloy finds included needle fragments. The flint artifacts recovered were probably used in compound tools, perhaps to cut the reeds or to harvest local grains. One arrowhead fragment was recovered. Outside the excavated area, a suite of groundstone tools were recovered in the general surface collection of Field VI. It is likely that this type of site materiel would have remained here on a semipermanent basis. The groundstone tools were probably used for food processing.

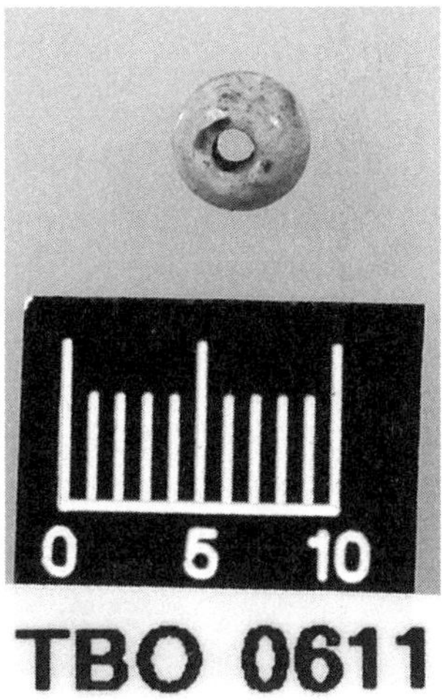

Fig. 7.48. Faience bead, TBO 0611.

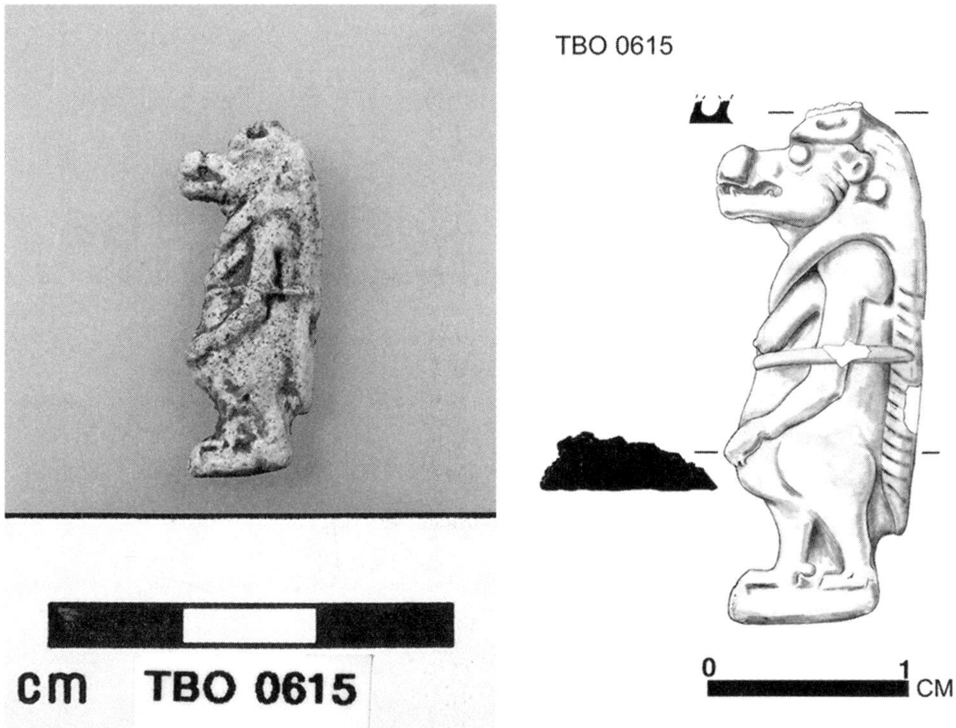

Fig. 7.49a and b (right). Faience Taweret amulet, TBO 0615.

Fig. 7.50a and b (left). Sandstone grindstone (?) fragment, TBO 0539.

Personal items include a variety of beads and a small but elegant and detailed fertility amulet showing Taweret, the hippopotamus goddess (TBO 0615).[7] A number of deliberately rounded, small circular sherds were recovered from the surface of Field VI Area 1. Although these sherds may have a variety of uses, they could have been used as gaming pieces, and if so, are evidence of leisure activity carried on by the hut occupants.

The main occupation phase of Field VI Area 1 provided some evidence of animal husbandry in the flotation material recovered from Locus 003, the main walls of Hut 1. This was not surprising: it was initially assumed that the features were the product of seminomadic peoples with associated domestic flocks. It is certainly possible that animals were penned nearby. The fires all

7. Depicted below in fig. 7.49. For a discussion of this amulet and others associated with fertility and childbearing from Tell el-Borg, see James K. Hoffmeier, "Deities of the Eastern Frontier," in *Scribe of Justice: Egyptological Studies in Honour of Shafik Allam* (ed. Z. A. Hawass, Kh. A. Daoud, and R. B. Hussein; Cairo: Supplement aux Annales du Service des Antiquités de l'Egypte, Cahier 42, 2011) 197–216.

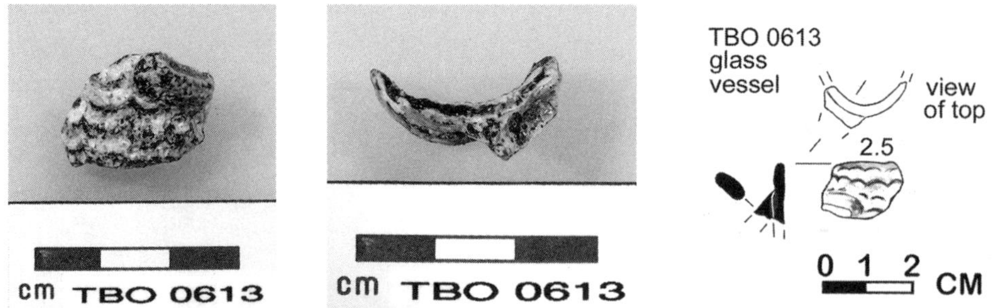

Fig. 7.51. Glass jar fragment, TBO 0613. a–b. photos; c. drawing by Lyla Pinch-Brock.

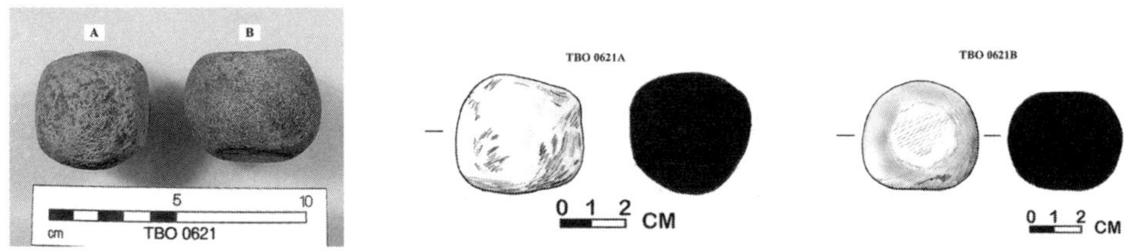

Fig. 7.52. Granite and granodiorite pounders, TBO 0621A and B. a. photos; b–c. drawings by Lyla Pinch-Brock.

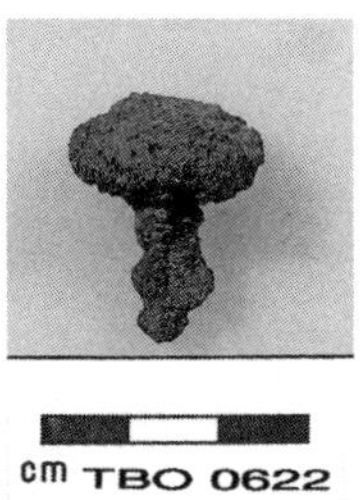

Fig. 7.53 (left). Copper/copper alloy nail, TBO 0622.

Fig. 7.54 (right). Two pieces of copper/copper alloy pin, TBO 0625.

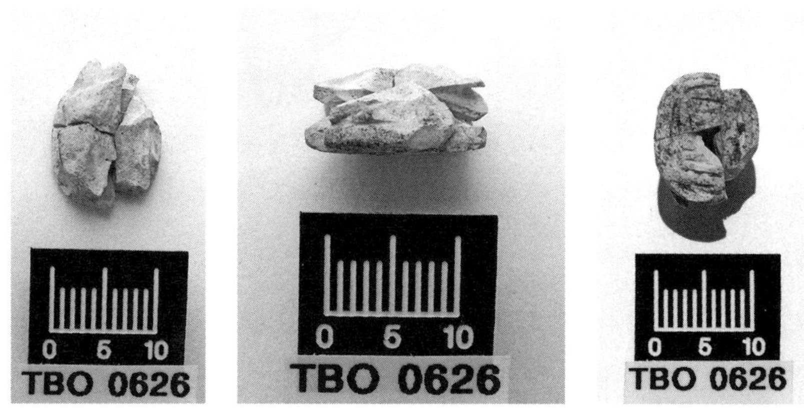

Fig. 7.55. Scarab, TBO 0626. a. top view; b. end view; c. bottom view.

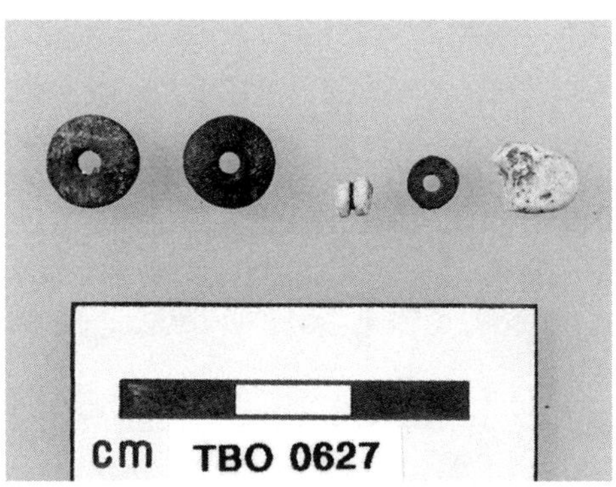

Fig. 7.56. Five beads, TBO 0627.

Fig. 7.57a–b. Glazed faience bowl fragment, TBO 0629.

yielded fish bones but no animal remains. Animal products were almost certainly used on site, but have left no evidence, other than the use of dung as fuel. It is probable that the earliest use of this area was to pen animals. The faint early phase stain alignments could represent a series of light

Fig. 7.58a–c. Clay cobra plaque, TBO 0598.

Fig. 7.58d. Cobra plaque from the British Museum (photo courtesy of the Trustees of the British Museum).

Fig. 7.59. Granodiorite pestle, TBO 0641.

Fig. 7.60. Granite pounder, TBO 0642.

Fig. 7.61a–b. Basalt jar fragment, TBO 0644.

animal pens that were periodically replaced. In this scenario, the occupational space would have been elsewhere, perhaps under the current military defenses.

Discussion of Small Finds from Units R and S

Units R and S were located east and south, respectively, of Unit AA, where the reed and grass habitat were discovered. R was a 2 × 30 m trench that was intended to probe the area south of Unit AA to determine if traces of the huts could be found. While there were some ashy spots, no clear structures were documented. Similarly, Unit R was devoid of any type of architecture. Consequently, it is impossible to know the original provenance of the small finds uncovered in these units. It is probable that the space in Area 1 surrounding Unit AA was domestic space. Reed huts or mud-brick houses may have been used, but they are completely lost due to a combination of natural deflation and the bulldozing of the area during modern military activity. As noted above, Area 1 was covered with a myriad of shells (fig. 7.2). Their presence is the signature of bricks that have been eroded or deflated.

The small finds in Units R and S are consistent with objects one would expect to find in domestic and funerary contexts—specially pounders, a pestle, beads, and fragments of copper/copper alloy tools. Some of these finds deserve further comment.

Table 7.5. Small Finds from Field VI Area 1, Units R and S

TBO	*Unit/Locus*	*Object Type*	*Material*	*Measurements*
0592	Unit R Locus 001	circular, shaped stone	limestone	2.1 × 1.6 cm
0613	Unit R Locus 001	bottle/jarlet	variegated glass	2.3 × 1.6 × .25 cm
0616	Unit R Locus 001	3 beads	faience	n/a
0621a	Unit R Locus 001	pounder/grinder	granite	4.8 × 5.0 dia cm
0621b	Unit R Locus 001	pounder/grinder	granodiorite	4.8 × 5.5 dia cm
0622	Unit R Locus 001	nail (?)	copper/copper alloy	3 × 2.3 (head) × 0.6 (stem) dia cm
0625	Unit R Locus 001	fragments of pin (?)	copper/copper alloy	1.5 × 0.3 dia cm; 0.9 × 0.3 dia cm
0626	Unit R Locus 001	scarab	faience	1.3 × .48 × .61 cm
0627	Unit R Locus 001	5 beads	faience, stone	n/a
0628	Unit R Locus 001	worked sherd game piece (?)	clay	0.8 × 2.6 dia cm
0629	Unit R Locus 001	sherd of dish or bowl	glazed faience	4 × 3 × 0.9 cm
0634	Unit R Locus 001	flat bead	faience	0.1 × 0.5 dia cm
0643	Unit R Locus 001	2 chipped stone tool fragments	chert	5.3 × 4.1 × .11 cm; 3.4 × 2.4 × .12 cm
0630	Unit S Locus 001	flat bead	bone (?)	0.1 × 0.7 dia cm
0571	Unit S Locus 002	flat bead	faience	0.1 × 0.6 dia cm
0598	Unit S Locus 002	cobra plaque	clay	5.5 × 4.4 × 2.7 cm
0632	Unit S Locus 002	flat bead	faience	0.6 × 0.2 dia cm
0638	Unit S Locus 002	bead	unknown stone	0.8 × 1.0 cm
0639	Unit S Locus 002	fragments of a needle or pin?	copper/copper alloy	1.6 and 2.2 × 0.3 dia cm
0641	Unit S Locus 002	pounder/pestle	granodiorite	5.9 × 5.2 × 4 cm
0642	Unit S Locus 002	pounder/grinder	granite	4.5 × 4.5 × 4 cm
0644	Unit S Locus 002	jar or plate (?) fragment	basalt	9.8 × 7.4 × 5.4 cm
0645	Unit S Locus 004	fragment of a needle or pin	copper/copper alloy	1.9 × 0.3 dia cm

- TBO 0623 = fig. 7.51a–b is a piece of elegant, variegated glass. Similar fragments of the same quality glass were documented in the cemetery area, Field III: TBO III 4 (fig. 4.15) and TBO III 15 (fig. 4.16a–b). See discussion in chapter 4.
- TBO 0626 = fig. 7.55a–c is a largely restored fragmentary scarab. Though the text on the stamp side is badly damaged, it could have a pair of *nb*-signs with Amun between them.[8]
- TBO 0598 = fig. 7.58a–c is a clay figurine that originally was included in a pottery basket. When examined by Rexine Hummel, she suspected that this object was a cobra plaque with uraeus mostly missing. Kasia Szpakowska confirmed that this object is a cobra plaque based on images we sent her to examine. She is presently engaged in a major study of more than 500 examples of clay cobra figurines. These clay images have been documented in domestic contexts such as Amarna but also in military settings such as Zawiyet Umm el-Rakham, Haruba (in North Sinai), and in Beth Shean in northern Canaan, where an Egyptian military garrison was stationed during much of the New Kingdom.[9] Now we can add the military establishment of Tell el-Borg to this list. A good

8. I am grateful for this very provisional reading by Daphna Ben-Tor, who is a specialist on scarabs.
9. Kasia Spakowska, "Playing with Fire: Initial Observations on the Religious Uses of Clay Cobras from Amarna," *JARCE* 40 (2003) 113–22.

example of a cobra plaque was found at Amarna (EA 55594) and is now in the British Museum (fig. 7.58d)

The precise function of these snake plaques remains uncertain, and which deity the cobra represents remains a challenge. These uraei probably represent one of several goddesses. Possibilities include Renenutet, Nehebkau, Meretseger, Wadjet, and even Nut.[10] Szpakowska has proposed that these figurines might have had a religio-magical function to protect individuals from nightmares, and their use may be in view in the magical spell recorded on Ostracon Gardiner 363, which prescribes placing uraei of pure clay at each of the four corners of a room where an individual sleeps.[11]

Further investigation of these cobra plaques and study of religious texts may help clarify some of the uncertainties,[12] but it is evident that Szpakowska's studies point to these objects as being protective objects used in personal religion.

Conclusions and Speculations

The ancient cultural features uncovered in Field VI Area 1 are the remains of a domestic quarter dating to the earliest occupation of the site. The first phase of occupation predates the first fosse fort, possibly as early as the seventeenth century B.C. The main domestic occupation probably was contemporary with the construction and use of the first fosse fort and dates to the 15th Century B.C. The huts and associated features appear domestic in nature, organized on a familial level, with animals quartered among the huts. It is possible that Hut 2A may have a wider communal role.

Bound reeds are a traditional building material in Egypt from Pre-Dynastic times up to the present day. As scholars have long recognized, the forms of reed architecture are echoed in more permanent materials, such as stone construction in temples and palaces. Vernacular architecture also made use of reed bundles and still does in the Delta and the Sinai (fig. 7.30). G. R. H. Wright, the late dean of Near Eastern architectural archaeologists, comments favorably on the building properties of reeds: "This is a very effective and versatile building material for light shelters. Some of these plants have very robust stems which serve as rigid frame members in themselves; others can be bundled together to form rigid members; still others can be latticed and interwoven. Above all, such elements can be woven into substantial and durable matting which, hung between frames, forms efficient wall paneling."[13] All of these elements were probably present in the hut features at Tell el-Borg. Bundled reeds are clearly used as buttressing along the walls of the huts and along the fence lines. Wright goes on to mention that reed architecture often employed mud plaster,[14] creating a form of wattle-and-daub construction; small fragments of daub were recovered from Locus 003, the outline stain of Hut 1 (fig. 7.27).

10. Ibid. Further on cobra goddesses, see Sally Johnson, *The Cobra Goddess of Ancient Egypt: Predynastic, Early Dynastic, and Old Kingdom Periods* (London: Kegan Paul, 1990).

11. Szpakowska, "Playing with Fire," 119–22.

12. For other works on this subject, see Szpakowska, "Snake Cults and Military Life in New Kingdom Egypt," in *Walls of the Prince: Egyptian Interactions with Southwest Asia in Antiquity: Essays in Honour of John S. Holladay Jr.* (ed. E. Banning, T. Harrison, and S. Klassen; Leiden: Brill, 2015) 274–91. K. Szpakowska and R. Johnston, "Snake Busters: Pilot Experiments in Making and Breaking Ritual Figurines," in *Mummies, Magic, and Medicine: Multidisciplinary Essays in Egyptology for Rosalie David* (ed. C. Price et al. (Manchester: Manchester University Press) 459–73.

13. G. R. H. Wright, *Ancient Building Technology*, vol. 1: *Historical Background* (Leiden: Brill, 2000) 50.

14. Ibid., 51.

A fire pit and nonstructural fence-lines mark the first, more temporary, occupation. These features probably were animal enclosures, not domestic dwellings, and they were probably sporadically used by the local transient population or by travelers passing through on the coastal route to Egypt, before the Egyptian garrison occupied the site.

The fragility of the features, the extensive modern military disturbances, and the shallowness of the features all combine to make any analysis problematic. The entire area made up of reed structures was destroyed in a fire. The fire may have been accidental, although the lack of evidence of a rebuild argues against this idea. The intact deposits are very limited in nature and difficult to identify. It is to be hoped that, when other sites along the Way of Horus are excavated, they may reveal similar features in a higher state of preservation.

Who Lived in the Huts in Field VI?

The archaeological record creates a mixed portrait of the occupancy of Field VI Area 1. The presence of ceramic materials, albeit in sherd form, not restorable pots, suggests more permanent use of the site. Nomadic, transient populations would have probably used goatskins for liquid containers, leaving a minimal archaeological signature. Postdepositional movement of the sherd material could account for some of the finds, such as the few coffin fragments found in Area 1; however, the ceramic subassemblage is too large and varied to be explained solely in this way. The large fire pit east of Hut 1 (Locus 002) evidences repeated use (fig. 7.26). The ground-stone artifacts are portable but could also have been deliberately left on site in a cycle of repeated occupation.

The likeliest candidates for the identity of the occupants that produced the main phase in Field VI Area 1 are the original inhabitants of Tell el-Borg, Shasu-Bedouin, although the precise length of their stay and the nature of their presence remain uncertain. The remains from Field VI probably represent the remains of a Shasu encampment on in the desert just outside of Egypt. Several scenarios are possible.

(1) The field-wide conflagration may have been deliberate, evidence of the arrival of the Egyptian garrison destroying the huts of the local "Asiatics" to eliminate a possible threat. Of course, the destruction may have been an accidental fire, although the lack of evidence of a rebuild argues against this. It is possible that the entire site may have been abandoned for a number of years when the garrison arrived and the fire was used to clear the site for subsequent usage.

(2) Another possibility is that the huts represent a seasonal occupation of this portion of the site by (temporarily) non-hostile Shasu, from as early as the 2IP (as the sherds and C^{14} suggest) and down to the early decades of the first fort, which we date to the reigns of Thutmose III and Amenhotep II.[15] They would have come for short periods of time to trade with the garrison or with the merchants who stopped off at this site, along the banks of the easternmost branch of the Nile. It is difficult to say whether or not the small campsites noticed by Eliezer Oren in his surveys in north Sinai represent habitat of such people or not.[16] The small amounts of Cypriote and Mycenaean wares could have come onto the site as the result of individualized, low-intensity trade from passing merchant vessels. Once the trade goods were exhausted or the local market saturated, the semi-nomadic occupants of the huts may have moved on, and the garrison may have burned the huts as a way of removing the refuse left behind.

15. Hoffmeier, *Tell el-Borg I*, 196–97.

16. Oren only mentions "campsites" in various articles but never elaborates. See, for example, "The Establishment of Egyptian Imperial Administration on the 'Ways of Horus': An Archaeological Perspective from North Sinai," in *Timelines: Studies in Honour of Manfred Bietak* II (ed. E. Czerny et al.; Leuven: Peeters, 2006) 279–92.

Trade with the garrison may not have been the only motivation of the hut occupants. They may have housed a small family group that was passing through the frontier posts. Traffic could have been seasonal with various groups settling down for a short time near the garrison during the summer to be close to a water source, or to gain the protection of the garrison in unsettled times.

A symbiotic relationship between Shasu/pastoralists and a military garrison, in addition to trade, is also worth considering. Bedouin throughout the millennia have served as scouts and/or guides for travelers and armies across north Sinai. The story of Sinuhe[17] reports that, when Sinuhe returned from his exile in the northern Levant, he stopped at the frontier town and military stronghold known as "the Ways of Horus"—that is, the site of Tjaru/Sile, Tell Hebua.[18] There Sinuhe was met by a *ṯs ỉm nty m-sꜣ pẖrt*[19] which has been variously translated: 'commander in charge of the patrol' by William Kelly Simpson,[20] while Miriam Lichtheim offered 'commander in charge of the garrison',[21] and Ellen Morris rendered it 'commander in charge of the frontier patrol'.[22] Sinuhe waited there until King Senusert I sent a ship to ferry him to the royal residence (Itjtawy), and with the ship gifts were sent "for the Asiatics (*sttyw*) who came with me to conduct me to the Ways of Horus" (B 245–46).

Sttyw is the term used in the Middle Kingdom for Levantine and Sinaitic bedouin.[23] Proof of the above suggestion is also found in the story of Sinuhe, in the account of his escaping Egypt and entering Sinai: he nearly died of thirst. Fortuitously, he was rescued by a *sttyw* who gave him drink[24]; the *sttyw* chief (*mtn*), who had been in Egypt, recognized Sinuhe. It is noteworthy that Simpson translates *mtn* 'bedouin chief'.[25] Moreover, Faulkner notes that the word *mtn/mtn* literally means 'path finder',[26] an apt name for a bedu. The *Wörterbuch* offers the same interpretation (*Wb* 2, 176).

It is known that Shasu-like people worked with the Egyptian military as scouts and trackers. When Ramesses II marched to Kadesh, he got intelligence from two Shasu, whose reports turned out to be false; the Hittites had planted them to mislead the Egyptians.[27] This account illustrates that the Egyptian military was accustomed to using Shasu for military intelligence and that the Hittites knew it as well!

---

17. The discussion of Sinuhe is based on the critical edition of A. M. Blackman, *The Story of Sinuhe*, (Bibliotheca Aegyptiaca 2; Brussels, 1932). Translations by Hoffmeier.
18. For a discussion of this identification and references, see James K. Hoffmeier and Stephen O. Moshier, "'A Highway out of Egypt': The main road from Egypt to Canaan," in *Desert Road Archaeology in Ancient Egypt and Beyond* (ed. F. Förester and H. Reimer; Africa Praehistorica 26; Cologne: Heinrich-Barth-Institut, 2013) 485–510. On the identification of "Ways of Horus" and Tjaru/Sile, see James K. Hoffmeier, *Ancient Israel in Sinai* (New York: Oxford University Press, 2005) 90–94.
19. B 242; Blackman, *Sinuhe*, 35.
20. William K. Simpson, *The Literature of Ancient Egypt* (New Haven: Yale University Press, 1973) 70.
21. Miriam Lichtheim, *Ancient Egyptian Literature I* (Berkeley: University of California Press, 1973) 81.
22. Ellen Morris, *The Architecture of Imperialism: Military Bases and the Evolution of Foreign Policy in Egypt's New Kingdom* (Leiden: Brill, 2005) 48.
23. *Styw* is clearly the word used in Sinuhe for the bedouin; it is a precursor to the New Kingdom term Shasu.
24. Sinuhe R 49–50; Blackman, *Sinuhe*, 14.
25. Simpson, *Literature of Ancient Egypt*, 71.
26. R. O. Faulkner, *Concise Dictionary of Middle Egyptian* (Oxford: Oxford University Press, 1962) 122.
27. KRI II, 108ff.

Later still, the Assyrians recognized the need to have friendly Arabs in north Sinai in anticipation of their conquest of Egypt. In his study of the Assyrian invasions of Egypt, A. Kirk Grayson, observed that as early as 732 B.C. Tiglath-Pileser III took the first steps toward the eventual conquest of Egypt when he seized "control over Sinai, the road to Egypt. He appointed an Arab sheik called Idi-bi'il as his representative in the area and installed him in a newly formed office with the appropriate title, 'Gate-keeper on the Border of Egypt'."[28]

Combining the evidence from Field VI and what we know of the desert dwellers of Sinai and the southern Levant leads us to conclude that a group of bedouin living so close to Egypt's frontier town (Tjaru/Sile) probably worked cooperatively with the Egyptian military. Then, too, since it appears that the occupational horizon of the hut community at Tell el-Borg continued into the period when the 18th Dynasty fort was constructed, they probably worked with the garrison at this fort.

FIELD INVESTIGATIONS, AREA 2

Area 2 of Field VI was opened at the end of the 2005 season, and excavation continued in 2006. It was hoped that by excavating approximately 50 m northeast of Area 1, the parameters of the domestic quarter (Field VI, Area 1) could be more precisely delineated. A 5 × 5 m square was initially laid out, designated Unit A, in order to determine whether there was domestic occupation in this part of the Tell (fig. 7.62). Square B was added—a 2 × 5 m extension to the east of Unit A (fig. 7.63a–b). Unit C was extended north 2.5 m and east 2.5 m from Unit A, on the opposite end of Unit B. Unit D extended 2 m east from the north wall of Unit C and then 4 m south. Another 2 × 4 m square was placed adjacent to Unit D, which was designated Unit E. Unit G, excavated in 2006, was a 3 × 5 m rectangle directly east of Unit E. Finally, a 3 × 5 m Unit F was placed approximately 30 m from Unit A (fig. 7.1), which yielded no indication of human activity.Initially, surface debris was removed to a depth of approximately 5 cm. When stains were encountered, excavation proceeded by hand troweling. Great care was taken to define and examine each stain. Each stain was also given its own locus number. Pits were treated as a discreet locus in order better to assess each pit's nature—whether modern, ancient, or a combination of both. The material of each pit was screened 100% until its nature was determined. If ancient debris was discovered, screening continued, while modern features were closed. In this case of particularly large pits, multiple basket designation were given in case it was later determined that one pit was really two or three ancient pits.

Field Results, Area 2

A total of eight loci were identified in six squares in the inaugural season (2005) of excavation in Field VI, Area 2; seven additional loci were identified in 2006. Of particular importance is Locus 002, where the vast majority of ancient material was discovered, as will be discussed below.

Surface and Disturbed Fill (Locus 001)

This locus designation covers all squares and includes surface material, including objects from obvious modern disturbances such as robber pits. In this dry, loose sand (Munsell 10YR 4/3) were numerous heavily eroded sherds. Potsherds that were potentially diagnostic or decorated were kept, cleaned, and examined more thoroughly. (In addition to the survey of the ceramic re-

28. A. Kirk Grayson, "Assyria's Foreign Policy in Relation to Egypt in the Eighth and Seventh Centuries B.C.," *JSSEA* XI no. 2 (1981): 86.

Fig. 7.62. Unit A, Locus 001.

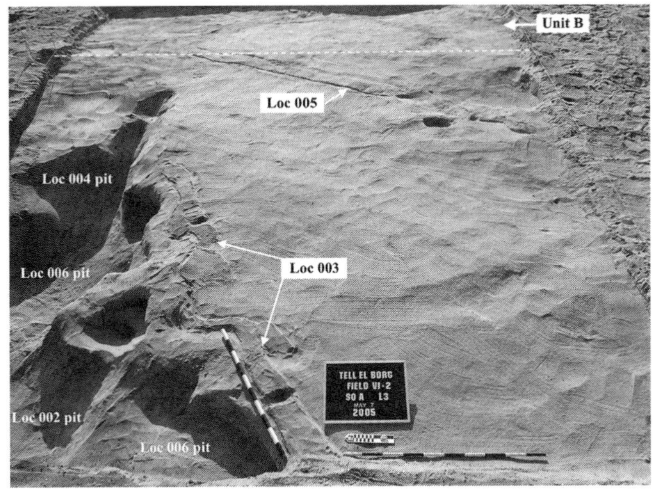

Fig. 7.63a. Unit A, Locus 003.

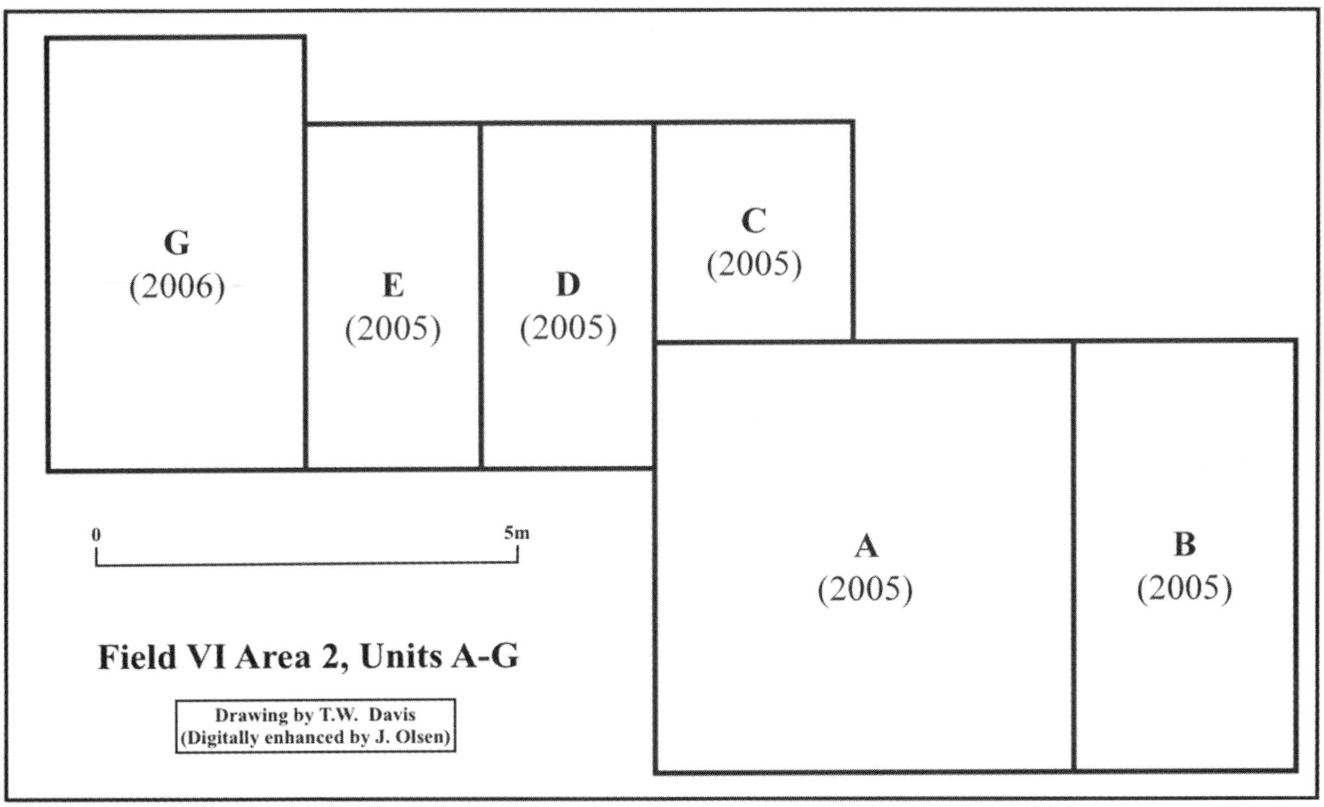

Fig. 7.63b. Plan of excavated units in Field VI Area 2.

mains reviewed here, see the treatment and distribution of the Egyptian, Levantine, Cypriote, and Mycenaean wares from Field VI in *Tell el-Borg I*, chapters 8–11.)

In Unit A, a White Shaved juglet fragment and 2 Blue-painted fragments were found. A Blue-painted sherd, a Red-slip bowl, and a late New Kingdom ware were found in Unit B. Unit C contained one Mycenaean sherd and many New Kingdom wares and forms, with an abundance of red-slip sherds. Interestingly, basket 3 from Unit C in Locus 001 contained three Canaanite rims, as well as a blue-painted sherd. An additional blue-painted sherd was found on the surface of Unit F, as well as a Cypriot burnished handle. All pottery was dated to the New Kingdom.

After removing 10 cm of Locus 001 in Unit F, it was determined that there were no signs of ancient domestic occupation there. The sand was mixed with mud to form a yellowish-orange color, resulting in a swirled pattern, resembling the rings of a tree trunk. This pattern may be the impression left by the turning wheel of a front-loader or similar tractor. Thus, it was clear that despite the presence of surface potsherds, this square did not contain ancient features, and the square was subsequently closed.

Locus 001 of Unit A overlay Loci 002, 003, 005, 006, and 008. A modern fire-pit was uncovered and removed. Bits of limestone also were encountered near the surface. This is similar to other fields from Tell el-Borg, particularly those fields that contained the New Kingdom forts. In Unit G, Locus 001 overlay 002, 009, 010, and 011.

Small finds recovered from the surface and Locus 001 of Area 2 included a wide variety of objects and materials, many suggestive of funerary contexts. A broken fragment of a mud seal impression (see below) indicates the one-time presence of papyrus documents, now disintegrated. Stone vessel fragments of calcite, limestone, and gneiss indicate high-status items. Twelve faience beads included scalloped, seed beads, and a larger disk-shaped bead (4 mm). More utilitarian objects included two flint sickle blades and a sheep/goat bone (for an analysis of the faunal remains, see chapters 13 and 14).

Indeterminate Dark Stains (Locus 003, Locus 005)

Two dark stains (Munsell: 10YR 5/3) were found in Unit A and each was given its own Locus number (fig. 7.63a). These dry, firm stains were initially treated as potentially ancient and occupational, much like the stains in Area 1. However, further work on them proved that they were not. Unlike the stains from Area 1, these stains did not contain any reed material, ash, fish bone, or any other ancient identifier. Underneath both of these stains was soft, dry, loose sand (Munsell 10YR 6/6–6/4), designated Locus 008. This layer served as a stopping point for the excavation in Area 2.

Locus 003 begins approximately 2 m from the southwest corner along the western wall. It then travels northeast at a slight angle for 3 m. The stain is roughly 25 cm thick in most places. Near the center of the stain, a circle (0.50 m diameter) was formed, with two separate small square stains appearing to the south of the circle. These were treated as part of Locus 003, and the most likely explanation is that this feature is modern and military in nature (figs. 7.62–7.63). One suggestion is that the circle and small squares are the pivot point and anchor points for a towed heavy artillery gun. A cross-section of the stain revealed that it was only 5 cm thick. A modern military crest from an Egyptian army uniform was found on the surface in this area (fig. 7.64a–b).

Locus 005 began halfway down the eastern wall of Unit A, and traveled southwest for 1.5 m before breaking off for approximately 40 cm. It then was attested extending 60 cm from the southern wall. This stain is also modern, most likely a vehicle track of some sort. In order to test this hypothesis, L005 was traced into Square B, where it curved to the north. It was also crossed by rodent tracks.

If these stains were the remains of some ancient structure, perhaps a fence, then no construction material remained: the stains are merely impressions in sub-soil, filled with surface/upper sand. The uniform shallow depth (less than 5 cm) suggests that the stains are the outline of something even less permanent than a fence, because (ancient or modern) cultural remains are completely absent.

Modern Pits (Locus 004, Locus 006)

In the northwest corner of Unit A, two modern pits were uncovered (Locus 004 and Locus 006) (figs. 7.62 and 7.63a). Locus 006 contained two major sections. The first extended from the west wall approximately 0.75 m in a semicircle. The second section was considerably larger, 1.5 m × 1 m, and extended from the north wall. The first section's depth was 15 cm, while the second was 45 cm at its deepest point. A third, smaller section lay between the two larger ones and was circular in shape, with a diameter of 35 cm and a depth of 27 cm. All three sections were composed of firm, dry sand (Munsell 10YR 3/4). Clean cutlines (likely from a shovel) were evident in all three sections, meaning that these three pits show evidence of more recent looting. However, a small sampling of pottery was found, including mostly New Kingdom marls, with one later New Kingdom and one Mycenaean sherd. This mix can easily be attributed to the generally disturbed nature of Tell el-Borg throughout this area.

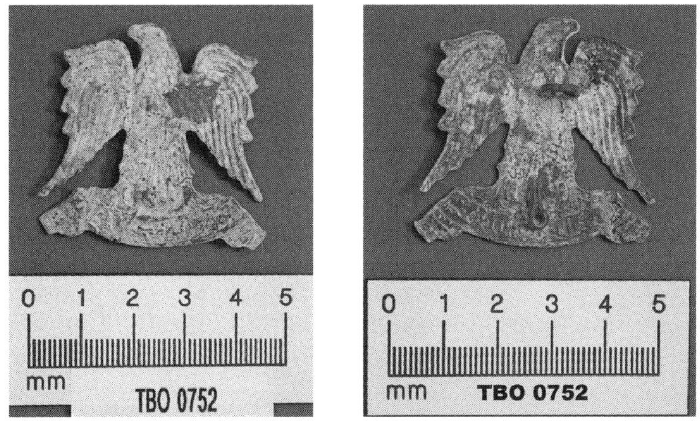

Fig. 7.64a–b. An Egyptian military officer's crest, TBO 0752.

The second and largest section of Locus 006 contained Locus 004, which actually cuts into Locus 006. Locus 004 sits on both the east and west ends of this section of Locus 006, with a width on each end varying from 10 cm to 50 cm. Initially, it was believed that both portions of Locus 004 were part of an ancient pit, but further work quickly revealed that it was in fact a modern pit. The pit lines were very clean; while there were few fish bones present, concrete and burned plaster were evident. Clearly, this is a modern military pit that was chopped through in numerous places by looters. It was also composed of soft, dry sand, which was of a lighter color than the sand of Locus 006 (Munsell 10YR 4/6). All pottery forms from this locus were New Kingdom rims, composed of 50% silt and 40% marl.

Massive Disturbed Pit (Locus 002, Locus 007)

A large pit containing numerous ancient materials was uncovered in the northwest corner of Square A (to be discussed below). This pit was overlain by Locus 001 and underlain by Locus 008. Locus 007 also extended into Units C and D. Generally, it was comprised of soft, loose, dry sand (10YR 4/4) mottled with ancient materials and modern disturbances. The pit is approximately 1.25 m wide in Unit A, and it runs for 1.5 m north along the western wall of Unit A before continuing into Unit C to the north and into Units D and E. In fact, Units C–E were opened solely for the purpose of expanding and defining the pit and the ancient materials in it. The northern extremity of the pit was reached approximately 1 m into Unit C. Moving west, the pit continued through Unit D and into E, which was opened to try to encompass the pit. In 2006, Square G was laid to complete the excavation of the pit. The western edge of Locus 002, was delineated within Square G. The total size of the pit was a massive 4.5 × 7.3 m (fig. 7.65).

As work continued, it became clear that this pit was also heavily disturbed and modern in date. The depth levels of the pit fluctuated between 44 cm and 72 cm in Unit A. In Unit C, the levels vary from 29 cm to 64 cm deep. At its deepest point (Unit D), the pit was 1.4 m below the surface. At the base of the pit in Unit A, three clear shovel cuts were found. Four similar shovel cuts were revealed at the base of Locus 007 in Unit D. Furthermore, approximately 90 cm deep in Unit D, the remains of Israeli army sandbags were found (fig. 7.66a–b). Square G contained

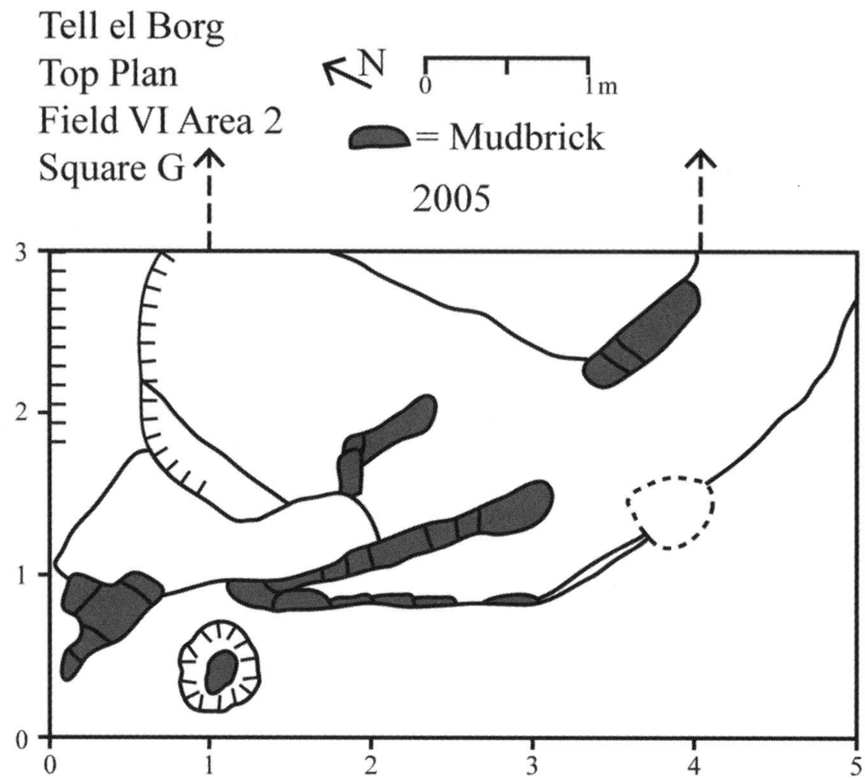

Fig. 7.65. Plan of Unit G (drawing by T. Davis, digitally enhanced by Joshua Olsen).

22 modern robber pits in and around the edges of Locus 002. The high quantity of pottery and ancient material present in the screening indicated the richness of the occupation before the site was abandoned and subsequently deflated. When a potentially undisturbed portion of the large pit was encountered, a new basket designation was assigned. All of the soil matrix from this pit, in each square, was screened.

Excavations in Unit C revealed a mottled, dry sand (10YR 4/3), which was treated as Locus 007. In the NE corner of this square, Locus 007 was 36 cm deep and 60cm deep in the center of the square. Locus 007 continued on into Unit D, as well, before being cut into by yet another modern pit. The discovery of fish bones next to a modern piece of wire demonstrates the complicated nature of these pit features. Furthermore, at its base Locus 007 contained four modern shovel cuts.

Pottery Sub-Assemblage

From Locus 007 came one blue-painted sherd and a proliferation of New Kingdom forms, 80% Silt, 15% Marl, with 12 rims, 3 bases, and 1 handle. As table 7.6 illustrates, the vast majority of pottery from this large pit feature was Egyptian, with a few Levantine and Mycenaean foreign wares. Silt ware predominates at a roughly 3:1 ratio, and rims are much more common than bases or handles.

Discussion of Small Finds from Field VI, Area 2, Units A–E (Ancient Pit)

Because the pit in Field VI, Area 2 was used for discarding waste, in addition to the range of sherds it contained, many small finds were documented. Since the ancient pit was cut into an even older tomb (#14, see further below), it is impossible to differentiate objects originally from the tomb from those tossed subsequently into the pit. Thanks to screening all the material from the

Fig. 7.66a. Modern pit with Israeli army sandbag (Unit D).

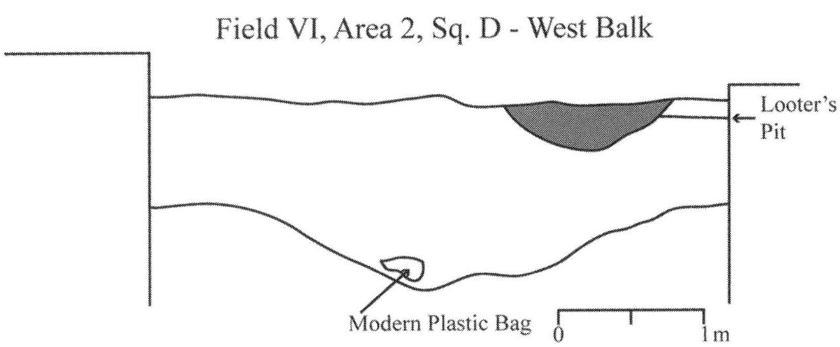

Fig. 7.66b. Section drawing of west baulk (Unit D) (drawing by Mark Janzen, digitally enhanced by Joshua Olsen).

Table 7.6. Field VI, Area 2 Pottery from Loci 002 and 007

Unit	*Silt*	*Marl %*	*Rims*	*Bases*	*Handles*	*Diagnostics*	*Comments*
A	0	25	34	8	10	1 White-shaved sherd	13 Levantine sherds; the rest are NK shapes and forms
A	0	15	45	4	—	1 Mycenaean body sherd; 1 White-slip milk bowl; 3 Cypriot BR II; 1 blue-painted body sherd	
A	0	15	9	—	lid		Red slip on silt bowls; variety of NK Marls, early and late
A	5	25	6	3	6	6 blue-pained sherds; 2 Cypriot BR	Some strange wares
C	—	—	—	—	—	1 Mycenaean sherd	Keeping only diagnostics
C	0	15	28	6	9	Blue-paint on slips; 1 small basket handle	NK forms
G/1	8	21	18	0	4	9% Levant origin	High number of red-slip bowls
G/2	31	16	121	15	19	9 Blue-painted; 1 Mycenaean; 6 BR-Cypriot; 1 White-shaved cup; 3 White-slip cups.	

Table 7.7. Small Finds from Field VI, Area 2, Units A–E

TBO	*Unit/Locus*	*Object Type*	*Material*	*Measurements*
0855	VI, 2 surface	knob of a jar lid (?)	travertine	1.7 × 1.2 cm dia
0261	A Locus 001	bead	carnelian	0.3 × 0.3 cm dia
0562	A Locus 002	stone	geode (?)	n/a
0556	A Locus 002	6 beads	5 faience, 1 carnelian	n/a
0565	A Locus 002	stamped amphora handle	Marl D	n/a
0572	B Locus 001	3 beads	faience	n/a
0568	C Locus 001	jar rim fragment	travertine	2.3 × 2.0 × 1.4 cm
0584	C Locus 001	flat white bead	faience	0.2 × 0.6 cm dia
0585	C Locus 001	red bead	faience	.15 × 0.3 cm dia
0567	C Locus 002	bulla w. seal impression	mud	1.3 × 1.0 × 0.6 cm
0575	C Locus 002	9 beads	faience	n/a
0583	C Locus 002	flat bead	clay	0.3 × 1.4 dia cm
0580	C Locus 007	4 beads	3 faience, 1 glass	n/a
0577[a]	D Locus 001	chipped stone tool	chert	49.9 × 4.70 × 14.96 mm
0693	D Locus 001	fragment of plate (?)	travertine	6.1 × 5 × 2.1 cm
0578	D Locus 002	white, flat bead	faience	0.2 × 0.5 dia cm
0586	D Locus 002	flat disk	uncertain	0.3 × 1.6 dia cm
0587	D Locus 002	fragment of a ring (?)	faience	1.0 × 0.2 cm
0589	D Locus 002	game pieces (?)	clay	n/a
0590	D Locus 002	piece of foil	gold	less than 1 gram
0591	D Locus 002	jar fragment	travertine	3.3. × 0.6 × 0.3 cm
0662	D Locus 002	jar fragment	glass	2 × 1.6 × .35 cm
0665	D Locus 002	38 beads	faience	10 various shapes
0668	D Locus 002	ring bezel w cartouche	faience	1.8 × 1.2 × 0.3 cm
0673	D Locus 002	stone fragment	limestone	2.1 × 1.7 × 1.2 cm
0674	D Locus 002	44 beads	mostly faience	n/a
0675	D Locus 002	small scarab	faience	0.7 × 0.5 × 0.4 cm
0677	D Locus 002	decorated ring bezel	faience	1.4 × 1 × 0.3 cm
0678	D Locus 002	ring	faience	0.5 × 3.2 dia cm
0679	D Locus 002	Arabic seal impression	copper	2 × 1.6 × 0.2 cm
0680	D Locus 002	broken ring	travertine	0.7 × 3.5 dia cm
0681	D Locus 002	circular lid	limestone	1.1 × 9.3 dia cm
0683	D Locus 002	bulla w. seal impression	mud	1.7 × 1.5 × 1.1 cm
0684	D Locus 002	fragments of a ring	faience	n/a
0688	D Locus 002	fragment of a whetstone	limestone	4.6 × 4.4 × 2 cm
0689	D Locus 002	decorated ring bezel	faience	1.8 × 1.1 × 0.3 cm
0778	D Locus 002	stamped amphora handle	Marl D	n/a
0779	D Locus 002	legs of a figurine	clay	5.8 × 3.2 × 1.9 cm
0685	E Locus 002	41 beads	faience, carnelian	n/a
0686	E Locus 002	50 beads	faience, copper/copper alloy, carnelian	n/a
0687	E Locus 002	4 pieces of rings	faience	n/a
0690	E Locus 002	tear-shaped pendant	faience	1.8 × 0.8 dia cm
0691[b]	E Locus 002	chipped stone tool	chert	5.8 × 4.6 × 1.2 cm
0695	E Locus 002	shaped stone	limestone	3.7 × 2.5 × 0.7 cm
0696	E Locus 002	2 fragments of rings	travertine, faience	n/a
0697	E Locus 002	2 fragments from 2 jars	travertine	A. 3.2 × 3.2 × 0.7 B. 3.6 × 3.0 × 0.4

a. TBO 0577 is catalogued in chapter 10, p. 375.
b. TBO 0691 is catalogued in chapter 10, p. 375.

Fig. 7.67. Collection of six beads, TBO 0556.

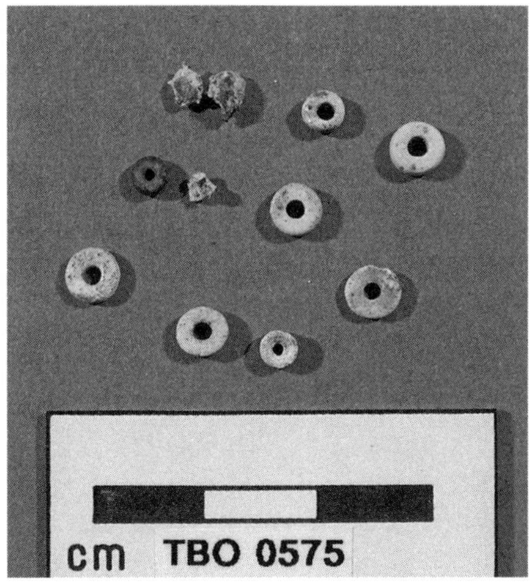

Fig. 7.68. Collection of nine beads, TBO 0575.

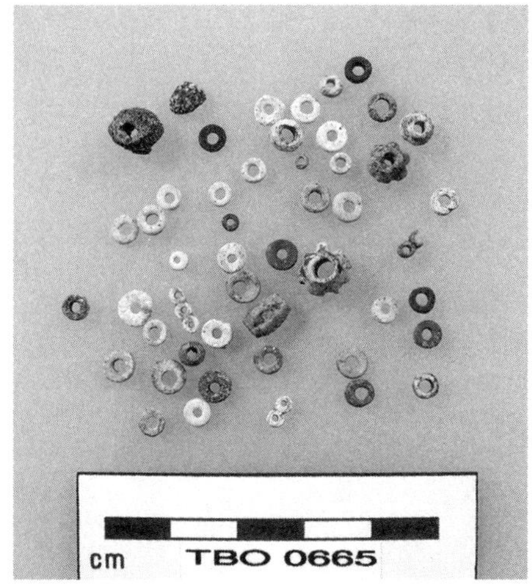

Fig. 7.69. Collection of 38 beads, TBO 0665.

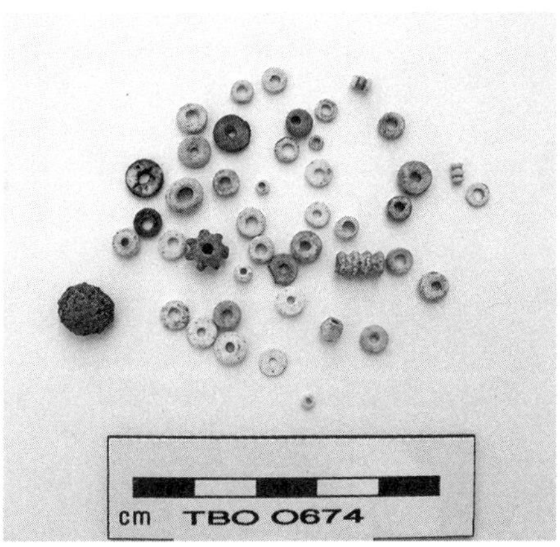

Fig. 7.70. Collection of 44 beads, TBO 0674.

Fig. 7.71. Collection of 41 beads, TBO 0685.

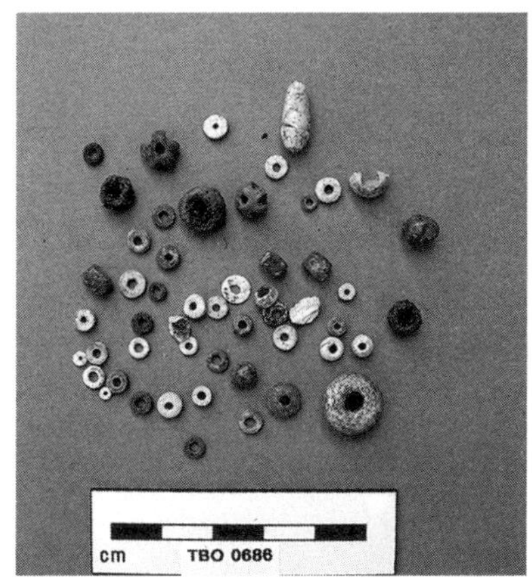

Fig. 7.72. Collection of 50 beads, TBO 0686.

large pit, a significant number of small objects, such as beads, were found in large numbers. They were mostly faience, with a few being made of carnelian and one of glass. These groupings include TBO 0556, six beads (fig. 7.67); TBO 0572, nine beads (fig. 7.68); TBO 0665, 38 beads (fig. 7.69); TBO 0674, 44 beads (fig. 7.70); TBO 0685, 41 beads (fig. 7.71); and TBO 0686, 50 beads (fig. 7.72).

Objects reflecting the elite status of the owner were also documented in this pit: travertine fragments from assorted vessels: TBO 0568 (fig. 7.73); TBO 0591(fig. 7.74); TBO 0697 (fig. 7.75); TBO 0855 (fig. 7.76). Several travertine rings were uncovered that are too large to be finger rings and too small to be bracelets: TBO 0678 (fig. 7.77); TBO 0680 and 0696 (fig. 7.78 and 7.79); are they possibly a hair ring? TBO 0680A is larger and could be a bracelet; a fragment of a glass jar, TBO 0662 (fig. 7.80a–b), and a small piece of gold foil, TBO 0590 (fig. 7.81). A tear-shaped faience pendant, TBO 0690 (fig. 8.82) seems to have a glaze covering and likely was a part of necklace.[29]

29. For comparenda for this tear-shaped pendants and beads, see Cyril Aldred, *Jewels of the Pharaohs: Egyptian Jewelry of the Dynastic Period* (New York: Ballantine, 1978) pls. 7, 8, 10, 11, 29, 30, 57.

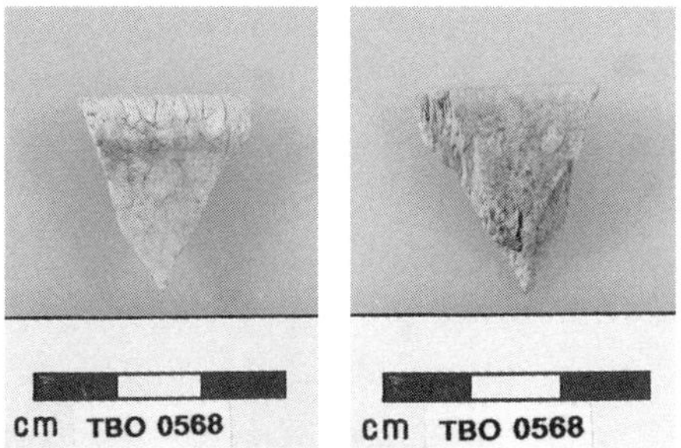

Fig. 7.73a–b. Rim fragment of a travertine jar, TBO 0568.

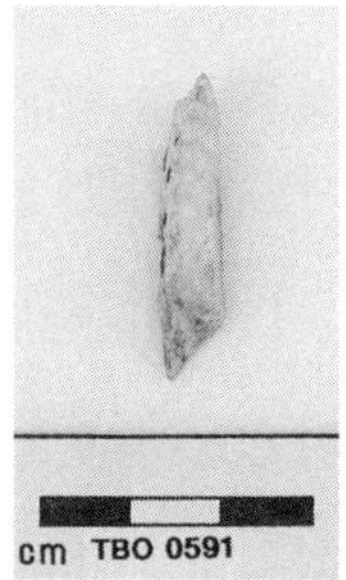

Fig. 7.74. Fragment of travertine vessel, TBO 0591.

Fig. 7.75a–b. Two fragments of travertine vessels, TBO 0697.

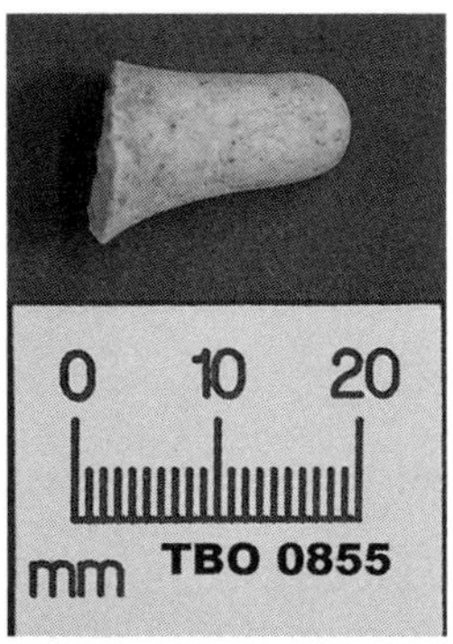

Fig. 7.76. Travertine knob from jar, TBO 0855.

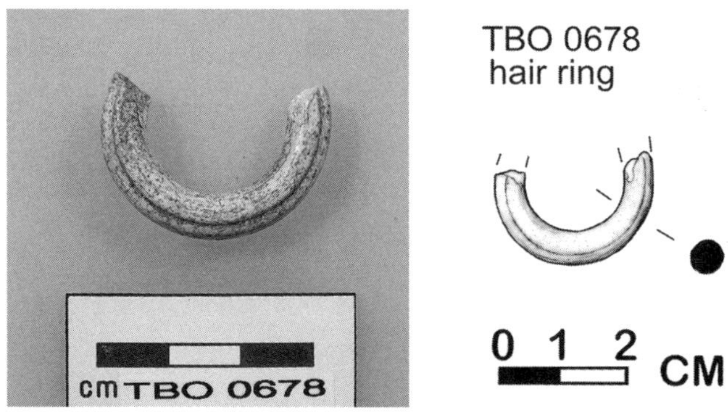

Fig. 7.77. Travertine (hair?) ring, TBO 0678. **a (left)**: photo; **b** (right): drawing by Lyla Pinch-Brock.

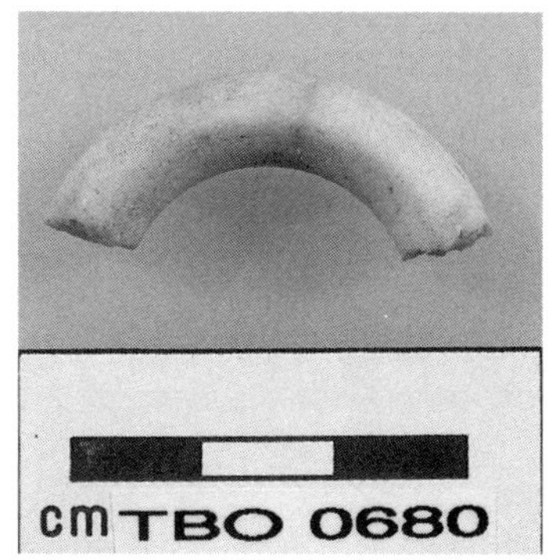

Fig. 7.78. Travertine (hair?) ring, TBO 0680.

One find appears to be a pair of legs of a clay figurine, TBO 0779 (fig. 7.83a–b). The back of the object is smooth, and the left side has a flange-like extension running parallel to the left leg, suggestive of clay that oozed out of the mold. If indeed this object is a molded figurine, it would have been 15–18 cm tall and likely represented a deity.

The pit also yielded a surprising number of glyptic objects. TBO 0675 is small faience scarab that is inscribed on the bottom and can be classified as a *rdỉ rʿ*-type (fig. 7.84a–d). Attested as early as the 1st Intermediate Period, continuing down to the 2nd Intermediate Period, which is the likely general period of this scarab.[30] A small object of this early date in Field VI is probably connected to the reed hut community in Field VI, Area 1 (see above).

TBO 0677 (fig. 7.85a–c) appears to be the bezel of a faience ring, although the breaks on either side of the object prevent one from seeing the arms of the ring. The decoration is sunken into the surface, but the motif is unclear. There appear to be two figures, possibly falcons or uraei, facing each other, with some sort of object between the figures. On a clay bulla (TBO 0773) found

30. I am grateful to Daphna Ben-Tor for this identification. For parallels and discussion, see Daphna Ben-Tor, *Scarabs, Chronology, and Interconnections: Egypt and Palestine in the Second Intermediate Period* (Orbis Biblicus et Orientalis, Series Archaeologica 27; Freiburg: Presses Universitaires, 2007) 20–21 and pls. 12:1–4, 84–85 and pl. 35:39–42.

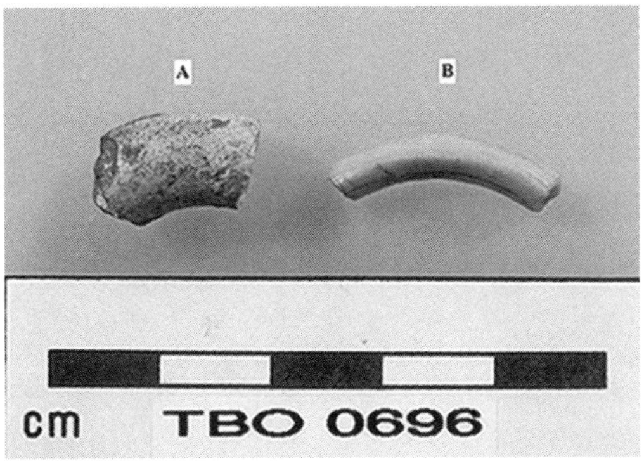

Fig. 7.79. **a**: Traver-tine bracelet(?) fragment, TBO 0680; **b**: Travertine (hair?) ring, TBO 0696

Fig. 7.80a–b. Glass jar fragment, TBO 0662.

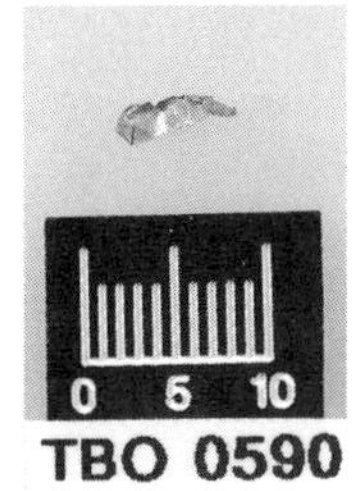

Fig. 7.81 (left). Small piece of gold foil, TBO 0590.
Fig. 7.82 (right). Tear-shaped faience pendant, TBO 0690.

Fig. 7.83. Molded clay figurine, TBO 0799. **a** (left): front view; **b** (right): side view.

Fig. 7.84. Scarab, TBO 0675. **a** (left): top view; **b** (middle, left): bottom view; **c** (middle, right): side view; **d** (right): drawing by Lyla Pinch-Brock.

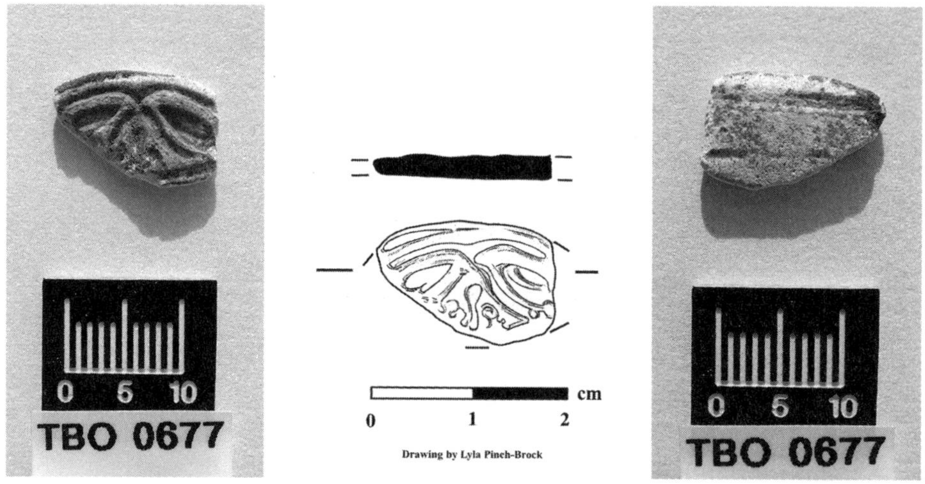

Fig. 7.85. Decorated bezel, TBO 0677. **a** (left): photo, top; **b** (middle): drawing by Lyla Pinch-Brock; **c** (right): photo, underside.

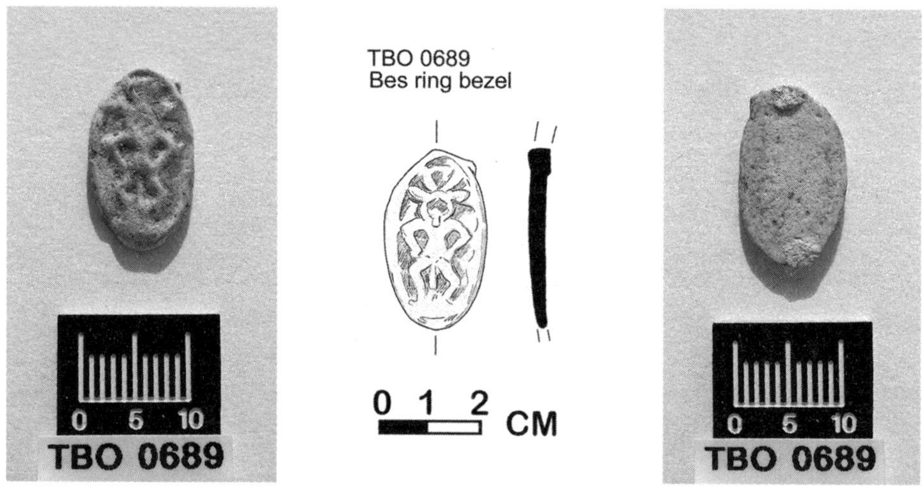

Fig. 7.86. Faience ring bezel with figure of Bes.

in the adjacent modern pit (Unit G Locus 1, see the next section), a pair of frogs are shown facing each other, with an *ankh*-sign standing between them. The figures on TBO 0677 might be employing a motif similar to this one.

TBO 0689 (fig. 7.86a–c) is a faience bezel or a ring whose arms have broken off and are missing. It has the figure of Bes on it.

This pit also yielded six royal seal impressions on amphora handles and bullae. Surprisingly, the later form of the name of Nefertiti was found on TBO 0565 (fig. 7.87a–b), a Marl D amphora handle. It reads *nfr nfrw ỉtn*, along with the epithet *ȝḫ.t n hy.s*, 'Nefer-neferu-Aten who is beneficial to her husband'. Jacobus van Dijk and James Hoffmeier published this inscription in 2010, observing: "This impression provides virtually the only complete, more or less undamaged and unusurped example of this intriguing name, the existence of which was rediscovered some years ago by Marc Gabolde."[31] Although scholars differ on the identity of this royal woman, we maintain that Akhenaten's principal wife, Nefertiti, is the queen in question, and she seems to be functioning as a coregent as suggested by the epithet.[32] The name of another Amarna royal ap-

31. James K. Hoffmeier and Jacobus van Dijk, "New Light on the Amarna Period from North Sinai," *JEA* 96 (2010) 201.

32. For a treatment of the other interpretations, see ibid., 201–2.

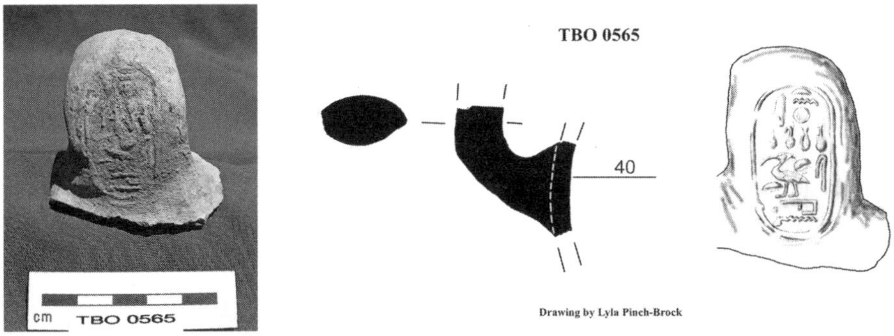

Fig. 7.87. Amphora handle with name of Nefer-neferu-aten, TBO 0565; **a** (left): photo; **b** (right): drawing by Lyla Pinch-Brock.

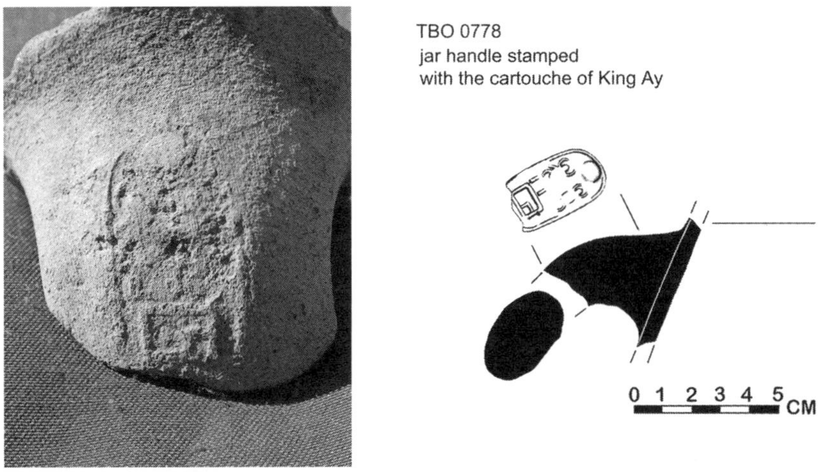

Fig. 7.88. Amphora handle with Aye's pre-nomen, TBO 0778; **a** (left): photo; **b** (right): drawing by Lyla Pinch-Brock.

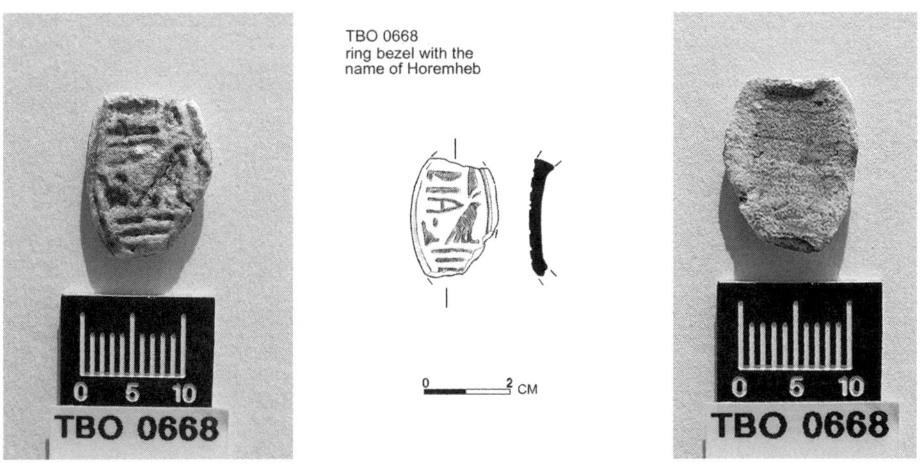

Fig. 7.89. Ring bezel with the name of Horemheb, TBO 0668: **a** (left): photo; **b** (middle): drawing by Lyla Pinch-Brock); **c** (right): photo of underside.

pears on TBO 0778 (fig. 7.88a–b)—namely, the pre-nomen of Aye. It reads *ḥwt ḫpr ḫprw rꜥ*: 'the Temple of Kheper-khepru-Re', meaning that the wine in the jar came from a temple estate of the successor to Tutankhamun. Last, the name of the final pharaoh of the 18th Dynasty, Horemheb, occurs on a ring bezel and two bullae. The bands of the faience ring, TBO 0668 (fig. 7.89a–c), were broken off, as the breaks on the verso of the bezel show. The inscriptions reads, *ḥr m ḥ[b] mry ỉmn*, 'Horemheb, beloved of Amun'. The very top and bottom of the more complete bulla, TBO 0683 (fig. 7.90a–d), is missing. It reads, *ḥr m [ḥb] mrỉ ⸢ỉm⸣n*, 'Horemheb, beloved of Amun'. On the sides of the bulla, one can see the fingerprints of the scribe who sealed the letter. On the back, the

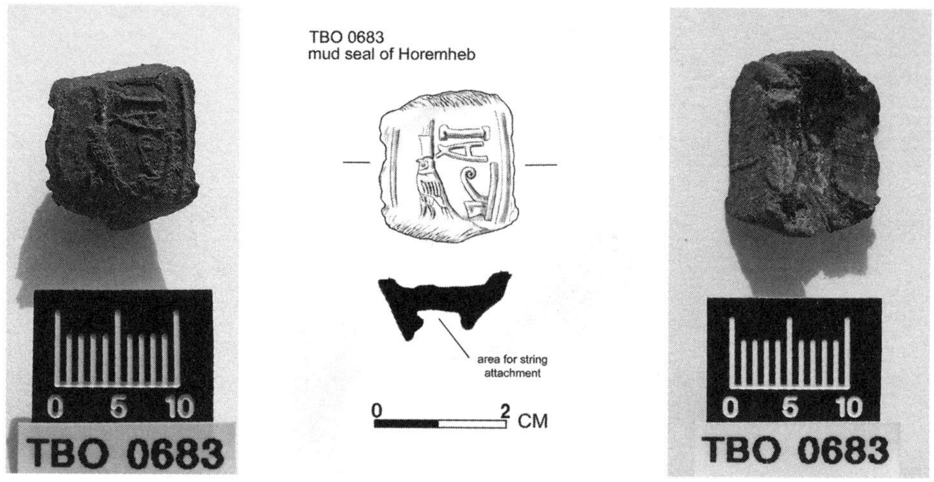

Fig. 7.90. Horemheb bulla, TBO 0683. **a** (left): top view; **b** (middle): drawing by Lyla Pinch-Brock; **c** (right): bottom view.

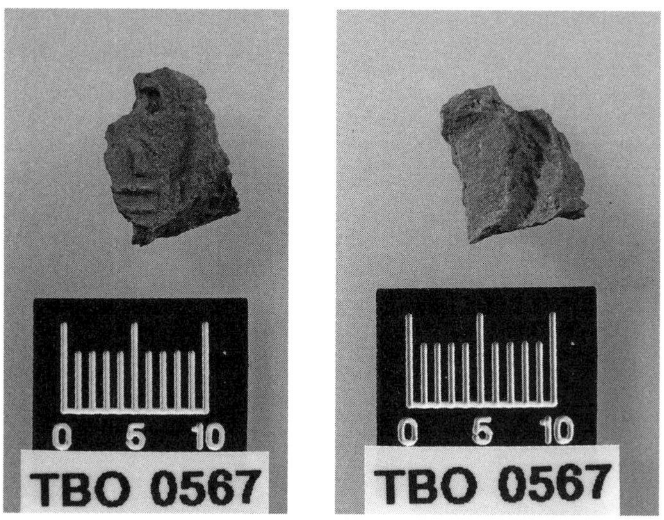

Fig. 7.91. Horemheb bulla, TBO 0567. **a** (left): top view; **b** (right): bottom view.

Fig. 7.92. Ummayad Period copper seal.

impressions of the string that bound the papyrus and the papyrus itself are visible (fig. 7.90c). Only the bottom right-hand side of the second bulla, TBO 0567 (fig. 7.91a–b), is preserved, but the lower section of the falcon is visible and beneath it the two arms of the ═ sign (the flat *m*) that is normally placed over the 𓎱 sign.

The presence of two bullae with Horemheb's name, even though found in a refuse pit in Field VI, is not insignificant. First, these are the only two royal seal impressions found on a bulla. The other royal names attested at Tell el-Borg are either on pottery (amphora handles or on a body sherd) or on architectural blocks and fragments. The bullae suggest that official documents or communiqués were dispatched to this fort either from nearby Tjaru or from Memphis. The second point is that the original provenance of the bullae at this site must have been an administrative facility of some sort. One might have expected that such an office would have been located within the fort located south of this area and across the Nile distributary (see *Tell el-Borg I*, chapters 5–6).

Table 7.8. Small Finds from Field VI Area 2, Unit G (Modern Pit)

TBO	*Unit/Locus*	*Object Type*	*Material*	*Measurements*
0754	G Locus 001	1 nail and 1 nail head	copper/copper alloy	1.2 × 0.6 dia cm; 0.3 × 0.7 dia cm
0859	G Locus 001	fragment of bulla	mud	2.6 × 1.7 × 0.7 cm
0783[a]	G Locus 001	chipped stone blade	chert	20.3 × 26.7 × 4.1 mm
0801	G Locus 001	5 beads	faience, stone	n/a
0756	G Locus 002	2 reworked sherd, tokens	clay	0.5 × 2 dia cm 0.7 × 0.3 dia cm
0753	G Locus 002	stone plate/bowl fragment	travertine	0.7 × 10 cm dia
0755	G Locus 002	4 disc-shaped beads	2 faience, 1 glass, 1 stone	n/a
0758	G Locus 002	28 beads	varied	n/a
0773	G Locus 002	fragment of bulla	mud	1.2 × 0.9 cm
0776	G Locus 002	fragment of stone vessel (?)	limestone	6.4 × 3.2 × 1.8 cm
0802	G Locus 002	2 disc-shaped beads	faience	0.15 × 0.4 dia cm
0804	G Locus 002	4 beads	faience, stone	n/a
0806	G Locus 002	5 fragments of metal tool	copper/copper alloy	n/a
0772	G Locus 009	2 beads	faience	0.2 × 0.4 cm dia 0.3 × 1.0 cm dia
0803	G Locus 009	11 beads	varied	n/a
0825	G Locus 009	3 metal fragments	copper/copper alloy	2.8 × 2.1 × 0.2 cm 0.9 × 0.6 × 0.4 cm 0.7 × 0.6 × 0.3 cm
0857	G Locus 009	blue-grey, ridged sherd	faience	0.8 × 0.8 × 0.2 cm
0871	G Locus 009	reworked sherd, tokens	clay	3.2 × 2.7 × 0.7 cm
0771	G Locus 011	bulla	mud	2.8 × 2.6 × 1.5 cm
0854	G Locus 011	leaf pendant or inlay	faience	1.2 × 0.7 × .15 cm
0866	G Locus 012	disc-shaped bead	faience	0.1 × 0.5 dia cm

a. This blade is treated in chapter 10.

TBO 0679 is a small copper seal impression with Arabic writing on it (fig. 7.92a–b). Tareq Ramadan[33] examined an image of this unique seal impression and believes that it is Umayyad, dating from the late 7th to mid-8th century A.D. While the world *allah* is clearly legible on the bottom line of the three lines of the inscription, the remainder of the text will require additional study. How this early Islamic period seal ended up at this site and in this particular locus is a complete mystery, although the disruption of the adjacent modern pit might explain how this object was uncovered among finds two millennia older. No other clearly identifiable finds from the early Islamic era were discovered at Tell el-Borg.

Discussion of Small Finds from Field VI Area 2, Unit G (Modern Pit)

TBO 0859 is a mud bulla (fig. 7.93a). The stamped impression is oval shaped and possibly a cartouche. No signs, however, are discernible. The back (fig. 7.93b) is rough, somewhat undulating, possibly revealing the indentation left by the string that was wrapped around the papyrus scroll. The blackened area of the bulla suggests that it had been in a fire. Another bulla, TBO 0771 (fig. 7.94a), lacks a stamped surface, but some illegible scratching into the surface is evident. The

33. Hoffmeier contacted Dr. Donald Whitcomb of the Oriental Institute for assistance with this object. He, in turn, referred him to Tareq Ramadan, a Jordanian scholar. He examined images of this seal and made the preliminary observations mentioned here. He will conduct further research on the inscription in the future.

Fig. 7.93. Clay bulla, TBO 0859. **a** (left): front; **b** (right): back.

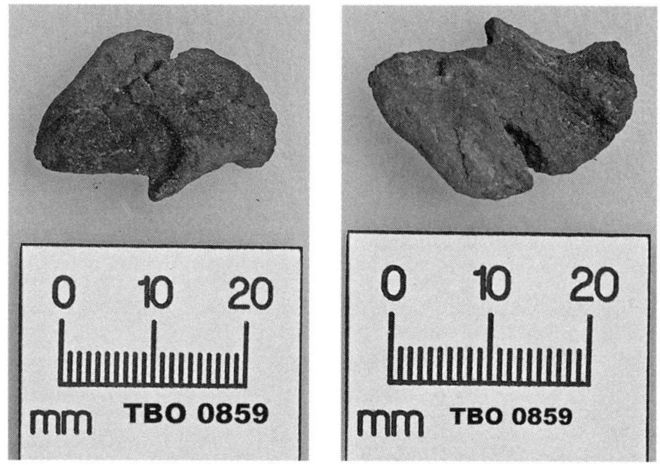

Fig. 7.94. Clay bulla, TBO 0771. **a** (left): front; **b** (right): back.

Fig. 7.95. Clay bulla with pair of frogs, ☥-sign between them, TBO 0773.

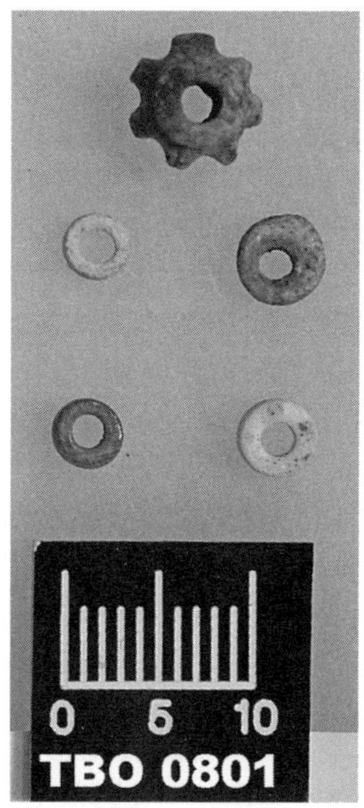

Fig. 7.96. TBO 0801.

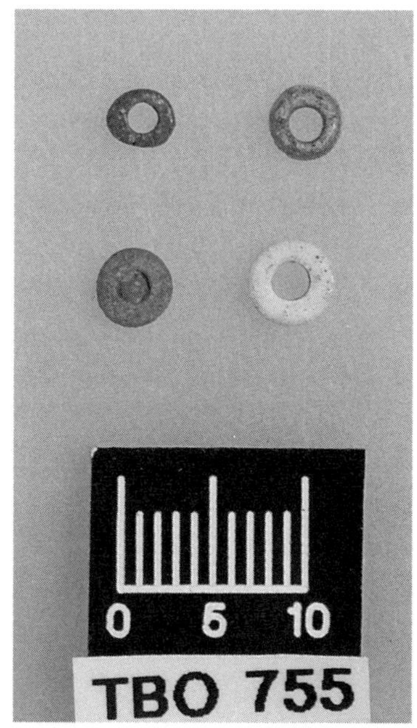

Fig. 7.97. TBO 0755.

underside (fig. 7.94b) has the impression of the string of the original document, and shortly after discovery, the conservator noted that fibers from the string were still intact. This pit yielded yet a third clay seal impression, TBO 0773 (fig. 7.95a–b). This one is unique, with a pair of frogs facing a standing ☥-sign between them. No parallels to this motif can be cited.[34] The association of frogs and life reminds one of the divine birthing scenes (e.g., Hatshepsut, Amenhotep III) where the frog-headed goddess lifts the *ankh*-sign (life and/or breath) to the nostrils of the image of the

34. This conclusion was reached based on an email exchanged with Daphna Ben-Tor.

Fig. 7.98. TBO 0772.

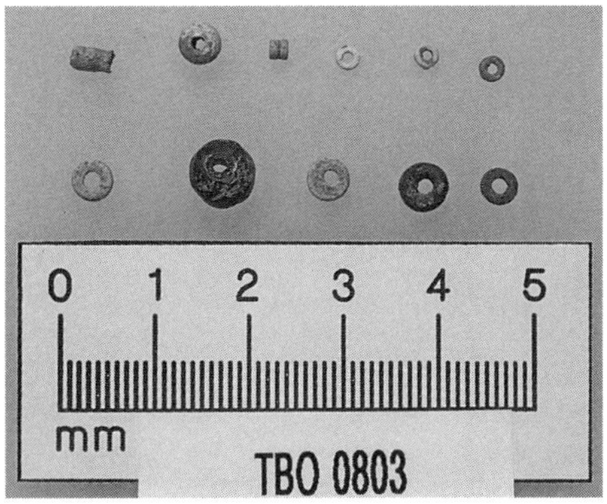

Fig. 7.99. TBO 0803.

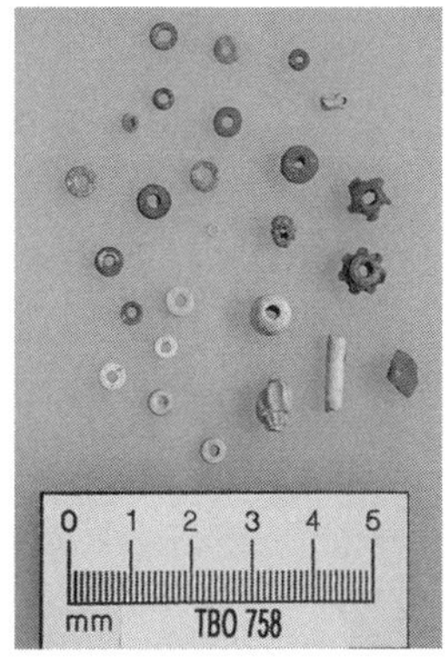

Fig. 7.100. TBO 0758.

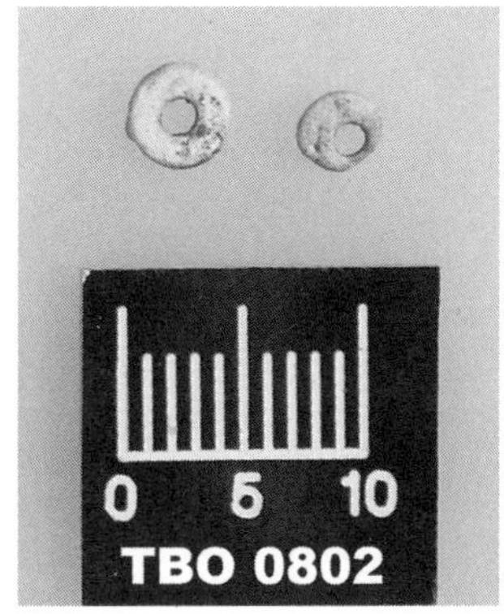

Fig. 7.101. TBO 0802.

ruler being formed on Khnum's potter's wheel.[35] What this birth or life icon is doing on a bulla that sealed a document is curious indeed.

The discovery of three clay bullae within the Unit G pit along with the two royal seal impressions of Horemheb from the ancient pit in adjacent units, within a few meters of each other, is remarkable. The discovery of five seal impressions in Field VI Area 2 (Units A–G), along with the fact that no other bullae were recovered at Tell el-Borg, might indicate that there was an administrative center (now completely lost) nearby, where scribes were active.

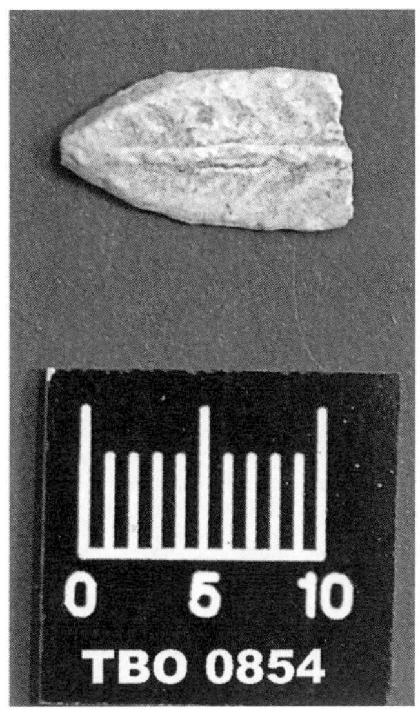

Fig. 7.102. Faience pendant or inlay, TBO 0854.

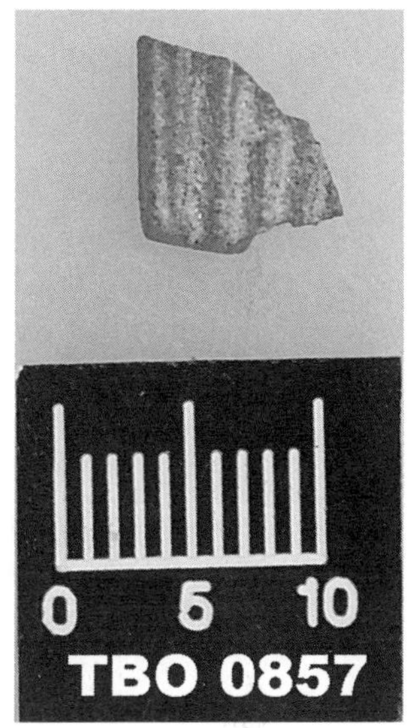

Fig. 7.103. Faience sherd, TBO 0857.

More than four dozen beads were uncovered, largely by sifting. These include TBO 0801 (fig. 7.96), TBO 0755 (fig. 7.97), TBO 0758 (fig. 7.98), TBO 0803 (fig. 7.99), TBO 0758 (fig. 7.100), TBO 0802 (fig. 7.101), and TBO 0866. The beads may well have originated in nearby Tomb 14 (see below). A faience leaf fragment, possibly a pendant or piece of inlay, was also recovered in this pit, TBO 0854 (fig. 7.102), along with a blue-gray faience rippled sherd, TBO 0857 (fig. 7.103).

Tomb 14 (Loci 010, 011, 012, 013, 014, 015, 016)

The removal of the surface soil (Locus 001) in Square G in 2006 revealed the remains of a mud-brick tomb, heavily disturbed both in antiquity and during the modern military occupation. The entire east side of the tomb had been destroyed by the large pit (Locus 002), an ancient pit (Locus 009, which was cut into and mostly removed by the modern excavation of Locus 002), and, at least 22 modern shovel cuts or robber pits (fig. 7.104). The surviving structure measured 2.40 m (east–west) by 3.20 m (north–south) × 1.60 m high (figs. 7.105, 7.106).

35. TBO 012 was a frog figurine uncovered in the cemetery area in Field III (fig. 4.119a–b). See the discussion of the frog and references in chapter 4.

Fig. 7.104. First appearance of the outline of Tomb 14, with recent signs of robbing.

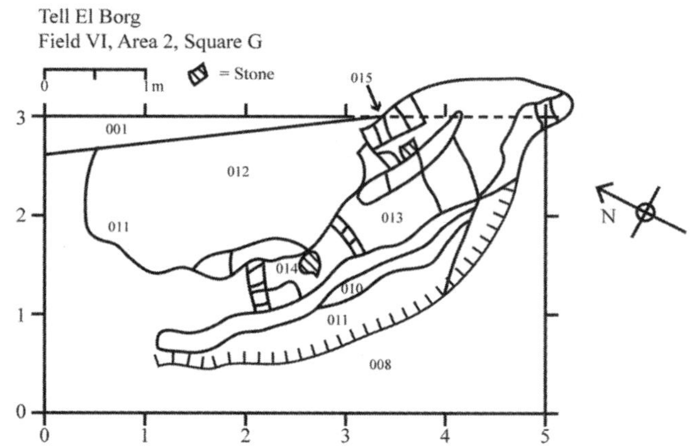

Fig. 7.105. Top plan of Unit G with Tomb 14.

Fig. 7.106. Tomb 14 in Field VI.

The tomb was constructed below ground-level in a man-made pit (Locus 011). The surviving pit edge is curved to the southeast and probably was larger than 4 m across in its original form. The western edge of the pit, the only surviving side, was heavily disturbed with modern robber/shovel pits. The limited fill between the tomb wall and the pit edge yielded few sherds. The brick wall of the tomb was placed directly against the pit edge at the base but became freestanding for the top 50–70 cm of surviving wall (Locus 010). The level of the original ground surface is unknown, because the interior of the crater has been heavily disturbed. The basal sand forms the surviving surface west of the tomb.

Fig. 7.107. Inside wall (west), with stepped entrance.

Fig. 7.108a–b. **a** (top right): Patch of lime plaster flooring in Tomb 14; **b** (below): closeup of limestone patch in Tomb 14.

The tomb was constructed as a series of chambers descending into the ground (fig. 7.106). The initial entry to the tomb is heavily disturbed, with only remnants of the brick wall surviving on the west side. This is the highest surviving point of the tomb wall, just below the modern surface. A modern robber pit destroyed the northern edge. The remnant wall (north end of Locus 010) is placed directly on and against undisturbed basal sand (fig. 7.104).

The next chamber (Locus 014) starts approximately 1 m south of the initial construction. Locus 014 is walled on 3 sides, with a step down from the basal sand of the initial entry area (fig. 7.107). An ancient pit heavily disturbed the east side of the chamber (Locus 009) along with a modern robber cut. This severed the apparent connection between the mud brick of the eastern and southern walls. A modern shovel cut extended all the way through the western wall of the chamber at the northwest corner. A patch of white lime plaster measuring 26 cm (east–west) × 33 cm (north–south) extended from the west wall in the northwest corner (fig 7.108a–b). This 1-cm-thick lime plaster overlay 5 cm of mud plaster, on clean fill sand. The plaster was cut by the robber pits and probably originally extended out 45 cm to overlie a step 3 courses high (mud brick, stone, mud brick). This step, 14 cm wide, was built on the basal sand and bonded into the main wall (Locus 010) (fig. 7.106). Against the step, the base was flat mud brick laid into the sterile sand. The remnant east wall of Locus 014 was bonded by the constructed step into the main wall of the tomb, Locus 010. This was built into the basal sand and then cut by the ancient pit (Locus 009). A later cross-wall, abutting Locus 010, was not bonded, just one brick thick, and measured 60 cm high, forming the south end of the chamber. When the chamber was cleared of disturbed fill, the step structure showed clearly on the west wall, indicating that the tomb was designed to have a stepped entry. The closing wall was probably built after the body had been laid in the tomb. The wall did not have the internal strength to function as a support wall, since it was abutting and not anchored into the existing structure. The west wall of the chamber had a slight rising curve, suggesting that the tomb may have had a domed roof, just like the larger tombs in Field III (see chapter 4). The internal chamber measured 60 × 75 cm.

South of Locus 14 was a lower entry chamber, Locus 13. The tomb chamber floor formed the bottom of the entry chamber, which was delineated by a separate cross-wall, Locus 15, creating a 60-cm-wide entry space. A sloping ramp led down to the floor of the tomb from the base of Locus 014. This ramp started at 108 cmbs and terminated on the surviving floor level at 190 cmbs. The cross wall, Locus 015, was constructed to rest on the floor. The cross wall was also heavily damaged by looting pits and is isolated on both the north and south ends. The entire southern tip of the tomb structure is missing as well.

The floor of the tomb was constructed very solidly, at least 40 cm thick, of mud bricks and limestone (3 blocks). The blocks were not squared-off but appear to be leftover waste from other construction. The floor was truncated by the ancient and modern pits, and no material was found on its surface. One Base Ring II sherd was found among the materials on the floor. The base of the floor was laid into the sand and composed of fragmentary mud bricks.

Tomb 14 Summary

The original design of the tomb had a three-stepped sequence of chambers. The lowest one, presumably the burial chamber, was originally at least 120 cm wide. After the initial construction was complete, the lowest step became a ramp, and a cross-wall was placed to block the top of the ramp. The second chamber may then have been used for offerings or a stele placed on the plastered floor. Many of the small finds found in the disturbed pits may have come from the tomb. The high number of beads recovered from the pits in Area 2 may have been adornment on the now-disappeared body. The clay bulla TBO 0771 (fig. 7.94a–b) seems to have originated in the tomb itself. It had no identifiable seal impression, but some string fibers and string impressions indicate that at least 1 document was placed in the tomb. The tomb was clearly robbed in ancient

Table 7.9. Pottery Recovered from Tomb 14

Locus/ Basket	*Silt*	*Marl*	*Levant*	*Cypriot*	*Rims*	*Bases*	*Handles*	*Lids/ Misc*	*Remarks/ Decoration*
009/1	192	28	15	3	36	4	2	2	combing (or mat ting) on one rim; 4 blue paint; rope decoration
009/3	193	30	32	0	36	2	2	0	1 blue paint; 1 huge basin/tub
009/4	150	24	9	1	14	2	0	0	1 white-shaved burned Nile silt; 1 decorated red sherd with red bands on cream slip
009/5	60	4	5	1	3	2	0	1 import	2 blue-painted sherds; 1 Token (Marl D) 1 Cypriot Base-Ring
011/1	72	17	2	1	8	1	0	0	2 blue painted; 1 Cypriot Milk Bowl
011/2	21	0	1	0	2	1	0	0	Fragments of red-slipped jar (no rim or base)
012/1	160	21	8	0	21	1	0	0	2 Blue-painted
012/2	134	7	6	0	18	0	0	0	Base fill of pit tomb
013/1	18	2	2	0	3	0	0	0	Dot and band dec.; mid-18th dyn. black paint on marl A; 1 blue-painted
013/2	7	15	6	1	8	0	2	1 Cypriot body	1 Cypriot WS milk bowl, black dec. on white
014/1	6	0	0	0	1	0	0	0	Scant data
016/1	1	9	3	1	10	1	0	2 body sherds	1 Cypriot Base-Ring II, white bands on black, 1 Blue-painted sherd; 1 "strange" sherd, vessel body, pale gray, no core, fine angular sand, evenly distributed, some fine red particles

times and disturbed again during the modern military occupation. The provenance of four bullae was from the intrusive pit, not from Tomb 14.

Area 2 Summary

The material recovered from Area 2 evidences later activity in Field VI, down to the end of the 18th Dynasty: a stamped jar handle from Nefer-neferu-aten and a scarab and seal impressions from Horemheb were found. It is a strong possibility that the Horemheb mud sealings were originally placed around documents deposited among the grave offerings in the tomb, which provided them added protection from weathering. If so, then this tomb dates from the end of the 18th Dynasty, which is consistent with the in situ ceramics.

Fieldwork in Area 2 did not uncover any traces of domestic structures. The discovery of the remains of Tomb 14 indicates that the cemetery district extended this far west, but probably at a later date. However, the material recovered from the modern/ancient disturbed pits points to what life may have been like on this part of the tell during the early New Kingdom. The high percentage of small finds from this feature makes it clear that ancient people continued to use this area after the burning of the huts early in the New Kingdom. The pit could have simply been a dump pit, holding refuse from the robbing of the tomb, or there could have been domestic buildings nearby, evidence of which simply did not survive the deflation and modern interference, particularly martial activities. Modern interference on top of burned reed stains or similar features would likely remove such features altogether.

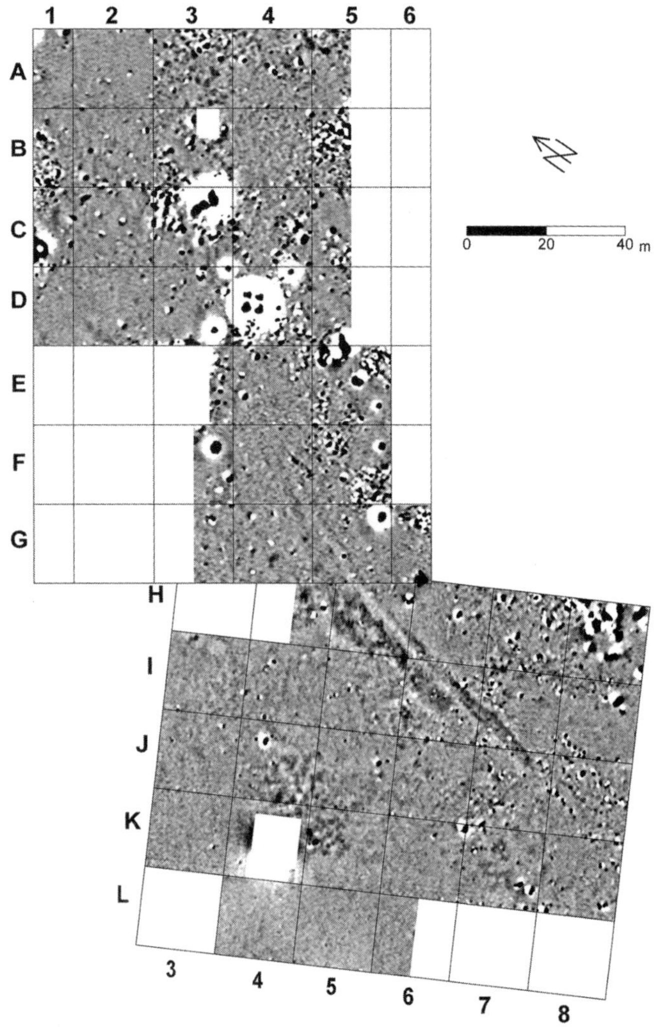

Fig. 7.109. Magnetometer image of Field VI Area 3.

Field Investigations in Area 3: The Field VI Fosse

The initial investigation of Field VI in 2002 included the hand-stripping of a 5 × 5 m block in what would later be designated Area 3, about 60 m southwest of Area 2 (fig. 7.1). No subsurface features were identified: subsoil was encountered immediately beneath the surface. It was assumed that the area had been completely deflated and/or mechanically stripped during the military occupation, and no surface material from the stripped area was kept. The southern portions of Area 3 had originally been identified as part of Field VII when Square D was placed here in 2002 (in 2007, Field VII Square D was redesignated as Field VI Area 3 Square D). No features were identified in Square D, which lay close to the Egyptian military trench line, and no pottery was retained from the surface collection after it was initially sorted. As it turned out, the northwest corner of the 5 × 5 m probe was about 2 m east of the long mud-brick feature that would come to light five years later.

During the 2007 field season, Field VI was examined again and subject to a remote-sensing survey using a Fluxgate Gradiometer Geoscan Research FM 256. The four large survey blocks in Field VI were not oriented to the site grid to enable the widest coverage between the roadway separating Field VI and Field VII and the military trenches dividing up Field VI into areas (*Tell el-Borg I*, 351, 356–57). The block in Area 1 measured 60 × 120 m and included the hut stains, which did not appear as distinctive magnetic anomalies. Area 2 coverage included an 80 × 80 m block just south of "the borg" and a smaller offset block measuring 60 × 50 m. This overlapped the Area 3 block, which measured 80 × 80 m. A linear magnetic anomaly (+100 m) was detected in the survey of Field VI Area 3, curving to the northeast; because this is the direction of the crater (fig. 7.109), it was thought this might be a modern military road. Unit B was placed across the anomaly to determine its nature. (For results, see the next section.) Other test units were placed to examine the moat at various intervals. Five other isolated anomalies were tested within Field VI; none were caused by ancient cultural features.

Unit B

A test trench, Unit B (Square A was the 5 × 5 m sterile probe excavated in 2002), originally measuring 2 × 10 m, was laid out along the same grid as the magnetic survey, with a midpoint at one of the survey stakes, to cross the linear anomaly. This was expanded to eventually measure

4 × 10.5 m, with a small 2 × 1.5 m extension east along the north wall. Surface material and three robber pits were removed as Locus 001; no material was retained from this Locus. The westernmost robber pit had a depth of 26 cmbs and the central pit was two shovel probes together measuring 59 cmbs at its deepest point; a small third shovel cut 18 cmbs was removed from the eastern third of the unit. Upon surface clearance, the source of the magnetic anomaly became clear: a more than 2-m-wide, mud-brick lined, sand-filled moat, cutting across the unit in a northwest–southeast direction (figs. 7.1, 7.110–7.111).

Immediately beneath the surface, west of the moat at the west edge of the unit, was Locus 002: a very mottled dark brown (10YR 3/2 – 3/3) mud layer with distinctive parallel markings in white sand. This was initially thought to be bricks, but if so, they were precisely uniform and very long, measuring 50 × 20 cm (fig. 7.112). On the surface of the mud were sherds showing heavy weathering and/or

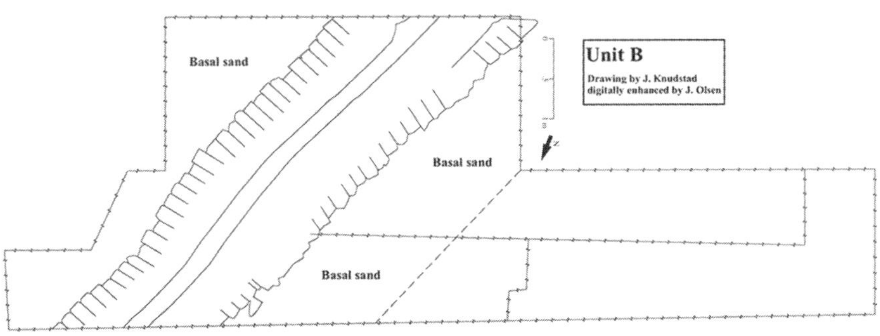

Fig. 7.110. **a** (above left): Mud-brick fosse in Field VI Area 3, Unit B; **b** (left): Top plan of Unit B section of fosse.

Fig. 7.111. Unit B fosse section looking east.

Fig. 7.112. Impressions of bulldozer tracks immediately west of Unit B.

Fig. 7.113. Part of equid head found in fosse (Unit B)

modern brick fragments pressed into the "brick" surface. When cleaned, the "bricks" are clearly not bricks; a modern military brick fragment was pressed across a joint and under the sand of the "mortar." This formation must be the result of some sort of heavy military vehicle traffic across the surface. The impressed mud stain was 11 cm in depth and extended along the northern edge of the unit for more than 5 m, running diagonally across the unit to the southwest and cut by two of the robber pits. When scraped, Locus 002 lifted cleanly off of the underlying brown sandy fill, which was designated Locus 003.

Locus 003 was a fill layer above a hard-packed surface (Loci 011/007), which rose to the east. It was general tell occupational sand fill and contained bone and some sherds. A 1 × 2 m window was placed to reach the base of Locus 003. This was marked by a hard-packed mud surface (Locus 011) above basal sand at 62 cmbs. Basket 3 from the window yielded a disarticulated concentration of large equid bones, which may relate to the horse skull recovered in the moat fill (fig. 7.113). This probably represents occupational/natural debris that has been leveled first by deflation and then by bulldozing. Immediately east of Locus 003 was a section of sterile basal sand with a slope down to the west, which Locus 003 filled.

Below Locus 003 was a very hard-packed surface (Locus 007) with some sherds, which rose to the east and became a humped accumulation of mud and "mud-bricky" detritus; 2 substantive mud-brick fragments were visible in the north section of Unit B (fig. 7.114). This is in a pit cutting into the subsoil unevenly and may represent mud-brick collapse of a wall accompanying the moat, which is now gone. Any connection between Locus 007 and the fosse is severed by deflation. This surface underlies Locus 003 and may account for its formation. It is very thick, nearly 50 cm, at the eastern edge. The very top is uneven; perhaps it was exposed to the wind and weather. This does not appear to be a constructed surface but is, rather, a slump. The best hypothesis is that this is either a mixing base for mud bricks or, more likely, the remains of a wall that slumped. The original link to the moat has weathered away.

Locus 003 is probably tell occupational material deposited after the moat went out of use, and it provided the source of the mud fill as the moat walls decayed and were spread by wind and rain. Unfortunately, the exposure was too limited to determine actual role or function. Immediately

Fig. 7.114. Northern baulk of Unit B with mud and brick detritus that may be a portion of original inside enclosure wall.

Fig. 7.115. Top view of fosse in Unit B.

west of Square B, the area had been mechanically disturbed and mixed down to the basal sands by large tracked vehicles.

The main feature exposed by the excavation of Unit B was the source of the magnetic anomaly: a Pharaonic moat constructed of mud bricks (figs. 7.110, 7.111, 7.114–7.123). The mud-brick west wall (Locus 005) of the moat was placed into a small foundation trench (Locus 013), an irregular cut into the basal sand (Locus 004) through occupational debris. The foundation trench was very uneven in width, measuring from 30 cm to 10 cm. It was fully excavated in the north half of the unit, and it almost disappears as one goes farther south along the fosse wall, eventually becoming too hard to distinguish from the basal sand. A few nondiagnostic sherds were found in the fill. The fill appears to stop at about 60 cmbs, at which point the bricks are placed fully within it and envelop the entire space. The mud-brick moat wall was placed into the sand on the base as headers, with only a very few stretchers visible. The wall was one brick thick (9–10 × 17–18 × 38–42 cm, 10YR 5/4) and used very fine mud plaster (10YR 8/2–7/3) between joints and as a leveler on the basal bricks. The bottom row was placed directly on the basal tell sand, with no apparent plaster base; bricks were then built up and stepped back, creating an angled surface with a sloping plaster cover; runoff and slump obscured the actual face of the plaster and made discovery of the brick face difficult (fig. 7.115). The east wall of the fosse (Locus 008) was also placed in a small foundation trench (Locus 009) and built in the same way as the west wall. Different individuals or labor teams may have built separate sections: some bricks appear to be better and are more evenly laid then others. The top of the moat within Unit B had an internal width of 165 cm at the top and was 25 cm at its base. The wall survived to a height of 90 cm. The bottom was coated with a 3–5 cm accumulation of darker brown sand and mud.

The east-side foundation trench (Locus 009) yielded more cultural material than the west-side foundation trench. Locus 009 also was very uneven in width, from 50 cm to 1–2 cm at the point where it becomes impossible to identify along the north portion of the exposed fosse wall. This locus yielded 30 sherds, including 2 Cypriot Base Ring sherds. The horn from a Base Ring bull figurine was found directly against the mud brick of the western wall of the fosse in the foundation trench. Cypriot Base Ring figurines have a relatively long use span and may on occasion

Fig. 7.116 (above). Badly denuded northern portion of the Field VI fosse.

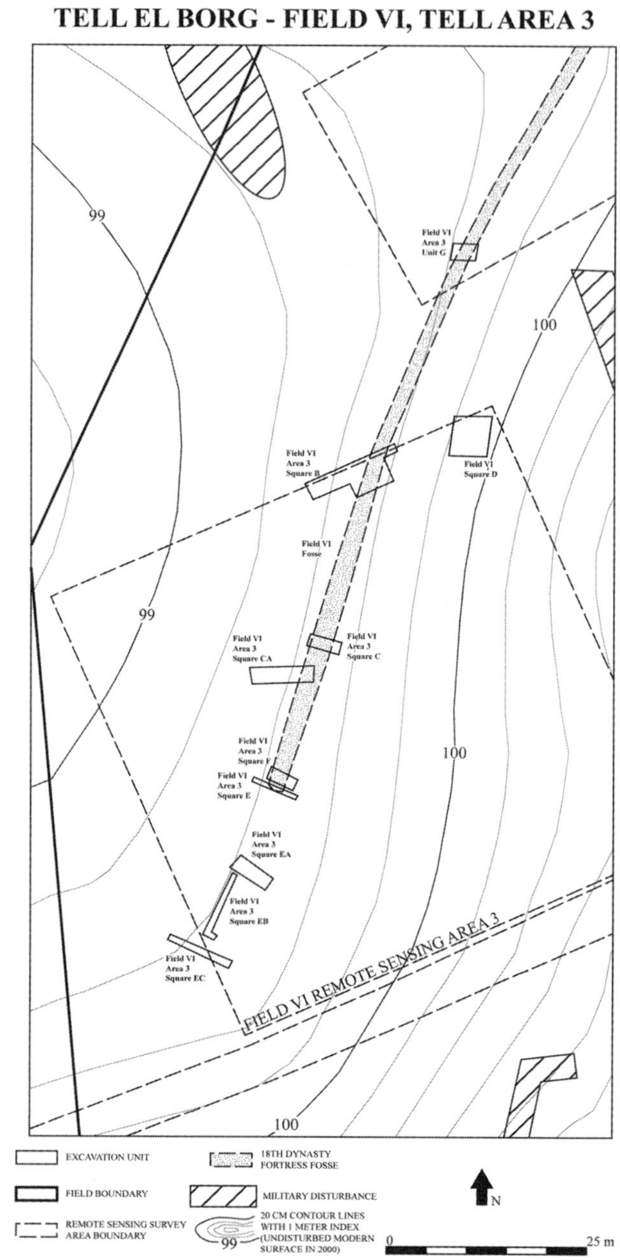

Fig. 7.117 (right). Plan of Field VI Area 3, by D. Olney, digitally enhanced by Joshua Olsen.

even be an heirloom piece. Consequently, it provides little aid in dating the fosse, except to place its construction in the New Kingdom after 1500 B.C.

The moat fill was separable into three loci in Unit B: the upper fill, Locus 006, mostly brownish-yellow (10YR 6/8) sand and mud-brick detritus with a loose consistency; overtop of Locus 010, with a relatively even surface and clear texture change to a much harder yellowish-brown (10YR 5/4–4/3) sand and clay detritus; and Locus 014, a large section of collapsed mud-brick detritus and yellowish-brown (10YR 5/4) sand also lying above Locus 010 in the south section of the exposed moat. Flat-lying sherds marked the top surface of 010 at an average depth of 50 cmbs.

The Locus 006 matrix contained fragments of mud brick and what appeared to be slope-washed mud intermixed with wind-deposited sands. This material was most likely deposited after the moat went out of use. Included in the fill was the aforementioned equid skull, without any

Fig. 7.118 (left). Remnant of fosse in Units H and I, with collapsed bricks in the bottom.

Fig. 7.119**a** (below, left). Section of fosse in Unit C.

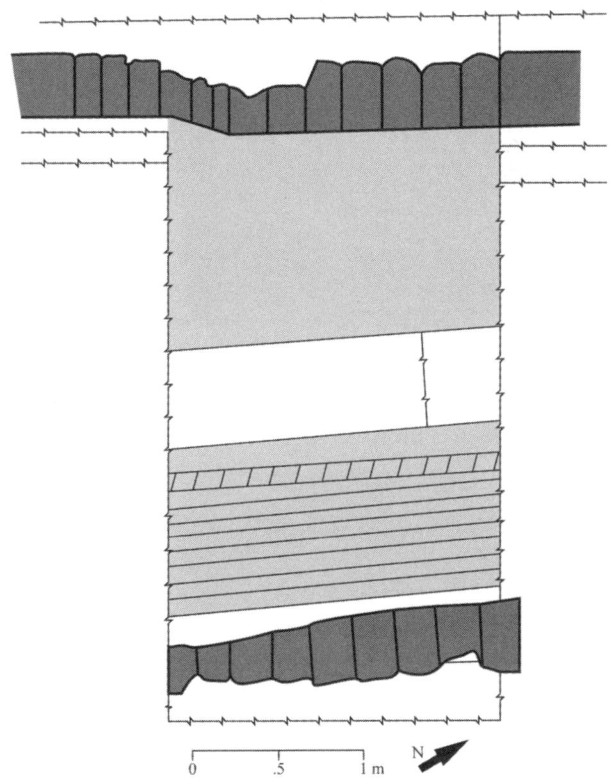

Fig. 7.119**b** (below). Plan of fosse in Unit C. Drawing by J. Knudstad, digitally enhanced by Joshua Olsen.

other bone elements (fig. 7.113). Locus 010 is hard-packed, with mud lenses and sand mixed and hardened by sun and wind. The profile of Locus 010 shows a slight bowl effect, indicating that it was not an artificial fill but the product of natural erosion. Periodic rains would have washed mud off of the plaster-lined walls and deposited them inside the moat, mixing with wind-blown sand and baking to a hard consistency during the dry season. Locus 003 may be contemporary with the filling of the moat, but this cannot be demonstrated, because the deflation of the area has removed the connection.

Fig. 7.120. South end of fosse in Unit F.

Fig. 7.121. South end of fosse in Unit F.

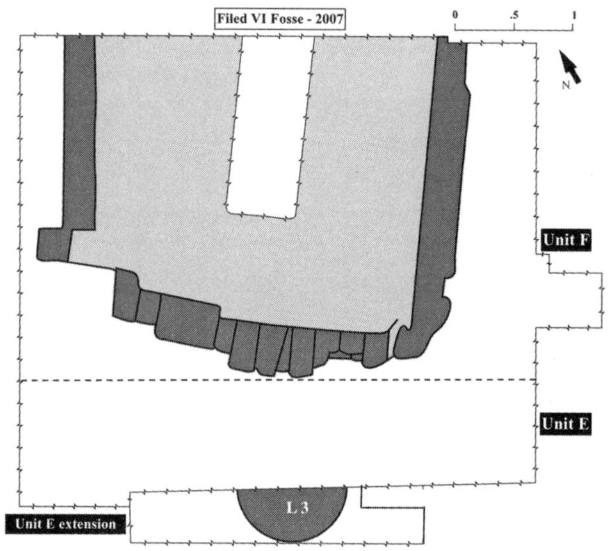

Fig. 7.122. Plan of south end of fosse in Unit F. Drawing by J. Knudstad, digitally enhanced by Joshua Olsen.

Fig. 7.123. Ceramic vessels in fosse fill of Unit F.

Extent of the Field VI Fosse: Units C, E, and G

The surviving sections of this New Kingdom fosse measured approximately 176 m long (figs. 7.116–7.117). In a few sections in this long section, the bottom of the moat contained bricks that apparently had collapsed from the upper moat walls and now lay in the trough at the bottom (fig. 7.118). The southeast terminus was marked by a constructed end (Unit F), with a built mud-brick closing wall. Repeated test units placed along the projected alignment to the southern end the moat (Units Ea, Eb, and Ec) revealed no indication of any further construction on what must have been the original gateway or where its construction was anticipated. Unit Ec is located 25 m southwest of Unit F. No constructed northern end was found: the fosse alignment simply petered out, with a very thin mud smear being the remaining signature at the 176 m mark. Because the final 100 m of the northern end was adjacent (west) to the heart of the 1960s Israeli military

Fig. 7.124. Closeup of vessels in fosse fill of Unit F.

Fig. 7.125. TBP 0810. Bowl from fosse fill in Unit F.

camp, no doubt whatever survived of the fosse after millennia of deflation was mostly bulldozed to create the modern camp. The surviving depth of the eastern end of the fosse, nearly 1.5 m high, clearly indicates that Field VI has been deflated to at least that degree. A *khamseen*, in April 2007, interrupted work on the fosse and eroded at least 20 cm of the exposed walls in one afternoon, indicating the fragile nature of the surviving feature.

Eighteen meters south of Unit B, a small window was opened to trace the fosse. Unit C (1.5 × 4 m) exposed a section of the mud-brick moat that was preserved to a higher level than in Unit B (fig. 7.119). After the fill was cleared, a depth of 1.36 m was reached. The inside width at the top was 2.36 m, while the surviving outside width of the top of the fosse was 3.05 m. As with the section exposed in Unit B, there was no evidence for a stone or fired-brick foundation for the sloping mud-brick walls, as was the case of the moats associated with the18th Dynasty and 19th Dynasty forts in Fields IV, V, and VIII (see *Tell el-Borg I*, 128–82, 218–21, and 228–38). The type of brick and sandy mortar that was noted in Unit B was found in the section of the fosse in this unit.

Moving 18 m farther south from Unit C, a 1 × 3.5 m trench was laid across the line of the fosse (Unit E), hoping to intersect with the end of the fosse as revealed in the magnetometer images (fig. 7.109). Although we overshot the mark slightly, the remains of half of a circular mud pillar base(?) was exposed (figs. 7.120–7.122). Built on basal sand, about half of this feature was lost in the course of excavation because it looked just like the surrounding mud and detritus mud-brick material of Locus 1. The radius of this Locus 3 feature is 43 cm; it was brown to dark gray color (10YR 5/3 to 10YR 3/1). In order to determine if this pillar base had a counterpart to the south, an extension of Unit E and additional probes and trenches were excavated south of Unit E (extension)—that is, Units Ea, Eb, and Ec—but these were sterile. No further trace of the moat on the other side of the entranceway was discovered, which was consistent with the magnetometer data.

The constructed, southern end of the long Field VI fosse was exposed immediately north of Unit E in Unit F, a 3 × 3.5 m unit. The construction technique used for the fosse here was the same as that found in Units B and C: it had the same size and type of bricks and sandy white mortar (see above). The maximum width of the fosse at the preserved height is 2.25 m and the depth, like that found in Unit C, was approximately 1.35 m. It seems likely that the sections uncovered in Units C and F do not represent the original height.

POTTERY FROM FIELD VI AREA 3 FOSSE

Rexine Hummel
ROYAL ONTARIO MUSEUM

A few nearly complete vessels and diagnostic sherds were recovered in Unit F (figs. 7.123, 7.124, 7.125), mostly in Loci 2 and 3, a muddy-sand mix fill (10YR 7/6) about 30 cm from the bottom of the moat. This placement means that these ceramic remains date to the terminal phase of the use of the fort.

Pottery Plate 7.3

Red-Slipped Bowls

Most noticeable in the assemblage was the predominance of bowl fragments that had been coated with red slip, many of which had been burnished on all surfaces. A total of ten diagnostic sherds from bowls were burnished red inside and out, three of which are illustrated here. Another nine bowl rims were described but not drawn, of which four were simply slipped red and five were left uncoated.

3:1 Saucer. TBP 810. Rim diam: 14 cm. Ware: Nile B1. Surface: Thick red slip[36] inside and out, burnished.
Parallel: Bourriau 2010: Appendix 2, p. 488. Type: 4.2.5. Memphis. This long-lived bowl begins in the early to mid-18th Dynasty and continues up to the late 19th Dynasty. Bourriau notes that burnishing inside and out is very popular from the mid-18th Dynasty into the early Ramesside Period.

3:2 Bowl. Sherd: 10. Rim diam: 20 cm. Ware: Nile B2. Surface: red slip inside and out, burnished.
Parallels: Bourriau 2010: Appendix 2, p. 488. Type: 4.2.5. Memphis. This long-lived bowl begins in the early to mid-18th Dynasty and continues up to the late 19th Dynasty into the early Ramesside Period. Aston 1998: 113:123. Qantir, Ramesside Period.

3:3 Bowl. Sherd: 9. Rim diam: 35 cm. Ware: Nile B2. Surface: red slip inside and out, burnished.
Parallel: Bourriau 2010: Appendix 2. Pg. 488. Type: 4.2.5. Memphis. This long-lived bowl begins in the early to mid-18th Dynasty and continues up to the late 19th Dynasty.

3:4 Carinated bowl. Sherd 3. Rim diam: 25 cm. Ware: Marl A4. Surface: red slip in and out, black horizontal bands on the exterior above the carination.
Parallels: Aston 2014: 27, pl. 4:28. Valley of the Kings, KV 47. Popular in the reign of Thutmosis III to reign of Amenhotep III. Hummel and Shubert 1994: pl. LXXII: 2, East Karnak, New Kingdom.

3:5 Cypriot bowl. Sherd 4. Rim diam: 17 cm. Ware: Cypriot White Slip II. Surface: White-slipped background with brownish-black painted ladder design on exterior.
Parallel: Swiny 2014: 487, fig. 564, Tell el-Borg, 13th century B.C.

3:6 Bowl. Sherd 6. Rim diam: 32 cm. Nile B2. Surface: Uncoated.
Parallel: Bourriau 2010: Appendix 2, p. 477. Type: 3.8.2. Memphis. This long-lived bowl begins in the early to mid-18th Dynasty and continues up to the late 19th Dynasty.

3:7 Bowl. Sherd 8. Rim diam: 30 cm. Well-fired Nile B2. Surface: Uncoated.
Parallel: Bourriau 2010: Appendix 2, p. 479. Type: 3.10.8. Memphis. This long-lived bowl begins in the early to mid-18th Dynasty and continues up to the late 19th Dynasty

3:8 Large, carinated bowl. TBP 816. Rim: 45 cm. Ware: Nile B2. Surface: Cream slip. (Munsell 5YR 7/4) One row of rope impressions decorates outer wall.

---

36. The red slip is Munsell 10R 4/6.

Parallels: Bourriau 2010: Appendix 2, p. 488. Type: 4.18.5. Memphis. Clusters in the early to mid-18th Dynasty. Aston, 2004, Pl 214–215: Group 221 and group 259. Tell el-Dab'a, 17th Dynasty. Aston, 1998: 91:42, Qantir, Late 2IP.

Pottery Plate 7.4

4:1 Small jar. TBP 814, Rim diam: 5 cm. Ware: Nile B1. Surface: red slip, burnished.
Parallel: Rose 2007: 237, Type: SH3.1, fig. 381. Amarna. 18th Dynasty.

4:2 Jar. Sherd 1. Rim diam: 10 cm. Ware: Nile B2. Surface: red slip, burnished.
Parallel: Bourriau 2010: Appendix 2, p. 496. Type: 11.15.2. Memphis. early to mid-18th Dynasty

4:3 Jar. Sherd 12. Rim diam: 10 cm. Ware: Nile B2. Surface: red slip, burnished.
Parallels: Bourriau 2010: Appendix 2, p. 491. Type 10.8.4. Memphis. This form occurs in the early to late 18th Dynasty. Rose 2007: 256, Type: SH14.1, fig. 467. Amarna, 18th Dynasty.

4:4 Amphora . Sherd 2. Rim diam: 10 cm. Ware: Marl D. Surface: Thick cream slip.
Parallels: Bourriau 2010: Appendix 2, p. 470. Type: 10.8.8. Memphis. This long-lived jar begins in the mid- to late 18th Dynasty and continues up to the Ramesside Period. Rose 2007: 278, Type: MF 3.4, fig. 609. Amarna, 18th Dynasty.

4:5 Meat jar. Sherd 5. Rim diam: 30 cm. Ware: Mixed clay. Surface: Thick pink-cream slip.
Parallels: Rose 2007: 276, Type: MF 1.4, fig. 600. Amarna, 18th Dynasty. Aston, 1998: 533, fig. 2175. Qantir, Ramesside Period.

Blue-Painted Jars

Many Blue-Painted sherds were found in the mud and were sent to the conservation laboratory. Consequently, three Blue-Painted funnel-neck jars were partially restored. Funnel-neck jars were very common at New Kingdom sites and range in date from mid- to late 18th to the end of the 19th Dynasty.[37] The ancient artist took advantage of the natural curve of the shoulder to feature a register of pendant blue petals. This motif on funnel-necked jars is characteristic of the late 18th Dynasty.

4:6 Body of funnel-neck jar. TBP 812. Ware: Nile B2. Surface: Peach-colored slip. A typical blue petal frieze broken only by a red horizontal line encircles the shoulder of the jar. A combination of a red line framed by blue and black lines delineates the shoulder area from the neck. Below the frieze, traces of a trio of "nefer"(?) glyphs is drawn in black paint on the peach background, perhaps indicating very fine wine.
Parallel: Hope 1999: fig. 3:c. Colin Hope has categorized all the marks found on blue-painted pottery from several sites and their relative frequency. While a single "nefer" glyph appears frequently, the triple "nefer" glyph is much less popular.

4:7 Body of funnel-neck jar. TBP 813. Ware: Nile B2. Surface: Cream slip. A typical blue petal frieze broken only by a red horizontal line encircles the shoulder of the jar. A combination of a red line framed by blue and black lines delineates the shoulder area from the undecorated neck.
Parallel: Rose 2007: 245, Type: SH 9.3, fig. 425. Amarna, 18th Dynasty.

4:8 Body of jar (probably a funnel-neck jar) TBP 813. Ware: Nile B2. Surface: cream slip. A panel of long, narrow blue petals broken only by red-and-black horizontal lines encircles mid- to base section of the of the jar. A combination of a red line framed by blue and black lines delineates the bottom of the decorated area.
Parallel: Rose 2007: 244, Type: SH 9.3, fig. 422. Amarna. 18th Dynasty.

The mud at the bottom of the fosse produced a large number of diagnostic sherds. Most noticeable was the predominance of both open and closed vessel fragments that had been coated with red slip, many of which had been burnished, suggesting a date in the mid- to late 18th Dynasty.[38]

37. Aston, 1998: 188

38. Bourriau (2010: 139) says: "during the mid to late 18th Dynasty there is a distinct rise in the use of red slip in conjunction with burnishing inside and out."

Most of the diagnostic sherds that were recovered are illustrated here. However, because of the small size of some of the rims and bases, a few have been described but not drawn. In cases where the forms were known, the sherds were typed to an existing prototype in the Borg ceramic typology. In addition, some tiny decorated or foreign body sherds were registered but not drawn. They include: a fragment of a Marl D amphorae, one Marl A2 flask fragment with painted black and red-brown concentric circles, a large sherd from an Oasis-ware amphora, and rims from three large bowls. Although parallels for some of the pot forms occur as early as the 2IP and as late as the 19th Dynasty, the bulk of the Borg assemblage resembles levels IIIA and IIIB at Memphis[39] and therefore fits comfortably into the mid- to late 18th Dynasty.

Works Cited

Aston, David

1998 *Die Keramik des Grabungsplatzes. Q I.* Teil 1: *Corpus of Fabrics, Wares and Shapes.* Mainz: von Zabern.

2004 *Tell el-Dabʿa XII: A Corpus of the Pottery of the Late Middle Kingdom and Second Intermediate Period.* 2 volumes. Vienna: Austrian Academy of Sciences.

2014 *Pottery Recovered near the Tombs of Seti I (KV 17) and Siptah (KV47) in the Valley of the Kings.* Aegyptica Helvetica 24. Basel: Schwabe.

Bourriau, Janine

2010 *The Survey of Memphis IV, Kom Rabia: The New Kingdom Pottery.* Excavation Memoir 93. London: Egypt Exploration Society.

Hope, Colin

1999 "Some Remarks on Potmarks of the late Eighteenth Dynasty." Pp. 121–46 in Anthony Leahy and John Tait (eds.), *Studies on Ancient Egypt in Honour of H. S. Smith.* London: Egypt Exploration Society.

Hummel, R., and Steven B. Shubert

1994 "Kom el Ahmar: Ceramic Analysis." Pp. 30–82 in Donald Redford (ed.), *The Akhenaten Temple Project*, Vol. 3: *The Excavations of Kom el-Ahmar and Environs.* Toronto: Akhenaten Temple Project.

Rose, Pamela,

2007 *The Eighteenth Dynasty Pottery from Amarna.* London: EES.

Stuart Swiny

2014 "The Cypriot Pottery." Pp. 482–94 in James Hoffmeier (ed.), *Tell el-Borg I: Excavations in North Sinai.* Winona Lake, Indiana: Eisenbrauns.

39. Bourriau 2010: appendix 2.

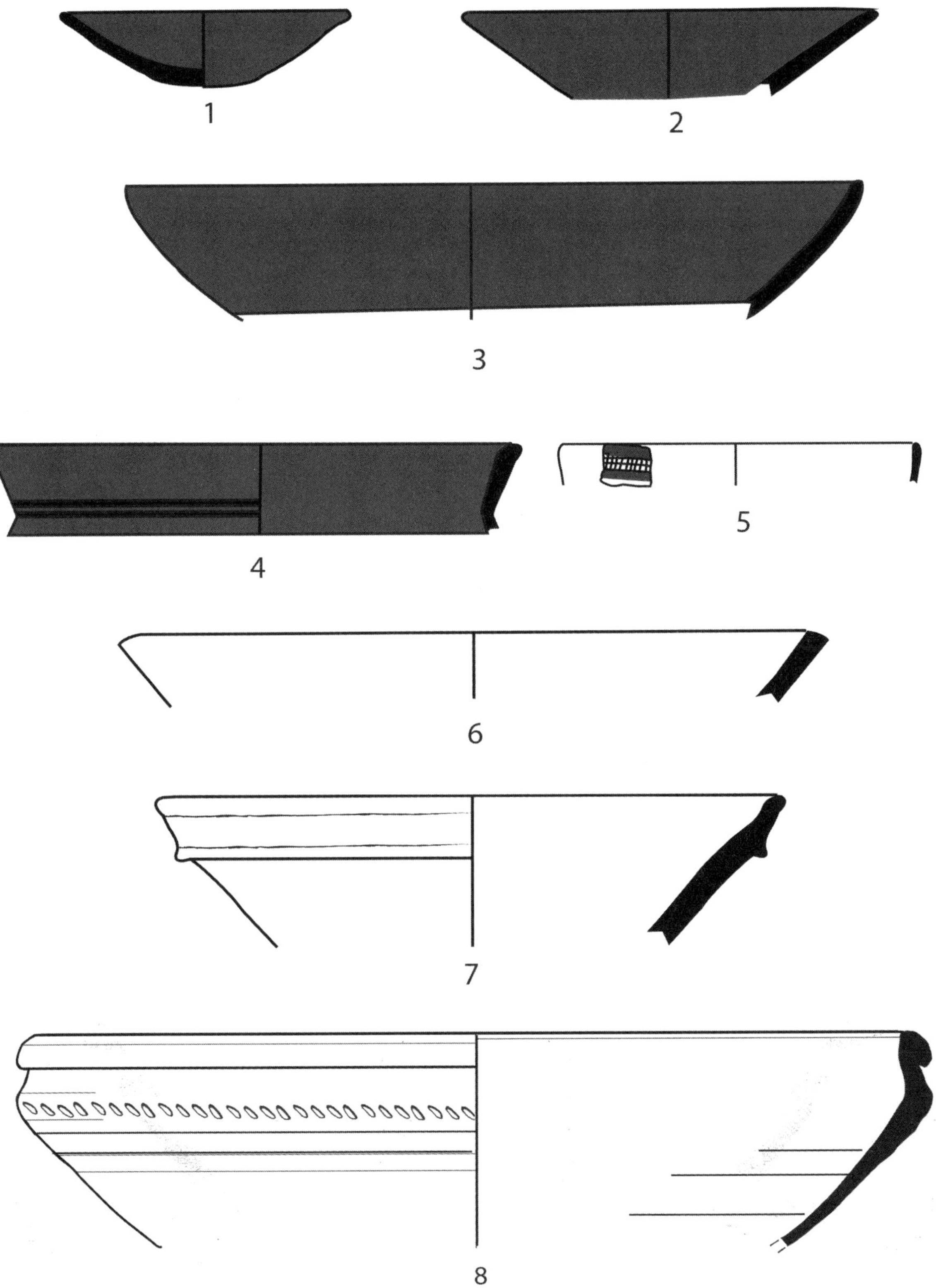

POTTERY PLATE 7.3 1:3

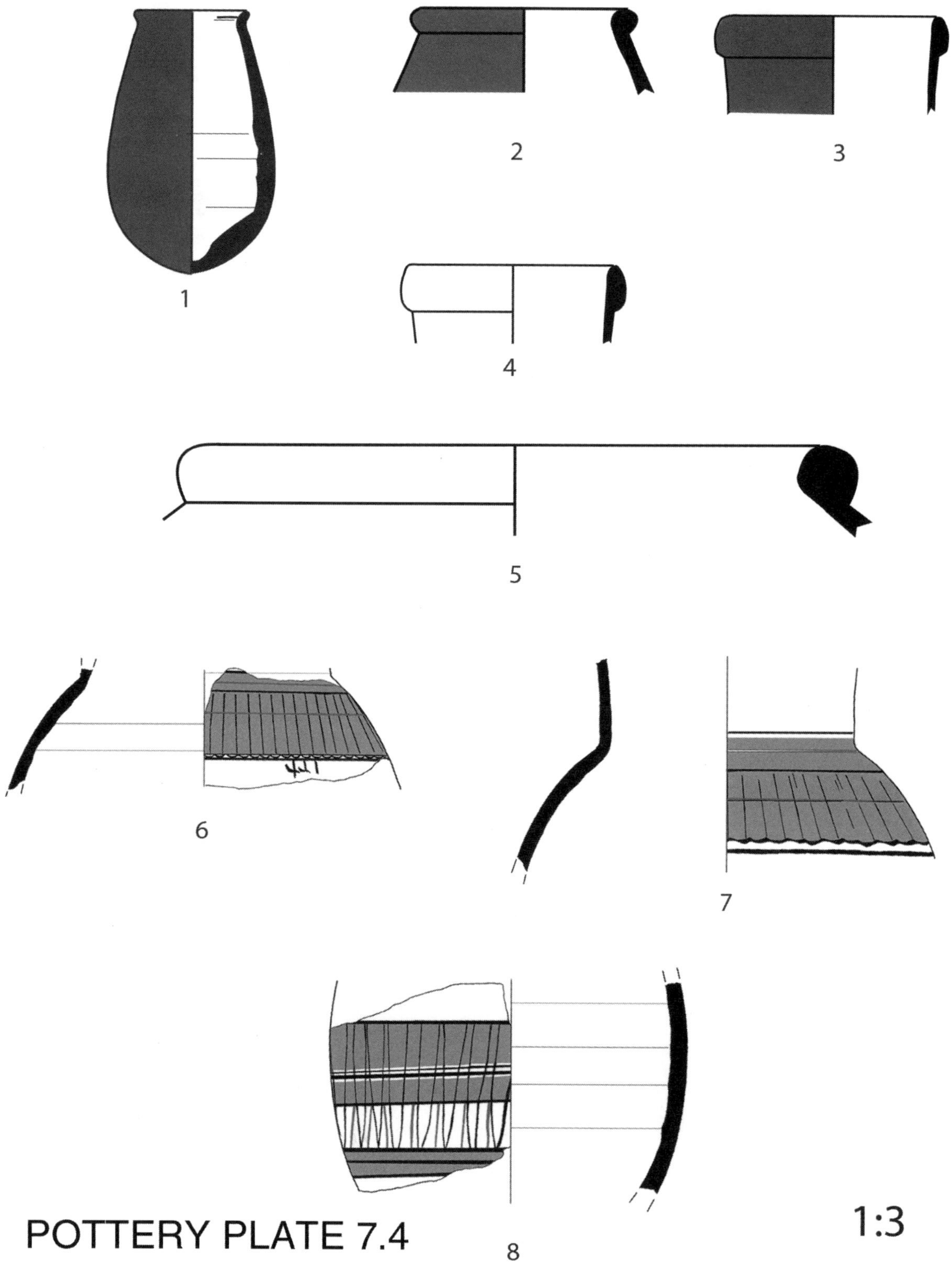

POTTERY PLATE 7.4

1:3

Discussion and Significance of the Field VI Fosse

A comparison with the moats discovered in Fields IV, V, and VIII and the one uncovered in Field VI is called for. The mud-brick fosse associated with the 18th Dynasty fort was well constructed, laid on a foundation of fired (red) brick that varied (depending on elevation) from 8 to 14 courses, and seems to have been in use from the reign of Thutmose III or Amenhotep II (ca. 1450–1400 B.C.) to the end of the Amarna period (see *Tell el-Borg I*, chapter 5). The incomplete moat associated with the second, or Ramesside period, fort employed a mix of reused stones of various sizes as its foundation. It appears to have been constructed late in the 18th to early 19th Dynasty to judge from the pottery associated with it (*Tell el-Borg I*, 380–81), not to mention the inscribed blocks in the foundation that were subject to Atenist iconoclasm (*Tell el-Borg I*, 244–52).

The earlier moat with fired-brick foundations was 8 m wide at the top and was about 3 m deep (Fosse E) (*Tell el-Borg I*, 146, fig. 186). Similarly, Fosse N in Field V, associated with the Ramesside-era fort, was about 8 m wide at the top (*Tell el-Borg I*, 253). The depth of both moats ranged between 2.5 and 3 m. The Field VI fosse, whose surviving dimensions are 2.5 m wide at the top and 1.35 m deep, most likely is not preserved to its original height. One can easily leap across such a narrow trough. No trace of an internal wall was discovered as a result of excavation, nor is there any hint of one in the geophysical data (fig. 7.109), but surely a wall was required if the fosse was to have any defensive value.

The discovery of a mud-brick-lined moat in Field VI—though its entire extent is not known nor is it known whether it encircled the area north of the Nile distributary—is significant for understanding the strategic nature of this military site and how it was defended. The presence of a moat-fortified structure in Field VI means that both sides of the river were protected. Although the evidence is scant, it is thought that the central area of the site, including Field VI, was largely domestic, while Field II was public space. The area defended by the moat probably did not include the burial zones of Fields II and III.

Chapter 8

Mapping an Ancient Egyptian Highway of North Sinai: The Ways of Horus

Hesham M. Hussein
Inspector of Archaeology – North Sinai

Roads played an important role connecting places and regions in both the modern and ancient world; they were remarkable tools that linked civilizations and communities through trade, travel, colonialism, and imperialism. Overland routes were very important for the function of Egypt's economy and culture. During the Late Bronze Age/New Kingdom, Egypt had a strong relationship and connection with the ancient Near East via vital desert roads. Sinai was a strategic corridor and a key bridge between Egypt, the Levant, and ancient Near East. "The Way(s) of Horus"[1] passed through the coastal line of North Sinai. It was one of the most important land bridges in antiquity, as it assisted in important economic, military and political roles throughout Egyptian history, controlled people and trade, witnessed military campaigns, and, unfortunately, facilitated invasions and occupations of Egypt. The modern international road across north Sinai from Al-Qantara to El-Arish closely corresponds to the route of the ancient "Ways of Horus."

Egyptians used different long-distance ways through the Sinai desert in order to reach North Sinai, South Sinai, and the Levant by land or by maritime routes.[2] Actually, there were two main land routes: one starts at the Wadi Tumilat and passes through the middle of the Sinai Peninsula to the copper mines of Timna in the southern Levant and ends in the Oasis of Tayma in northeastern Saudi Arabia.[3] The other road was the Ways of Horus through North Sinai to the Levant.

Clédat proposed that the origin of such desert routes in North Sinai dated back to the Early Dynastic period, as testified by archaeological evidence and the earliest contacts between Egypt and Southern Levant.[4] However, little is known about the caravan route through North Sinai as

1. Alan H. Gardiner, "The Ancient Military Road between Egypt and Palestine," *JEA* 6 (1920) 99–116; D. Valbelle, "La(les) rout(s) d'Horus," in C. Berger-el-Naggar, G. Clère, and N. Grimal (éds.), *Hommages à Jean Leclant* (Cairo: IFAO, 1994) 379–86. James K. Hoffmeier and Stephen O. Moshier, "'A Highway out of Egypt': The Main Road from Egypt to Canaan," in *Desert Road Archaeology in Ancient Egypt and Beyond* (ed. F. Förester and H. Reimer; Africa Praehistorica 26, Cologne: Heinrich-Barth-Institut, 2013) 485–510.

2. Pierre Tallet, "Ayn Sukhna and Wadi el-Jarf: Two Newly Discovered Pharaonic Harbors on the Suez Gulf," *British Museum Studies in Ancient Egypt and Sudan* 18 (2012) 147–68

3. Claire Somaglino and P. Tallet, "Une mysterieuse route sud-orientale sous le regne de Ramses III," *BIFAO* 111 (2011) 361–69; Somaglino Claire and Pierre Tallet, "A road to the Arabian Peninsula in the Reign of Ramesses III," in *Desert Road Archaeology in Ancient Egypt and Beyond* (ed. F. Förster, Frank and Heiko Reimer; Africa Praehistorica 26, Cologne: Heinrich-Barth-Institut, 2013) 511–18

4. J. Clédat, "Les Vases de El-Béda," *ASAE* 13 (1914), 115–21; Yuval Yekutiel, "Settlement and Subsistence Patterns in North Sinai during the Fifth to Third Millennia B.C.E," In *Egypt and Levant: Interrelation*

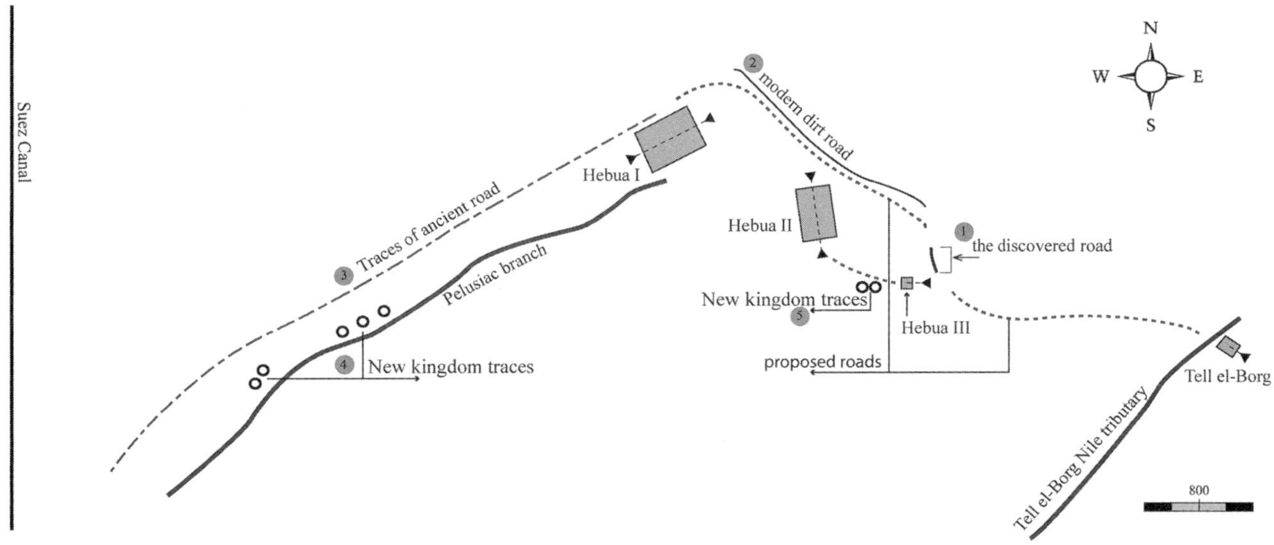

Fig. 8.1. A map of the Tell Heboua Region based on a Google earth image (drawing by H. Huessein).

Fig. 8.2. Field photograph of the discovered road section.

Fig. 8.3**a**. Photographic cross-section of the discovered road.

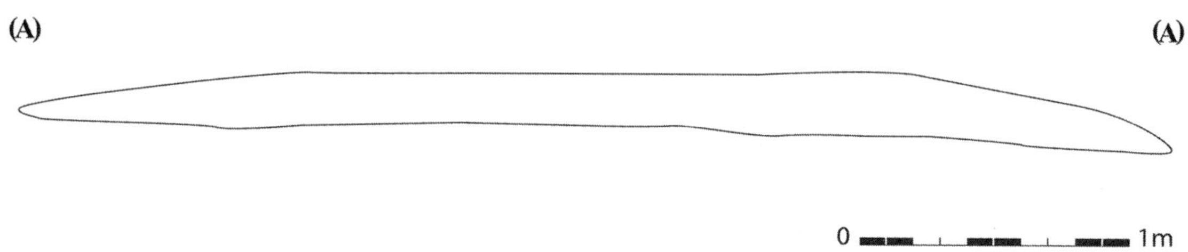

Fig. 8.3**b**. Drawing of the cross-section of the discovered road (H. Huessein).

the evidence is scant. In fact, in the area of the flood-plain, ancient unpaved routes are often difficult to trace, and dune activity in northern Sinai further complicate the search. Additionally, modern reclamation and development projects throughout the region create further obstacles for identifying and tracing many ancient routes. Few paved roads from ancient Egypt have been discovered.[5]

from the 4th through the Early 3rd Millennium B.C.E. (ed. E. Van Den Brink and T. Levy: London, 2002), 115–21; Cédric Meurice and Yann Tristant, "Jean Clédat et le site de Béda: Données nouvelles sur une découverte protodynastique dans le Sinaï septentrional," *BIFAO* 104 (2004), 457–75.

5. S. Vinson, "Transportation," in *UCLA Encyclopedia of Egyptology* (ed. Willeke Wendrich; Los Angeles, 2013, 9), http://digital2.library.ucla.edu/viewItem.do?ark=21198/zz002hczw6.

Fig. 8.4. The road delineated, looking south.

During my regular archaeological duties[6] at the Qantara inspectorate office in 2010, I noticed some dark, dried mud patches, mixed with sea shells, over a sandy area in the vicinity of Tell Heboua.[7] I examined the surface and exposed a cross-section of a portion of the mud traces, which appeared to be a man-made mud feature. Upon further examination, it is clearly part of an ancient mud road (figs. 8.1, 8.2, 8.3a, 8.4, and 8.5) in the desert sands, located just northeast of Heboua III.[8] It is reasonable to conclude that it was constructed as a link between the chain of forts on the Ways of Horus, extended from north and turning southeast, linking Tell Heboua and Tell el-Borg.

The technique used to construct this section of road is like that used in some construction at Tell Heboua. The newly discovered portion of the road was constructed of mud, mixed with sea and Nile shells, lying on the sand dunes. There were numerous Holocene mud deposits (with shells) in the area, as documented by Stephen Moshier,[9] and they are likely the source for the

6. The author did regular survey at the northwestern part of Sinai Peninsula (Sahl el-Tina) after *khamaseen* and heavy rains in order better to observe the archaeological sites and surrounding landmarks of the ancient landscape.

7. For more information about Tell Heboua: M. Abd el-Maksoud and D. Valbelle, "Tell Heboua-Tjarou: L'apport de l'épigraphie," *RdE* 56 (2005), 1–43; M. Abd el-Maksoud and D. Valbelle, "Tell Heboua II: rapport préliminaire sur le décor et l'épigraphie des éléments architectoniques découverts au cours des campagnes 2008–2009 dans la zone central du Khetem de Tjarou," *RdE* 62 (2011), 1–39.

8. Tell Heboua III is one of the important New Kingdom archaeological sites in the northeastern part of Sinai and was part of the ancient New Kingdom city Tjaru, capital of the 14th lower Egyptian nome. The archaeological investigation revealed various mud-brick architectural features that were part of a small Egyptian community. According to recent excavation at the site, it seems to be dated back to the middle of the 8th Dynasty.

9. *Tell el-Borg I*, 69–74.

Fig. 8.5. The road delineated, looking south.

mud. Shells gave this construction a white color on top of the yellow sand.[10] It is 4 m wide, and it has a thickness of 25 cm (fig. 8.3a–b). I was able to trace this road section 25 m to the north. Unfortunately, the rest of the road was destroyed by the excavations for the el-Salam irrigation and reclamation project.[11]

10. This technique, "mud plus Nile and sea shells," is known and very much used during the New Kingdom at Tell Heboua. Shells played an important role as a straw to consolidate the composition. For more information, see Mohamed Abd el-Maksoud, *Tell Heboua (1981–1991): Enquête Archéologique sur la Deuxième Période Intermédiaire et le Nouvel Empire à l'Extrémité Orientale du Delta* (Paris: Éditions Recherche sur les Civilisations, 1998) 48.

11. At the beginning of 1992, The Supreme Council of Antiquities launched the North Sinai Archaeological Salvage Project as a response to the pending impact of the northern Sinai Agricultural and Irrigation Project, which aimed to map, rescue, and protect more than 30 endangered archaeological sites dating to different periods, and especially to deal with the sites most seriously affected by planned irrigation canals and drainage system. Unpublished reports: The Supreme Council of Antiquities, North Sinai Archaeological Salvage Project report (1992–1995); Steven Snape, "el-Salaam Canal," in *Encyclopedia of the Archaeology of Ancient Egypt* (ed. Kathryn A. Bard and Steven B. Shubert; New York: Routledge, 1999) 689–90.

Fig. 8.6. Israeli military road from the 1960s–1970s.

As an example of another road-building project in Sinai, the Israeli army built a network of roads and paths using a similar technique during the Sinai occupation from 1967 until 1973 (fig. 8.6).[12] People who live in Sinai still used the same method to reach their farms in sand dune areas: they create thick mud layers over the sand to facilitate the way for their animals, carts, and vehicles.

The width of the road (4 m) and material for building (mud mixed with sea shells) was appropriate for different categories of wheeled vehicle that were used in ancient Egypt and other parts of the Ancient Near East.[13] Moreover, it was adequate to be used by donkeys and horses so that they did not have to cross sand dunes, which were more difficult.[14]

12. The Israeli army had bulldozed materials and debris from archaeological sites especially Pelusium in order to build a network of paths and routes at Sahl el-Tina, i.e. the "mud plain" and high hills south of Gilbana (Gabel Abu Asab), Balouza and other villages, to facilitate movement for vehicles and soldiers.

13. Joost Crouwel, "Studying the six chariots from the tomb of Tutankhamun – an update," in Chasing Chariots, proceedings of the first international chariot conference (Andre J. Veldmeijer and Salima Ikram (eds.); Cairo: American University Cairo, 2013) 73.

14. See similar consideration: F. Förster et al., "Tracing linear structures: Remote sensing, landscape classification and the archaeology of desert roads in eastern Sahara," in *Towards Interdisciplinarity: Experiences of the Long-Term ACACIA Project* (ed. W. J. G. Möhlig, O. Bubenzer, and G. Menz; Cologne, 2010), 49–75.

Fig. 8.7. Bedouin road.

Here, a map (made by the author) is offered, based on a recent Google-Earth image (fig. 8.1), showing the geographical locations and entrances of Tell Heboua I, II, III,[15] and Tell el-Borg's[16] defensive walls, as well as the archaeological sites and scattered New Kingdom traces and remains in the Heboua region.[17] The location of these archaeological sites and remains mark the ancient way to Canaan—that is, the "Ways of Horus."

A modern dirt road used by Bedouins and farmers (figs. 8.1, 8.2, and 8.7), located to the north of Heboua II, may be part of the ancient road that linked Heboua I and II. Additionally, ancient traces of a road built from a mix of mud and limestone chips runs north of Heboua I, extending to the west, and likely ran parallel to the north bank of the defunct Pelusiac Nile Branch (figs. 8.1, 8.3, and 8.4).

Archaeological sites and ancient traces adjacent to the discovered road help date the road to the New Kingdom.[18] This period, of course, marks the greatest period of military and economic activity in this critical area of ancient Egypt.

15. The 1990–1991 survey of northwestern part of Sinai (Tell Heboua survey map) identified many New Kingdom traces in the Heboua region that are thought to mark the ancient way to Egypt (D. Valbelle et al., "Reconnaissance archéologique à la pointe oriental du delta rapport préliminaire sur les saisons 1990 et 1991," *CRIPEL* 14 [1992], fig. 2).

16. *Tell el-Borg I* (ed. James K. Hoffmeier; Winona Lake, IN: Eisenbrauns, 2014), see especially chapters 5–6.

17. For more information about the Tell Heboua archaeological complex, see: D. Valbelle et al., "Reconnaissance archéologique à la pointe oriental du delta rapport préliminaire sur les saisons 1990 et 1991," fig. 2.

18. The recently discovered road is located 150 m to the northeast of Tell Heboua III; recent archaeological investigation (Supreme Council of Antiquates, Season 2010) helped date the site to the New Kingdom (18th Dynasty); D. Valbelle et al., "Reconnaissance archéologique à la pointe oriental du delta rapport préliminaire sur les saisons 1990 et 1991," 17.

CHAPTER 9

Identification and Provenance of Elite Stones Found at Tell el-Borg

Stephen O. Moshier
WHEATON COLLEGE

INTRODUCTION

The excavation of Tell el-Borg yielded a variety of stones that had been imported to the site. These include varieties of igneous granite and basalt, metamorphic quartzite and metaconglomerate, sedimentary sandstone, limestone, travertine, chert, agate, and volcanic pumice. The most commonly occurring stones are described in this chapter, along with attempts at interpreting their provenance. As an outpost defending the eastern frontier of the New Kingdom along the Sinai coast, Tell el-Borg was situated far from natural outcropping of the stones encountered at the site, with the exception of some sandstones of local origin.

METHODS

Stones were identified and documented as they were found on the surface in the field or after they were returned from the field to the study and storage area. Photographs were taken of representative samples, and chips were removed for thin-section production. Field and petrographic descriptions of the stones were compared with descriptions of geological materials in the region such as documented by Issawi, Aston, Harrell, and Shaw, and Harrell.[1]

TYPES OF STONE

Granite

Granite is an igneous rock that forms by the cooling of silica-rich (felsic) magmas intruded in deep continental crust (>10 km). Pink granite at Tell el-Borg is composed of coarse crystals of

1. B. Issawi, M. El Hinnawi, M. Francis, and A. Mazhar, *The Phanerozoic Geology of Egypt: A Geodynamic Approach* (Cairo: Egyptian Geological Survey Special Publication 76, 1999); B. Aston, J. A. Harrell, and I. Shaw, "Stones" in *Ancient Egyptian Materials and Technology* (ed. P. T. Nicholson and I. Shaw; Cambridge: Cambridge University Press, 2000) 5–77; J. A. Harrell, *Topographical and Petrological Survey of Ancient Egyptian Quarries*, http://www.eeescience.utoledo.edu/Faculty/Harrell/Egypt/Quarries/Survey_Info.html (updated 2007).

quartz, plagioclase feldspar, and potassium microcline feldspar (pl. 9.1 A and B). One massive block, estimated to weigh 11 metric tons, was encountered in Field II. The block lacked inscriptions and may have served as a statue base (pl. 9.1 C). Several large, uninscribed granite slabs were found on the surface nearby. Hundreds of smaller (hand-sized) fragments were recovered throughout the site. The gate area of Field V contained enough fragments to make a significant pile of rocks (pl. 9.1 D) that were derived from a pair of stelae mounted at the entrance of the fort's gate. Black gneissic granite or granodiorite exhibits very weak foliation, porphyritic texture, and contains medium and coarse crystalline quartz and feldspar with coarse biotite (pl. 9.1 E and F). The red and black granites are identical to granites from numerous localities from Aswan to Shellal in Upper Egypt that were quarried by ancient Egyptians.[2]

Basalt, Dolerite

Mafic igneous rocks recovered at Tell el-Borg include both dense dolerite and vessicular basalt. Fragments of vessicular basalt (pl. 9.2 A) were found at the surface and in at least one loci of excavation (Field IV, Area 1, Unit D-2 Locus 5a). Vesicular basalt was used in the Levant for grinding stones, however, there is no known quarry for the rock in the Red Sea region and it has not been reported from other Egyptian Bronze-Age sites.[3] Vesicular basalt at Tell el-Borg may have been derived from eastern sources in the Levant or Arabia.

Fragmented dolerite was also encountered at the surface at Tell el-Borg (pl. 9.2 B and C). The rock contains abundant fine-crystalline, lath-shaped, plagioclase feldspar with pyroxene and minor olivine. Dolerite is also known as diabase and is similar in composition to basalt, except for having slightly coarser crystals than basalt. Dolerite occurs in dikes cutting through Precambrian granites in the Aswan region and was used by ancient Egyptians as a pounding tool in quarrying operations.

Limestone

Limestone is a carbonate sedimentary rock abundant in outcroppings along the middle to northern Nile Valley and in the Red Sea regions. Large blocks of limestone were used and reused at Tell el-Borg for wall foundations, paving, and building stone, including inscribed doorframes and wall-panels containing mural displays. *Talatat* blocks were encountered in Fields II, IV, and V. Most of the limestone is a chalky, microcrystalline variety classified as biomicrite or lime mudstone (pl. 9.2 D and E). Matrix microporosity contributes to the chalky character of the rock. Microfossils include globigerinid foraminifera. These limestones appear to have been quarried from the Mokattam Formation (Middle Eocene) that forms prominent escarpments from the northern Nile Valley, Eastern Desert, and Sinai.[4] The typical biomicrite at Tell el-Borg is identical to building stones at Saqqara and less similar to dolomitic biomicrites found along the Sinai–Gulf of Suez coast. A fragment of light brown, dense biomicrite (pl. 9.2 F and G) found in Field 2 (Area 1, Unit F, Locus 37) compares with material used for New Kingdom statues, but a source and quarry for the rock is unknown.[5]

---

2. Aston, Harrell, and Shaw, "Stones," 35–37.
3. Personal communication, James Harrell, 2007.
4. B. Issawi et al., *The Phanerozoic Geology of Egypt: A Geodynamic Approach*, 251.
5. James Harrell, personal communication, 2007.

A well-preserved specimen of fossil foraminifer *Nummulites gizihensis,* 1.8 cm in diameter, was recovered as a "small find" artifact in Field IV (Square G-1, Locus 1). The surface appears polished and may have been used as a game piece or inlay ornament (pl. 9.3 A). Building stones of the Giza Pyramids contain similar-sized fossils of this species, derived from grainstone facies of the Mokattam Formation.

Travertine (Egyptian "Alabaster")

Travertine is composed of coarse, bladed to fibrous, calcite crystals. Travertine is usually associated with limestone, forming in pools on cave floors (flowstone), precipitating around springs, or filling fissures in limestone strata. Travertine fragments are abundant on the ground in Field II, an area that is thought to have been the center of religious activity. Some fragments are several centimeters thick, forming slabs 10 cm or more in diameter, consistent with the use of travertine for pavements or wall linings (pl. 9.3 B). Sources of travertine from the Nile Valley and Eastern Desert include quarries in Eocene limestone outcroppings south of Cairo, Wadi Gerrawi near Helwan city, and localities between El Minya and Assiut.[6]

Chert and Chalcedony

Chert and chalcedony are chemically precipitated sedimentary rocks composed of microcrystalline quartz that is most often found as thin beds or nodules embedded in limestone. Chert is composed of equant (equi-dimensional) microcrystalline quartz and tends to be gray, black, white, or brown in color. Dark-colored chert is known as flint. The physical properties of hardness and concoidal fracture in chert led to its almost ubiquitous use by ancient cultures for cutting tools and weapons. Gray and black cherts were recovered from Tell el-Borg, typically showing evidence of working (tool-making). Chalcedony is composed of fibrous microcrystalline quartz that is typically translucent, colored, and banded. Diverse patterns and colors in the varieties of chalcedony led to its use in jewelry, religious objects, and small vessels. Varieties of chalcedony found at the site include agates and carnelian. Chert was quarried in the northern region of the Nile Valley and agates are found as pebbles in many places in the Eastern Desert. Agates are also found in the Sinai, but they have not been investigated in detail. These stones fall under the category of "lithics." Carol McCartney presents a thorough description of lithics from Tell el-Borg in this volume (chapter 10)

Sandstone

Quartz arenite is the most typical variety of sandstone, a siliciclastic sedimentary rock, at Tell el-Borg. Fragments of hard, coarse-grained, red, brown, and gray quartz arenites are very common throughout the site (pl. 9.3 C–E). The red color results from coatings of very fine hematite (iron oxide) crystals on quartz grains in the rock. Some of the fragments appear to have been shaped, but with no obvious use. There are no fragments large enough to indicate that sandstone was used for building. More likely, the sandstone was used for tools (e.g., grindstone, querns) or perhaps statuary. These rocks appear to derive from the Oligocene-age Gebel Ahmar Formation, which forms outcroppings between Cairo and the Suez.[7] A soft (easily broken, weakly cemented),

6. Aston, Harrell, and Shaw, "Stones," 59–60.
7. B. Issawi et al., *The Phanerozoic Geology of Egypt: A Geodynamic Approach*, 278–82.

porous, fine-grained, light-gray sandstone collected on the surface (pl. 9.3 F) is similar to sandstones of the Nubia Group, Late Cretaceous–Early Paleocene, widely distributed in Egypt and quarried by ancient Egyptians along the Nile Valley.[8]

Metamorphosed sedimentary rocks at Tell el-Borg include quartzite and conglomerate. Metagreywacke (a form of quartzite derived from an original rock of quartz sand and clay) was shaped into hand-sized spherical pounders (pl. 9.4 A). Weathering revealed internal laminae in one specimen. Chlorite, the metamorphic product of detrital clay in the original sediment, contributes to the green-gray color of the rock. A large stone of red metaconglomerate (characterized by rounded rock pebbles and coarse sand) were recovered from the surface (pl. 9.4 B). Greywacke and conglomerate of similar composition were quarried by ancient Egyptians from the late Precambrian-age Hammamat Series at Wadi Hammamat in the Eastern Desert, but the conglomerate from that locality is greenish in appearance.[9]

Importation of Elite Stones

Elite stones associated with New Kingdom culture at Tell el-Borg must have been transported great distances from disparate sources along the Nile Valley and Eastern Desert to the eastern frontier in the north Sinai and possibly from the Levant or Arabia. The most practical means of transporting heavy rock in ancient Egypt was by water routes, both natural channels and engineered canal systems. The Pelusiac Nile flowed past the New Kingdom capital at Pi-Ramesses and via Hebua I and II (Tjaru) to Tell el-Borg. Redmount explored the existence and utility of the so-called "Canal of the Pharaohs" in Wadi Tumilat, which would have linked the Red Sea and the Nile.[10] Sneh and his team interpreted linear features on air photos as the remains of an ancient canal system heading north from Lake Timsah toward the ancient Ballah Lakes.[11] Based upon our paleogeographic survey of the region, we believe that a natural channel of the Pelusiac Nile distributary system flowed into the depression that includes the Ballah Lakes and turned northeastward to Tell el-Borg, where it emptied into an adjacent, ancient lagoon.[12]

Texts from the Ramesside era report on the transportation of granite blocks to the east frontier region. Pap. Anastasi V (24.4–25.1) refers to the shipment of granite stelae and their plinths from Pi-Ramesses in the Delta to the eastern frontier, stating, "we passed the Fortress of Rammes[su Belov]ed of Amun which is in Tjaru/Sile in regnal year 33, second month of summer, day 23. We will go to unload the boats at the Dwelling of Ramessu Beloved of Amun."[13] Clearly,

8. Aston, Harrell and Shaw, "Stones," 54–56; B. Issawi et al., *The Phanerozoic Geology of Egypt: A Geodynamic Approach*, 174–75.

9. Aston, Harrell and Shaw, "Stones," 58.

10. C. A. Redmount, "The Wadi Tumilat and the 'Canal of the Pharaohs'," *Journal of Near Eastern Studies* 54 (1995), 127–35.

11. A. Sneh, T. Weissbrod, and I. Perath, "Evidence for an Ancient Egyptian Frontier Canal," *American Scientist* 63 (1975), 542–48.

12. S. O. Moshier,"Geologic Setting of Tell el-Borg with Implications for Ancient Geography of the Northwest Sinai." In *Excavations in North Sinai: Tell el-Borg* I, ed. J. K. Hoffmeier (Winona Lake, Indiana: Eisenbrauns, 2014), 62–83; S. O. Moshier and B. Gayed, "Geological Investigation of the Ballah Depression, Northern Suez Canal Zone, Egypt," chapter 2 in this volume.

13. The text is found in Alan Gardiner, *Late Egyptian Miscellanies* (Brussels: Queen Elizabeth Foundation of Egyptology, 1937) 70; translation courtesy of James K. Hoffmeier.

the point of delivery was the Dwelling of Ramesses/Lion (of Seti I), beyond the frontier town and fort of Tjaru/Sile. We have proposed that this site might be equated with Tell el-Borg.[14]

Locally Sourced Calcareous Sandstones

Excavation in the gate area of Field V (second-phase fortress) revealed pavers of calcareous sandstone (*Tell el-Borg I*, 285–87). The rock is composed of medium-grained quartz sand cemented by brown, microcrystalline calcite.[15] A natural outcropping of calcareous sandstone forms part of the western flank of the topographic high that defines the northern half of Tell el-Borg. This area of the tell includes Field VII, where excavations revealed New Kingdom(?) tombs that were dug into this hard unit of unknown thickness (see chapter 6). The texture and composition of the rock compares with typical beach rock.[16] Beach rock forms by the cementation of sand just below the surface of the intertidal zone of a beach.[17] By implication, Tell el-Borg may represent the relict topographic expression of a raised beach or Kurkar ridge that formed during the Pleistocene high sea-level stand some 125,000 years ago.

A stone of muddy calcareous sand was recovered from Field 2 (Area 1, Unit F, Locus 25) with an embedded New Kingdom pottery sherd (pl. 9.4 C and D). The composition and texture of scattered quartz sand and silt in a porous matrix of lime mud (micrite and microspar) is typical of carbonate cemented soils also known as "caliche" (pl. 9.4 E and F). Tubular pores may reflect decayed plant roots or insect burrows.

Pumice and the Problematic Association with Mediterranean Volcanoes

Pumice, a porous, glassy, volcanic rock, was recovered in several of the excavation fields of Tell el-Borg. Pumice excavated at other Bronze Age sites across the Delta and now north Sinai, particularly associated with the 17th to 18th Dynasties, has been linked to the catastrophic Thera (Santorini) eruption during the second millennium B.C.[18] Thera is located north of Crete in the Aegean Sea. Microscopic shards from the Thera eruption have been detected in sediment cores from the eastern Mediterranean Sea and from the Delta region.[19] This ash was deposited from airborne clouds of pyroclastic material ejected from the volcano. The Tell el-Borg samples have

14. James K. Hoffmeier and Mohamed Abd el-Maksoud, "A New Military Site on 'the Ways of Horus' — Tell el-Borg 1999–2001: A Preliminary Report," *Journal of Egyptian Archaeology* 89 (2003) 195–97; *Tell el-Borg I*, chapter 2.

15. See fig. 65 in S. O. Moshier, "Geologic Setting of Tell el-Borg," 69.

16. See ibid., fig. 64 on p. 68.

17. J. S. Hanor, "Precipitation of Beachrock Cements; Mixing of Marine and Meteoric Waters vs. CO2-degassing," *Journal of Sedimentary Research* 48 (1978), 489–501.

18. M. Bietak, "Science versus Archaeology: Problems and Consequences of High Aegean Chronology," in *The Synchronisation of Civilisations in the Eastern Mediterranean in the Second Millennium B.C.–II* (ed. M. Bietak; Vienna: Austrian Academic of Sciences, 2000) 23–33; W. L. Friedrich et al., "Santorini Eruption Radiocarbon Dated to 1627–1600 B.C.," *Science* 312 (2006) 548.

19. D. J. Stanley and H. Sheng, "Volcanic Shards from Santorini (Minoan Ash) in the Nile Delta, Egypt," *Nature* 320 (1986) 733–35.

not yet received chemical analysis that would tie the material to the Thera eruption, but the association is very likely.

Pumice was ejected from the Thera volcano during the eruption and accumulated in massive rafts that drifted on the Mediterranean Sea surface.[20] The pumice rafts would have followed the surface current circulation patterns of the sea and reached the Nile Delta and Sinai Coasts many weeks after the eruption. The discovery of pumice in ancient Egyptian archaeological sites along the Sinai coast has been reported in the international news media, promoting the mistaken idea that pumice was transported to the sites by tsunami waves following the Thera eruption.[21] Tsunamis move water at the shoreline and landward with great force, but the waves at sea would be ineffective to transport material floating on the surface from the source. Furthermore, it is likely that Thera pumice circulated in the Mediterranean Sea for decades after the eruption. Pumice was used as an abrasive tool; typical excavated specimens have one or more flattened sides. Since the arrival of pumice along the Sinai coast spanned considerable time and the material may have been used and reused by generations of ancient Egyptians, linking the appearance of pumice with the precise date of the eruption is very problematic.

Conclusions

Geological artifacts at Tell el-Borg represent typical New Kingdom sources from the Nile Valley and Eastern Desert, including granite, sandstone, limestone, travertine, and agates. Vesicular basalt must have been derived from sources in the Levant or Arabia. Soft sandstone composed of cemented Pleistocene quartz sand of local origin was used in limited quantities for paving floors in the second-phase fortress. Pumice recovered at Tell el Borg is very likely from the second millennium eruption of Thera (Santorini). The presence of elite stones such as granite, sandstone, and travertine attest to the significance of Tell el-Borg and is an indication of royal sponsorship at this military site.

20. F. W. McCoy and G. Heiken, "Tsunami Generated by the Late Bronze Age Eruption of Thera (Santorini), Greece," *Pure and Applied Geophysics* 157 (2000) 1227–56.

21. K. Kratovac, "Sinai Pumice Linked to Ancient Eruption," Associated Press 4/2/2007.

Plate 9.1. **A**. Red granite specimen (3 cm scale). **B**. Thin section photomicrograph (cross-polarized light) of red granite: m- microcline feldspar, p–plagioclase feldspar, q – quartz (1 mm scale). **C**. Field photograph of massive red granite block in Field II (meter scale). **D**. Field photograph of black gneissic granite in Field V. **E**. Black gneissic granite specimen (3 cm scale). **F**. Thin section photomicrograph (cross-polarized light) of black gneissic granite: m- microcline feldspar, p–plagioclase feldspar, q – quartz, b – biotite mica (1 mm scale).

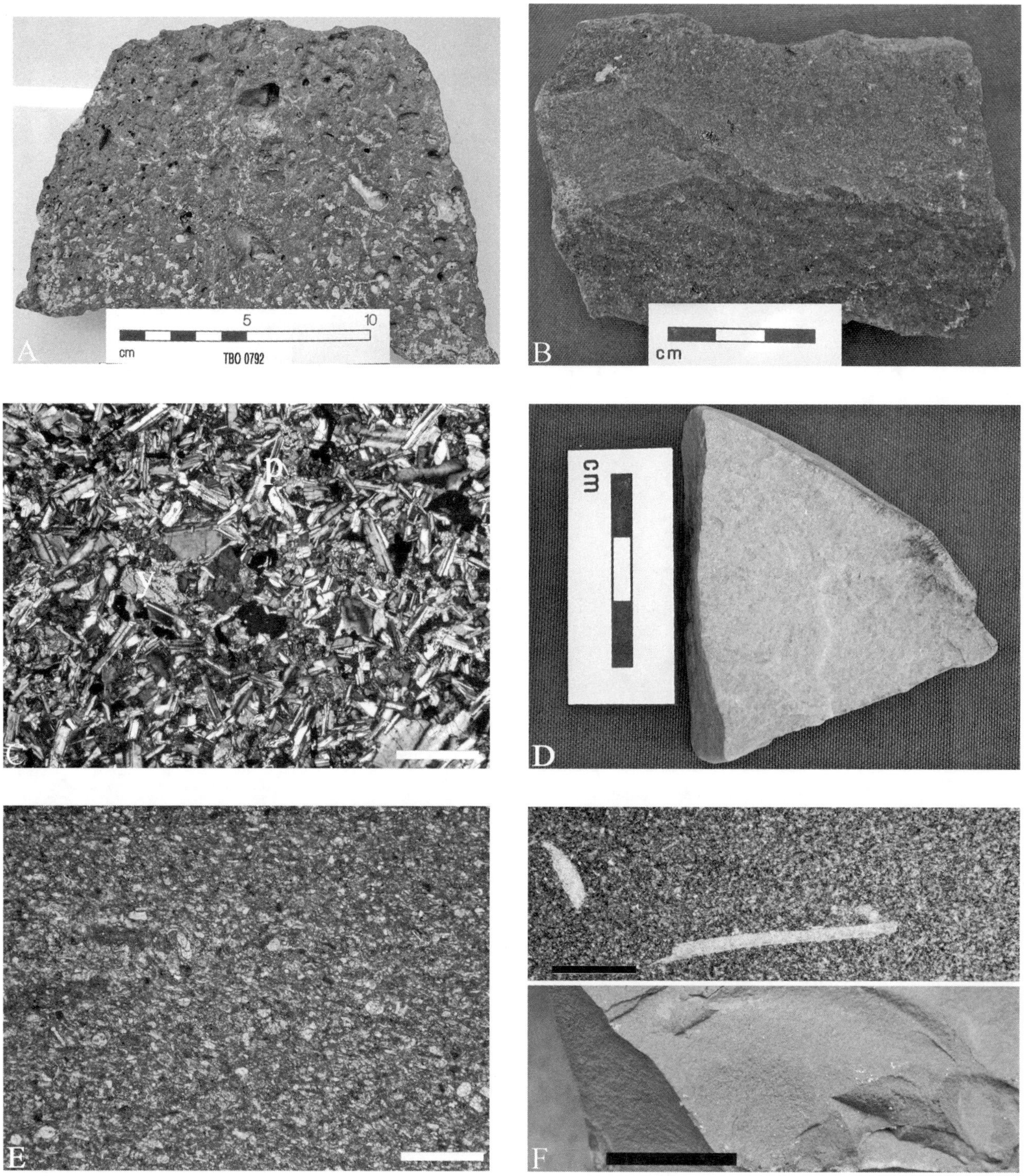

Plate 9.2. **A**. Vesicular basalt specimen (10 cm scale). **B**. Dolerite (diabase) specimen (3 cm scale). **C**. Thin section photomicrograph (cross-polarized light) of dolerite: p – plagioclase feldspar, y – pyroxine. **D**. Chalky, cream colored, fine crystalline limestone (biomicrite) (3 cm scale). **E**. Thin section photomicrograph (plane-polarized light) of biomicrite showing microcrystalline calcite (lime mud or micrite) matrix and medium sand-size skeletons of foraminifera (1 mm scale). **F**. Bottom: brown, fine crystalline limestone (micrite) specimen (1 cm scale). Top: thin section photomicrograph (plane-polarized light) of brown, fine crystalline limestone showing microcrystalline calcite (lime mud or micrite) matrix and thin shell (bivalve mollusk) fragments (1 mm scale).

Plate 9.3. **A**. Single specimen of polished foraminifer fossil *Nummulites gizihensis* (1 cm scale). **B**. Fragment of travertine (3 cm scale). **C**. Red sandstone specimen (3 cm scale). **D**. Thin section photomicrograph (cross-polarized light) of red sandstone showing medium and coarse quartz sand (1 mm scale). **E**. Gray sandstone specimen (1 cm scale). **F**. Thin section photomicrograph (plane-polarized light) of gray sandstone showing fine, angular quartz sand with abundant inter-particle porosity (1 mm scale).

Plate 9.4. **A**. Two spherical pounding stones composed of meta-greywacke. Parallel mm-laminae evident in specimen, left (3 cm scale). **B**. Meta-conglomerate specimen (3 cm scale). **C**. Calcareous crust with potsherd (right of 3 cm scale bar). **D**. Thin section photomicrograph (plane-polarized light) of calcareous crust (specimen in C) showing microcrystalline calcite matrix, thin shell fragments (probably terrestrial snails), quartz sand (q) and large pores (v) (1 mm scale). **E**. Field photograph of a caliche surface on Pleistocene sand encountered along a railroad bed south of Qantara city, Sinai (inset shows close-up). **F**. Thin section photomicrograph (plane-polarized light) of caliche crust (collected from area photographed in E) (1 mm scale).

CHAPTER 10

Lithics / Chipped Stone Implements from Tell el-Borg

Carole McCartney
CYPRUS AMERICAN ARCHAEOLOGICAL RESEARCH INSTITUTE

INTRODUCTION

This report documents the chipped-stone assemblage recovered at Tell el-Borg. The total sample of 271 artifacts is varied and includes both in situ and derived material.[1] Of the former, the most interesting is the relatively large sample collected in Field VI, where a number of reed huts were constructed and are considered to be a domestic field outside the fort.[2] As such, this sample (n=95) is most likely to demonstrate the utilization of chipped-stone tools at Tell el-Borg. A smaller (n=28) sample came from Field III, a part of the site that has also been considered to be domestic in function, in addition to its use as a cemetery. However, the location of Field III, which is adjacent to Field VI, may simply be an extension of the latter (*Tell el-Borg I*, Site map 1, p. 12). The other substantial sample (n=88) comes from Field V, where construction of the Ramesside-period fort incorporated sediments containing lithic artifacts from elsewhere on the site. Given the relatively close correspondence between the Field V and VI samples, it is likely that at least some of the Field V sample came from Field VI or another Field designated for domestic use at the site. A similar pattern is documented by the incorporation of lithic material in the construction of the early fort in Field IV (n=39). More negligible amounts of similarly derived material were recovered in Fields II, VII, and VIII, though differences in the artifact types and raw materials utilized suggest that these samples were incorporated in sediments derived from other fields on the site. All aspects, including core reduction and tool manufacture, are indicative of the on-site production of a flake-based ad hoc industry. Intrusive, possibly imported, items, such as a number of Canaanean blade fragments and tabular scrapers, represent the likely reutilization of tools introduced to Sinai from Palestine during the Early Bronze Age, which were not, therefore, manufactured at the site. Finally, a number of potentially older intrusive tool types demonstrate the incorporation of prehistoric materials into the construction matrix of the forts. The latter indicate a background Palaeolithic, Neolithic, and Early Bronze Age presence that corresponds with

1. For images of individual objects by TBO numbers, see chapter 10 figures on the OCHRE database: http://ochre.lib.uchicago.edu/publish?project=Borg.

2. James K. Hoffmeier, "Tell el-Borg on Egypt's Eastern Frontier: A Preliminary Report on the 2002 and 2004 Seasons," *JARCE* 41 (2004) 90–91.

in situ prehistoric evidence documented elsewhere in the Sinai Peninsula. The small sample size, the derived nature of the majority of the lithic sample (typical of later prehistoric and early historic sites), and the lack of sieving precludes any attempt at a detailed analysis of chaîn opératoir, demanding that the analysis be done at a relatively coarse scale. That said, there are a number of interesting patterns belonging to the sample of chipped stone recovered at Tell el-Borg that are of interest to the functioning of daily life in a desert fort.

Raw Materials

The raw materials utilized at Tell el-Borg were identified by James Phillips and Thomas Davis based on the extensive field survey work in the Sinai Peninsula conducted by the former.[3] The cherts used at Tell el-Borg were grouped into four categories used to designate the geographic origin. Material from the Sinai group represents local stone that includes typically opaque cherts, which are red, yellow, and gray-brown, some of which is banded. A smaller number of red translucent cherts were also incorporated in this group. Perhaps understandably, these materials dominate the lithic sample at Tell el-Borg (table 10.1). Remaining cortex on Sinai group materials is water rolled and indicates the use of secondary river cherts. Alluvial gravels in the immediate vicinity of the site, however, also provided a source for ad hoc flake tools manufactured at the site. Stone coming from the west in the field of the Nile include high quality translucent and semi-translucent chalcedonic materials and agate as well as banded brown or red-brown to yellow-brown cherts. The latter typically exhibit a water-rolled cortex indicative of a secondary river source context. In contrast, materials assigned to the Palestinian group typically show a chalk cortex, though this too is rolled and indicative of a secondary source context. The latter cherts are light to pale brown, yellow-brown, red-brown, or gray in color and opaque or less frequently semitranslucent. Negev cherts are also opaque and range in color from brown to purple-gray. The latter are not common at Tell el-Borg.

As table 10.1 demonstrates, the chipped stone artifacts from Tell el-Borg were predominantly made of chert types regularly found in Egypt, whether locally in the Sinai Peninsula or imported to the site from the Nile valley. This is particularly true in Field VI, where the knapping of wadi cobbles for the production of flakes for ad hoc tool use from local materials is evidenced. In contrast, cherts belonging to the Palestine group appear to represent imported tools, which may have been exchanged for copper by local Sinai pastoralists during the Early Bronze Age and were later scavenged by the fort's Late Bronze Age occupants. Sites in southern Sinai demonstrate clear influences from southern Palestine during the early part of the Bronze Age.[4] A small number of reworked Canaanean blade fragments and two tabular scrapers are likely to be residual tools or scavenged materials that belong to this period. Of interest in this context are surface finds, including ground-stone tools, vessels, and fragments of clay coffins that include objects made on stone types that may derive from the Southern Sinai.[5] Geometric glossed segments were also made on

3. J. Philips, "Sinai During the Paleolithic: The Early Periods," in *Prehistory of Arid North Africa* (ed. A. Close; Dallas: Southern Methodist University, 1987) 105–21.

4. I. Beit-Arieh, "A Pattern of Settlement in Southern Sinai and Southern Canaan in the Third Millennium B.C." *BASOR* 243 (1981) 50; I. Finklestein and A. Perevolotsky, "Processes of Sedentarization and Nomadization in the History of Sinai and the Negev," *BASOR* 279 (1990) 74–75; S. Rosen, *Lithics After the Stone Age* (Walnut Creek, CA: Altamira, 1997) 58.

5. J. K. Hoffmeier and M. Abd El-Maksoud, "A New Military Site on the 'Ways of Horus': Tell el-Borg 1999–2001, A Preliminary Report," *JEA* 89 (2003) 175.

Table 10.1. Raw Material Distribution by Field of Origin: Numbers and Percentage

Source	Field II	Field III	Field IV	Field V	Field VI	VII and Surface	Field VIII	Total
Sinai	3\42.86%	6\21.43%	10\25.64%	32\36.36%	49\51.58%	3\33.33%	1\20.00%	104\38.38%
Palestine	2\28.57%	10\35.71%	6\15.38%	19\21.59%	20\21.05%	2\22.22%	1\20.00%	59\21.77%
Negev	—	1\3.57%	—	—	2\2.11%	—	—	3\1.11%
Egypt	1\4.29%	9\32.14%	8\20.51%	21\23.86%	14\14.74%	2\22.22%	2\40.00%	57\21.03%
Other	1\4.29%	2\7.14%	15\38.46%	16\18.18%	10\10.53%	2\22.22%	1\20.00%	48\17.71%

cherts assigned to the Palestine material group, but these tools were produced on a range of materials, including materials from the Nile Valley and local Sinai cherts, suggesting the possible presence of both imported and locally made sickles. Rather than indicating directional influence from Palestine, they concur with other evidence, suggesting a dynamic system of trade between Egypt and Palestine during the Late Bronze Age, and they are likely to indicate the continued interaction between nomadic groups and the large urban centers at this time.[6]

Technology

The distribution of artifact categories is shown in table 10.2. Within the group of artifacts likely to be contemporary with the use of the forts, two distinct chaînes opératoires may be documented. The first provides evidence of a local expedient core technology aimed at the production of small flakes and chips (flakes less than 15 mm) on site. Amorphous flake cores as well as simple cores-on-flakes represent the only core types recovered at the site. These cores typically made on small wadi cobbles were simply prepared (if prepared at all) by the removal of cortex for the establishment of the striking platform. No formal shaping of the core face took place, while evidence for the core maintenance is limited to the correction of the striking platform. Flake butts are typically plain or facetted though a significant number retain cortex, as do the dorsal surfaces of many irregular flakes (table 10.3). Dorsal scar patterns are mainly unidirectional or crossed at 90 degrees and indicate a simple unidirectional to change-of-orientation flaking rhythms.

Core data are restricted to Fields IV, V, and VI of the site, where evidence for domestic huts or materials likely derived from domestic contexts for fortress construction are found. Significant amounts of debris and unworked flake blanks from these fields agree with the more limited core data in documenting a simple core technology. In contrast, Fields II and III show high percentages of tools but comparatively little evidence of corereduction activity. The tools from these fields include artifact types such as geometric glossed elements that appear to have been imported to the site, as well as likely derived specimens. None of the corereduction materials recovered at Tell el-Borg can be attributed to the latter artifact types. Geometric glossed segments were made on large flakes struck from large regularly shaped unidirectional or change-of-orientation cores, unlike those found at Tell el-Borg. No evidence for striking platforms type is preserved on these intensively retouched tools shaped in part by the truncation of the bulbar end of the flake (see below). Blade technologies are present only in the form of derived tools that can be attributed to the Neolithic or Bronze Ages (for type detail, see below) with no evidence for blade/bladelet manufacture on site. Blades are defined as any blank with a length twice the width, while bladelets are diminutive blades not larger than 12 mm wide and 40 mm long. Both blades and bladelets were

6. Finkelstein and Perevolotsky, "Processes of Sedentarization and Nomadization," 76–77.

Table 10.2. Artifact Category Counts and Percentages by Field

Category	*Field II*	*Field III*	*Field IV*	*Field V*	*Field VI*	*VII and Surf.*	*Field VIII*	*Total*
Cores	—	—	4\10.26%	6\6.82%	3\3.16%	—	—	13\4.80%
Debris	2\28.57%	7\25.00%	15\38.46%	29\32.95%	35\36.84%	5\55.56%	4\80.00%	97\35.79%
Blanks	—	3\10.71%	10\25.64%	21\23.86%	20\21.05%	—	—	54\19.93%
Tools	5\71.43%	18\6.29%	10\25.64%	32\36.36%	37\38.95%	4\44.44%	1\20.00%	107\39.48%
Total	7\100%	28\100%	39\100%	88\99.99%	95\100%	9\100%	5\100%	271\100%

Table 10.3. Technical Variables (Measured from a Sample of 134 Tools and Blanks)

Dorsal Scar Pattern	*Flakes (n=97)*	*Blades (n=21)*	*Bladelets (n=6)*	*Chips (n=11)*
Crossed at 90-degrees	41/42.27%	3/14.29%	—	6/54.55%
Unidirectional	41/42.27%	15/71.43%	5/83.33%	3/27.27%
Bidirectional	8/8.25%	—	—	1/9.09%
Cortical	7/7.22%	3/14.29%	1/16.67%	1/9.09%
Butt Types	*Flakes (n=62)*	*Blades (n=2)*	*Bladelets (n=4)*	*Chips (n=11)*
Plain	19/30.65%	—	—	4/36.36%
Facetted	15/24.19%	1/50.00%	1/25.00%	1/9.09%
Cortical	23/37.10%	1/50.00%	—	2/18.18%
Compression	4/6.45%	—	1/25.00%	3/27.27%
Punctiform	—	—	1/25.00%	1/9.09%
Filliform	1/1.61%	—	1/25.00%	—

made more exclusively on regular unidirectional cores, while the preservation of two finely prepared filliform butts on bladelets indicates a prismatic blade technology (table 10.3). Canaanean blade fragments are similarly unidirectional and exhibit typical trapezoidal sections indicating a prismatic blade core technology, which replication studies have attributed to the use of either pressure or indirect percussion techniques.[7]

TOOLS

Table 10.4 shows the distribution of the major tool classes by excavation Field. The distribution of the tools like that of the entire sample generally shows the predominance of lithic items in Fields V and VI. While tools found in Field VI are likely to provide a glimpse of the local uses of chipped stone tools, those found in other fields probably represent derived material incorporated into the building fills. Glossed tools clearly dominate the formally retouched tools, while the more numerous utilized implements demonstrate the primarily expedient nature of the local industry. Other tool classes include flake tools that correspond to the simple flake-based industry utilized at the site and correspond well with those found in Bronze Age assemblages elsewhere in the Near East.[8] Derived types imply the presence of potential Palaeolithic, Late Neolithic and Early Bronze Age occupations in the Field predating the construction of the Late Bronze Age forts.

7. Rosen, *Lithics after the Stone Age*, 44–46; P. Anderson, J. Chabot and A. van Gijn, "The Functional Riddle of 'Glossy' Canaanean Blades and the Near Eastern Threshing Sledge," *Journal of Mediterranean Archaeology* 17 (2004) 94.

8. See Rosen's *Lithics after the Stone Age* for an extensive review of post-Neolithic chipped stone.

Table 10.4. Tool Classes by Field

Tool Class	*Field II*	*Field III*	*Field IV*	*Field V*	*Field VI*	*Field VII*	*Field VIII*	*Total*
Arrowhead	—	—	—	2/6.25%	1/2.70%	—	—	3/2.80%
Backed	—	—	1/10.06%	1/3.13%	1/2.70%	—	—	3/2.80%
Biface	—	—	—	1/3.13%	2/5.41%	—	—	3/2.80%
Denticulate	—	1/5.56%	—	2/6.25%	1/2.70%	—	—	4/3.74%
Glossed	2/40.00%	7/38.89%	2/20.00%	10/31.25%	7/18.92%	1/25.00%	—	29/27.10%
Notch	—	—	—	1/3.13%	—	1/25.00%	—	2/1.87%
Perforator	—	1/5.56%	3/30.00%	2/6.25%	3/8.11%	—	—	9/8.41%
Retouched	1/20.00%	2/11.11%	—	2/6.25%	5/13.51%	—	—	10/9.35%
Scraper	1/20.00%	—	—	4/12.50%	2/5.41%	—	—	7/6.54%
Truncation	—	—	1/10.00%	—	3/8.11%	—	—	4/3.74%
Utilized	1/20.00%	7/38.89%	3/30.00%	7/21.88%	12/32.43%	2/50.00%	1/100.00%	33/30.84%

Arrowheads (N=3)

The three arrowheads in the assemblage belong to types typically assigned to the Late Neolithic and that are, therefore, possibly to be intrusive at Tell el-Borg (pl. 10.3). TBO 0507 is a well-defined but fragmentary Harparsa point tang, with wings delineated by small notches created by bifacial pressure retouch on both lateral edges. TBO 0745 is a complete Nizzanim point exhibiting a tang showing pronounced shoulders, which was created by covering bifacial pressure retouch. TBO 0841 is a smaller example of the Nizzanim style but exhibits only unifacial retouch. Similar points are commonly found in Late Neolithic sites across the Near East but persist in both Negev and Sinai into post-Neolithic periods. In post-Neolithic assemblages in particular, however, they typically occur with transverse arrowheads, which eventually replace them, a type that has not been found at Tell el-Borg. Both small tanged arrowheads and transverse arrowheads persisted together in Egypt into the Old Kingdom and continue even later in the western desert until the first millennium B.C., while metal versions with similar morphologies were in use during the New Kingdom.[9] However, given the small number of stone arrowheads and the more common occurrence of larger metal arrowheads at Tell el-Borg (*Tell el-Borg I*, pp. 514–20), it seems likely that the fort's inhabitants had already switched to the use of metal for their military purposes. Nevertheless, the recent discoveries of the same types of arrowheads at Pi-Ramesses from the 19th Dynasty demonstrate that this ancient style of blade was still in use in the Late Bronze Age.[10]

Table 10.5. Arrowheads

TBO	*Field/Locus*	*Technology*	*Length*	*Width*	*Thickness*
0507	VI 1, AA Locus 18	Bifacial bilateral pressure retouch	10.98 mm	9.50 mm	2.50 mm
0745	V 1, BB2 Locus 5	Bifacial covering pressure retouch	27.24 mm	9.72 mm	2.56 mm
0841	V 1, Ua Locus 3	Unifacial covering pressure retouch	18.24 mm	9.10 mm	3.40 mm

9. A. Gopher, *Arrowheads of the Neolithic Levant* (Winona Lake, IN: Eisenbrauns, 1994) 222–25, with references.

10. Andreas Tillman, *Neolithicum in der Später Bronze Zeite: Steingeräte des 2. Jahrtausend aus Auaris-Pi-Ramesse* (Hildesheim: Gerstenberg, 2007)., 216–17.

Table 10.6. Backed Pieces

TBO	*Field/Locus*	*Technology*	*Length*	*Width*	*Thickness*
0555	IV G4 Locus 2	Unidirectional blade segment – with abrupt retouched back and truncations	43.94 mm	18.86 mm	5.42 mm
Unregistered	VI Locus 2	Bidirectional flake with basal truncation and inverse bilateral backing retouch	37.36 mm	39.26 mm	7.16 mm
Unregistered	V Locus 2	Unidirectional blade fragment–with direct abruptly back and inverse truncation	17.76 mm	17.16 mm	5.16 mm

Table 10.7. Bifaces

TBO	*Context*	*Technology*	*Length*	*Width*	*Thickness*
0601	VI AA Locus 11	Bifacial covering pressure retouch—fragmentary	32.96 mm	19.70 mm	6.88 mm
0663	V Z3 Locus 04	Handaxe with heavy patina	90.30 mm	52.98 mm	29.26 mm
Unregistered	VI E Locus 02	Bifacial retouch—fragmentary	17.60 mm	27.12 mm	8.44 mm

Backed Pieces (N=3)

TBO 0555 appears to belong to the Egyptian tradition of double-truncated (and backed) blades ascribed to the Early Bronze period.[11] This tool exhibits semi-abrupt to abrupt retouch on relatively narrow blade segments. These items could represent performs for use as glossed tools but exhibited no visible gloss with a 20× magnification. This type of tool appears to be residual and to belong to earlier activity in the field during the Early Bronze period. The unregistered items, one of which is made on the distal end of a flake from Field VI, are consistent with an ad hoc flake-based industry. The latter are likely to belong to a late period of lithic tool use but represent a common tool type; thus, more specific attribution to any particular period is not possible.

Bifaces (N=3)

Bifaces form a small component of the Tell el-Borg chipped-stone assemblage. The two registered examples appear to be intrusive items, which are not indicative of the New Kingdom context. TBO 0601 is fragmentary but exhibits one intact, finely denticulated lateral edge that was shaped by covering pressure retouch (pl. 10.3). Though fragmentary, the piece probably represents a lateral edge of a larger bifacial knife, because it exhibits larger preliminary retouch overlain by the finer denticulated pressure retouch. In Egypt, these tools are restricted to the Early Bronze I period.[12] TBO 0663 is a small bifacial hand-axe. This artifact is covered in a heavy gray-brown patina indicative of considerable time depth and provides the clearest evidence (together with a similarly heavily patinated denticulate) of a Palaeolithic presence in the field.

Denticulates and Notches (N=6)

Both denticulates and notches represent nonformal tools produced with a simple flake-based core technology (pl. 10.2). Such tools are typical of lithic assemblages that belong to the Bronze Age.[13] TBO 0412 was made on a nonprismatic bladelet segment and does not represent evidence of deliberate bladelet production. A heavily denticulated flake exhibiting a thick surface patina is intrusive and likely to correspond to the hand-axe TBO 0663 noted above.

11. Rosen, *Lithics after the Stone Age*, 60–65.
12. Ibid., 81–83.
13. Ibid., 90

Table 10.8. Denticulates and Notches

TBO	*Context*	*Technology*	*Length*	*Width*	*Thickness*
III 64	III Aa Locus 13	Proximal flake fragment with well prepared plain butt	68.10 mm	48.26 mm	6.14 mm
0416	V U Locus 2	Unidirectional medial flake fragment with side-blow truncations and direct retouch on lateral edge	23.90 mm	31.69 mm	7.12 mm
0425	V H Locus 3	flake fragment with inverse fine retouch on pronounced hinge termination and polish on dorsal	19.84 mm	36.44 mm	8.06 mm
Unregistered	VI AA Locus 1	Heavily patinated flake with denticulate retouch	27.12 mm	28.80 mm	9.20 mm
0412	V B Locus 1	Unidirectional medial bladelet segment with inverse lateral notch	21.94 mm	11.18 mm	4.28 mm
0421	Surface	Distal flake fragment with lateral notch – reused fragment of a tabular scraper	32.86 mm	37.76 mm	9.52 mm

Glossed Pieces (N=29)

The glossed tools represent the most highly diagnostic artifacts belonging to the Tell el-Borg assemblage. There is no evidence for the manufacture of glossed tools at the site, and given the very standardized character of the various segment types, these tools probably arrived as complete sickles. The sample contains two major types—namely, backed and/or truncated segments produced on prismatic blades and larger geometric glossed segments manufactured on flakes or broad blades. Glossed segments produced on relatively narrow prismatic blades that exhibit truncation and backing retouch have been recorded in Early Bronze Age contexts in Egypt.[14] According to Rosen,[15] there is a lack of a chronological overlap between these glossed tools and the larger geometric segments, which suggests that the former are residual tools that were not in active use at Tell el-Borg. The presence of Early Bronze Age residual glossed tools accords well with the presence of a few reused relatively narrow Canaanean blade fragments and the tabular scrapers mentioned within the glossed tool table (table 10.9) and below. Geometric glossed segments are the most common type at Tell el-Borg, occurring most frequently in rectangular or subtriangular forms, types that have been found elsewhere in Egypt and throughout the Levant.[16] These segments were intensively retouched, using both backing and truncations, and typically show the creation of a denticulated working edge frequently remodified by extensive resharpening retouch. Gloss on the geometrics is typically invasive and well developed and clearly demonstrates the use of a curvilinear haft in a number of cases, as does the distinction between rectilinear and subtriangular morphologies. Working edges frequently also exhibit extensive edge rounding and striations visible with a 20× magnification, occasionally with the naked eye. Alternatively, the gloss is very bright and very narrow, being restricted to a few millimeters parallel to the working edge. The presence of reed huts in Field VI suggests one possible functional requirement for the presence of sickles at the site though use-wear analysis is required in order to confirm the suggestion of reed cutting at the site (see pp. 278–98).

14. Ibid., 50–51.
15. Ibid., 60
16. Manfred Bietak, "Tell el-Dabᶜa," *Archiv für Orientforschung* 32 (1985), 367; E. Coqueugnoit, "Outillage de Pierre Taillée au Bronze Récent: Ras Shamra 1978–1988," in *Ras Shamra-Ougarit VI: Arts et Industries de la Pierre* (ed. M. Yon; Paris: Éditions Recherche sur les Civilisations, 1991), 162.

Table 10.9. Glossed Pieces

TBO	Context	Type	Technology	Length	Width	Thickness
0009	II.2 D Locus 16	Geometric glossed segment	Distal blade fragment with slightly convex bifacial basal truncation – inverse slightly convex backing and bifacial gloss over direct denticulated retouch on the left lateral edge	55.04 mm	27.80 mm	5.20 mm
0101	IV D2 Locus 5A	Backed and truncated glossed segment	Prismatic medial blade segment with basal truncation and inverse convex back on right lateral – opposite left has continuous direct denticulated retouch – no visible gloss	42.60 mm	14.42 mm	4.64 mm
0165	III.2 D Locus 1	Geometric glossed segment	Distal flake fragment with inverse basal truncation, direct flat retouch lower left lateral and distal end and bifacial backing retouch on right lateral edge – no visible gloss, resharpened	22.12 mm	32.74 mm	4.54 mm
0173	V surface	Geometric glossed segment	Distal blade fragment – alternating direct and inverse baking retouch, flat retouch distal truncation and direct denticulated retouch and invasive bifacial gloss on right lateral edge	63.40 mm	30.70 mm	10.78 mm
0204	IV D17 Locus 4	Truncated glossed segment	Prismatic medial blade segment with distal truncation– fine bilateral retouch with gloss restricted to left lateral	43.98 mm	11.44 mm	5.70 mm
0243	III.2 L Locus 1	Backed glossed blade	Prismatic distal blade fragment with side-blow basal truncation and partial retouched back on the lower left lateral – narrow bright gloss on right lateral	60.10 mm	20.80 mm	10.58 mm
0236	II.3 surface	Geometric glossed segment	Medial flake fragment with bifacial basal truncation opposite heavy bifacial gloss on denticulated retouch on distal end	26.92 mm	45.74 mm	5.70 mm
III 17	III D surface	Prismatic glossed blade	Medial Blade segment with snapped proximal and distal ends – left lateral edge with gloss–finely denticulated	42.00 mm	15.00 mm	0.50 mm
0349	III Ab Locus 1	Truncated glossed fragment	Prismatic medial blade segment with basal inverse truncation adjacent to glossed left lateral edge	9.36 mm	18.30 mm	4.80 mm
0362	V surface	Geometric glossed segment	Distal flake fragment with direct basal truncation, direct right lateral backing and direct denticulated retouch with invasive bifacial invasive gloss on distal end	22.70 mm	41.22 mm	5.70 mm
0363	V surface	Geometric glossed segment	Medial flake fragment with inverse and bi- facial basal truncation, direct denticulated retouch and bright narrow inverse gloss on distal end	22.40 mm	27.74 mm	2.72 mm
0372	V.1 L Locus 1	Geometric glossed segment	Medial flake fragment with direct distal truncation, direct right lateral backing and direct denticulated retouch with bright narrow invasive bifacial gloss on left lateral edge	37.82 mm	23.84 mm	5.50 mm
III 73	III Ab Locus 1	Geometric glossed segment	Distal flake fragment with bifacial basal truncation, direct left lateral backing and gloss with resharpening inverse retouch on distal end	26.40 mm	52.56 mm	7.70 mm
III 86	III B Locus 1	Geometric glossed segment	Medial flake fragment with bifacial basal truncation, bifacial backing on right lateral and left lateral with invasive bifacial gloss over denticulated retouch	27.02 mm	22.91 mm	5.36 mm
0391	IV D18 Locus 5A	Geometric glossed segment	Distal flake fragment with inverse basal truncation, direct concave backing on right lateral, and direct denticulated retouch with bright disbursed bifacial invasive gloss on distal end	31.30 mm	46.10 mm	7.86 mm
0397	III.2 Locus 1	Geometric glossed segment	Medial blade segment with direct basal and distal truncations, bifacial backing on right lateral and inverse resharpening retouch over bright but diffuse inverse gloss on left lateral	52.94 mm	27.76 mm	8.90 mm
0442	VI AA Locus 1	Canaanean glossed blade	Medial blade segment with trapezoidal section, unretouched – with narrow very bright gloss on the right lateral edge	27.46 mm	18.10 mm	5.22 mm
0464	VI AA Locus 1	Geometric glossed segment	Distal flake fragment with direct basal truncation and retouch on distal edge, direct backing on left lateral, and basal end bifacial gloss with distal end denticulated retouch on right lateral	46.18 mm	27.56 mm	6.88 mm
0477	Between VI and VIII surface	Geometric glossed segment	Distal blade fragment with bifacial basal truncation, direct flat retouched distal, bifacial backing on left lateral edge, with bright diffuse bifacial gloss and direct denticulated retouch on right lateral edge	6.58 mm	47.50 mm	24.52 mm

Table 10.9. Glossed Pieces

TBO	*Context*	*Type*	*Technology*	*Length*	*Width*	*Thickness*
0483	VI surface	Canaanean glossed blade	Medial blade segment with trapezoidal section – unretouched – bilaterally glossed–with narrow bright gloss on left lateral edge	31.26 mm	17.28 mm	6.38 mm
0501	VI.1 AA/E loc 9	Geometric glossed segment	Distal flake fragment with bifacial backing on left lateral, an inverse basal truncation made by flat retouch and heavy right lateral bifacial gloss	54.22 mm	25.76 mm	8.10 mm
0574	V A Locus 2	Geometric glossed segment	Medial flake fragment with direct basal and distal truncations, bifacial backing retouch on left lateral and direct denticulated retouch with narrow bright but disbursed invasive bifacial gloss on the right lateral	39.26 mm	23.50 mm	6.98 mm
0610	VI G4 Locus 2	Backed and truncated glossed segment	Prismatic medial blade segment with direct rectilinear basal and distal truncations and right lateral back – gloss with find denticulation on left lateral edge	31.18 mm	16.48 mm	4.74 mm
0676	V.1 W3 loc FT.4	Geometric glossed segment	Distal flake fragment with basal truncation, bi- facial left lateral backing opposite denticulated retouch with invasive bifacial gloss on right lateral edge	24.54 mm	36.44 mm	4.10 mm
0742	V.1 Z Locus 3	Denticulated glossed fragment	Medial blade segment exhibiting gloss over fine inverse denticulated scarring on left lateral	26.98 mm	13.46 mm	4.70 mm
0783	VI.2 G Locus 1	Geometric glossed segment	Distal flake fragment broken at the proximal end – with bilateral backing retouch and heavy gloss with denticulated resharpening retouch on the distal working end	20.32 mm	26.72 mm	4.14 mm
0800	V.2 B Locus 9	Geometric glossed segment	Distal blade fragment with direct distal trun- cation, direct right lateral backing and direct denticulated retouch with bifacial bright gloss	38.22 mm	21.82 mm	7.44 mm
0842	V.1 Ub Locus 2	Backed and truncated glossed segment	Prismatic medial blade segment with convex left lateral backing, bifacial distal truncation and denticulated retouch right lateral with gloss	47.76 mm	16.34 mm	4.24 mm
0872	VI.1 surface	Geometric glossed segment	Medial blade segment with bifacial basal and distal truncations, bifacial backing on right lateral and bifacial gloss over denticulated retouch on left lateral	64.02 mm	23.84 mm	7.96 mm

Table 10.10. Perforators

TBO	*Context*	*Technology*	*Length*	*Width*	*Thickness*
0096	IV D2 Locus 5a	Bidirectional medial segment – finely ground with facetted lateral edge – polish and striations are visible on the pointed tip formed by the inter-section of the distal and proxiumal breaks	10.10 mm	33.74 mm	3.06 mm
0259	III.2 L Locus 1	Proximal Bladelet fragment with polish and striations on corner of distal break	51.36 mm	9.02 mm	11.18 mm
0449	IV E.1 Locus 1	Reused glossed blade fragment with trapezoidal section – possible Canaanean blade – inverse retouch and wear on distal lateral corners	28.96 mm	15.02 mm	5.02 mm
0463	VI AA Locus 1	Reused medial Canaanean blade segment – oblique retouch on distal break with wear on pointed tip formed where the break intersects the left lateral edge	35.60 mm	22.06 mm	7.58 mm
0468	VI surf	Proximal flake fragment with wear and polish on corner of distal end break	29.30 mm	7.56 mm	13.52 mm
0824	V.1 BB2 Locus 3	Cortical flake with wear encircling right basal corner	27.16 mm	22.40 mm	9.50 mm
Unregistered	V.1 Ia Locus 3	Distal flake fragment with wear encircling pointed distal end	36.46 mm	21.48 mm	6.34 mm
Unregistered	VI AA Locus 1	Flake with fine were encircling pointed distal end	31.22 mm	12.30 mm	4.02 mm
Unregistered	VI E Locus 2	Bidirectional Distal flake fragment with wear and polish on left lateral corner	10.50 mm	25.82 mm	8.26 mm

Perforators (N=9)

Perforators are relatively frequent in the Tell el-Borg assemblage, a fact that is likely to be related to the numerous stone beads found at the site (pl. 10.2). The presence of the perforators

Table 10.11. Retouched

TBO	*Context*	*Technology*	*Length*	*Width*	*Thickness*
0070	II.2 I Locus 15	Fragmentary medial Canaanean blade segment–trapezoidal section –with abrupt direct retouch on both lateral edges	30.50 mm	31.24 mm	8.30 mm
0340	III D Locus 2	Medial flake fragment with direct lateral retouch	19.60 mm	15.02 mm	5.02 mm
0399	III B Locus 1	Medial flake fragment with inverse lateral retouch and polish on dorsal surface	28.26 mm	24.70 mm	7.30 mm
Unregistered	V.1 Ia Locus 3	Medial flake fragment with fine direct retouch on lateral edge	17.30 mm	33.20 mm	8.86 mm
Unregistered	VI BB Locus 11	Distal flake fragment with abrupt direct lateral retouch	15.16 mm	6.64 mm	2.30 mm
Unregistered	VI R Locus 1	Medial flake fragment with miscellaneous lateral retouch	22.36 mm	41.88 mm	6.30 mm
Unregistered	V.1-Ua Locus 3	Medial flake fragment with inverse lateral retouch	17.70 mm	20.70 mm	5.60 mm
Unregistered	V.1-BB.4 Locus 5	Medial flake fragment with coarse alternating retouch on the distal end	21.64 mm	26.76 mm	8.44 mm
Unregistered	VI.2 E Locus 2	Proximal fragment with miscellaneous retouch	8.70 mm	9.02 mm	2.86 mm
Unregistered	VI AA Locus 1	Cortical flake with direct lateral retouch	40.24 mm	52.0 mm	9.44 mm

Table 10.12. Scrapers

TBO	*Context*	*Technology*	*Length*	*Width*	*Thickness*
0057	II.2 H Locus 1	Unidirectional medial flake segment with scraper retouch on basal end break	69.68 mm	37.78 mm	10.10 mm
0671	V Z3 Locus 4	Reused thick tabular scraper fragment – abrupt lateral scraper retouch and inverse steep retouch on opposite lateral – inverse retouch off distal break forms backing	68.86 mm	61.84 mm	15.30 mm
0782	Surface	Proximal end of tabular flake scraper with bilateral direct retouch	61.30 mm	36.94 mm	10.10 mm
0847	V.1 BB6 Locus 3	End scraper on reused medial Canaanean blade segment	36.30 mm	20.44 mm	6.58 mm
Unregistered	VI E Locus 2	Scraper resharpening flake	19.62 mm	12.06 mm	5.56 mm
Unregistered	V.1 BB3 Locus 3	Side scraper on unidirectional distal blade fragment	40.54 mm	21.98 mm	12.96 mm
Unregistered	VI A Locus 6	Side scraper on unidirectional proximal flake fragment	38.36 mm	41.08 mm	14.10 mm

in the lithic sample suggests that at least some bead production occurred on site. While the majority of the perforators were produced on expedient flakes or flake fragments, both TBO 0449 and TBO 0463 are reused Canaanean blade fragments. Some perforators exhibit abrupt or semi-abrupt retouch, but the majority of these tools are defined by the presence of wear that encircles a distal tip or corner created by the intersection of a break with a lateral edge. Such edge damage is typically accompanied by visible polish and occasionally striations. One example, TBO 0096, is unique. This tool, which is made on a medial flake fragment, was finely ground and facetted on both dorsal and ventral surfaces, as well as both lateral edges. The pointed tip formed by the intersection of the distal and proximal breaks is well rounded and exhibits fine striations created during both manufacture and use.

Retouched (N=10)

Marginally retouched pieces are relatively common at Tell el-Borg. The majority of these artifacts represent fragmentary tools with direct edge retouch. Most of the retouched tools were made on flakes and are consistent with the expedient character of the local industry. One exception, TBO 0070, is a fragmentary, bilaterally-retouched Canaanean blade segment, which like other Canaanean blade fragments is intrusive in the fort contexts (table 10.11).

Table 10.13. Truncations

TBO	Context	Technology	Length	Width	Thickness
0458	VI AA Locus 1	Unidirectional medial flake segment with basal and distal truncations – wear on corner created by inter- section of basal truncation and lateral edge may indicate use as a perforating tool	23.70 mm	31.82 mm	6.88 mm
0544	VI AA Locus 1	Unidirectional Blade – with abrupt bilateral retouch and distal truncation	41.20 mm	15.32 mm	424 mm
0635	VI Locus 1	Naturally backed medial flake segment with basal and distal truncations	25.36 mm	32.60 mm	8.56 mm
0655	IV D20 Locus 4	Reused Canaanean blade segment with basal and distal truncations	25.60 mm	22.66 mm	6.78 mm

Table 10.14. Utilized

TBO	Context	F	B	BL	Edge wear	Polish	Abrasion	Length	Width	Thickness
0033	II.2 E Locus 1	×			×			59.60 mm	47.40 mm	9.26 mm
0159	III.2 C Locus 1	×			×			40.18 mm	39.54 mm	6.24 mm
0223	III.2 F Locus 1	×			×			22.30 mm	33.70 mm	5.96 mm
0229	III D Locus 1	×			×	×		40.18 mm	22.26 mm	5.50 mm
0275	III.2 M Locus 1	×			×		×	17.64 mm	59.80 mm	4.92 mm
0288	IV D.1 Locus 2	×			×			17.60 mm	29.22 mm	9.02 mm
0315	Surface	×			×			38.50 mm	51.30 mm	6.24 mm
0320	Surface	×			×	×		48.14 mm	32.24 mm	13.18 mm
0332	III.2 TT2 surface			×	×			25.08 mm	8.64 mm	2.10 mm
0329	III.2 TT2 Locus 1	×			×			31.48 mm	21.84 mm	8.54 mm
III 63	III B Locus 2	×			×			66.22 mm	96.78 mm	8.26 mm
0378	IV D15 Locus 3	×			×	×		41.02 mm	23.46 mm	8.50 mm
0466	VI AA Locus 1	×			×		×	42.50 mm	51.64 mm	12.20 mm
0577	VI D Locus 1		×		×			49.90 mm	14.96 mm	4.70 mm
0636	VI surface	×			×			23.54 mm	34.26 mm	4.60 mm
0643	VI R2 Locus 1	×			×			53.40 mm	41.52 mm	11.32 mm
0691	VI.2 E Locus 2	×			×			58.18 mm	46.40 mm	11.92 mm
0786	V.1 BB3 Locus 3	×			×			17.90 mm	13.90 mm	2.14 mm
0840	V.1-BB6 Locus 2	×			×			36.48 mm	23.76 mm	6.58 mm
0864	V 2 A Locus 9a	×			×			19.14 mm	15.22 mm	4.42 mm

Scrapers (N=7)

Tell el-Borg scrapers form two distinct groups: simple flake scrapers and intrusive tabular scrapers (pls. 10.2 and 10.3). The latter again indicate the possibility of an Early Bronze Age occupation in the field. TBO 0671 was substantially reworked, indicating the reuse of scavenged earlier material in the Late Bonze Age context. TBO 0782, while not heavily modified, shows similar scavenging activity. The four flake scrapers are typical of an industry based on a simple core technology that characterizes lithic assemblages of the Bronze Age.

Truncations (N=4)

A small number of truncations belong to the local flake-based industry (pl. 10.2). Three of these artifacts are double truncations, one of which reuses a Canaanean blade segment. TBO 0458 may have been used as a perforating tool, but the corner wear suggestive of this function

Table 10.14. Utilized

TBO	*Context*	*F*	*B*	*BL*	*Edge wear*	*Polish*	*Abrasion*	*Length*	*Width*	*Thickness*
Unreg	VI R2 Locus 1	×			×		Water rolled over wear	30.98 mm	29.14 mm	5.32 mm
Unreg	V.1 Ia Locus 3	×			×			42.94 mm	31.28 mm	8.70 mm
Unreg	V I Locus 3	×			×			20.40 mm	8.36 mm	5.50 mm
Unreg	VI B Locus 1	×			×	×	×	25.54 mm	29.16 mm	7.56 mm
Unreg	VI.2 G Locus 1	×			×	×		33.74 mm	26.50 mm	5.56 mm
Unreg	V.1 Ha Locus 3	×			×			18.94 mm	11.28 mm	4.32 mm
Unreg	V.2 A Locus 2	×			×	×		32.64 mm	19.84 mm	6.62 mm
Unreg	VI.2 E Locus 2	×			×	×		35.30 mm	24.36 mm	5.20 mm
Unreg	VIII.2 C Locus 12	×			×			28.16 mm	19.24 mm	6.98 mm
Unreg	VI surface	×			×			24.80 mm	35.10 mm	7.16 mm
Unreg	VI.1 AA Locus 1	×			×	×		54.52 mm	48.54 mm	6.18 mm
Unreg	IV F2 Locus 2	×			×		Incised cortex	61.32 mm	33.72 mm	14.50 mm
Unreg	VI.2 G Locus 1	×			×			18.32 mm	17.20 mm	5.96 mm

was poorly developed. Truncations may have functioned as scraping edges, but edge damage on the lateral edge(s) delineated by the truncations shows the use of the unretouched edge as well.

Utilized (N=33)

Utilized pieces represent ad hoc implements employed for their sharp edges and corners (pl. 10.2). They represent the most expedient element facet of the local industry employed at the forts. The presence of visible light polish and abrasion suggests the possibility that these tools were employed in the manufacture of ornaments, while continuous lengths of angular fine edge chipping (frequently associated with light polish) implies the use of these flakes as cutting edges. However, use-wear analysis is required to formally document tool function.

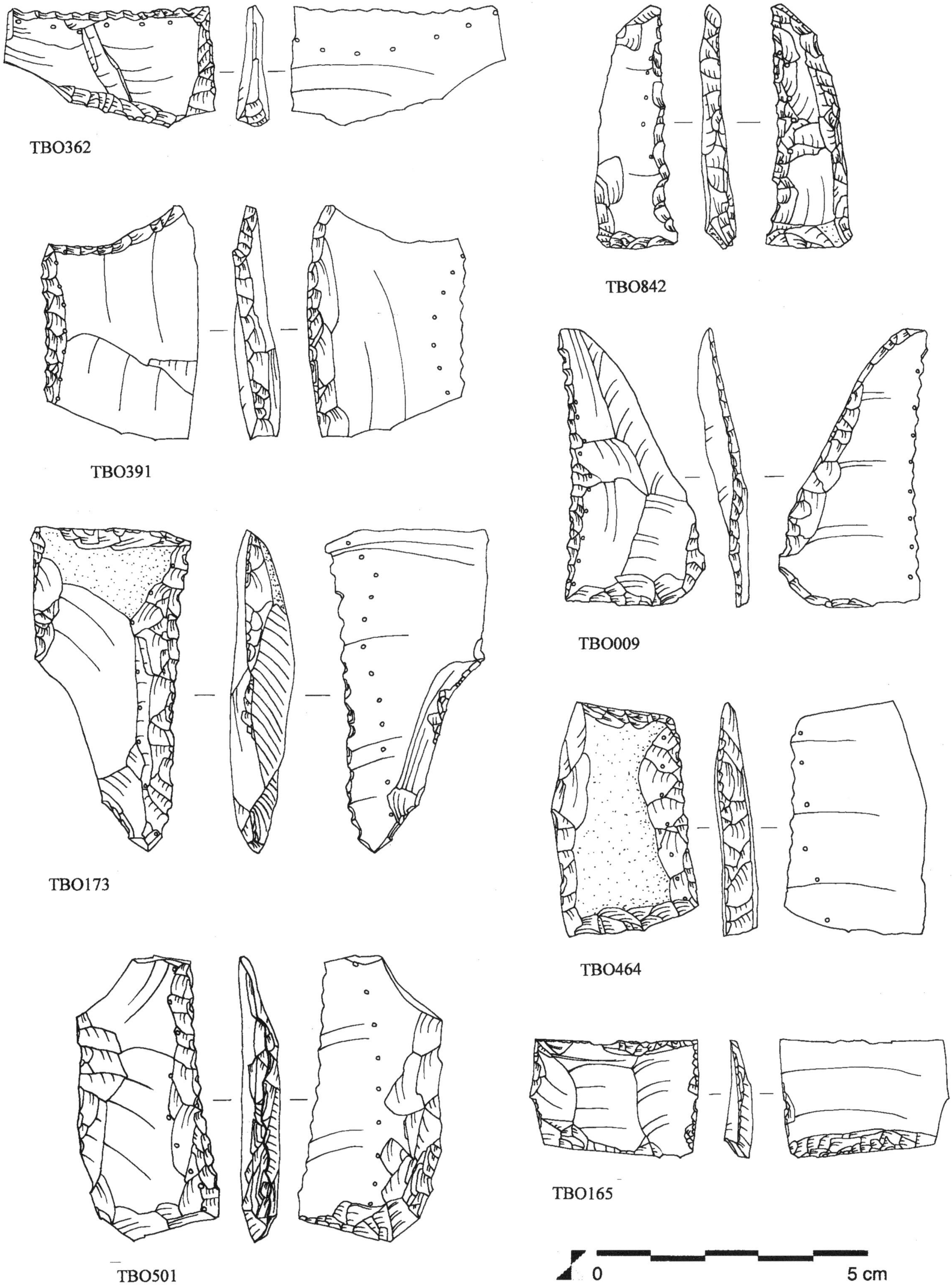

Plate 10.1. Glossed Tools (Scale 1:1).

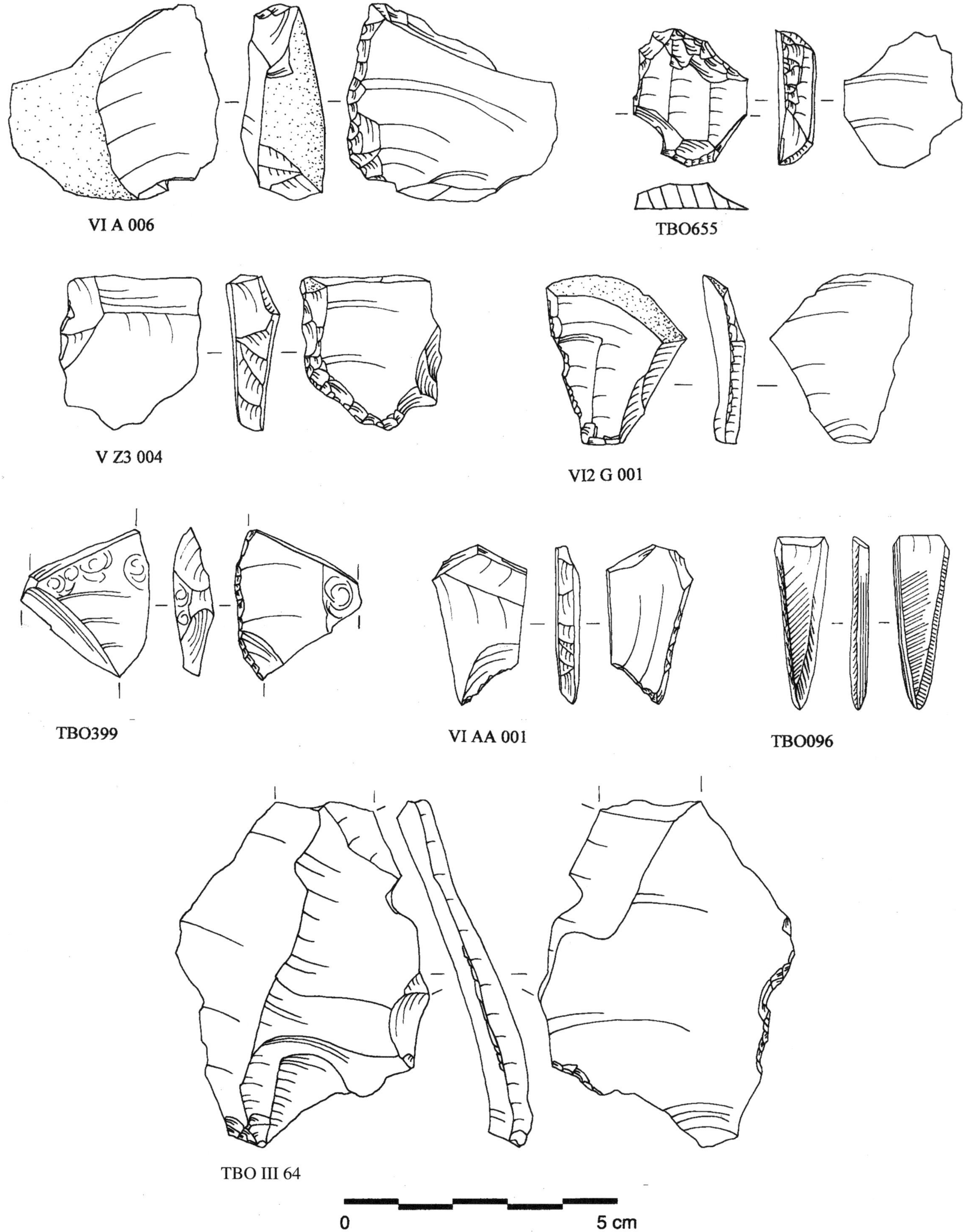

Plate 10.2. Flake Tools (Scale 1:1).

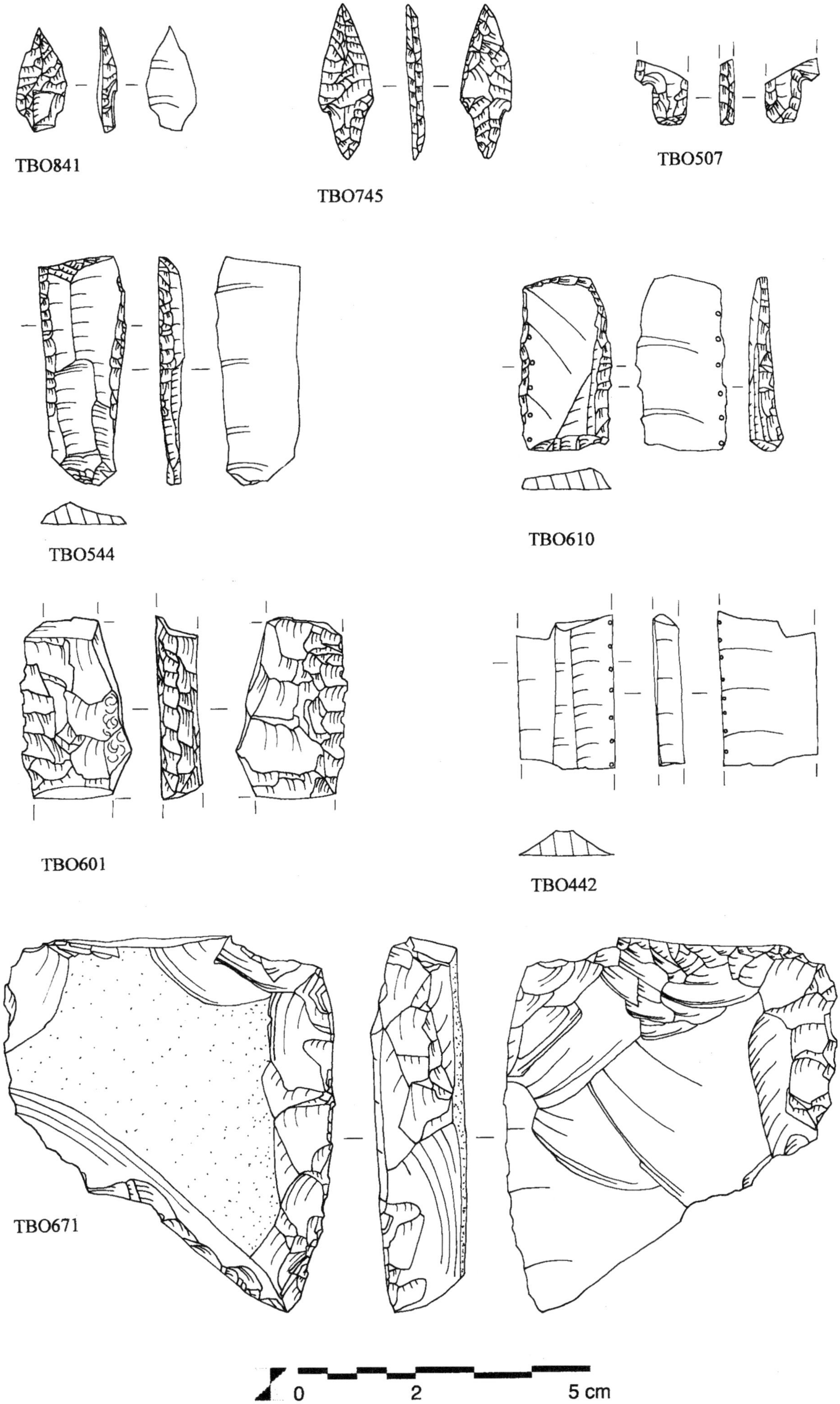

Plate 10.3. Derived Tools (Scale 1:1).

CHAPTER 11

Report on the Charred Plant Remains at Tell el-Borg

Claire Malleson
American University Beirut

Introduction

During the 2007 season of work at Tell el-Borg, the archaeobotanical material recovered in previous excavations was analyzed.[1] A total of 46 separate samples had been taken, and two additional samples were recovered during the season. The majority of these samples had been processed prior to 2007 by team members using the bucket flotation method[2] and window screen mesh (all that was available easily to the team). As noted by Wagner,[3] window screen ranges in size from 1–1.8 mm mesh; the mesh used at Tell el-Borg was 1.5 mm. Thirteen of the samples were floated using the same method by the author in 2007, using a 0.125 mm mesh (Endecott sieve). The larger sieve mesh size will have affected the recovery of smaller seeds and grains. However, it was observed during initial sorting that there was still a considerable quantity of material smaller that 1.5 mm retained in the dried sample, and the results show that some smaller-seeded species were indeed retrieved. The volume of the soil was not measured; where a count "per ml" is given, it is based on the volume of the light fraction. Only charred macro-remains are preserved in this assemblage.

Twenty of the samples contained no plant remains; of the remaining 28 samples, only 9 had sufficient quantities of plant remains to justify inclusion in this report.[4] The samples taken have all been dated to the 18–19th Dynasties based on general dating for the site.

1. Thanks to Dr. M. A. Murray (University College London, U.K.) for the loan of equipment and invaluable advice, and to Dr. M. Nesbitt (Kew Gardens, U.K.) for his advice on the contents of this report.

2. In this process, the soil sample is placed in a bucket of water and agitated in order to release the light charred plant remains, which are then collected in a fine sieve mesh. The unsorted charred plant remains are known as the light fraction.

3. G. E. Wagner, "Comparability Among Recovery Techniques," in *Current Palaeoethnobotany* (ed. C. A. Hastorf and V. S. Popper; Chicago: University of Chicago Press, 1988) 21.

4. The 18 samples with minimal quantities of plant remains each contained no more than 5 fragments in total of either *Lolium* sp., *Triticum* sp., or unidentifiable vesicular fragments. The sample from TBP 155

Due to the short period available for the study of this material, several questions remain unanswered. Much of the material from Field VI was exceptionally well preserved and has the potential for identification to species level, but in this report identification is only to species level where this was possible on first inspection.

Analysis of Samples

A range of different species was found to be present in the samples from the site. Cereals dominated the assemblage: *Triticum turgidum* ssp. *dicoccon* (emmer wheat), *Hordeum vulgare* (hulled barley), as well as some possible *T.aestivum* (free-threshing wheat), and a very tentative identification of *T. monococcum* (einkorn). Several species of wild grasses (crop weeds) were present: *Lolium* sp. (rye grass), *Bromus* sp. (brome grass), *Phalaris* sp. (canary grass), as well as other weed species from the Fabaceae family (Trifolieae tribe (clover), Viceae tribe (vetch), and *Scorpiurus* sp.), *Chenopodiaceae, Lamiaceae, Cyperaceae* (*Eleocharis* sp. and *Cyperus* sp. (sedge), *Malvaceae* (mallow), *Polygonaceae* (*Rumex* sp. (dock)), and *Portulacaeae* (*Portulaca* sp. (purslane)) families. A small number of fruit and pulse food crop species were also found: *Lens culinaris* (lentils), *Ficus carica* (common fig), and *Vitis* sp. (grape). In general, the specimens were well preserved and there were very few vesicular fragments.

Results

Table 11.1. Sample, Field III Area D Locus 4: Contents of Pot TBP 0156

Species	*Count*	*Per ml*	*Percentage* [a]
T. turgidum ssp. *dicoccon* glume base	4	4	4.17
T. dicoccon spikelet fork	11	11	11.46
Lolium sp.	81	81	84.37
TOTAL	**96**	**96**	**100**

a. This indicates the percentage of the entire sample represented by the species.

Table 11.2. Sample, Field III Area B Locus 1: Contents of Pot TBP 0173

Species	*Count*	*Per ml*	*Percentage*
T. dicoccon glume base	8	8	11.94
T. dicoccon spikelet fork	4	4	5.97
Lolium sp.	20	20	29.85
Poaceae indeterminate	3	3	4.48
Vitis sp.	1	1	1.49
Vesicular fragments	31	31	46.27
TOTAL	**67**	**67**	**100**

(Field III Locus 4) contained one complete example of *Vitis* sp. One sample from Field VI (Area S3 Locus 3) did contain a large quantity of charred plant remains, but the excavators noted that this deposit was a mix of modern and ancient material, so it has been excluded from this report.

Table 11.3. Sample: Field III Area 2/BB Locus 2, Dump Layer

Species	*Count*	*Per ml*	*Percentage*
T. dicoccon grain	1	0.03	1.11
T. dicoccon glume base	5	0.15	5.56
T. dicoccon spikelet fork	5	0.15	5.56
Lolium sp.	41	0.43	45.56
Phalaris sp.	1	0.03	1.11
Trifolieae tribe	3	0.09	3.33
Viceae tribe	1	0.03	1.11
Rumex sp.	1	0.03	1.11
Vesicular fragments	32	0.98	35.55
TOTAL	**90**	**2.77**	**100**

Table 11.4. Sample: Field VI Locus 2, Reed Hut Wall

Species	*B (109ml)*		*AA/E (53ml)*		*2007 (91.5ml)*		*Total (253.5ml)*	
	Count	*Per ml*	*Count*	*Per ml*	*Count*	*Per ml*	*Count*	*Per ml*
T. *dicoccon* grain	178	**1.63**	23	**0.43**	17	**0.18**	218	**0.86**
T. *dicoccon* spikelet			2	**0.04**			2	**0.008**
T. *dicoccon* glume base	238	**2.18**	175	**3.0**	20	**0.22**	433	**1.71**
T. *dicoccon* spikelet fork	351	**3.22**	171	**2.44**	35	**0.38**	557	**2.2**
T. *dicoccon* spikelet fork w. rachis	134	**1.23**	53	**1**	6	**0.06**	193	**0.76**
Triticum sp. rachis fragments	110	**1.01**	47	**0.89**	3	**0.03**	160	**0.63**
Triticum sp. (cf *T. monococcum?*)	20	**0.18**	14	**0.26**	1	**0.01**	35	**0.14**
Triticum cf *aestivu*	2	**0.02**	1	**0.02**			3	**0.011**
Triticum cf *aestivu* rachis	7	**0.06**	7	**0.13**			14	**0.05**
H. *vulgare* grain	24	**0.22**	8	**0.15**	8	**0.09**	40	**0.16**
H. *vulgare* internode	38	**0.35**	12	**0.23**			50	**0.2**
Cereal indeterminate	13	**0.12**	5	**0.09**	2	**0.02**	20	**0.08**
Cereal indeterminate glume base	4	**0.04**					4	**0.015**
Cereal culm node	28	**0.26**	6	**0.11**			34	**0.13**
Lolium sp.	1346	**12.35**	488	**9.21**	256	**2.8**	2090	**8.24**
Lolium sp. spikelet	180	**1.65**	14	**0.26**	2	**0.02**	196	**0.77**
Phalaris sp.	10	**0.09**	6	**0.11**	7	**0.08**	23	**0.09**
Bromus sp.	1	**0.009**					1	**0.004**
Poaceae indeterminate	25	**0.23**	1	**0.02**	4	**0.04**	30	**0.12**
Poaceae indeterminate spikelet fork	21	**0.19**	12	**0.25**	1	**0.01**	34	**0.13**
Poaceae indeterminate rachis fragments	6	**0.05**					6	**0.024**
Poaceae indeterminate rachis chain	3	**0.03**	2	**0.04**			5	**0.02**
Poaceae embryo	1	**0.009**					1	**0.004**
Trifoliae tribe	259	**2.38**	105	**1.98**	33	**0.36**	397	**1.57**
Viceae tribe	2	**0.02**	3	**0.06**			5	**0.02**
Scorpiurus sp.	2	**0.02**					2	**0.008**
cf *Lens culinaris*			2	**0.04**			2	**0.008**
Fabaceae	2	**0.02**					2	**0.008**
Chenopodiaceae			2	**0.04**			2	**0.008**
Lamiaceae			1	**0.02**			1	**0.004**
cf *Cyperus* sp.	8	**0.07**	4	**0.07**	5		17	**0.07**
Portulaca sp.					2		2	**0.008**
Ficus carica			1	**0.02**			1	**0.004**

Table 11.4, continued. Sample: Field VI Locus 2, Reed Hut Wall

Species	*B (109ml)*		*AA/E (53ml)*		*2007 (91.5ml)*		*Total (253.5ml)*	
	Count	*Per ml*	*Count*	*Per ml*	*Count*	*Per ml*	*Count*	*Per ml*
Vitis sp.	13	**0.12**	4	**0.07**	1	**0.01**	18	**0.07**
Nut shell fragment			1	**0.02**			1	**0.004**
cf Root/Tuber	2	**0.02**					2	**0.008**
Indeterminate seeds	8	**0.07**	3	**0.06**	15	**0.16**	26	**0.1**
Dung fragments <2 mm	376	**3.45**	134	**2.53**	10	**0.11**	520	**2.05**
TOTAL	3412	**31.3**	1307	**24.66**	428	**4.68**	5147	**20.3**

Table 11.5. Sample: Field VI Locus 3, Fire Pit

Sample	*Level 1 (23 ml)*		*Level 2 (13.5 ml)*		*Total (36.5 ml)*	
	Count	*Per ml*	*Count*	*Per ml*	*Count*	*Per ml*
T. dicoccon	55	**2.39**	29	**2.15**	84	**2.3**
T. dicoccon glume base	29	**1.26**	28	**1.33**	57	**1.56**
T. dicoccon spikelet fork	20	**0.87**	24	**1.78**	44	**1.21**
T. dicoccon spikelet fork with rachis	12	**0.52**	4	**0.3**	16	**0.44**
Triticum sp. rachis fragments	7	**0.3**	3	**0.22**	10	**0.27**
Triticum sp. (? cf *T.monococcum*?)	12	**0.52**	2	**0.15**	14	**0.38**
Triticum cf *aestivum*	2	**0.09**	4	**0.3**	6	**0.16**
Triticum cf *aestivum* rachis	1	**0.04**	1	**0.07**	2	**0.05**
H. vulgare	4	**0.17**	8	**0.59**	12	**0.33**
H. vulgare internode	15	**0.65**	5	**0.37**	20	**0.55**
Cereal indeterminate	8	**0.35**			8	**0.22**
Cereal culm node	11	**0.48**			11	**0.3**
Lolium sp.	677	**29.43**	304	**22.52**	981	**26.88**
Lolium sp. spikelet	9	**0.39**	6	**0.44**	15	**0.41**
Phalaris sp.	10	**0.43**			10	**0.27**
Poaceae indeterminate	14	**0.61**	25	**1.85**	39	**1.07**
Poaceae indeterminate spikelet fork	21	**0.91**	1	**0.07**	22	**0.6**
Poaceae indeterminate rachis chain	2	**0.09**	1	**0.07**	3	**0.08**
Trifoliae tribe	231	**10.04**	34	**2.52**	265	**7.26**
Viceae tribe	3	**0.13**	1	**0.07**	4	**0.11**
cf *Lens culinaris*			1	**0.07**	1	**0.03**
Fabaceae	2	**0.09**	2	**0.15**	4	**0.11**
cf Cyperaceae	5	**0.22**	1	**0.07**	6	**0.17**
Eleocharis sp.	1	**0.04**			1	**0.03**
cf Malvaceae	2	**0.09**			2	**0.05**
Rumex sp	2	**0.02**				
Vitis sp.	11	**0.48**			11	**0.3**
Seed head indeterminate	1	**0.04**			1	**0.03**
Indeterminate seeds	5	**0.22**			5	**0.14**
Dung fragments <2 mm	142	**6.17**	80	**5.92**	222	**6.08**
TOTALS	1302	**56.61**	564	**41.78**	1866	**51.12**

DISCUSSION

Field III

Two samples are from intact pots: TBP 156 (*Tell el-Borg I*, 371, pl. 2:2 on p. 411) (fig. 11.1a–b) and TBP 173 (fig. 11.2a–b). The context from which pot TBP 156 derived contained other general debris, such as animal bone, potsherds, and ash, with intact pots at the base,[5] and clearly represents the initial tomb collapse. TBP 173 came from a large pit filled with general waste and many intact pots as well as potsherds.[6] Grains placed in jars for funerary use (in ancient Egypt) are usually uncharred,[7] and it seems unlikely that these remains represent such an offering, because the charred remains clearly consist entirely of crop-processing waste: cereal chaff and crop weed seeds[8] (see the later discussion for Field VI for more details on the components of cereal-processing waste). It is possible that the fill in the pots is contemporary with this early dumping/destruction phase of the cemetery rather than being related to the placement of the pots in the tombs.

The third sample analyzed from this area (Field III, Area 2, Square BB, Locus 2) derived from a dumping context.[9] This sample, along with all other samples from this area may well represent a background noise of general waste-dumping in the area after the construction of the tombs, possibly during the occupation of either the 18th or 19th Dynasty fortress.

The samples from Field III had a relatively high proportion of fragmented specimens of rye grass, some smaller weed seeds, and just one fragment of a cereal grain (emmer wheat). From this it could be suggested that this waste is the product of (post-threshing) sieving (through a small mesh),[10] charred by its use as a domestic fuel.

Field VI

There were two features in Field VI that produced large quantities of well-preserved charred plant remains: a feature that was interpreted as being the charred remains of a reed hut and a charred pit/hearth adjacent to the hut.[11]

THE REED "HUT 1"

The "wall" of the hut feature was sampled on three occasions in different places. Several things must be taken into account when examining these results. The volume of material retained during flotation varied between samples, (unfortunately the precise volume of soil sieved is

5. See chapter 4, figs. 4.31–4.33.

6. See p. 242 and pl. 4.7.

7. Examples roughly contemporary to the samples from Tell el-Borg are known from the tomb of Tutankhamun.

8. Examples from Old Kingdom Saqqara contained mainly cereal grains, with some weed seeds: T. I. Rzeuska, "The Case of Beer Jars with Ashes" in *Timelines: Studies in Honour of Manfred Bietak, Volume I* (ed. E. Czerny et al.; Leuven: Peeters, 2006) 291–98.

9. See chapter 2 in this volume.

10. M. A. Murray, "Cereal Production and Processing" in *Ancient Egyptian Materials and Technology* (ed. P. T. Nicholson and I. Shaw; Cambridge: Cambridge University Press, 2000), 526.

11. See James K. Hoffmeier, Thomas W. Davis, and Rexine Hummel, "New Archaeological Evidence for Ancient Bedouin (Shasu) on Egypt's Eastern Frontier at Tell el-Borg," *ÄuL* 26 (2016) 285–311 and chapter 8 in this volume.

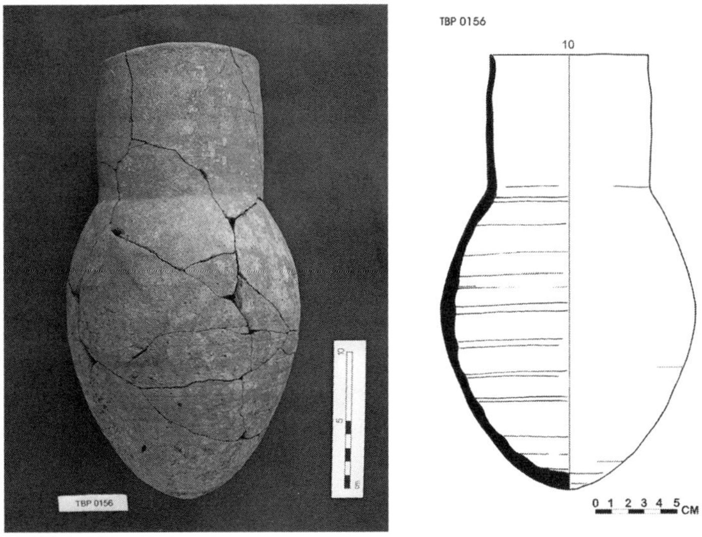

Fig. 11.1. TBP 156. **a** (left): Photo; **b** (right): drawing by L. Pinch-Brock.

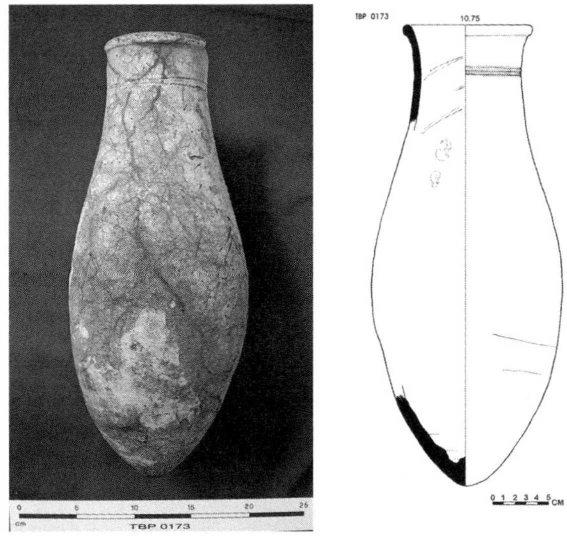

Fig. 11.2. TBP 173. **a** (left): Photo; **b** (right): drawing by L. Pinch-Brock.

Table 11.6. Analysis

Species	*Wall Feature*	*Fire Pit*
Cereal chaff % of Cereal elements	81.96	57.82
Cereal chaff % of whole assemblage	28.07	9.08
Cereal grain % of whole assemblage	6.18	6.62
Weeds/wild % of whole assemblage	54.67	71.28
Triticum spp. elements % of all cereal	91.61	75.17
T. dicoccon % of Triticum spp.	96.78	90.95
T. dicoccon grain % of *T. dicoccon*	13.95	38.01
T. dicoccon glume/forks % of *T. dicoccon*	75.37	57.47
T. dicoccon rachis % of *T. dicoccon*	10.24	4.52
cf *T. aestivum* % of *Triticum spp.*	1.11	3.29
cf *T. aestivum* rachis % of cf *T. aestivum*	77.77	33.33
H.vulgare % of cereal elements	5.11	10.88
H. vulgare rachis % of *H.vulgare*	55.55	62.50
Poaceae % of whole assemblage	80.59	71.76
Cereal % of Poaceae	42.50	21.88
Non-cereal % of Poaceae	57.50	78.13
Lolium sp. % of Poaceae	55.11	74.11
Lolium sp. % of non-Cereal Poaceae	95.85	94.86
Lolium sp. spikelets % of Lolium sp.	8.57	1.51
Phalaris sp. % of non-cereal Poaceae	0.96	1.90

unknown;[12] the volumes given here refer to the volume of light fraction). The sample excavated in 2007 had been taken as an attempt to provide a fully quantifiable example from this feature. However, the feature had been severely damaged by natural elements since its original exposure; the charred plant material was in considerably poorer condition than the other samples. It should also be noted that this sample was excavated from the very base of the feature and most

12. With the one exception of the sample taken in 2007 (4.45 liters).

probably represents the bottom 5 cm of the 20/25-cm-deep locus or at worst the shadow or stain of the feature rather than the original structure itself. Interpretation of the real function of this structure can only be tentative, given that the only loci sampled were this wall and the adjacent pit; the internal structures and surfaces were not sampled.

There was some question regarding the dating of the reed hut during excavation, due to its exceptional state of preservation. However, the feature certainly pre-dates the Greco-Roman period, due to the dominance of emmer over free-threshing wheat in the assemblage; during the Greco-Roman period, emmer was almost totally replaced by free-threshing wheat.[13] Based on ceramic analysis, this feature seems to date from the 18th–19th Dynasties.[14]

The material in samples BB and AA/E was exceptionally well preserved; in many cases, the epidermis was mostly intact, and occasionally some hairs were preserved, while all the specimens had at least some epidermis present. The sample taken in 2007 was less well preserved, containing some vesicular fragments and a higher percentage of fragmented specimens.

The dominance of cereal chaff elements cannot be a direct result of the charring process: experiments by Boardman and Jones[15] have shown that the grains of glume wheats (*T. turgidum* ssp. *dicoccon*) survive charring better than the glumes.[16] Therefore, the fact that in these samples the glumes represent between 70–85% of the emmer wheat elements suggests that this material is likely to represent crop-processing waste rather than grain storage.[17] This is also supported by the fact that the rachises of the free-threshing cereals (*H. vulgare* and cf *T. aestivum*) represent more than 60% of the free-threshing cereal elements.[18]

The identification of a low presence of *T. monococcum* grains is tentative. There have been other identifications of *T. monococcum* in Egypt and, if present, then the species was most likely to be a weed of other cereal crops.[19] It should be noted that the identification of this species is widely questioned among archaeobotanists working in Egypt.[20]

The condition of the identifiable specimens is exceptionally good and indicative of the fact that it originates from within the construction material of, or very closely adjacent to, a structure of some kind, rather than a floor surface; in the latter case, the material would be expected to have become more trampled and fragmented. Initial interpretation in the field suggested that the charred material was the remains of the reeds used as the walls of a temporary hut or shelter that burned down. Therefore, when it became clear that many of the plant remains were not reed or straw components, as was initially expected, but cereal crop-processing waste and dung fragments, the interpretation of the structure and the taphonomy of the locus became more complex.

There were a very high proportion of dung fragments in the samples. Counts of fragments are provided above (table 11.4), but this is not representative of the fact that the samples were actually dominated by tiny fragments of fine straw that were observed to be identical to the ma-

---

13. D. Samuel, "Brewing and Baking," in *Ancient Egyptian Materials and Technology* (ed. P. T. Nicholson and I. Shaw; Cambridge: Cambridge University Press, 2000) 538.

14. *Tell el-Borg I*, 371.

15. S. Boardman and G. Jones, "Experiments on the Effects of Charring on Cereal Plant Components," in *Journal of Archaeological Science* 17 (1990) 1–11.

16. Boardman and Jones, "Charring on Cereal Plant Components."

17. The proportion of rachis to glumes in the glume wheat is dominated by glumes (70–80% glumes and 4–10% rachis); this may be a result of the fact that the rachis does not survive the charring process as well as the glume. Boardman and Jones, "Charring on Cereal Plant Components," 4.

18. See Boardman and Jones, "Charring on Cereal Plant Components," 6.

19. Murray, "Cereal Production and Processing," 513.

20. Personal communication, M. Nesbitt, 2007.

terial within the larger dung fragments. In one instance, a complete coprolite was preserved and identifiable as belonging to *Ovi-caprid* (Sheep/Goat).

Dung can be preserved through charring in several ways: by accidental burning (for example an animal pen burning down), by accidental burning of a structure that has used dung as a building material, or by deliberate burning of dung as a fuel. Cereal crop-processing waste is often a component of dung because it is frequently used as animal fodder, but this waste can also become mixed with dung through the creation of dung-cakes for use as a fuel[21] or by mixing the chaff with dung for use as a building material. The dung material at Tell el-Borg was comprised mainly of straw chaff; none of the identifiable plant elements were found in a dung matrix, and the seeds and grains were in good condition, showing no obvious signs of having been chewed. Unlike the material in these samples, grains, chaff, and wild plant seeds deriving from animal dung are badly distorted.[22] In this case, therefore, it is probably safe to state that very few of the plant remains derive directly from their use as animal fodder and may be more likely to represent domestic fuel.

The charred plant seeds, grains, and chaff elements in this feature must represent cereal crop-processing waste. These remains must derive either from the burning-down of an animal pen (the charred remains from around the reed walls representing uneaten fodder mixed with dung), or a post-"habitation" use of the space as a dump—the chaff and dung having been cleared from a hearth or the nearby fire-pit, then naturally collected around the walls of the abandoned hut.

The Fire Pit

This feature is contemporary with the reed hut. Given the interpretation of this feature in the field as a fire pit and the species and elements present, there can be little doubt that the charred plant remains represent the use of cereal crop-processing waste as domestic fuel (table 11.5). The samples from the fire pit contained a higher density of charred seeds and grains than the sample from the reed hut walls: an average of around 51 seeds/grains per ml of light fraction (reed hut = average of 20 seeds/grains per ml). The explanation for this could well be simple: this feature is clearly an area of deliberate burning and very likely to have been a domestic cooking installation fuelled with wood, chaff, and dung, whereas the reed hut sample may represent accidental burning of some loose fodder and animal waste.

The fire pit contained a higher percentage of wild and weed species, while the wall feature contained more chaff elements. This may well indicate the use of different chaff products from different stages of processing for two different purposes: larger sieving waste for fodder and small sieving waste for fuel.

General Comments

The predominance of emmer is unsurprising, given that it was the dominant cereal crop in Egypt during the New Kingdom.[23] The low quantities of cf *T. aestivum* at Tell el-Borg fits the

21. S. M. Valamoti and M. Charles, "Distinguishing Food from Fodder through the Study of Charred Plant Remains: An Experimental Approach to Dung-Derived Chaff," in *Vegetation History and Archaeobotany* 14 (2005) 529.
22. Valamoti and Charles, "Distinguishing Food from Fodder," 530.
23. Murray, "Cereal Production and Processing," 512.

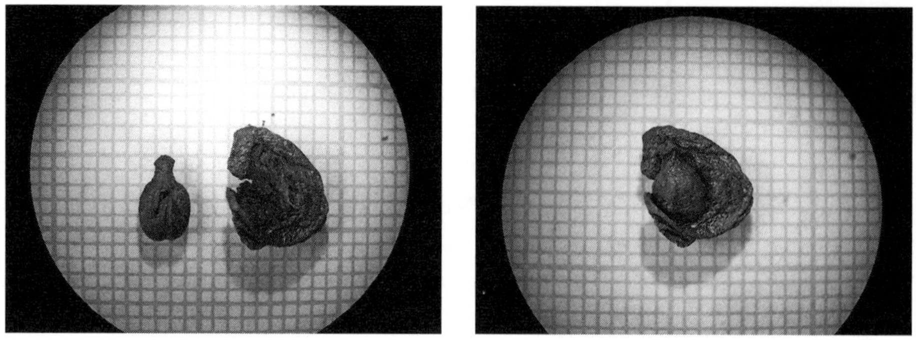

Fig. 11.3a–b. Charred grape, *Vitis vinifera* seed with fruit flesh fragment

hypothesis that, along with *T. monococcum*, it was present as a "weed" in Egyptian cereal crops.[24] Bread wheat appears not to have been cultivated in Egypt until the Ptolomaic period (after which emmer began to decline in importance)[25] despite the fact that Egypt had contact with the Levant where the less labor-intensive free-threshing wheat predominated during the Middle and Late Bronze Ages. Samuel suggests that rye grass infested emmer crops in ancient Egypt,[26] a theory that is upheld by results from Tell el-Borg; *Lolium* sp. is the most frequent species present at the site (see tables 11.1–11.5). However, given the small quantity of samples recovered from secure contexts at the site, these results may simply reflect recovery bias.

Bread and beer were the staples of the ancient Egyptian diet.[27] Both emmer wheat and barley are known to have been ingredients of beer,[28] while bread was generally made from wheat (although there are some reports that bread at Deir el-Medina was made from barley).[29] The presence of flint/chert sickle blades and quern stones at Tell el-Borg combines with the archaeobotanical evidence to suggest strongly that agriculture was taking place nearby. This fits well with the geoarchaeological evidence for the presence of an ancient branch of the Nile close to the site of Tell el-Borg.[30] It is likely that the 18–19th Dynasty inhabitants of North Sinai were practicing agriculture along this river branch in a similar fashion to the rest of the Nile Valley.

Within the ceramic corpus from Tell el-Borg, beer jars (in funerary contexts) are well represented, while there is only one certain fragment of a bread mould (*Tell el-Borg I*, 400–401 and pl. 20, p. 429). Although bread and beer may well have been imported to Tell el-Borg, the evidence for local arable farming suggests that these industries were taking place at the site; however, without any evidence for baking or brewing installations, it is impossible to draw any solid conclusions at this stage.

Wine from grapes was not a staple of the ancient Egyptian diet but would have been available at festivals and for funerary purposes,[31] and the Pelusiac/Tjaru region was respected for the

24. M. A. Murray, personal communication, 2007; and "Cereal Production and Processing," 513.

25. Ibid., 513.

26. Samuel, "Brewing and Baking," 559.

27. W. J. Darby, P. E. Ghalioungui, and L. Grivetti. *Food: The Gift of Osiris, Volume II* (London: Academic Press, 1977) 501–50.

28. Samuel, "Brewing and Baking," 546.

29. Ibid., 558.

30. J. K. Hoffmeier and S. O. Moshier, "New Paleo-Environmental Evidence from the North Sinai to Complement Manfred Bietak's Map of the Eastern Delta and Some Historical Implications," in *Timelines: Studies in Honour of Manfred Bietak, Volume II* (ed. E. Czerny et al.; Leuven: Peeters, 2006) 168.

31. M. A. Murray, "Viticulture and Wine Production," in *Ancient Egyptian Materials and Technology* (ed. P. T. Nicholson and I. Shaw; Cambridge: Cambridge University Press, 2000) 577.

quality of the wines it produced.[32] Much of the textual evidence relating to Tjaru is in the form of wine jar labels, and despite the lack of archaeobotanical evidence for vineyards or wine processing from any of the North Sinai sites, there is a very strong case for this region being a center of wine production during the early New Kingdom.[33] The 32 grape pips from Tell el-Borg could indicate that this fortress was engaged in the cultivation of grapes and/or the production of wine (fig. 11.3a–b).

Other foods were consumed and/or cultivated at the site, such as lentil and fig, but the small number of different species and the low numbers of specimens makes it difficult to draw any conclusions. These low numbers may well be a direct result of the sample processing.

Summary

The archaeobotanical evidence, when studied in combination with the archaeological evidence from Tell el-Borg and relevant textual evidence, indicates that the inhabitants of the site were probably engaged in the processing and/or cultivation of cereal crops (principally emmer wheat) for the production of bread and beer, as well as animal fodder, and possibly the cultivation of grapes for the production of wine. Cereal crop processing waste and animal dung were important commodities for use as domestic fuel.

32. Darby, Ghalioungui, and Grivetti, *Food: The Gift of Osiris, Volume II*, 600; and E. F. Morris. *The Architecture of Imperialism* (Leiden: Brill, 2005) 280.

33. Wine of Tjaru is known from wine dockets from Tutankhamun's tomb; see Jaroslav Černy, *Hieratic Inscriptions from the Tomb of Tutʿnkhamun* (Oxford: Griffith Institute the University Press, 1965) 2.

Chapter 12

Faunal Report on the First Three Seasons of Excavations (2000–2002)

Michelle A. Loyet
Webster University

Introduction

The faunal assemblage from Tell el-Borg consists of some 2,439 pieces, of which 50.3% are identifiable (table 12.1). While this may appear to be a large percentage of unidentifiable bone, it is not dissimilar to other assemblages that are collected through a mix of screening and collection by eye.[1] It is typical of most Near Eastern and Egyptian sites to forgo screening on many loci for the sake of expediting excavation. Given the massive size of many of these sites, it is impossible to fully screen all loci and still collect a worthwhile amount of archaeological information. As a result, only sediments from secure loci are screened, yet artifacts, including fauna, are collected from these different types of loci. Ultimately, this does introduce a certain bias into the faunal record, but that bias will generally affect the smallest animals (less than 140 grams), although many of these animals will be lost even when screening with ¼" mesh.[2]

In the case of the Tell el-Borg assemblage, the fauna is dominated by two types of taxa: large domestic fauna (35.6%) and fish (38.9%) (table 12.2). Collection practices will surely bias the representation of the fish, most especially smaller fish, although the larger animals should remain largely unaffected. Given the potential under-representation of fish in the Tell el-Borg assemblage, it seems that either fishing or fish in the form of rations sent to the fort played a major role in the Tell el-Borg diet. On the other hand, cattle also represent a large percentage of the assemblage (14.8%). While this is by no means as great a percentage as fish, the relative size of cattle should be considered. If a fish, even a large one, provides, say, 1 kilogram of meat, that is only a small percentage of the meat provided by an average cow. A number of researchers

1. Michelle A. Loyet, "Small Ungulate Butchery in the Islamic Period (A.D. 632–1260) at Tell Tuneinir, Syria," *Journal of Near Eastern Studies* 58 (1999) 33–45; eadem, "The Potential for Within-Site Variation of Faunal Remains: A Case Study from the Islamic Period Urban Center of Tell Tuneinir, Syria," *Bulletin of the American Schools of Oriental Research* 320 (2000) 23–48.

2. Brian S. Shaffer, "Quarter-Inch Screening: Understanding Biases in Recovery of Vertebrate Faunal Remains," *American Antiquity* 57 (1992) 129–36; J. P. N. Watson, "Fragmentation Analysis of Animal Bone Samples from Archaeological Sites," *Archaeometry* 14 (1972) 221–28.

Table 12.1. Total Assemblage

	# of Pieces	*Percentage*
Unidentifiable	1,213	49.7
Identifiable	1,226	50.3
Total	2,439	100

Table 12.2. Total Identifiable Fauna

Common Name	*Taxon*	*# of Pieces*	*Percentage*
Cattle	*Bos taurus*	182	14.8
Sheep/Goat	Ovicaprines	98	8.0
Pig	*Sus scrofa*	107	8.7
Donkey	*Equus asinus*	28	2.3
Horse	*Equus caballus*	2	0.2
Indet. Equid	*Equus* spp.	20	1.6
Goose		8	0.7
Duck		24	2.0
Indet. Bird	Aves	14	1.1
Turtle		2	0.2
Crocodile		3	0.2
Nile Catfish	*Clarias* spp,	35	2.9
	Synodontus spp.	5	0.4
Nile Perch	*Lates niloticus*	25	2.0
Tilapia	*Tilapia* spp.	42	3.4
Indet. Fish		370	30.2
Dog	*Canis*	13	1.1
Ostrich Eggshell		117	9.5
Shell (marine?)		124	10.1
Indet. Rodent		7	0.6
	Total	1,226	100

have attempted to provide meat estimates for domestic animals;[3] however, "consumable" meat is a culturally contingent category and varies from situation to situation (consider most middle-class Americans' aversion to organ meat). The problems are compounded by intra-specific and ontogenetic variation as well as sexual dimorphism. Furthermore, researchers have developed meat yield estimates ranging from 18–45 kilograms for sheep and goat and 226–454 kilograms for cattle. The most conservative estimates come from Clark,[4] who estimates an average of 226 kilograms per individual for cattle and 27 kilograms for sheep and goat. However, even given these potential problems in the estimation of meat weights, it is clear that the most meat consumed at

3. G. Clark, "The Faunal Remains," in *Fouilles du Forum de Cherchel 1977–1981* (ed. N. Benseddik and T. W. Potter: 6e Supplément au Bulletin d'Archéologie Algérienne; Algiers: Agence Nationale d'Archéologie et de Protection des Sites et Monuments Historiques, 1993) 159–95; Brian Hesse and Dexter Perkins Jr., "Faunal Remains from Karataş Semayük in Southwest Anatolia: An Interim Report," *Journal of Field Archaeology* 1 (1974) 149–60; R. Lee Lyman, "Available Meat from Faunal Remains: A Consideration of Techniques," *American Antiquity* 44 (1979) 536–46; Dexter Perkins Jr. and Patricia Daly, "A Hunters' Village in Neolithic Turkey," *Scientific American* 219 (1968) 97–106.

4. Clark, "The Faunal Remains."

Tell el-Borg would have been provided by cattle. The next most important meat resource would be pig, followed by sheep and goat.

Sheep and goat are problematic members of the faunal assemblage. While it is possible to determine the difference between sheep and goat on the basis of metric data or bone morphology,[5] these methods were developed using modern, complete skeletons. The fragmentary nature of the archaeological record makes it possible to distinguish sheep from goat in only a small portion of the faunal assemblage. Due to the problems in determining sheep from goat, other faunal analysts[6] have resorted to combining the two taxa. Given the focus and range of this analysis, little added information would be gained by separating the two taxa, so the two genera are treated as a single taxa, ovicaprines.

Other animals that play minor roles in the Tell el-Borg faunal assemblage are waterfowl and other riverine fauna (turtle, crocodile). This may indicate that the branch of the Nile that at one time flowed through the site was a focus of subsistence activity. Also present in the assemblage, although not likely consumed, are horse and donkey, as well as canids. A large number of fragments of ostrich eggshell were also found, but it is unclear whether the eggs were consumed or used as a kind of container and discarded when broken. Shells, many obviously marine, are also quite common in the assemblage. However, given the depositional history of the site, the presence of these shells should not be assumed to be the result of human behavior. In the same vein, the small number of rodents is also most likely intrusive to the site or at least should not be considered a resource.

MAMMALIAN REMAINS

Among the mammalian remains in the Tell el-Borg faunal assemblage, we find cattle, sheep, goat, pig, donkey, horse, and dog (table 12.3), all of which are domesticates. The most common of the mammalian fauna is cattle (39.8%), followed by approximately equal numbers of pig and ovicaprines (23.4% and 21.4%, respectively). Of the mammalian fauna, these are most likely the only animals consumed. Other taxa present include horse and donkey, which probably served as traction animals, and dog, which would have been used for companionship or as a watchdog or herding animal.

Cattle

Domestic cattle were of paramount economic importance in Dynastic Egypt.[7] The earliest evidence for domestic cattle in Egypt dates to 4800 B.C., giving cattle production a long history.

5. Joachim Boessneck, Hanns-Hermann Müller, and Manfred Teichert, "Osteologische Unterscheidungsmermale Zwischen Schaf (Ovis Aries Linné) und Zeige (Capra Hircus Linné)," *Kühn-Archiv* 78 (1964) 5–129; Wietske Prummel and Hans-Jörg Frische, "A Guide for the Distinction of Species, Sex and Body Side in Bones of Sheep and Goat," *Journal of Archaeological Science* 13 (1986) 567–77.

6. Gil J. Stein, "Producers, Patrons, and Prestige: Craft Specialists and Emergent Elites in Mesopotamia from 5500–3100 BC," in *Craft Specialization and Social Evolution: In Memory of V. Gordon Childe* (ed. Bernard Wailes; Philadelphia: University of Pennsylvania Museum of Archaeology and Anthroplogy, 1996) 25–38; Melinda A. Zeder, "The Archaeobiology of the Khabur Basin," *Bulletin of the Canadian Society for Mesopotamian Studies* 29 (1995) 21–32; eadem, "Environment, Economy, and Subsistence on the Threshold of Urban Emergence in Northern Mesopotamia," in *Espace Naturel, Espace Habité en Syrie Nord (10e-2e Millénaire Av. J.-C.)*, (ed. Michel Fortin and Olivier Aurenche; Bulletin of the Canadian Society for Mesopotamian Studies 33; Quebec: Canadian Society for Mesopotamian Studies, 1998) 55–67.

7. Patrick F. Houlihan, *The Animal World of the Pharaohs* (Cairo: The American University of Cairo Press, 1996).

Table 12.3. Mammalian Fauna

Common Name	Taxon	# of Pieces	Percentage
Cattle	*Bos taurus*	182	39.8
Sheep/Goat	Ovicaprines	98	21.4
Pig	*Sus scrofa*	107	23.4
Donkey	*Equus asinus*	28	6.1
Horse	*Equus caballus*	2	0.5
Indet. Equid	*Equus* spp.	20	4.4
Dog	*Canis*	13	2.8
Indet. Rodent		7	1.6
	Total	457	100

Initially it was thought that domestic cattle were an import from the Near East, as were barley, wheat, and other herd animals. However, it is now thought that cattle in Egypt originated from an independent domestication of the indigenous wild aurochs (*Bos primigenius*) of North Africa.[8] Cattle production was generally left to specialized herdsmen. These herdsmen would not only drive the cattle north to the Delta during the drier part of the year but would also oversee their breeding and other aspects of their maturation.[9]

Cattle would have been used for a number of purposes, for traction as well as for milk and meat. It is interesting that most authors contend[10] that beef was a luxury food—a prerogative of the wealthy. Yet it is a common component of the Tell el-Borg assemblage, an assemblage associated with a military outpost. It is possible that these cattle were not intended for primary usage as food. Records from Dynasty 18 indicate that cattle were used in military campaigns to haul wagons.[11] This may be the initial reason for the presence of the cattle at Tell el-Borg. As the cattle age and are no longer useful for cartage, or as they breed and the herd increases, excess animals would have certainly been consumed.

Sheep and Goats

Unlike cattle, all Egyptian sheep and goats are descended from an Asian progenitor and share a similar Levantine origin.[12] Records of privately owned flocks show that sheep easily numbered in the hundreds but are rarely depicted in tombs nor are they listed in the offering-list menus.[13] There does seem to be some restriction on sheep consumption, although their usefulness as a producer of wool and dairy products was certainly exploited by ancient Egyptians. Large herds that were reported to have been kept during the New Kingdom were most likely used as a source of secondary products, and the animals would have been slaughtered for their flesh after their productivity waned.[14] Goat is similarly widespread, and unlike sheep, is depicted in tomb

8. Douglas J. Brewer, Donald B. Redford, and Susan Redford, *Domestic Plants and Animals: The Egyptian Origins* (Warminster: Aris & Phillips, 1994).
9. Ibid.
10. Ibid.; Philippe Germond and Jacques Livet, *An Egyptian Bestiary* (London: Thames and Hudson, 2001); Houlihan, *The Animal World of the Pharaohs.*
11. Ibid.
12. Ibid.
13. Ibid.
14. Brewer, Redford, and Redford, *Domestic Plants and Animals: The Egyptian Origins.*

and tomb chapel paintings and likely was consumed by the upper classes.[15] Goats were used for their meat, skin, and milk, although meat would have been their primary purpose.[16]

Ovicaprines are less in evidence in the Tell el-Borg assemblage than cattle, representing only 21.4% of the mammalian fauna. Germond and Livet[17] contend that only the ordinary people of the country consumed mutton as a food resource. It is surprising, then, that it is not more in evidence in the Tell el-Borg faunal assemblage. It is possible that the ovicaprines at Tell el-Borg were used as a ready resource for dairy products rather than for meat production.

Pigs

Although some[18] contend that pigs share an Asiatic origin with sheep and goat, others[19] find it more likely that Egyptian pig were independently domesticated from local populations of wild boar that were present in the Nile Valley and Delta. The aggressive nature of the males and the physical stature of swine make it even more unlikely that they were brought from Mesopotamia to Egypt.[20]

Pigs are versatile in their feeding habits and consume much of what humans discard, making them easy to produce, even in urban settings.[21] The chief role of pig is meat and fat for the kitchen. They produce no secondary products but do mature very quickly and produce two litters a year.[22] One of the most important discoveries relating to pig production is the discovery of pigpens in the Amarna workmen's village. These pens are associated with a complex where the animals were slaughtered, butchered, salted, and the meat packed in pottery jars.[23] It is in the New Kingdom that the production of pig expands dramatically, and the mention of pig in economic texts expands as well.[24] The pigs present in the Tell el-Borg assemblage are certainly there as a result of consumption practices, because they serve no other purpose.

Donkeys and Horses

Donkeys and horses in Egypt are strictly working animals. It is likely that donkeys were domesticated in Africa, although not in the Nile valley itself, as the earliest remains are associated with nomadic cultures.[25] By the Old Kingdom, the donkey was regularly employed as a beast of burden, and this usage extends throughout Egyptian history.[26] Unlike modern Egyptians, there does not seem to be any evidence that ancient Egyptians rode on the backs of donkeys, and only foreigners depicted in tomb paintings are shown mounted.[27]

---

15. Houlihan, *The Animal World of the Pharaohs*.
16. Brewer, Redford, and Redford, *Domestic Plants and Animals: The Egyptian Origins*.
17. Germond and Livet, *An Egyptian Bestiary*.
18. Ibid.
19. Brewer, Redford, and Redford, *Domestic Plants and Animals: The Egyptian Origins*; Houlihan, *The Animal World of the Pharaohs*.
20. Brewer, Redford, and Redford, *Domestic Plants and Animals: The Egyptian Origins*.
21. Ibid.
22. Ibid.
23. Barry J. Kemp, *Ancient Egypt: Anatomy of a Civilization* (London: Routledge, 1991).
24. Houlihan, *The Animal World of the Pharaohs*.
25. Brewer, Redford, and Redford, *Domestic Plants and Animals: The Egyptian Origins*.
26. Ibid.
27. Houlihan, *The Animal World of the Pharaohs*.

There is no evidence for domesticated horses in Egypt before 1800 B.C. The horse was likely domesticated in Eurasia, and the earliest horse remains in the Near East do not appear until the fourth millennium B.C. in Mesopotamia.[28] All available evidence suggests that the horse was introduced into Egypt on a large scale at the time of the Hyksos invasion.[29] Unlike the donkey, horses do not seem to be used merely as a beast of burden but almost exclusively for pulling chariots. Most horses in Egypt were the property of the state.[30] Possessing a horse was a symbol of prestige because of the high cost of ownership, which was limited to the king, the aristocracy, and the military.[31]

Dogs

The earliest dogs in Egypt appear ca. 4800 B.C. at Mermide Beni Salame and likely entered Egypt along the same path as the early domestic ungulates.[32] Most dogs in Egypt were likely pariahs, rather than pets, although tomb scenes showing pets and hunting dogs indicate that these particular animals were well cared for and were sometimes provided with elaborate burial.[33] There is no evidence that dogs were consumed, but they would have been employed in hunting, herding, or as guard animals.[34]

Fish Remains

Fish and fishing were integral to not only the secular and religious spheres of Egyptian life but were also essential to the economy. Nile fish provided an inexpensive and nutritious source of protein.[35] Fish bone and fishing equipment have been recovered from Egyptian archaeological sites from the Predynastic period onward.[36] Fish and fishing are also depicted in tomb reliefs, paintings, and votive offerings throughout Egyptian history.[37] Tomb paintings include scenes of fishermen hauling heavy nets full of fish, the gutting and drying of fish, angling, catching fish with traps and weirs, and fishmongers selling fish at open-air markets.[38] Although there is abundant evidence for fish utilization by ancient Egyptians, including fish remains from archaeological sites and artistic depictions, it is unclear to what extent the Egyptian diet relied on fish. Taphonomic processes and the difficulty of identification have adverse effects on the processing of archaeological fish remains, resulting in a potentially biased analysis. While artistic depictions are plentiful, the contexts in which they occur (tombs, religious contexts) indicate that we should be cautious in assuming that this is reflective of the everyday diet in ancient Egypt. However, it

28. Brewer, Redford, and Redford, *Domestic Plants and Animals: The Egyptian Origins*.
29. Ibid.; Houlihan, *The Animal World of the Pharaohs*; Germond and Livet, *An Egyptian Bestiary*.
30. Brewer, Redford, and Redford, *Domestic Plants and Animals: The Egyptian Origins*.
31. Houlihan, *The Animal World of the Pharaohs*.
32. Brewer, Redford, and Redford, *Domestic Plants and Animals: The Egyptian Origins*.
33. Ibid.
34. Houlihan, *The Animal World of the Pharaohs*.
35. Ibid.
36. Douglas J. Brewer and Renée F. Friedman, *Fish and Fishing in Ancient Egypt* (Warminster, England: Aris & Phillips, 1989); Houlihan, *The Animal World of the Pharaohs*.
37. Ibid.
38. Ibid.

is believed that Egyptian peasants fished as much as they cultivated, and that, by the New Kingdom, fishing activities were organized on a vast scale and state controlled.[39]

Taphonomy and Identification of Fish Bone

Two aspects of the nature of fish remains render them a problematic indicator of ancient diet. Differential survival of the delicate bones of certain fish can bias the zooarchaeological record.[40] The variable relative density of cranial elements compared to postcranial elements has led, in some cases, to the inaccurate interpretation of fish preparation and storage practices.[41] These problems are further compounded by the fact that, as cold-blooded animals, fish continue to grow throughout their lifetimes.[42] As they grow, relative density of body parts can change, and in the case of assemblages that have undergone the effects of density-mediated destruction, different body parts will represent larger fish than smaller fish of the same taxa.

Second, fish bones as a group are extremely difficult to identify to genus level. Among the most difficult to identify are vertebral elements. For example, cranial elements of the Nile catfish (*Clarias* spp.) are quite distinctive and can easily be identified even when only small fragments occur in the zooarchaeological record. A single *Clarias* cranium, broken and distributed over an area of a site, could potentially produce hundreds of identifiable fragments.[43] The vertebral columns of fish, on the other hand, given the same degree of breakage and distribution, would not be nearly as identifiable. In fact, in most cases, the identification would be limited to "fish vertebrae."[44] Due to the problems associated with the identification of fish remains, plentiful artistic representations of fishing and fish preparation in Egyptian art become a valuable resource in interpreting and supplementing the zooarchaeological record.

Representations of Fish in Egyptian Art

In interpreting fishing scenes as historic evidence, care must be taken. In the case of tomb reliefs and paintings, the purpose of the reliefs is not to record the use of fish in daily life. These representations were expressly related to religion and magic[45] and the provisioning of the tomb owner in the afterlife. Although it is ultimately not possible to determine relative importance of certain fish taxa from these reliefs, the artistic representations may provide us with a sample, or a range of species, that were utilized by ancient Egyptians. Artistic representations can also assist in the identification of fishing tools and techniques, as a variety of nets, hooks, harpoons, and weirs are depicted Egyptian art.[46]

39. Germond and Livet, *An Egyptian Bestiary*.
40. Brewer and Friedman, *Fish and Fishing in Ancient Egypt*.
41. Ibid.; Virginia L. Butler, "Natural Versus Cultural Salmonid Remains: Origin of the Dalles Roadcut Bones, Columbia River, Oregon, U.S.A.," *Journal of Archaeological Science* 20 (1993) 1–24; Virginia L. Butler and James C. Chatters, "The Role of Bone Density in Structuring Prehistoric Salmon Bone Assemblages," *Journal of Archaeological Science* 21 (1994) 413–24.
42. Douglas J. Brewer, "Seasonality in the Prehistoric Faiyum Based on the Incremental Growth Structures of the Nile Catfish (Pisces: Clarias)," *Journal of Archaeological Science* 14 (1987) 459–72; Douglas J. Brewer, "Incremental Growth Structures in Nile Fish and Molluscs from Archaeological Sites as Indicators of Holocene Environmental Change in Egypt," *The Holocene* 2, no. 1 (1992) 30–36.
43. Brewer and Friedman, *Fish and Fishing in Ancient Egypt*.
44. Ibid.
45. Ibid.
46. Ibid.

Table 12.4. Fish

Common Name	*Taxon*	*# of Pieces*	*Percentage*
Nile Catfish	*Clarias* spp,	35	7.3
	Synodontus spp.	5	1.0
Nile Perch	*Lates niloticus*	25	5.2
Tilapia	*Tilapia* spp.	42	8.8
Indet. Fish		370	77.7
	Total	477	100

Fish Depiction and Use

Artistic depictions of fish extend as far back as the Predynastic period, and continue to be represented in both stationary and portable art throughout Egyptian history.[47] A great variety of fish have been depicted in the art, including catfish (*Clarias* and *Synodontus*), mullets (*Mugil*), mormyrids, *Tilapia* (also known by its Arabic name, bulti), puffer fish (*Tetrodon*), carp (*Labeo*), eel (*Anguilla vulgaris*), moonfish (*Citharinus*), and electric catfish (*Malapterurus electricus*).[48]

During the New Kingdom, fish are depicted in tomb art more frequently than in any prior period.[49] They are also mentioned in a number of New Kingdom texts. Fish were a part of the rations given to the troops of Seti I.[50] Documents referring to the artisans' village of Deir el-Medina at the Valley of Kings indicate that, during the reign of Ramesses II, twenty fishermen were employed to supply the workmen.[51] Fish that were recorded as having been supplied to the workmen include: *Tilapia*, *Synodontus*, and *Mormyrus*.[52] There are also records of fish rations given to officers of the royal court and the priests of Karnak,[53] but these may not be as comparable to the remains from Tell el-Borg, because status may play a role in the rations provided. The soldiers and the families associated with the fort at Tell Borg may be more comparable to the Deir el-Medina workmen.

Fish Use at Tell el-Borg

Of those fish remains that can be positively identified, it is clear that *Lates niloticus* (Nile perch), *Clarias* spp. (Nile catfish), *Tilapia* sp., and *Synodontus* sp. (another type of catfish) are present in the Tell el-Borg faunal assemblage (table 12.4). The most common fish is *Tilapia* spp., at 8.8% of the assemblage, closely followed by *Clarias* spp. (7.3%). However, unidentifiable fish remains (77.7%) dominate the vast majority of the assemblage.

47. Brewer and Friedman, *Fish and Fishing in Ancient Egypt.*
48. Houlihan, *The Animal World of the Pharaohs.*
49. Brewer and Friedman, *Fish and Fishing in Ancient Egypt.*
50. James Henry Breasted, *Ancient Records of Egypt*, vol. 2 (5 vols.; Chicago: University of Chicago Press, 1906).
51. Brewer and Friedman, *Fish and Fishing in Ancient Egypt.*
52. Ibid.
53. Norman de Garis Davies, *The Rock Tombs of El Amarna, Part I* (London: Egypt Exploration Fund, 1903); Angela von den Driesch, "Some Archaeozoological Remarks on Fishes in Ancient Egypt," in *Animals and Archaeology 2. Shell Middens, Fishes and Birds* (ed. Caroline Grigson and Juliet Clutton-Brock; British Archaeological Reports, International Series 183; Oxford: British Archaeological Reports, 1983), 87–110.

Lates niloticus

This type of fish has a wide distribution and has been recovered throughout the Nile and from most East African lakes. It can grow to tremendous size, reaching as much as 70 kilograms, and an exceptional specimen from Lake Nasser was measured at 2 m in length, weighing 175 kilograms. *Lates* can easily be caught by net but is a fierce fighter when caught by hook and line. They prefer deeper, oxygenated waters. Behavior and feeding habits of this species change with age: the fry feed on underwater insects; juveniles on small fish, eggs, and shrimp; and the large fish mainly on other fish. Younger *Lates* are more often observed, because older fish prefer rock crevices or other secure places and only dart out of these sanctuaries to attack prey and breed.[54]

Clarias spp.

There are two species of *Clarias* present in the Nile, but they are not distinguishable from one another by any traits other than aspect of the gills; modern Egyptian fishermen do not distinguish between the two. *Clarias* can tolerate conditions that would kill most other fishes, and they prefer shallow, deoxygenated waters, although they can also survive in deeper waters. Their ability to survive in stagnant water is due to an accessory breathing organ that enables these fish to use atmospheric oxygen. *Clarias* can easily be collected by hand, especially during spawning season.[55]

Synodontus sp.

Synodontus is one of the most abundant fishes in the Nile. These fish are well known for their serrated spines, which can inflict painful wounds. Modern Nile fishermen sometime use wire cutters to remove the spines before taking the fish from the nets. Lake Nasser fishermen are said to dislike the fish because it causes damage to their nets, although Nile fishermen utilize it regularly. As opposed to *Clarias*, *Synodontus* prefers deeper water, and can be described as an omnivorous bottom feeder.[56]

Tilapia

Three species of *Tilapia* occur regularly in the Nile, but separation on the basis of osteological characteristics is not possible. They typically inhabit inshore waters and sheltered bays and prefer shallow-water areas where abundant vegetation exists. Tomb scenes often show *Tilapia* caught in nets or by spear. *Tilapia* are most abundant in the swampy, shallow waters of the Delta.

The presence of these types of fish in the Tell el-Borg faunal assemblage may speak to the character of the branch of the Nile that at one time ran near the site. *Tilapia* and *Clarias* both prefer shallower water, while *Lates* and *Synodontus* prefer deeper water. This seems to indicate that the river environs adjacent to the fort provided a number of different niches, in order for these species to survive—that is, of course, if these fish are in fact coming from the river adjacent to the site. It must be considered that, because this is a fort, a portion of the faunal remains found at the site may come from provisions brought from other parts of Egypt, because the storage and redistribution of fish was a common practice. The 18th Dynasty tomb of Meryre at Amarna shows a scene displaying royal storehouses, well stocked with dried fish awaiting distribution.[57] The Harris papyrus from the 20th Dynasty records that during his reign Ramesses III delivered 474,200 fish and 440 jars of pickled fish to Theban temples alone.[58]

54. Brewer and Friedman, *Fish and Fishing in Ancient Egypt.*
55. Ibid.
56. Ibid.
57. Houlihan, *The Animal World of the Pharaohs.*
58. Ibid.

Table 12.5. Avian Fauna

Common Name	*Taxon*	*# of Pieces*	*Percentage*
Goose		8	17.4
Duck		24	52.2
Indet. Bird	Aves	14	30.4
	Total	46	100

Avian Remains

Egyptians kept and reared a number of species of bird, principally waterfowl.[59] Geese (*Anser anser*) and duck (*Anas* spp.) were the most common, but they also bred other birds, including swans, cranes, pigeons, doves, quail, and pelican.[60] Chicken is unknown in Egypt until the Persian Period, although an ostracon with a drawing of a chicken was recovered from Tutankhamun's tomb (Dynasty 18).[61] Duck dominates the avian remains at Tell el-Borg at 52.2% of the avian assemblage. Goose is also present, as well as a number of smaller indeterminate fowl (see table 12.5). In addition to the osteological remains of the birds, a large amount of ostrich eggshell was also recovered (see tables 12.2 and 12.6), although, as stated earlier, it is unclear whether the eggs were used as containers or as food. There is no evidence that the ostriches themselves were ever present at the site.

Duck

There is no evidence to suggest that ducks were domesticated in Egypt, but they were certainly captured and held in captivity, probably as a means of maintaining a local population and to prevent migration.[62] Whether or not the birds in the Tell el-Borg assemblage were kept or hunted cannot be determined, because the adjacent river would have supplied a large number of fowl for hunting.

Geese

Although geese are less common than duck at Tell el-Borg, this is not the case with other Egyptian sites, where the goose is often the most common avian taxa.[63] However, less stock should be put in this distribution, because avian bones are in general uncommon in the Borg assemblage (only 3.8% of the entire identified assemblage). A much larger avian sample would be necessary to make any reliable assessments of use. Unlike duck, geese were domesticated in Egypt.[64] As is the case with duck, these animals could have been obtained either through hunting or could have been kept as barnyard animals.

59. Germond and Livet. *An Egyptian Bestiary.*
60. Ibid.
61. Brewer, Redford, and Redford, *Domestic Plants and Animals: The Egyptian Origins.*
62. Ibid.
63. Ibid.
64. Ibid.

Table 12.6. Distribution Throughout Site

	Field II		Field III		Field IV	
Common Name	#	%	#	%	#	%
Cattle	81	27.4	34	11.1	59	13.9
Sheep/Goat	13	4.4	33	10.8	47	11.1
Pig	71	24	8	2.6	15	3.5
Donkey	2	0.7	15	4.9	9	2.1
Horse	2	0.7	0	0	0	0
Aves	6	2.0	14	4.6	8	1.9
Turtle	0	0	0	0	2	0.5
Crocodile	0	0	0	0	3	0.7
Fish	59	19.9	163	53.3	134	31.5
Dog	0	0	11	3.6	1	0.2
Ostrich Eggshell	6	2.0	17	5.5	94	22.1
Shell (marine?)	56	18.9	11	3.6	53	12.5

Distribution of Fauna Throughout the Site

Differential distribution of fauna throughout a site can give clues as to the different functional areas of a site. In the case of Tell el-Borg, fauna from three areas was examined. Locus numbers beginning with Field II (Area/Unit 1E, 1F, 1G, 1H, 1I, 2J) were sorted into one group; those from Field III were sorted into a second group (Area/Unit 2A, 2C, 2D, 2E, 2F, 2G, 2H, 2I, 2J, 2K, 2L, 2M, 2P, 2Q, 2R, 2S); and those from Field IV were assigned to a third group (Area/Unit D, E, F). As can be seen from table 12.6, there is some differential distribution of fauna throughout the site of Tell el-Borg. Cattle are most common in Field II (27.4%), with a significantly lower relative percentage in the other two areas. Fish remains are most common in Field III (53.3%), as are avian remains (4.6%). Ostrich eggshell most commonly occurs in Field IV. It is also significant that horse only occurs in Field II (but see chapter 14 for subsequent equid remains), while crocodile and turtle only occur in Field IV. Upon completion of analysis of other artifact classes (ceramics, architecture, etc.), it should be possible to provide hypotheses regarding the causal factors for the differential distribution of fauna at the site.

Mortality Profiles

In the case of both cattle and ovicaprines, mortality patterns can be indicative of pastoral herd management and production strategies and will reflect what products (meat, milk, wool, traction) consumers required. This will only be visible, however, in cases where optimization of a particular product is a focus. In the case of sheep, for example, *all* herds of sheep will produce milk, wool, and meat. It is only with conscious optimization of a particular product or products that mortality patterns will indicate which product is being optimized. The herd will still produce all products, but one product will be produced more efficiently. Given optimization, if meat production was the aim, sheep and goats would be culled near full maturation, when their weight gain begins to slow and it becomes more costly to keep them. Milk production, on the other hand, creates a much older mortality profile: ewes would be kept for long periods of time, although male lambs will be slaughtered once milk production is stimulated. Wool production creates the oldest mortality profile, as all animals, regardless of sex, would be retained for wool production.[65] However, it is unlikely that administered herds will produce only one product but may be structured for the optimal production of a number of resources. Optimized, diversified production may indicate a greater level of administrative control. This, however, may be more difficult to discern than other traits. One problem is that, dependent upon herding strategy, males and females may be culled at different times. In the case of milk production, young males are culled but females are retained for further production and increase of the herd. Even when only meat production is the goal, males will often be culled at the age of maximum weight gain (between one and two years in modern herds) and females kept as breeding stock (average of six to eight years in modern herds). Since it is not always possible to determine sex based on most body parts, the actual culling practices may not be entirely clear. A second problem is that in all cases younger animals may be underestimated in faunal assemblages, because the bones of juveniles are less dense than the bones of adult animals. For this reason, these bones are more likely to be lost to taphonomic processes than are the bones of older animals.[66]

In the case of the Tell el-Borg faunal assemblage, epiphyseal fusion was used to determine the age at death, using data from Silver and Noddle.[67] Because the epiphyses of long bones fuse at a fairly predictable and known rate over time, it is possible to determine the approximate age of animals at death based on the characteristics of their bones. The construction of the resulting survivorship curves was done using those methods outlined in Zeder and Redding.[68] Long bone survivorship curves were computed using a method developed by Redding[69] that calculates fusion scores based on the proportion of bones that are fused or fusing, versus those that are unfused, in each age class. Bones that have the same latest age at fusion are combined in to a single age class (table 12.7).

There are potential problems, however, with the construction of such survivorship curves. In all cases, methods for age estimation were developed using modern populations of sheep and goat. First, the necessary conflation of sheep and goat into a single taxon may affect the accuracy of assignment of absolute ages. There is also no guarantee that the dates of bone fusion in modern breeds are the same as those in ancient breeds. While absolute ages may not be determinable, the *order* of bone fusion is more likely to be constant between present and past breeds. Therefore, a fusing distal femur still came from an older animal than did a fusing distal humerus; the problem occurs in being able to assign the exact age of the animal given the available data.

65. Pam J. Crabtree, "Zooarchaeology and Complex Societies: Some Uses of Faunal Analysis for the Study of Trade, Social Status, and Ethnicity," in *Archaeological Method and Theory* (ed. Michael B. Schiffer; Tucson: University of Arizona Press, 1990) vol. 2: 155–205; Roger L. D. Cribb, "The Logic of the Herd: A Computer Simulation of Archaeological Herd Structure," *Journal of Anthropological Archaeology* 6 (1987) 376–415; Sebastian Payne, "Kill-off Patterns in Sheep and Goats: The Mandibles from Asvan Kale," *Anatolian Studies* 23 (1973) 281–303.

66. R. Lee Lyman, *Vertebrate Taphonomy* (Cambridge Manuals in Archaeology; New York: Cambridge University Press, 1994).

67. I. A. Silver, "The Ageing of Domestic Animals," in *Science in Archaeology* (ed. Don Brothwell and Eric Higgs; New York: Praeger, 1969) 283–302; Barbara Noddle, "Ages of Epiphyseal Closure in Feral and Domestic Goats and Ages of Dental Eruption," *Journal of Archaeological Science* 1 (1974) 195–204.

68. Melinda A. Zeder, *Feeding Cities: Specialized Animal Economy in the Ancient Near East* (Washington: Smithsonian Institution Press, 1991); Richard Redding, "The Faunal Remains," in *An Early Town on the Deh Luran Plain: Excavations at Tepe Farukhabad* (ed. Henry T. Wright; Museum of Anthropology Memoirs 13; Ann Arbor: University of Michigan Press, 1981) 233–61.

69. Ibid., 248.

Table 12.7. Ages of Epiphyseal Fusion for Three Domestic Taxa Present in Faunal Assemblages[70]

Element	*Age at Fusion*		*Age at Fusion*		*Age at Fusion*	
	Age Class	*Ovis/Capra*	Age Class	*Bos*	Age Class	*Sus*
Distal Humerus	A	10m	A	12–18m	A	1y
Proximal Radius		10m		12–18m		1y
Proximal First Phalanx	B	13–16m		18m	B	2y
ProximalSecond Phalanx		13–16m		18m		
Distal Tibia	C	18–24m	B	2–2.5y		2y
Distal Metapodial	D	18–28m	C	2.5–3y	C	2.5y
Proximal Femur	E	30–36m	D	3.5y	D	3.5y
Distal Radius		36m	E	3.5–4y		3.5y
Proximal Tibia	F	36–42m		3.5–4y		3.5y
Distal Femur		36–42m		3.5–4y		3.5y
Proximal Humerus		36–42m		3.5–4y		3.5y

In the case of the survivorship curves produced for this study, I have maintained the "ages" provided by the various researchers. I have done this to maintain comparability between my research and the research of others. However, I note again that these ages are merely an estimate, and what is important is the relative abundance of individuals in each stage/class, not the "age" of those individuals at death. A second reason that I have maintained the absolute ages rather than converting wear stages to I, II, III, etc., is that, if such stages are used, it would mask the fact that the maturation intervals are not equal; stages may be separated by anywhere from 4–8 months in the case of sheep and goat and 6 months to 1 year in the case of cattle.

The interpretation of mortality profiles and survivorship curves also may present difficulties. Most interpretations[71] assume an optimization of one or more products. However, there is no reason to believe that past pastoralists abided by the ideal patterns developed for the purpose of interpretation. For example, it is assumed that if meat production is the aim of a pastoral manager, young males will be harvested when they reach an optimum point in weight gain, before the cost of maintaining their weight increases in the second year of life.[72] It is assumed that these culled animals will be sent to consuming centers, while older breeding stock, as well as some younger animals, are retained in order to maintain the herd, given natural attrition.[73] If milk production is the aim, surplus lambs are slaughtered once production is not in danger. In the case of wool, emphasis is shifted to adult animals, and mortality profiles will show a large number of animals slaughtered when they are past maturity.[74]

70. B. Noddle, "Ages of Epiphyseal Closure in Feral and Domestic Goats and Ages of Dental Eruption," *Journal of Archaeological Science* 1 (1974) 195–204; I. A. Silver, "The Ageing of Domestic Animals," in *Science in Archaeology* (ed. D. R. Brothwell and E. S. Higgs; New York: Praeger, 1969) 283–302.

71. Cribb, "The Logic of the Herd: A Computer Simulation of Archaeological Herd Structure"; Payne, "Kill-off Patterns in Sheep and Goats: The Mandibles from Asvan Kale"; Gil J. Stein, "Medieval Pastoral Production Systems at Gritille," in *The Archaeology of the Frontier in the Medieval Near East: Excavations at Gritille, Turkey* (ed. Scott Redford; AIA Monographs, New Series 3; Philadelphia: University Museum, University of Pennsylvania, 1998) 181–209.

72. Payne, "Kill-off Patterns in Sheep and Goats."

73. Stein, "Medieval Pastoral Production Systems at Gritille," 181–209.

74. Payne, "Kill-off Patterns in Sheep and Goats."

These patterns, however, are idealized. They were developed using modern herding practices as an analog, and this may or may not be representative of past pastoral practices, even given the similar production goals. These problems are further compounded by the fact that animals are rarely kept for a single product,[75] and in the case of ovicaprines, the inability to distinguish between the two species results in the mixing of two taxa that produce dissimilar products. However, mortality profiles can still be useful in general, especially in comparisons between the various assemblages or taxa.

Table 12.7 illustrates the survivorship patterns for ovicaprines, showing that significant numbers of sheep and goat survived beyond 3 years. This seems to indicate a production strategy that is not focused on meat but rather on secondary products such as milk. This table further illustrates the survivorship pattern for cattle, which also shows significant numbers of animals surviving into adulthood and beyond (3.5–4 years). This also indicates a production strategy that is not focused on meat but on secondary products such as milk and in the case of cattle, traction.

Conclusions

This analysis of the Tell el-Borg faunal assemblage is merely a preliminary analysis. As excavation continues and a larger amount of faunal material is available for analysis, the conclusions may be bolstered or may change all together. At this stage, it seems that the faunal assemblage from Tell el-Borg indicates a lifestyle in many ways identical to that of the Nile Valley, which is not surprising considering the source of the population. The Tell el-Borg residents were subsisting on a diet of domestic fauna and their secondary products (milk) and bolstering that diet with riverine resources in the form of fish and perhaps waterfowl. Mortality profiles for the major domestic fauna indicate a generalized culling strategy, designed to maximize as many products as possible.

75. Payne, "Kill-off Patterns in Sheep and Goats."

CHAPTER 13

The Faunal Remains from the 2004–2007 Excavations at Tell el-Borg

Louise Bertini
AMERICAN RESEARCH CENTER IN EGYPT

INTRODUCTION

The assemblage of archaeozoological remains analyzed in this chapter comprises 2,658 bone fragments discovered between 2004–2007, while those recovered from 2000–2002 were studied in the previous chapter by Michelle Loyet (above, chapter 12). The data that is presented here represents Fields V, VI, VIII, and IX, in addition to completion of Fields II, III, and IV (table 13.1), which were partly analyzed by Loyet. Of those, 590 elements are identifiable to genus and anatomical element. The total of bones identified as belonging to limbs, ribs, vertebrae, or skull fragments of large (e.g., cattle, horse), medium to large (e.g., younger cattle), medium (e.g., sheep, goat, pig), and small (e.g., hare) mammals is 1,857.

The faunal material from the sample examined is, in general, in fairly good condition, although a majority of the sample is very fragmented, making species identification difficult at times beyond mammal size. The preservation, however, due to the dry desert environment of North Sinai,[1] did cause a majority of the bones to have large amounts of sand encrustation, which took a great amount of time to clean off in order to ensure correct identification.

METHODOLOGY

All bone fragments were examined, with information being recorded for each on its taxon, element, portion, side, age, butchery marks, being worked, gnawed, burn marks, erosion, and breakage patterns. Established protocols for aging bones based on both tooth eruption/wear and epiphyseal fusion were used.[2] Measurements were also taken on all adult (fused) mammalian

1. While the landscape of Tell el-Borg today consists of loose, windblown sand over much of the surface, in antiquity the landscape was very different and considerably wetter, including an ancient paleo-lagoon to which the site was constructed next to. For further discussion, see S. Moshier, "The Geological Setting of Tell el-Borg with Implications for Ancient Geography of Northwest Sinai," in *Tell el-Borg I*, 62–83.

2. R. Barone, *Anatomie comparée des mammifères domestiques* (Paris: Vigot Frères, 1965); A. Grant, "The Use of Tooth Wear as a Guide to the Age of Domestic Ungulates," in *Ageing and Sexing Animal Bones*

Table 13.1. Animal Taxa from Tell el-Borg from all Analyzed Contexts

Numbers refer to the amount of number of individual specimens (NISP)

Species	*Field II*	*Field III*	*Field IV*	*Field V*	*Field VI*	*Field VIII*	*Field IX*	*Total*	*%*
Crocodilus niloticus (Crocodile)	0	2	1	8	8	4	16	**39**	—
Total identified Reptiles	**0**	**2**	**1**	**8**	**8**	**4**	**16**	**39**	—
Anas crecca (Teal)	0	0	0	22	0	0	0	**22**	—
Struthio camelus- shell (Ostrich)	2	2	55	4	16	0	0	**79**	—
Total identified Birds	**2**	**2**	**55**	**26**	**16**	**0**	**0**	**101**	—
Chiroptera (Bat)	0	0	0	2	0	0	0	**2**	**0.34**
Bos taurus (Cow)	3	18	21	24	34	13	11	**124**	**21.02**
Canis familiaris (Dog)	1	0	1	6	12	1	0	**22**	**3.73**
Capra hircus (Goat)	0	0	0	2	0	0	0	**2**	**0.34**
Equus asinus (Donkey)	0	1	1	1	0	0	0	**3**	**0.51**
Equus caballus (Horse)	1	0	0	14	19	0	4	**38**	**6.44**
Equus (Unidentified Equid)	5	2	3	69	12	1	15	**107**	**18.14**
Felis catus (Cat)	1	0	0	8	0	0	1	**10**	**1.69**
Gazella (Gazelle)	0	0	0	1	0	0	0	**1**	**0.17**
Hippopotamus amphibious	0	0	0	0	0	0	1	**1**	**0.17**
Ovis aries (Sheep)	0	0	3	3	0	0	0	**6**	**1.02**
Ovis/Capra (Sheep/Goat)	12	9	25	58	40	16	5	**165**	**27.97**
Rodentia sp. (Rodent)	0	4	2	33	3	4	0	**46**	**7.80**
Crocidura sp. (Shrew)	0	0	0	10	12	0	0	**22**	**3.73**
Sus scrofa (Pig)	6	1	5	3	13	7	6	**41**	**6.95**
Total identified mammals	**29**	**35**	**61**	**234**	**145**	**42**	**43**	**590**	**100**
Small mammal	5	0	0	2	3	1	0	11	—
Medium mammal	31	31	97	274	719	111	27	1291	—
Medium-large mammal	0	19	2	20	58	2	13	114	—
Large Mammal	10	24	111	88	103	16	89	441	—
Total identified mammals based on size	**46**	**74**	**210**	**384**	**883**	**130**	**129**	**1,857**	—
Unidentified Bird	4	4	6	37	18	1	1	71	—
TOTAL ASSEMBLAGE	**81**	**117**	**333**	**689**	**1070**	**177**	**189**	**2,658**	—

fragments, as described by von den Driesch.[3] Human bone and shell fragments were found throughout the animal bone assemblage and were identified and counted, but are not part of this

from Archaeological Sites (ed. B. Wilson, C. Grigson, S. Payne; Oxford: BAR, 1982) 91–108; E. Hambleton, "A Method for Converting Grant Mandibular Wear Stages to Payne Style Wear Stages in Sheep, Cow, and Pig," in *Archaeological Sciences 1997: Proceedings of the Conference Held at the University of Durham, 2nd–4th September 1997* (ed. A. Millard; Oxford: Archaeopress, 2001) 103–8; R. A. McCance, E. H. R. Ford, and W. A. B. Brown, "Severe Under Nutrition in Growing and Adult Animals: Development of the Skull, Jaw, and Teeth in Pigs," *British Journal of Nutrition* 15 (1961) 213–24; I. A. Silver, "The Ageing of Domestic Animals," *Science in Archaeology* (ed. D. Brothwell and E. Higgs; New York: Basic Books, 1963) 250–68; S. Payne, "Kill-off Patterns in Sheep and Goats: The Mandibles from Asvan Kale," *Anatolian Studies* 23 (1973) 281–303.

3. A. von den Driesch, *A Guide to the Measurement of Animal Bones from Archaeological Sites* (Harvard University Peabody Museum Bulletin 1; Boston: Peabody Museum, 1976).

report. Fish bones are also excluded from this report, because they were put aside to be identified in a future season. The majority of the fish bones, however, appear to be Nile Catfish (*Synodontis* and *Clarias sp.*), followed by Nile Perch (*Lates niloticus*), and Bulti (*Tilapiini)*.

Although there are various problems with different quantification methods,[4] due to the various taphonomic issues associated with understanding a faunal assemblage,[5] the number if individual specimens (NISP) is the quantification method that will be used in this paper. NISPs are the easiest to calculate, are readily available for comparative sites, and have the best results for both inter- and intra-site comparison.[6]

THE FAUNA

A wide variety of animal remains were present at Tell el-Borg, including cattle, sheep/goat, pigs, equids, gazelle, dogs, cats, mice, crocodiles, birds, fish, and shells. The most numerous of the identified mammals were sheep/goats, followed closely by cattle.

Sheep and Goats

Sheep and goats represent the largest identified group of elements from the analyzed sample. The ratio of sheep/goats to cattle is 1.4 : 1, indicating an almost equal dependence on both large and small cattle. Of the 173 sheep/goat elements, only 8 elements could be identified to species, with 6 identified as sheep, and 2 as goat. Unfortunately, this sample is too small to calculate any accurate sheep-to-goat ratios in order to investigate their possible differing management practices. Despite the difficulty distinguishing between sheep and goat morphologically,[7] given the heavy use of cattle, it is possible that the majority of the sheep/goat remains are most likely goat, because sheep compete more directly with cattle for food, while goats make use of plants in waste areas making them a more logical complement to the cattle.[8] From this sheep–goat sample, no sex estimations could be made.

4. A. Gautier, "How do I count you, let me count the ways: Problems of Archaeozoological Quantification," in *Animals and Archaeology 4: Husbandry in Europe* (eds. C. Grigson and J. Clutton-Brock; Oxford: BAR, 1984) 237–51.

5. E. Reitz and E. Wing, *Zooarchaeology* (Cambridge: Cambridge University Press, 2008).

6. Gautier, "How do I count you, let me count the ways."

7. J. Boessneck, H. H. Müller, and M. Teichert, "Osteologische Unterscheidungmerkmale zwischen Schaf (*Ovis aries* Linné) und Zeige (*Capra hircus* Linné)," *Kühn-Archiv* 78 (1964) 1–29; J. Boessneck, "Osteological Differences between Sheep (*Ovis ariea* Linné) and Goats (*Capra hircus* Linné)," in *Science in Archaeology* (ed. D. Brothwell and E. Higgs; New York: Basic Books, 1963) 331–58; F. Hole, K. V. Flannery, and J. A. Neely, "Prehistory and Human Ecology on the Deh Luran Plain," in *Memoirs of the Museum of Anthropology, No.1* (Ann Arbor, MI: University of Michigan Press, 1969); W. Prummel and H-J. Frisch, "A Guide for the Distinction of Species, Sex, and Body Size of Sheep and Goat," *Journal of Archaeological Science* 14 (1986) 609–14; Balasse Marie and Stanley H. Ambrose, "Distinguishing Sheep and Goats Using Dental Morphology and Stable Carbon Isotopes in C4 Grassland Environments," *Journal of Archaeological Science* 32 (2005) 691–702; M. A. Zeder and S. E. Pilaar "Assessing the Reliability of Criteria Used to Identify Mandibles and Mandibular Teeth in Sheep, *Ovis*, and Goats, *Capra*," *Journal of Archaeological Science* 37 (2010) 225–42.

8. R. W. Redding, "The Role of the Pig in the Subsistence System of Ancient Egypt: A Parable on the Potential of Faunal Data," *Animal Use and Culture Change MASCA Research Papers in Science and Archaeology, Supplement 8* (Philadelphia: University of Pennsylvania Museum, 1991).

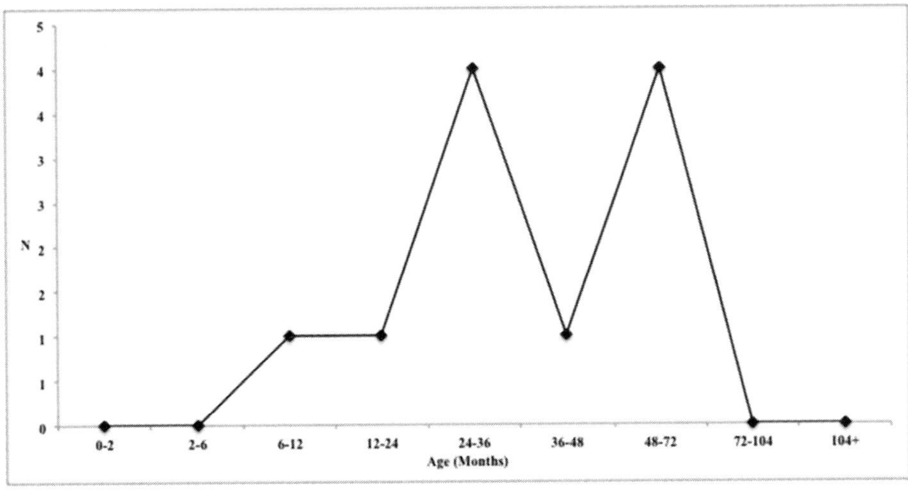

Fig. 13.1. Caprine survivorship based on tooth eruption/wear after Payne (see n. 2) for all contexts.

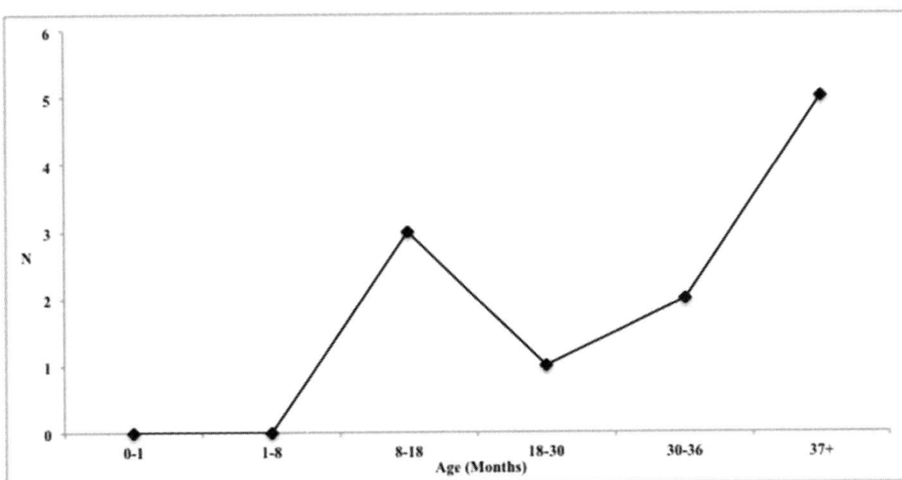

Fig. 13.2. Cattle survivorship based on tooth eruption/wear after Grant (see n. 2) and Hambleton (see n. 2) for all contexts.

Table 13.2. Number and Percentage of Sheep/Goat Fused vs. Unfused Limb Bones

Bone Element	*Fused*	*Unfused*	*% Fused*
Px. Humerus	0	2	0%
Ds. Humerus	2	0	100%
Ds. Radius	0	1	0%
Ds. MP	8	2	80%
Px. Phalanx 1	4	1	80%
Px. Phalanx 2	7	1	88%
Px. Tibia	1	2	33%
Ds. Tibia	3	5	38%
Px. Femur	1	2	33%
Ds. Femur	0	1	0%

From the analyzed sample, there are 43 limb bone elements (table 13.2) and eleven mandibles (fig. 13.1) from which age distributions could be calculated. Tooth wear/eruption shows two peaks: one at 24–36 and a second at 48–72 months. This points to sheep/goat use for secondary products including milk and possibly even wool to supply the inhabitants of the fort.

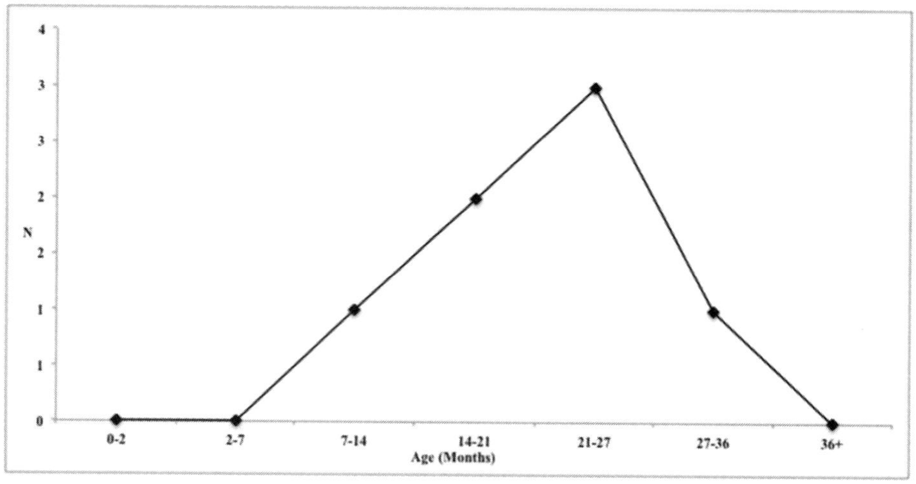

Fig. 13.3. Pig survivorship based on tooth eruption/wear after Grant and Hambleton for all contexts.

Table 13.3. Number and Percentage of Cattle Fused vs. Unfused Limb Bones

Bone Element	*Fused*	*Unfused*	*% Fused*
Px. Humerus	0	2	0%
Ds. Humerus	1	0	100%
Ds. Radius	1	0	100%
Px. Radius	1	0	100%
Ds. MP	3	3	50%
Px. Phalanx 1	2	2	50%
Px. Phalanx 2	1	0	100%
Ds. Tibia	2	1	67%
Px. Femur	1	4	20%
Ds. Femur	1	0	100%
Px. Calcaneous	0	2	0%

Cattle

Cattle are represented by a total of 124 fragments. The ratio of sheep/goats to cattle based on NISP's is 1.4 : 1 for all of the areas analyzed in this chapter. Although the ratio seems to point to a more sheep/goat based economy, cattle do provide more meat per unit of bone[9] and thus are a major source of animal protein, yielding twice as much meat as sheep/goats. Loyet (chapter 12) also points to a heavy reliance on cattle, with a complete reversal of ratios, having a 1.8 : 1 cattle-to-sheep/goat ratio based on Areas II, III, and IV. It is therefore possible that the inhabitants of Tell el-Borg relied significantly on cattle for both meat and their secondary products. From the present sample of cattle elements, no sex estimations could be made.

Based on tooth eruption/wear, the age distribution of cattle ranges from 8 months to more than 4 years, with the vast majority of the sample peaking at 37+ months (fig. 13.2). There are twenty-seven limb bone fragments exhibiting different stages of fusion (table 13.3).

9. G. Dahl and A. Hjort, *Having Herds: Pastoral Herd Growth and Household Economy* (Stockholm: Stockholm Studies in Social Anthropology, 1976).

Table 13.4. Number and Percentage of Pig Fused vs. Unfused Limb Bones

Bone Element	*Fused*	*Unfused*	*% Fused*
Ds. Humerus	1	1	50%
Px. Radius	1	0	100%
Ds. MP	0	1	0%
Px. Phalanx 1	3	1	75%
Px. Phalanx 2	1	0	100%
Px. Tibia	0	2	0%
Ds. Tibia	1	0	100%

Pigs

Pigs are represented by a total of 41 elements. Similar to the Old Kingdom, large state-supported centers such as the Giza Workmen's Village, the pig was simply found not to be a valuable provisioning resource. This interpretation is most likely due to the fact that pigs possess very few secondary resources (mainly fat and hides), and they are unsuitable for large-scale feeding.[10] However, it is well known that many people in ancient Egypt reared pigs as an additional source of protein,[11] as is borne out by the Tell el-Borg assemblage.

While the sample of pig elements from which age data could be estimated is quite small, limb bone fusion (table 13.4) and tooth eruption/wear (fig. 13.3) data could still be calculated. Tooth eruption/wear (fig. 13.3) shows a peak at 21–27 months. This is an age slightly older than what is expected of pig remains, since typically most pigs are slaughtered between six and ten months,[12] because once they reach reproductive maturity they become difficult to care for, often competing with humans for food resources.

Donkeys and Horses

Equids (donkeys, horses, and possibly even mules or hinnies) are the third most common identified taxa (N=148), of which 3 elements could be confirmed as donkey and 38 as horse. Employed as a beast of burden and warfare, it is expected that equids played a central role in the daily activities of the fort. A curious find at Tell el-Borg in the eastern fosse of square A and B in Area V was the complete burial of multiple equids, from which the vast majority of equid remains (N= 84) discussed in this report derive. This is a find that is discussed by Salima Ikram in greater detail in the next chapter.

10. R. W. Redding, "Status and Diet at the Workers' Town, Giza, Egypt," in *Anthropological Approaches to Zooarchaeology: Complexity, Colonialism, and Animal Transformations* (ed. D. Campana et al.; Oxford: Oxbow, 2010) 65–75.

11. L. Bertini, "How Did the Nile Water System Impact Swine Husbandry Practices in Ancient Egypt?" in *A History of Water, Series 3, Volume 3: Water and Food: From Hunter-Gatherers to Global Production in Africa* (ed. T. Østigård and T. Tvedt; London: I. B. Tauris, 2016) 75–100; H. M. Hecker, "Preliminary Report on the Faunal Remains from the Workmen's Village," *Amarna Reports 1* (ed. B. Kemp; London: Egypt Exploration Society, 1984) 154–64; S. Ikram, *Choice Cuts: Meat Production in Ancient Egypt* (Leuven: Peeters, 1995); R. L. Miller, "Hogs and Hygiene," *The Journal of Egyptian Archaeology* 76 (1990) 125–40; Redding, "The Role of the Pig"; M. A. Zeder, "Pigs and Emergent Complexity in the Ancient Near East," *Ancestors for the Pigs: Pigs in Prehistory* (MASCA Research Papers in Science and Archaeology 15; Philadelphia: University of Pennsylvania Museum, 1988) 109–22.

12. Redding, "The Role of the Pig," 65–75.

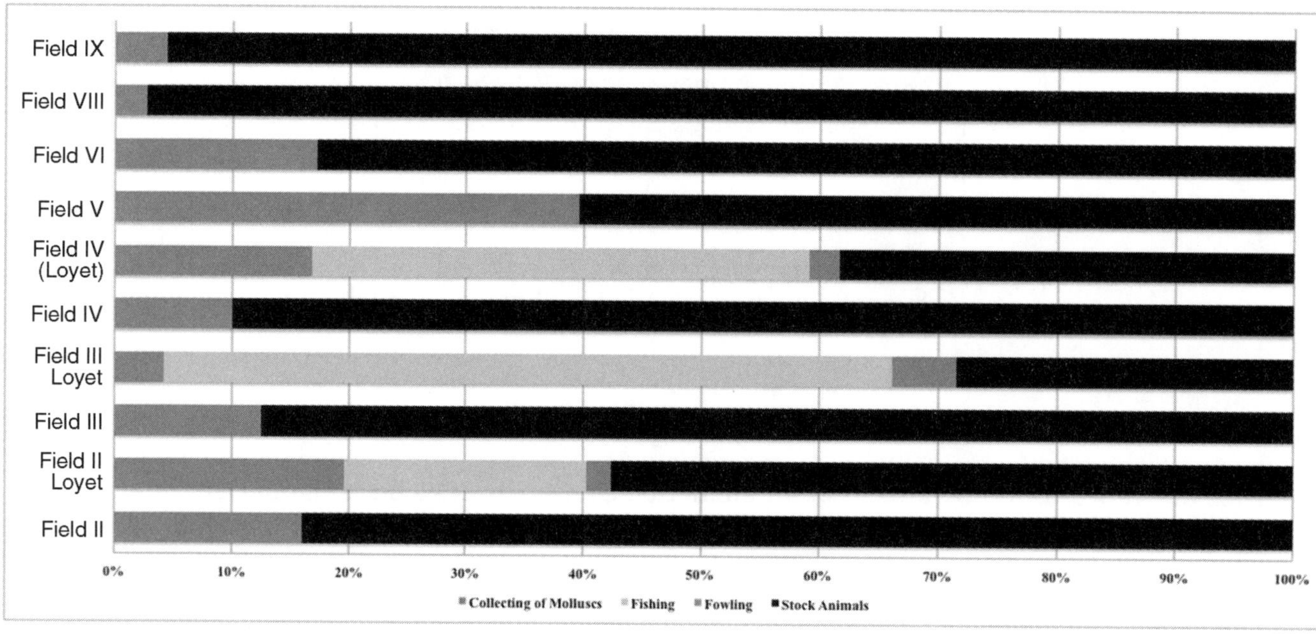

Fig. 13.4. Relative importance (%) of different economic activities used to obtain food at Tell el-Borg.

Crocodile

Several crocodile bones (N=39) were identified. The majority of the crocodile elements identified were scales (osteoderm/scute) and vertebrae. It has been noted that crocodiles were a source of food for the early dwellers of the Nile Valley,[13] since their remains have been found at Predynastic settlements such as Merimde, Omari, and Maadi.[14] Most likely, crocodiles were not being eaten here, because the inhabitants of Tell el-Borg probably depended on consumption of meat from cattle, sheep/goat, pigs, and the occasional duck. It is possible that the soldiers hunted them, and there might have been some activity using their skins/scales for weaponry.[15] Of course, the crocodile remains may simply be natural deposits, because these creatures were omnipresent in the surrounding environment. To that end, it is worthy of note that the greatest concentration of crocodile bones is in Area IX, where the ancient canal flowed through the site.

Hippopotamus

A distal end of a humerus from a hippopotamus was also recovered in Area IX. Since this is the first element of a hippopotamus to be identified at the site, it is difficult to say if there were hippopotami in the surrounding environment and/or they were hunted. Certainly these animals were present in antiquity and have been identified at the nearby site of Tell el-Dabᶜa.[16]

---

13. S. Ikram,"Crocodiles: Guardians of the Gateways," in *Thebes and Beyond: Studies in Honor of Kent R. Weeks* (ed. Z Hawass and S. Ikram; Cairo: SCA, 2010) 85–98.

14. J. Boessneck, *Die Tierwelt der Alten Agypten* (Munich: Beck, 1988); J. Rowland and L. Bertini, "The Neolithic within the Context of Northern Egypt: New Results and Perspectives from Merimde Beni Salama," *Quaternary International* 410a (2016) 1–13.

15. Roman Period crocodile armor at the British Museum (EA5472) is said to be from Egypt.

16. J. Boessneck and A. von den Driesch, *Tell el-Dabᶜa VIII: Tiere und Historische Umwelt im Nordost-Delta im 2 Jahrtausend V. Chr. Anhand der Knochenfunde der Ausgrabungen 1975–1986* (Vienna:

Avians and Avian Shells

A total of 93 bird remains were analyzed, of which 22 could be identified to the genus level and were identified as *Anas crecca* or the common teal (freshwater duck). All of the identified teal remains came from Area V, as seen in table 13.1. Most of the unidentified bird remains are bone shaft fragments, thus rendering identification difficult to impossible.

In addition, 79 ostrich eggshell fragments were also identified. The largest concentration of eggshell fragments came from Area IV (N=55). No complete eggs were found, and the excavated fragments were all small in size. The fragments are all tan in color and display no evidence of incised decoration or painting. Although it is possible the eggs were consumed, the more likely scenario is that they were used as objects or vessels.[17] Although the ostrich is known to have been present throughout the region,[18] no bones of the bird were identified at the site, which points to either food production and/or object use of the eggs only.

Discussion

The most important factor influencing the choice of food production is the environment of the site's location. Given the marshy lagoon locale of the site, it is ideal for many types of herding regimes.[19] As such, the Tell el-Borg faunal assemblage shows an overwhelming reliance on stock animals (fig. 13.4). While Loyet's work on Fields III and IV does show a significantly higher percentage of fish remains as compared to the same areas analyzed in this chapter, since there are fish remains that still need to be analyzed, this distribution should be used with caution. There is, however, a clear reliance on older cattle and sheep/goats (figs. 13.1 and 13.2; tables 13.2 and 13.3) signifying the use of secondary resources such as milk and wool by the inhabitants of Tell el-Borg. Given the older age distribution of both species, it is probable that the inhabitants of Tell el-Borg were utilizing a mixed strategy of both animals. The bimodal distribution of the cattle age distribution (fig. 13.1) supports that while some were killed for meat between 8–18 months, the vast majority were killed at an older age, thus making use of their secondary products. Sheep/goats rather seem to be used for both milking and wool, with very few killed at a younger age (fig. 13.2). These data point to a clear exploitation of these two species, most probably corresponding with the volume of troops that is expected to have either passed through the fort or that were stationed there. Because the fortress of Tell el-Borg seems to have played an important defensive role on the Ways of Horus, one can thus expect that the strong reliance primarily on cattle and sheep/goats, with a specific mortality profile, is evidence of state provisioning at the site.

The percentages of cattle and sheep/goat are in stark contrast to a different fort site of the same time period, Kom Firin[20] in the western Nile Delta (table 13.5) where pigs far outnumber both cattle and sheep/goat combined. At Tell el-Borg, pigs make up a significantly smaller percentage of the total identified faunal remains. The reason for this difference is twofold. The first

Verlag der Österreichischen Akademie der Wissenschaften, 1992).

17. P. F. Houlihan, *The Birds of Ancient Egypt* (Warminster, England: Aris & Phillips, 1986). B. Laufer, *Ostrich Egg-shell Cups of Mesopotamia and the Ostrich in Ancient Modern Times* (Anthropology Leaflet 23; Chicago: Field Museum of Natural History, 1926).

18. N. Manlius, "The Ostrich in Egypt: Past and Present," *Journal of Biogeography* 28 (2001) 945–53.

19. S. Moshier, "The Geological Setting of Tell el-Borg with Implications for Ancient Geography of Northwest Sinai," in *Tell el-Borg I* (ed. J. Hoffmeier; Winona Lake, Indiana: Eisenbrauns; 2014), 62–83.

20. L. Bertini, "Faunal Remains at Kom Firin," in *Kom Firin II: The Urban Fabric and Landscape* (ed. Neal Spencer; London: British Museum, 2014) 306–311.

Table 13.5. Relative Importance (%) of Domestic Cattle, Ovicaprines, and Pigs at Tell el-Borg (both Bertini and Loyet's Analysis) as Compared to Kom Firin

	% Tell el-Borg	% Tell el-Borg (Loyet)	% Kom Firin (Bertini 2014)
Cattle	37%	47%	6.8%
Ovicaprines	51%	25%	10.6%
Pig	12%	28%	82.6%
N	338	387	587

reason has to do with Tell el-Borg being a crucial location on the Ways of Horus, where there probably was a higher volume of troops passing through and/or stationed there. Troops were thus provisioned with food, thanks to the state, explaining the heavy dependence on stock animals, particularly sheep/goat and cattle. However, the environment and available raw materials seem to have also been taken into consideration at these New Kingdom fortresses. While pigs could potentially have survived in the marshy environment of Tell el-Borg, the one area analyzed where there is a slightly higher percentage[21] of pig remains at the site is Field VI. Whether or not the pigs were associated with the residents of the burned reed huts is unclear.[22] The presence of pigs in this area seems to point to a long-term settlement, not a transient population. Although it is possible that there may have been transitory soldiers at this location, the pigs and their keepers were clearly not transient, because they need constant access to water and an area to wallow in order to keep cool due to their inability to sweat.[23] It is likely that this confirms that pigs were serving as an additional source of protein for the soldiers, who most likely reared the species because the fort's central authority was not likely provisioning them.

At Kom Firin, on the other hand, pigs overwhelmingly dominate the faunal assemblage (table 13.5). Because the environment at Kom Firin was very wet, being located between 2 branches of the Nile,[24] the site is an ideal environment for pigs, providing easy access to fresh water, compared to the more likely semi-salty marshy lagoon at Tell el-Borg. Given these different environmental locations, there was no need for the state to provide for the inhabitants at Kom Firin; they could provide for themselves.

CONCLUSIONS

The faunal material examined in this report indicates several mammal and avian species, of which cattle and sheep/goat seem to have been the most commonly maintained and consumed animal. While cattle and sheep/goat were primarily utilized for their secondary resources (milk, wool

21. While the overall percentage of identified pig remains at Tell el-Borg analyzed in this chapter is 6.95%, the percentage of identified pig remains from Area VI is 9%.

22. It appears to the excavators of Field VI (see chapter 7) that the amount of deflation in this area was considerable, reflected in the fact that sherds spanning a couple of centuries were found on the surface. Whatever structures were constructed after (or over) the reed huts were completely eroded away, leaving only the later pottery or stone tools.

23. M. Harris, *Cows, Pigs, Wars, and Witches: The Riddles of Culture* (New York: Vintage, 1974).

24. J. Bunbury, E. Hughes, and N. Spencer, "Ancient Landscape Reconstruction at Kom Firin," in *Kom Firin II: The Urban Fabric and Landscape* (ed. Neal Spencer; London: The British Museum Press, 2014) 11–13.

etc.) in order to maximize their potential gains, individuals more likely kept pigs as an additional source of protein separate from the centralized provisions of the fort. Horse and donkey were highly valued and intensely utilized. Additional mammals/reptiles present in the surrounding environment include crocodiles, typical carnivores (cats and dogs), rodents, and even hippopotamus.

Future work is expected to yield more evidence on sheep/goat butchering practices and herding strategies and may also help to confirm if goats are in fact more common at the site, possibly indicating intensive agriculture in the surrounding environments. Additionally, additional analysis is required on the fish remains to understand their role in both the diet and economic functions of the site.

In sum, the analysis of faunal data from both Tell el-Borg and other surrounding fort sites has the potential to contribute to our understanding of the economic functions and provisions for New Kingdom frontier forts, specifically those along the "Ways of Horus," and possibly even environmental reconstruction of the surrounding areas. Only continued and future work will help to shed more light on these issues.

CHAPTER 14
The Equid Remains from Tell el-Borg

Salima Ikram
AMERICAN UNIVERSITY CAIRO

During the 2005 and 2006 seasons at Tell el-Borg, three deposits of equid burials were found in the eastern fosse (or moat): the first in Field V Area 2, Unit A; the second in Unit B. A third deposit was uncovered in Field VI Area 3 (also in a fosse) was not examined by the author but only seen in photographs. The former was partially excavated when the equid in the easern fosse was first discovered in 2005, carefully photographed, and then covered over and left for a year until the archaeozoologist could come to examine the skeleton in 2006. The second find was discovered and dug in 2006 and the final one in 2007.

After thorough photo documentation, the skeletons were excavated as a group, with the bones numbered as they were extracted. Due to the fragility of the deposit, whenever possible, measurements were taken in the field after brushing off the bone, but because of accretions and the bones' fragility, the measurements are not always as precise as one might wish. Measurements were retaken where possible in the laboratory, after the dried bones had been brushed completely clean. The bones were stored in paper bags that were placed in boxes in order to ensure that they remained as complete as possible.

The damp, very salty and sandy matrix in which the animals were found had affected the bones badly. For the most part, the bones could not be removed intact from the matrix: either they crumbled or they had large chunks of sandy soil adhering to them like concrete, making it difficult to see them clearly. It was impossible to note any other taphonomy on the bones (gnawing, burn marks, etc.), save for a pinkish tinge on some bones, presumably from a fungus that flourishes in sandy soil that excavators and archaeozoologists have encountered on bones from other sites having similar conditions.

FIELD V AREA 2, UNIT A

The larger of the two deposits was found in Field V Area 2, Unit A (see *Tell el-Borg I*, 235–38 and in this volume fig. 14.1). It consisted of an assemblage of semiarticulated equid bones that seem to have come from a group of at least four animals—it is possible that a part of another animal also formed a part of the assemblage, but because many of the bones were so damaged, it is difficult to determine this accurately. Presumably, the burial had been made at or toward the end of the fosse's active use: these animals did not lie at the bottom of the pit; they rested on a layer of compacted sand some 1.30 m from the bottom of the fosse. The dead animals had been thrown in,

Fig. 14.1. Jumble of equid remains in Ramesside period moat (photo by NSAP).

Fig. 14.2. Close-up of equid remains in Ramesside period moat (photo by NSAP)

rather than carefully buried, and lay one on top of the other, their limbs entangled (fig. 14.2). They had different orientations: the head of one pointed south, while the head of another pointed east. It is quite possible that the skeletons are a result of a single depositional incident, with a series of animals being thrown in one general area, one after the other. Certainly, very little mud or sand lay between the different individuals, and their skeletons were, in some cases, mixed up with one another. However, it is also possible that this assemblage might be a result of a series of deposits, made over extremely short intervals consisting of days rather than minutes or even hours.

The bodies of all these animals are not complete; curiously, the heads of two of these creatures are missing, although the majority of the limb bones are present. Possibly, the bodies were thrown down without the heads, although it is difficult to imagine why their heads had been severed, unless this was the result of military (or other violent) activity. It is possible that some carnivore dragged away the heads, although this is unlikely, given the limited amount of edible flesh on the head and the remaining relatively well articulated skeletons. Darker soil near the bones was indicative of the area where the flesh and internal organs (and their contents) disintegrated and left a mark.[1]

1. I am grateful to Marsha Levine, Simon Davis, Angela von den Driesch, Johanna Sigl, Richard Redding, Nadja Poellath, and Fiona Marshall for all their help with references and opinions on the identifications of these bones. Members of the Zooarch list-serve have also been tremendously helpful in pointing me in the right direction for articles and theses, most of which are unavailable in Cairo. S. Turner's tenacity was instrumental in helping complete this project. It is unfortunate that due to reasons beyond my control and that of Director James Hoffmeier, who kindly invited me to work on these bones, I was unable to reexamine the equid bones after doing more reading and research on equids; hopefully, future researchers will be able to derive even more information from these bones. Additionally, since the time of initial study and recording of the bones, several hard drives expired, taking with them the detailed images of bone and teeth.

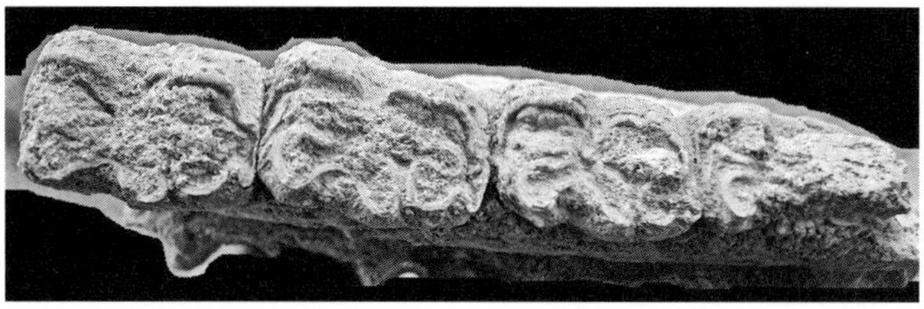

Fig. 14.3. Teeth from Equid 1 (photo by NSAP).

Fig. 14.4. Skull with teeth of Equid 2 (photo by NSAP).

One animal was situated east–west, with its head to the east, twisted backward, up to the sky (Equid 1). It was lying on its left side. The limbs were spread out and in considerable disarray; not all the bones were recovered. Although its lumbar vertebrae were too damaged to count properly and use to determine the species,[2] the overall bone and teeth measurements and the internal folds of the mandibular teeth all point to its identification as a horse (fig. 14.3).[3] It is possible that it might be a mule, because morphologically mules and hinnies resemble horses more closely than asses.[4] The fusion of the bones that clearly formed a part of this skeleton and what could be determined from the teeth indicates that the animal was well over five years of age when it died.[5]

Another creature was oriented north–south, lying on its left side, with its head facing south (Equid 2). It was most probably a male donkey or possibly a young horse (fig. 14.4). It has canine teeth, indicative of its sex. Their presence also indicates that the animal was probably over five years of age when it died. The age is confirmed by the presence of the third molar in the mandible. Because its teeth could not be separated or accurately measured without damaging them, and their occlusal surfaces were too destroyed to see, these could not be relied upon to determine the species. Although it is not totally clear, it seems that the animal had five lumbar vertebrae. The presence of five rather than six lumbar vertebrae suggests that the animal is a donkey,[6] although its overall size gave the impression of being a bit bigger than that associated with donkeys; unfortunately, clear measurements for most of what was definitely part of the skeleton were not possible. The animal could be a small horse or large donkey or, indeed, mule, and thus it is difficult to classify the animal securely.

The other two animals' heads were not found (Equids 3 and 4), although most of their limb bones were preserved, after a fashion. The bones were all fused, indicating that the animals were

2. R. M. Stetcher, "Anatomical Variations of the Spine in the Horse," *Journal of Mammalogy* 43.2 (1962) 205–19.

3. S. Davis, "Late Pleistocene and Holocene Equid Remains from Israel," *Zoological Journal of the Linnaen Society* 70 (1981) 289–312. Horse and donkey are separated on the basis of Davis's work.

4. V. Eisenmann and S. Beckouche, "Identification and Discrimination of Metapodials of Pleistocene and Modern *Equus*, Wild and Domestic," in *Equids in the Ancient World* (ed. R. H. Meadow and H-P. Uerpmann; Wiesbaden: Reichert, 1986) 117–63.

5. I. A. Silver, "The Ageing of Domestic Animals," in *Science in Archaeology* (ed. D. Brothwell and E. S. Higgs; London: Thames and Hudson, 1963) 282–302.

6. Stetcher, "Anatomical Variations."

Fig. 14.5. The equid in situ in Field V Area 2, Unit B.

adults, more than 4.5 years of age when they died. Equid 3 lay on its left side and Equid 4 on its right. A tentative identification of donkey was made for Equid 3 on the basis of the size of its limbs (although it is a little larger than those of earlier donkeys from Egypt)[7] and the general bone morphology. Equid 4 might possibly be a horse or a mule: its bones seemed to be larger than those of a donkey or, indeed, Equid 3. Unfortunately, insufficient vertebrae were preserved, so a distinction could not be made on that basis.

Tables 14.1 and 14.2 provide a list of the measurable bones from all the animals in this deposit, using von den Driesch's system.[8] It was not always possible to determine, based on position, which limb went with which animal, because the limbs were very mixed up in some of the areas, which is why they have not been organized by equid number—although when fairly certain the equid number is provided with the bone. Measurements were taken using callipers and, in the absence of a measuring board, improvised wooden blocks and a tape measure. The accretions and general fragility of the bones made it very difficult to take accurate measurements; thus, there are one or two instances where a + sign indicates that the bone might have been a bit larger than the measurement given, or a ? marks imprecision.

7. J. Boessneck, A. von den Driesch, and A. Eissa, "Eine Eselsbestattung der 1. Dynastie in Abusir," *MDAIK* 48 (1992) 1–10; S. Rossel et al., "Domestication of the Donkey: Timing, Processes, and Indicators," *PNAS* 105.10 (2008) 3715–20 (www.pnas.org_cgi_doi_10.1073_pnas.0709692105).

8. A. von den Driesch, *A Guide to the Measurement of Animal Bones from Archaeological Sites* (Cambridge, MA: Peabody Museum/Harvard University, 1976).

Table 14.1. Measured Limb Bones (in mm) from Trench A

No.	*Element*	*GL(1)*[a]	*Bp*	*BFp*	*Dp*	*BFd*	*BT*	*Bd*	*Dd*	*GH*	*GB*	*LmT*	*LA*
85/0	Humerus	295[b]=Withers 1436.465	N	N	N	N	N	78	N	N	N	N	N
32	Humerus EQ 2	N	N	N	N	N	N	53	N	N	N	N	N
68	Humerus EQ 1	310[b]=Withers 1509.7	71	N	N	N	78	N	N	N	N	N	N
69	Humerus EQ 1	N	N	N	N	N	78	84	N	N	N	N	N
66	Radius	N	84	79	N	N	N	N	N	N	N	N	N
91/0	Radius	328	N	N	N	N	N	N	N	N	N	N	N
29	RadiusEQ 3	N	N	N	N	47	N	56	N	N	N	N	N
64	Radius	N	N	N	N	46	N	53	N	N	N	N	N
27	RadiusEQ 3	N	N	N	N	46	N	56	N	N	N	N	N
67	RadiusEQ 4	349[b]=Withers 1515.66	86	N	N	N	N	77	N	N	N	N	N
39	Metacarpal III EQ 4	280?[b]=1708.58	35	N	N	N	N	33	N	N	N	N	N
52	Metacarpal III EQ 2?	228[b]=1391.256	52	N	N	N	N	51	N	N	N	N	N
80/0	Metacarpal III	N	37.5	N	N	N	N	N	N	N	N	N	N
87/0	Metacarpal III	205[b]=1250.5	N	N	N	N	N	N	N	N	N	N	N
55	Metacarpal IIIEQ 4	230[b]=1474.3	55	N	N	N	N	48+	N	N	N	N	N
28A	Metacarpal IIIEQ 3	220?[b]=1410.2	37	N	27	N	N	34	N	N	N	N	N
26	Metacarpal IV	72	37.5	N	N	N	N	33.5	N	N	N	N	N
89/0	Acetabulum	N	N	N	N	N	N	N	N	N	N	N	56
27	AcetabulumEQ 3	N	N	N	N	N	N	N	N	N	N	N	61
45	AcetabulumEQ 4?	N	N	N	N	N	N	N	N	N	N	N	67
84/0	FemurEQ 1?	410?	N	N	N	N	N	N	N	N	N	N	N
61	FemurEQ 2?	275	N	N	N	N	N	N	N	N	N	N	N
5	Patella	65	N	N	N	N	N	N	N	N	68+	N	N
18	Tibia	N	N	N	N	N	N	47	N	N	N	N	N
38	Tibia	N	N	N	N	N	N	42	30	N	N	N	N
82/0	Tibia	N	N	N	N	N	N	66	40	N	N	N	N
25	TibiaEQ 3	N	N	N	N	N	N	51	32	N	N	N	N
20	Metatarsal III	N	35.5	N	N	N	N	N	N	N	N	N	N
15	Metatarsal III	N	49	N	N	N	N	N	N	N	N	N	N
88/0	Metatarsal III	260[b]=1362.14	N	N	N	N	N	N	N	N	N	N	N
95/0	Navicular	N	N	N	N	N	N	N	N	N	47.5	N	N
60	AstragalusEQ 4??	N	N	N	N	N	N	N	N	44	43	39	N
81/0	Astragalus	N	N	N	N	N	N	N	N	41	62?	N	N
24	AstragalusEQ 3	N	N	N	N	N	N	N	N	42	44	N	N
8	CalcaneusEQ 4?	108	N	N	N	N	N	N	N	N	N	N	N
19	CalcaneusEQ 3	80	N	N	N	N	N	N	N	N	N	N	N
3	Phalange 1EQ 4?	86	51	N	N	N	N	41	N	N	N	N	N
12A	Phalange 1	84	50	N	N	N	N	N	N	N	N	N	N
90/0	Phalange 1	80	N	N	N	N	N	N	N	N	N	N	N
2	Phalange 1EQ 2	65	35	N	N	N	N	26	N	N	N	N	N
13	Phalange 1EQ 1	84	54	N	31	N	N	40	N	N	N	N	N
51	Phalange 1EQ 4	87	58	N	33	43	N	46	N	N	N	N	N
54	Phalange 1EQ 4?	84	57	N	N	N	N	45	N	N	N	N	N
28B	Phalange 1EQ 3	68	N	34	27	36	N	33	N	N	N	N	N
30	Phalange 2	35	36	33.4	23	N	N	33	N	N	N	N	N
12B	Phalange 2EQ 1?	46	N	N	N	N	N	N	N	N	N	N	N
14	Phalange 2	52	44	41	N	N	N	N	N	N	N	N	N
50	Phalange 2EQ 4?	N	52	N	N	N	N	N	N	N	N	N	N
53	Phalange 2EQ 2?	45	48	N	N	N	N	N	N	N	N	N	N

Table 14.2. Additional Measured Limb Bones (in mm) from Trench A

No.	*Element*	*GL(1)*	*BFcd*	*GLP*	*LG*
72	Atlas	94	89	N	N
46	Scapula	N	N	N	51
92/0	Scapula	N	N	88?	N

Measurement Abbreviation Key
(based on von den Dreisch)[a]

GL	Greatest length
GL(1)	Greatest length of the lateral part
GB	Greatest breadth
GH	Greatest height
GLP	Greatest length of the glenoid process
LA	Length of acetabulum
LG	Length of the glenoid cavity
LmT	Length of medial part of the Trochlea tali
Bp	Proximal breadth
Bd	Distal breadth
BFp	Proximal articular breadth
BFd	Distal articular breadth
BFcd	Greatest breadth of the caudal articular surface
BT	Greatest breadth of trochlea
Dd	Depth of distal end
Dp	Depth of proximal en

a. Shoulder and withers height estimates are based on A. von den Driesch and J. Boessneck ("Kritische Anmerkungen zur Widerristhohenberechnung aus Langenmassen vor- und fruhgeschichtlicher Tierknochen," *Säugetierkundliche Mitteilungen* 22 [1974] 325–48); and E. May (published by Johnston in 2004: C. J. Johnston, *A Biometric Study of Equids in the Roman World* (Unpublished thesis, University of York, Department of Archaeology, 2004; http://www/york.ac.uk/depts/arch/ (pgstudents/Johnsone.html) where GL of the metacarpal is multiplied by 6.102, and that of the metatarsal by 5.239. Humeri are multiplied by 4.87 and radii by 4.34. The reliability in height estimation using these measurements for donkeys is less secure than for horses.

b. A. von den Dreisch, *A Guide to the Measurement of Animal Bones from Archaeological Sites* (Cambridge, MA: Peabody Museum/Harvard University, 1976).

Field V Area 2, Unit B

The second equine deposit came from Unit B, Locus 7, and morphologically seems to belong to a donkey (*Equus asinus*) (fig. 14.5); this is particularly clear from the mandibular teeth (fig. 14.6).[9] The bones were found some 1.5 m from the bottom of the fosse, and possibly had been thrown in after the *original* active life of the fosse. The deposit was spread out and the bones were very broken and eroded due to the natural activity of sand, wind, salt, and water. The skeleton lay on its left side, and consisted of a skull, facing north, and its limbs aligned east-west. The elements recovered included a part of the pelvis (broken), parts of the two forelegs (right humerus and right first phalanx, right and left radii and ulnae and metacarpal III), and most of the two hind-legs (right and left femurs, tibiae, metatarsals, and the right patella). The vertebrae, ribs, and most of the hooves are missing. The way in which the bones are positioned, with the fore- and hind-limbs roughly in anatomically correct position, although a bit spread apart, suggests that the creature had been deposited as an entire animal, and then portions had been dragged off by animals. All the limb bones appeared to be fused, and the teeth seem to have all erupted, and those that were visible, were quite worn. Thus, the animal must have been at least 5 years old when it died, but

9. S. Davis, "Late Pleistocene and Holocene."

more likely much older. The sex of this particular creature could not be established as the pelvis was very damaged. No canine teeth were visible, but this does not argue conclusively for a female rather than a male animal

Due to the fragile nature of the deposit, only some of the bones could be measured (see table 14.3). The occlusal surface of the teeth could be examined, but were too damaged at the edges to measure with any accuracy. The measurements for this donkey are a little larger than those recorded for donkeys from earlier periods (see n. 7), but this animal is definitely a donkey, based on the morphology of the teeth.

Field VI Area 3, Unit B

An isolated equid head, apparently without the maxilla, was found in this area (fig. 14.7), like those in Field V, in an abandoned moat 400 m to the east, on the south side of the Nile distributary. Unfortunately, it was not possible to determine whether it was a horse or donkey, though the sizes of the teeth suggest that it was a horse, although by no means is this identification secure.

Discussion

It is difficult to distinguish between different types of equids, because there are few morphological differences in the bones and teeth, and experts only agree about some of these.[10] Size is a criterion that is sometimes used, with horses being larger than donkeys,[11] and mules (male donkey [jack] and a female horse [mare], more horse-like tails) falling between the two, with hinnies (male horse [stallion] and a female donkey [jennet]) being smaller than mules, but both horses and mules might share measurements of horses. Furthermore, Egyptian horses, particularly those from the early New Kingdom, are quite small and gracile and can be difficult to distinguish from donkeys based on size alone, save for some bones, such as the metapodia. Certain anatomical elements that are now regarded as acceptable to distinguish between these animals are teeth and the occiput. Tooth morphology can distinguish between horses and donkeys, particularly the shape of the double knots on the occlusal (chewing) surface of the tooth: asses tend to have V shapes and horses U-shaped.[12] Another distinguishing feature is the ability of a horse skull to balance vertically on its occipital condyles.[13] However, only two very fragile skulls were recovered, and the teeth were quite worn and eroded and also encrusted with the concrete-like dirt and thus were difficult to examine and measure, particularly the occlusal (biting) surfaces. In this paper, when teeth are not available, size has been used as a basic distinguishing characteristic

10. M. A. Zeder. "The Equid Remains from Tal-e Malyan, South Central Iran," in *Equids in the Ancient World*, Vol. 1 (ed. R. Meadow and H.-P. Uerpmann; Wiesbaden: Ludwig Reichert, 1986), 366–409; S. Bökönyi, "Once More on the Osteological Diffrences of the Horse, the Half-Ass, and the Ass," Appendix A in *The Caspian Miniature Horse of Iran* (ed. L. Firouz; Miami: Field Research Projects 64 [1972]): 12–17; P. Ducos, "A New Find of an Equid Metatarsal Bone from Tell Mureybet in Syria and Its Relevance to the Identification of Equids from the Early Holocene of the Levant," *Journal of Archaeological Science* 2 (1975): 71–73; V. Eisenmann, *Les Chevaux (Equus sensu lato) fossils et actuels: Cranes et dents jugales supérieures* (Cahiers de Paléontologie; Paris: CNRS, 1980); Davis, "Late Pleistocene and Holocene"; to cite just a few.

11. Size was the basis for differentiating equids in the chapter by Bertini (chapter 13 in this volume). It is interesting to note the variations in measurements between the animals in the fosse and those found in the settlement.

12. Davis "Late Pleistocene and Holocene."

13. Personal communication from F. Marshall.

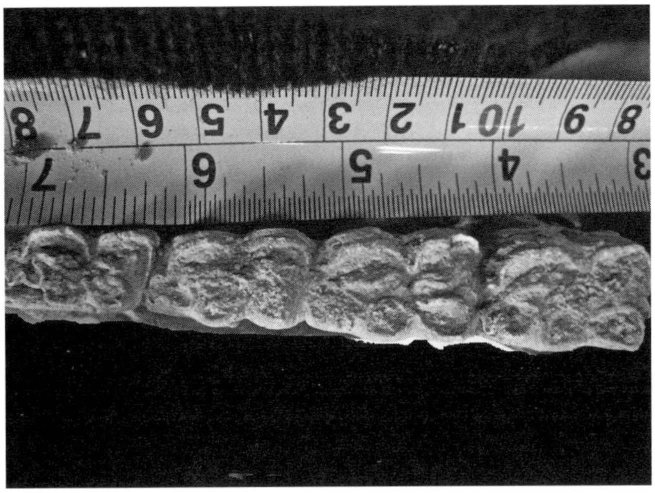

Fig. 14.6. The row of mandibular teeth from the animal that identify it as a donkey.

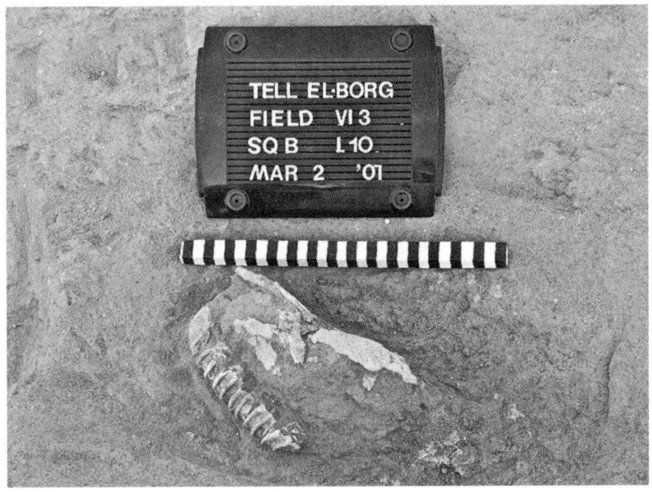

Fig. 14.7. Remains of one of the equid skulls in Field VI Fosse.

Table 14.3. Measurements (mm) of Equid Bones from Unit B

Element	*Side*	*GL*	*GB*	*Bp*	*BFp*	*Bd*	*BFd*	*LA*
Radius	R	N	N	64	58	N	N	N
Radius	L	280	N	N	N	58	51	N
Patella	R	N	50	N	N	N	N	N
Metatarsal	L	N	N	N	N	40	N	N
Metatarsal	R	N	N	37	N	N	N	N
Acetabulum	L	N	N	N	N	N	N	59

between horse and donkey, with the latter having smaller limb bones. This, however, does not take mules or hinnies into account. Both of the latter animals appear in tomb art—for example, in the Memphite tomb of Horemheb[14]—and would have played a significant role in military as well as domestic contexts. These animals, together with the issue of different-sized horse breeds and size further confuse the identification of equids.

All the creatures found at Tell el-Borg were mature animals, because their epiphyses (long bones and vertebrae) were fused. The examples of teeth that were found indicated older animals whose dentine had worn down (which also made it difficult to use these to separate species). The sex of most of these creatures could not be securely determined, because the pelvic areas were not well preserved and the teeth were also not sufficiently well preserved, save in one case, where the canine teeth indicated a male, with the remaining animals being females. Thus, it seems that the equids at Tell el-Borg included three donkeys (Equids 2 and 3 from Unit A and the equid in Unit B), one horse (Equid 1), and two animals whose identity is unclear (Equid 4 and the one from Area VI). Equid 4 might be a horse, although it is also possible that it is a mule/hinnie or, perhaps, a large donkey. It is conceivable that portions of other equids formed a part of the whole assemblage, but due to the dissolved nature of some of the deposit, this is difficult to determine.

14. G. T. Martin, *The Memphite Tomb of Horemheb* (London: Egypt Exploration Society, 1989), pls. 28–29.

From the time of Egypt's early history, donkeys were the primary beast of burden for both people and goods. Donkey remains are known from Egypt from the earliest times from sites such as Abusir, Tarkhan, and Abydos.[15] Horses, introduced with or subsequent to the Hyksos domination of Egypt, and the resulting hybrid equids (mules and hinnines), remain rare in the archaeozoological record, partly due to the relative youth of the field of archaeozoology in Egypt, the difficulty in distinguishing them, and partly due to the elite nature of and limited use of horses.[16] Thus, the discovery of horse bones at Tell el-Borg, both in the fosse as well as in other areas of the site remains a valuable find. Horses feature more commonly in the royal and elite art from the New Kingdom onward than they do in the form of skeletal remains.[17] Even Tell el-Borg boasts a stela sporting an image of the goddess Astarte seated upon a horse, dedicated by one Betu, whose chief title was "the overseer of horses," presumably at the fortress at el-Borg.[18] This too was found in the fosse, albeit at a lower level than the equids. Nonetheless, it is tempting to think that these animals might have been under Betu's care.

Horse remains that have been found in Egypt come from primarily military, and, to a lesser extent, civil contexts, most dating from the late Second Intermediate Period and early New Kingdom, soon after their introduction from the Levant by the Hyksos. As far as we know, these animals were used to pull chariots, although they also might have been ridden. Although there are few representations showing this in the New Kingdom, these images proliferate from the Late Period onward. A mummified mare, possibly a "pet," covered with a saddle blanket was found in a coffin in the courtyard of Senenmut's upper tomb (TT71).[19] Another group of horses was found at Saqqara; one of the animals was in its own wooden coffin. The dating of these animals is not secure, but this group almost certainly was buried later than the New Kingdom, particularly the encoffined one.[20] The remaining horse finds come from more formally royal contexts. These include teeth found at Tell el-Dabʿa (middle Hyksos period) as well as bones,[21] teeth and bones from the late New Kingdom and Late Period at Kom Firin (L. Bertini, pers. comm.), some possible bone and tooth fragments from the Ramesside fort at Zur Umm Rakkam (L. Bertini, pers. comm.), a

15. Respectively, J. Boessneck, A. von den Driesch, and A. Eissa, "Eine Eselsbestattung," 1–10; W. M. F. Petrie, *Tarkhan* II (London: Quaritch, 1914), 6, pl. XIX 1–3; and S. Rossel et al., "Domestication of the Donkey."

16. F. Braunstein-Sylvestre, "Quand le cheval arrive-t-il en Egypte?" in *Origin and Early Development of Food-Producing Cultures in North-Eastern Africa* (ed. L. Krzyzaniak and M. Kobusiewicz; Poznan: Polska Akademia Nauk-Oddzial w Poznaniu, 1984) 271–75.

17. C. Rommelare *Les chevaux du Nouvel Empire égyptien: Origines, races, harnachement* (Etude no. 3; Brussels: Connaissance de l'Egpte ancienne, 1991).

18. J. Hoffmeier and K. Kitchen, "'Reshep and Astarte in North Sinai: A Recently Discovered Stela from Tell el-Borg" *Ägypten und Levante/Egypt and the Levant* 17 (2007) 132.

19. S. Ikram and N. Iskander, *Catalogue Général of the Non-Human Mummies in the Cairo Museum* (Cairo: SCA, 2002) 46; A. Lansing and W. Hayes, "The Museum's Excavations at Thebes 1935–36," *Bulletin of the Metropolitan Museum of Art* 32.1 (1937) 7–11; D. E. Derry and B. Boulgakow's unpublished examination of the skeleton; J. Boessneck, "Ein altägyptisches Pferdeskelett," *MDAIK* 26 (1970) 43–47.

20. J. E. Quibell and A. Olver, "An Ancient Egyptian Horse," ASAE 26 (1926) 172–76.

21. J. Boessneck, Tell el-Dabʿa III (Vienna: Österreichischen Akademie der Wissenschaften, 1976) 25; J. Boessneck and A. von den Driesch, *Tell el-Dabʿa VII. Tiere und historische Umwelt im Nordost-Delta im 2. Jahrtausend v. Chr. Anhand der Knochenfunde des Ausgrabungen 1975–1986* (Vienna: Österreichischen Akademie der Wissenschaften, Denkschriften der Gesamtakeademie, XI, 1992); A. von den Drieschand and J. Peters, "Frühe Pferde- und Maultierskelette aus Auaris (Tell el-Dabʿa), Östliches Nildelta," *Egypt and the Levant* 11 (2001) 301–11; M. Bietak and I. Forstner-Müller, "Der Hysospalast bei Tell el-Dabʿa: Zweite und Dritte Grabungskampagne (Frühling 2008 und Frühling 2009)," *Egypt and the Levant* 19 (2009) 98–100, fig. 8.

horse skeleton at Buhen (tentatively dated to Second Intermediate Period), another at Soleb (ca. 1580–1350 B.C.), one in the Sinai (Hyksos period), and at Tell Hebua.[22]

This last example provides the closest parallel to the equids of Tell el-Borg in terms of geographical proximity, although it is earlier in time than the Tell el-Borg equids: it is stratigraphically dated to between the end of the Second Intermediate Period and the very beginning of the New Kingdom, while the Tell el-Borg horse dates to after 1300 B.C., more in keeping with the mummified mare from Senenmut's tomb. Later examples of horse burials have been found in Nubia (Qustul and Ballana), as well as in Kurru,[23] to list some of the best-known examples of horse-finds from the Pharaonic era. The equid remains from Tell el-Borg complement the finds at other fort sites, such as Zawiyet Umm el-Rakham and Tell Hebua and emphasize the important role played by both donkeys and horses in the provisioning and defence of Egypt.

22. Respectively: J. Clutton-Brock, *Horse Power* (London: Natural History Museum, 1992) 80–83; J. Clutton-Brock, "The Buhen Horse," *Journal of Archaeological Science* 1 (1974) 89–100; P. Ducos, "Le Cheval de Soleb" in *Soleb II Les Necropoles* (ed. M. S. Giorgini; Florence: Sansone, 1971) 260–65; Clutton-Brock, *Horse Power*, 83. I have been unable to trace the original site report for this animal; L. Chaix, "An Hyksos Horse from Tell Heboua (Sinai, Egypt)" in *Archaeozoology of the Near East* IVB (ed. M. Mashkour et al.; Groningen: Centre for Archeological Research and Consultancy, 2000) 177–86.

23. S. Ikram and N. Iskander, *Catalogue Général of the Non-Human Mummies in the Cairo Museum* (Cairo: SCA, 2002) 47; S. Bökönyi, "Two Horses Skeletons from the Cemetery of Kurru, Northern Sudan," *Acta Archaeologica Academiae Sceintiarum Hungaricae* 45 (1993) 301–16. Also see the unpublished (at the time of writing) 2016 dissertation of Susan Turner, Macquarie University, *The Horse in New Kingdom Egypt: Its Introduction, Nature, Role and Impact.*

CHAPTER 15

Reflections on a Decade of Research and Excavations at Tell el-Borg and Its Environs (1998–2008)

James K. Hoffmeier
TRINITY INTERNATIONAL UNIVERSITY

INTRODUCTION

This volume marks the final major publication of our decade of work in North Sinai. The published data amassed in two major excavation reports and in more than two dozen reports and studies have shed much light on northwestern Sinai, both on the ancient landscape and also on the military history of this strategic zone. The purpose of this final chapter is to reflect on these data and to take stock of some of the interpretations that have already been advanced, as well as offer some proposals for future study. The current unrest and security issues in north Sinai, sadly, will inhibit further exploration for some time to come.

THE PALEO-ENVIRONMENT OF NORTHWESTERN SINAI

We recognized from the inception of this project that the area of northwestern Sinai was ancient Egypt's eastern military frontier zone. During an initial visit to the region in 1994, we recognized the need to understand clearly the interrelationship between the ancient landscape or paleoenvironment and the forts already uncovered (Tell el-Herr, Tell Qedua, and Hebua I at that time) and those that would be discovered and explored in the years to come (e.g., Hebua II, Tell el-Borg, and Tell Abyad). After some initial coring in the low, flat plane between Hebua I and II in 1995 (see *Tell el-Borg I*, 6–7), which demonstrated that a body of water separated the two sites; Hebua II subsequently turned out to be home to the fort of Tjaru, *ḫtm n ṯꜣrw*. In 1998, geologist Stephen Moshier joined the team and, along with colleagues from the Geological Survey of Egypt, did remarkable work that has forever altered the map of this area.[1]

1. James K. Hoffmeier and Stephen O. Moshier, "New Paleo-Environmental Evidence from North Sinai to Complement Manfred Bietak's Map of the Eastern Delta and Some Historical Implications," in *Timelines: Studies in Honour of Manfred Bietak II* (Leuven: Peeters, 2006) 167–76; and Stephen O. Moshier and Ali el-Kalani, "Late Bronze Age Paleogeography along the Ancient Ways of Horus in Northwest Sinai,

The As-Salam irrigation project is currently transforming the desert region, east and south of the present-day northeastern edge of the Delta, into farmland. Indeed, one of the original considerations in choosing to work in this area east of the Suez Canal, between Qantara and Baluza (Pelusium), was to salvage archaeological sites before they were lost forever.

We now know that two eastern branches of the Nile flowed across northwest Sinai, te one distributary passing between Hebua I and II,[2] while the southern counterpart went by Tell el-Borg (fig. 2.11 above; *Tell el-Borg I*, fig. 77). The latter was uncovered during our excavations in 2000.[3] These branches predate the course of the Pelusiac branch, which reached the first-millennium site of Pelusium. Traces of the Pelusiac were discovered in the early 1970s by members of the Israel Geological Survey, north of the coastal ridge formed by the Pelusium line.[4] These two earlier distributaries emptied into the paleo-lagoon 2–3 km east of Tell el-Borg and Hebua, respectively (for the present discussion, see figs. 2.1, 2.4, and 2.11 above and *Tell el-Borg I*, chap. 3, pp. 74–83).

The region of northwest Sinai was indeed a wet area throughout the period of Tell el-Borg's occupation. There were numerous bodies of water and wetlands: the Balah Lake system,[5] the Paleo-lagoon, and two Nile branches. During the Nile's annual inundation, the low-lying areas were flooded wetlands full of grasses, reeds, and rushes. Seeds of various grasses and water plants were documented by our paleo-botanist, Claire Malleson (see chapter 11), and reeds were used to construct the earliest habitations on the site (see chapter 7).[6] The surrounding wetlands likely were the sources for brick used in the various constructions at Tell el-Borg.

We concur with Manfred Bietak's now nearly 40-year-old proposal[7] that the waters of the two main bodies of water in this region, the paleo-lagoon and the Ballah Lakes are the Lake of Horus (*š-ḥr*) and the Lake or Sea of Reeds/Rushes (*pꜣ ṯwfy*), respectively.[8] They are mentioned parallel

Egypt," *Geoarchaeology* 23 (2008) 450–73; Stephen O. Moshier in *Tell el-Borg I*, 62–83; Stephen O. Moshier and James K. Hoffmeier, "Which Way Out of Egypt? Physical Geography Related to the Exodus Itinerary," in *Israel's Exodus in Transdisciplinary Perspective: Quantitative Methods in the Humanities and Social Sciences* (ed. Thomas Levy et. al.; New York: Springer), 101–8.

2. This branch was identified through satellite imagery by Dominique Valbelle and Bruno Marcolongo; see D. Valbelle et al., "Reconnaissance Archéologique à la Pointe Orientale du Delta Rapport Préliminaire Sur Les Saisons 1990 et 1991," *CRIPEL* 14 (1992) 11–31; B. Marcolongo, "Évolution du paléo-environnement dans la partie orientale du Delta du Nil depuis la transgression flandrienne (8000 B.P.) par rapport aux modèles de peuplement anciens," *CRIPEL* 14 (1992) 23–31.

3. James K. Hoffmeier and Mohamed Abd el-Maksoud, "A New Military Site on 'the Ways of Horus': Tell el-Borg 1999–2001, A Preliminary Report," *JEA* 89 (2003) 195.

4. Amihai Sneh, Tuvia Weissbrod, and Itamar Perath, "Evidence for an Ancient Egyptian Frontier Canal," *American Scientist* 63 (1975) 542–48. Previously they had discovered the Pelusiac Nile from the Greco-Roman period; see Amihai Sneh and Tuvia Weissbrod, "Nile Delta: The Defunct Pelusiac Branch Identified," *Science* 180 (1973) 59–61.

5. For a complete study of the geological history of the Ballah lakes, Moshier's work in this volume is essential (chapter 2).

6. In addition to the treatment of the reed huts in this volume, see J. K. Hoffmeier, T. W. Davis and R. Hummel, "New Archaeological Evidence for Ancient Bedouin (Shasu) on Egypt's Eastern Frontier at Tell el-Borg," *Ägypten und Levante* 26 (2016) 285–311.

7. M. Bietak, *Tell El-Dab'a* (Vienna: Österreichischen Akademie der Wissenschaften, 1975) vol. 2, figs. 10, 23. Subsequently, Bietak has continued to maintain this identification; see Bietak, "Comments on the Exodus," in *Archaeological and Historical Relationships in the Bible Period* (ed. A. F. Rainey; Tel Aviv: Tel Aviv University Press, 1987) 165; Bietak, *Avaris: The Capital of the Hyksos* (London: The British Museum, 1996) fig. 1.

8. A. Gardiner, *Late-Egyptian Miscellanies* (Brussels: Fondation égyptologique Reine Élizabeth, 1937) 22.

to each other in Pap. Anastasi III (2.11–12). Thus, the nearby royal residence of Pi-Ramesses is blessed with the products of these adjacent wetlands, as the text itself declares: "the papyrus-marshes (*pꜣ ṯwfy*) comes with rushes to it (Pi-Ramesses) and the Lake of Horus (*š-ḥr*) with reeds." Not surprisingly, we discovered that the fish and fowl that were a rich part of the diet of the residents of Tell el-Borg likewise came from the neighboring bodies of water.

In between these channels, lakes, and wetlands were stretches of sand, and it was on these solid surfaces that both the military road ran and the forts were built. The route that ran from the Delta to Hebua I and beyond, also known as the Ways of Horus, connected the various military establishments.[9] Thus, the forts at Tell el-Borg were strategically located to protect the intersection of the land road and river course that guarded access to Egypt.[10]

Due to a number of factors, including lower Nile levels and possible tectonic tilting of northwest Sinai along the Pelusium Line (i.e., a transcontinental linear structure along the Central Plate, which is moving northward, and the Northwest African Plate),[11] the water levels of the paleo-lagoon were lowered.[12] By the Third Intermediate Period, the old coastal ridge that once marked the Mediterranean coast, but had been opened to the sea at the northern end of the lagoon in the 2nd millennium and earlier, silted up. This change in landscape made it possible to traverse the area where the lagoon waters previously emptied into the sea. Archaeological proof of this development is the location of the site Tell Ghaba at the center of the earlier mouth of the lagoon and the military site to the east, Tell Qedua, with its Saite period fort, and Hebua I to the west, which also had a fort in the Third Intermediate Period. Thus, a new land route was established between Pelusium (and points east) to Tanis in the Delta.[13] As a consequence, the New Kingdom and earlier route around the southern end of the lagoon, which passed by Tell el-Borg, fell out of use (fig. 15.1).

Because this area of northwest Sinai (Egypt's northeast frontier zone) was so moist, with Nile distributaries, lakes, and wetlands, it served as a natural defense that, when coupled with the forts and naval operations at Hebua and Tell el-Borg, made Egypt virtually impenetrable from the east.

THE IDENTIFICATION OF THE SITE

We have believed from the earliest days of our work at Tell el-Borg that it should be identified with the New Kingdom military site "The Dwelling (*tꜣ ʿt*) of the Lion/ Ramesses/Sessy," first

9. Concerning the road out of Egypt to Canaan, see James K. Hoffmeier and Stephen O. Moshier, "'A Highway out of Egypt': The Main Road from Egypt to Canaan," in *Desert Road Archaeology in Ancient Egypt and Beyond* (ed. F. Förester and H. Reimer; Africa Praehistorica 26; Cologne: Heinrich-Barth-Institut), 485–510.

10. James K. Hoffmeier, "Reconstructing Egypt's Eastern Frontier Defense Network in the New Kingdom (Late Bronze Age)," in *The Power of Walls: Fortifications in Ancient Northeastern Africa* (ed. Friederike Jesse and Carola Vogel; Africa Praehistorica; Cologne: Heinrich-Barth-Institut), 163–94; and *Tell el-Borg I*, 34–61.

11. D. Neev, "The Pelusium Line: A Major Transcontinental Shear," *Tectonophysics* 38 (1977): T1–T8; David Neev, N. Bakler, and K. O. Emery, *Mediterranean Coasts of Israel and Sinai: Holocene Tectonism from Geology, Geophysics, and Archaeology* (New York: Taylor and Francis, 1987).

12. For a discussion of the desiccation of this region and the more northerly course taken by the Pelusiac late in the 2nd and into the 1st millennium, see James K. Hoffmeier, "The Curious Phenomenon of Moving Military Sites on Egypt's Eastern Frontier," *JSSEA* 36 (2016/17; The Edwin Brock Memorial Volume).

13. Hoffmeier, "The Curious Phenomenon of Moving Military Sites on Egypt's Eastern Frontier."

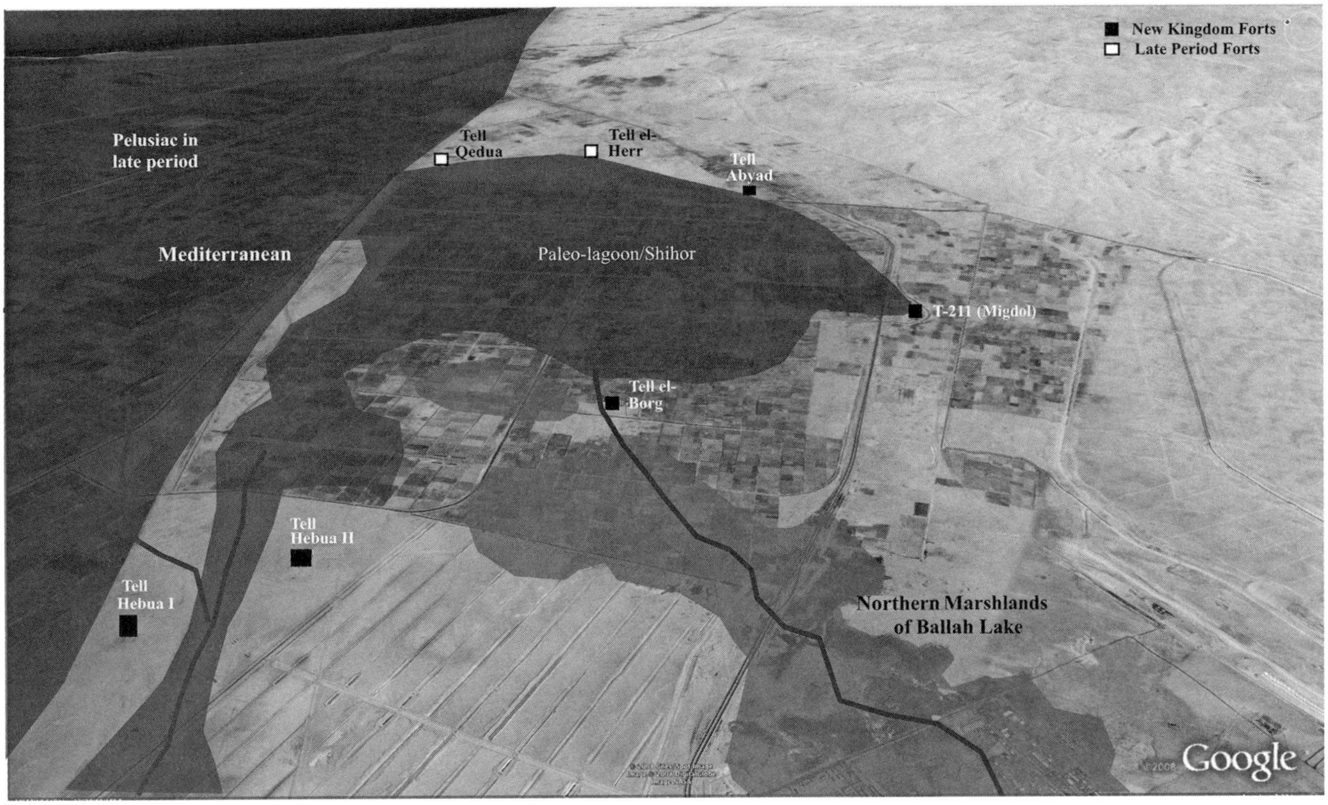

Fig. 15.1. Paleo-environmental map with sites with forts marked (Google Earth image with data overlaid by S. O. Moshier).

attested in the famed Karnak war reliefs of Seti I.[14] Even though the site had a dynamic military presence in the 18th Dynasty (see next section), the name of the site prior to the Ramesside period is yet to be discovered. Given the tendency for military toponyms to continue, with only the royal name changing to reflect the current reign, one might think that the name had been "Dwelling (*tꜣ ꜥt*) of the Lion"—that is, the lion representing any pharaoh, or *tꜣ ꜥt* + ROYAL NAME.

With the identification of Tjaru/Sile with Hebua I and II now a settled fact,[15] establishing the sequence of sites that followed, especially with the excavations at Tell el-Borg and Tell Abyad (on the eastern side of Shi-Hor), can now be determined. Here is the proposed sequence, and fig. 15.2 presents this material on a Google earth image combined with the paelo-environmental data gathered by Mosier.[16]

14. Hoffmeier and Abd el-Maksoud, "A New Military Site on 'the Ways of Horus'," 195–97. See also *Tell el-Borg I*, chapter 2, and Hoffmeier, "The Curious Phenomenon of Moving Military Sites on Egypt's Eastern Frontier."

15. M. Abd el-Maksoud and D. Valbelle, "Tell Héboua-Tjarou l'apport de l'épigraphie," *Rd'É* 56 (2005) 7–8, 18–21. Regarding Hebua II, see Mohamed Abd el-Maksoud and Dominique Valbelle, "Tell Héboua II: Rapport Préliminaire sur le décor et l'épigraphie des elements architectoniques découverts au cours des campagnes 2008–2009 dans la zone centrale du Khétem de Tjarou," *Rd'É* 62 (2011) 1–39. The title of this article (and the contents) indicates that Valbelle and Abd el-Maksoud believe that Hebua II is "the fortress of Tjaru."

16. Hoffmeier, "The Curious Phenomenon of Moving Military Sites on Egypt's Eastern Frontier."

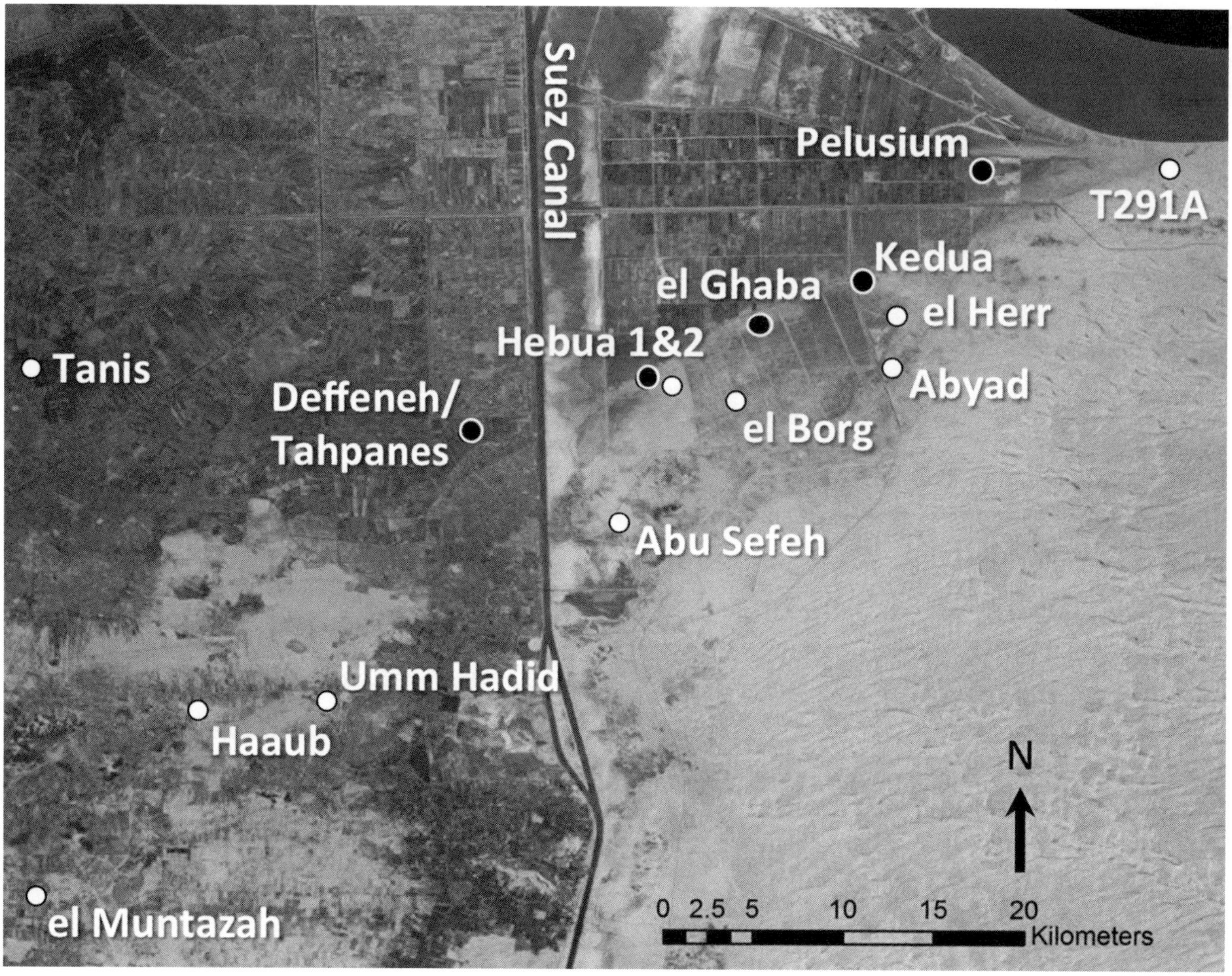

Fig. 15.2. Archaeological sites of the Northeast Delta and East Frontier. Saite Period sites are marked in black. ArcGIS (ESRI) map prepared by S. O. Moshier.

Egyptian Name	*Archaeological Site*
Tjaru/The Ways of Horus[17]	Hebua I
Tꜣ dnỉt	Hebua distributary (early Pelusiac)
ḫtm n ṯꜣrw	Hebua II
The Dwelling of the Lion/Ramesses II	Tell el-Borg
Migdol of Menmaatre/Ramesses III	T-211
Wadjet District of (Ramesses II)	Tell Abyad

17. Since every fort had a name, it stands to reason that the fort at Hebua I was named, even though presently we do not know what it was; *ḫtm n ṯꜣrw* (as suggested by the placement of the label on the Seti I scene) was likely the recently discovered fort at Hebua II. Since we do not know the name of the fort at Hebua I, I have simply called it "Tjaru/Ways of Horus."

History of Occupation of Tell el-Borg

A pair of flint Nizzanim blades (TBO 0741 and 841) may represent the earliest human presence at the site (see *Tell el-Borg I*, 517–18, figs. 581 and 582, and further discussion in this volume, chapter 10). These are late Neolithic period tips, a style that continued into the Old Kingdom in Egypt, and in the western desert they are found as late as the 1st millennium B.C. A handful of Nizzanim arrowheads were found at Pi-Ramesse, which suggests that they may have enjoyed use in Egypt into the New Kingdom.[18] Likewise, some were found at Tell el-Dabᶜa in a New Kingdom context.[19] Thus, their presence at Tell el-Borg remains a mystery. Hunters in the area preceding the Pharaonic period could have left these tips, but we cannot rule out that they may be later revivals of a classic type used in the New Kingdom.

The earliest inhabitants are associated with the reed huts found in the highest area of the tell: Field VI Area 1.[20] Based on C^{14} and early ceramic markers, a date in the 2nd Intermediate Period through early 18th Dynasty is most likely for these residents. Ceramic remains for the earlier period were documented in *Tell el-Borg I*, 376–78. We have wrestled with the ethnicity of this group and lean toward identifying them with as desert dwellers, or Shasu, but we cannot rule out that they were Egyptian soldiers stationed here prior to the first fort's construction.

The earliest royal name discovered is that of Thutmose III, found on a reused block that was churned up when the drainage canal was dug through the site (TBO I 2 = figs. 92A and 93A in *Tell el-Borg I*, 91–92). This is the lone witness to his name,[21] however, and for his son and successor, Amenhotep II, there are numerous attestations. Amenhotep II's name occurs on six doorjambs that experienced the expunging of Amun's name during the Amarna period (*Tell el-Borg I*, 245–47, figs. 353a–358b). These jambs no doubt graced the doorways of structures at the time of the 18th Dynasty fort, though none of those structures survived. Amenhotep's cartouche also was found on several impressions on ceramic vessels. TBO 0071 (fig. 4.82a–b) is a body sherd with the prenomen, *ꜥꜣ ḫprw rꜥ* stamped on it. A second body sherd, TBO 0364, has the same partial cartouche (fig. 4.147a–b).

It may well be that the first fort at Tell el-Borg was commissioned and begun during the reign of Thutmose III but certainly by the reign of Amenhotep II (to judge from the architectural pieces) the fort was functioning and continued in use until late in the Amarna Period (*Tell el-Borg I*, 128–97). No other earlier royal 18th Dynasty person is documented at Tell el-Borg until the name of Queen Tiye, wife of Amenhotep III, whose name is found on a faience ring in the Field

18. Edgar Pusch, "Pi-Ramesses-beloved-of-Amun' Headquarters of the Chariotry," in *Pelizaeus-Museum Hildesheim Guidebook* (ed. A. Eggebrecht; Mainz: von Zabern, 1996) 135, s. 133. See further Andreas Tillmann, "Neolithikum in der Späten Bronzezeit: Steingeräte des 2. Jahrtausend aus Auaris," *Die Grabungen des Pelizaeus Museums Hildesheim in Qantir-Piramesse/4* (Mainz: von Zabern, 2007), 216–17, who demonstrates that Neolithic type arrowheads were used in the Late Bronze Age. I am grateful to Manfred Bietak for drawing this study to my attention.

19. M. Bietak and I. Hein (eds.), *Pharaonen und Fremde: Dynastien im Dunkel* (Katalog der 194. Special Exhibition of the Historisches Museum of the city of Vienna in collaboration with the Institute of Egyptology of the University of Vienna and the Austrian Archaeological Institute Cairo, in the City Hall of Vienna, Volkshalle, 8. September bis 23. Oktober 1994; Vienna, 1994) 257, nos. 348, 349. I am grateful to Manfred Bietak for drawing this study to my attention.

20. See chapter 7 in this volume and Thomas Davis, James Hoffmeier, and Rexine Hummel, "New Archaeological Evidence for Ancient Bedouin (Shasu) on Egypt's Eastern Frontier at Tell el-Borg," *Ägypten und Levante* 26 (2016) 285–311.

21. One other badly preserved inscription could contain the cartouche of Thutmose III (TBO 0130 = *Tell el-Borg I*, 105–6) but is too incomplete to be certain.

III cemetery (TBO 0252; fig. 4.125a–b). From this point on, the royals of the Amarna Period are well represented:[22]

- Akhenaten (TBO 0309 = *Tell el-Borg I*, fig. 174)
- Neferneferuaten who is beneficial to her husband (TBO 0565 = fig. 7.87a–b)
- Ankhkheperura, 2 (TBO 0077 = *Tell el-Borg I*, fig. 173 and TBO II 37 = *Tell el-Borg I*, fig. 175)
- Tutankhamun, 2 (TBO II 36 = fig. 3.5a–b and TBO II 61 = fig. 15 in reference in n. 22 below
- Kheperkheperura, Aye (TBO 0778 = fig. 7.88a–b)
- Horemheb, 3 (TBO 0567 = fig. 7.91a–b; TBO 0683 = fig. 7.90a–d; TBO 0668 = 7.89a–c)

The royal names, Akhenaten to Aye, are on amphora vessels, whereas two cartouches of Horemheb are on mud bullae that sealed official documents, and the third (TBO 0668) is on the bezel of a faience ring. Clearly, during the Amarna period, official and military activity at the fort was robust, because the wine jars demonstrate that they had been furnished to the officers (and troops?) out of the royal largess, possible from the vineyards of Tjaru, whose famous vintage is mentioned in the tomb of Tutankhamun and the newly discovered KV 63.[23] The military activity at this fort throughout the Amarna Period also demonstrates that there was no weakening of Egypt's border defenses in response to Akhenaten's religious revolution. Indeed, the above-mentioned iconoclasm of Amun's name on the Amenhotep II blocks assures us of ongoing military presence; as Van Dijk has argued, such a widespread program of defacing images and the writings of Amun (and other deities) "can only have been carried out with the support of the army."[24]

The presence of the stamped handles of Akhenaten and Ankhkheperura in the fill of the 18th Dynasty moat, and the latter being at the top of that fill, suggests that the fort with the fired brick moat of the Thutmose III–Amenhotep II era continued in use until late in the Amarna Period, 1450–1330 B.C. (see *Tell el-Borg I*, 137–43). The complete loss of the back or west side, and signs of flood damage to the areas of the moat called Fosse E and G, led the archaeologists and our geologist to agree that a high-flooding Nile must have demolished this end of the fort, thus requiring the building of the second fort (*Tell el-Borg I*, 147–83 and 197–98). The evidence seems to suggest that the second or "Ramesside" fort was constructed during the reign of Horemheb or early in the 19th Dynasty (*Tell el-Borg I*, chapter 5).

Surprisingly, Seti I's name was not found at Tell el-Borg, even though he was militarily active in North Sinai, as the Karnak war reliefs attest, and then, before he became pharaoh, he had been the commandant of the nearby Fortress Tjaru, the central command post for the region.[25] Ramesses II's name, however, is widely attested (more than 20 occurrences) at Tell el-Borg, on blocks and fragments from the destroyed limestone covered gateway (*Tell el-Borg I*, 97–99, 103, 105, 108–9, 114, 117, 284, 298, 300, 303, 304, 307, 309, 313), not to mention the pair of Ramesses II stelae that stood in front of the same gate (*Tell el-Borg I*, 329–45). No doubt, Ramesses II

22. For a complete study of the seal impressions from this period and their significance, see James K. Hoffmeier and Jacobus van Dijk, "New Light on the Amarna Period from North Sinai," *JEA* 96 (2010) 191–205.

23. For a discussion of these references, see Hoffmeier and van Dijk, "New Light on the Amarna Period from North Sinai," 197.

24. Jacobus van Dijk, "The Amarna Period and Later New Kingdom," in *The Oxford History of Ancient Egypt* (ed. I. Shaw; New York: Oxford University Press, 2001) 270.

25. See the 400-year Tanis Stela, which reports that Seti had been *ỉmy-r ḫtm n ṯ3rw* (KRI II, 288.7, 9).

originally decorated this gate,[26] and, subsequently, Merneptah's name was added to the gate (*Tell el-Borg I*, figs. 475a–b, 482a–b, and possibly 487a–b).

The last royal name found at Tell el-Borg, also among the limestone fragments in the shattered gate area, is that of Ramesses III (*Tell el-Borg I*, 298–99, fig. 457a–b). We have proposed that the gate of the fort did experience a military attack and was at least partially damaged and burned, along with the stelae from the entrance.[27] How much longer the site continued in use after this possible Sea Peoples assault on the gate remains uncertain. No pottery was found for the Third Intermediate Period. The 12th century B.C. seems to align with the last known reference to the Dwelling of the Sesu in a broken stela from Serabit el-Khadim (no. 300), which contains the epithet: "Amun Lord of the Thrones of the Two Lands of 'the Dwelling (at) of Sesu'."[28] Just recently, Meindert Dijkstra matched stela no. 300 with no. 297, which has provided an important clue to dating the stela, likely to the reign of Ramesses IV (1153–1147 B.C.).[29] This datum indicates that "the Dwelling of Sesu" continued to play a military role past the middle of the 12th century B.C., but before the end of the 20th Dynasty it appears to have been abandoned.

After the New Kingdom, evidence of human presence is limited. Two Scythian trilobe-style arrowheads were surface finds, TBO 0094 and 0322 (*Tell el-Borg I*, 514–15), and date to the Hellenistic period. A limited number of late-period sherds were recovered from the site. We noticed that fired bricks had been mined for reuse in Field VIII Unit A-5, and some Hellenistic period pottery was discovered there (*Tell el-Borg I*, 177–78). This led the excavator to believe that brick removal should be dated to this late period. In all, about 30 sherds from the Greek and Roman periods were collected. No other remains from this period were discovered, which suggests that occupation, if permanent was limited, and most likely was from transients.

From the Greco-Roman period to the modern era, the only datable object recovered was a 7th–8th century A.D. Umayyad copper seal impression with an Arabic inscription; it was found in a pit (chapter 7, fig. 7.92a–b). After the 1967 war, the Israeli army took control of Tell el-Borg, establishing a military camp on this site, which was elevated and therefore strategic, within sight of the Suez Canal, 10 km to the west. Sandbag enforced bunkers remained from the Israeli army operations (*Tell el-Borg I*, fig. 17). One such sandbag was found at the bottom of a pit (chapter 7, fig. 7.66a). The Israeli army withdrew during the October or Yom Kippur War of 1973, and the Egyptian army set up camp at the site. Early in our excavations, a large section of an Al-Ahram newspaper dated to October 1973 was found, confirming the time when the Egyptians reclaimed this territory. Fired brick (with the name of the brick company stamped in Arabic!) trenches and bunkers were constructed, and they zigzagged through the area of what would become Field VI and VII (figs. 6.12 and 7.1). A further sign of the Egyptian military was the discovery of an eagle insignia from an officer's hat (fig. 7.64a–b). Sometime after the Camp David accords were signed in 1978, the Egyptian military moved farther east (closer to the Israeli border) and the various installations were razed (*Tell el-Borg I*, fig. 18). Interestingly, the three different armies who de-

26. There is evidence of an earlier mud-brick gate that could date back to Horemheb or Seti I: the Z-4 mud-brick structure, adjacent to the south side of the stone gate (*Tell el-Borg I*, 291–94).

27. First proposed in James K. Hoffmeier, "Tell el-Borg on Egypt's Eastern Frontier: A Preliminary Report on the 2002 and 2004 Seasons," *JARCE* 41 (2004) 100–103. See also, *Tell el-Borg I*, 325–29, and James K. Hoffmeier, "A Possible Location in Northwest Sinai for the Sea and Land Battles between the Sea Peoples and Ramesses III," *BASOR* 380 (2018) 1–25.

28. A.H. Gardiner and T. E. Peet, *The Inscriptions of Sinai Part I* (London: EEF, 1917) pl. LXXVII; A. H. Gardiner and T. E. Peet, *The Inscriptions of Sinai Part II* (London: EEF, 1955) 193–94.

29. Meindert Dijkstra, "A Chief of the Bowmen, Overseer of Foreign Lands at Serabit el-Khadim (Sinai 300+297) and the 'Dwelling of Sesu' (Tell el-Borg)," *Ägypten und Levante* 19 (2009) 121–26.

fended this elevated landscape recognized its strategic nature during the 2nd millennium B.C. and also in modern times.

THE MILITARY NATURE OF THE DWELLING OF THE LION/RAMESSES

The strategic nature of this ancient military site has already been noted in detail, primarily as seen in its architecture. The 18th Dynasty fort is largely represented by the impressive and unique fired-brick moat, which measured ca. 117 × 80 m, yielding a 9600 m^2 footprint. Little else of this fort survived, save the large D-19 structure located just inside the entrance of the fort in Field IV, along with a small stretch of the defense wall that was integrated into the enclosure wall of the second fort (*Tell el-Borg I*, 184–90). Otherwise, the enclosure wall, along with the entire gate system was lost.

The aforementioned Amenhotep II door-jambs stood in the doorways of important buildings, such as the commander's quarters, a temple, or storage magazines. The 18th Dynasty stela of Betu, the overseer of horses (*ỉmy-r ssmt*), demonstrates that a unit of chariotry was stationed at "the Dwelling."[30] Betu appears to be a Hurrian name, and Hurrians were experts in horsemanship. It is not surprising, therefore, that he was the stablemaster. Whether Betu was in Egypt voluntarily or had been conscripted as a prisoner-of-war (or was the son of one) we may never know, but clearly the appropriate Syro-Canaanite deities associated with horses and chariots, Astarte and Resheph, are honored on this stela (*Tell el-Borg I*, figs. 362–365). Fittingly, Astarte is perched on a chair and seated on the back of a horse, while Resheph is identified by the epithet "Lord of the horse stable" (*ršp nb pr ỉḥw*). Other signs of chariotry at Tell el-Borg include a pair of cheek bridle bits and a limestone saddle finial (*Tell el-Borg I*, 414–16). Then, too, there are the equine remains found in association with the second fort, as well as one from the Field VI moat (see chapter 14).

One last indication of the presence of chariotry is the discovery of a stretch of mud/mud-brick road between Hebua II (the Khetem of Tjaru) and Tell el-Borg by Dr. Hesham Hussein, a member of the North Sinai Inspectorate who worked many years with us at the site. He graciously agreed to publish his finding in this volume (chapter 8). The fact that there was a road across the sand dunes between Tjaru, the area's central command post, and "The Dwelling" meant that carts with supplies and chariots could move back and forth between the sites.

Weapons of various sorts were also discovered. A sword (TBO 0395) and an Aegean type lance blade (TBO 0177), unparalleled in Egypt, are among the prize finds (*Tell el-Borg I*, 510–14, figs. 570 and 193–194, fig. 257a–b). The lance was apparently used in chariot warfare to attack the enemy's horses. Copper/copper alloy spear/javelin tips and arrowheads were also found (*Tell el-Borg I*, 514–20). These weapons are further testimony to the military nature of the site.

The second or Ramesside-era fort was originally designed to include a moat around the mud-brick enclosure wall, the wall measuring from 3.6 to 4.1 m wide. For reasons that are unclear, the moat sections found in Field IV A (Fosse A) and Field V Area 2 (Fosse N) were only partially constructed (*Tell el-Borg I*, 217–21 and 228–30). Of the former, only 18.5 m survived. It was likely longer, but a section was lost when the modern canal was dug (*Tell el-Borg I*, 119–20, figs. 137a–b). The mud-brick walls of the fosse were laid on a foundation made of various stone fragments and pieces of fired brick. Many of the limestone blocks were *talatat* from an Akhenaten era temple, which proved to be an important criterion for dating this feature. Fosse N, on the other hand had

30. James K. Hoffmeier and Kenneth A. Kitchen, "Reshep and Astarte in North Sinai: A Recently Discovered Stela from Tell el-Borg," *Ägypten und Levante* 17 (2007) 127–36. See also *Tell el-Borg I*, 251–53.

a wider array of stone blocks in the foundations, including the Amenhotep II door-jambs and the Betu Stela, and in the matrix of the fill, the equine remains had been tossed (*Tell el-Borg I*, 229–54). Approximately 18 m of the structure remained, and 23 m additional of trench continued west of the end of the constructed moat, but the brick walls were not laid into the trench. This demonstrates that the construction of the fosse was abruptly stopped.

The gate of the Ramesside fort was pylon-like, covered in limestone and extensively decorated (*Tell el-Borg I*, 318–25 and fig. 519). The royal names were recited in the previous section. It is likely that the blocks found in Field I were originally on this gateway and that Ramesses II is the king portrayed pursuing Shasu enemies, firing arrows from his chariot.[31] The other side of the gate may have contained a triumph scene in which the deity (Amun-Re?) extended his arm and offered a sword to the king with the order to extend the borders of Egypt.[32] A pair of walls extended from the stone gate to form an open court. At the end of the walls stood a pair of stelae of Ramesses II, perhaps signaling that this fort marked a section of Egypt's border.[33]

The familiar war scenes of the Seti I relief at Karnak contain stylized icons of the forts across north Sinai, and their names are typically recorded. Pap. Anastasi I records a version of the names of this sequence of forts and wells or watering holes. Also shown at Karnak are the wells and cisterns associated with the forts, and often their names are included (*Tell el-Borg I*, fig. 1). In the case of the Seti I panorama, "the Dwelling of the Lion" has a rectangular pool in front of it and a pair of trees by the front corners, but no name is recorded. At Tell el-Borg, two stone-lined water installations were uncovered that were fed by the high water table in the area due to the proximity of the Nile. The first one was in Field II and was located near (north of) the Nile distributary (for a thorough treatment, see chapter 3). This water installation was somewhat oval in shape, with stairs of reused *talatat* that descended to water level. The other well or cistern ("the Fosse D well") was located within the walls of the Ramesside fort on the south side of the Nile. This well was at least 7 m long on the western side and at least 2 m deep, with stone steps at the northwest and southwest corners (the northeast and southeast corners were not reached) (*Tell el-Borg I*, figs. 387–391). Since the eastern side was not excavated, it is uncertain whether the structure was originally square or rectangular. By locating the well inside the fort, the troops would have had access to water should they be under siege, an important military consideration. If this square or rectangular well be the one depicted in the Seti I relief, its placement outside of the fort (rather than inside) may have been so that its presence could be illustrated in the relief.

There is some evidence for the military organization of this fort. A small inscribed limestone block, thought to be a name-plate (TBOX 27 = *Tell el-Borg I*, 108–11 and figs. 123 a–d and 124), contains the name of an officer, "the Weapons bearer (*t̠ȝỉ-ḫʿw*)" named Shesep, who was attached to the "Great Company (*sȝ ʿȝ*) (of) Amun, 'Amun appears gloriously and victoriously for Usi-mare Setepenre (=Ramesses II).'" A *sȝ*, company or regiment, is typically made up of 250 soldiers, and 20 regiments made up an army division of 5,000. Further, a regiment had three senior officers, the highest ranking of which is the "standard-bearer" (*t̠ȝy sryt*).[34] The weapon-bearer Shesep was

31. James K. Hoffmeier and Lyla Pinch Brock, "A New Royal Chariot Scene from Tell el-Borg," *JSSEA* 32 (2005) 81–92; James K. Hoffmeier, "The Gate of the Ramesside Period Fort at Tell el-Borg, North Sinai," in *Ramesside Studies in Honour of K. A. Kitchen* (ed. M. Collier and S. Snape; Bolton: Rutherford) 207–19.

32. TBO I 1 shows the male deity extending his arm (*Tell el-Borg I*, figs. 88–90), while TBO I 6 portrays another a male figure (deity?) with arm extended, under which the text reads "I give (or have given) to you [///]. . . your boundaries, there (?) [///]. . ." (*Tell el-Borg I*, 94–95 and fig. 98a–b).

33. See *Tell el-Borg I*, 325 and especially nn. 134–38.

34. For the organization structure of a *sȝ*, see Alan R. Schulman, *Military Rank, Title, and Organization in the Egyptian New Kingdom* (Berlin: Bruno Hessling, 1964) 26–30.

possibly an aide to one of the officers. If our fort was home to this regiment, then at least 200 and possibly 250 soldiers were stationed there.

One curious datum that might elucidate the military organization of the Borg fort and its relation to the nearby central command of Tjaru is on the Serabit Stela 297/300, introduced previously. There, an unnamed military officer is depicted with the titles [*ḥ*]*ry* [*p*]*ḏt ỉmy-r ḫ3swt nb t3.wy*, "the commander of the host, overseer of foreign lands," who stands before an image of "Amun-Re Lord of the Thrones of the Two Lands of the Dwelling of Sesu."[35] Unfortunately, the name of the officer is not given, but Dijkstra, following Eileen Hirsch, identifies him as Usikau, who has the same titles on other Serabit stela from the reign of Ramesses IV.[36] Regardless of the identity of this military commander, it seems doubtful that his command center was based at "the Dwelling." Nevertheless, the depiction on Stela 297/300 may be commemorating a visit of this officer to this fort and might suggest that the commanding officers at "the Dwelling" reported to this *ḥry pdt* who was stationed at Tjaru. Because the regiment stationed at Tell el-Borg, bearing the name "Amun appears gloriously and victoriously," is from the Division of Amun, it makes sense that this *ḥry pdt* stands in presence of Amun-Re Lord of the Thrones of the Two Lands. This epithet of Amun-Re was also written on a pair of the Amenhotep II door-jambs previously discussed (*Tell el-Borg I*, figs. 353–54). Perhaps this form of Amun-Re was the patron deity of the Dwelling of the Lion/Ramesses.

Similarly, some marine units were surely attached to "the Dwelling." Given the presence of the Nile, this is not unexpected. New evidence supports our suspicion. Recently, Orly Goldwasser has shown that some of the royal cartouches found on vessels in North Sinai include a hieroglyph for *boat*, indicating that these are the names of marine units that served in the area. She has pointed to one of the Tutankhamun amphora impressions from Tell el-Borg, TBO II 0061 (fig. 3.9), as having a boat sign (see discussion in chapter 3, Excursus I). This writing demonstrates that in the late 18th Dynasty there was a marine unit at Tell el-Borg. This new interpretation of TBO II 0061 makes perfect sense, given the location of the site on the distributary and the proximity of the paleo-lagoon, which had direct access to the Mediterranean. It is now evident that the military makeup of this fort was rather complex, with infantry, chariotry, and navy all being present at "the Dwelling."

LIFE ON THE EASTERN FRONTIER

The soldier's life is lampooned by scribes as filled with drudgery and danger. Nebmare-nakht, the scribe who authored Pap. Lansing, offers a lengthy appraisal of the life of the soldier, recognizing the obvious differences between officers and soldiers. He says:

> Come, ⟨let me tell⟩ you the woes of the soldier, and how many are his superiors: the general, the troop-commander, the officer who leads, the standard-bearer, the lieutenant, the scribe, the commander of fifty, and the garrison-captain. They go in and out in the halls of the palace, saying: "Get laborers!" He is awakened at any hour. One is after him as (after) donkey. He toils until the Aten sets in his darkness of night. He is hungry, his belly hurts; he is dead while yet alive.

35. Gardiner and Peet, *The Inscriptions of Sinai Part I*, pl. LXXVII; Gardiner and Peet, *The Inscriptions of Sinai Part II*, 193–94.

36. Dijkstra, "A Chief of the Bowmen, Overseer of Foreign Lands," 122; Eileen Hirsch, "Ramesses III. und Sein Verhältnis zur Levante," in *Das Konigtum der Ramessidenzeit: Voraussetzungen – Verwirklichung – Vermachtnis. Akten des 3. Symposions zur aguptischen akonigsideologie in Bonn 7. -9.6.2001* (ÄAT 36; ed. Rolf Gundlach and Ursula Roßler-Kohler; Wiesbaden: Harrassowitz, 2003) 150.

> When he receives the grain-ration, having been released from duty, it is not good for grinding.
>
> He is called up for Syria. He may not rest. There are no clothes, no sandals. The weapons of war are assembled at the fortress of Sile. His march is uphill through mountains. He drinks water every third day; it is smelly and tastes of salt. His body is ravaged by illness. The enemy comes, surrounds him with missiles, and life recedes from him. . . . If he comes out alive, he is worn out from marching. . . . Be a scribe, and be spared from soldiering![37]

It is recognized that this New Kingdom writer elevates his own scribal craft above all other trades and forms of employment, a literary tradition that can be traced back at least to the "Satire of the Trades."[38] In this possibly Middle Kingdom document, however, soldiering is not mentioned. Nebmare-nakht especially draws attention to the hardships of a soldier on campaign. Noteworthy is the mention of nearby Tjaru/Sile as the rallying and launching point for expeditions across Sinai. This point is confirmed in the Annals of Thutmose III and in the Ramesses II Kadesh inscriptions.

Conditions for soldiers at Tell el-Borg—at a stationary location near the frontier—obviously were different from those traveling and bivouacking farther east in Sinai or in the Levant. Due to the fact that the interiors of both forts have been completely lost, we do not know if the soldiers and officers lived within the fortifications or in what we believe were residential areas, possibly in Field VI (see chapter 7). The only obvious habitats discovered at the site were the reed huts in Field VI, which predate the earliest fort. Tents were certainly used on foreign campaigns,[39] but it seems unlikely that they served as permanent dwellings, given the fact that our fort was located just 4 km south of the Mediterranean coast, making this area subject to cold, wind, and rain during the winter months. Our own experience over a decade of work, typically in March–April, confirmed just how cold and wet this season can be. In January 2000, when we began surveying, we lived in a nearby building, and I experienced the coldest overnight of my life!

More promising is information about diet. The location of "the Dwelling" by the Nile distributary, along with surrounding wetlands and adjacent lagoon meant that there was an abundance of fish and waterfowl available for consumption (not to mention reeds for basketry, mats, and arrows). Indeed fish—perch, tilapia, and catfish—bones were the most common faunal remains at the site. Consequently, fish was probably the most frequently consumed meat (see chapters 12 and 13). Faunal remains of 22 genuses of birds were identified, the most common being the freshwater duck. Sheep/goats and pig bones were also found. Pigs served no other purpose than their meat, it is clear that pork was eaten here. Most unexpected was the significant number of bovine remains. Louise Bertini has concluded that the residents of Tell el-Borg "relied significantly on cattle for both meat and their secondary products." The faunal assemblage analyzed suggests that the diet of the troops stationed at this fort was quite robust, perhaps reflecting the importance and strategic nature of "the Dwelling of the Lion." The troops were well fed!

The paleo-botany further indicates that a typical Egyptian diet was enjoyed at the site. Bread and beer are the staples of any Egyptian diet. The discovery of emmer wheat and free-threshing wheat (chapter 13), along with the presence of bread molds and beer jars, numerous grindstones and mortars, are testimony to the dietary essentials. The presence of sickle blades may indicate that some planting and harvesting of grains occurred at or near the site (chapter 10).

---

37. Miriam Lichtheim, *Ancient Egyptian Literature* (Berkeley: University of California Press, 1976) 2.172.

38. Wolfgang Helck, *Die Lehre des Dwꜣ-ḫtjj* (Wiesbaden: Harrassowitz, 1970); Miriam Lichtheim, *Ancient Egyptian Literature* (Berkeley: University of California Press, 1973) 1.184–92.

39. James K. Hoffmeier, "Tents in Egypt and the Ancient Near East," *Society for the Study of Egyptian Antiquities Newsletter* 7.3 (1977) 13–28.

Other botanical remains include lentils, fig, and grape seeds. The grapes of the Tjaru region were highly valued for the wine produced.[40] A significant number of wine amphorae, both Egyptian (*Tell el-Borg I*, 424–25) and Levantine (*Tell el-Borg I*, 457–59), were documented. Twenty-six amphorae were discovered in the cemetery area in a pit thought to have been from funerary ritual meals (chapter 4, Excursus I). The appearance of royal names from the 18th Dynasty on jar handles and other vessels shows that the Crown was responsible for keeping the wine flowing for the troops! The soldiers at Tell el-Borg seem to have enjoyed a rich and healthy diet and wine for special occasions.

RELIGIOUS LIFE

Evidence for religious practices and cult at Tell el-Borg are scant. On the architectural front, in what we have labeled as "public" space in Field II, the mud-brick floor of a structure thought to be a temple was uncovered. Measuring 7.60 m wide and at least 6.75 long, the floor is just one brick thick. At the eastern end of the structure are three constructed rectangles counter-sunk through the floor and into the basal sand (figs. 3.37–3.38). These may have had plinths set in them, on which statues were placed. In this scenario, this preserved eastern section was the holy of holies, and the western section of the edifice did not survive (chapter 3). If this poorly preserved building had been a small temple or shrine, it is the only religious structure uncovered, but there is no indication who was the patron deity.

Elsewhere I have written in detail about the various gods and goddess whose names or iconographic images were documented at Tell el-Borg and in the immediate area.[41] The dominate role of Horus in the eastern frontier is evident from the geographical names, such as the Way(s) of Horus and Shi-Hor and the epithet Horus of Mesen that is thought to somehow be related to Tjaru.[42] A small copper-alloy statuette of a falcon headed figure (fig. 4.148a–b) could be the only representation of Horus at the site, although one cannot rule out that Ra-Harakhty or Montu is the intended deity. Amun-Re's name occurs on the Amenhotep II door-jambs already mentioned and another one where he is identified as "Amun-Re who is within Tjaru" (*Tell el-Borg I*, 245–48). Nut's name is also found on two of these blocks (*Tell el-Borg I*, figs. 355a–b, 357a–b), including the epithet "Great one, foremost of Tjaru." The connection to nearby Tjaru might indicate that there were major cult centers of these two deities just a few kilometers away.

Deities associated with childbirth, child-rearing, and protection—popular religion—are represented by Tawert, Hekat, and Bes.[43] These deities remind us that despite Tell el-Borg being a military site, families were present and life moved on from generation to generation with the appropriate protective amulets. Foreign deities were also documented. Astarte and Reshep have been already mentioned in this chapter and studied in detail elsewhere.[44] Another Canaanite goddess, "Anat lady of heaven," occurs on an inscribed block. Given how little survived at this relatively remote site that had undergone so much damage in modern times, it is striking that two

40. Hoffmeier and van Dijk, "New Light on the Amarna Period from North Sinai," 197.

41. James K. Hoffmeier, "Deities of the Eastern Frontier," in *Scribe of Justice: Egyptological Studies in Honour of Shafik Allam* (ed. Z. A. Hawass, Kh. A. Daoud, and R. B. Hussein; Supplement aux Annales du Service des Antiquités de l'Egypte, Cahier 42; Cairo: Service des Antiquités de lEgypte, 2011) 197–216.

42. See Hoffmeier, "Deities of the Eastern Frontier," 197–99 for a review of the various uses of Horus on texts from the region.

43. Hoffmeier, "Deities of the Eastern Frontier," 202–4.

44. Hoffmeier and Kitchen, "Reshep and Astarte in North Sinai."

sky-goddesses' names survive. It might be that the protection of these sky-deities (and we can add Horus as the male counterpart) was particularly needful in this frontier location, as was true of the martial deities Reshep, Astarte, and Seth.[45]

Death at Tell el-Borg

More than a dozen burials of the New Kingdom period were excavated in Field III and the "Western Cemetery" revealed two and possible three pits, dug into the kurkar sandstone, that were used as tombs (chapter 4). No doubt there were dozens more in Field VII that went unexplored due to the massive modern robbing in that area (chapter 6), and possibly just as many were destroyed in Field III during the recent construction of the modern drainage canal and adjacent service roads. Given that the site was occupied continuously for more than 250 years, a large number of burials would be expected. We must allow for the possibility that some of the residents, be they officers, soldiers, or adjuncts and their families, may have returned to their ancestral homes for burial or retired there. The fact that large burials such as Tombs 1, 2, and 4 contained the remains of men, women, and children means that entire families lived at Tell el-Borg. The tradition of son following father in his trade or profession extended to the military, too.[46] It may be that families lived for generations at a site such as this, and sons followed their fathers in military service.

Burial practices on the frontier mirrored those elsewhere in Egypt. The size of the tomb, whether for a single interment or a family mausoleum, directly corresponded to one's economic status or, in the case of the military, one's rank. While it could be an accident of survival, no wooden coffins were uncovered. The clay coffin was the sarcophagus of choice (chapter 5), and sherds were associated with the single occupant burial and the multi-occupant tomb in Field III and in what we deemed to be the poorer burials in Field VII. It may be that the high (and fluctuating) water table necessitated a water-resistant container to protect the remains of the deceased. No tombs were found intact, but the fragmentary remains indicate that the burials were well-stocked with vessels that contained food and drink, and there is some evidence for mummification.

The tombs were uniformly oriented, with the head pointing west, thus having all the Osirian connections one would expect. A structure found among the tombs in Field III, Area 2 may have been used to prepare the dead for burial, and the large pit containing nearly 100 vessels points to burial commemoration ceremonies.

Concluding Remarks

The archaeological and geological work done at Tell el-Borg and its environs have contributed significantly to our understanding of the east frontier defense network in the New Kingdom. And yet in many ways, this effort represents only a couple of steps forward on a long path. Thanks to the ongoing work at Hebua I and II, much more will come to light in years to come. It was our team's belief, especially after the extensive magnetometer survey work done in 2006 and 2007 (*Tell el-Borg I*, chapter 7), that we had obtained sufficient data from the excavations to form

45. A copper-alloy image of Seth (TBO 0669 = *Tell el-Borg I*, figs. 322a–d and 323).

46. A classic illustration of this is found in the biography of Ahmose son of Abena: he refers to his father having been a soldier under Seqenenre Tao II and Ahmose and reports, "I became a soldier in his stead on the ship" (Lichtheim, *Ancient Egyptian Literature*, 2.12)

Fig. 15.3. CORONA Image with paleo-environmental features and archaeological site noted (prepared by S. O. Moshier).

some firm conclusions about the history and function of the site. The survey yielded a number of anomalies that we investigated and concluded that, due to deflation over the centuries and the extensive damage done by two recent armies between 1967 and 1984, not to mention the widespread damage to the site from the as-Salam irrigation project in the 1990s, little more could be gleaned by further excavation.

It was our hope to investigate other military sites in the region. One obvious goal was to locate the next site on the highway after Tell el-Borg. From Eliezer Oren's survey, we learned of T-211, located at the southern tip of the paleo-lagoon, Shi-hor, which he described as a New Kingdom site based the sherds and stone fragments scattered around an area of 6 acres. Our effort to locate the site in 2007, despite having the coordinates, failed due to the area having been developed for a fruit farm. In so doing, the private property had been covered with up to a meter of sand, because it was a low and somewhat marshy spot. A grove of sickly-looking fruit trees was present. Apparently, this low area and high water table was so salinized that growth was very difficult. This failure to yield fruit may mean that, in the future, archaeological work can take place, with the aid of magnetometer, and thus we may be able to determine the exact location of the fort beneath the sands. I have elsewhere proposed that this site is Migdol of Menmaatre.[47]

Another site that could prove beneficial for elucidating the east frontier defense system in the New Kingdom is T-278, located just east of Pelusium and very close to if not on the ancient coastline (fig. 15.3). Visited in 2007 by a member of our staff, this site is reported to be completely untouched by the As-Salam irrigation project and other modern development, but sand dune activity could create challenges for exploration. Nevertheless, T-278 needs to be investigated: its strategic location suggests that it served militarily for both naval and land operations.

Insha'allah, as one would say in Egypt, the security situation in north Sinai will improve soon and exploration at T-211 and T-278 can proceed and build on the work done at Hebua I and II, Tell el-Borg, and Tell Abyad (T-116) and answer many more questions about the military and economic history of this important eastern region of Egypt.

47. James K. Hoffmeier, "The Search for Migdol of the New Kingdom and Exodus 14:2: An Update," *Buried History* 44 (2008) 3–12; idem, "The Curious Phenomenon of Moving Military Sites"; idem, "A Possible Location in Northwest Sinai for the Sea and Land Battles between the Sea Peoples and Ramesses III," *Bulletin of the American Schools of Oriental Research* 380 (2018) 2–25.